Advance Praise for

"*Head First Networking* takes network concepts that are sometimes too esoteric and al technical people to understand without difficulty and makes them very concrete ai done."

—Jonathan Moore, Owner, Forerunner Design

"*Head First Networking* is a comprehensive introduction to understanding, building, and maintaining computer networks. The book offers practical guidance on how to identify and repair network connection problems, configure switches and routers, and make your network secure. It is useful as a textbook for computer networking classes and as a resource for network professionals."

— Dr. Tim Olson, Chair of the Division of Sciences, Salish Kootenai College

"The big picture is what is often lost in information technology how-to books. *Head First Networking* keeps the focus on the real world, distilling knowledge from experience and presenting it in byte-size packets for the IT novitiate. The combination of explanations with real world problems to solve makes this an excellent learning tool."

— Rohn Wood, Senior Research Systems Analyst, University of Montana

Praise for other *Head First* books

"Kathy and Bert's *Head First Java* transforms the printed page into the closest thing to a GUI you've ever seen. In a wry, hip manner, the authors make learning Java an engaging 'what're they gonna do next?' experience."

—Warren Keuffel, Software Development Magazine

"Beyond the engaging style that drags you forward from know-nothing into exalted Java warrior status, Head First Java covers a huge amount of practical matters that other texts leave as the dreaded "exercise for the reader..." It's clever, wry, hip and practical—there aren't a lot of textbooks that can make that claim and live up to it while also teaching you about object serialization and network launch protocols. "

—Dr. Dan Russell, Director of User Sciences and Experience Research IBM Almaden Research Center (and teaches Artificial Intelligence at Stanford University)

"It's fast, irreverent, fun, and engaging. Be careful—you might actually learn something!"

—Ken Arnold, former Senior Engineer at Sun Microsystems Coauthor (with James Gosling, creator of Java), *The Java Programming Language*

"I feel like a thousand pounds of books have just been lifted off of my head."

—Ward Cunningham, inventor of the Wiki and founder of the Hillside Group

"Just the right tone for the geeked-out, casual-cool guru coder in all of us. The right reference for practical development strategies—gets my brain going without having to slog through a bunch of tired stale professor-speak."

—Travis Kalanick, Founder of Scour and Red Swoosh
Member of the MIT TR100

"There are books you buy, books you keep, books you keep on your desk, and thanks to O'Reilly and the Head First crew, there is the penultimate category, Head First books. They're the ones that are dog-eared, mangled, and carried everywhere. Head First SQL is at the top of my stack. Heck, even the PDF I have for review is tattered and torn."

— Bill Sawyer, ATG Curriculum Manager, Oracle

"This book's admirable clarity, humor and substantial doses of clever make it the sort of book that helps even non-programmers think well about problem-solving."

— Cory Doctorow, co-editor of Boing Boing
Author, *Down and Out in the Magic Kingdom*
and *Someone Comes to Town, Someone Leaves Town*

Praise for other *Head First* books

"I received the book yesterday and started to read it...and I couldn't stop. This is definitely très 'cool.' It is fun, but they cover a lot of ground and they are right to the point. I'm really impressed."

— Erich Gamma, IBM Distinguished Engineer, and co-author of *Design Patterns*

"One of the funniest and smartest books on software design I've ever read."

— Aaron LaBerge, VP Technology, ESPN.com

"What used to be a long trial and error learning process has now been reduced neatly into an engaging paperback."

— Mike Davidson, CEO, Newsvine, Inc.

"Elegant design is at the core of every chapter here, each concept conveyed with equal doses of pragmatism and wit."

— Ken Goldstein, Executive Vice President, Disney Online

"I ♥ Head First HTML with CSS & XHTML—it teaches you everything you need to learn in a 'fun coated' format."

— Sally Applin, UI Designer and Artist

"Usually when reading through a book or article on design patterns, I'd have to occasionally stick myself in the eye with something just to make sure I was paying attention. Not with this book. Odd as it may sound, this book makes learning about design patterns fun.

"While other books on design patterns are saying 'Buehler… Buehler… Buehler…' this book is on the float belting out 'Shake it up, baby!'"

— Eric Wuehler

"I literally love this book. In fact, I kissed this book in front of my wife."

— Satish Kumar

Other related books from O'Reilly

Network Warrior

DNS and Bind, 5th Edition

802.11 Wireless Networks

Security Warrior

Other books in O'Reilly's *Head First* series

Head First Java™

Head First Object-Oriented Analysis and Design (OOA&D)

Head First HTML with CSS and XHTML

Head First Design Patterns

Head First Servlets and JSP

Head First EJB

Head First PMP

Head First SQL

Head First Software Development

Head First JavaScript

Head First Ajax

Head First Physics

Head First Statistics

Head First Rails

Head First PHP & MySQL

Head First Algebra

Head First Web Design

Head First Networking

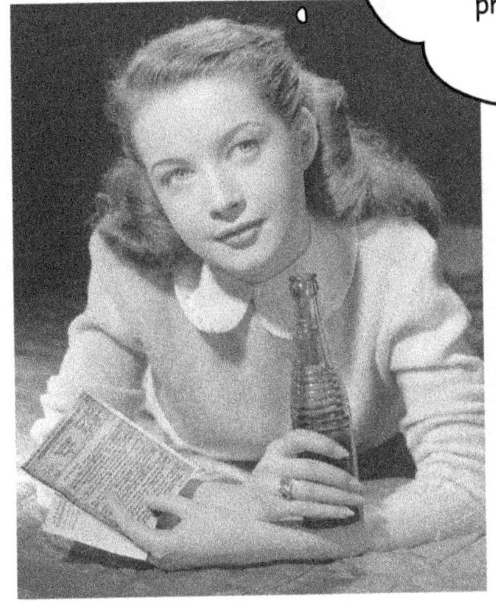
Wouldn't it be dreamy if there was a book on networking that didn't ask you to memorize the OSI Layer model by page 3? But it's probably just a fantasy...

Al Anderson
Ryan Benedetti

Beijing • Boston • Farnham • Sebastopol • Tokyo

Head First Networking

by Al Anderson and Ryan Benedetti

Published by O'Reilly Media, Inc., 1005 Gravenstein Highway North, Sebastopol, CA 95472.

O'Reilly Media books may be purchased for educational, business, or sales promotional use. Online editions are also available for most titles (*oreilly.com/safari*). For more information, contact our corporate/institutional sales department: (800) 998-9938 or *corporate@oreilly.com.*

Series Creators:	Kathy Sierra, Bert Bates
Series Editor:	Brett D. McLaughlin
Design Editor:	Dawn Griffiths
Cover Designers:	Louise Barr, Steve Fehler
Production Editor:	Brittany Smith
Indexer:	Julie Hawks
Brain Image on Spine:	Eric Freeman
Page Viewers:	Al: Emily, Ella, and Austin; Ryan: Josefina, Vincenzo, Shonna

Printing History:

May 2009: First Edition.

No routers were harmed in the making of this book (but some CAT-5 cables were).

ISBN: 978-0-596-52155-4

[LSI]

[10/14]

We dedicate this book to the first person who ever said, "Hey, let's connect this one to that one and get them to talk to each other . . ."

And for making networking complex enough that people need a book to learn it.

Al: To Emily, Ella, and Austin

Ryan: To my three miracles: Josie, Vin, and Shonna

Authors of Head First Networking

Al Anderson

Ryan Benedetti

Al Anderson is grateful that his family gave him the time and space to write this book. He is also grateful to have Ryan as co-author. Al is the Director of Academic IT Services at Salish Kootenai College. He also teaches such classes on networking services, network operating systems and programming for the IT program.

Al has also produced training videos on Ruby, Ruby on Rails, and RealBasic. If that was not enough, he recently finished his Bachelor's in Computer Engineering after starting 20 plus years ago.

This book adventure started over a year and half ago when Ryan and Al were flown to Boston to attend training at O'Reilly's Cambridge office. They were not under contract yet, and they were not sure where the journey would take them. It turned out to be a great adventure. Thank you O'Reilly!

Ryan Benedetti holds a Master of Fine Arts degree in creative writing from the University of Montana and teaches in the Liberal Arts Department at Salish Kootenai College (SKC) on the Flathead Indian Reservation.

For seven years, Ryan served as Department Head for Information Technology and Computer Engineering at SKC. Prior to that, he worked as editor and information systems specialist for a river, stream, and wetland research program in the School of Forestry at the University of Montana.

Ryan's poems have been published in *Cut Bank* and Andrei Codrescu's *Exquisite Corpse*. He loves painting, cartooning, playing blues harmonica, making Flash learning toys, and practicing zazen. He spends his best moments with his daughter and son in the Mission Mountain Valley of Montana, and with his sweetheart, Shonna, in Portland, OR.

Table of Contents (Summary)

	Intro	xxv
1	Walking on Wires: *Fixing Physical Networks*	1
2	Networking in the Dark: *Planning Network Layouts*	51
3	Into the Wire: *Tools and Troubleshooting*	85
4	You've Been Framed: *Packet Analysis*	125
5	How Smart is Your Network?: *Network Devices and Traffic*	175
6	Bringing Things Together: *Connecting Networks with Routers*	205
7	It's a Matter of Protocol: *Routing Protocols*	243
8	Names to Numbers: *The Domain Name System*	291
9	Listen to Your Network's Troubles: *Monitoring and Troubleshooting*	329
10	Working Without Wires: *Wireless Networking*	363
11	Get Defensive: *Network Security*	399
12	You Gotta Have a Plan!: Designing Networks	437
i	Leftovers: The *Top Ten Things (We Didn't Cover)*	469
ii	Looking Things Up: ASCII Tables	479
iii	Getting a Server to talk DNS: Installing BIND	485

Table of Contents (the real thing)

Intro

Your brain on networking. Here *you* are trying to *learn* something, while here your *brain* is doing you a favor by making sure the learning doesn't *stick*. Your brain's thinking, "Better leave room for more important things, like which wild animals to avoid and whether naked snowboarding is a bad idea." So how *do* you trick your brain into thinking that your life depends on knowing networking.

Who is this book for?	xxvi
We know what you're thinking	xxvii
Metacognition	xxix
Bend your brain into submission	xxx
Read Me	xxxii
The technical review team	xxxiv
Acknowledgments	xxxv

fixing physical networks

1 Walking on Wires

Just plug in that cable and the network's up, right?

Network cables silently do their job, pushing our data from here to there, faster than we can blink. But what happens when it all goes wrong? Organizations rely on their networks so much that the business falls apart when the network fails. That's why knowing how to fix physical networks is so important. Keep reading, and we'll show you how to troubleshoot your networks with ease and fix physical problems. You'll soon be in full control of your networks.

Coconut Airways has a network problem 2
How do we fix the cable? 5
Introducing the CAT-5 cable 6
The CAT-5 cable dissected 7
So what's with all the colors? 8
Let's fix the broken CAT-5 cable 11
A closer look at the RJ-45 connector 12
So what are the physical steps? 17
You fixed the CAT-5 cable 19
Coconut Airways has more than one network 20
Introducing the coaxial cable 23
Coaxial networks are bus networks 24
So can we fix the cable? 25
The network's still not working 26
What about connectors and terminators? 29
No sound means no electrons 31
You've fixed the coaxial cable 37
Introducing fiber-optic cables 38
The Coconut Airways cable's over-bent 39
How to fix fiber-optics with a fusion splicer 40
A fiber-optic connector needs fitting too 42
We're nearly ready to fix the connector 44
There are two types of fiber 45
Which mode fiber should you use? 46
Let's fit the connector on the fiber-optic 47
Coconut Airways is sky high 49

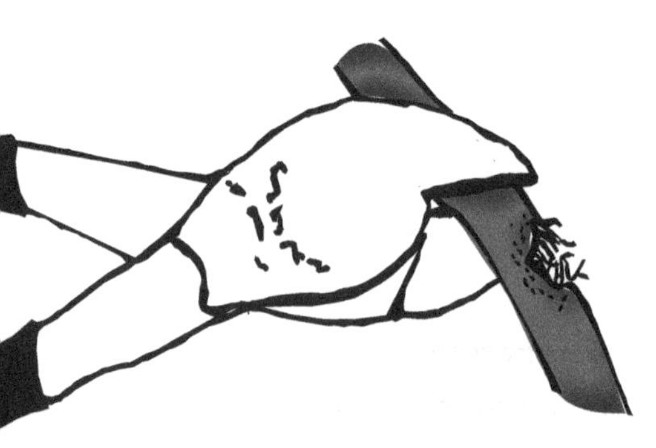

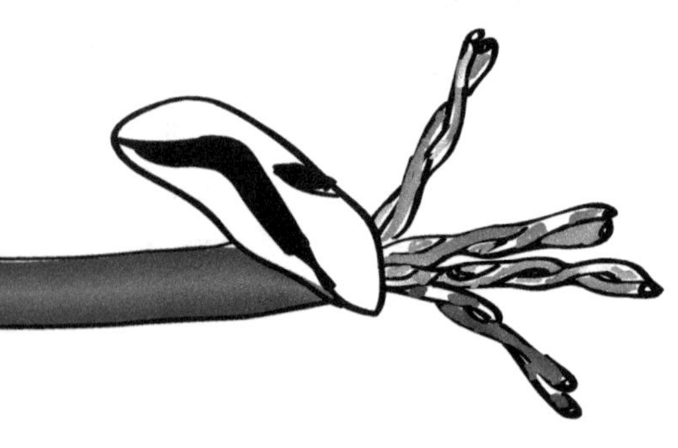

planning network layouts

Networking in the Dark

2

Tired of tripping over wires and getting mauled by your electrical closet? When you build a network without planning, you end up with a big mess—wires running every which way, wires connected to who knows what? In this chapter, you'll learn how to plan a physical network layout that will save your bacon down the road. You will also learn how to use proper network hardware to contain and help manage all those wires.

Ghost Watch needs your help!	52
Every good network needs a good plan	53
How to plan a network layout	55
Let's plan the cabling with a floorplan	56
Ready to plot some network cables?	60
We need to decide on the cable management hardware	64
Uh oh! The cabling is a mess	65
Ghost Watch needs cable management hardware	66
Things that go bump...	68
Let's start by labeling the cables	74
But there are still lots of cables	75
So what's a patch panel?	76
Behind the scenes of a patch panel	77
The wires go into a punch down block	78
Roll the cameras!	83

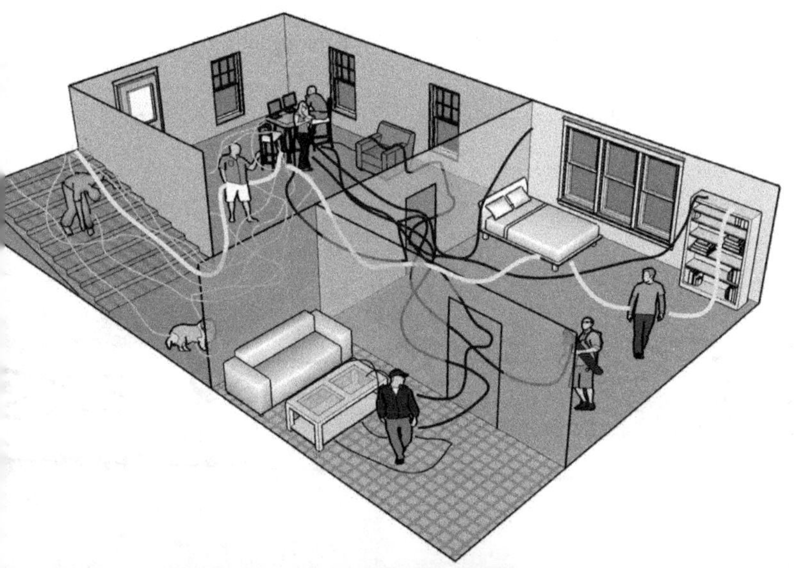

tools and troubleshooting

Into the Wire

3

How do you know when a network signal isn't getting through a network cable? Often the first thing you'll hear about it is when the network stops working effectively, but the trouble is, it's hard to tell what's wrong by just looking at a cable. Fortunately, there's a raft of tools you can use that let you see deep into the heart of your network cables, down to the signal itself. Keep reading, and we'll show you how to use these tools to troubleshoot your networks, and how to interpret the secrets of the signal.

Mighty Gumball won the Super Bowl contract	86
A toner and tracer can check for a signal...	
...but can't check for signal quality	88
Introducing the multimeter	92
So what's resistance?	93
So how well did the multimeter do?	99
An oscilloscope shows voltage changes	101
Voltage is really electrical pressure	102
Where does noise on network cables come from?	103
So how well did the oscilloscope perform for Mighty Gumball?	108
A logical analyzer uses voltage too	110
When is a logical analyzer useful?	115
So which tool is best?	115
A LAN analyzer combines the functions of all the other tools	118
A LAN analyzer understands the network traffic in the signal	119
So which tool is best?	120
The Mighty Gumball problems are sorted	123

packet analysis

You've Been Framed

It's time to go under the hood.

Network devices send data down the cable by converting the data into a signal. But how do they do this? And what else might be hiding in the signal? Just like a doctor needs to look at blood cells to identify blood-borne diseases, a network pro needs to look at what's in the network signal to detect network intrusions, perform audits, and generally diagnose problems. And the key to all of this is packet analysis. Keep reading while we put your network signal under the microscope.

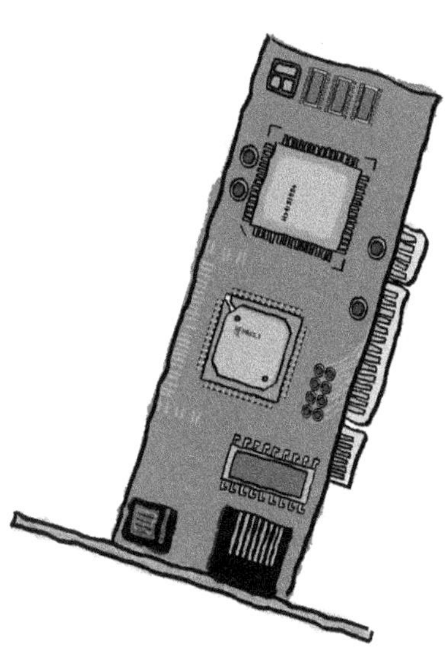

What's the secret message? 126
Network cards handle encoding 130
To get the message, reverse the encoding 131
The Ethernet standard tells hardware how to encode the data 132
A quick guide to binary 136
Computers read numbers, humans read letters 142
Hexadecimal to the rescue 144
We can convert to ASCII using hex 145
Back at the spy agency... 152
Protocols define the structure of a message 153
Network frames have lots of layers 161
Your friendly packet field guide 162
So can we decode the secret message? 168
We've got all the right packets... but not necessarily in the right order 169
The packet tells you the correct order 170

network devices and traffic

How Smart is Your Network?

A network can never be too smart.

Networks need as much intelligence as you can pack into them, but **where does that intelligence come from**? The answer is from its network devices. In this chapter, we'll look at how **hubs, switches and routers** use their innate **intelligence** to move packets around a network. We'll show you how these devices **think**, why they're so **useful**, and we'll even take a peek at what network traffic looks like using **packet analyzing software**. Keep reading, and we'll show you **how to super-charge your network**.

You've decoded the secret message... 176
The packet information tells us where the packet came from 179
So who's the mole? 180
There's more to networks than computers 181
Hubs are dumb 182
Hubs don't change the MAC address 183
A hub sends signals, and sends them everywhere 184
So what passed the signal to the hub? 185
A switch sends frames, and only sends them where they need to go 186
Switches store MAC addresses in a lookup table 188
The switch has the information... 192
We can use software to monitor packets 194
Let's hook Wireshark up to the switch 195
Wireshark gives us traffic information 196
Routers have MAC addresses too 199
Routers are really smart 200
You've found the mole! 203

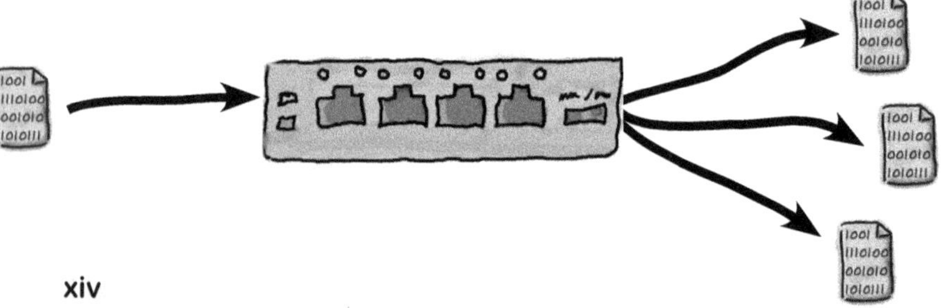

Bringing Things Together

Need to a get a network connection to a place far, far away?

So far, we've shown you the ins and outs of how you get a single network up and running. But what do you do if you need to share resources with some other network? That's where routers come into their own. Routers specialize in seamlessly moving network traffic from one network to another, and in this chapter you'll learn exactly how they do that. We'll show you how to program your router, and how the router itself can help you troubleshoot any problems. Keep reading, and you'll find it's out of this world...

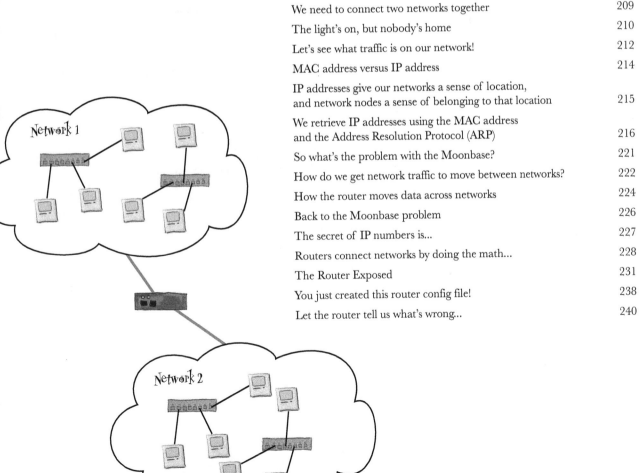

Networking on the moon 206
We need to connect two networks together 209
The light's on, but nobody's home 210
Let's see what traffic is on our network! 212
MAC address versus IP address 214
IP addresses give our networks a sense of location, and network nodes a sense of belonging to that location 215
We retrieve IP addresses using the MAC address and the Address Resolution Protocol (ARP) 216
So what's the problem with the Moonbase? 221
How do we get network traffic to move between networks? 222
How the router moves data across networks 224
Back to the Moonbase problem 226
The secret of IP numbers is... 227
Routers connect networks by doing the math... 228
The Router Exposed 231
You just created this router config file! 238
Let the router tell us what's wrong... 240

routing protocols

It's a Matter of Protocol

To build big networks, you need to use routers and they have to talk to each other.

Routers need to exchange routes with each other. They use various routing protocols to exchange routes. In the chapter, you will first see how to manually enter a route, then you will learn how to implement the simple RIP routing protocol. Finally you will learn how to setup EIGRP, an advanced routing protocol.

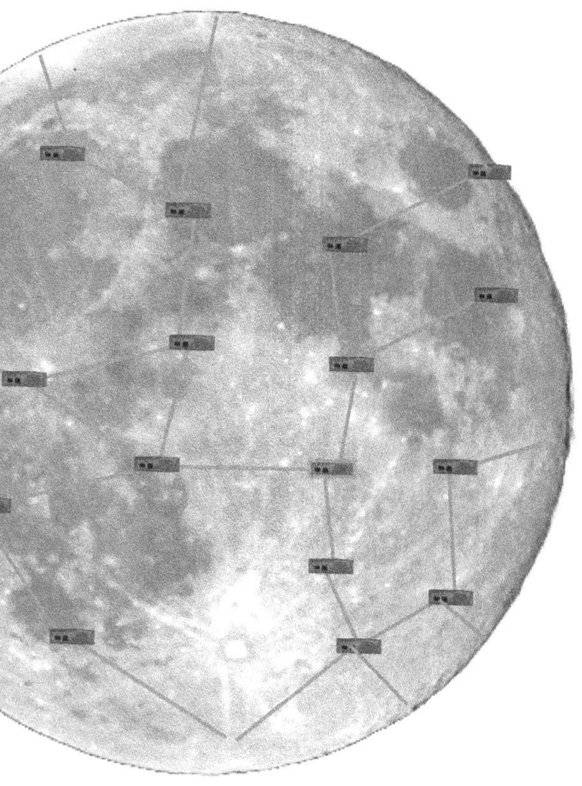

Houston, we have a problem...	244
Routing tables tell routers where to send packets	245
Each line represents a different route	246
So how do we enter routes?	248
Routes help routers figure out where to send network traffic	249
So are the moonbases now connected?	253
Back on the moon...	255
So how do we troubleshoot bad routes?	256
The traceroute command is useful too	257
So what's the problem with the network connection?	261
The network address changes keep on coming...	262
Use RIP to get routes to update themselves	264
So how do we set up RIP?	270
There are too many hops	272
The routing protocol zoo	276
So how do we setup EIGRP?	282
We have lift off!	288

the domain name system
Names to Numbers

You probably don't even think about it, but when you type a URL into a browser, how does your computer find an IP address for that server?

In this chapter you will discover the world of Internet domains. You will find out how there are 13 root servers that deal out domain name information for the entire Internet. You will also install and configure your own DNS server.

The Head First Health Club needs a website	292
Hello, my domain name is...	293
Let's go buy a domain name	294
Uh-oh! We're in trouble	296
Introducing the DNS	298
The DNS relies on name servers	298
How the DNS sees your domain	299
So how does this affect the Health Club?	304
First install a DNS name server...	306
...then configure the name server	307
The Nameserver Exposed	313
The anatomy of a DNS zone file	314
Here's what the DNS zone file tells us about the Health Club servers	315
The Health Club can't send emails	317
Email servers use RDNS to fight SPAM	318
Check your sources with reverse DNS	319
The dig command can do a reverse DNS lookup	320
Your name server has another important zone file...	322
The emails are working!	327

monitoring and troubleshooting

9 Listen to Your Network's Troubles

Listening to your network can save you lots of heartache!

Well, you have your network up and running. But like anything, it needs to be monitored and maintained. If it's not, one day it will just stop working, and you will have no idea why. You will discover in this chapter various tools and techniques to help you listen to your network and understand what is going on with it, so you can deal with any problem before it becomes a bigger problem.

Pajama Death are back on tour	330
So where would you start troubleshooting a misfiring network?	331
Start troubleshooting your network problems by checking in with your network devices	333
Troubleshoot network connectivity with the ping command	334
If the ping fails, check the cables	335
Get started with the show interface command	341
Cisco Show Command Exposed	342
The ticket network's still not fixed	345
SNMP to the rescue!	346
SNMP is a network admininistrator's communication tool	347
How to configure SNMP on a Cisco device	348
Get devices to send you their problems	354
How to configure syslogd on a Cisco device	355
How do you tell what's in the logs?	356
Too much information can be just as bad as not enough	359
How do you know which events are important?	360
Pajama Death's a sell-out!	361

10 wireless networking

Working Without Wires

Surfing the Internet without wires is great!

This chapter will show you all the things that you need to think when setting up a wireless access point. First you need to consider the physical location, because radio waves can be blocked. Second, we introduce some more network acronyms, NAT and DHCP. But don't worry, we'll explain them, so at the end of the chapter you will be able to have one great wireless network up and running.

Your new gig at Starbuzz Coffee 364
Wireless access points create networks using radio waves 365
Let's fit the wireless access point 366
What about the network configuration? 373
So what's DHCP? 374
First make sure the client has DHCP turned on... 376
Second, make the wireless access point a DHCP server... 376
...and then specify an acceptable range of IP addresses 377
So has setting up DHCP solved the problem? 378
Secrets of the DHCP Server 378
This time it's personal 379
We've run out of IP addresses 380
NAT works by reallocating IP addresses 381
So how do we configure NAT? 382
There's more than one wireless protocol 386
The central Starbuzz server needs to access the cash register 390
Port mapping to the rescue! 392
Let's set up port mapping on the Starbuzz access point 394
The wireless access point is a success! 398

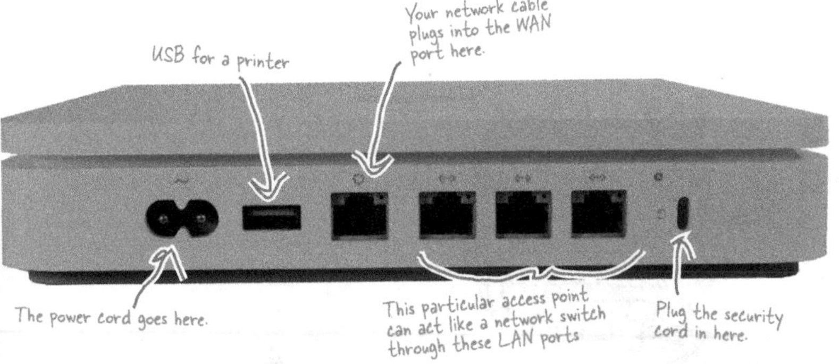

USB for a printer
Your network cable plugs into the WAN port here.
The power cord goes here.
This particular access point can act like a network switch through these LAN ports
Plug the security cord in here.

11

network security

Get Defensive

The network's a dangerous place to make a living. Attackers lurk around every corner: rootkits, and script kiddies, and bots... oh my! You've got to buck up and harden your network, or the barbarians will crash the gates. In this chapter, we expose you to the seedy underworld of the network, where attackers spoof MAC addresses, poison your ARP cache, infiltrate your internets, sneak packets into your network, and trick your co-workers into coughing up their passwords. Get defensive, dude! Let's keep our precious data in and the interlopers out.

The bad guys are everywhere 400
And it's not just the network that gets hurt... 401
The big four in network security 402
Defend your network against MAC address spoofing 405
So how do we defend against MAC address spoofing? 410
Defend your network against ARP poisoning attacks 411
So what can we do about ARP poisoning attacks? 412
It's all about the access, baby! 414
Set up your router's Access Control Lists to keep attackers out 415
So how do we configure the Access Control List? 417
Firewalls filter packets between networks 420
Packet-filtering rules! 421
Master the static packet filter 422
Get smart with stateful packet-filters 426
Humans are the weakest link in your security chain 429
So how do social engineers operate? 430
Smash social engineering with a clear and concise security policy 432
You've hardened your network 435

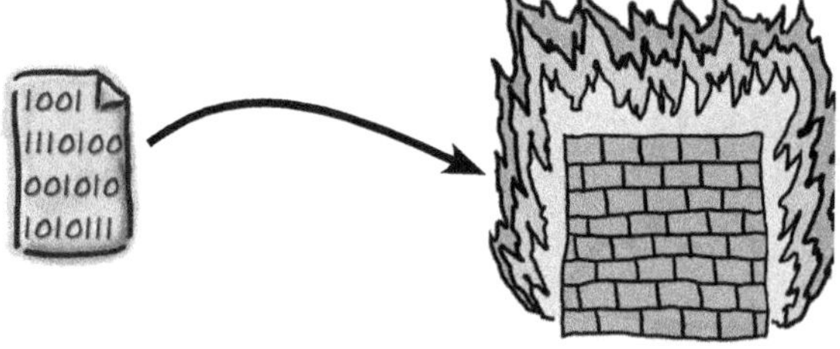

12 designing networks

You Gotta Have a Plan!

When it comes to networks, a good plan means everything. You've learned an awful lot about networking since those early days in Chapter 1. You've learned how to implement physical cable networks, how wireless access points work, how to make the most of your intelligent network devices, and all sorts of troubleshooting techniques to get you out of the hairiest network dilemmas. It's now time for you to put everything you've learned into practice and see just how far you've traveled on your networking journey. We know you can do it!

Now you have to plan a network from scratch!	438
You have to know what the needs are before you can plan	441
So you've developed your questions, now what?	443
The Plan	443
Look at your action plan	444
So you have a physical layout, what's next?	447
Blueprints show everything in a building's design	448
You may have to modify your network design based on what you see in the blueprints!	449
So you've got your physical network layout, what's next?	456
Finally, you need an implementation plan	464

i leftovers

The Top Ten Things (we didn't cover)

Networking is such a huge subject, we couldn't hope to cover everything in just one book.

But before we turn you loose on the world, we want to add a few more things to your toolbox. Some of these things are in all the network books, so we thought we could squeeze them in here. Some of these things are higher level, and we want you to at least be familiar with the terminology and basic concepts. So before you put the book down, take a read through these tidbits.

#1 Network topologies 470

#2 Installing Wireshark 472

#3 How to get to the console or terminal 474

#4 The TCP Stack 475

#5 VLANS 476

#6 Cisco IOS Simulators 476

#7 BGP 477

#8 VPN 477

#9 Intrusion Detection Systems 478

#10 Cisco Certification 478

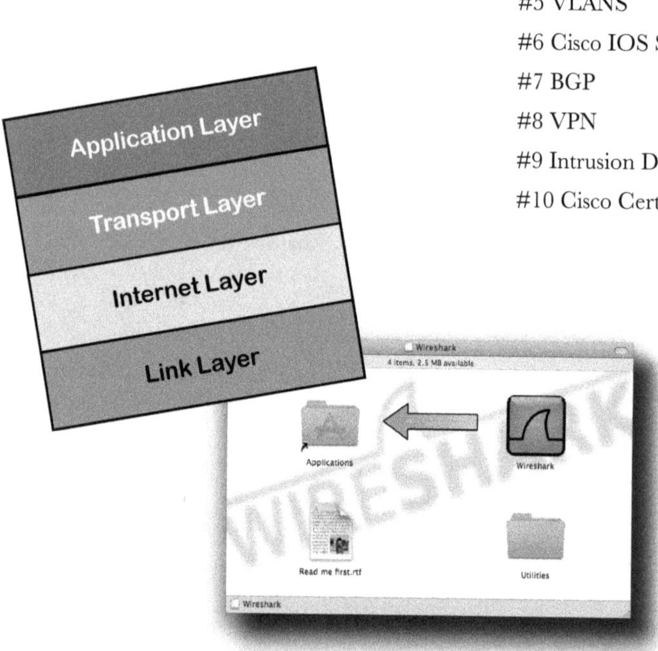

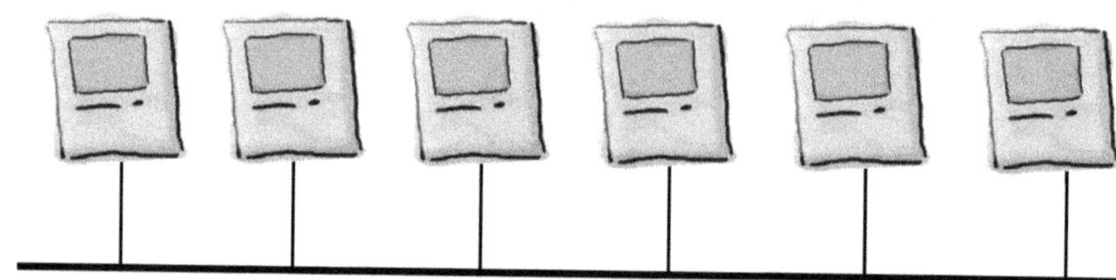

ascii tables

Looking Things Up

Where would you be without some trusty ASCII tables?

Understanding network protocols isn't always enough. Sooner or later, you're going to need to look up ASCII codes so you can understand what secrets are being passed around your network. In this appendix, you'll find a whole bunch of ASCII codes. Whether you prefer binary, hexadecimal, or good old decimal, we've got just the codes you need.

ASCII tables 0-28 480
ASCII code tables 29-57 481
ASCII code tables 58-87 482
ASCII code tables 88-117 483
ASCII code tables 118-127 484

installing bind

Getting a Server to talk DNS

Every good network professional needs a good DNS server. And the most commonly used DNS server on the Internet is BIND. Installing BIND is fairly simple, but just in case you need some extra reassurance, here are some handy instructions on how to do it.

#1 Installing BIND on Windows (XP, 2000, Vista) 486
#2 Installing BIND Mac OS X Server 487
#3 Installing BIND Mac OS X Client & Linux 487

Intro

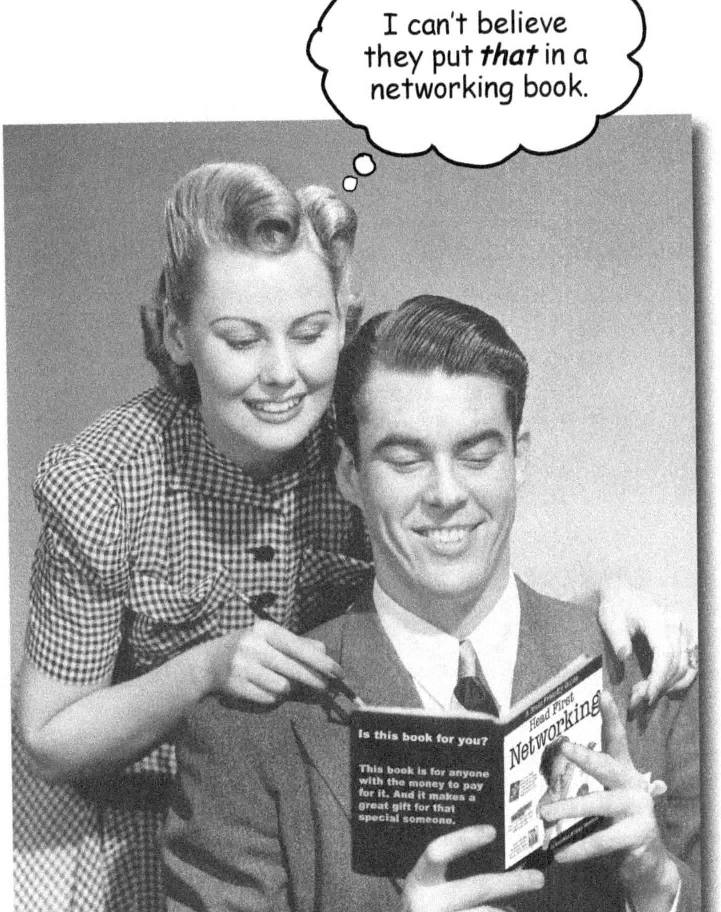

In this section we answer the burning question: "So why DID they put that in a networking book?"

Who is this book for?

If you can answer "yes" to all of these:

1. Do you need to learn networking for a job, for a class (like CCNA), or just because you think it's about time you learned the difference between a switch and a router?
2. Do you want to learn, understand, and remember how to run an industrial-strength packet sniffer, set up a Domain Name System server, build firewall packet filters, and configure routing protocols like EIGRP?
3. Do you prefer stimulating dinner party conversation to dry, dull, academic lectures?

this book is for you.

Who should probably back away from this book?

If you can answer "yes" to any of these:

1. Are you completely new to computers?
2. Are you a CCNA or CCNP looking for a reference book?
3. Are you afraid to try something different? Would you rather have a root canal than mix stripes with plaid? Do you believe that a technical book can't be serious if it anthropomorphizes multimeters and oscilloscopes?

this book is not for you.

[Note from marketing: this book is for anyone with a credit card.]

We know what you're thinking

"How can *this* be a serious networking book?"

"What's with all the graphics?"

"Can I actually *learn* it this way?"

We know what your *brain* is thinking

Your brain thinks THIS is important.
Great. Only 488 more dull, dry, boring pages.
Your brain thinks THIS isn't worth saving.

Your brain craves novelty. It's always searching, scanning, *waiting* for something unusual. It was built that way, and it helps you stay alive.

So what does your brain do with all the routine, ordinary, normal things you encounter? Everything it *can* to stop them from interfering with the brain's *real* job—recording things that *matter*. It doesn't bother saving the boring things; they never make it past the "this is obviously not important" filter.

How does your brain *know* what's important? Suppose you're out for a day hike and a tiger jumps in front of you, what happens inside your head and body?

Neurons fire. Emotions crank up. *Chemicals surge.*

And that's how your brain knows...

This must be important! Don't forget it!

But imagine you're at home, or in a library. It's a safe, warm, tiger-free zone. You're studying. Getting ready for an exam. Or trying to learn some tough technical topic your boss thinks will take a week, ten days at the most.

Just one problem. Your brain's trying to do you a big favor. It's trying to make sure that this *obviously* non-important content doesn't clutter up scarce resources. Resources that are better spent storing the really *big* things. Like tigers. Like the danger of fire. Like how you should never have posted those "party" photos on your Facebook page. And there's no simple way to tell your brain, "Hey brain, thank you very much, but no matter how dull this book is, and how little I'm registering on the emotional Richter scale right now, I really *do* want you to keep this stuff around."

We think of a "Head First" reader as a learner.

So what does it take to *learn* something? First, you have to *get* it, then make sure you don't *forget* it. It's not about pushing facts into your head. Based on the latest research in cognitive science, neurobiology, and educational psychology, *learning* takes a lot more than text on a page. We know what turns your brain on.

Some of the Head First learning principles:

Make it visual. Images are far more memorable than words alone, and make learning much more effective (up to 89% improvement in recall and transfer studies). It also makes things more understandable. **Put the words within or near the graphics** they relate to, rather than on the bottom or on another page, and learners will be up to *twice* as likely to solve problems related to the content.

Use a conversational and personalized style. In recent studies, students performed up to 40% better on post-learning tests if the content spoke directly to the reader, using a first-person, conversational style rather than taking a formal tone. Tell stories instead of lecturing. Use casual language. Don't take yourself too seriously. Which would *you* pay more attention to: a stimulating dinner party companion, or a lecture?

Get the learner to think more deeply. In other words, unless you actively flex your neurons, nothing much happens in your head. A reader has to be motivated, engaged, curious, and inspired to solve problems, draw conclusions, and generate new knowledge. And for that, you need challenges, exercises, and thought-provoking questions, and activities that involve both sides of the brain and multiple senses.

Get—and keep—the reader's attention. We've all had the "I really want to learn this but I can't stay awake past page one" experience. Your brain pays attention to things that are out of the ordinary, interesting, strange, eye-catching, unexpected. Learning a new, tough, technical topic doesn't have to be boring. Your brain will learn much more quickly if it's not.

Touch their emotions. We now know that your ability to remember something is largely dependent on its emotional content. You remember what you care about. You remember when you *feel* something. No, we're not talking heart-wrenching stories about a boy and his dog. We're talking emotions like surprise, curiosity, fun, "what the...?" , and the feeling of "I Rule!" that comes when you solve a puzzle, learn something everybody else thinks is hard, or realize you know something that "I'm more technical than thou" Bob from engineering *doesn't*.

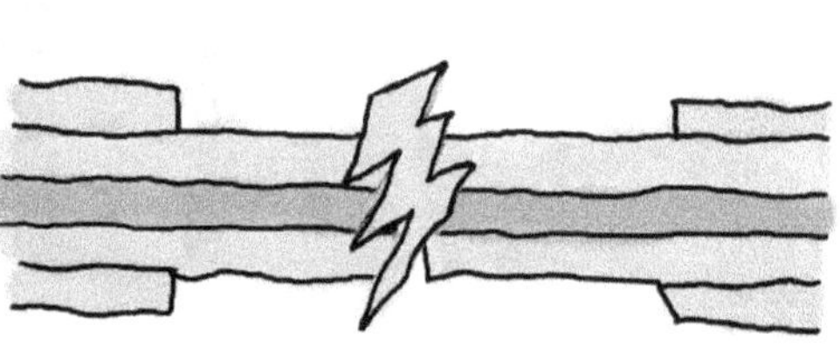

Metacognition: thinking about thinking

If you really want to learn, and you want to learn more quickly and more deeply, pay attention to how you pay attention. Think about how you think. Learn how you learn.

Most of us did not take courses on metacognition or learning theory when we were growing up. We were *expected* to learn, but rarely *taught* to learn.

But we assume that if you're holding this book, you really want to learn networking. And you probably don't want to spend a lot of time. If you want to use what you read in this book, you need to *remember* what you read. And for that, you've got to *understand* it. To get the most from this book, or *any* book or learning experience, take responsibility for your brain. Your brain on *this* content.

The trick is to get your brain to see the new material you're learning as Really Important. Crucial to your well-being. As important as a tiger. Otherwise, you're in for a constant battle, with your brain doing its best to keep the new content from sticking.

I wonder how
I can trick my brain
into remembering
this stuff...

So just how *DO* you get your brain to treat networking like it was a hungry tiger?

There's the slow, tedious way, or the faster, more effective way. The slow way is about sheer repetition. You obviously know that you *are* able to learn and remember even the dullest of topics if you keep pounding the same thing into your brain. With enough repetition, your brain says, "This doesn't *feel* important to him, but he keeps looking at the same thing *over* and *over* and *over*, so I suppose it must be."

The faster way is to do ***anything that increases brain activity,*** especially different *types* of brain activity. The things on the previous page are a big part of the solution, and they're all things that have been proven to help your brain work in your favor. For example, studies show that putting words *within* the pictures they describe (as opposed to somewhere else in the page, like a caption or in the body text) causes your brain to try to makes sense of how the words and picture relate, and this causes more neurons to fire. More neurons firing = more chances for your brain to *get* that this is something worth paying attention to, and possibly recording.

A conversational style helps because people tend to pay more attention when they perceive that they're in a conversation, since they're expected to follow along and hold up their end. The amazing thing is, your brain doesn't necessarily *care* that the "conversation" is between you and a book! On the other hand, if the writing style is formal and dry, your brain perceives it the same way you experience being lectured to while sitting in a roomful of passive attendees. No need to stay awake.

But pictures and conversational style are just the beginning…

Here's what WE did:

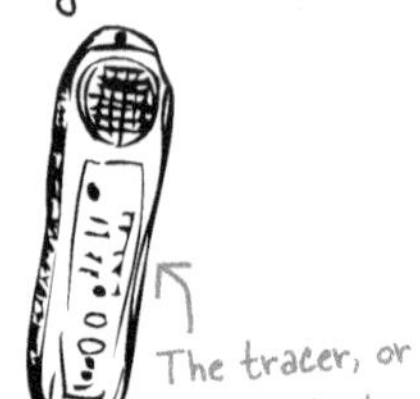

<Boop> Hey, I hear you! Electrons live and active round here. <Boop>
The tracer, or tone-detector.

We used ***pictures***, because your brain is tuned for visuals, not text. As far as your brain's concerned, a picture really *is* worth a thousand words. And when text and pictures work together, we embedded the text *in* the pictures because your brain works more effectively when the text is *within* the thing the text refers to, as opposed to in a caption or buried in the text somewhere.

We used ***redundancy***, saying the same thing in *different* ways and with different media types, and *multiple senses*, to increase the chance that the content gets coded into more than one area of your brain.

We used concepts and pictures in ***unexpected*** ways because your brain is tuned for novelty, and we used pictures and ideas with at least *some* ***emotional*** *content*, because your brain is tuned to pay attention to the biochemistry of emotions. That which causes you to *feel* something is more likely to be remembered, even if that feeling is nothing more than a little ***humor***, ***surprise***, or ***interest.***

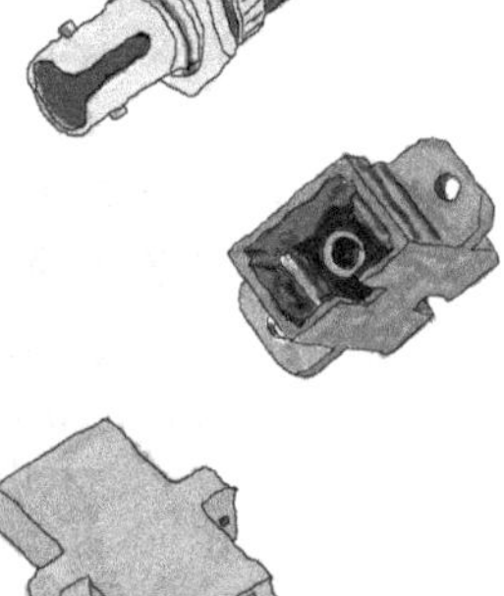

We used a personalized, ***conversational style***, because your brain is tuned to pay more attention when it believes you're in a conversation than if it thinks you're passively listening to a presentation. Your brain does this even when you're *reading*.

We included more than 80 ***activities***, because your brain is tuned to learn and remember more when you ***do*** things than when you *read* about things. And we made the exercises challenging-yet-do-able, because that's what most people prefer.

We used ***multiple learning styles***, because *you* might prefer step-by-step procedures, while someone else wants to understand the big picture first, and someone else just wants to see an example. But regardless of your own learning preference, *everyone* benefits from seeing the same content represented in multiple ways.

We include content for ***both sides of your brain***, because the more of your brain you engage, the more likely you are to learn and remember, and the longer you can stay focused. Since working one side of the brain often means giving the other side a chance to rest, you can be more productive at learning for a longer period of time.

And we included ***stories*** and exercises that present ***more than one point of view,*** because your brain is tuned to learn more deeply when it's forced to make evaluations and judgments.

We included ***challenges***, with exercises, and by asking ***questions*** that don't always have a straight answer, because your brain is tuned to learn and remember when it has to *work* at something. Think about it—you can't get your *body* in shape just by *watching* people at the gym. But we did our best to make sure that when you're working hard, it's on the *right* things. That ***you're not spending one extra dendrite*** processing a hard-to-understand example, or parsing difficult, jargon-laden, or overly terse text.

We used ***people***. In stories, examples, pictures, etc., because, well, because *you're* a person. And your brain pays more attention to *people* than it does to *things*.

Here's what YOU can do to bend your brain into submission

So, we did our part. The rest is up to you. These tips are a starting point; listen to your brain and figure out what works for you and what doesn't. Try new things.

Cut this out and stick it on your refrigerator.

---

1 **Slow down. The more you understand, the less you have to memorize.**

Don't just *read*. Stop and think. When the book asks you a question, don't just skip to the answer. Imagine that someone really *is* asking the question. The more deeply you force your brain to think, the better chance you have of learning and remembering.

2 **Do the exercises. Write your own notes.**

We put them in, but if we did them for you, that would be like having someone else do your workouts for you. And don't just *look* at the exercises. **Use a pencil.** There's plenty of evidence that physical activity *while* learning can increase the learning.

3 **Read the "There are No Dumb Questions"**

That means all of them. They're not optional sidebars, ***they're part of the core content!*** Don't skip them.

4 **Make this the last thing you read before bed. Or at least the last challenging thing.**

Part of the learning (especially the transfer to long-term memory) happens *after* you put the book down. Your brain needs time on its own, to do more processing. If you put in something new during that processing time, some of what you just learned will be lost.

5 **Talk about it. Out loud.**

Speaking activates a different part of the brain. If you're trying to understand something, or increase your chance of remembering it later, say it out loud. Better still, try to explain it out loud to someone else. You'll learn more quickly, and you might uncover ideas you hadn't known were there when you were reading about it.

6 **Drink water. Lots of it.**

Your brain works best in a nice bath of fluid. Dehydration (which can happen before you ever feel thirsty) decreases cognitive function.

7 **Listen to your brain.**

Pay attention to whether your brain is getting overloaded. If you find yourself starting to skim the surface or forget what you just read, it's time for a break. Once you go past a certain point, you won't learn faster by trying to shove more in, and you might even hurt the process.

Feel something.

Your brain needs to know that this *matters*. Get involved with the stories. Make up your own captions for the photos. Groaning over a bad joke is *still* better than feeling nothing at all.

9 **Get your hands dirty!**

There's only one way to learn to network: get your hands dirty. And that's what you're going to do throughout this book. Networking is a skill, and the only way to get good at it is to practice. We're going to give you a lot of practice: every chapter has exercises that pose a problem for you to solve. Don't just skip over them—a lot of the learning happens when you solve the exercises. We included a solution to each exercise—don't be afraid to peek at the solution if you get stuck! (It's easy to get snagged on something small.) But try to solve the problem before you look at the solution. And definitely get it working before you move on to the next part of the book.

Read Me

This is a learning experience, not a reference book. We deliberately stripped out everything that might get in the way of learning whatever it is we're working on at that point in the book. And the first time through, you need to begin at the beginning, because the book makes assumptions about what you've already seen and learned.

We begin by teaching basic concepts like cabling and physical layout, then we move on to signals and hardware, and then onto stuff like wireless networking, security, and network design.

While it's important to create well-designed networks, before you can, you need to understand the basic components and concepts of networking. So we begin by having you physically layout simple networks and work with network cables. Then, a bit later in the book, we show you good network design practices. By then you'll have a solid grasp of the basic information and can focus on the advanced aspects of network design.

We don't cover every networking technology on the planet.

While we could have put every single networking technology in this book, we thought you'd prefer to have a reasonably liftable book that would teach you the networking technologies that will get you up and running. We give you the ones you need to know, the ones you'll use 95 percent of the time. And when you're done with this book, you'll have the confidence to go research that hot new technology and implement on your kickass network.

We intentionally cover things differently than the other networking books out there.

Trust us. We've read a lot of networking books. We decided to write a book that our students could use, a practical book that didn't start out with the OSI layer model. We like it when our students stay awake in class. We also cover stuff we couldn't find in other books: all that structural stuff that keeps your cables neat and out of sight; how signals get encoded into binary, hex, and ascii; and how reading blueprints can help you lay out your network.

The activities are NOT optional.

The exercises and activities are not add-ons; they're part of the core content of the book. Some of them are to help with memory, some are for understanding, and some will help you apply what you've learned. ***Don't skip the exercises.*** The crossword puzzles are the only thing you don't *have* to do, but they're good for giving your brain a chance to think about the words and terms you've been learning in a different context.

The redundancy is intentional and important.

One distinct difference in a Head First book is that we want you to *really* get it. And we want you to finish the book remembering what you've learned. Most reference books don't have retention and recall as a goal, but this book is about *learning*, so you'll see some of the same concepts come up more than once.

The book doesn't end here.

We love it when you can find fun and useful extra stuff on book companion sites. You'll find extra stuff on networking at the following two urls:
http://www.headfirstlabs.com/books/hfnw/
http://www.hfnetworking.com

The Brain Power exercises don't have answers.

For some of them, there is no right answer, and for others, part of the learning experience of the Brain Power activities is for you to decide if and when your answers are right. In some of the Brain Power exercises, you will find hints to point you in the right direction.

The technical review team

Jonathan Moore

Tim Olson

Rohn Wood

Technical Reviewers:

Johnathan Moore has ten years of experience as a network technical consultant and contractor. He owns Forerunner Design, a Web design and development business located in Wenatchee Washington.

Tim Olson teaches computer engineering and physics at Salish Kootenai College and is on the science team for the NASA Mars Science Laboratory mission. He enjoys skiing and horseback riding with his family in the mountains of western Montana.

Rohn Wood lives and works in Montana trying to bring high performance computing to the old West. A full time employee of the University of Montana and half-time employee of the University of Washington, he makes his living off his UNIX chops and works remotely from his home in the Bitterroot Mountains with a view down into the valley a few miles from Travelers Rest where Lewis and Clark laid over with Corps of Discovery two hundred years ago. An 18 year user of Linux and a veteran of RS232 Gandalf Boxes, ThinNET, and Token Ring, Rohn appreciates the need for learning the hard way and RTFM.

Acknowledgments

Brett McLaughlin

Our editor:

Thanks to our editor, Brett McLaughlin, who dove into this project when he had a massive load of other things to do. Brett helped us by putting our ideas on trial, opening our eyes to things we didn't see, and pushing us to produce the best book we possibly could. Brett, you are a juggernaut of production! Ryan would especially like to mention that his sessions with Brett and Al kept him going during a difficult life transition. Thanks, guys!

The O'Reilly Team:

Thanks to Dawn Griffiths for the excellent and magical work she did to shape this book up and make it look beautiful.

Thanks to Catherine Nolan for taking a chance on two "fliers" from Montana.

Thanks to Laurie Petrycki for gambling on us and welcoming us to Boston and O'Reilly Media as if we were long-lost family.

Thanks also to the Head First folks we met in Boston, especially our brothers and sisters-in-arms: David Griffiths, Dawn Griffiths, Lynn Beighley, Cary Collett and Louise Barr. Thanks to Karen Shaner, Brittany Smith, and Caitrin McCullough.

We will never forget the day we discovered the Head First series at the bookstore. Thanks to Kathy Sierra and Bert Bates for lighting up the neurons of geeks everywhere.

Thanks to Tim O'Reilly for his vision in creating the best geek press ever!

Al's Friends and Family:

Without Emily, my wife, I would have not been able to write this book. She took care of business while I hunkered down in the den all those countless weekends and evenings. I love you honey! Without Ella and Austin's patience with their dad, this would have been a much harder project to accomplish. I love you guys too! Finally, my faithful dog CC, she was always with me in the den, sleeping of course.

Ryan's Friends and Family:

Thank you to my daughter, Josefina, and my son, Vincenzo, who love books as much as I do. Thanks to my sweetie, Shonna Sims, who believed in me just when I was about to give up on this book. Thanks also to my Mom and Pops, my brother Jeff, my nieces Claire and Quinn, Dr. Tracee Jamison, Yumi Hooks, Dr. Giuseppi Onello, Curtis Cladouhos, Garret Jaros, Henrietta Goodman, and Dr. Paul Hansen (without whom I never would have gotten into technology in the first place). A huge thanks to my co-author, Al, about whom people often ask, "Is that your brother?" In many ways, he is.

A Special Thank You from Al and Ryan:

Thanks to the IT students of Salish Kootenai College, without whom we would never have been inspired to write this book in the first place.

Safari® Books Online

When you see a Safari® icon on the cover of your favorite technology book that means the book is available online through Safari Books Online.

Safari offers a solution that's better than e-books. It's a virtual library that lets you easily search thousands of top tech books, cut and paste code samples, download chapters, and find quick answers when you need the most accurate, current information. Try it for free at `http://safaribooksonline.com`.

1 fixing physical networks

Walking on Wires

Just plug in that cable and the network's up, right? Network cables silently do their job, pushing our data from here to there, faster than we can blink. But what happens when it all goes wrong? Organizations rely on their networks so much that the business falls apart when the network fails. That's why knowing how to fix physical networks is so important. Keep reading, and we'll show you how to troubleshoot your networks with ease and fix physical problems. You'll soon be in full control of your networks.

Coconut Airways has a network problem

There's no better way to travel between islands than by seaplane, and Coconut Airways has an entire fleet. They offer scenic tours, excursions and a handy shuttle service between the islands. Their service is proving popular with tourists and locals alike.

Demand for flights is sky-high, but Coconut Airways has a problem—whenever staff try to use the flight booking system, they're presented with a network error message:

Coconut Airways depends on their flight booking system. Without it, passengers can't book seats, and it's bringing their flights to a standstill. What's more, no passengers means no money.

Coconut Airways needs to get their network up and running again, and fast. Think you can help them out?

Here's the wiring closet for Coconut Airways. What sort of problems do you see? Circle each one.

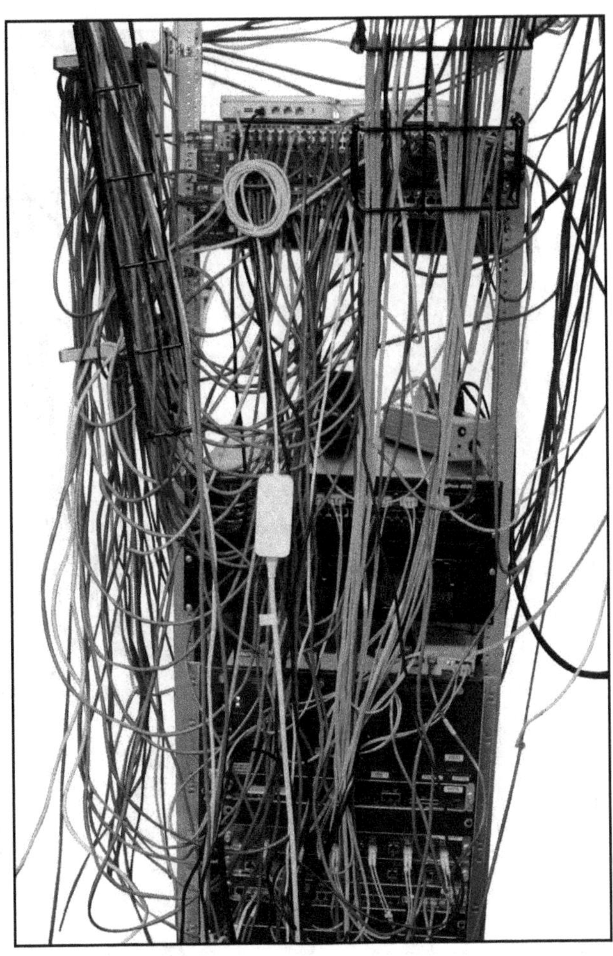

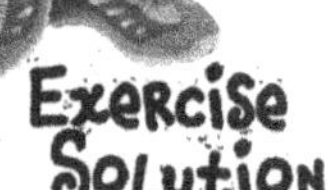

Here's the wiring closet for Coconut Airways. What sort of problems do you see? Circle each one.

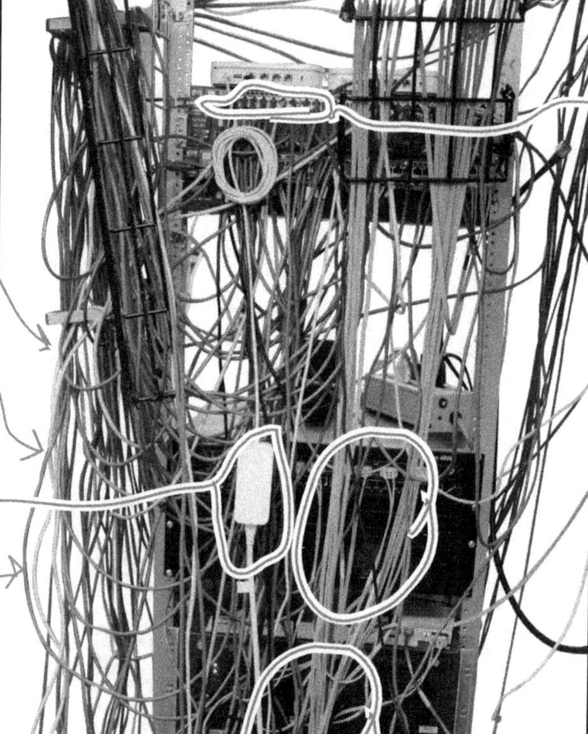

Bind your cables and run them along a stable surface. That way you reduce tangling, snags, and confusion.
Which cable goes where? Label your wires so that you can troubleshoot problems more efficiently.
Don't dangle your power supplies. Gravity and a little nudge could drop your power.
Label your devices on the front and the back.
You don't want fiber-optic cables to bend much. All of the weight of the cables resting on one another might cause problems in the long run.
Check your connectors and ports regularly. You never know when a connector will pop, especially when you have dangling cables.
Looks like there's a break in the flight booking network cable. That's probably what's causing the network error message on the flight booking system.
Put your fiber optic devices closer to where the cables come in to the rack. In this case, the top of the rack would be best.

The booking system network cable is busted

It looks like a break in the flight booking network cable is giving the Coconut Airways staff network errors. If we can fix the network cable, that should get rid of the messages, and Coconut Airways will be able to book passengers on their flights again.

So how do you think we should fix the network cable?

How do we fix the cable?

There are two key things we need to do in order to mend the cable and get the flight booking system up and running again.

We need to cut out the broken part of the cable.
It's the break in the cable that's causing us the problem, so let's get rid of it.

RJ-45 connector
The jacket and the wires inside appear to have been chewed.

We need to attach a connector.
By cutting out the broken part of the cable, we lose the connector on the end. We need the connector so that we can plug the cable into things, so we'll need to put a new one on.

But how do we do this?

At the moment we don't know anything about the sort of cable it is, and the type of cable has an effect on how we go about things.

So what sort of cable are we dealing with here?

What sorts of network cables do you already know about? How do you think they are different from one another? Why?

Introducing the CAT-5 cable

The sort of cable running the main Coconut Airways network is called a Category 5 cable for Ethernet, or ***CAT-5*** cable. It has two distinguishing features. First of all, it has an unshielded twisted pair cable or ***UTP*** cable. Secondly, it takes an ***RJ-45*** connector on either end. Most Ethernet networks run on CAT-5 cables.

CAT-5 cables have print on the outside giving you important information about the cable. As an example, you can look on the outside of the cable to see what type it is, what the speed is, and any relevant standards.

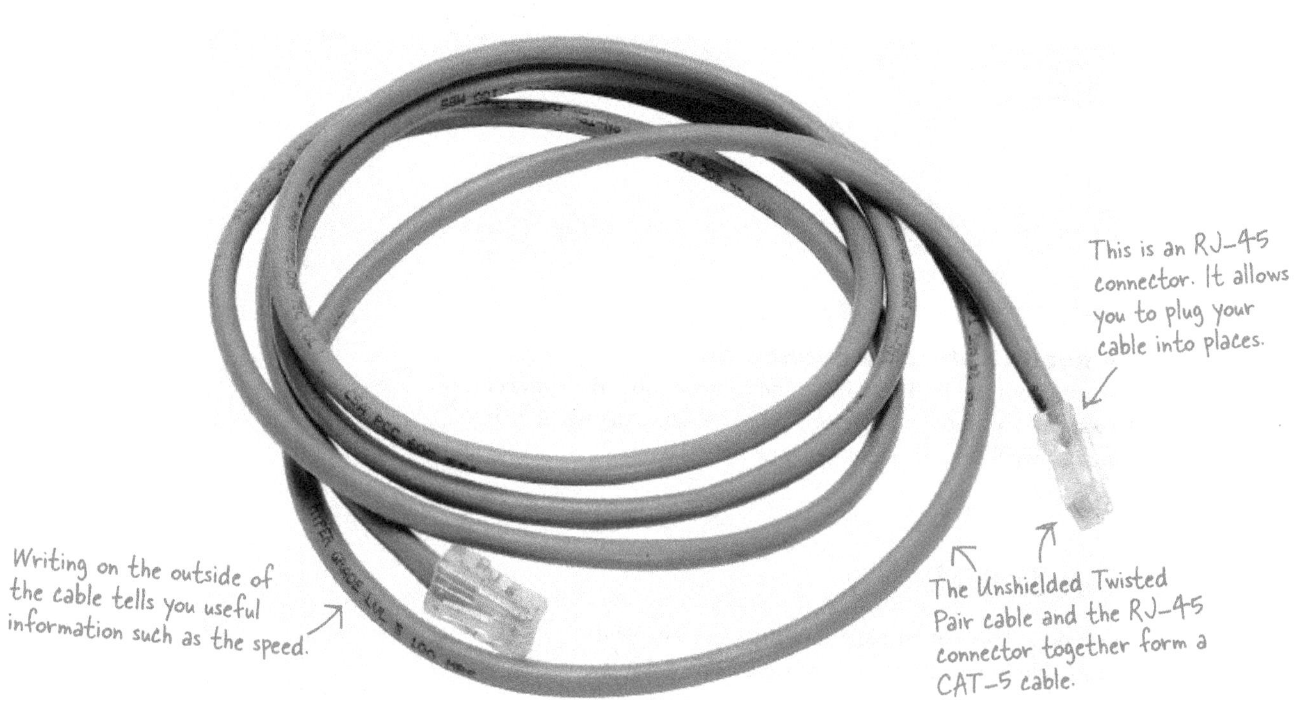

This is an RJ-45 connector. It allows you to plug your cable into places.
Writing on the outside of the cable tells you useful information such as the speed.
The Unshielded Twisted Pair cable and the RJ-45 connector together form a CAT-5 cable.

So what's inside a CAT-5 cable? Let's take a look.

The CAT-5 cable dissected

If you open up a CAT-5 cable, you'll find eight colored wires twisted into four pairs. One pair is brown, another pair is blue, another pair is green, and the final pair is orange. Each pair consists of one plain and one striped wire.

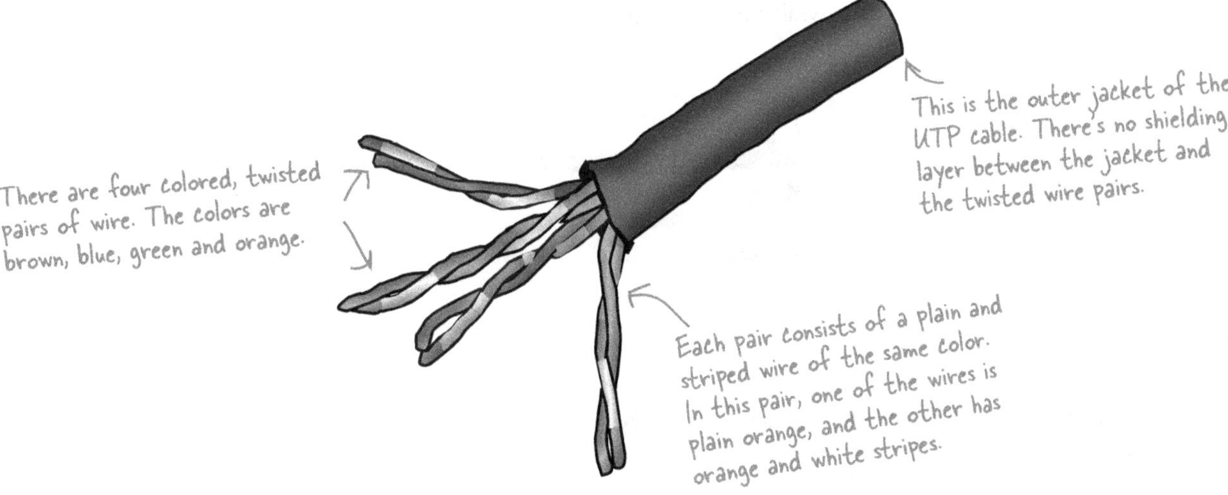

There are four colored, twisted pairs of wire. The colors are brown, blue, green and orange.
This is the outer jacket of the UTP cable. There's no shielding layer between the jacket and the twisted wire pairs.
Each pair consists of a plain and striped wire of the same color. In this pair, one of the wires is plain orange, and the other has orange and white stripes.

So why are the pairs twisted?

The problem with wires that aren't twisted is that they generate magnetic fields that interfere with the signal carried on the wire. This means that you can get electromagnetic interference and crosstalk—both of which are bad for your network data.

When the wires are *twisted*, the magnetic field around the wire is effectively disrupted so that any interference is reduced. The more twists there are in the pairs, the better.

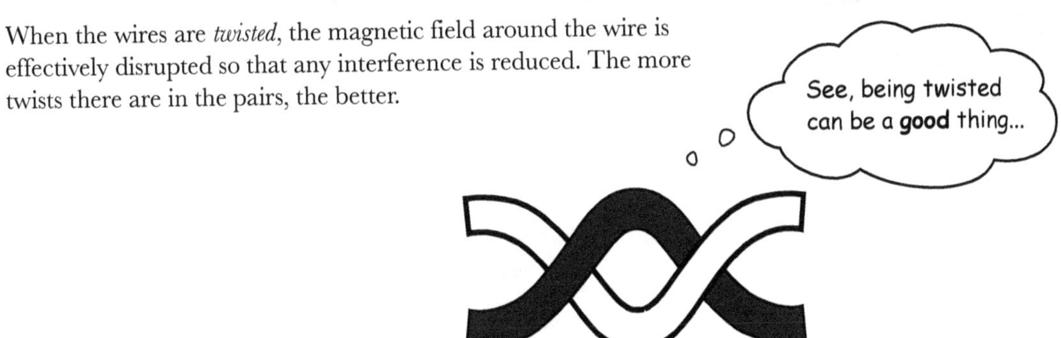

See, being twisted can be a **good** thing...

It's not just the twists in the wires that are significant, the colors are important too. Let's take a closer look.

So what's with all the colors?

The paired wires in a CAT-5 cable are colored for a reason. Each color has a specific meaning, and so does the solidity of the color.

Orange and green wires send and receive data.
The orange pair sends data, while the green pair receives data.

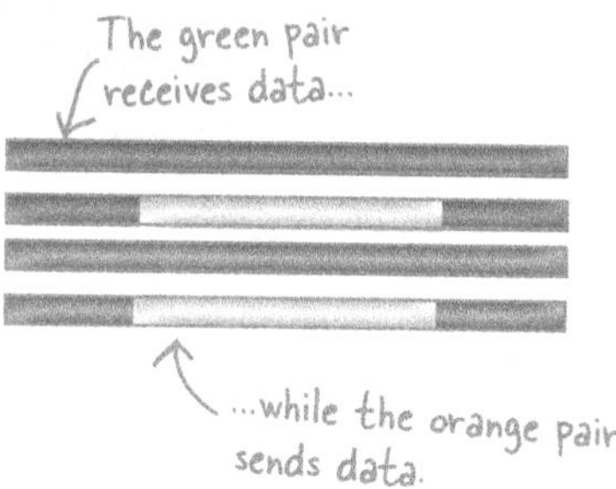

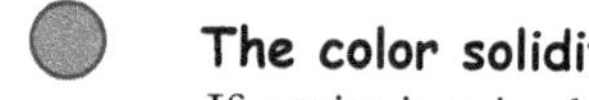

The color solidity shows the wire polarity.
If a wire is striped, then this means that it is positive. If a wire is solid, then the wire is negative.

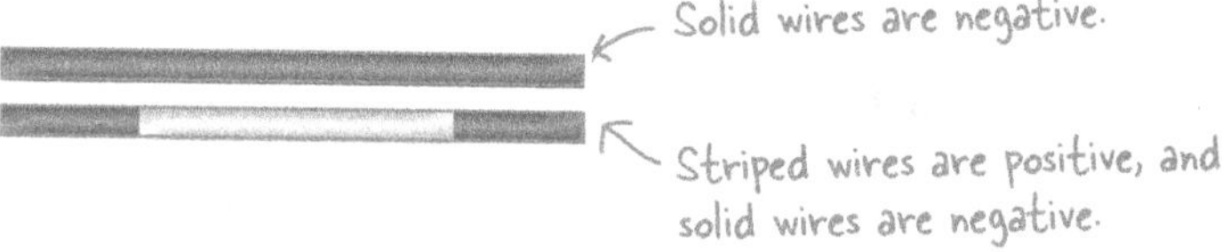

Solid wires are negative.
Striped wires are positive, and solid wires are negative.

Blue and brown wires are reserved for future bandwidth capacity.
Blue and brown wires don't do anything yet, but they will in the future. The cable standards folks designed CAT-5 with the extra colored wires so that they could be used for higher bandwidths in the future.

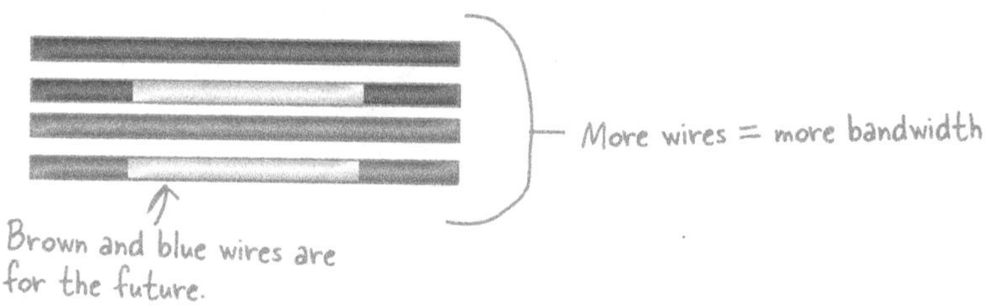

Brown and blue wires are for the future.

Bandwidth tells us how much data can flow through the wires on a cable. Network speed tells us the rate at which data can move on a wire. To get an idea about bandwidth and network speed, visit the following site and test the connection you're using: **http://www.speedtest.net/**

Press the "Begin Test" button on speedtest.net...

...and you get a report on your download and upload capacity.

Mb/s stands for megabits per second..

BRAIN POWER

What's the difference between bandwidth and speed on a network cable?

....

....

the Scholar's Corner

bandwidth: the transmission capacity of a computer network or telecommunication system.

speed: the rate at which something is able to move.

there are no Dumb Questions

Q: What's the difference between bandwidth and speed?

A: Bandwidth is a capacity; speed is a rate. Bandwidth tells you the maximum amount of data that your network can transmit. Speed tells you the rate at which the data can travel. The bandwidth for a CAT-5 cable is 10/100 Base-T. The speed of a CAT-5 cable changes depending on conditions.

Q: What is Base-T?

A: Base-T refers to the different standards for Ethernet transmission rates. The 10 Base-T standard transfers data at 10 megabits per second (Mbps). The 100 Base-T standard transfers data at 100 Mbps. The 1000 Base-T standard transfers data at a massive 1000 Mbps.

Q: What's the difference between megabits per second (Mbps) and megabytes per second (MBps)?

A: Megabits per second (Mbps) is a bandwidth rate used in the telecommunications and computer networking field. One megabit equals one million bursts of electrical current (aka binary pulses). Megabytes per second (MBps) is a data transfer rate used in computing. One megabyte equals 1, 048, 576 bytes, and one byte equals 8 binary digits (aka bits).

Q: Aren't there newer, faster cable standards like CAT-5e and CAT-6?

A: CAT-5e and CAT-6 cables are newer standards for cables. We cover CAT-5 because it's the base framework for the higher cable standards. CAT-5e and CAT-6 have bandwidths of 10/100/1000 Base-T.

Q: Can I build my own CAT-5e and CAT-6 cables?

A: Building a CAT-5e cable is generally no more difficult than building a CAT-5 cable. We don't recommend building your own CAT-6 cables because of the precision needs of the cable.

Let's fix the broken CAT-5 cable

Now that we know more about how CAT-5 cables work, let's see if you can fix the Coconut Airways network cable. All you need is a pair of wire cutters, a utility knife, a crimping tool, and an RJ-45 connector.

1. 
Cut the broken part out.
Cut the cable well before the break to ensure that you have a good set of wire ends. Make the cut as straight as possible so that the individual wires are the same length.

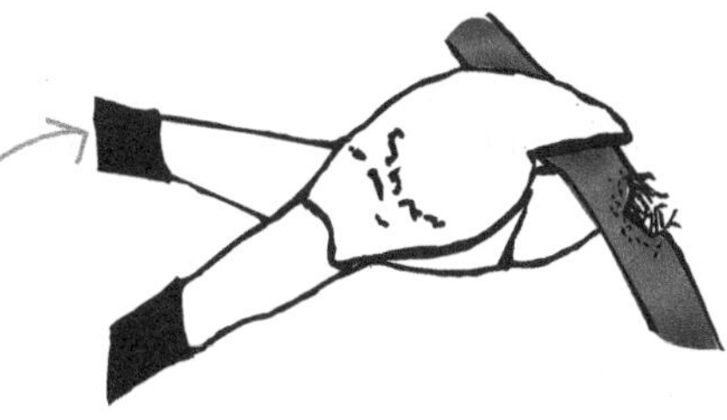

2. 
Strip the cable cover back on the good end.
Cut carefully along the length of the jacket with a blade, making sure you don't cut into the insulation of the bundled wires inside the jacket. A good cut length is somewhere between 1/2 and 1 inch. Once you've done that, pull the cable jacket apart and peel it back to expose the twisted pairs.

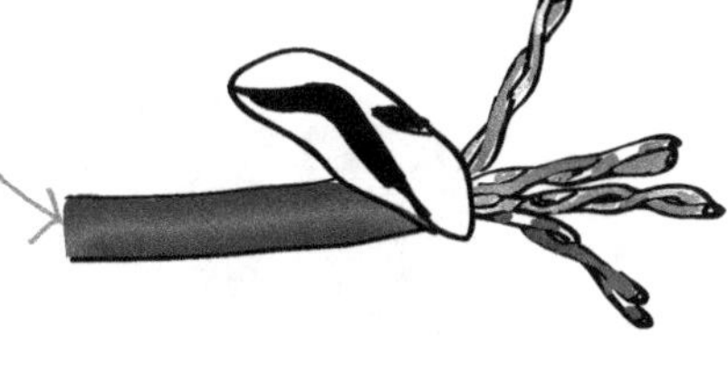

3. 
Untwist and flatten the individual wires.
Untwist the wires so that you can line them up with the slots on the RJ-45 connector. Generally you need about1/2 inch of the wire to fit into the connector.

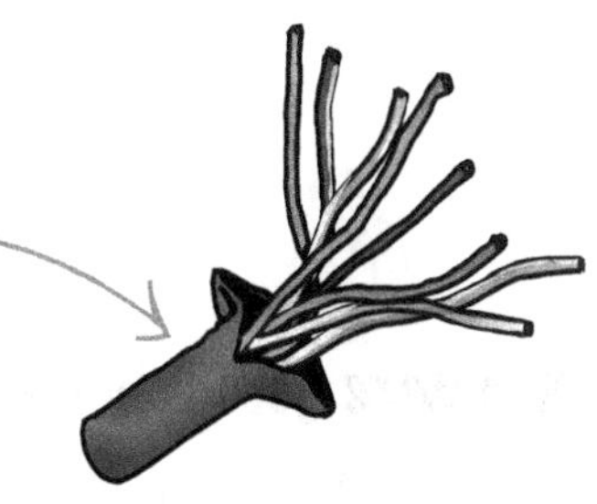

4. **Place each wire into the RJ-45 connector.**
Each wire fits into a slot in the RJ-45 connector. Just line up each wire with the relevant slot and you're good to go.

Now stop right there! Are you trying to get me **electrocuted** or something? How do I know which position each wire goes in? Do you expect me to just **guess**???

Where you put each wire is important.

Each wire needs to go into a particular slot in the RJ-45 connector, but at the moment we don't know which wire goes where. We need to know more about what's inside the RJ-45 connector.

A closer look at the RJ-45 connector

As we saw earlier, the connector at the end of a CAT-5 cable is called an RJ-45 connector. It allows you to plug your cable into a wall jack or the network port of a network device like a computer.

Each wire in the cable goes into a slot inside the RJ-45 connector, and this connects it to a pin in the connector.

Each wire in the cable goes into a slot in the RJ-45 connector. This fixes the wire to a pin in the connector.

So which wire goes where?

The position of each wire is important.

When you plug an RJ-45 connector into a jack, the pins on the connector make contact with pins in the jack. If the wires are in the correct position, this allows information, in the form of electrons, to flow. If the wires are in the wrong position, the information won't be able to get through.

The order of the wires in an RJ-45 connector conforms to one of two standards. These standards are ***568A*** and ***568B***.

568A and 568B Wiring Standards Up Close

568A and 568B are cabling standards that tell you which order your wires need to go in when fitting an RJ-45 cable.

The 568A wire order

If you're following the 568A wiring standard, you use the following wire order:

Striped green, solid green, striped orange, solid blue, striped blue, solid orange, striped brown, solid brown.

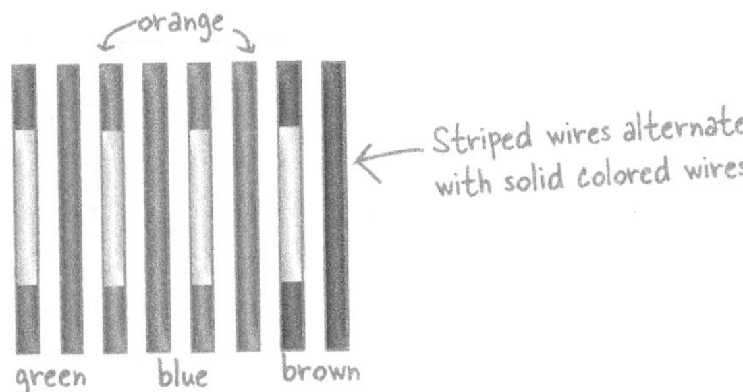

The 568B wire order

If you're following the 568B wiring standard, you use the following wire order instead:

Striped orange, solid orange, striped green, solid blue, striped blue, solid green, striped brown, solid brown.

green

The 568B wire order is like the 568A wire order but with the position of the green and orange wires switched around.

orange blue brown

Can you see any similarities between the 568A and 568B wire orders? The order for each standard is basically the same except the orange and green wires are switched over.

So which standard should you use?

When you attach an RJ-45 connector, the key thing is that both ends of the cable use the same standard. Before fitting a new RJ-45 connector, take a look at the other end of the cable. If the other end of the cable uses standard 568A for the RJ-45 wire order, then fit your new RJ-45 connector using the 568A standard. If it uses 568B, then use this standard instead.

Sharpen your pencil

The good end of the broken Coconut Airways network cable has an RJ-45 connector wired up using standard 568B. What should the wire order be on the other end? Draw a line between each wire and its rightful slot.

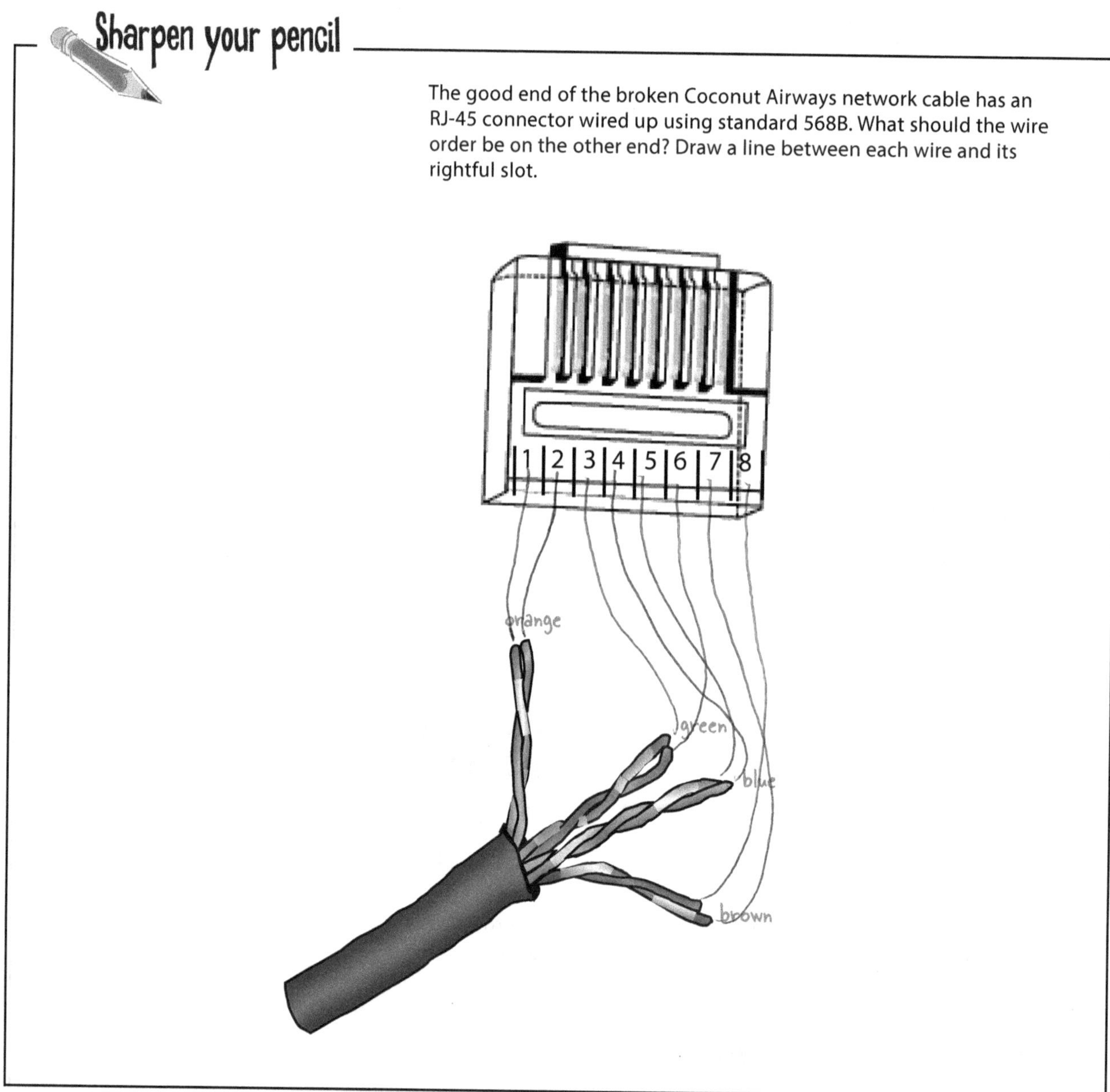

The Case of the Meteorologist and the RJ-45 Connector

Stranded in a remote research station after a heavy storm, Jack has to repair a CAT-5 cable that uses cabling standard 568B. Normally, he could jump on his favorite search engine to find the pin and wire color arrangement, but the storm has taken out his connection to the Internet.

Five Minute Mystery

Jack's in a panic. What can he do? If he doesn't repair the network soon, he'll lose crucial research data from his weather-monitoring instruments.

Suddenly, Jack has an idea and leaves the room armed with a pair of scissors. Five minutes later, the network's back up.

How did Jack solve the problem without looking up Standard 568B?

He opened up the RJ-45 connector to look at the wiring standard

Sharpen your pencil Solution

The good end of the broken Coconut Airways network cable has an RJ-45 connector wired up using standard 568B. What should the wire order be on the other end? Draw a line between each wire and its rightful slot.

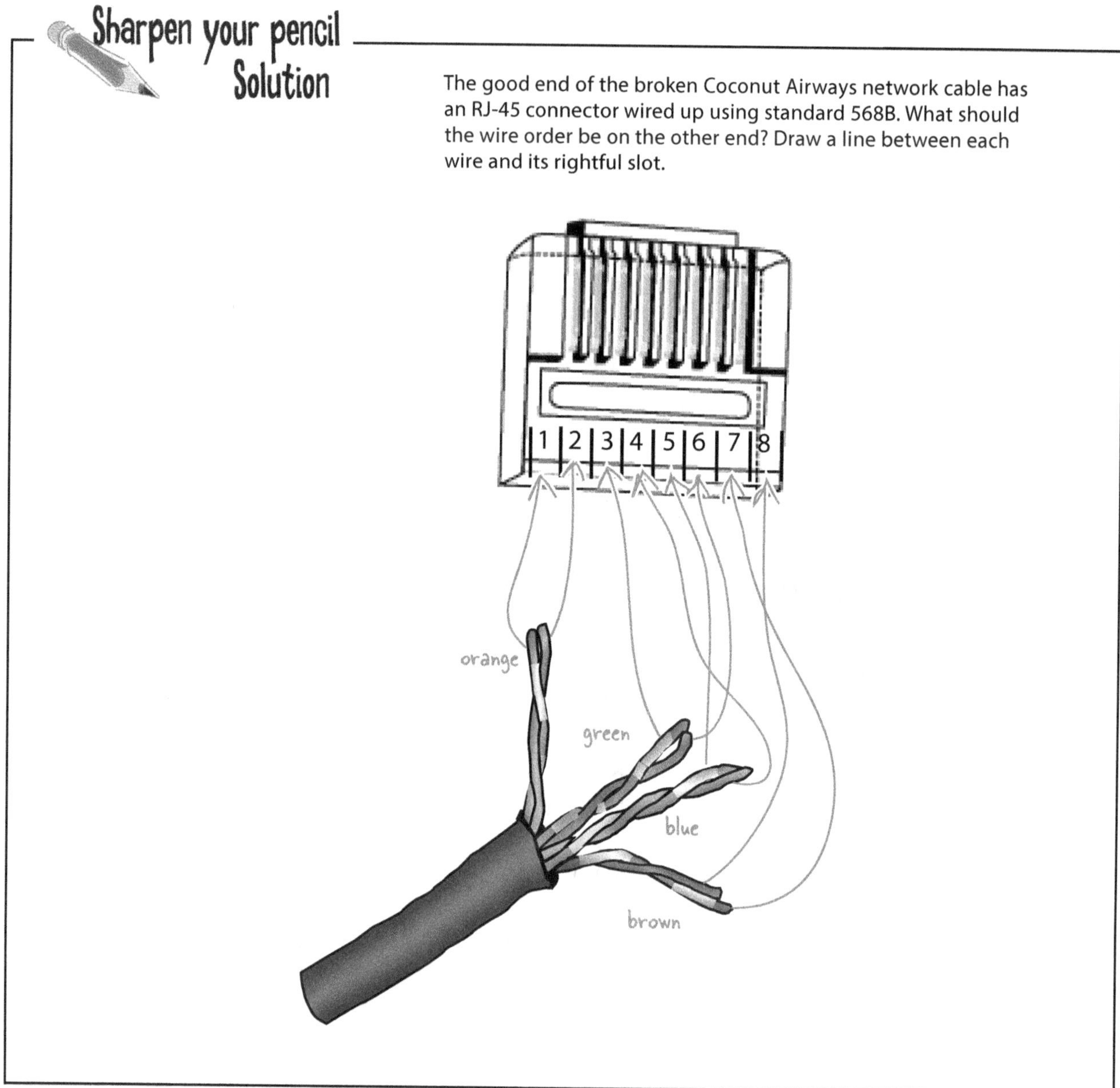

So what are the physical steps?

Now that we know how the wiring standards for the RJ-45 connectors work, let's have another go at fixing the broken CAT-5 network cable for Coconut Airways.

1. **Cut the broken part out.**
   Cut the cable well before the break to ensure that you have a good set of wire ends. Make the cut as straight as possible so that the individual wires are the same length.

2. **Strip the cable cover back on the good end.**
   Cut carefully along the length of the jacket with a blade, making sure you don't cut into the insulation of the bundled wires inside the jacket. A good cut length is somewhere between 1/2 and 1 inch. Once you've done that, pull the cable jacket apart and peel it back to expose the twisted pairs.

3. **Untwist and flatten the individual wires.**
   Untwist the wires so that you can line them up with the slots on the RJ-45 connector.

These are the steps we went through earlier.

4. **Check whether the other end of the cable follows wiring standard 568A or 568B.**
   Both ends of the cable need to follow the same wiring standard, so make a note of what the other end uses.

5. **Place each wire into the RJ-45 connector using the same standard as the other end.**

6. **Attach the connector to the cable with a crimping tool.**
   Once the lines are in their proper slots, place the RJ-45 into the crimping tool, and then squeeze the tool to crimp the RJ-45 snugly onto the cable. Check the end of the RJ-45 connector to ensure that the wire is seated correctly in each slot.

The Case of the Meteorologist and the RJ-45 Connector

How did Jack solve the problem without looking up Standard 568B?

After he left with the scissors, Jack found an old RJ-45 end that used Standard 568A. He cut off the connector, traced the wires to their pins and wrote down the order for Standard 568B by trading the orange and green wires' position in the wiring order.

there are no Dumb Questions

Q: Are you sure that a CAT-5 connector is called "RJ-45"? I've read that it's called an "8P8C" connector?

A: Through common use, we have come to call an 8P8C connector an RJ-45 connector. The acronym 8P8C stands for 8 positions, 8 contacts. The RJ-45 connector looks a lot like an 8P8C connector, so over time, many folks mislabeled the connector. Now, through that common but incorrect use, more people call an 8P8C connector an RJ-45 connector. Say "8P8C" to a network pro, and you may get a funny look.

Q: Why should I always use the same wiring standard on both ends of the cable?

A: If we don't use the same standard on both ends of the cable, we won't have a "straight-through" or patch cable; we'll have what's called a "crossover cable." In other words, we'll flip-flop the green and the orange wire pairs, and the send wires and receive wires will trade purposes. Always check the opposite end of the cable and match the wire pair configuration.

Q: What is a crossover cable used for?

A: Suppose you want to connect a laptop to a desktop computer. One way of doing this would be to use a crossover cable, a cable that can send and receive data on both ends at the same time. A crossover cable is different from a straight-through cable in that a straight-through cable can only send or receive data on one end at a time.

You could also use a switch or a hub to connect the two devices—but you'll see more about these later in the book.

Q: How long should I make my CAT-5 cable?

A: The general rule of thumb is that you measure the distance between the devices you want to connect and add one to two feet for flexibility of movement. The maximum length of CAT-5 is 328 feet (100 meters).

You fixed the CAT-5 cable

Thanks to you, the Coconut Airways flight bookings system is back in business. Before too long, all of their scheduled flights are fully booked and ready for take-off.

Hey, not so fast! Do you think I'm gonna fly these planes without being **paid**?
The Coconut Airways Pilot

BRAIN POWER

We fixed the flight booking network, but it looks like the network troubles aren't over for Coconut Airways. What do you think might have gone wrong?

Coconut Airways has more than one network

You've done a great job of fixing the flight booking system. Unfortunately, that's not the only network at Coconut Airways.

The Coconut Airways accounts and payroll systems run off a coaxial network down in the basement, and they've recently had a problem with the local wildlife getting into the building. It looks like a hungry critter has taken a good chunk out of one of the coaxial cables, and the damaged cable has brought things to a standstill.

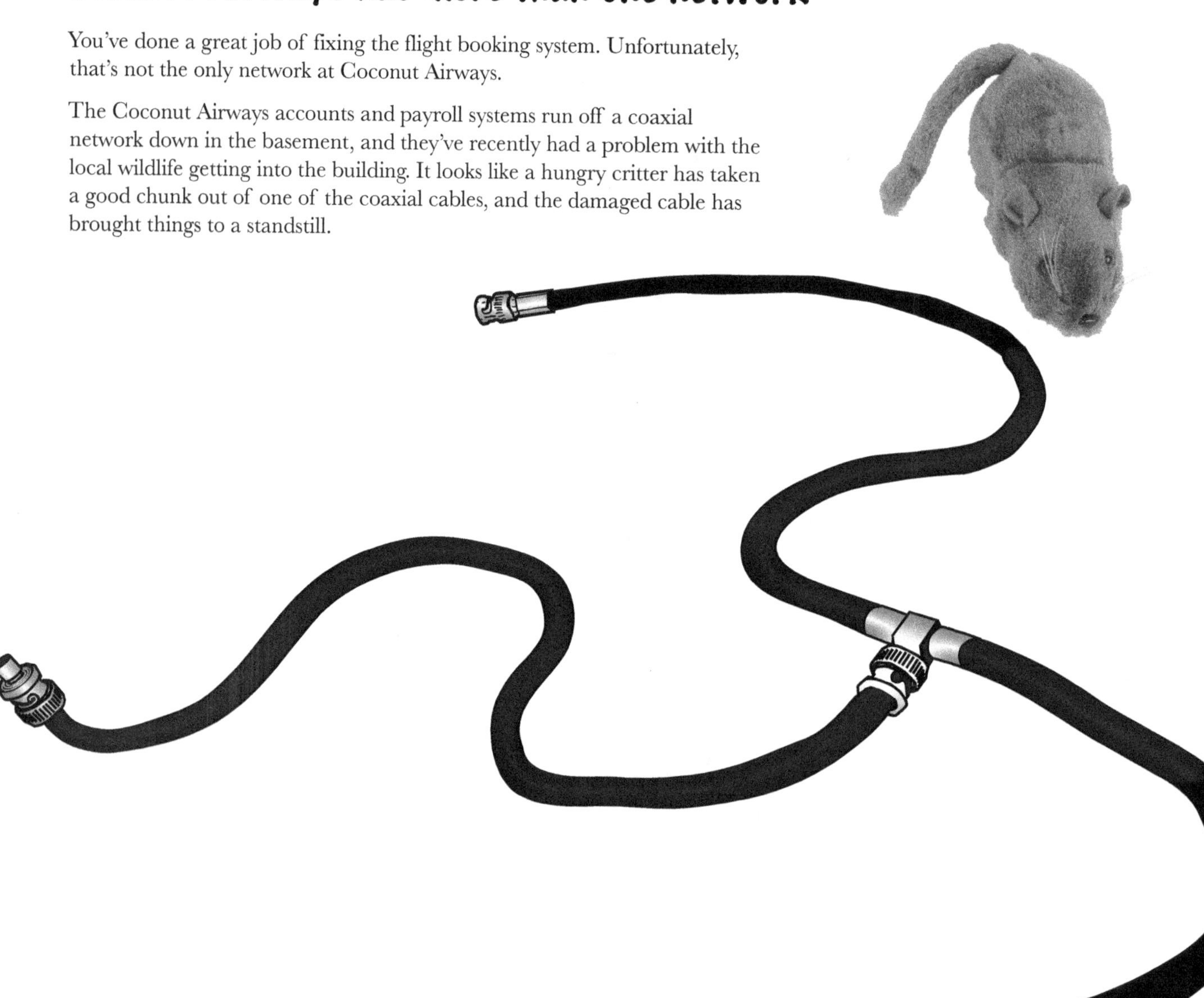

Without the coaxial network, Coconut Airways can't process payments from customers and can't pay the pilots to fly the planes.

They need you to save the day for them again.

Here's a sketch of the Coconut Airways flight bookings network, and the coaxial network in the basement. What differences do you see between the two networks? Why do you think they are different?

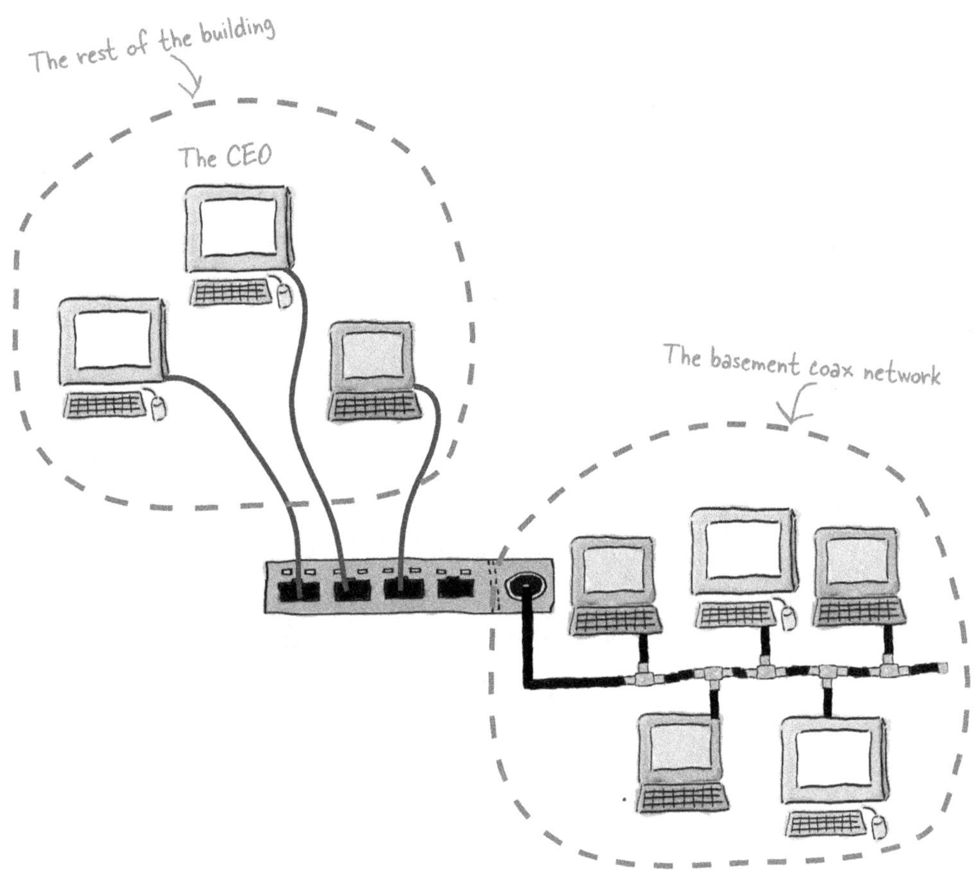

Here's a sketch of the Coconut Airways flight bookings network, and the coaxial network in the basement. What differences do you see between the two networks? Why do you think they are different?

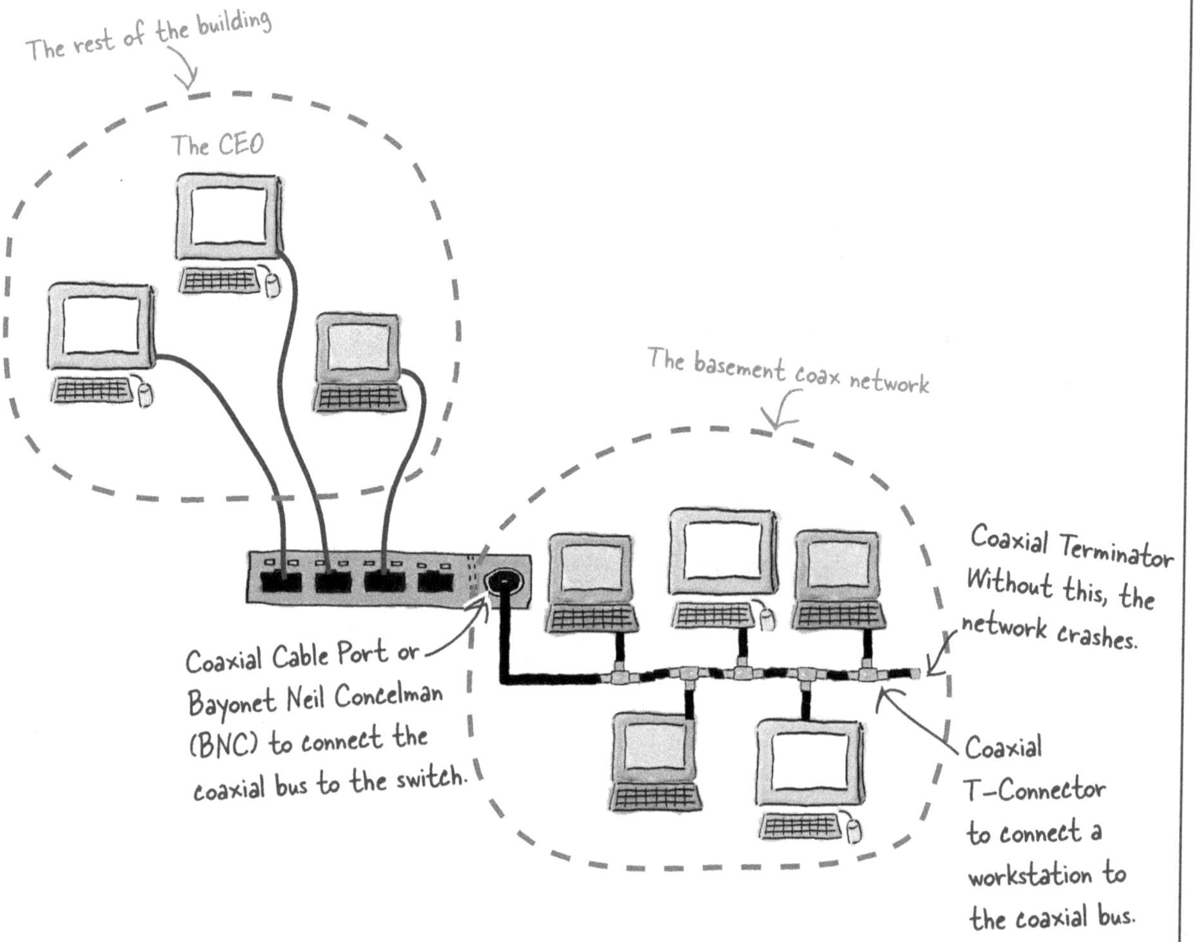

The rest of the building

The CEO

The basement coax network

Coaxial Terminator Without this, the network crashes.

Coaxial Cable Port or Bayonet Neil Concelman (BNC) to connect the coaxial bus to the switch.

Coaxial T-Connector to connect a workstation to the coaxial bus.

Introducing the coaxial cable

The Coconut Airways network in the basement runs on coaxial cables rather than CAT-5. So what's the difference?

Just like CAT-5 cables, coaxial cables are used to create networks. There are two key differences between them.

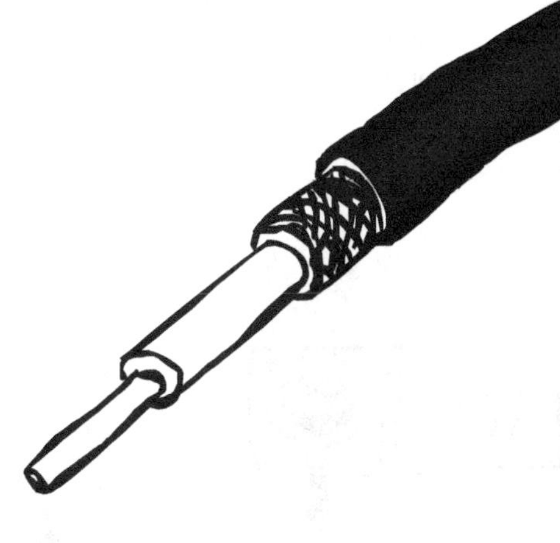

1. **The cable contains one big copper wire rather than four twisted pairs.**
   A coaxial cable has a jacket on the outside, just like a CAT-5 cable. Inside the cable, however, there's just the one wire. It has a copper core or conductor, with a layer of insulation made of plastic and other materials.

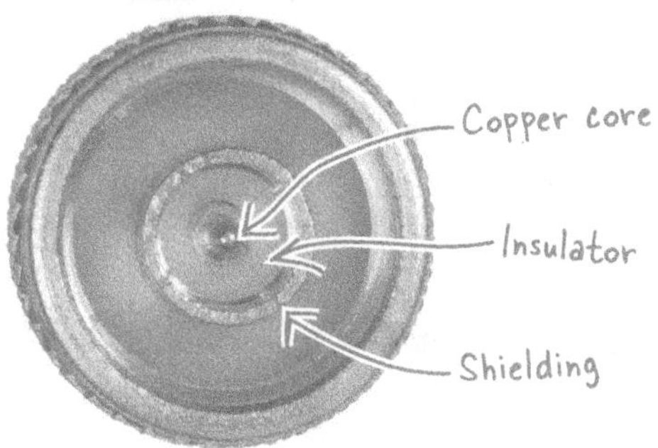

2. **The cables use different sorts of connectors and terminators.**
   CAT-5 cables use RJ-45 connectors. Coaxial cables, on the other hand, use BNC connectors, T-connectors, and terminators. The sort of connector you use depends on why you need it.

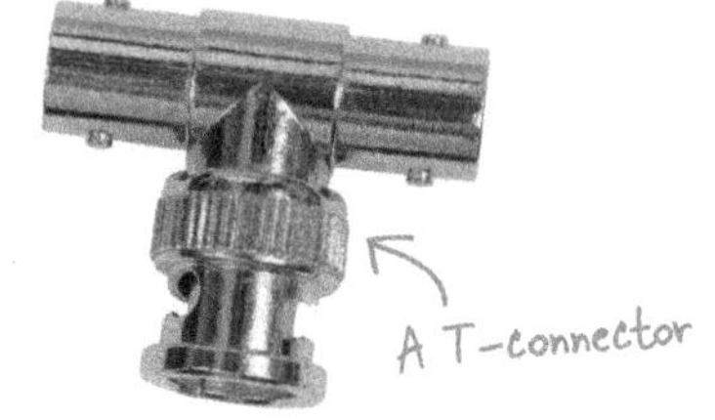

Now we've looked at the cables, what about the network?

Coaxial networks are bus networks

Coaxial networks (aka RG-62 networks) count on a central line, called a ***bus***. The bus functions as the spine of the network.

Each workstation on the network or ***node*** must be connected to the network with a T-Connector. The T-Connector attaches the node's network cable to the main bus. If the bus is broken, unterminated, or has a broken T-Connector, the entire network will go down.

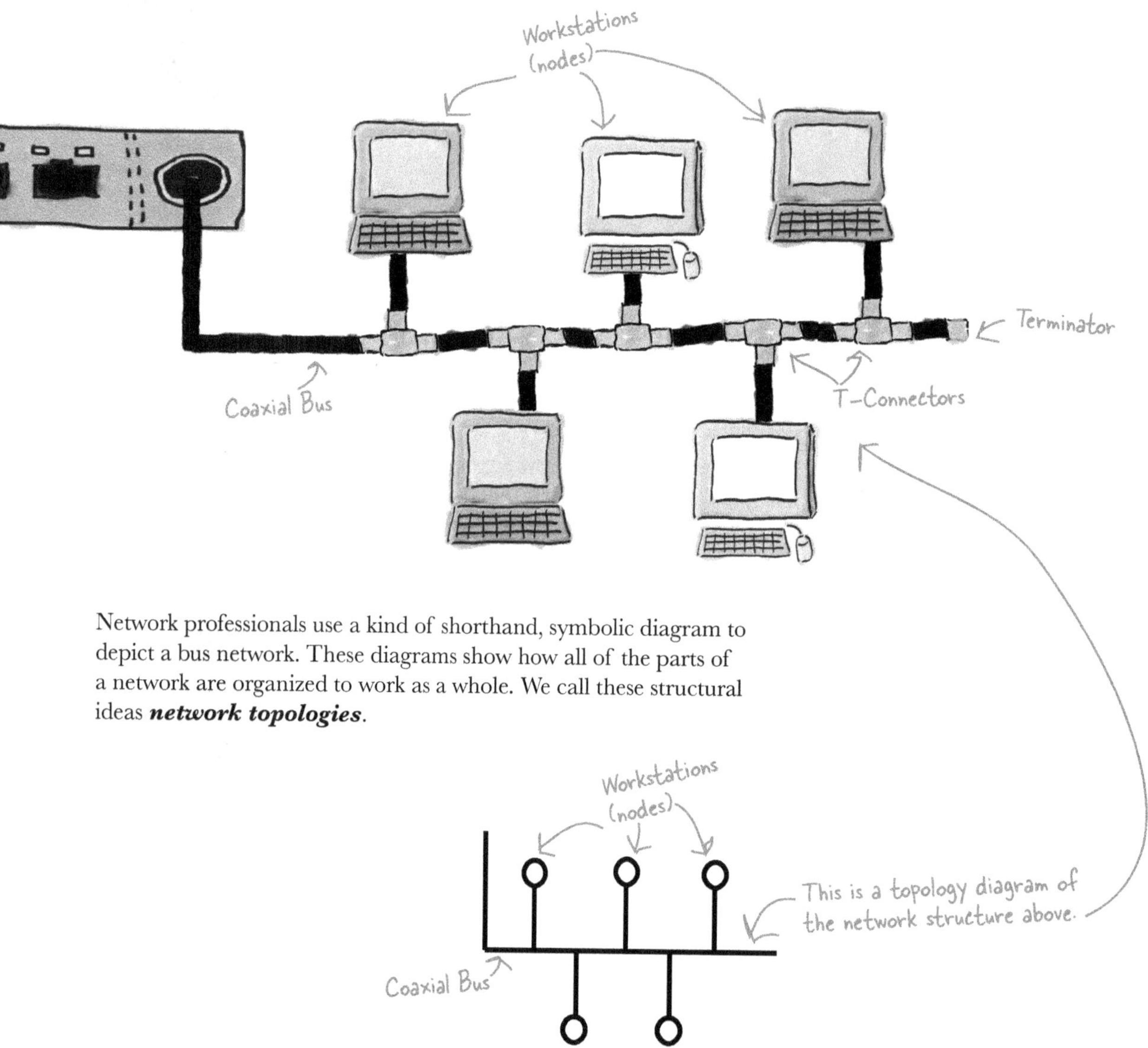

Network professionals use a kind of shorthand, symbolic diagram to depict a bus network. These diagrams show how all of the parts of a network are organized to work as a whole. We call these structural ideas ***network topologies***.

So can we fix the cable?

We've found out a bit more about coaxial cables and networks. Does this give us enough knowledge to fix the Coconut Airways coaxial network?

The rodents must have chewed through the bus. If we cut out the chewed part of the cable and stick on another connector, that should fix it. Right?

Let's see if she's right.

1. **Cut the broken part out.**
   Cut the cable well before the break to ensure that you have a good set of wire ends.

2. **Strip and prepare the new end.**
   Strip back the cable covering shield and insulator so that you leave a 1/2 to 1-inch portion of the copper core protruding.

3. **Place a BNC connector on the new end.**
   You can either crimp or solder the new connector onto the end of the cable.

So has that fixed the network?

The network's still not working

Unfortunately, cutting out the chewed bit of network cable and fitting a connector hasn't worked. The Accounts staff are still seeing network error messages whenever they try to access their systems.

So why didn't our fix work?

Hmm, I wonder. We fixed the part of the cable that was visibly damaged, but that hasn't gotten rid of the network problems. But what if the cable's damaged elsewhere too? What if we can't see which bit is damaged?

Not all cable damage is visible from the outside.

Even though we've fixed the part of the cable that's visibly damaged, there may be further damage inside the cable.

So how can we detect this sort of damage? To do that, we need to dig a bit deeper into how coaxial cables actually work.

there are no Dumb Questions

Q: Do many organizations still use coaxial networks now?

A: Coaxial networks are being phased out by most network administrators. However, the principles behind coaxial network are important for a network professional to understand. No one can predict when all the coaxial networks will become extinct.

Q: If coax is being phased out, why do I still need to know about it?

A: Knowing how coaxial networks work is essential for troubleshooting. You never know when you'll come across "legacy" infrastructure—cable and network devices that are old but still functioning.

Q: Why does a coaxial network need a terminator?

A: Great question! Keep reading, and we'll show you.

So what goes on inside a coaxial cable?

As we've seen, coaxial network cables are made up of a jacket, an insulator, and a metal conductor in the center. The metal conductor allows electrons to move through it, and the electrons carry your network data. Electrons can't pass through the insulator.

As long as the path of the conductor is complete and unbroken, electrons can flow through it and the network data can travel along the cable. We say that it's ***continuous***.

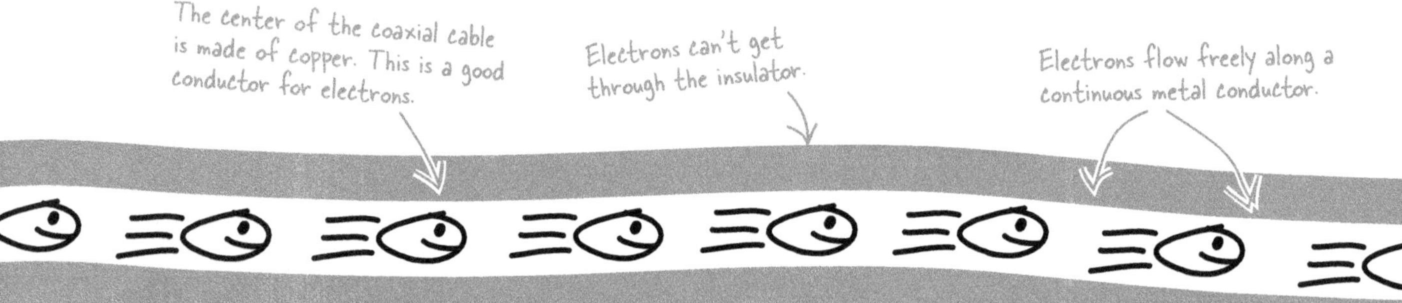

The center of the coaxial cable is made of copper. This is a good conductor for electrons.
Electrons can't get through the insulator.
Electrons flow freely along a continuous metal conductor.

But what if there's a break in the conductor?

If there's a break in the conductor, this means that electrons can't flow along the length of the cable. We said earlier that electrons carry your network data, so if the electrons can't go through the cable, neither can the network data.

This means that if there's a break in the coaxial conductor of the bus, Coconut Airways will get network error messages.

What about connectors and terminators?

Connectors conduct electrons, so adding connectors to coaxial network cables helps to maintain continuous electrical flow. Connectors allow electrons to bridge the gap between cables, or between cables and network devices, and this allows your network data to get through.

As we've seen, a coaxial network cable is made up of one big conductor core. When the conduction is not looped back through the copper core, we say that it is not ***terminated***. When a wire isn't terminated, the network loses the flow of electrons and, therefore, the flow of network data.

A terminator ensures that the signal in the cable keeps moving. The terminator does this by ensuring that the electrons stay in an electrical loop. A resistor in the terminator redirects electrons to the shielding layer, which effectively keeps them looping back along the cable without interfering with the network's signal. If the main cable is not terminated, the network will not function.

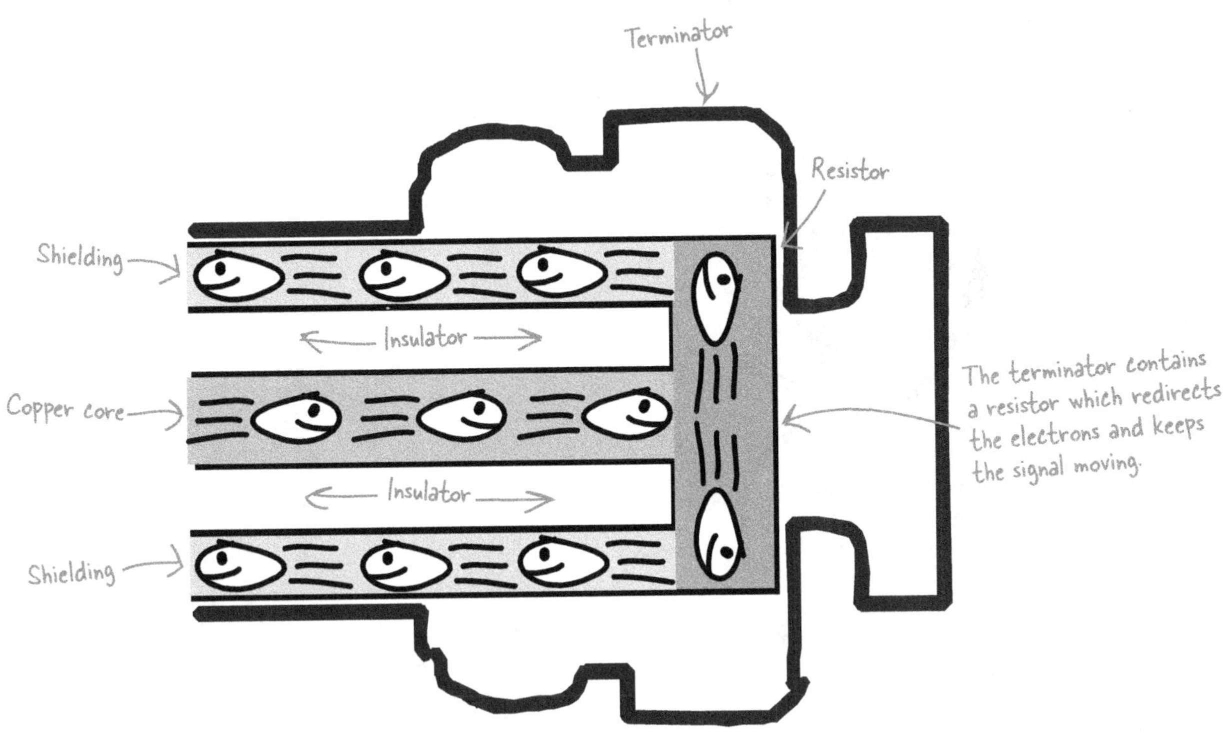

So how do we find a break in continuity in a coaxial cable network? We need to listen to electrons...

Use toner-tracer sets to listen to electrons

As we've seen, continuity breaks in a coaxial cable network stop electrons flowing. As electrons carry our network data, this means that the network data can't get through either.

One way of finding a continuity break in a coaxial cable is to listen for signs of life from the electrons, and we can do this using a ***toner-tracer set***. So what's that?

A toner-tracer set is a tool used by network professionals to detect noises from electrons. You attach the toner part of the toner-tracer set to the network cable, and the toner then sends a generated signal along the cable. You then use the tracer to listen for the signal by placing it on the cable. The tracer sounds when it hears electrons carrying the signal. It amplifies the signal.

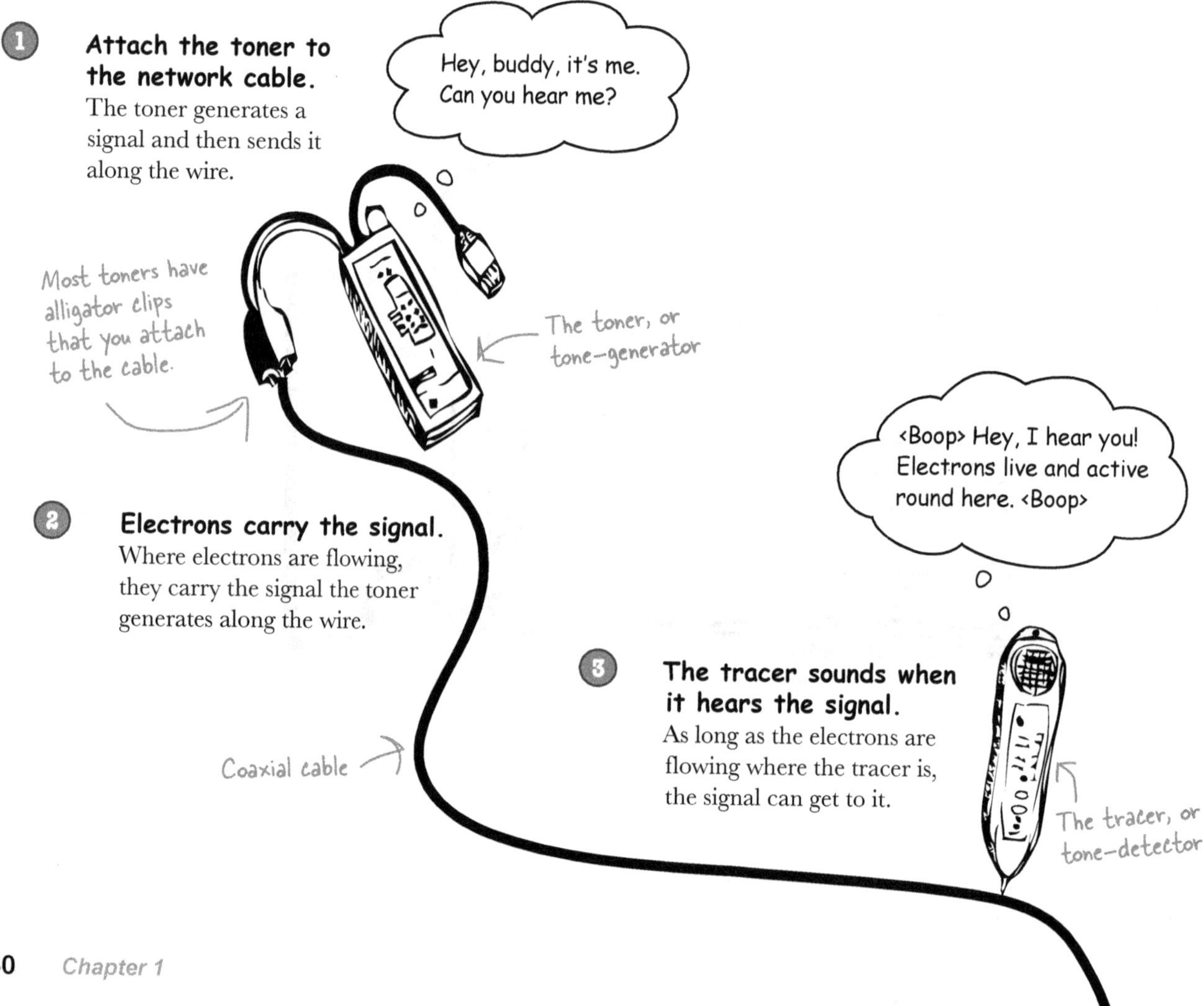

1
Attach the toner to the network cable.
The toner generates a signal and then sends it along the wire.
Hey, buddy, it's me. Can you hear me?
Most toners have alligator clips that you attach to the cable.
The toner, or tone-generator
2
Electrons carry the signal.
Where electrons are flowing, they carry the signal the toner generates along the wire.
<Boop> Hey, I hear you! Electrons live and active round here. <Boop>
Coaxial cable
3
The tracer sounds when it hears the signal.
As long as the electrons are flowing where the tracer is, the signal can get to it.
The tracer, or tone-detector

No sound means no electrons

We can use toner-tracer sets to identify breaks in continuity by listening out for when the electrons go quiet. If the tracer is unable to pick up a signal from the toner, this means there's a break between the toner and where the tracer is currently positioned.

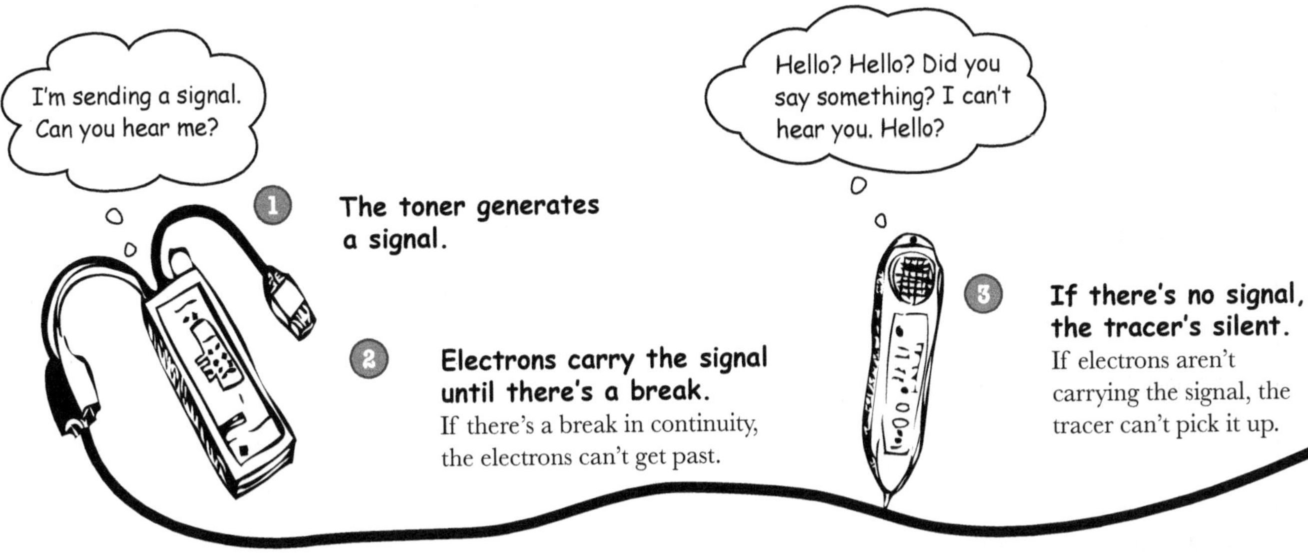

I'm sending a signal. Can you hear me?
1 The toner generates a signal.
2 Electrons carry the signal until there's a break.
If there's a break in continuity, the electrons can't get past.
Hello? Hello? Did you say something? I can't hear you. Hello?
3 If there's no signal, the tracer's silent.
If electrons aren't carrying the signal, the tracer can't pick it up.

So how do we find the continuity break?

We've said that up until the break, electrons are active, but after the break, they're silent. The break in continuity is **the point where the electrons go quiet**. This means that you can find the continuity break by repositioning the tracer until you find the point where the electrons go silent. And when you've pin-pointed where the break in continuity is, you can fix it.

Dude, are you reading me?

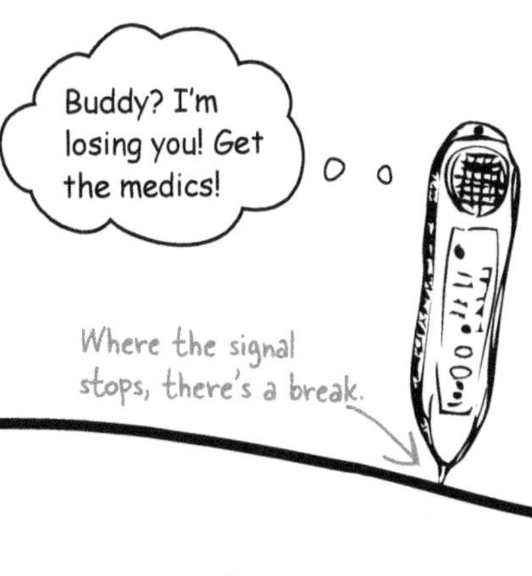

Buddy? I'm losing you! Get the medics!
Where the signal stops, there's a break.

Let's use this to fix the Coconut Airways network.

The Coconut Airways coaxial cable network is on the next page. A toner is attached to the network cable, and so are several tracers. Assume that each T-connector goes to a functioning workstation. Where do you think the continuity break is if:

1. Only Tracer F is silent.

2. Only Tracers G and H are silent.

3. None of the tracers are silent.

4. All of the tracers are silent.

5. Only Tracers E, F, G and H are silent.

6. Only Tracers F and H are silent.

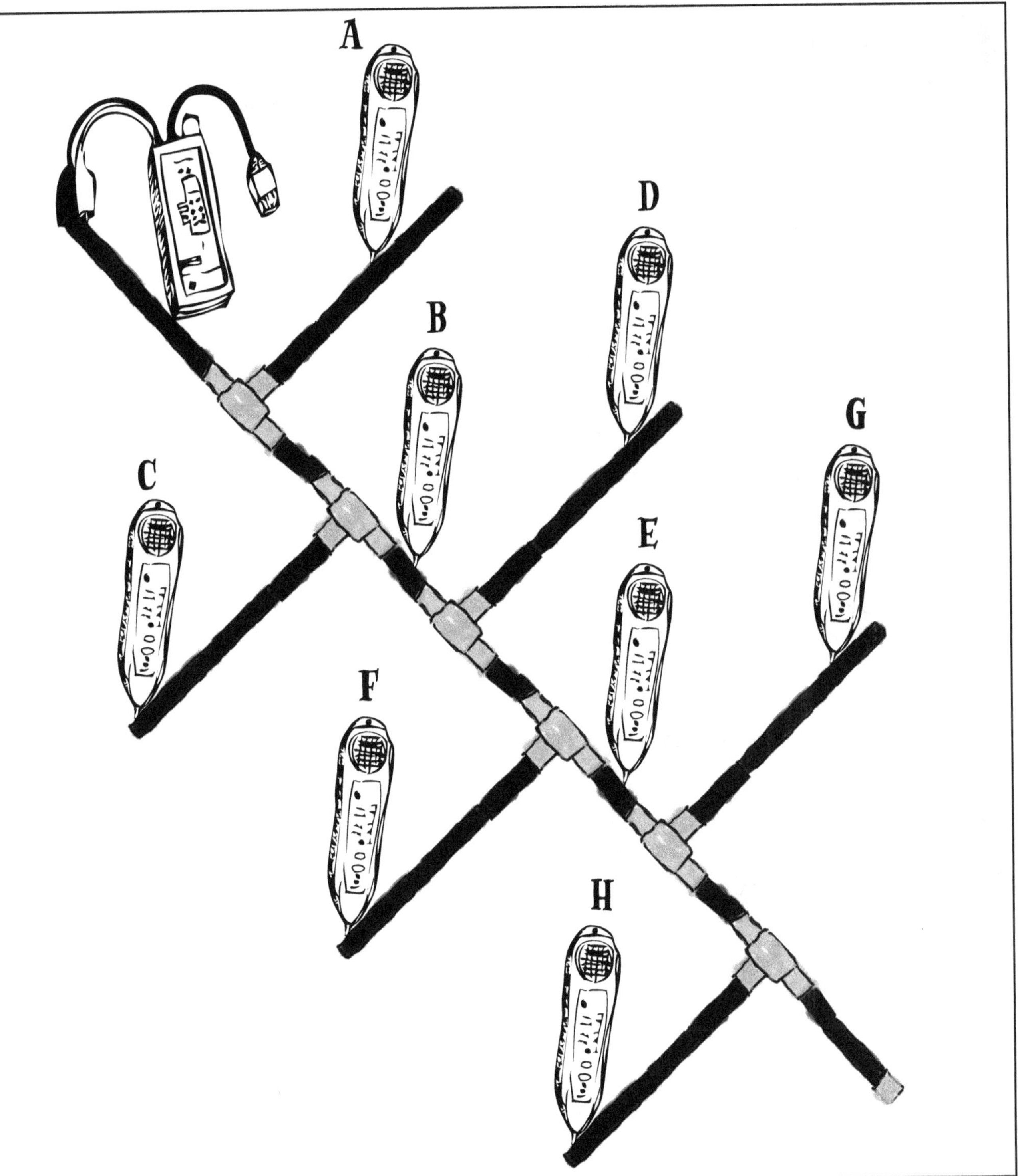
A
B
C
D
E
F
G
H

The Coconut Airways coaxial cable network is on the next page. A toner is attached to the network cable, and so are several tracers. Assume that each T-connector goes to a functioning workstation. Where do you think the continuity break is if:

1. Only Tracer F is silent.

2. Only Tracers G and H are silent.

3. None of the tracers are silent.

4. All of the tracers are silent.

5. Only Tracers E, F, G and H are silent.

6. Only Tracers F and H are silent.

There are actually TWO breaks here, as toners E and G can pick up a signal.

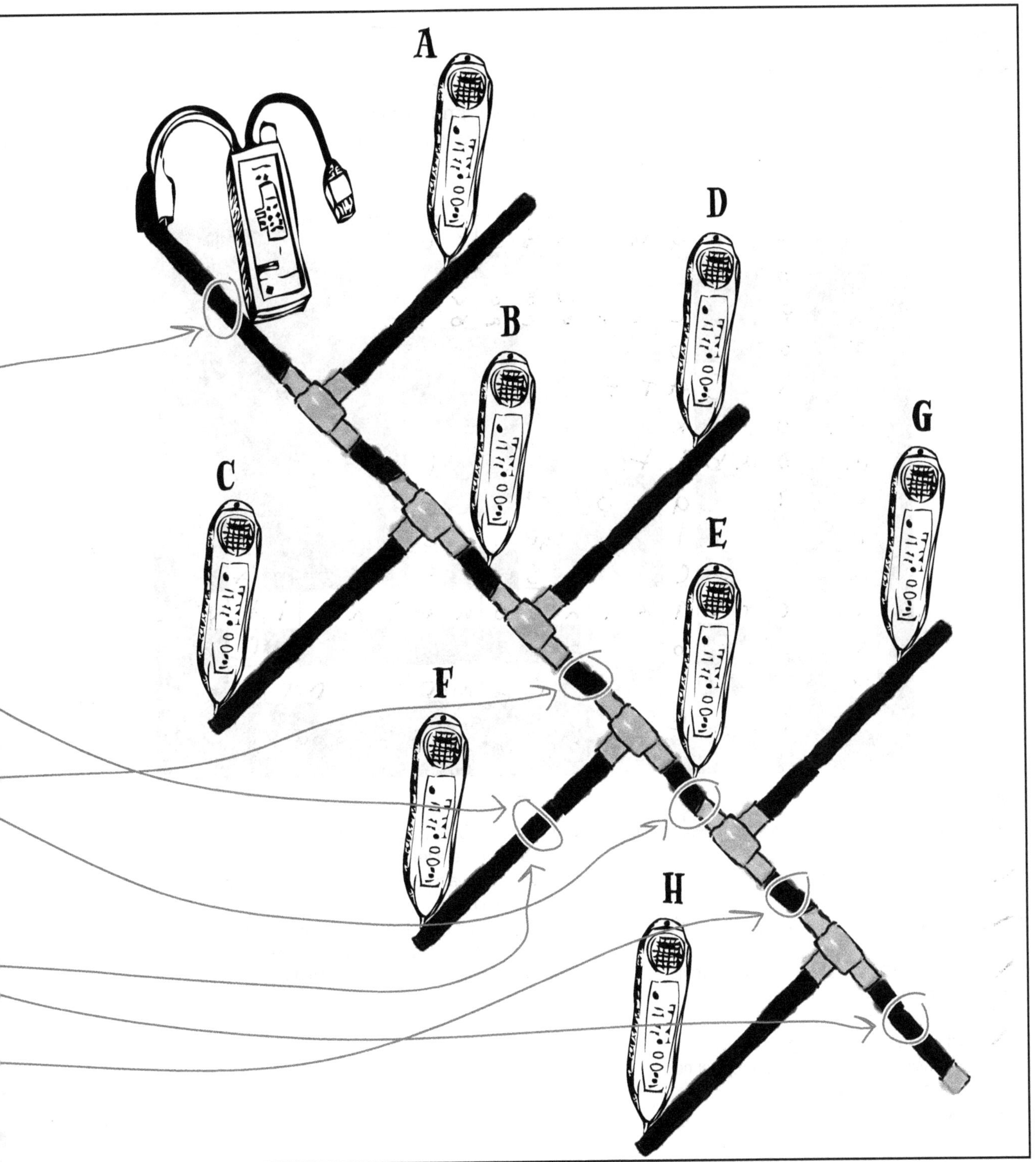
A
B
C
D
E
F
G
H

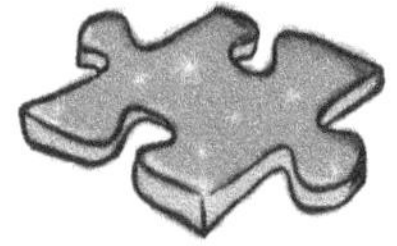

Cablecross

Answers on page 48.

Time to give your right brain a break and put that left brain to work. All the words are related to the stuff we've studied so far.

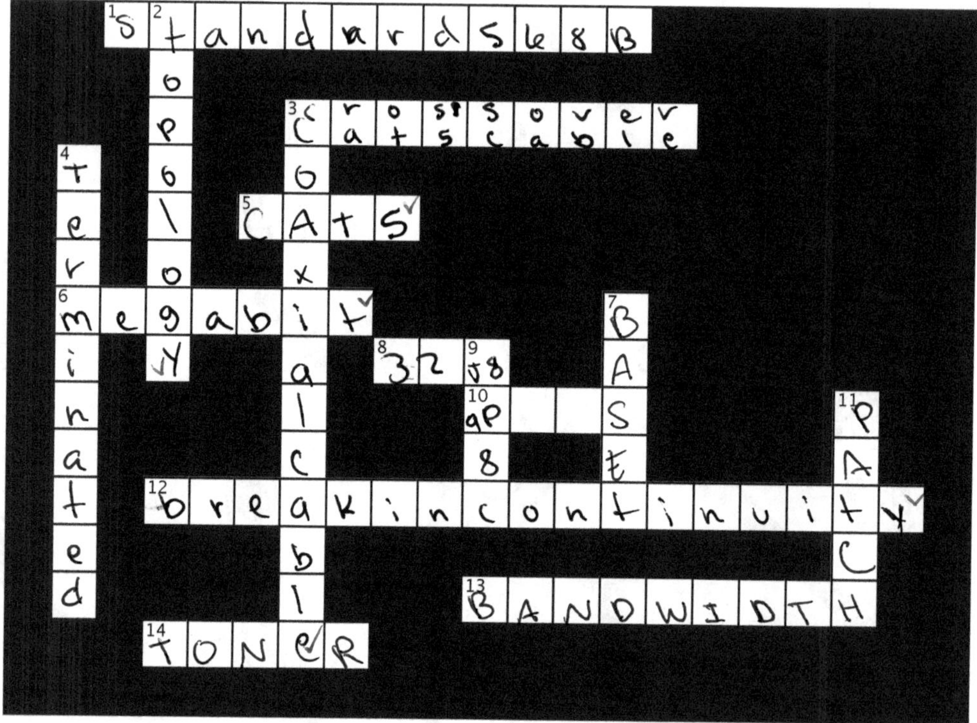

Across

1. Striped orange, solid orange, striped green, solid blue, striped blue, solid green, striped brown, solid brown...
3. A cable that can send and receive on both ends at the same time.
5. UTP cable with 8 wires usually terminated with an RJ-45 connector.
6. Equals one million bursts of electrical current.
8. Maximum length of a CAT-5 cable (in feet).
10. Contact points on a jack.
12. Point where the electrons go quiet . . .
13. The transmission capacity of a computer network or telecommunications system.
14. Signal generator.

Down

2. A symbolic diagram that shows how a network works.
3. To make a true electrical bus network, use this media.
4. If the main cable is not __________, the network will not function.
7. Standards for Ethernet transmission rates.
9. The true name of the RJ-45 connector.
11. Another name for a "straight-through" cable.

You've fixed the coaxial cable

Well done, you've found the break in the Coconut Airways coaxial cable network! The Accounting department staff are able to use their systems again, and pay their pilots.

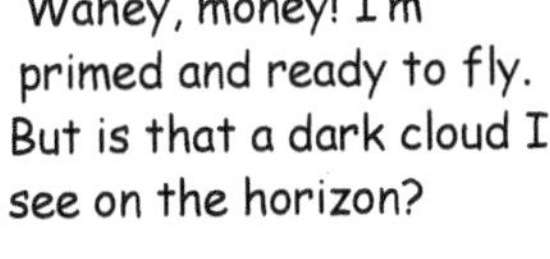

Wahey, money! I'm primed and ready to fly. But is that a dark cloud I see on the horizon?

We're in for a bumpy ride.

Tropical storms are a real problem out in the islands, and Coconut Airways have to carefully avoid flying their seaplanes when the weather gets too fierce. Normally it's not a problem as they get up-to-the-minute weather reports over the Internet.

Today things are different. Coconut Airways lost their Internet connection, and it's too dangerous for their pilots to fly without updated weather reports.

Coconut Airways are connected to the Internet via a fiber-optic line, and it looks like there might be a problem with it. But what can that problem be?

Let's start by taking a closer look at how fiber-optic cables work.

Introducing fiber-optic cables

Fiber-optic cables send network information using light rather than electrons. Light bounces through the inside of the cable, carrying the network signal.

The light passes through the transparent core of the fiber-optic cable. This core is made of transparent glass or plastic, which allows light to pass through it easily. The layer just outside of the core is called ***cladding***. Cladding acts a bit like a mirror, reflecting light so that it bounces along the core and doesn't escape.

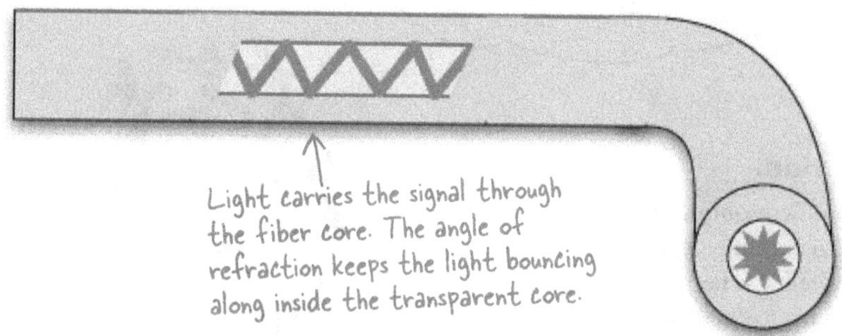

Light carries the signal through the fiber core. The angle of refraction keeps the light bouncing along inside the transparent core.

The outside of the cable is coated with polymer, and Kevlar® threads running between the core and the coating add strength and protection to the cable.

Fiber-optics have connectors too

Just like CAT-5 and coaxial cables, the ends of a fiber-optic cable have connectors. There's a variety of connector types that can be used.

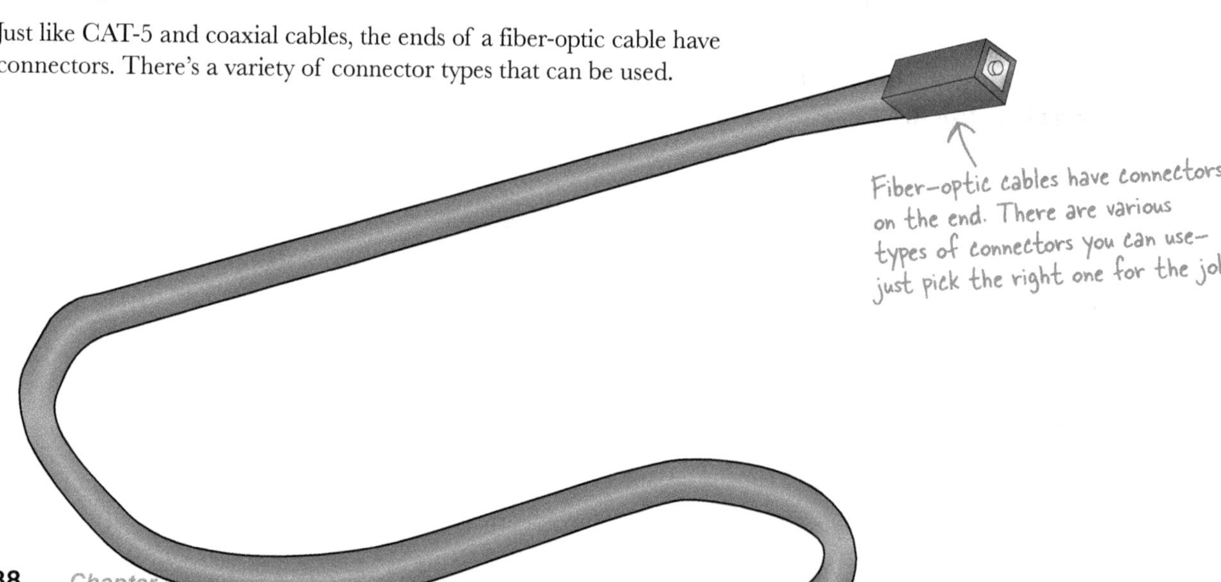

Fiber-optic cables have connectors on the end. There are various types of connectors you can use— just pick the right one for the job.

The Coconut Airways cable's over-bent

So what about Coconut Airways?

Here's the fiber-optic cable. Can you see how tightly it's bent?

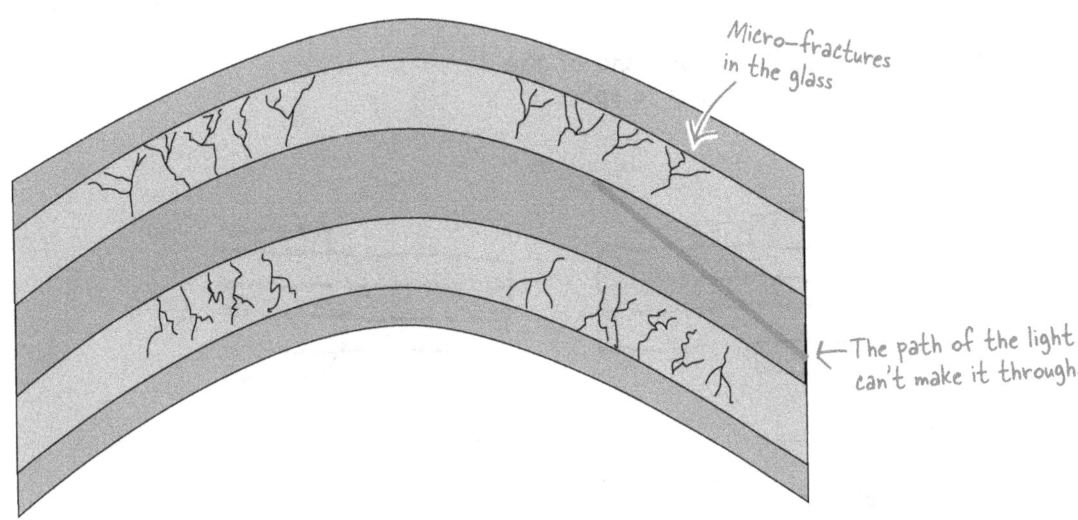
Micro-fractures in the glass
The path of the light can't make it through.

Fiber-optic cables usually have a minimum bend radius of 3.0 cm. If the cable's bent more than this, the fiber core can develop micro-fractures, real fractures, or severely leak light. And as it's the light that's carrying the network data, a loss of light means a loss of information and network errors.

So how do we fix damaged fiber-optic cables? Well, one way is with a ***fusion splicer***.

So what's a fusion splicer?

A fusion splicer allows you to fuse two pieces of fiber together. The splicer provides high-precision guides that allow you to line up the fiber. Once you've got the ends lined up, you heat the two ends with an electric arc and push them together. After you fuse the ends together, the fusion-splicer heat-shrinks a protective cover over your splice.

Let's take a closer look at the steps for splicing a fiber-optic cable.

You can use a fusion splicer to fix fiber-optic cables.

How to fix fiber-optics with a fusion splicer

Here are the steps you need to go through in order to fix a fiber-optic cable with a fusion splicer.

You need to train extensively on a fusion splicer before using one.

Fusion splicers are expensive and can be tricky to use, but they're well worth the money and effort.

1. **Strip the coating from each end of the fiber-optic cable you want to splice.**

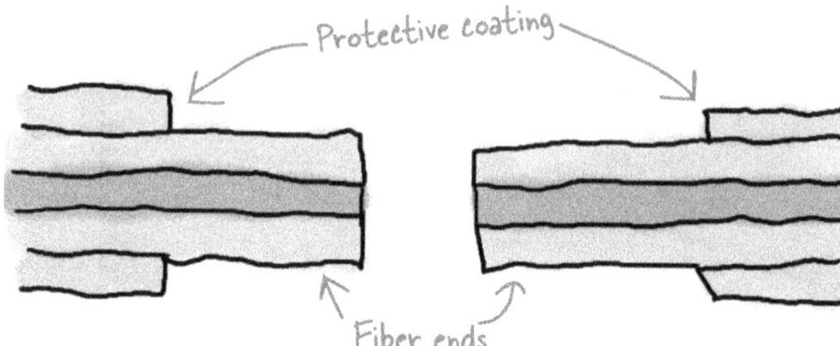

2. **Line up each end.**
The guides on the fusion splicer allow you to be really precise about this.

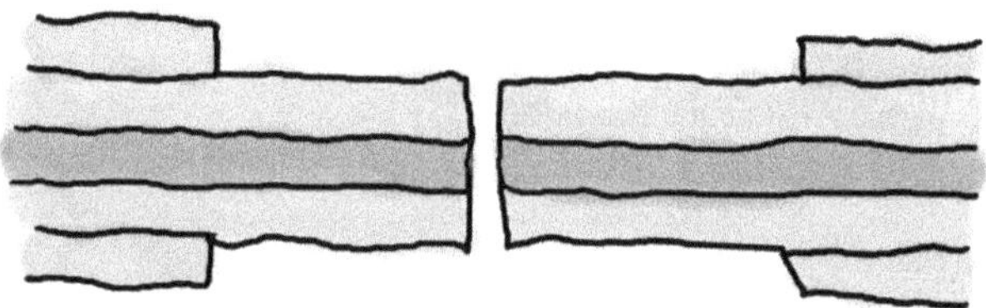

3. **Smooth the ends before fusing them.**
The fusion splicer creates an arc of electricity that makes the faces of the core super smooth so that they can align properly.

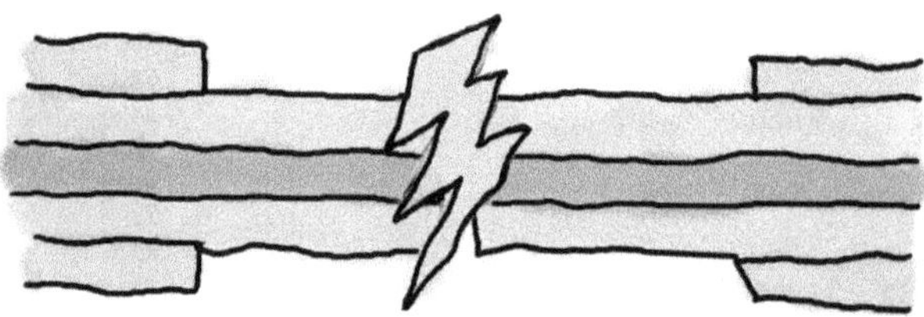

4. **Fuse the ends together.**
This is the main purpose of the fusion splicer. The electric arc melts the ends, fusing them together to create a spliced core.

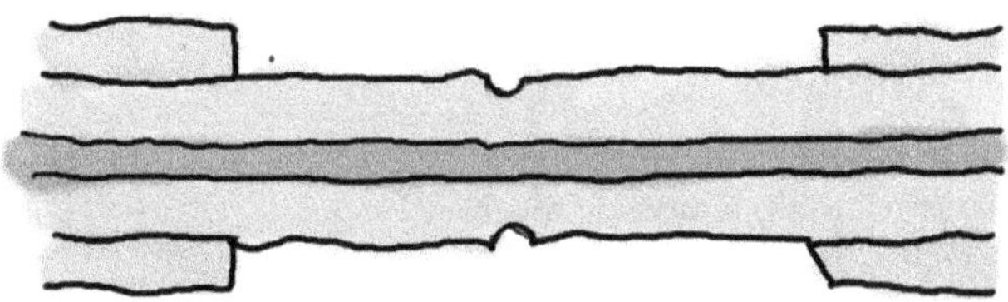

5. **Finish the splice by covering it with new coating.**
Your fiber-optic cable is now ready for testing.

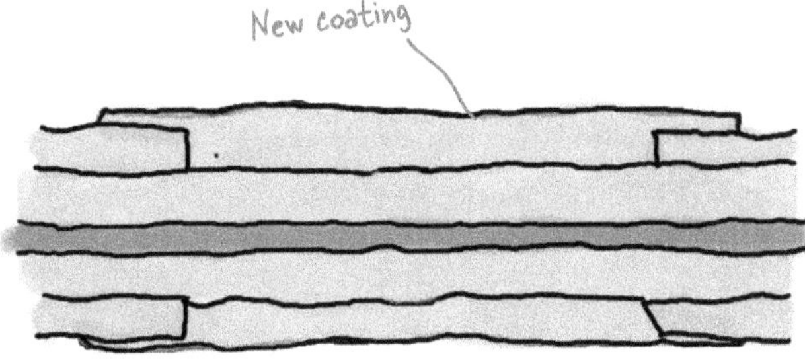

So has this fixed the Coconut Airways fiber-optic?

A fiber-optic connector needs fitting too

Coconut Airways has one more problem with their fiber-optic cable. We've fixed the over-bent cable, but one of the connectors is missing too, right near the wall jack. We need to fit a new connector so that we can plug the fiber-optic in at the wall.

Fiber-optic cables take various types of connectors, but they all do the same basic job: they bring the ends of two fiber-optic cables together, and allow light to flow through uninterrupted.

The differences between the connectors is all to do with their housing. In other words, the shape, color, how large or small, how close together another fiber connector can be, and how they attach.

Here are some of the fiber-optic connectors you might see around.

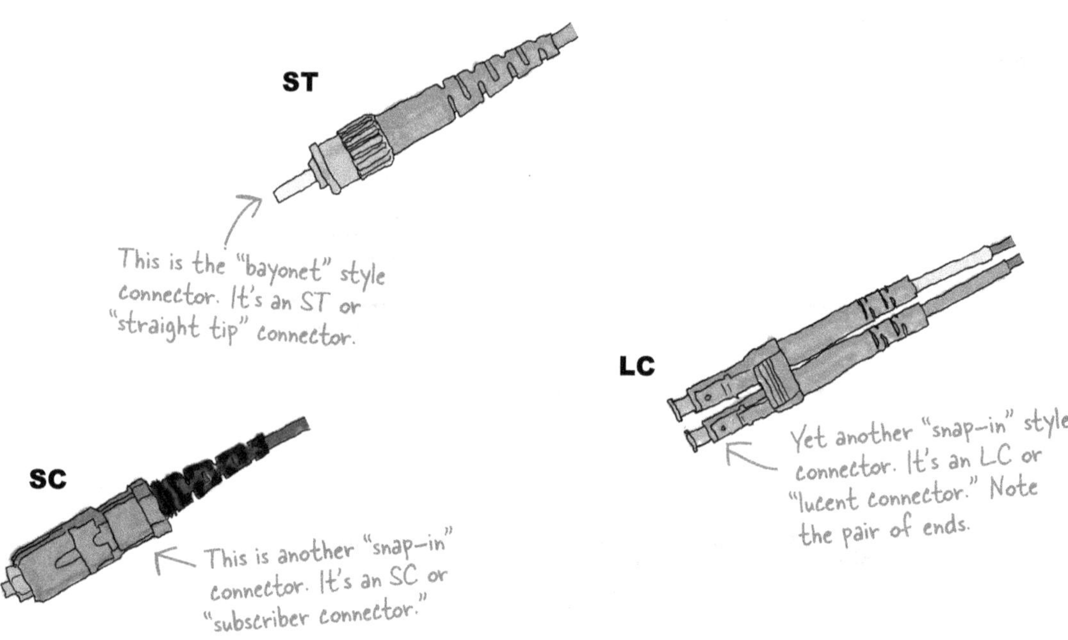

ST
This is the "bayonet" style connector. It's an ST or "straight tip" connector.
LC
Yet another "snap-in" style connector. It's an LC or "lucent connector." Note the pair of ends.
SC
This is another "snap-in" connector. It's an SC or "subscriber connector."

BRAIN POWER

Why do some of the connectors have a pair of fiber cores, where others have only a single core?

What's My Connector?

Connectors and receptacles must match in terms of type. Match each of the connectors below to the receptacle it fits into.

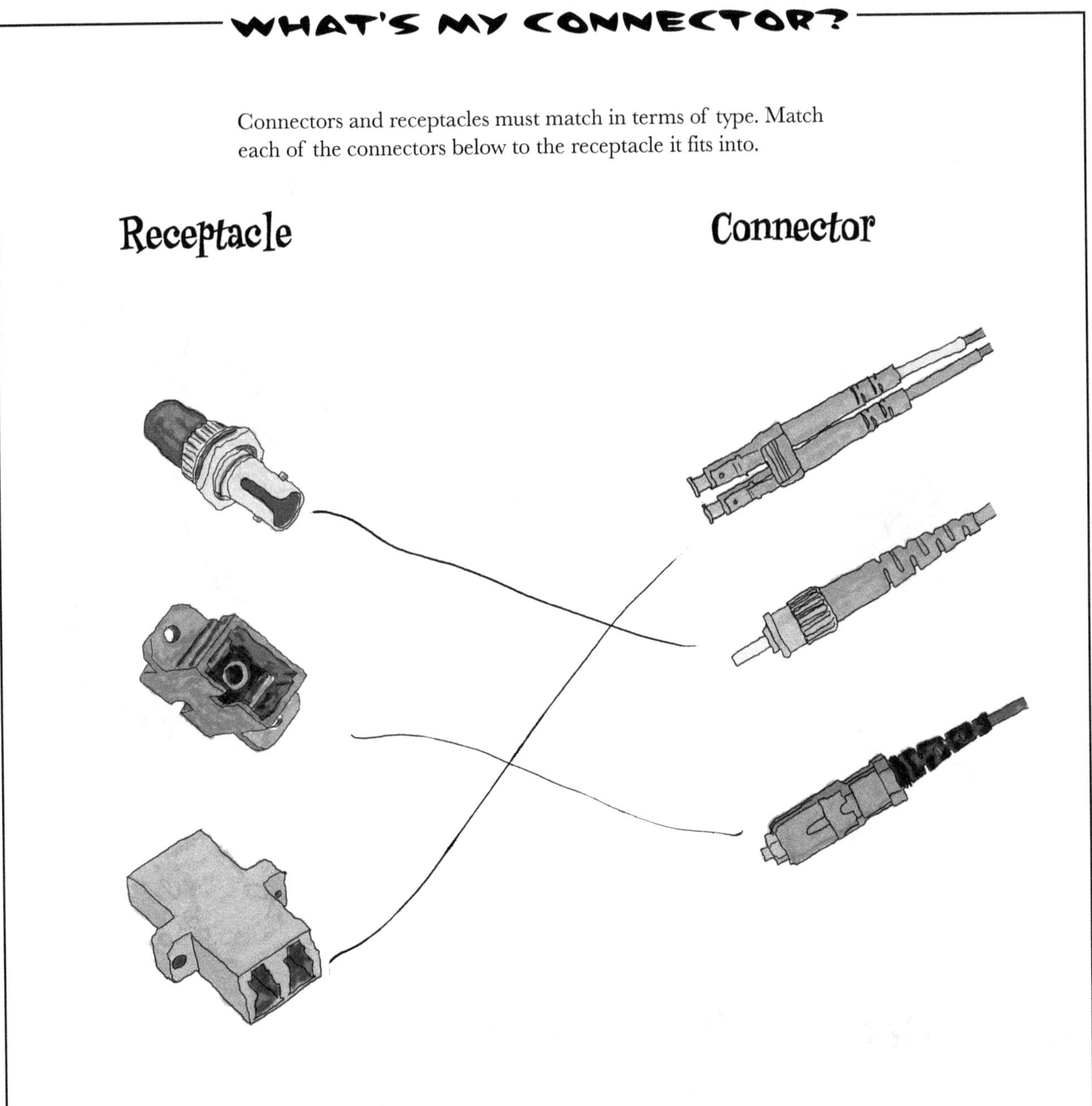

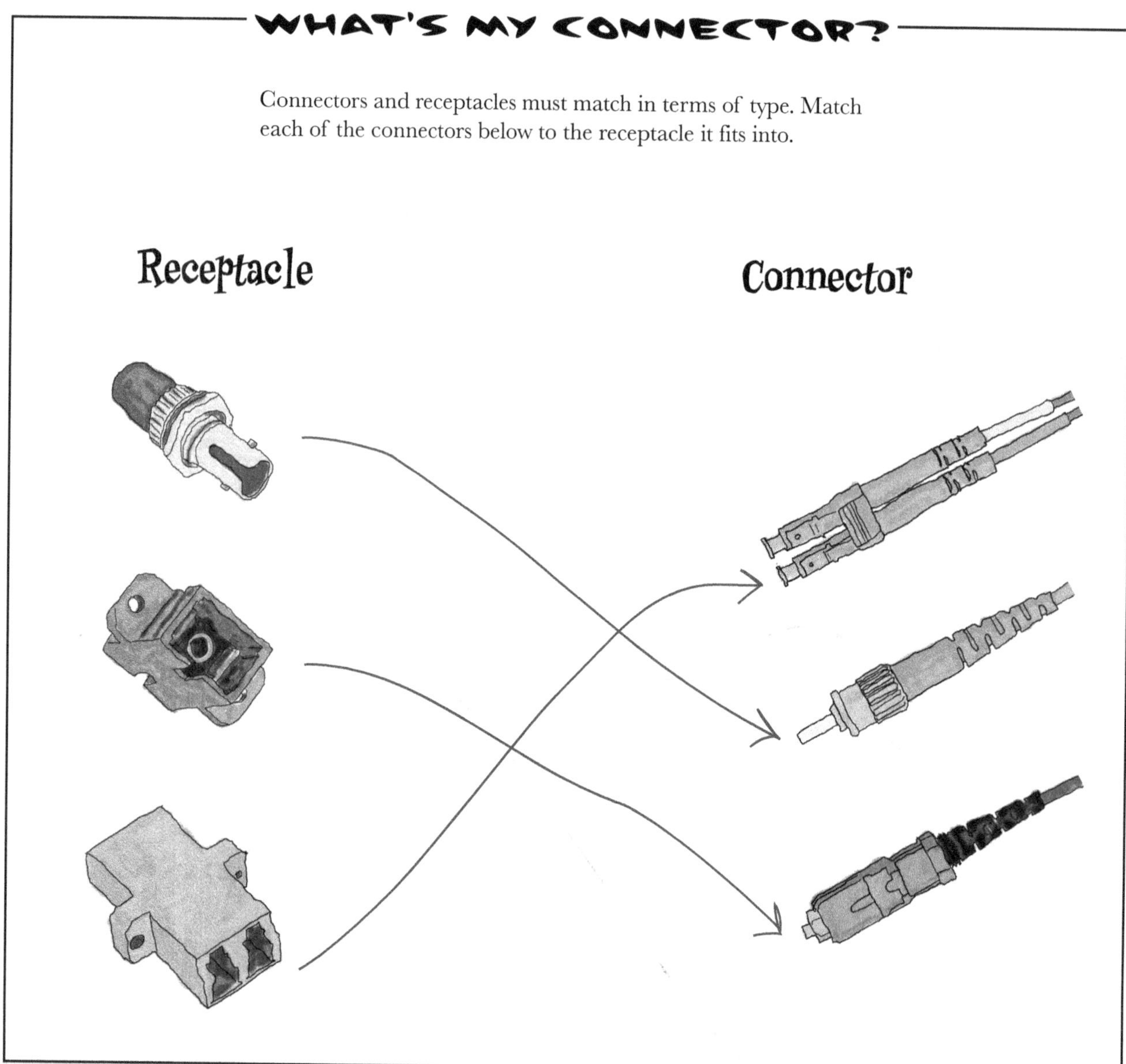
WHAT'S MY CONNECTOR?
Connectors and receptacles must match in terms of type. Match each of the connectors below to the receptacle it fits into.
Receptacle
Connector

We're nearly ready to fix the connector

There's just one more thing that can affect what sort of connector we choose to go on the end of the cable: there are two types of fiber. Let's take a look.

There are two types of fiber

Fiber comes in two flavors: ***single mode*** and ***multimode***. The word "mode" refers to the number of paths the light takes through the fiber.

Single mode fiber

In a single mode fiber, the light travels in a **single path**. It takes a laser light, and it has a very small core like this:

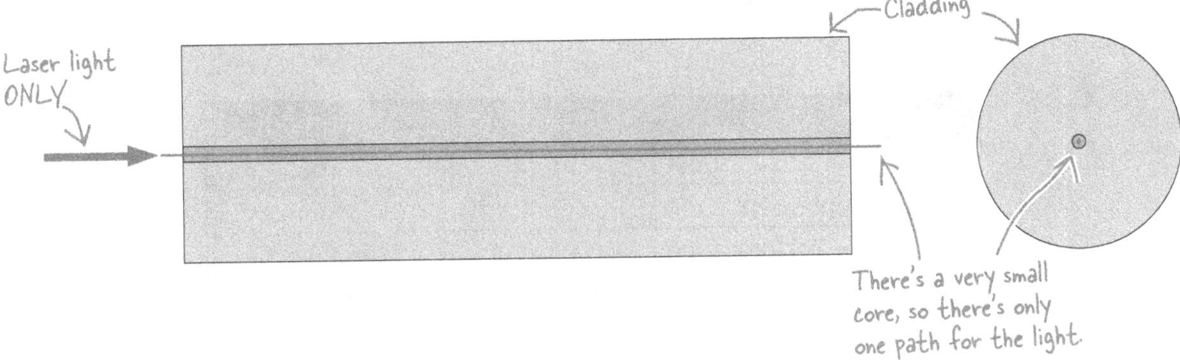

Multimode fiber

In a multimode fiber, the light travels **many paths**. It takes a laser or LED light, and has a much larger core like this:

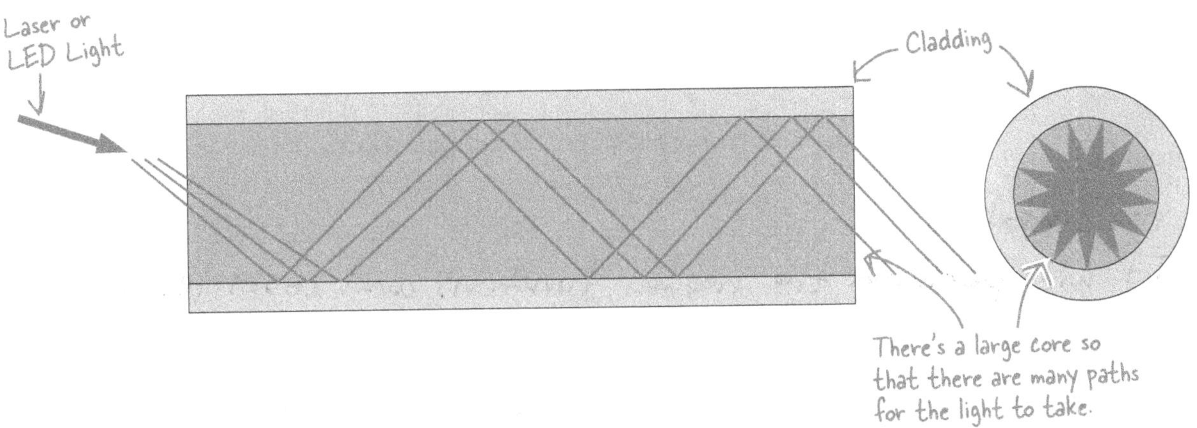

Laser or LED Light
Cladding
There's a large core so that there are many paths for the light to take.

So how do we choose between the two types of fiber?

Which mode fiber should you use?

The two types of fiber-optic cable have very different characteristics. There are differences in areas such as performance, speed, and possible distance. There are big differences in price, too, as it's harder to manufacture single mode fiber.

Here's a quick guide to the differences between single mode and multimode fiber-optic cable.

	Single Mode	Multimode
Cost	High	Low
Easy of Implementation	High	Low
Performance	14 Tbit/s	10 Gbit/s
LED Source	Laser Only	Laser or LED
Distances	10-100km	2000 m+
Signal Loss	+	-
Core Size	Small	Large

Exercise

You need to buy some fiber-optic cable and run a network 1300 meters with a speed of 1Gbit/sec. Choose single mode or multimode, and write your reasons for your choice.

multimode

It will perform the needed functions and costs less.

Let's fit the connector on the fiber-optic

There are two main ways that connectors are attached to fiber patch cables.

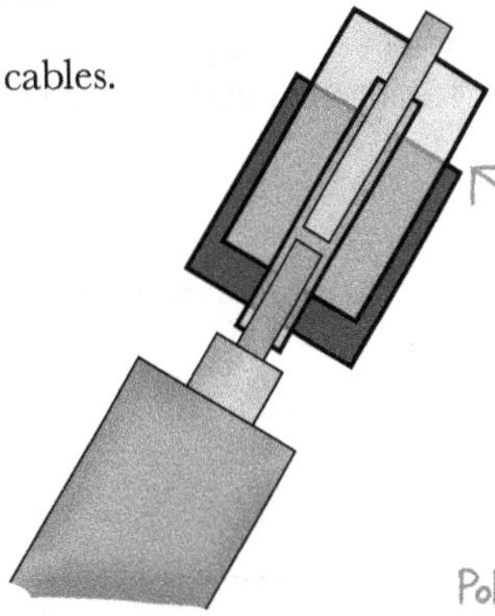

Pre-built Connector

Already has a fiber end epoxied in place.

1. **Use a pre-built connector and splice it to the exisiting patch cable.**
   This technique is faster and easier, but there is some light loss where the two fibers are pushed together.

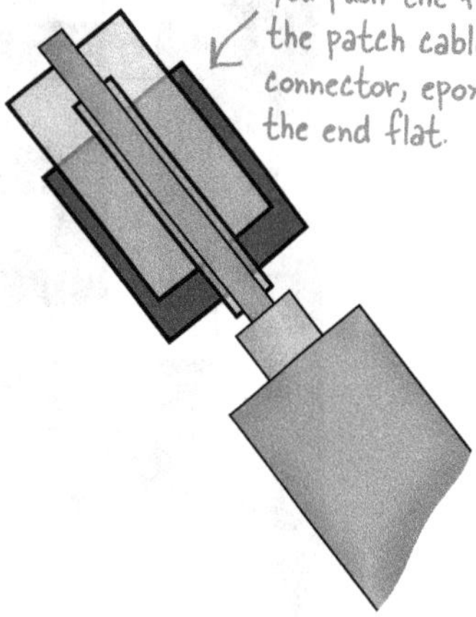

Polish & Epoxy Connector

You push the fiber from the patch cable into the connector, epoxy, then polish the end flat.

2. **Use a connector that does not have a fiber inside. You epoxy the fiber of the patch cable inside the connector, then polish the end of the fiber.**
   This technique is slower and more complicated, and you need special equipment and training. The advantage is that it makes a higher quality connection.

So which technique should we use?

While we could use either technique, let's go with the pre-built connector for now. Only a few tools are needed for this approach, and any network tech can learn to do them in less than 15 minutes—which means that Coconut Airways will get their Internet connection up and running pretty quickly. You can even get videos and quick guides on how to fit these from manufacturers.

So has this fixed the problem for Coconut Airways?

You need to buy some fiber-optic cable and run a network 1300 meters with a speed of 1Gbit/sec. Choose single mode or multimode, and write your reasons for your choice.

Single mode would be the best choice because of the length of the cable. Multimode won't work for the length at this speed.

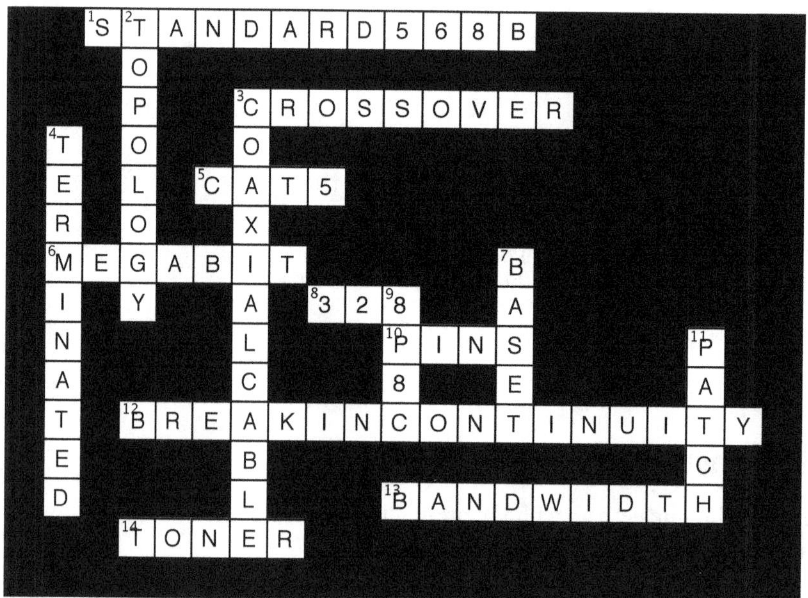

Across

1. Striped orange, solid orange, striped green, solid blue, striped blue, solid green, striped brown, solid brown... [STANDARD568B]
3. A cable that can send and receive on both ends at the same time. [CROSSOVER]
5. UTP cable with 8 wires usually terminated with an RJ-45 connector. [CAT5]
6. Equals one million bursts of electrical current. [MEGABIT]
8. Maximum length of a CAT-5 cable (in feet). [328]
10. Contact points on a jack. [PINS]
12. Point where the electrons go quiet . . . [BREAKINCONTINUITY]
13. The transmission capacity of a computer network or telecommunications system. [BANDWIDTH]
14. Signal generator. [TONER]

Down

2. A symbolic diagram that shows how a network works. [TOPOLOGY]
3. To make a true electrical bus network, use this media. [COAXIALCABLE]
4. If the main cable is not __________, the network will not function. [TERMINATED]
7. Standards for Ethernet transmission rates. [BASET]
9. The true name of the RJ-45 connector. [8P8C]
11. Another name for a "straight-through" cable. [PATCH]

Coconut Airways is sky high

Congratulations! You've successfully troubleshooted and fixed all of the network problems that Coconut Airways were experiencing, and they're back in full operation. All of their flights are fully booked, their cash-flow problems are no more, and the pilots can fly safely thanks to their up-to-date weather information.

You've learned a lot in this chapter. You've found out about the different types of network cable, you've learned some important troubleshooting techniques, and you've seen the steps you need to go through to fix various cabling problems.

2 planning network layouts

Networking in the Dark

Heavens, a CAT-5 in the doghouse. Who would've thought...

Tired of tripping over wires and getting mauled by your electrical closet? When you build a network without planning, you end up with a big mess—wires running every which way, wires connected to who knows what? In this chapter, you'll learn how to plan a physical network layout that will save your bacon down the road. You will also learn how to use proper network hardware to contain and help manage all those wires.

Ghost Watch needs your help!

The most popular reality TV show in Networkville is Ghost Watch. Every week the Ghost Watch team goes into an old building and records any strange sights and sounds they encounter using their high-tech equipment. The trouble is, the team's networking skills keep letting them down, and their footage ends up too distorted to use, or isn't even recorded.

This week the Ghost Watch team is in an old abandoned hotel, and they need you to help them set up their network. They need unobtrusive cabling with a clean signal, and they must be able to adapt quickly to whatever might happen. Here are their requirements:

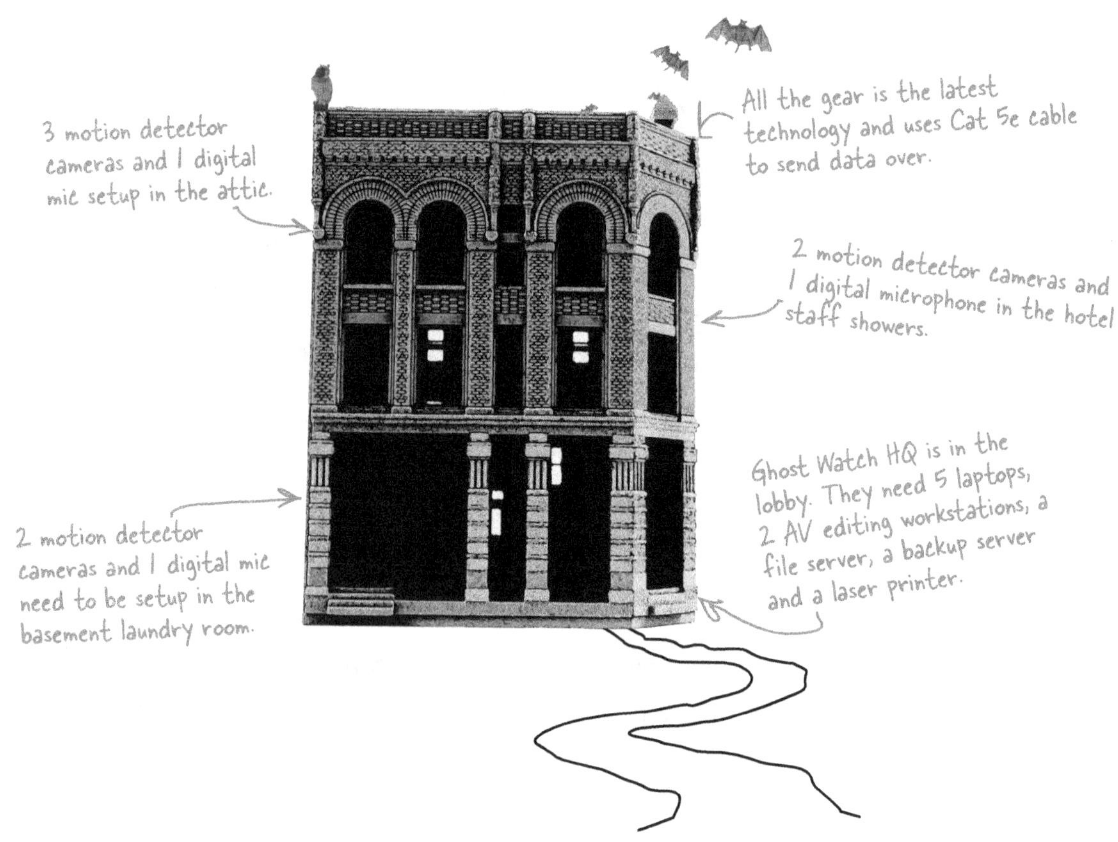

3 motion detector cameras and 1 digital mic setup in the attic.
All the gear is the latest technology and uses Cat 5e cable to send data over.
2 motion detector cameras and 1 digital microphone in the hotel staff showers.
Ghost Watch HQ is in the lobby. They need 5 laptops, 2 AV editing workstations, a file server, a backup server and a laser printer.
2 motion detector cameras and 1 digital mic need to be setup in the basement laundry room.

So where should we start?

Every good network needs a good plan

Networking involves much more than stringing cables around haphazardly. Before you start pulling lines all over the place, you need to figure out what you are connecting, where all these things are going to be located, and how best to network them.

Let's start by looking at all the devices that Ghost Watch need for this gig.

Sharpen your pencil

Write down a list of the devices that are needed, along with where they need to go.

Hint: take a look at the page opposite.

Devices	Physical area
2 motion detector cameras	Hotel showers, second floor

Write down a list of the devices that are needed, along with where they need to go.

Hint: take a look at the page opposite.

Devices	Physical area
2 motion detector cameras	Hotel showers, second floor
1 digital microphone	Hotel showers, second floor
5 laptops	First floor lobby
2 AFV editing workstations	First floor lobby
1 file server	First floor lobby
1 backup server	First floor lobby
1 laser printer	First floor lobby
2 motion detector cameras	Basement laundry room
1 digital microphone	Basement laundry room
3 motion detector cameras	Attic
1 digital microphone	Attic

So how does the device list help us plan a network?

The first step in planning a good network is to work out exactly what devices need to be included, and where they'll be located. Without it, you're effectively networking in the dark.

So what other steps are needed?

What other things do you need to consider when you're planning a network? Why?

How to plan a network layout

If you take a step-by-step approach and plan your network layout *before* running the cable, you'll save yourself a lot of time and money.

Here are the key steps you need to go through:

1. **List out the various network devices and where they will be located.** ← We've just done this step.
   Be sure you include what type of cable they need, for example, CAT-5.

2. **Adjust your plan for obstacles**

3. **Make a list of the hardware you will need to run the cable.**
   This includes things like cable trays, J-hooks, wire ties, and so on.

4. **Put your wire in!**
   Run your cables between the various devices.

So far we've completed one of these steps. We've made a list of all the Ghost Watch devices we need to wire up, along with where each of them needs to go. Let's move onto the next step.

Let's plan the cabling with a floorplan

Floorplans give you a way of picturing the floor space of the area in which you need to lay down network cables. They show you information such as floor layout, and also many of the networking obstacles that you need to plan for when you're laying down cables.

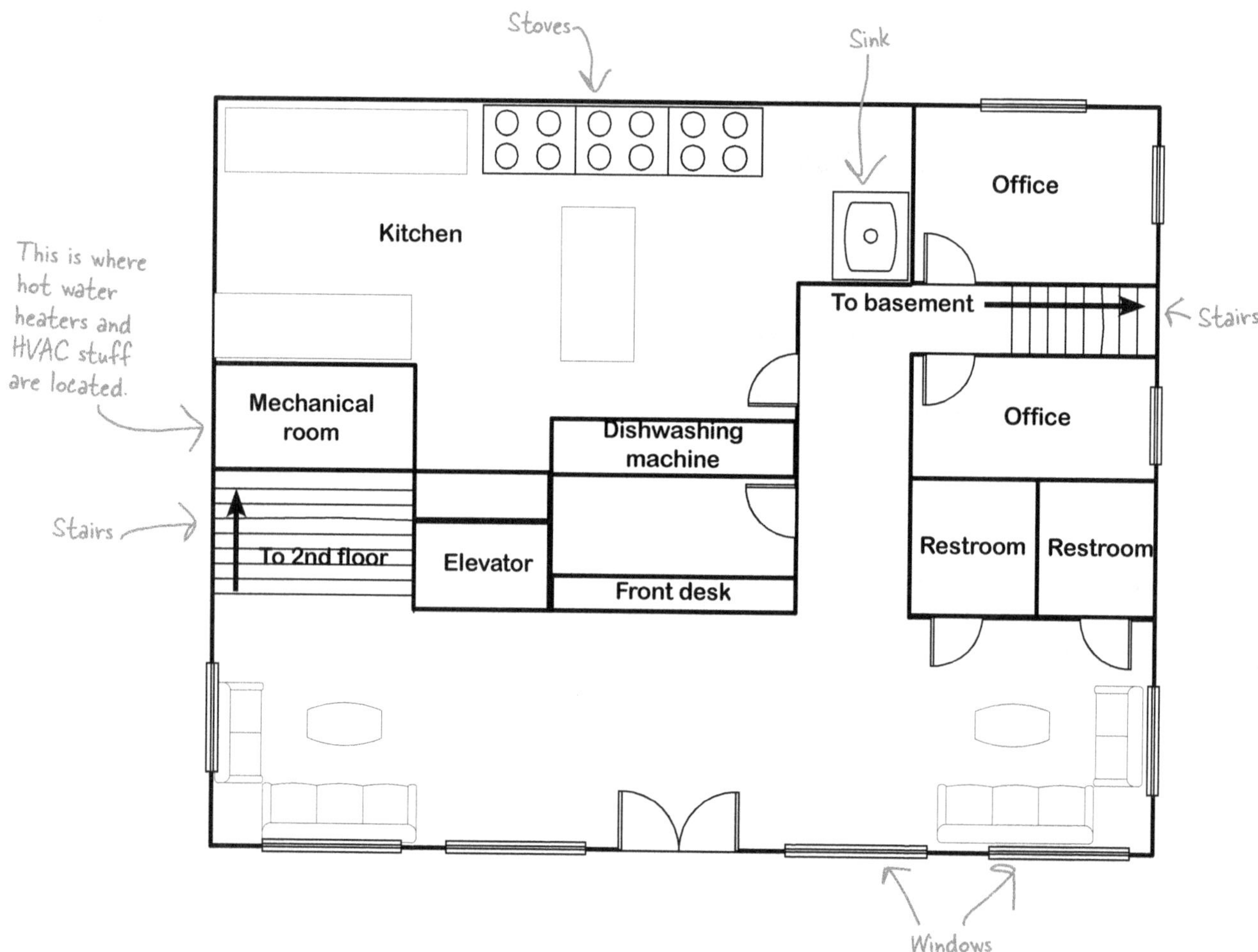

Ghost Watch has gotten hold of floorplans for each floor of the hotel they're investigating. We can use these to check for obstacles and plan where the network cables should go.

Here are the floorplans for the basement of the hotel.

Your task is to identify areas of the building that might pose problems in running cable or could damage the cable. Circle and make notes about five areas that might be problematic when the network cables are installed.

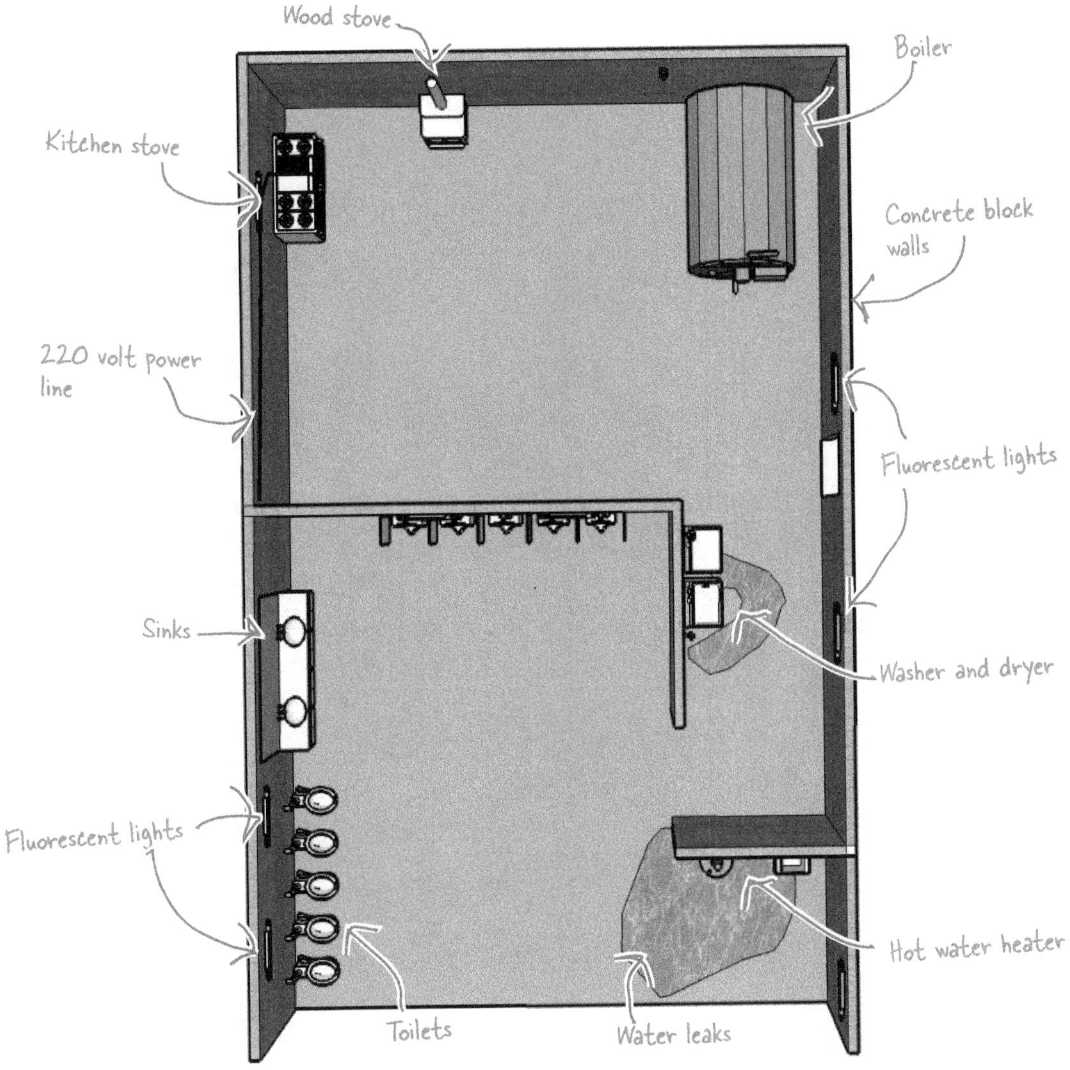

Wood stove

Boiler

Kitchen stove

Concrete block walls

220 volt power line

Fluorescent lights

Sinks

Washer and dryer

Fluorescent lights

Hot water heater

Toilets

Water leaks

Notes: The boiler may create heat and vibrations

Exercise Solution

Here are the floorplans for the basement of the hotel. We've drawn in the various recording devices that need to talk to one another.

Your task is to identify areas of the building that might pose problems in running cable or could damage the cable. Circle and make notes about five areas that might be problematic when the network cables are installed.

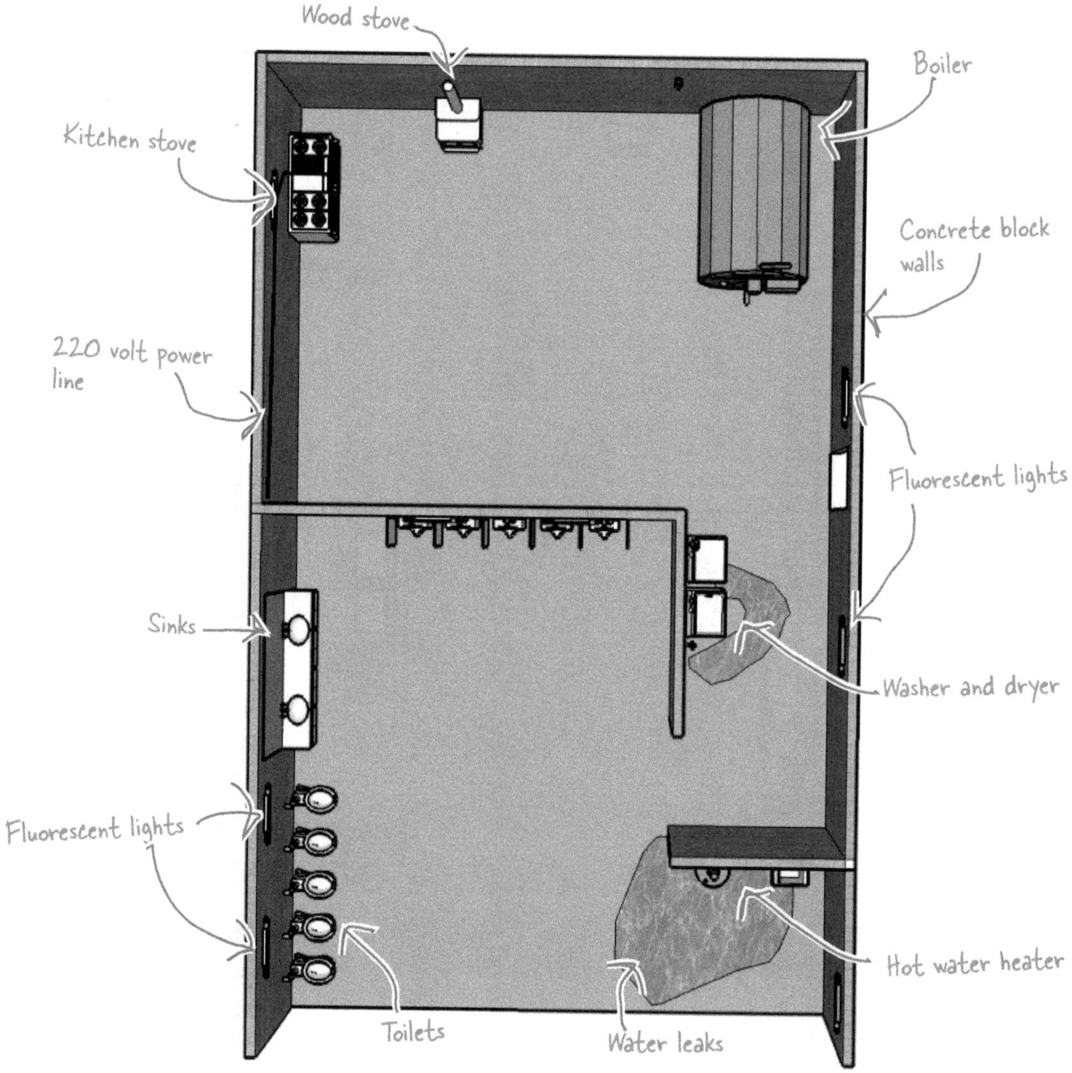

Wood stove
Boiler
Kitchen stove
Concrete block walls
220 volt power line
Fluorescent lights
Sinks
Washer and dryer
Fluorescent lights
Hot water heater
Toilets
Water leaks

Notes: The boiler may create heat and vibrations, so might the laundry equipment. There also may be water around the laundry equipment. The large electrical line needs to be avoided. The hot water heater and wood stove will be hot and need to be avoided. The fluorescent light may cause some interference.

Obstacles Up Close

So what should you do when you encounter obstacles in Networkville? Here's a quick guided tour.

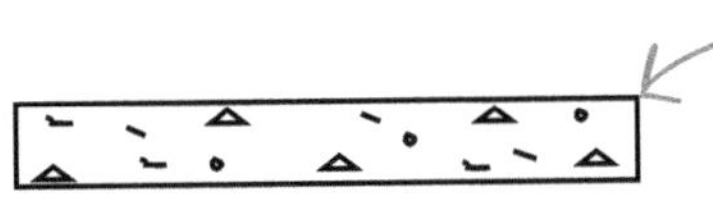

Walls

You can run your cables around walls, or drill through them instead. Pay attention to what your walls are made of. You need to be careful when you drill through concrete walls, and it can be hard to attach things to brick and concrete.

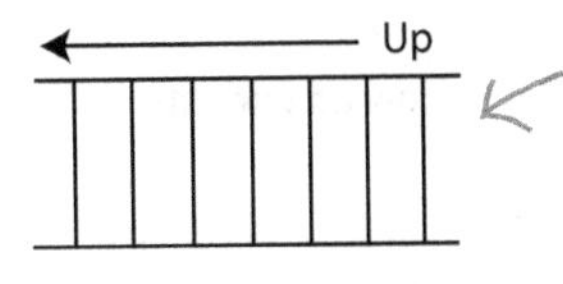

Stairs

You can use stairs as a way of getting cable from one floor to another, but make sure that it's out of the way of people using the stairs by using trays or J-Hooks.

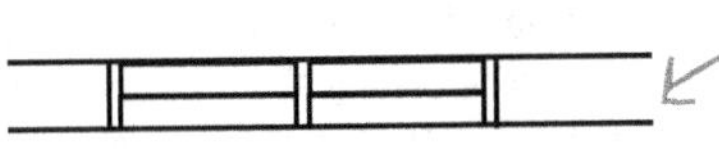

Windows

You can't run cables through or across windows. Run your cable above or below instead.

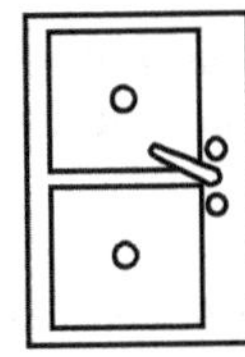

Sinks, showers, and all things wet

Water and cables don't mix. Water can corrode your cables or make them spark. Make sure you avoid running your cables near water, and in particular, don't run cables under sinks or showers.

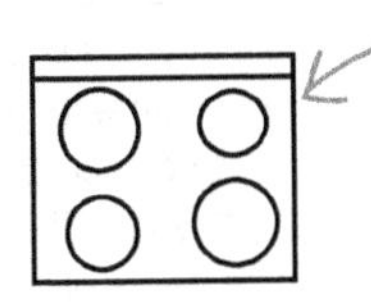

Stoves and all things hot

Network cables mustn't get too hot, so don't run network cables over or above stoves, or other obstacles that give off heat. Another problem with stoves is that electric stoves are supplied with 220VAC electrical lines, and this will cause noise in network cables that run too close.

Equipment with Electric Motors

As well as giving off heat, motors also give off vibrations and electromagnetic waves. Vibrations are bad for your network cables, so don't run cables over motors or similar devices. Electromagnetic waves can cause interference issues.

Ready to plot some network cables?

You've learned a lot about what obstacles can cause problems for your network layout. Let's see how you get on with planning the route the network cables should take for Ghost Watch.

there are no Dumb Questions

Q: Why will getting the list of devices wrong cost money down the road?

A: If a few devices are forgotten or added later in the project, that usually is not a big deal. But if a large number of devices are missed or misplaced, this can cause you to have to redo all your carefully planned wiring. Which means you just did the project twice.

Q: So should I make allowances in my plan for additional devices to be added?

A: Great idea! This will save you a tremendous amount of time, energy, and money down the road when other devices are added.

Q: How do I make those allowances?

A: First thing to do is to plan to run some extra cables. That way they are in place when you need them. You may need to run several types.

Second, add some length to the cables that are being run. That means if you plan calls for a 50' cable, add 5% to 10% or 2.5' to 7.5'. On longer runs, add 15%. Doing this will assure that you never come up short on cable.

Q: Do I need to worry about electrical power for the devices?

A: Good question. If the devices that you are dealing with need power, like computers, printers, or network devices, it would be a good idea to think about power. Often that is an afterthought. Even more, people tend to try to run too many devices from a particular electrical power source.

Q: How do I determine when I go through an obstacle versus going around it?

A: Many things impact this decision. First, is the network cabling being installed going to be permanent? If so, then you will want to use permanent solutions to get around obstacles. For example, if there is wall in your way, if the cable is going to stay in place, then you probably will want to go through the wall. If the cable is only temporary, then you will want to just go around the wall.

Q: How do I get through walls?

A: That depends on the type of wall. You can drill through a typical sheetrock covered wood or metal wall. These are the types of walls found in most homes. You will want to be careful about electrical lines inside the wall. Brick and concrete walls can be drilled through, but special drill bits and hammer-drills are needed.

Q: Should I talk with the building's owner or manager before running cables?

A: If the installation of the cables is going to be permanent, it is very important to include the people that live and own the space that you are running cable in. Sharing your plan with them can help you too. They may be able to suggest alternate routing of cables or other obstacles that you might not be aware of.

Sharpen your pencil

Take a stab at laying out the cables on this floor of the hotel. Draw cables from the cameras and mics to the monitoring desk, noting where you might go through walls.

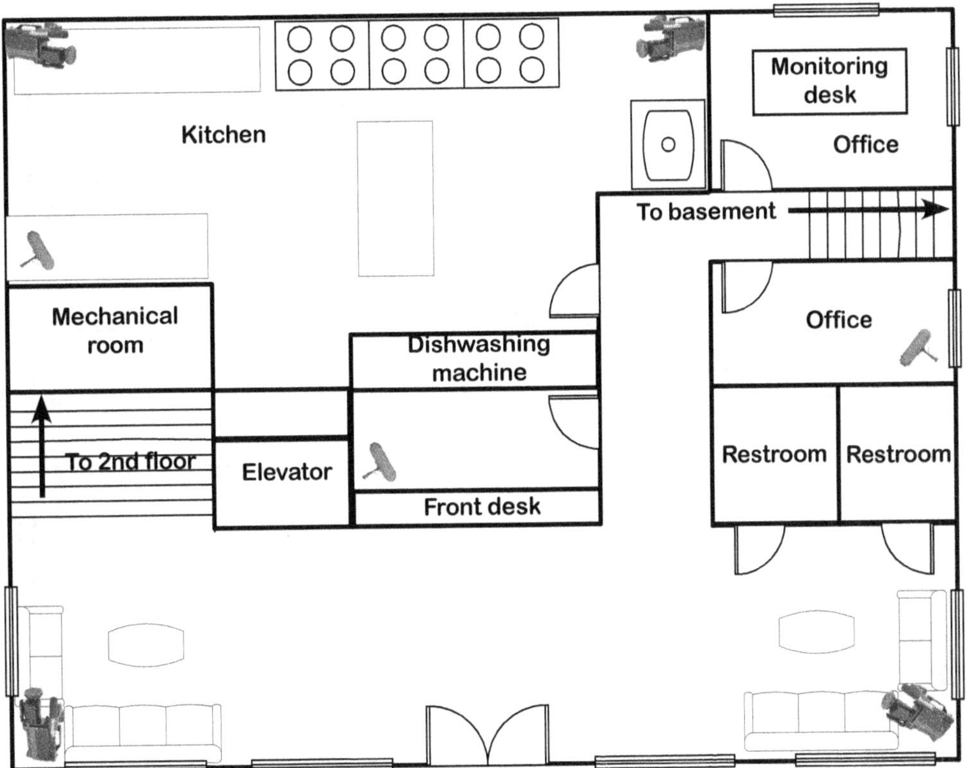

Sharpen your pencil Solution

Take a stab at laying out the cables on this floor of the hotel. Draw cables from the cameras and mics to the monitoring desk, noting where you might go through walls.

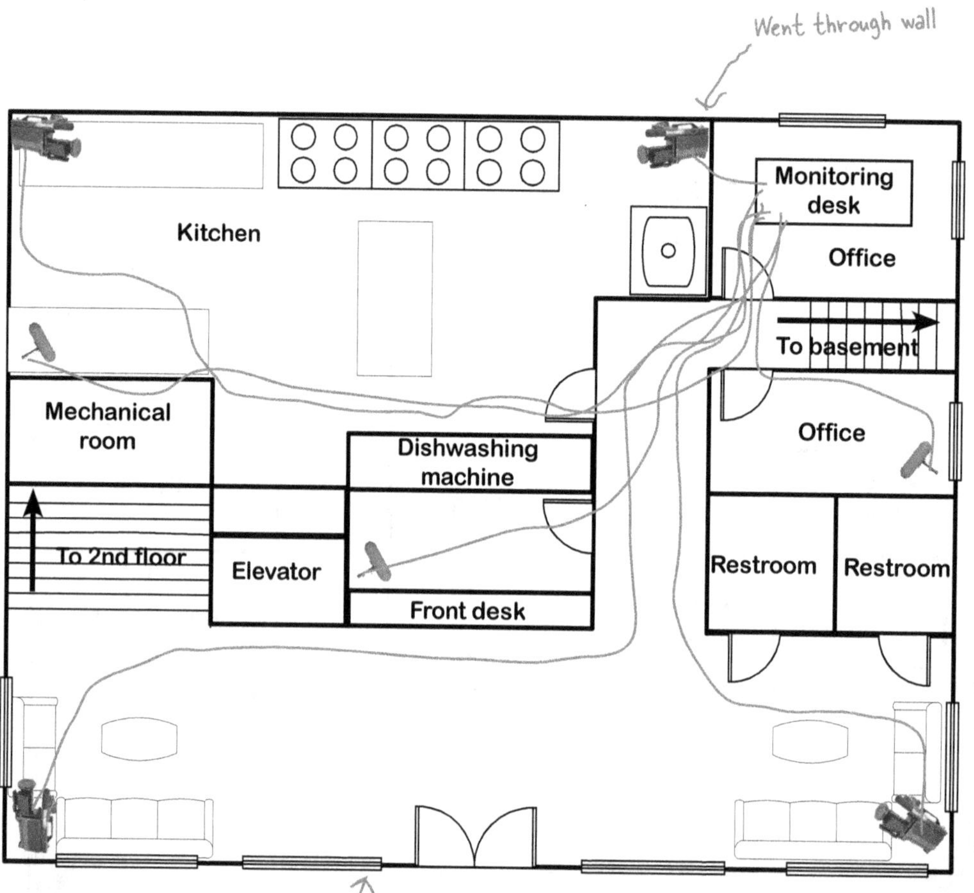

So where have we got to?

Let's take another look at the network planning steps and see how far along we are.

1. **List out the various network devices and where they will be located.**
Be sure you include what type of cable they need, for example, CAT-5.

2. **Adjusted your plan for obstacles**

3. **Make a list of the hardware you will need to run the cable.**
This includes things like cable trays, J-hooks, wire ties, and so on.

4. **Put your wire in!**
Run your cables between the various devices.

We've done the first two steps now.

Let's move onto the next step.

there are no Dumb Questions

Q: What do I do when there is solid concrete wall in the way?

A: You have a couple of solutions. Of course you could always figure out a way around the wall, but sometimes that is not an option. There are special drill bits and drills that will allow you to drill a hole through concrete. It is best to consult with the building manager before you do something like this.

Q: How do I deal with big electrical lines that are near where the network cable needs to go?

A: Avoid them! But you know that already. The worst thing to do is run the network cable parallel to the electrical line. If you have no choice but to run it parallel to an electrical line, then put a foot or two in between the network line and the electrical line.

Q: Should network cable ever run on the floor?

A: You need to avoid running network cables on the floor. You will see in many places that it is run that way. But it really becomes a hazard. People can trip on it. It can cause difficulties with wheelchair access. The cable can even be damaged from people walking on it. So try not to do this.

Q: How is network cable run in new buildings?

A: Good question. In new buildings, there are different types of conduits that are put in place when the building it under construction. Often it is the electrical contractor that will do this. This makes it very easy to run the network cables because you just pull them through the conduits that the electricians installed.

We need to decide on the cable management hardware

The next step on the plan is to take a look at the ***cable management hardware*** we need for the Ghost Watch network. So what's that?

So far, we've looked at all the routes our network cables should take, taking into account any obstacles and problem areas that might be in the way. Cable management hardware refers to all of the items we need to control how the cable goes where we want it to.

As an example, suppose we want to run a cable across the top of a doorframe. We can't just place the cable there; we need to hold it in place so that it stays where we want it to, stays out the way, and doesn't fall. Similarly, if we wanted to run cables along the side of a wall, we'd need cable management hardware to keep the cables out the way and stop them from straying.

I'm not sure we need cable management hardware on this gig; we're not going to be here for long. I've already used your plan to lay the network cables.

Even when the network's only short term, you still need cable management hardware.

Leaving stray cables around is dangerous—for people and for equipment. Sometimes poorly places cables are easy for people to trip on, and as we've seen, cables mustn't run through water or across obstacles that could damage the cabling. Even when you're setting up a temporary network, you still need to properly think it through.

So what does the cabling look like without the cable management hardware in place?

Uh oh! The cabling is a mess

Here's the network that's been laid out by the network guy. There are cables everywhere, and it's a hazard. So what can we do?

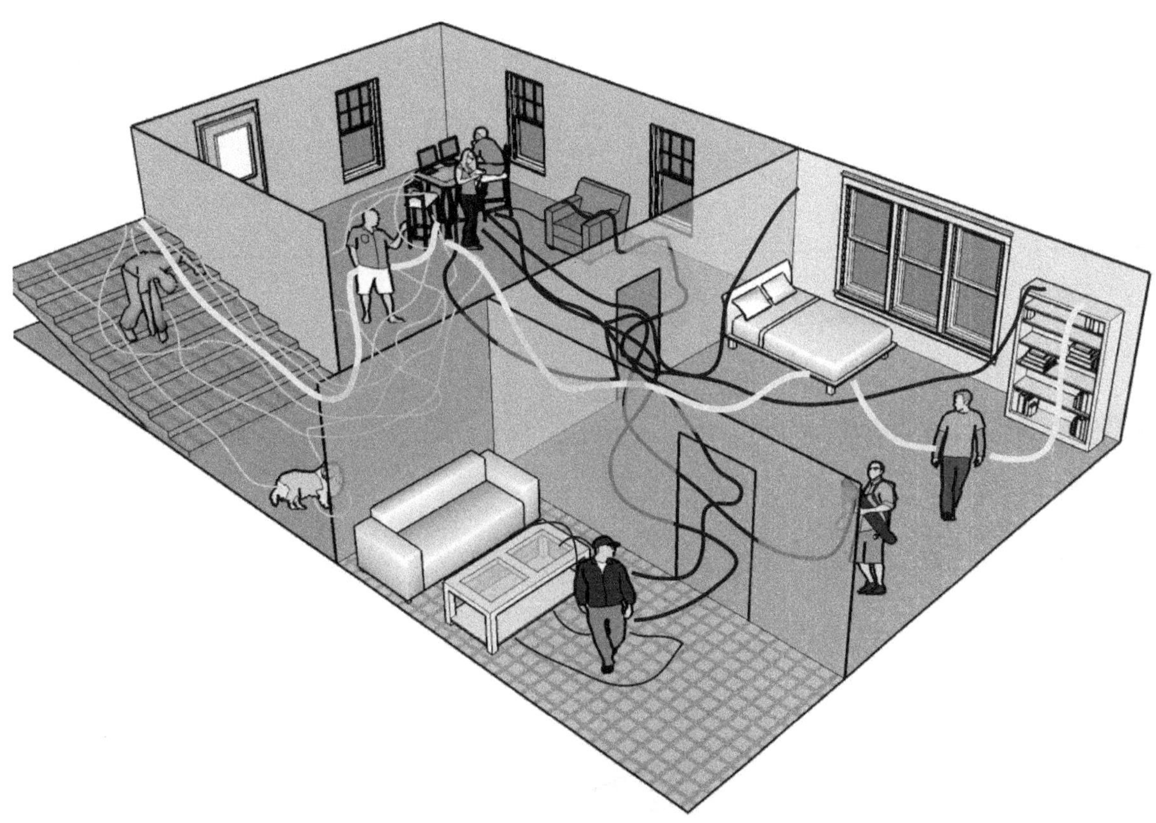

Sharpen your pencil

Take a look at the cabling efforts above. What sorts of problems do you see? How would you organize things differently?

Sharpen your pencil Solution

Take a look at the cabling efforts above. What sorts of problems do you see? How would you organize things differently?

We would use a j-hook to hang the cables coming down the stairs. We would put a cable tray in the back room where all the computers are located. All the cable could go into that tray. We would also use wire ties to bundle all the cables neatly.

Ghost Watch needs cable management hardware

As you can see, the cabling is hazardous without anything keeping the cables out of harms way. There are cables running from floor to ceiling, down the stairs, and haphazardly across the floor.

So what hardware is available to deal with these sorts of problems?

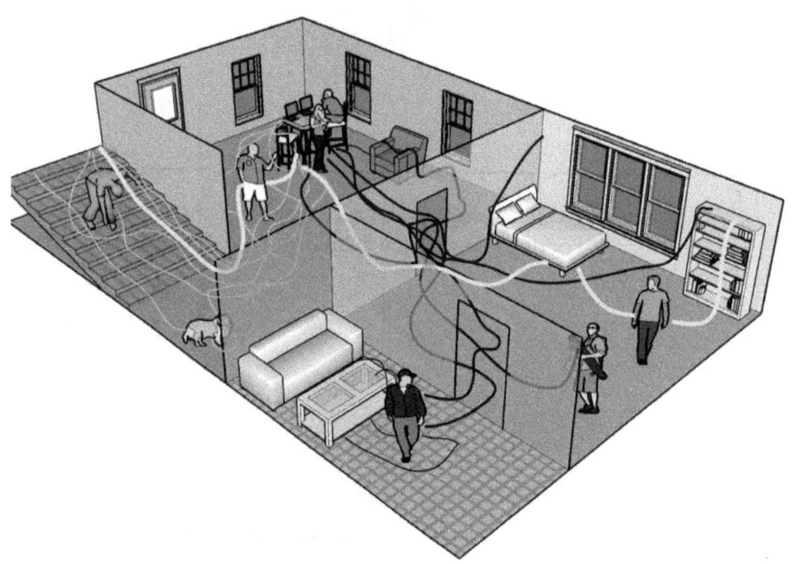

Cable Management Hardware Up Close

Let's take a closer look at what sorts of cable management hardware are around.

J-Hooks

J-hooks are used to hang cable from. These are usually attached to floor joists or beams.

Cable protectors

Cable Protectors are used to protect cables that have to run on floors. Great caution should be used when implementing these on a floor where there is a lot of traffic. The cable protector is a trip hazard and can create barriers for wheelchairs.

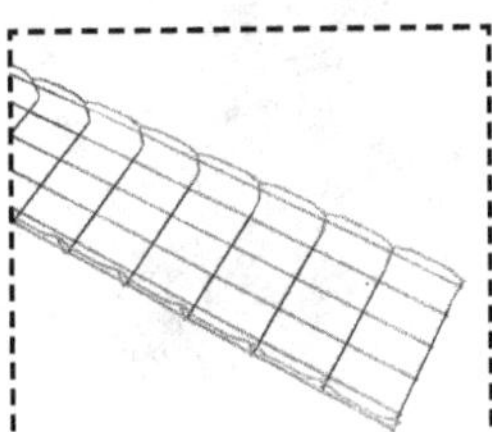

Cable trays

Cable trays are used to hold large numbers of cables that have to run relatively long distances. These are mostly used in basements, attics, and other hidden spaces because they are very industrial in appearance. Although, rooms that are network or computer specific often have trays running near the ceiling. Cable trays take a good deal of planning to install them correctly and some special tools.

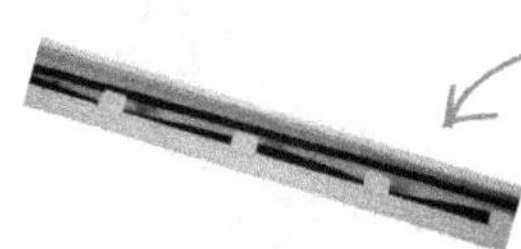

Raceways

A raceway is often used to run cable to workstations that do not have wall jack access. Often cubicle farms will have some form of raceway installed for phone and network cables.

Cable ties

Cable ties are a great way to keep cables neat. Just remember not to over tighten them. Overtightening a wire tie on Cat 5 cable can alter its twist and create problems with the cable.

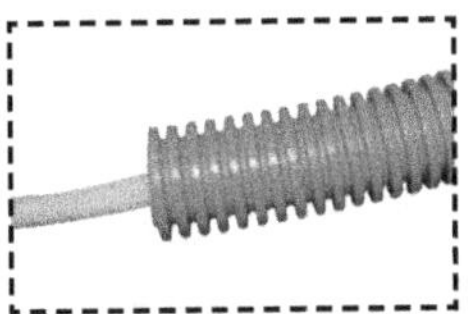

Smurf tubes

A smurf tube is generally run in new buildings inside the walls. One end attaching to a wall box, the other in some accessible but hidden place such as a basement or attic.

Things that go bump...

The microphones in the basement are picking up some strange noises. We need you to investigate if something is messing with the network cables and causing the noise.

Here is a diagram of the cable layout in the basement:

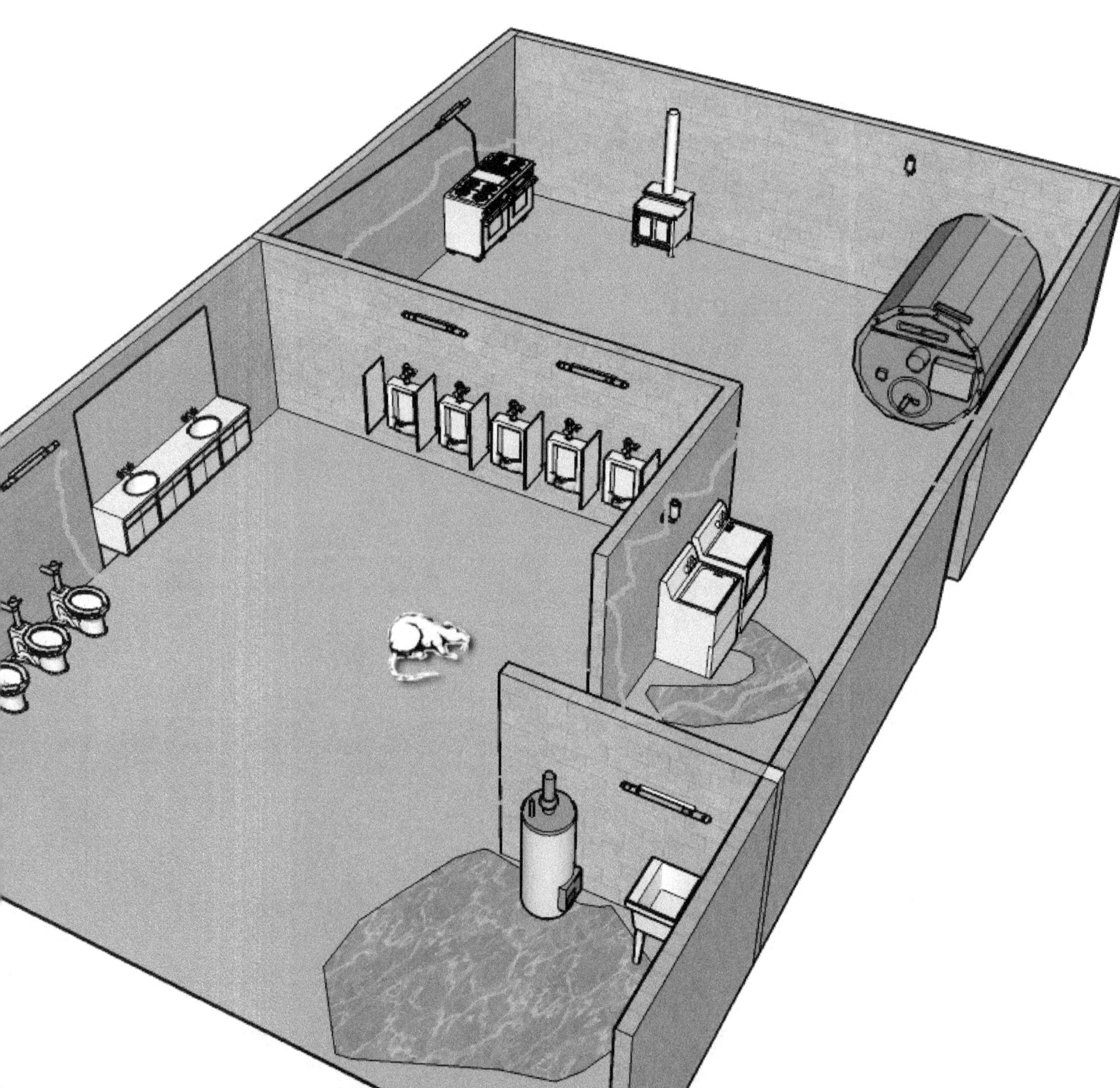

Noise can come from ghosts or from things messing with your cables.

Your cables are carrying electrical signals. Anything that affects the cables mechanically or electrically can create noise.

Please tell me that you heard that too!

Sharpen your pencil

Look at the cabling on the diagram to the left. Write down some things that could affect the cables and cause strange noises to be recorded.

Sharpen your pencil Solution

Look at the cabling on the diagram to the left. Write down some things that could affect the cables and cause strange noises to be recorded.

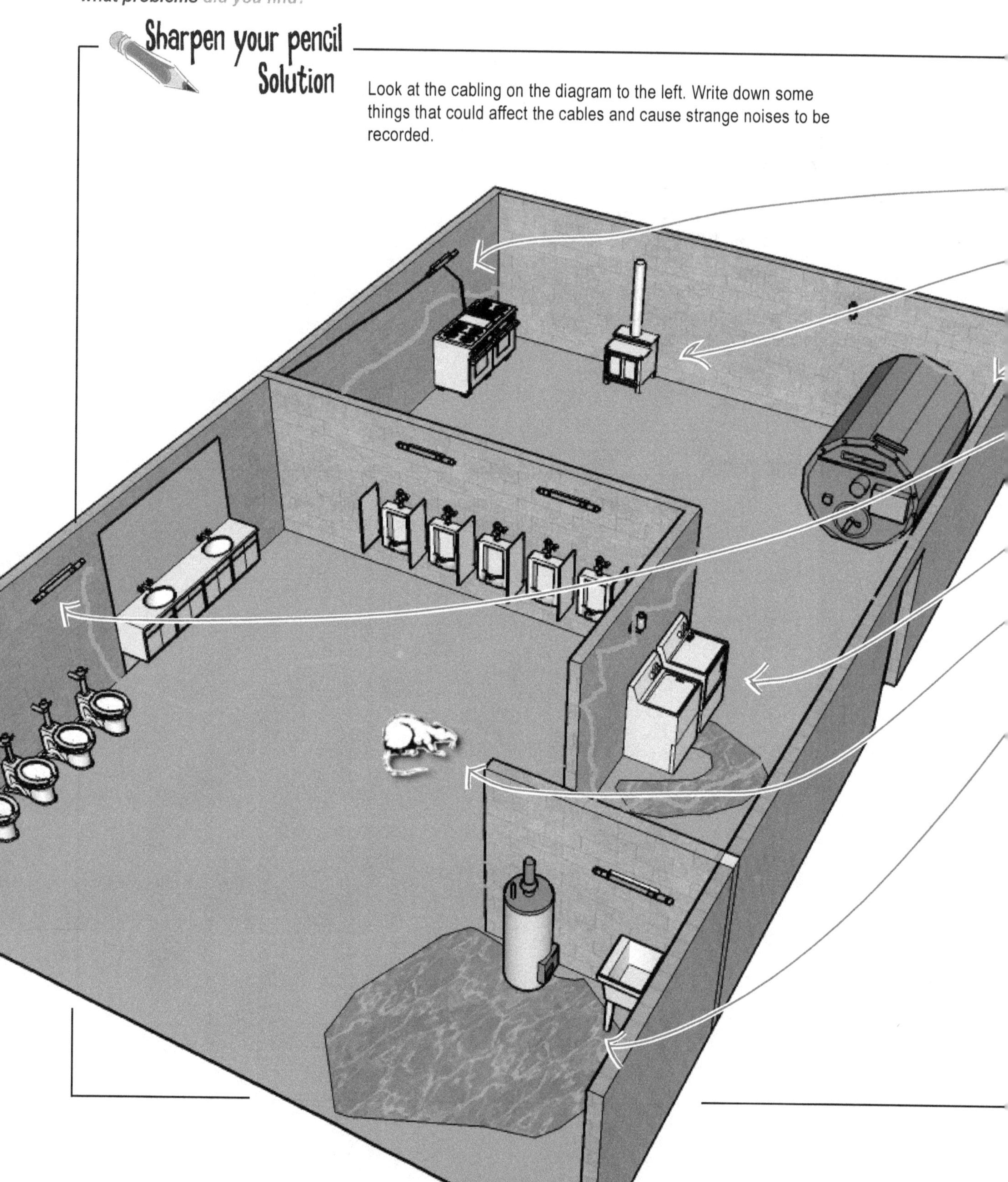

Be careful where you run cable. Power lines interfere with network cable signals.

Heat can really destroy cables.

Big pieces of industrial equipment like this boiler can destroy network cable with heat and vibration.

Fluorescent lights can cause noise in network cables

Big appliances can cause interference and vibration problems.

Rats and other vermin present big problems to network cables. They chew up wire, etc.

Water causes corrosion and shorts in cables.

So how is it going? Get that noise handled?

Frank: I think I got that noise taken care of by moving that cable near the stove. Are there other electrical things I should look out for?

Electrician: There are lots of things you need to look out for. First, some people that don't know any better run network cables in the same conduit as electrical line. That is a recipe for interference.

Frank: That is good to know. What are some other things?

Electrician: If you have the electricians run the smurf tube for your network gear, be specific about where you want it to run. If you let them decide, it may be hard to pull network cables to where you need it later on.

Frank: Should I visit with the electrician?

Electrician: You betcha! That is the best way to communicate what you need.

Plumber: Don't forget to visit with the HVAC and plumbing people as well.

Frank: Are there things I need to watch for with HVAC and plumbing?

Plumber: I would not run network cable under anything that holds water. Also, it is best if you run your trays after the HVAC and plumbing work is done in a new building. That way, things won't get moved after you have installed them to make way for some pipe.

Electrician: Remember too, if you need some tips on pulling lines and stuff, especially in difficult spots, visit with an electrician. He probably has run into a similar situation and knows a great solution.

You've really cleaned up that noise and straightened out MOST of the cables!

Well done! So far you've created an inventory of devices that Ghost Watch need, you've planned where the cables should run, and you've also used cable management hardware to really tidy things up around the hotel.

So what do we mean by most cables?

What's in the closet?

Unfortunately, some of our wiring runs through the hotels old wiring closet and it is a mess! There are cables everywhere, and it's impossible to tell which cable belongs to which device.

The Ghost Watch team may need to react quickly if their cameras pick up signs of activity, and they can't afford to miss valuable footage for their show. But how can they tell which cable is which?

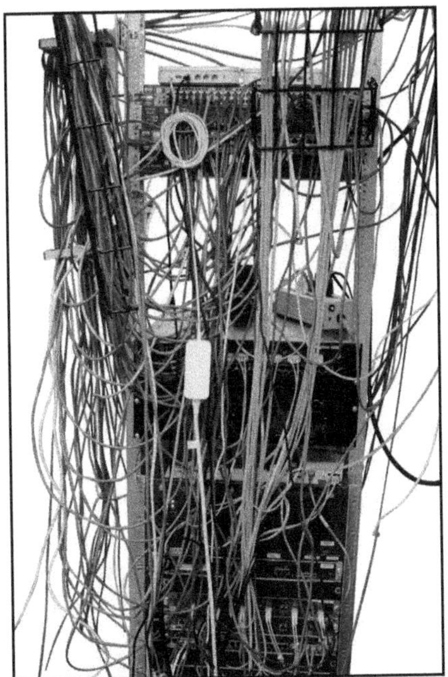

BRAIN POWER

How could you find out which cable is linked to which device?

Let's start by labeling the cables

One of the problems that Ghost Watch has is that it's difficult to tell which cable belongs to which device. There are so many cables, and each of them look identical. It would help if we labeled each cable, but we can only do that once we know where each cable is going and what it links to. So how do we do that?

Can you remember the toner and tracer set we saw in the last chapter? Well, we can cleverly use this equipment to make sense of our cables.

1. **Hook the toner up to the far end of the cable.**
   This is the end that's away from the wiring closet. It could be a wall jack or whatever's on the end.

Toners have alligator clips that are used to clip onto the wires.
Hey, buddy, you hear me?

2. **Use the tracer on the wiring closet side to check all the cables.**
   When you hear the tone, you know you've found the cable.

3. **Use a cable labeler to print out a label, then stick it on the cable.**
   Then repeat for all the unlabeled cables in the closet.

A cable labeler prints out labels that wrap around the cable. Some labels even have a protective coat.

But there are still lots of cables

Even when the cables are labeled, the closet still looks messy, with spaghetti-like structures falling in front of other things in the closet.

One thing we can do is gather the cables into manageable bundles, and tie them out of the way using plastic wire ties or velcro straps. This will make it clearer where each cable is going. The key thing here is not to tie the cables too tightly, as this can alter the electrical characteristics of the cables.

Cable management trays are also useful to keep cable from falling in front of other things in the closet.

Make sure not to put the wire ties on too tight; that can alter the electrical characteristics of the Cat 5 cable.

The horizontal cable management tray keeps cable from falling in front of other things in the rack.

But what else can we do?

Even though this helps, there's still a problem. There are still a lot of cables to search through when you're looking for one in particular, and the cable labels can be hidden or even fall off.

Sound impossible? Don't worry, there's something that will solve all of these problems and many more. It's called a ***patch panel***.

So what's a patch panel?

A patch panel is used to organize the cable and wire connections in your wiring closet. Cables coming from your network devices or wall jacks plug into the back of the patch panel, and these are connected to other devices using short patch cables at the front. It's typically mounted on a network rack, a specialized frame that forms the physical skeleton of your network closet like this:

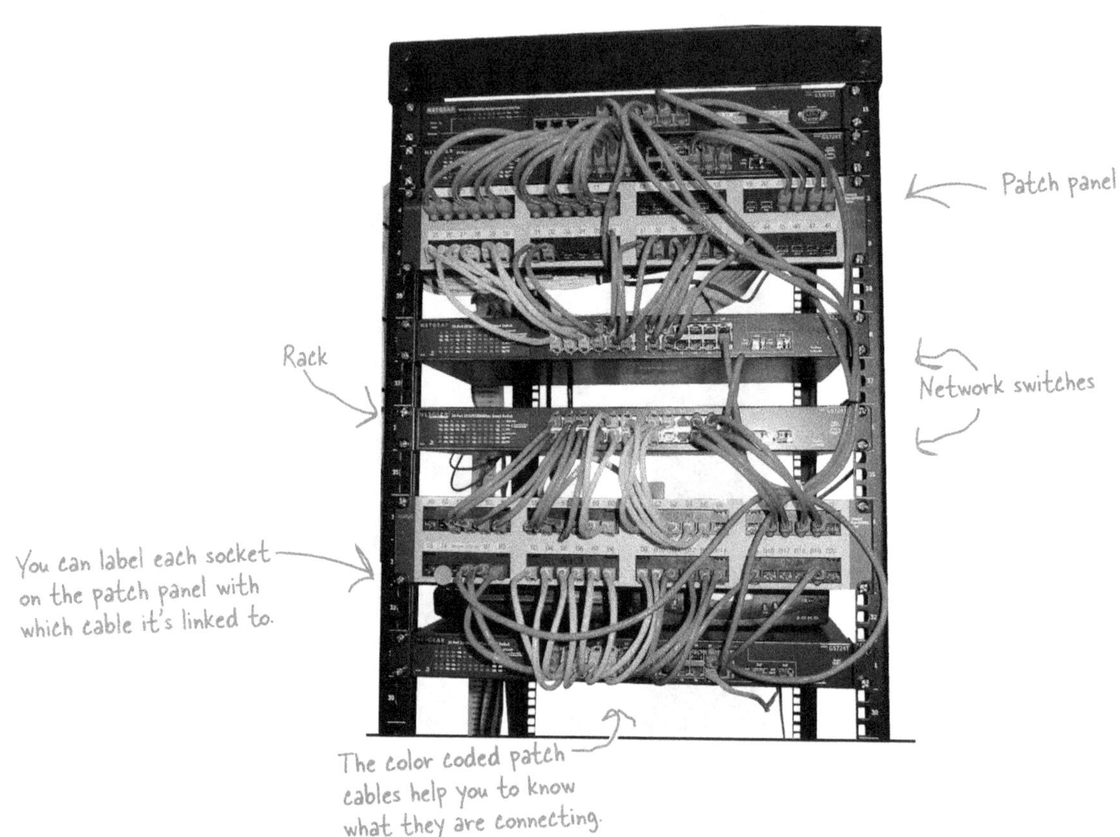

Patch panel
Rack
Network switches
You can label each socket on the patch panel with which cable it's linked to.
The color coded patch cables help you to know what they are connecting.

So how does a patch panel work?

** Image courtesy of Andrew Zadorozny, www.fastlinkcabling.com

Behind the scenes of a patch panel

So how do you connect devices together with a patch panel? Let's take a look.

A patch panel works like a telephone switchboard, but for cables.

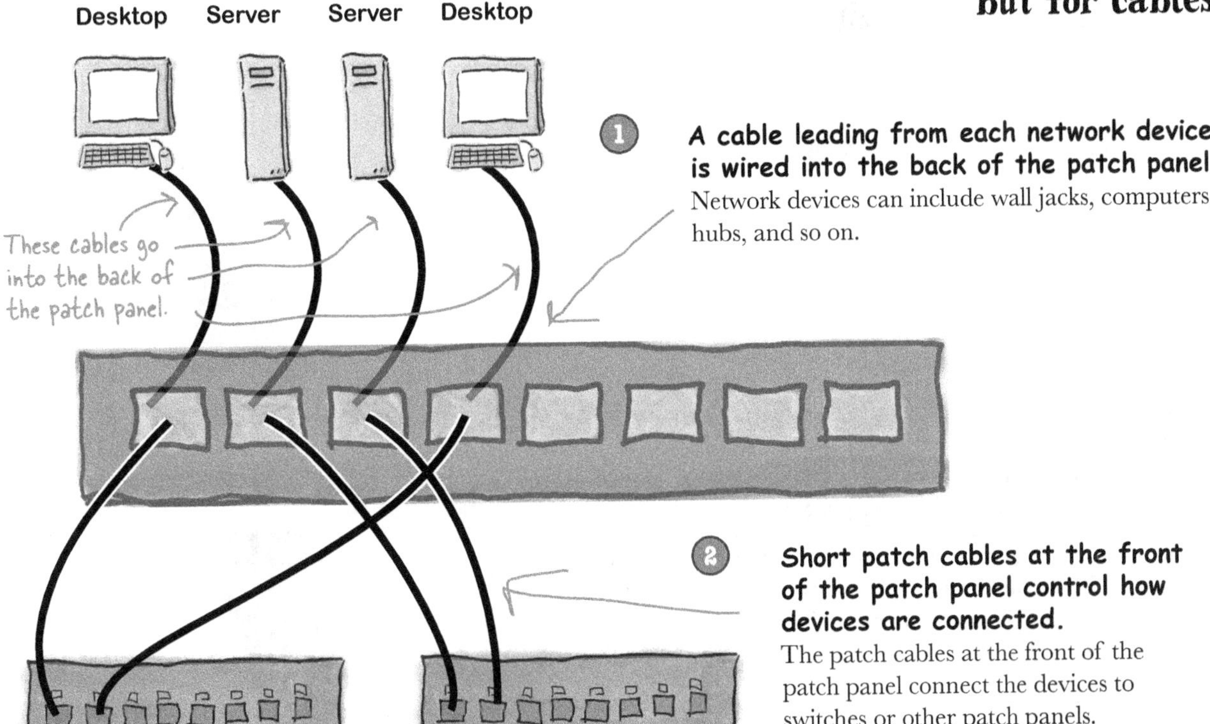
Desktop
Server
Server
Desktop
These cables go into the back of the patch panel.

1. **A cable leading from each network device is wired into the back of the patch panel.** Network devices can include wall jacks, computers, hubs, and so on.

2. **Short patch cables at the front of the patch panel control how devices are connected.** The patch cables at the front of the patch panel connect the devices to switches or other patch panels.

3. **To change the connection, simply change which socket the patch cable goes into.**

If you use a patch panel, it means that it's much easier to change the connection between two devices. All you need to do is change which socket the patch cables at the front are connected to, so the patch panel gives you an easier interface for managing connections.

Let's look in more detail at what goes on behind the patch panel.

The wires go into a punch down block

If you turn the patch panel over, you'll see a ***punch down block***. You punch individual wires into the block using an impact punch tool.

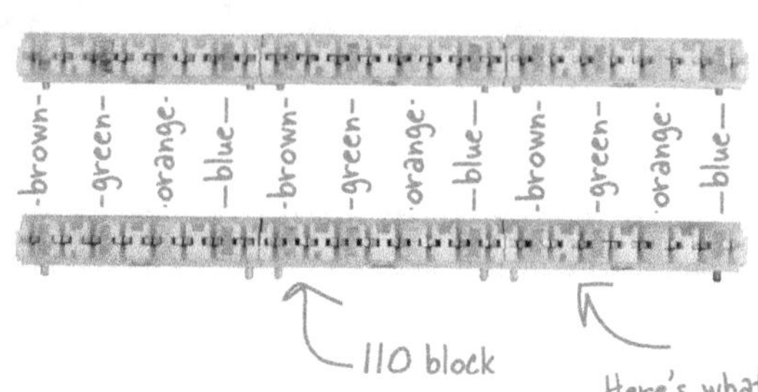

Here's what's behind a patch panel; it's a punch down block.

You install wires using an impact punch tool.

The way in which you install the wires is important. The wires follow a specific color pattern, and you need to follow this so that you can make connections between devices. The pattern depends on the type of block you're using and the type of wire you're punching into the block.

Each cable or set of wires corresponds to a socket on the front of the patch panel. If you label each socket with what it's connected to, you'll be able to tell at a glance what each of your network devices are connected to, and it will also be much easier to change the connections.

The general form for labeling the sockets on your patch panel is to use the room number followed by the jack or node number. As an example, you'd label the socket connected to room C node 1 as "C1."

66–block is an older block style.

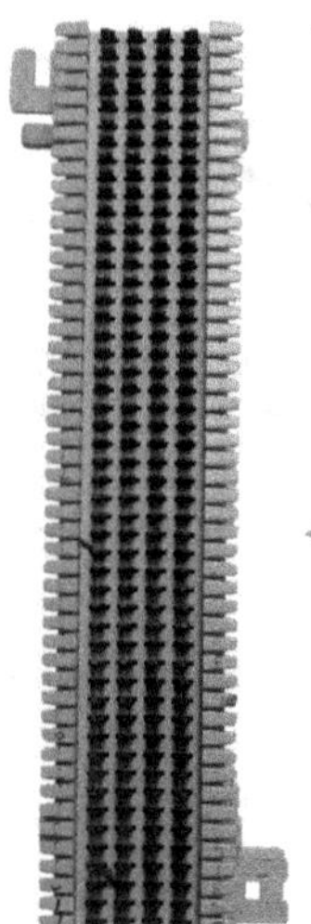

Use the information from the table below to connect the various servers, desktops and switches to the appropriate device. Draw a connection line from the patch panel to the end device.

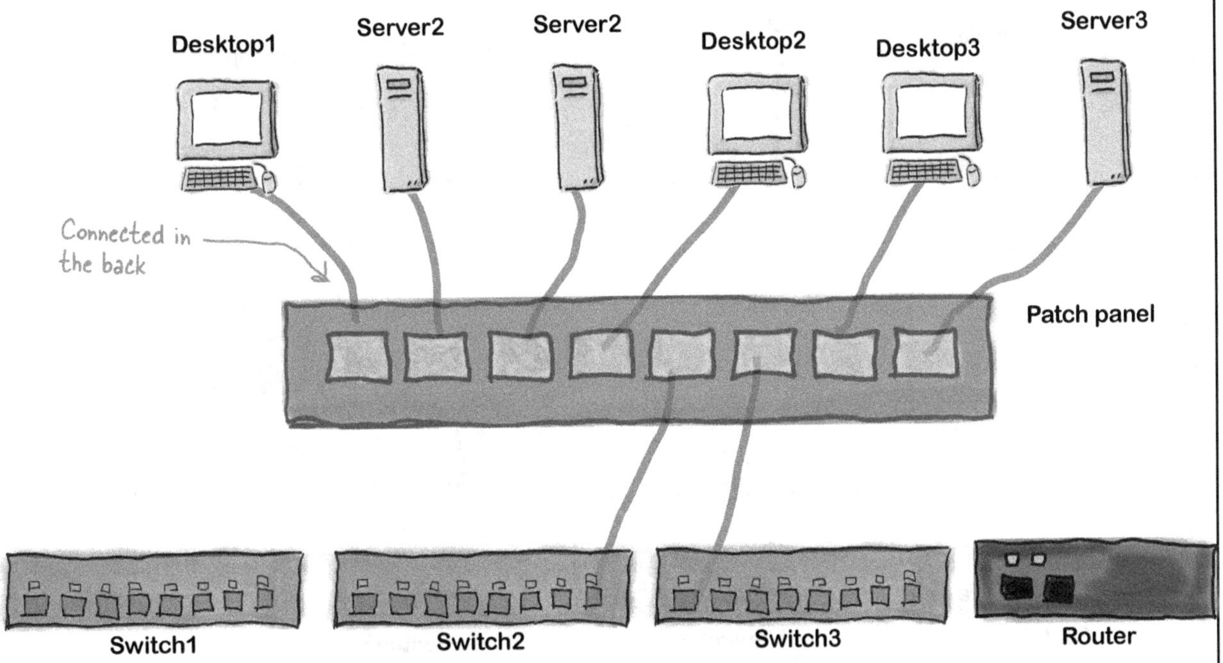

Device	Connect To
Desktop1	Switch1
Desktop2	Switch1
Desktop3	Switch3
Server1	Switch2
Server2	Switch2
Server3	Switch3
Switch3	Switch1
Switch2	Router

Exercise Solution

Use the information from the table below to connect the various servers, desktops and switches to the appropriate device. Draw a connection line from the patch panel to the end device.

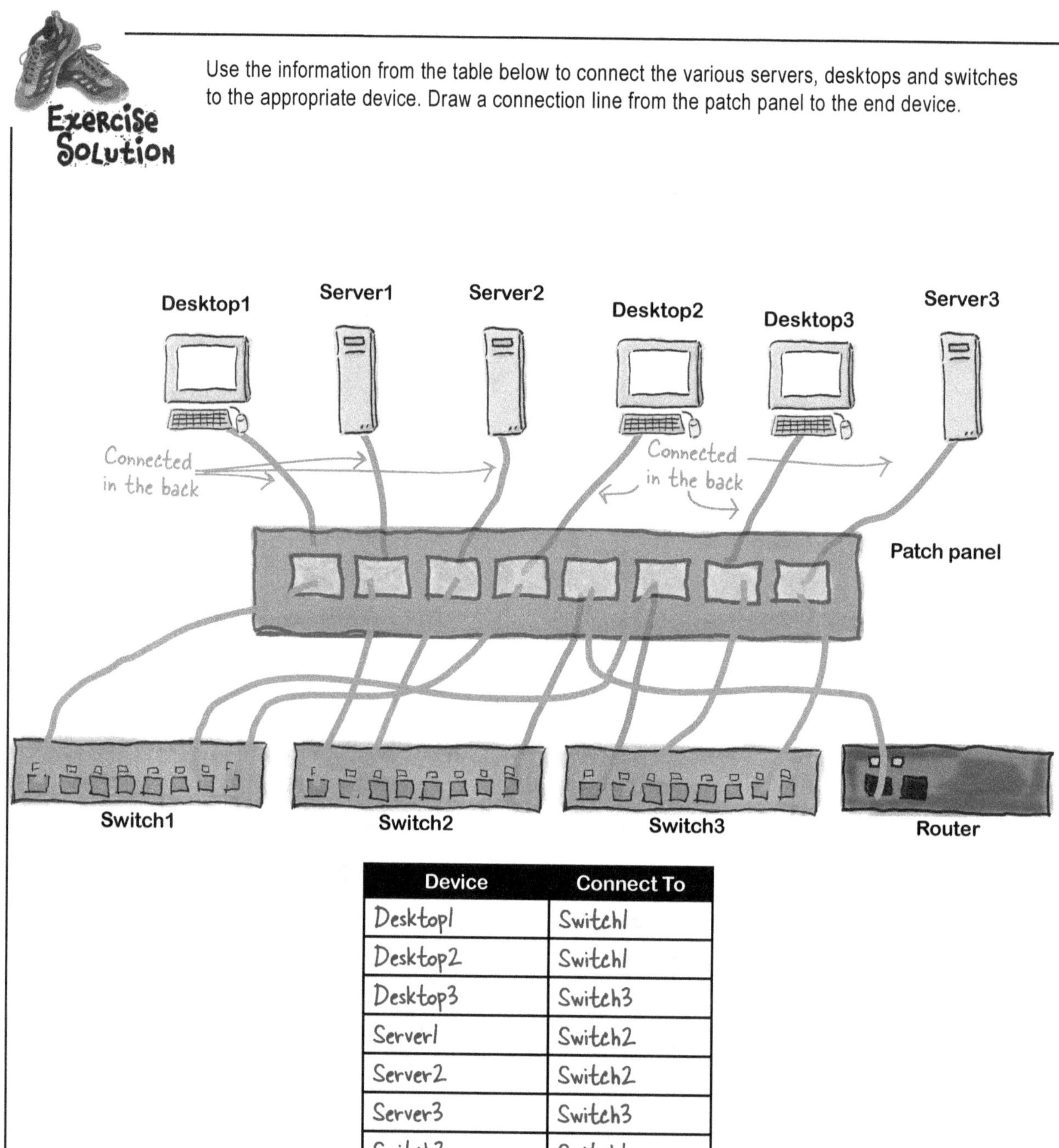

Device	Connect To
Desktop1	Switch1
Desktop2	Switch1
Desktop3	Switch3
Server1	Switch2
Server2	Switch2
Server3	Switch3
Switch3	Switch1
Switch2	Router

Take a look at these pictures of network hardware. For each one, say what it's called and whether it's a tool or cable management device.

	Name	Tool/Cable Management
	______________	______________
	______________	______________
	______________	______________
	______________	______________
	______________	______________
	______________	______________

Who Does What? Solution

Take a look at these pictures of network hardware. For each one, say what it's called and whether it's a tool or cable management device.

Name	Tool/Cable Management
Patch Panel	Cable Management
Punch Down Tool	Tool
Cable Ties	Cable Management
Cable Labler	Tool
Smurf Tube	Cable Management
J-Hook	Cable Management

Roll the cameras!

Thanks to you, Ghost Watch has an awesome network set up in the haunted hotel. Filming starts tonight, and the Ghost Watch team is confident they'll get all the spooky footage they need for their next program.

3 tools and troubleshooting

Into the Wire

How do you know when a network signal isn't getting through a network cable? Often the first thing you'll hear about it is when the network stops working effectively, but the trouble is, it's hard to tell what's wrong by just looking at a cable. Fortunately, there's a raft of tools you can use that let you see deep into the heart of your network cables, down to the signal itself. Keep reading, and we'll show you how to use these tools to troubleshoot your networks, and how to interpret the secrets of the signal.

Mighty Gumball won the Super Bowl contract

Mighty Gumball is the leading vendor of a wide variety of candies and chocolates, and they've just won an exclusive contract to sell their products at the next Super Bowl. With sales on the day and all the extra publicity, Mighty Gumball stands to make millions.

There's just one problem. Mighty Gumball has recently been plagued by network problems, and it's hitting gumball production. If they don't get their network errors fixed soon, they won't be able to produce enough gumballs in time for the Super Bowl, and they'll lose the contract.

We can't lose this contract; we've got to get our network sorted. I'll give $5,000 to whoever finds out what's wrong. I'll even throw in a year's supply of gumballs.
Mighty Gumball CEO

Am I missing the point here? Can't we just use a toner and tracer? Won't that find the problems?

Toner and tracer sets can't find every problem.

So far, we've only looked at network problems that toner and tracers can help us find, and while they're extremely useful, they can't root out every kind of network problem.

Here are some of the potential network problems that might be affecting Mighty Gumball. Can you see which ones a toner and tracer might not be able to detect?

Potential network cable problems

- Broken cables.
- Bad connectors.
- Mis-wired connectors.
- Too close to a power cable.
- Too long a cable.
- Wrong type of cable used.

Why is each of these a problem? Why do you think you can't use a toner and tracer set to detect all of these?

A toner and tracer can check for a signal...

As we saw earlier, we can use a toner and tracer to listen out for signs of life from electrons. The toner sends a signal along the cable, and provided you hook it up to the same cable, the tracer picks up the signal from the electrons. If the tracer can't pick up the signal at any point along the cable, this means there's a break at that point.

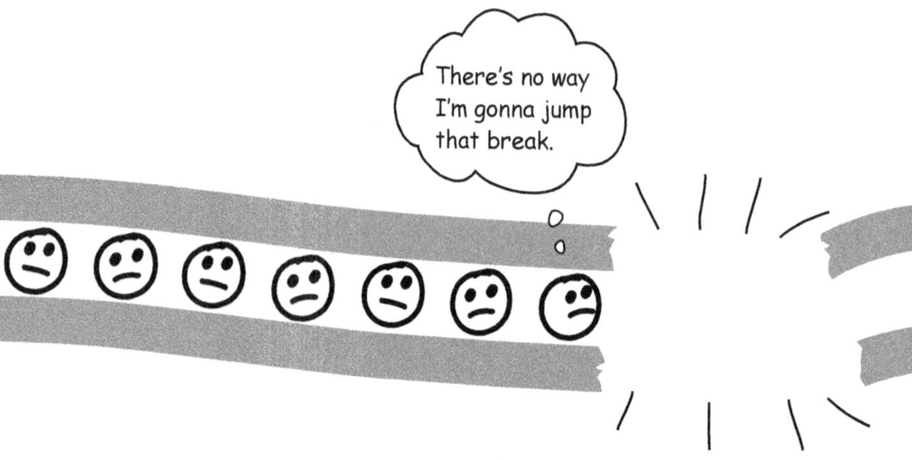

There's no way I'm gonna jump that break.
When there's a break in continuity, the electrons can't get through, so the tracer can't pick up the signal.

...but can't check for signal quality

If there's a connected wire going all the way through the cable, then the tracer will be able to pick up the signal along the entire length of the cable. The trouble is, it can't tell you anything about the quality of the signal, or the speed with which it moves along the cable. All it can tell you is that the wire is continuous.

If the wire's continuous, the tracer will pick up a signal all the way along the cable. What it can't tell you is anything about the signal quality.

So if the network problem's down to signal quality, you need something more than a toner and tracer. But what?

BE the Toner & Tracer

Your job is to play like you're the toner & tracer and imagine that you are facing the problems shown below. Say if you can help or not, and why or why not.

Problem	Can you help?	Tell us more
The wrong cable is plugged into a device.	☐ Yes ☐ No	....
The cable is wired improperly.	☐ Yes ☐ No	....
The cable is longer than the recommended maximum for Ethernet (100 meters).	☐ Yes ☐ No	....

BE the Toner & Tracer Solution

Your job is to play like you're the toner & tracer and imagine that you are facing the problems shown below. Say if you can help or not, and why or why not.

Problem	Can you help?	Tell us more
The cable is plugged to the wrong end.	☑ Yes ☐ No	You can hook the tracer on the correct wire and use the toner to find the correct plug on the opposite end.
The cable is wired improperly.	☑ Yes ☐ No	You can trace each wire of a cable and find the incorrect wires and fix them.
The cable is longer than the recommended maximum for Ethernet (100 meters).	☐ Yes ☑ No	A simple toner & tracer set will only tell you if there is a connected wire or not. You cannot tell the length with just a toner and tracer.

Well, I don't know about you guys, but I'm going after that $5,000 bonus.
Frank
Jim
Joe

Joe: Yeah? Me too. There must be some pretty hairy problems if the toner and tracer can't find them all.

Jim: Well, I'm going to set my multimeter to work on the cables. I'll soon be $5,000 richer.

Frank: A multimeter? Are you crazy? What's a multimeter going to tell you about the state of the cables?

Jim: Just wait and see. You might learn something.

there are no Dumb Questions

Q: Can a toner and tracer find a cable that is too long?

A: No. A toner and tracer can only check for whether there is a electrical connection. To check for the length, you need to measure the resistance of the cable.

Q: What signals can a toner send?

A: Generally, a toner can send a warbling type of signal that is used to trace or find the end of a cable.

A second signal is just a voltage that the tracer checks for on the other end. This is used to check a cable for breaks. This is called continuity.

Q: Does a tracer have to touch a cable to hear the warbling signal?

A: No, that is the nice thing about it. You can run it quickly over some wires and actually hear as you get closer to the wire that the toner is connected to.

Introducing the multimeter

As you can probably tell from its name, a multimeter is a versatile tool that measures multiple things, such as voltage and resistance along a cable. To use it, turn the selector knob on the multimeter to whatever it is you want to to measure, and then touch the probes to opposite ends of the wire you're testing. You then read the measurement off the multimeter display.

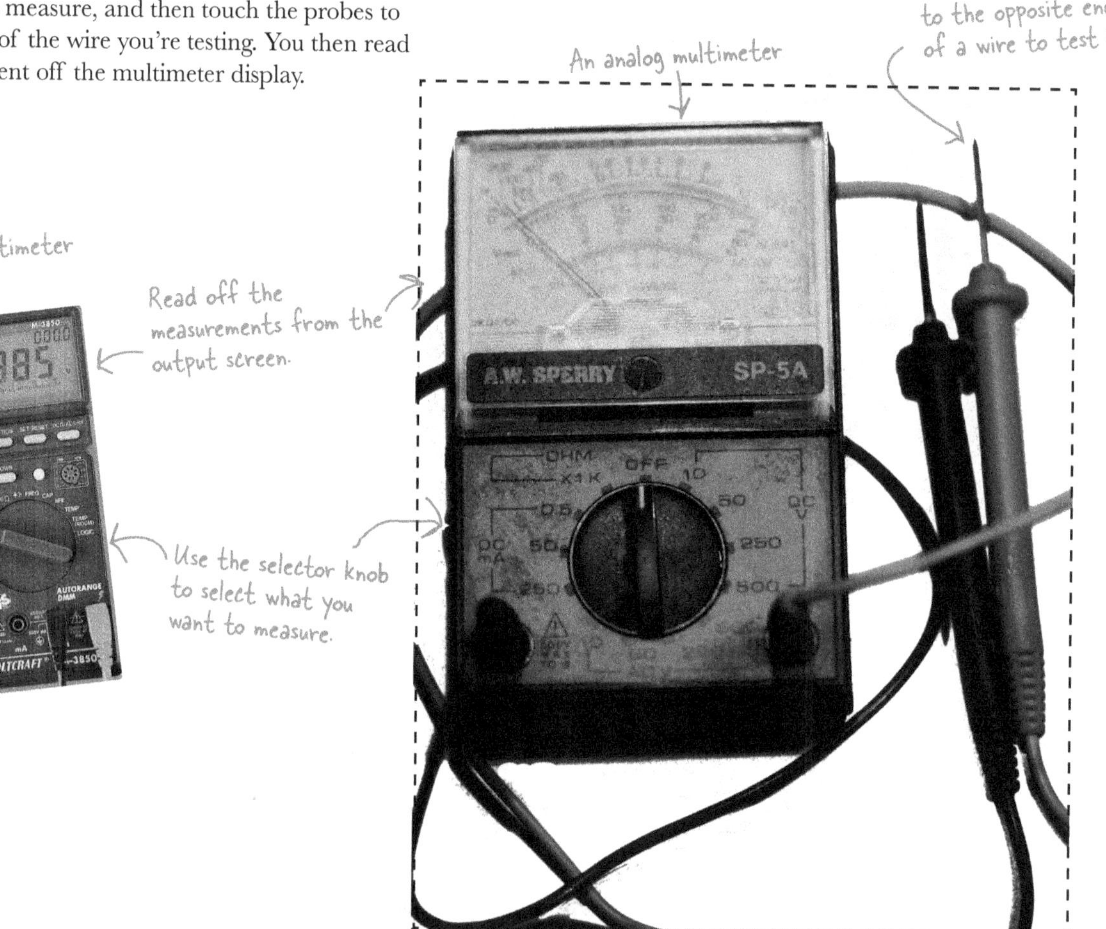
An analog multimeter
You touch the probes to the opposite ends of a wire to test it.
A digital multimeter
Read off the measurements from the output screen.
Use the selector knob to select what you want to measure.
0.385
VOLTCRAFT
A.W. SPERRY
SP-5A
OHM
OFF
DC V
DC mA

Use a multimeter to measure resistance

The thing that makes the multimeter really useful in networking is its ability to measure resistance along a cable. This is something that a toner and tracer can't tell you, and it can shed important light on how a cable is functioning.

So what's resistance, and what effect does it have on your network?

So what's resistance?

Resistance is a measurement of how hard it is for electrons to move through a wire. It's measured in ohms, and represented by the Greek letter omega, Ω. The higher the number of ohms, the harder it is for electrons to move through the wire.

When resistance is low

When a cable has low resistance, this means that it's easy for electrons to pass through the conductor. There's very little stopping the electrons from flowing, and so they move quickly and easily along the cable.

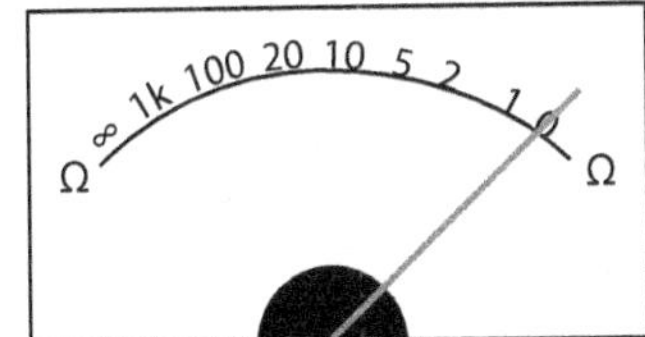

When resistance is low, electrons can move quickly and easily along the wire.

When resistance is high

When a cable has resistance that's high, this means that it's difficult for electrons to move through the wire. And if the electrons can't move well, your signal can't either.

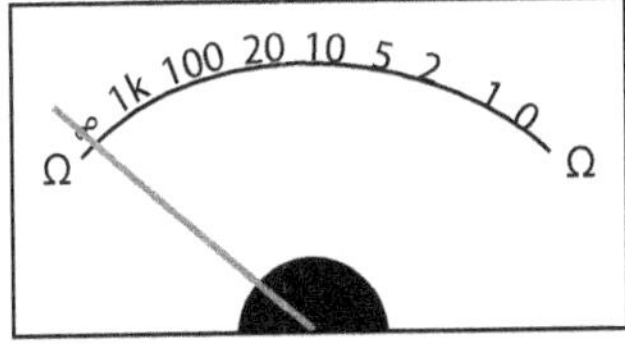

Oh man, this is like molasses; it's gonna take forever.

So if you're having network problems, you can use a multimeter to check out whether high resistance along the cable is slowing down your signal.

Fireside Chats

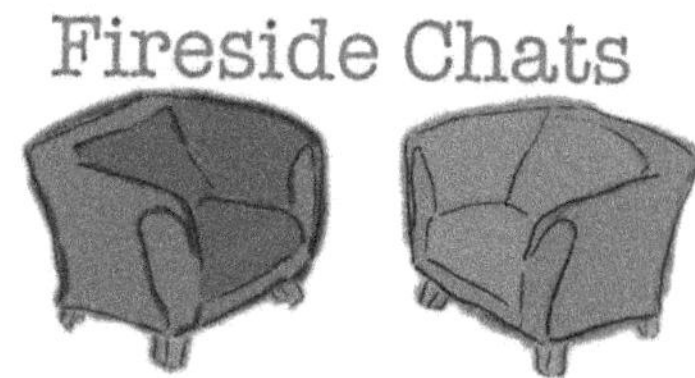

Tonight's talk: **Toner & Tracer vs. Multimeter**

Toner & Tracer:

Whoa, what are you doing here, Multimeter?

Multimeter:

What do you mean? I do networking too, you know.

Toner & Tracer:

I guess, like a screwdriver has uses in networking as well. We're made for finding broken cables and tracing cables. What can you possible add?

Multimeter:

Well I can tell how long a cable is by measuring its resistance. I can find broken cables as well!

Toner & Tracer:

That resistance thing is nice, but we don't think it's used very much. Your biggest problem is that both ends of the cable must be right next to you, how lame's that?

Multimeter:

You kind of got me there.

Toner & Tracer:

We even work on cables where the ends are in different buildings. Tracer doesn't even need to be touching the cable; we can keep tabs on each other with magnetic induction.

Multimeter:

But I have ways to measure cables like that. I can create a loop and then make measurements on that. Notice I said *measurements*.

Toner & Tracer:

What is that supposed to mean? Just because you give some number readout doesn't make you more useful. We're simple and effective at our job.

Multimeter:

Yeah, *your* job. Notice my name has multi in it. That means I can do multiple things, not like you. I can also measure how fast the electrons are flowing, or current. Can you do that? Can you?

Toner & Tracer:

Well...

Multimeter:

Anyway, gotta dash, I'm needed for some resistance training. See you around, guys.

Match up the wire with the resistance than an electron moving through these wires would feel.

A really long wire

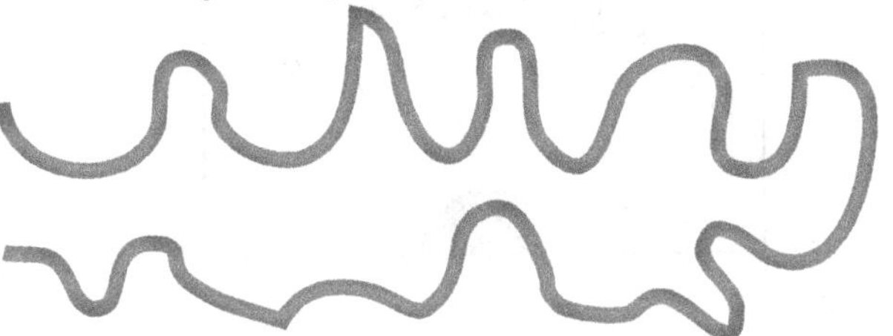

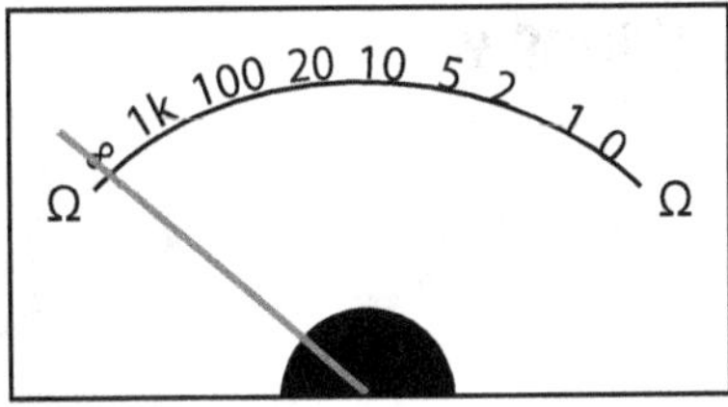

A really thick wire

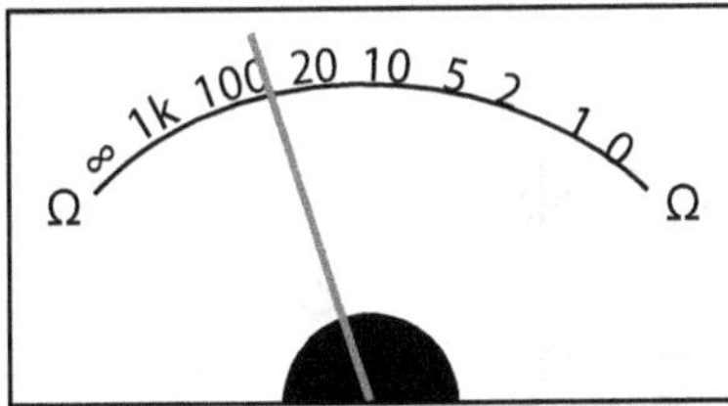

A broken wire

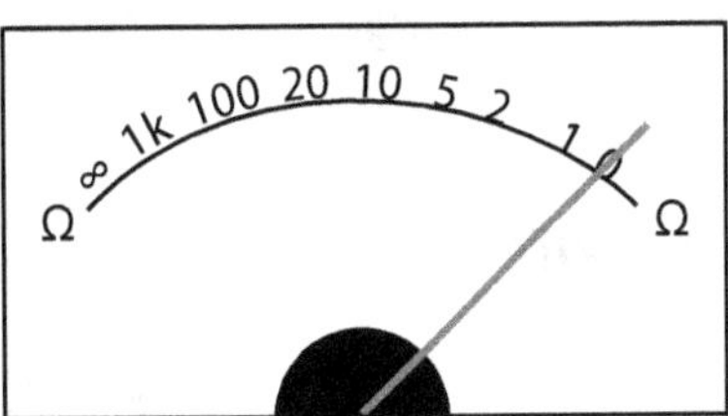

A short wire

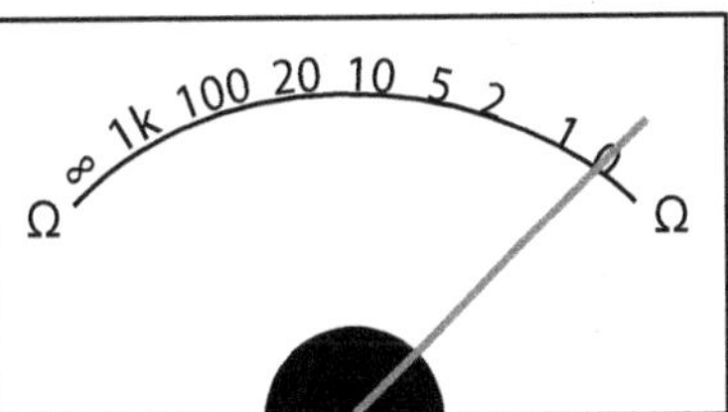

Exercise Solution

Match up the wire with the resistance than an electron moving through these wires would feel.

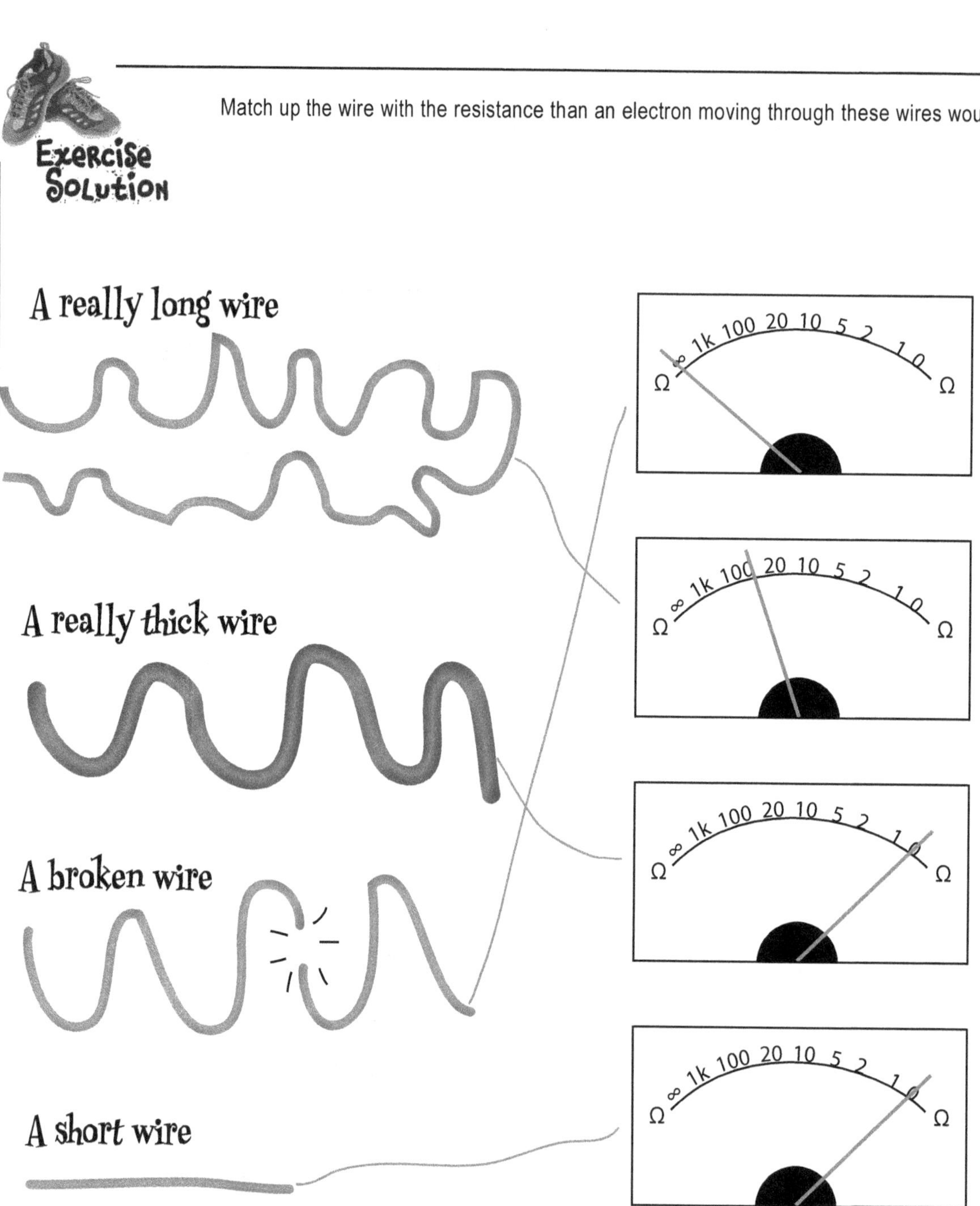

BE the Multimeter

Your job is to play like you're the multimeter and imagine that you are facing the problems shown below. Say if you can help or not, and why or why not.

Problem	Can you help?	Tell us more
The cable is longer than the recommended maximum for Ethernet (100 meters).	☐ Yes ☐ No	....
Noise on the cable produced by power, RF, loose connector, bare cables, and shorts.	☐ Yes ☐ No	....
Connector is mis-wired.	☐ Yes ☐ No	....

BE the Multimeter Solution

Your job is to play like you're the multimeter and imagine that you are facing the problems shown below. Say if you can help or not, and why or why not.

Problem	Can you help?	Tell us more
The cable is longer than the recommended maximum for Ethernet (100 meters).	☑ Yes ☐ No	You can use the resistance setting on the multimeter to read the resistance of the cable. A longer cable will have a higher resistance.
Noise on the cable produced by power, RF, loose connector, bare cables, and shorts.	☐ Yes ☑ No	The multimeter will not show noise on a line, with the exception of a higher than normal voltage.
Connector is mis-wired.	☑ Yes ☐ No	You can use the resistance setting on a multimeter to check for continuity, just like a toner and tracer, but with a readout instead of a tone.

So how well did the multimeter do?

Jim tested the cables at Mighty Gumball, and found six with mis-wired connectors, and twelve that were too long. So does this mean that Jim takes away the $5,000 bonus?

You're kidding me, right? We've still got a ton of network problems, and nobody's getting any money til they're all fixed.

So what's next?

there are no Dumb Questions

Q: So, it's called a multimeter. What else does it measure?

A: Great question! Most multimeters can measure voltages, both AC and DC, as well a current.

Q: What's AC & DC voltage?

A: DC stands for direct current. That is the type of voltage you get from a battery. It is just steady at one voltage, like 9 volts.

AC stands for alternating current. This current alternates in the direction it is flowing. Your house current is AC.

Q: What is current then?

A: If you think about voltage like the pressure in a water line, current is how fast the water flows. So electrical current is how fast the electrons are flowing in the wire.

Q: Are there any big differences between digital and analog multimeters?

A: Not really. In most cases, an analog multimeter uses just electrical components such as resistors, capacitors, and inductors.

The digital multimeters use integrated circuits along with the electrical components. This is why they are more expensive.

Q: Is a multimeter used that much by network people?

A: Not that much. We are using it here to show how to check cables and to show how resistance measurements work.

Sometimes, you will need to check for a specific voltage, and then they come in real handy.

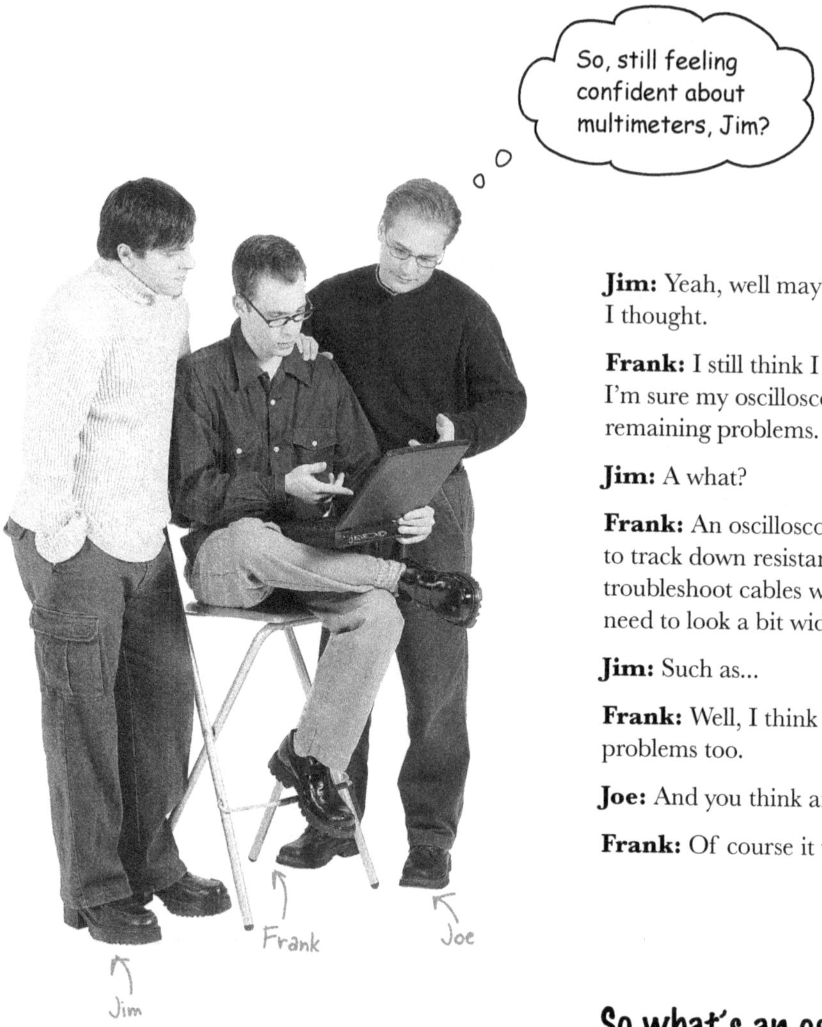

So, still feeling confident about multimeters, Jim?

Frank Joe Jim

Jim: Yeah, well maybe the problems are a bit bigger than I thought.

Frank: I still think I have a shot at the $5,000, though. I'm sure my oscilloscope will be able to sniff out the remaining problems.

Jim: A what?

Frank: An oscilloscope. You see, if you use a multimeter to track down resistance problems, you'll only be able to troubleshoot cables with that sort of problem. I think we need to look a bit wider than that.

Jim: Such as...

Frank: Well, I think we need to look for voltage problems too.

Joe: And you think an oscilloscope will find everything?

Frank: Of course it will. You just wait and see.

So what's an oscilloscope?

An oscilloscope shows voltage changes

An oscilloscope is another tool you can use to help you troubleshoot your network. It shows you the voltage changes on a wire over time, measured in milliseconds.

An oscilloscope takes some training to use properly.

An oscilloscope is a complex piece of test equipment requiring advanced training and some knowledge of electrical principles to use properly.

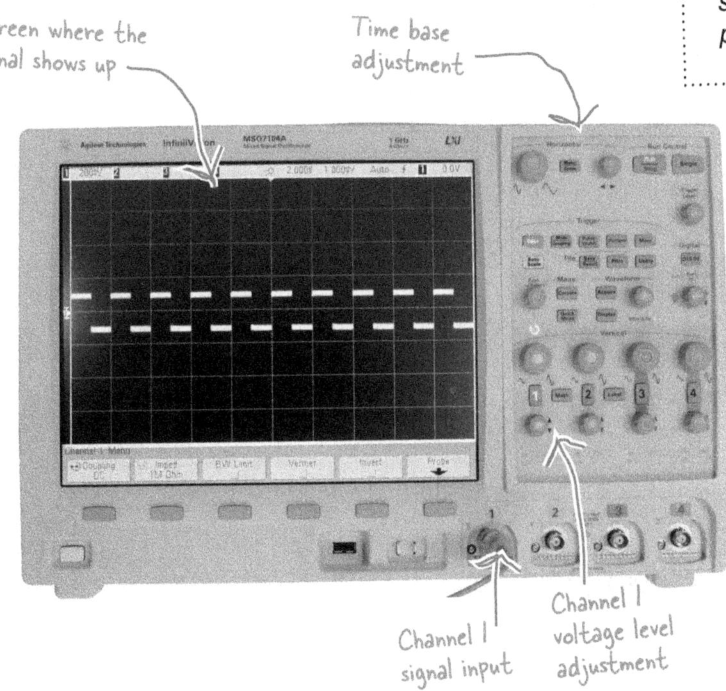

Here's an example readout from the oscilloscope showing you the voltage changes in a cable over time.

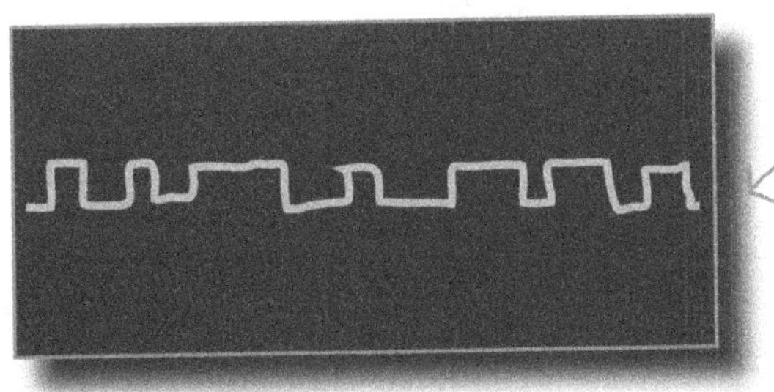

The highs and lows on the display correspond to the highs and lows of the voltage.

Being able to analyze the voltage changes in this way gives you important troubleshooting information about your cables. Let's see how.

Voltage is really electrical pressure

Let's start by taking a look at what voltage is.

In simple terms, voltage is the pressure that tries to make electrons flow. It's the push felt by the electrons. Think of voltage as the force that moves the electrons in a circuit, and resistance as anything that might slow them down, such as a broken wire.

If we compare electron flow in a cable to water flow down a garden hose, voltage is like the pressure of the water coming out the faucet, and resistance is like the width of the garden hose.

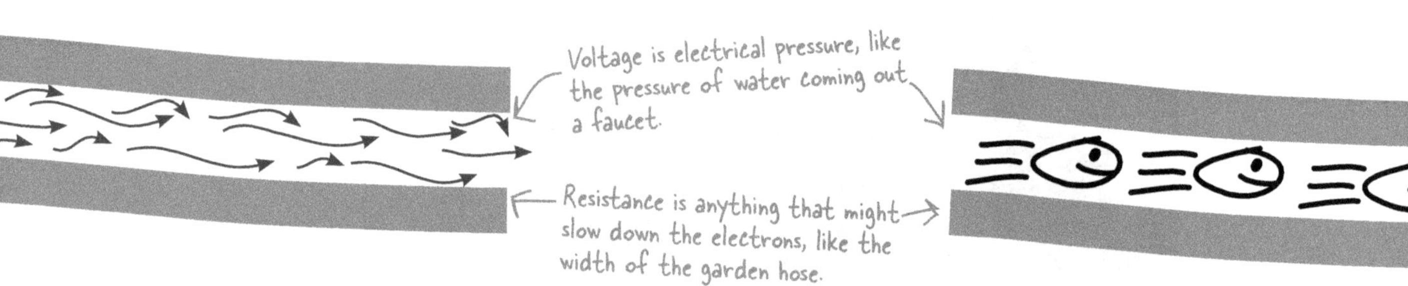

Voltage is electrical pressure, like the pressure of water coming out a faucet.
Resistance is anything that might slow down the electrons, like the width of the garden hose.

So how does this help us troubleshoot problems?

As we've seen, an oscilloscope allows us to see voltage changes over time. **The signal on a network cable is just the change in voltage over time**. This means that an oscilloscope effectively allows us to see a network signal. More importantly, it allows us to see how clear and distinct the network signal is, or whether there are any extraneous voltages changing the signal and causing network problems. We call extraneous voltages ***noise***.

A clear clean network signal...

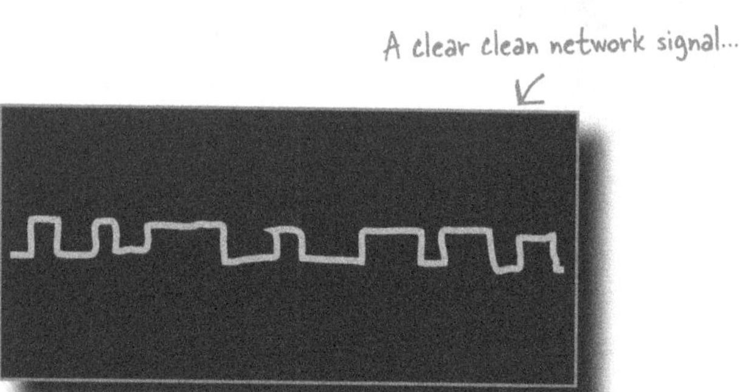

...and a network signal distorted by noise on the wire.

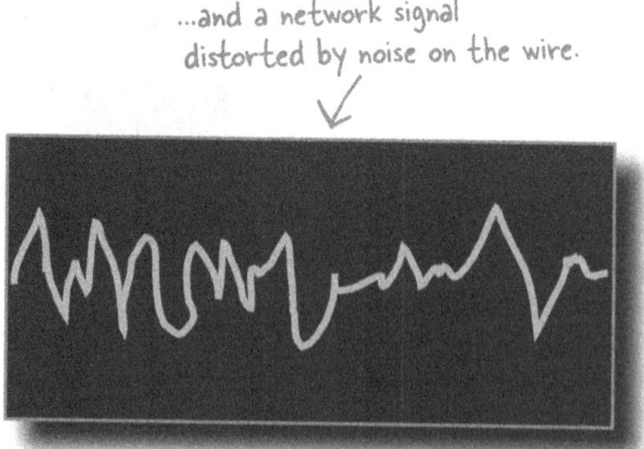

Where does noise on network cables come from?

Noise is unwanted signals on your network cables. It comes from lots of different sources of electronic energy. Most things that use electricity leak electromagnetic energy. This is especially true of electric things that move or have moving parts.

There are ways to take care of noise.

First make sure that you don't untwist your cable too much, that twist takes care of a lot of noise. Also, keep some distance between your network cables and things that create noise.

Match up the things that create noise on network lines with how they create noise.

Bad Grounding	I cause noise when I do not have a connection to what I am plugged into.
Radio Frequency Interference	I cause noise when I move cables.
Cable Crosstalk	I cause noise because I have revolving magnets.
Bad Connector	I cause noise by broadcasting waves of electromagnetic energy.
Physical Vibration	I cause noise when signals from me cable creep on to another cable next to me.
Electric Motor	I cause noise with voltage differences.

Answers on page 107.

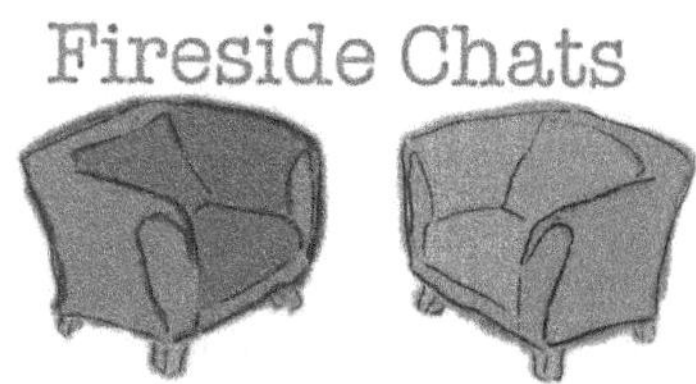

Tonight's talk: **Multimeter vs. Oscilloscope**

Multimeter:

Hey Oscilloscope, it is good to see another real electrical tool here.

Oscilloscope:

Did you have a bad morning or something?

Multimeter:

No, I just got done talking with Toner & Tracer. They were wondering why I was here. I guess you're in the same boat. We pretty much do the same thing.

Oscilloscope:

Hold your horses now. I think we do some different stuff. I mean, you can't really see a signal now, can you?

Multimeter:

I guess it's "pick on Multimeter" day. No, I can't do that trick of seeing the signal on a cable. I can measure the voltage, but that's about it. But I can tell how long a cable is, can you? It goes down well at parties.

Oscilloscope:

That resistance thing you do is cool. But seeing the signal is more than a trick. If there's noise or extraneous power on a cable I can help see that.

Multimeter:

Well, I can measure extraneous power as well, even AC power which is how noise shows up, right?

Oscilloscope:

True, but if it's transient or very quick, you won't catch it. I will.

Multimeter:

Well, only when you're setup correctly. Isn't it true that it takes some pretty special training to run you?

Oscilloscope:

I wouldn't say special training as such. But yes, someone using me will have to spend some time understanding all of my powerful skills. You're just a toy by comparison.

Multimeter:

I think I would rather be a "pick up and use" type of ***portable*** tool. Anyway, gotta go.

Exercise

Write down next to each oscilloscope screen what type of signal you think the green line represents and if it is not normal, what kind of network problem could cause the it to look like this.

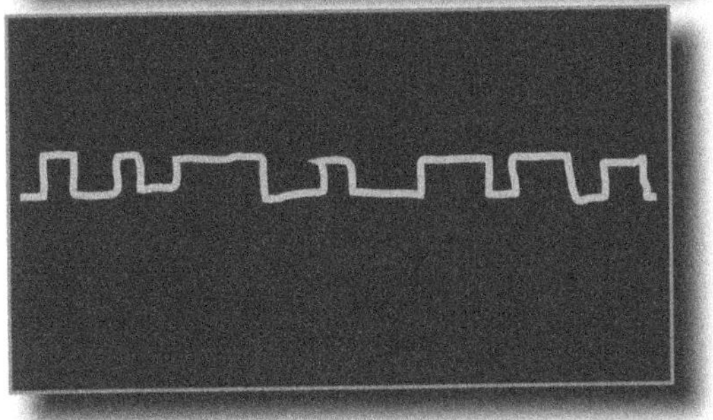

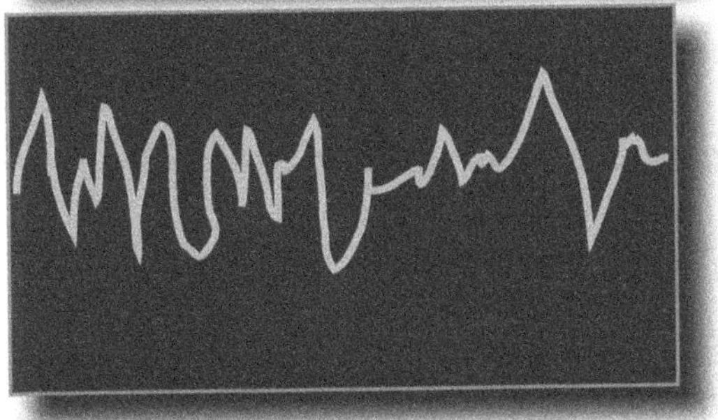

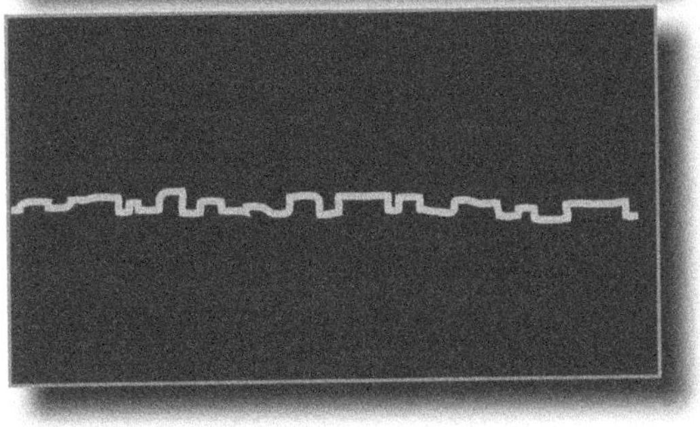

Exercise Solution

Write down next to each oscilloscope screen what type of signal you think the green line represents and if it is not normal, what kind of network problem could cause the it to look like this.

There is no signal here. So the cable could be broken or just not connected.

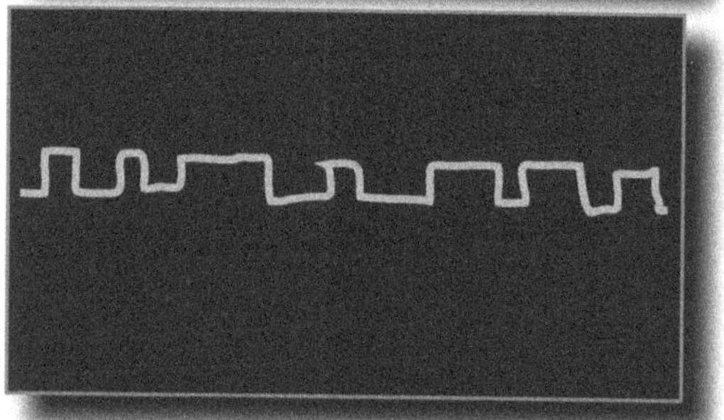

This is a real signal. It represents data in the form of 1's and 0's which correspond to the high and low voltages.

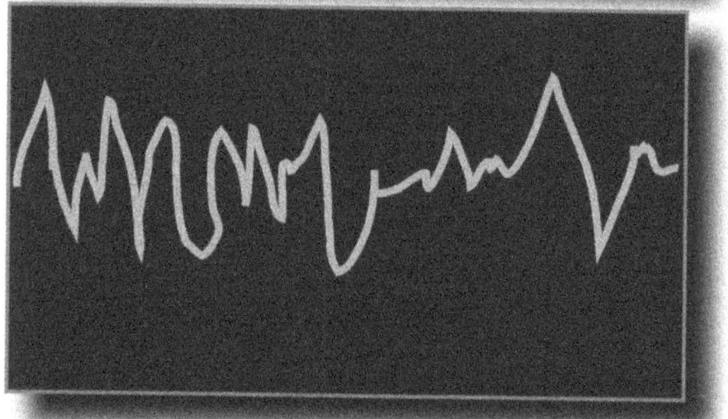

This is just noise. A cable too close to a power line or some other type of signal source could cause this. Even a bad or incorrect connection could cause this signal.

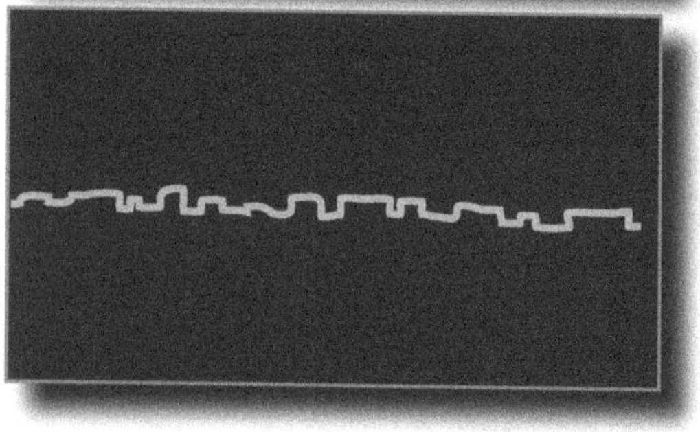

This is a real signal, but the voltage level is very reduced. A really long cable could cause this as well as bad connectors.

there are no Dumb Questions

Q: OK, given a choice, should I always choose an oscilloscope to check cables?

A: No, actually network professionals rarely use an oscilloscope. The toner & tracer is going to be your most useful tool. It will help you with many of the common jobs that a network person needs to do.

Q: What about the multimeter?

A: It's probably used more than an oscilloscope, but not often. It's useful when you need to measure a voltage on something, or check the resistance of a wire. It can be an OK stand in for a toner & tracer, but it can't take their place completely.

Q: So I should just use the toner & tracer to look for every problem?

A: No, they will only help you find and solve certain problems. If the problem is directly related to the physical cable, they are great tools to use. But if there is noise on the wire or network problems, they really aren't going to help you much. But keep reading, there are other tools we haven't covered yet that you can use to see what is really on the wire.

Q: Is that what noise really looks like on a wire then?

A: Definitely. The noisy signal shown on the previous page is exactly the kind of thing you will see.

Q: So is all noise on a network line just random voltages?

A: Not necessarily. Some stray voltages like the noise from overhead fluorescent lights is regular in nature. That is generally at 60 Hz.

Q: 60 Hz, what is that?

A: Hertz or Hz is cycles per second. For example, the AC power in your house (in the US) runs at 60 Hz, or it cycles from positive to negative 60 times per second.

Q: So why is noise so bad for a network signal?

A: If the noise reaches a voltage level high enough, it can mask data. There are different encoding techniques that you will learn in the next chapter that will reduce what noise can do to a signal, but at some point too much noise can kill any type of signal.

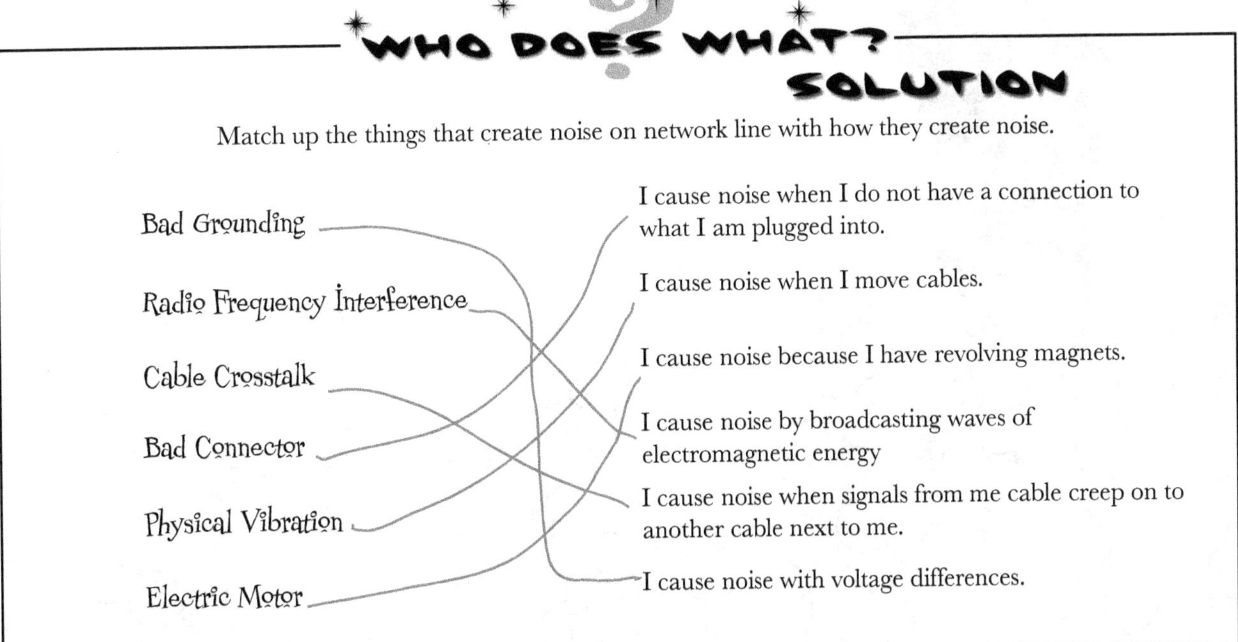

WHO DOES WHAT?
SOLUTION
Match up the things that create noise on network line with how they create noise.
Bad Grounding
Radio Frequency Interference
Cable Crosstalk
Bad Connector
Physical Vibration
Electric Motor
I cause noise when I do not have a connection to what I am plugged into.
I cause noise when I move cables.
I cause noise because I have revolving magnets.
I cause noise by broadcasting waves of electromagnetic energy
I cause noise when signals from me cable creep on to another cable next to me.
I cause noise with voltage differences.

So how well did the oscilloscope perform for Mighty Gumball?

Armed with his trusty oscilloscope, Frank managed to track down some more network problems at Mighty Gumball. It turns out that there was a large power cable lying across several cables, and this was creating noise in the network cables.

Unfortunately, there are still more network problems at Mighty Gumball to contend with. The machinery that makes the gumballs is back up and running, but the packaging conveyor belt keeps stopping.

This is outrageous! Can't anyone fix this? I'll increase the reward to $6,000 and throw in a free dental health plan...

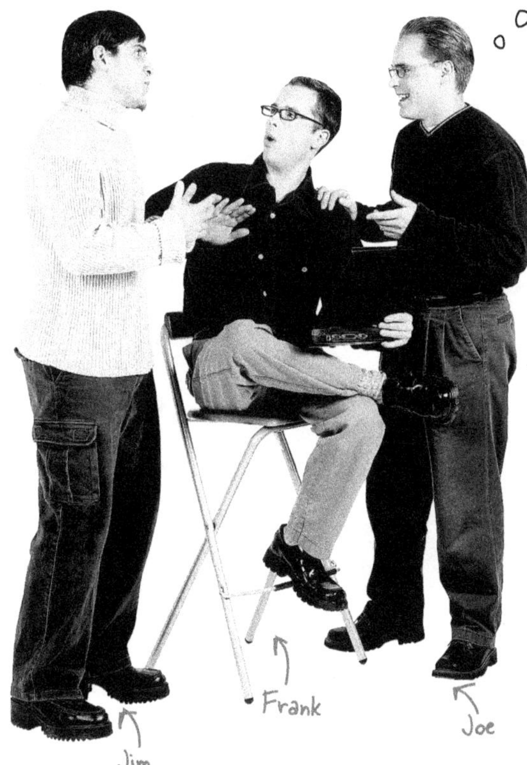

I thought you said your oscilloscope could solve all the world's problems, Frank.
Frank
Joe
Jim

Frank: OK, I admit it, I'm an idiot. I thought the remaining problems were to do with voltage, and I was wrong.

Joe: Well, actually I think you've got a point.

Frank: You think I'm an idiot too?

Joe: Not in that sense. Seriously, I think the network problems might well be something to do with voltage.

Jim: But that's crazy talk, Joe. Surely the oscilloscope would have picked up voltage problems.

Joe: Well, not necessarily, not if the problem's quite subtle.

Frank: So what are you suggesting?

Joe: I'm going to double-check those cables you looked at with a logical analyzer, and then I'll claim my $6,000 from the boss.

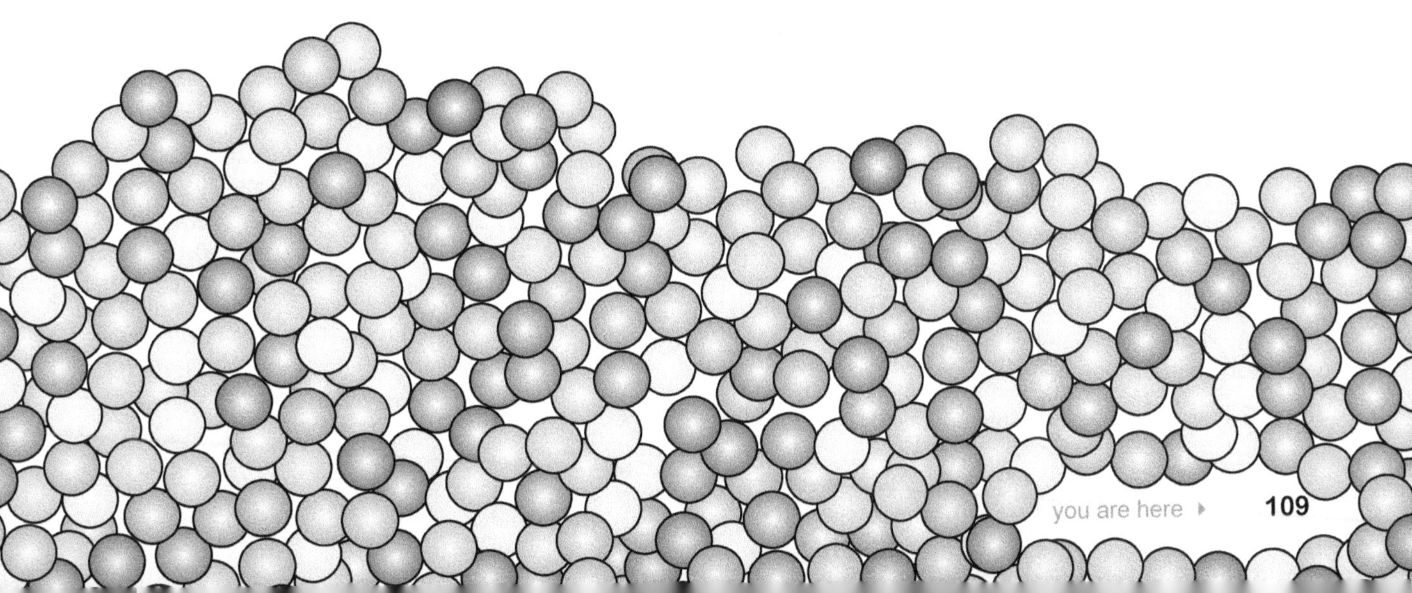

A logical analyzer uses voltage too

Just like an oscilloscope, a logical analyzer looks at changing voltage levels over time. Often high end oscilloscopes have the ability to function as a logic analyzer as well.

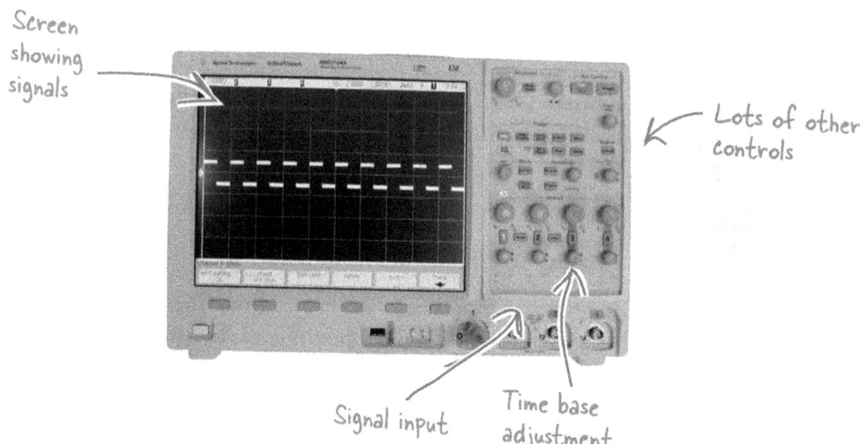

This is the same oscilloscope we saw earlier, but it can work as a logic analyzer as well. Yes, it's very expensive.

There's a key difference, though. Instead of reading the actual voltage, a logical analyzer reads the signal as a series of binary numbers, or 1's and 0's. When the signal goes higher than a set voltage level, the logical analyzer sees it as 1, and when the signal goes lower, the logical analyzer sees it as 0.

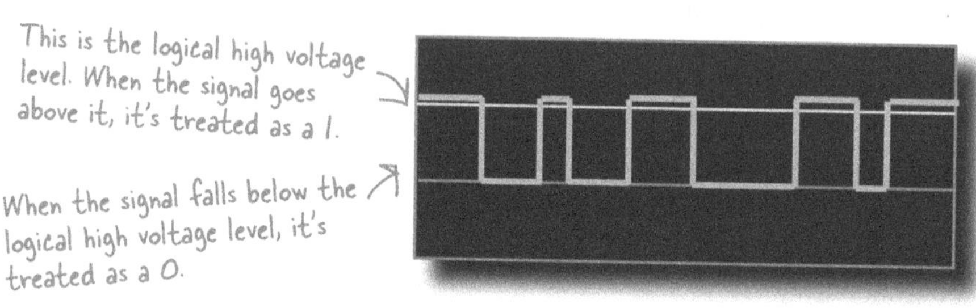

This is the logical high voltage level. When the signal goes above it, it's treated as a 1.
When the signal falls below the logical high voltage level, it's treated as a 0.
This is how the logical analyzer interprets the signal.
11001001100011011

The voltage changes in the signal represent data in the form of binary numbers, so a logical analyzer allows you to see the stream of data based on the logical voltage level. It effectively allows you to see the data in the signal.

So how does that help us troubleshoot network cables?

A logic analyzer takes lots of training to use properly.

A logic analyzer requires even more training than an oscilloscope to understand and use properly.

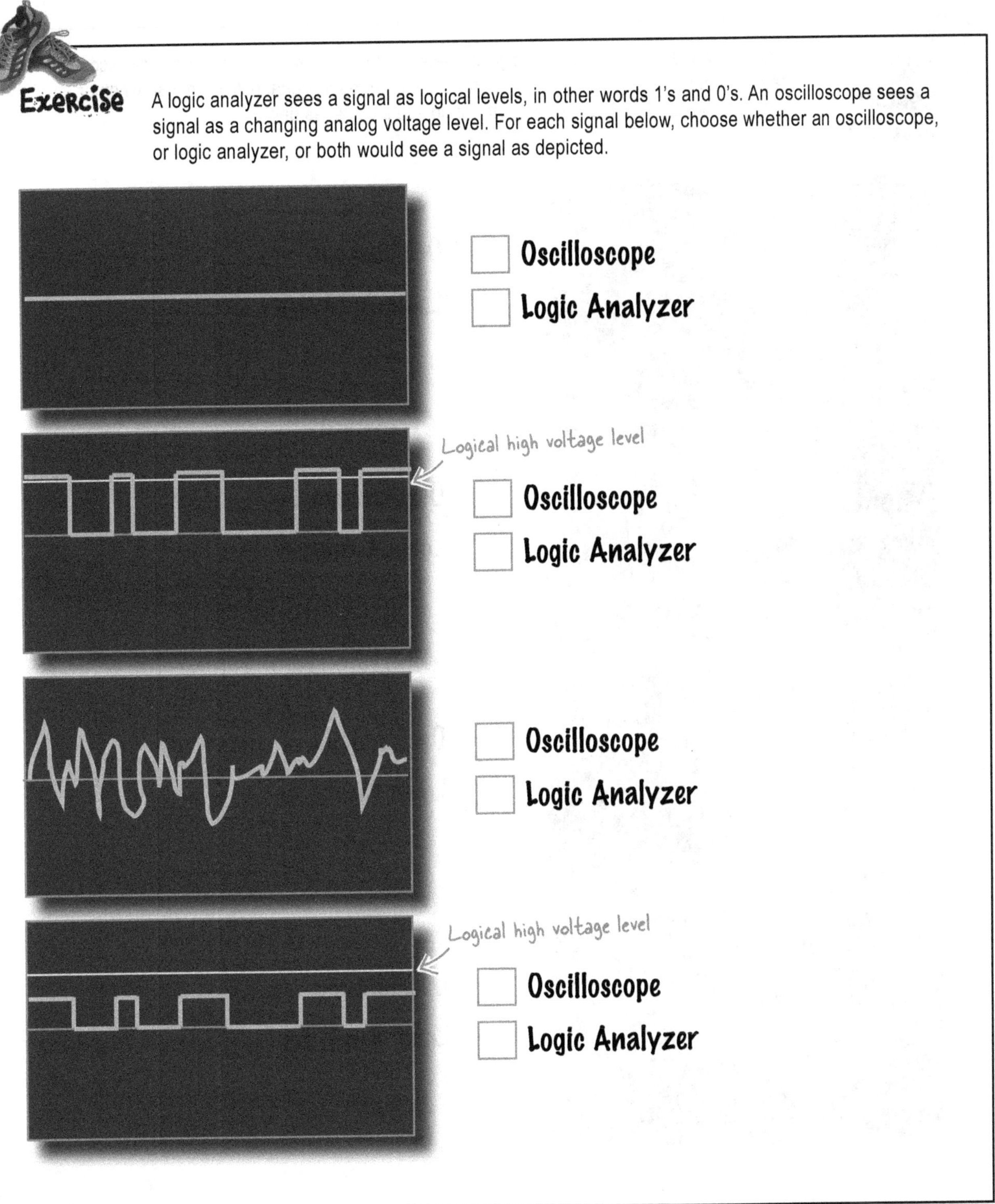
Exercise
A logic analyzer sees a signal as logical levels, in other words 1's and 0's. An oscilloscope sees a signal as a changing analog voltage level. For each signal below, choose whether an oscilloscope, or logic analyzer, or both would see a signal as depicted.
Oscilloscope
Logic Analyzer
Logical high voltage level
Oscilloscope
Logic Analyzer
Oscilloscope
Logic Analyzer
Logical high voltage level
Oscilloscope
Logic Analyzer

Exercise Solution

A logic analyzer sees a signal as logical levels, in other words 1's and 0's. An oscilloscope sees a signal as a changing analog voltage level. For each signal below, choose whether an oscilloscope, or logic analyzer, or both would see a signal as depicted.

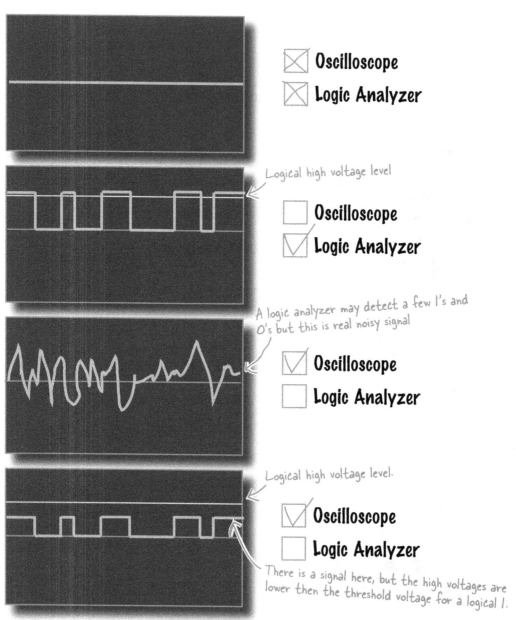

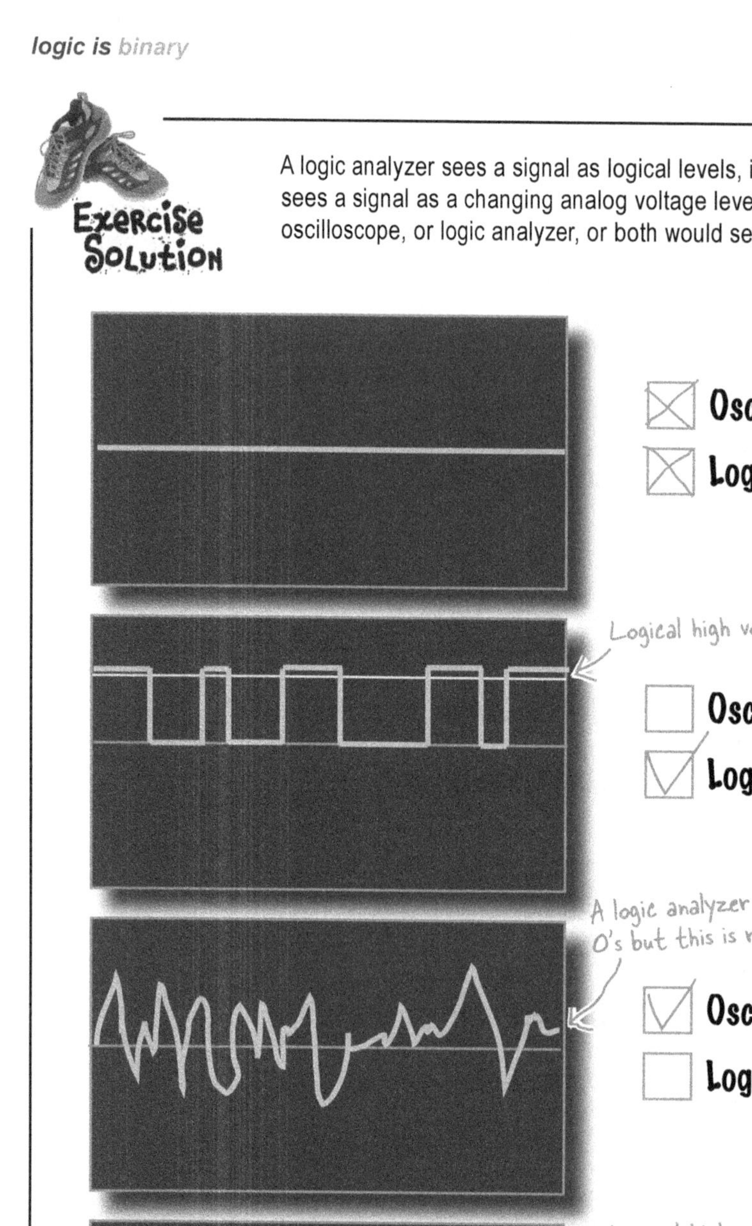

☒ Oscilloscope

☒ Logic Analyzer

Logical high voltage level

☐ Oscilloscope

☑ Logic Analyzer

A logic analyzer may detect a few 1's and 0's but this is real noisy signal

☑ Oscilloscope

☐ Logic Analyzer

Logical high voltage level.

☑ Oscilloscope

☐ Logic Analyzer

There is a signal here, but the high voltages are lower then the threshold voltage for a logical 1.

BE the Logic Analyzer

Your job is to play logic analyzer and convert the raw Ethernet signals shown below into data represented by 1's and 0's.

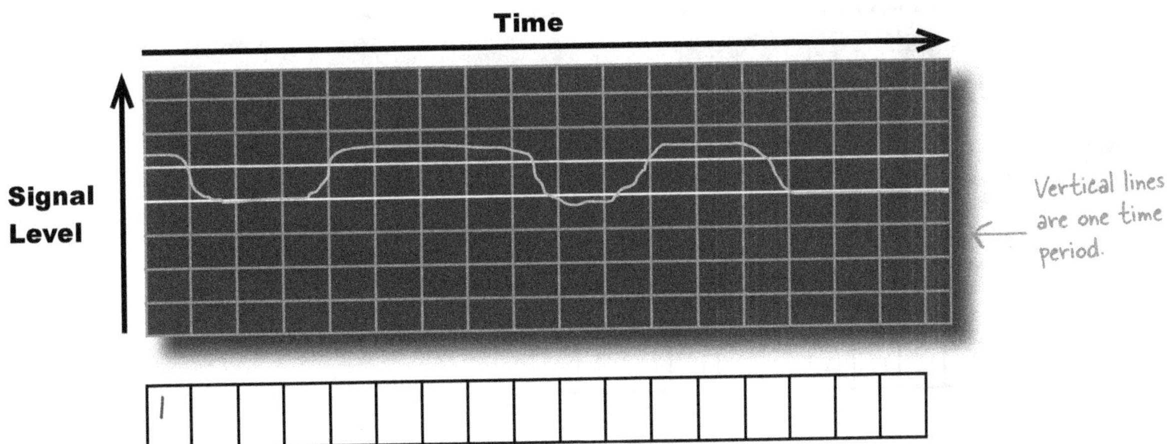

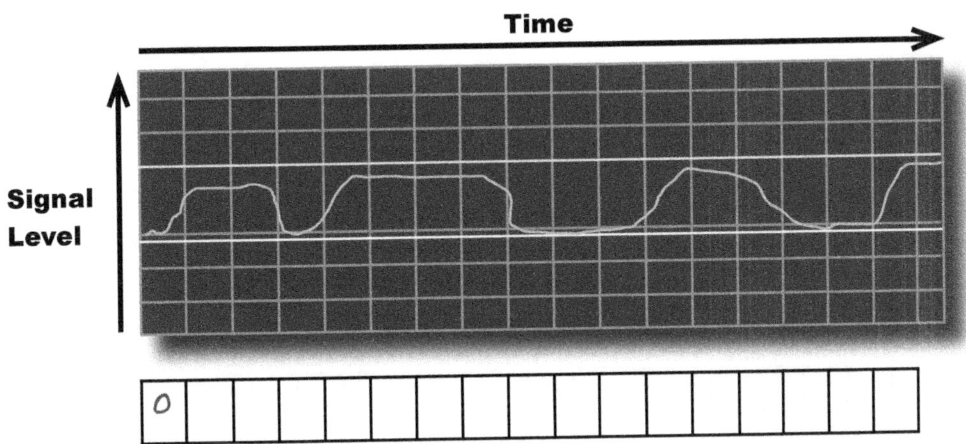

BE the Logic Analyzer Solution

Your job is to play logic analyzer and convert the raw Ethernet signals shown below into data represented by 1's and 0's.

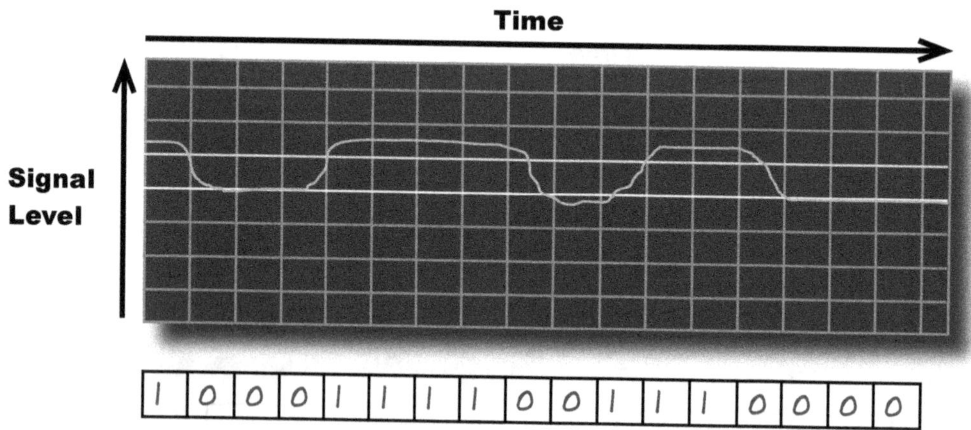

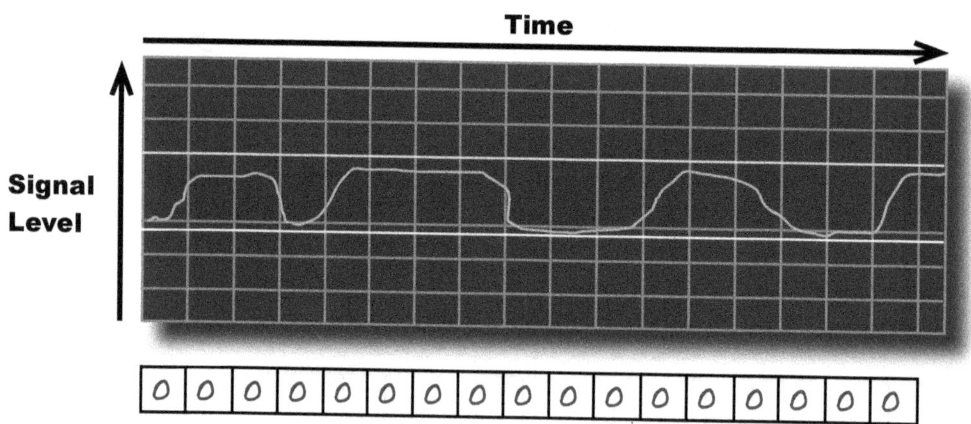

When is a logical analyzer useful?

As we've seen, an oscilloscope and a logical analyzer both measure changes in voltage over time. It's useful to compare how they both see the signal in a cable, as significant differences can indicate problems.

As an example, here's the display from an oscilloscope and a logical analyzer where the signal is clear, but the voltage change is small.

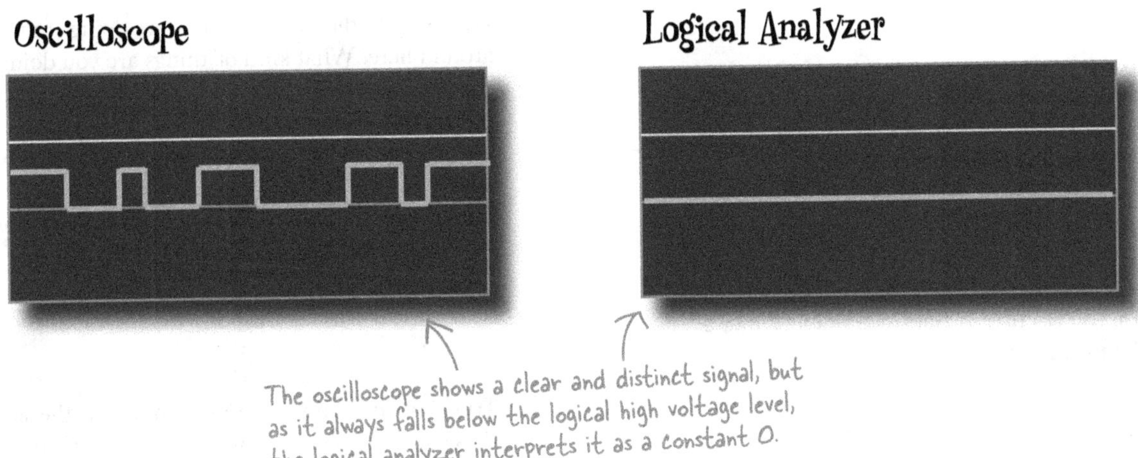

Oscilloscope
Logical Analyzer
The oscilloscope shows a clear and distinct signal, but as it always falls below the logical high voltage level, the logical analyzer interprets it as a constant 0.

Even though the signal looks well defined and clear on the oscilloscope, the voltage change is too small to register on the logical analyzer. In other words, the signal isn't strong enough to carry the network data.

So which tool is best?

So far we've looked at four tools you can use to help you troubleshoot your network cables. We've used a toner and tracer to listen to electrons, a multimeter to measure resistance, an oscilloscope to display changes in voltage over time, and a logical analyzer to interpret the signal into binary data. So which tool is the most effective?

Who should win the Mighty Gumball bonus?

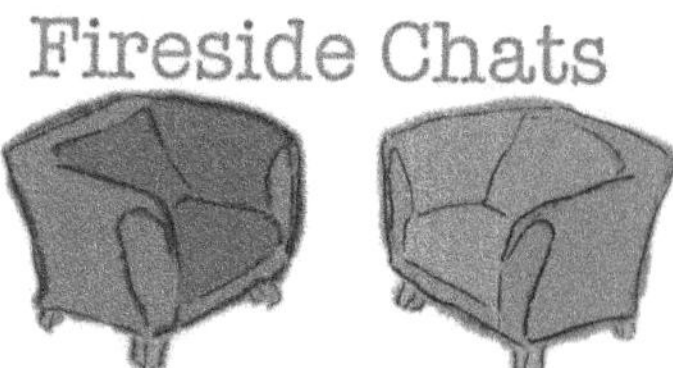

Tonight's talk: **Oscilloscope vs. Logic Analyzer**

Oscilloscope: Hey Bro! Good to see another high end electrical tool around here.

Logic Analyzer: What's up? I didn't know you were doing stuff around here. What kind of things are you doing?

Oscilloscope: Just like you, I'm looking at signals. I'm checking for noise, extraneous voltages, DC voltage levels, timing—you know the sort of thing.

Logic Analyzer: But let's get something clear here. You really don't know what the signal is, do you?

Oscilloscope: If you're saying that I can't turn a signal into 1's and 0's, you're correct. But I can still lock into a signal and show it.

Logic Analyzer: True, but you cannot store very much of the signal. Plus you can only see four or so signals at a time? I can see 64, or even more, signals.

Oscilloscope: Yes, I usually have four channels. But I am showing the analog value of the signal, the raw signal. That is a lot of information to store. You are storing a digital *interpretation* of the signal, right?

Logic Analyzer: Yes, I do represent the signal in a digital form and I store it that way. Very efficient, don't you think?

Oscilloscope: Right, efficient, but you lose all the non-digital information in the signal. Kind of hard for you to see different voltage levels, isn't it? I mean, if there are no standard logic voltage levels, then you're stuffed.

Logic Analyzer: I'll give you that one. I can't really see voltage levels outside of the normal logic level.

Oscilloscope: Not to rub it in, but I think that you're a lot more costly than me. It's true you can have lots of channels, but someone has to pay for them, right?

Logic Analyzer: Hey, I gotta run, I have a date with an FPGA.

The Mighty Gumball bonus went to Jill

Unbeknownst to Jim, Frank and Joe, Jill decided to try for the bonus too. She managed to pick up all the problems the other tools did, but with just the one piece of equipment.

Jill, how did you find so many problems—and so quickly?
Jill
Frank

Jill: I used a LAN Analyzer, which incorporates most of the tools that you guys were using into one device.

Frank: There's a toner & tracer, multimeter, oscilloscope, and logic analyzer in that thing?

Jill: Not exactly. It has the functions of those tools with regards to network cabling.

Frank: Can you give me an example?

Jill: Sure, instead of using a multimeter to find the resistance of a network cable and then calculating the length from that reading, this device does the calculation for you and gives you a readout.

Frank: WOW! That is awesome! What other things can it do?

Jill: I think it is best if you take it and play around with it for a while...

Let's take a closer look at what a LAN analyzer is, and how it works.

A LAN analyzer combines the functions of all the other tools

If you have to do any amount of troubleshooting and maintenance on a network, the LAN analyzer is a great tool to have. It has all the functions of the tools we previously covered in this chapter. You can use it to check and certify cables, and also watch and troubleshoot network traffic. Some units even help you deal with wireless networks.

LAN analyzers are expensive and require extensive training, but their flexibility makes them incredibly useful to network professionals.

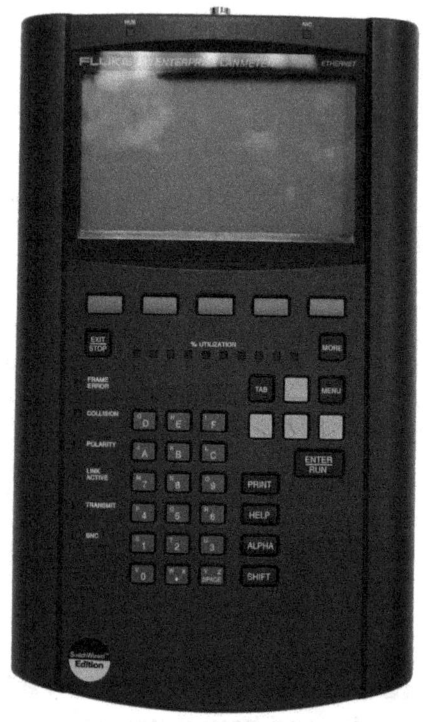

A LAN Analyzer has all the functions of the previous tools we looked at, but its output is geared to the network professional—you.

So how does a LAN analyzer actually work?

A LAN analyzer understands the network traffic in the signal

A LAN analyzer essentially acts as a computer on a network. It fully decodes the signals into actual network data. It takes the voltages, converts them to 1's and 0's, then understands that the 1's and 0's represent structured data. This data is in the form of **frames** on an Ethernet network.

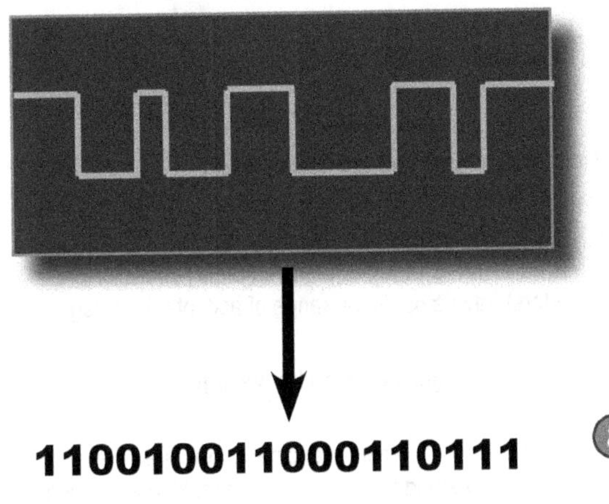

1 **The LAN analyzer starts by reading the voltage changes over time.**

110010011000110111

2 **The LAN analyzer then converts the voltages into 1's and 0's, depending on the voltage levels.** It does this in a similar way to a logical analyzer.

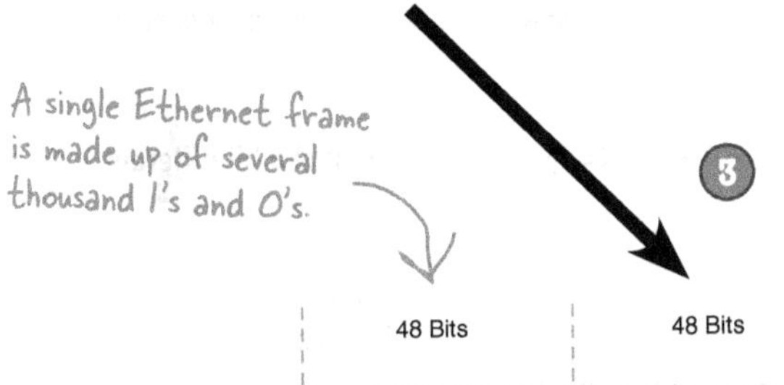

A single Ethernet frame is made up of several thousand 1's and 0's.

3 **The 1's and 0's represent structured data.** This data is in the form of ***frames*** on an Ethernet network.

	48 Bits	48 Bits	16 Bits	Variable 368 bits to 12000 bits	32 Bits
Packet Structure	Destination MAC Address	Source MAC Address	Ethernet Type	Data	CRC Checksum

4 **Inside the frames are the web pages, emails and other data traveling on your network.**

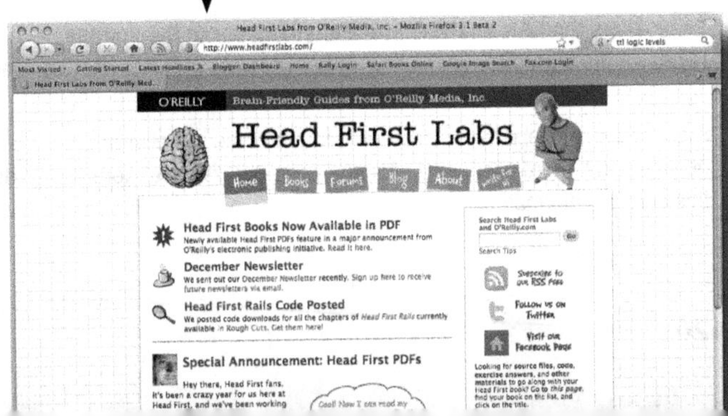

So which tool is best?

Well, it depends. If your problems are simple physical cabling problems, a good toner & tracer tool set is going to help you. Once the problems get more complex, i.e., more network related, you will need to use a tool like a LAN analyzer to get a idea of what is going on with your network.

there are no Dumb Questions

Q: So which is more powerful, a logic analyzer, an oscilloscope, or a LAN analyzer?

A: That depends on what you mean by powerful. An oscilloscope is certainly more versatile than a logic analyzer. Modern oscilloscopes can get pretty close in functionality to logic analyzers, and logic analyzers have many of the features of oscilloscopes, such as showing the raw signal. But for network professionals, the LAN analyzer is the ticket. It has most of the functions that you will need to troubleshoot and maintain a network.

Q: Does a LAN analyzer have the functions of a toner & tracer?

A: Yes, some LAN analyzers come with a small remote device that can be connected to the opposite end of a cable to test it or to help find it.

Q: So how much do these things cost?

A: A toner & tracer set can be purchased for less than $100. An oscilloscope can run from $1,000 to $20,000. A logic analyzer starts at about $3,000 and goes up, fast. A LAN analyzer is in the $1,000 to $15,000 range.

Q: Does the LAN analyzer know anything about the voltage levels of the signal?

A: At some level it has to in order to interpret the signal into network data. More expensive LAN analyzers will give you more of this detailed information.

Q: Does that logical voltage level change?

A: No, it is set by the type of integrated circuitry (ICs) that the hardware is built with. So CMOS (complementary-metal-oxide-semiconductors) have a particular range of acceptable voltages.

Q: Are these voltages common knowledge?

A: To any electrical or computer engineer, they are. These voltages are industry standards. So everyone making and using ICs agrees on what these voltage levels are so that components can work with one another in a circuit.

Q: So each of these tools view the signal a bit differently, huh?

A: That's a great way to think about it. The oscilloscope sees a raw voltage that is changing over time. The logic analyzer tries to make sense of this signal by decoding it into 1's & 0's.

The LAN analyzer has a whole different view. It actually tries looking at things from a "top-down" approach. It assumes that it is connected to a network cable and tries to decode the signal as a network signal.

Q: So how does a LAN analyzer know how to decode the network traffic?

A: In the next chapter we will take a look at encoding and decoding signals. You will learn about a couple of different ways this is done.

Draw a line from the problem to the **best** tool(s) that could help find the problem.

LAN Analyzer

Toner & Tracer

Oscilloscope

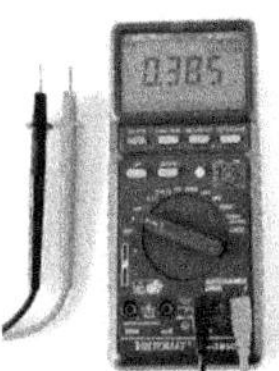

Multimeter

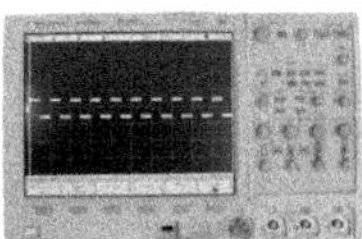

Logic Analyzer

Remember, this is a high end oscilloscope that also work as a logic analyzer.

Cable Break

Noise from power line

No signal on line

Continuity of cable OK, but resistance too high

Network storm from poorly configured switch

Cable too long, causing timing issues with Ethernet cable

Incorrect terminator on coax cable

RJ-45 connector wired incorrectly

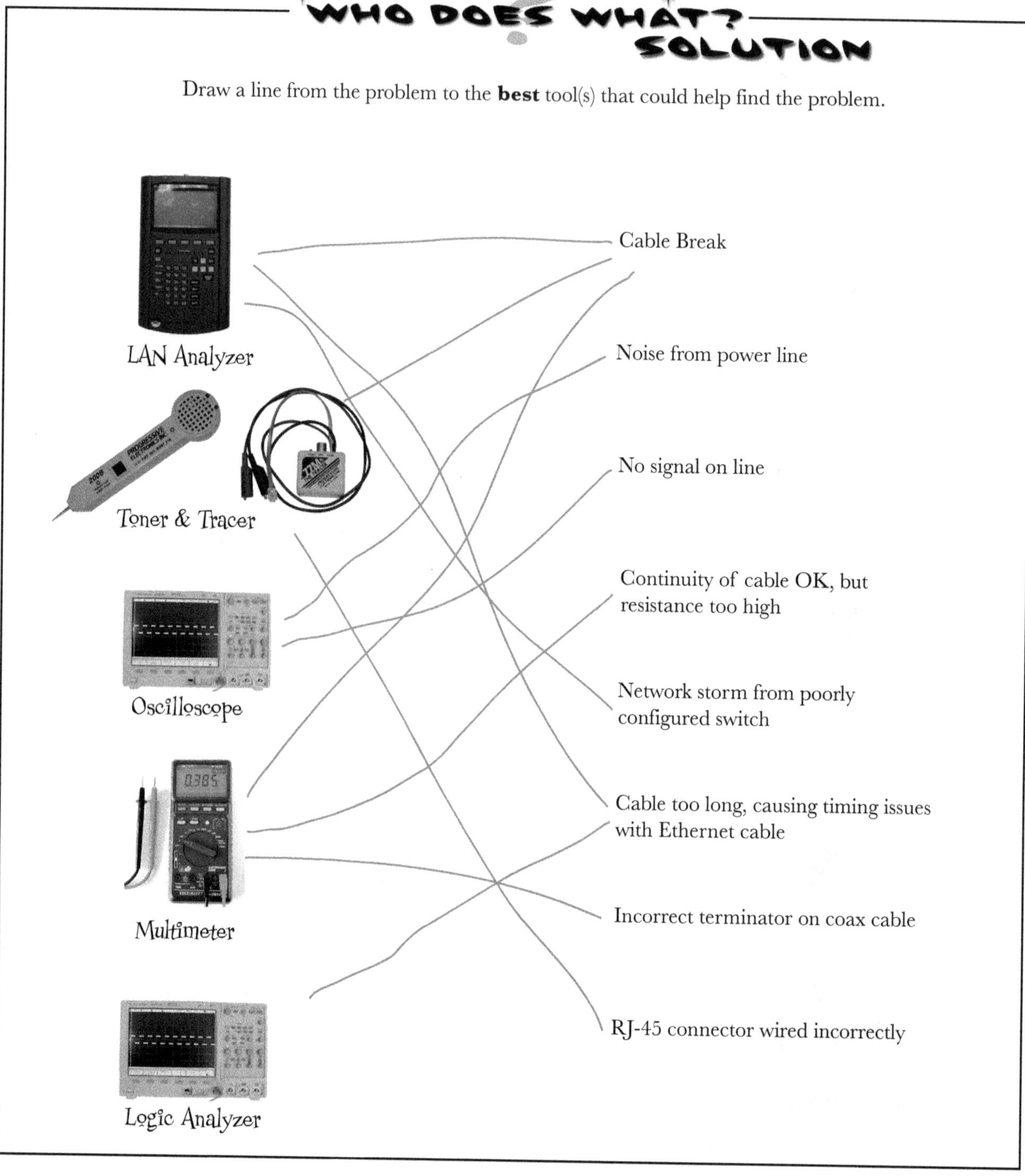
Who Does What? Solution
Draw a line from the problem to the **best** tool(s) that could help find the problem.
LAN Analyzer
Toner & Tracer
Oscilloscope
Multimeter
Logic Analyzer
Cable Break
Noise from power line
No signal on line
Continuity of cable OK, but resistance too high
Network storm from poorly configured switch
Cable too long, causing timing issues with Ethernet cable
Incorrect terminator on coax cable
RJ-45 connector wired incorrectly

The Mighty Gumball problems are fixed!

Thanks to the team's skilled use of network troubleshooting tools, all the problems with the Mighty Gumball network have been tracked down and corrected. It looks like Mighty Gumball is back on track to meet the demands of their Super Bowl contract after all.

Hooray, we've got it made! See you at the next Super Bowl!

4 packet analysis

You've Been Framed

It's time to go under the hood.

Network devices send data down the cable by **converting the data into a signal**. But how do they do this? And what else might be hiding in the signal? Just like a doctor needs to look at blood cells to identify blood-borne diseases, a network pro needs to look at **what's in the network signal** to detect network intrusions, perform audits, and generally **diagnose problems**. And the key to all of this is **packet analysis**. Keep reading while we put your network signal **under the microscope**.

What's the secret message?

The Head First Spy Agency specializes in conducting undercover investigations on behalf of their clients. No job is too big or too small, and they've just recruited **you** to their cause.

Here's your first assignment:

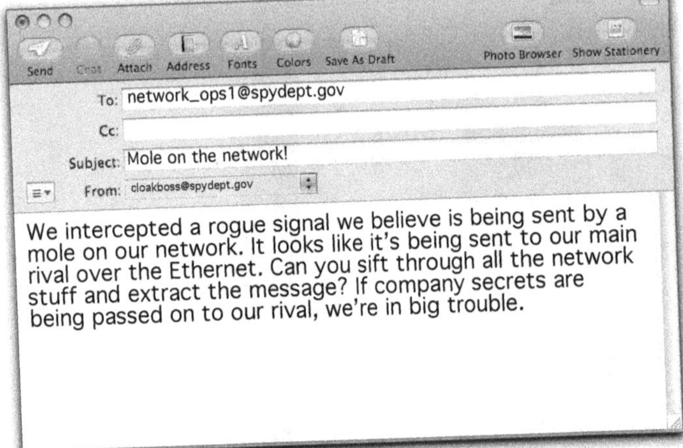

Send
Chat
Attach
Address
Fonts
Colors
Save As Draft
Photo Browser
Show Stationery
To: network_ops1@spydept.gov
Cc:
Subject: Mole on the network!
From: cloakboss@spydept.gov
We intercepted a rogue signal we believe is being sent by a mole on our network. It looks like it's being sent to our main rival over the Ethernet. Can you sift through all the network stuff and extract the message? If company secrets are being passed on to our rival, we're in big trouble.

Here's the mole – but what message is he sending?

So how do we extract a message from a signal?

We've seen before that network signals contain network data. This data is encoded into a format that computers can use, so if we can decode the signal, we should be able to extract the hidden message. But how do we do this?

Exercise

Think of three different ways the same signal could be converted into 1's and 0's. It's okay if you don't get them right. We've done the first one for you.

1 Start at 0. Where a high horizontal bar meets a vertical dotted line, we repeat the last number we got. Where a low horizontal bar meets the vertical dotted line we flip to the opposite number.

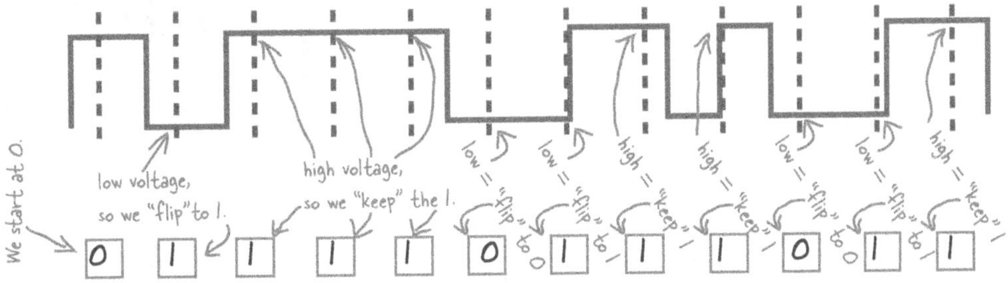

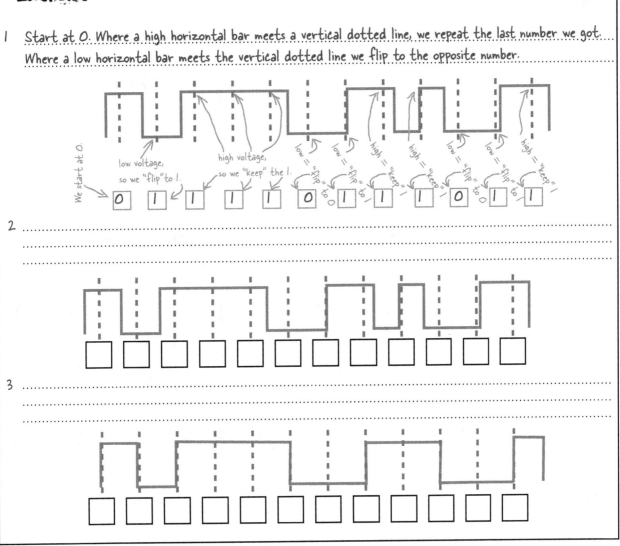

We start at 0.

low voltage, so we "flip" to 1.

high voltage, so we "keep" the 1.

low = "flip" to 0

low = "flip" to 1

high = "keep" 1

high = "keep" 1

low = "flip" to 0

low = "flip" to 1

high = "keep" 1

0	1	1	1	1	0	1	1	1	0	1	1

2 ....

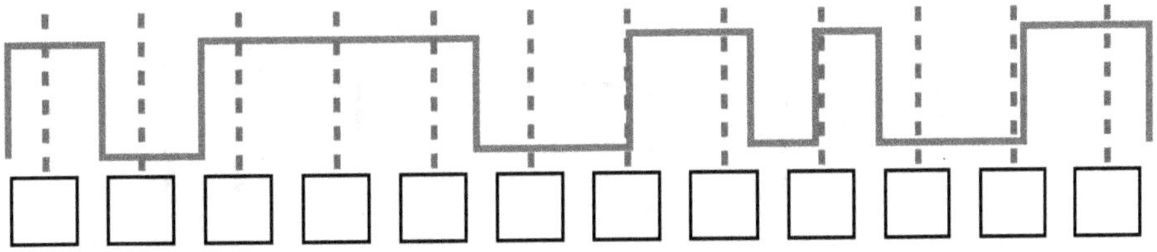

3 ....

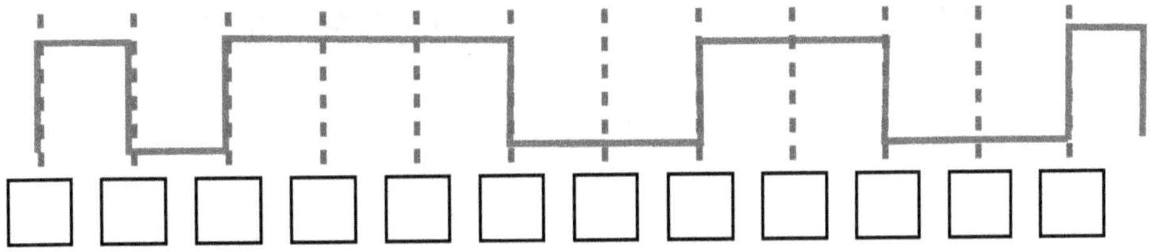

Could this signal represent something other than 1's and 0's?

Exercise Solution

Think of three different ways the same signal could be converted into 1's and 0's. It's okay if you don't get them right. We've done the first one for you.

1 Start at 0. Where a high horizontal bar meets a vertical dotted line we repeat the last number we got. Where a low horizontal bar meets the vertical dotted line we flip to the opposite number.

This encoding method is known in the industry as Non-Return Zero Inverted (NRZ-I).

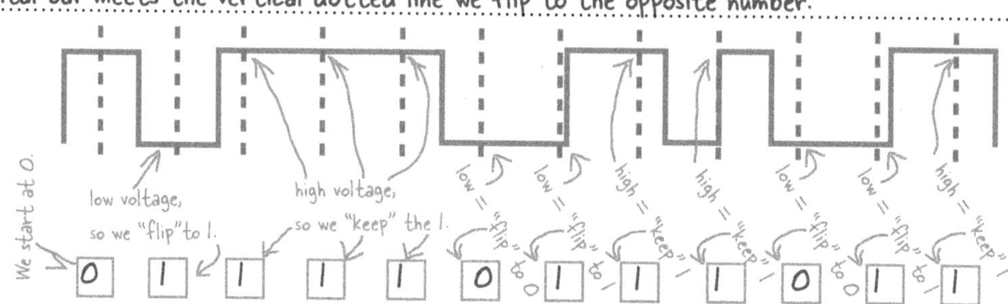

2 Where a high horizontal bar meets the vertical dotted line, we get a 1. Where a low horizontal bar meets a vertical dotted line, we get a 0.

This encoding method is known in the industry as Non-Return Zero.

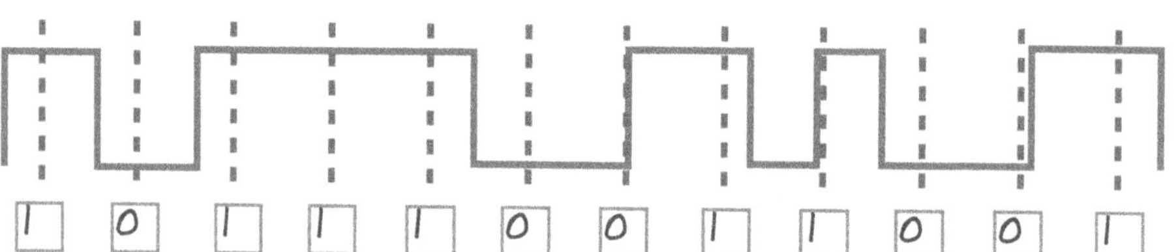

3 Whenever the signal changes, either from high to low or low to high, this signals a zero. If there is no change, then it is a one.

This is known as Non-Return Zero Space encoding.

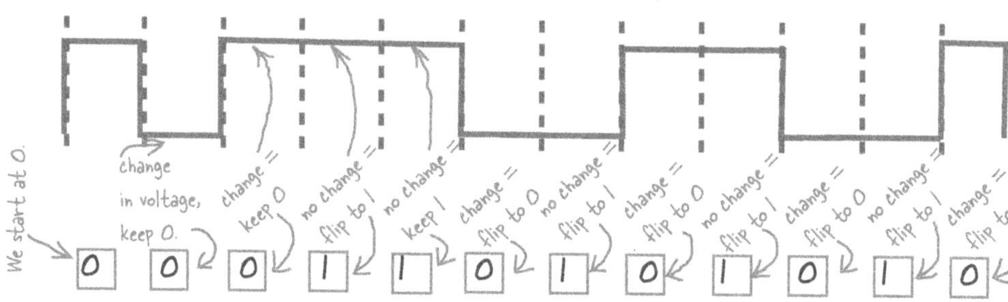

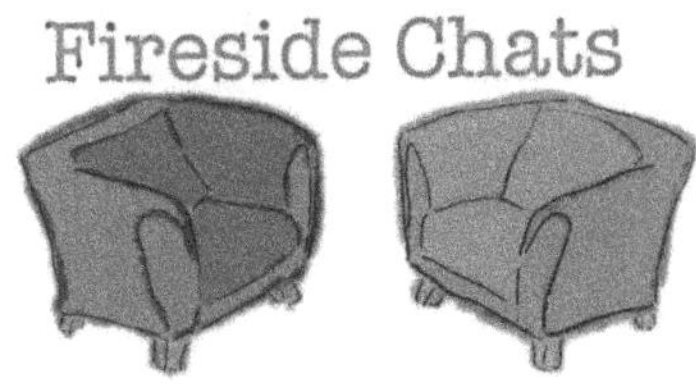

Tonight's talk:
Manchester Phase Encoding vs. Non-Return to Zero

Manchester Phase Encoding:

Welcome, Non-Return to Zero. Is there something I can call you for short?

Non-Return to Zero:

I prefer NRZ, but some folks call me NRZ-L for Non-Return to Zero Level. My name's nice and transparent. When I encode a signal, it starts at zero voltage, but it never gets to go back to zero voltage.

Manchester Phase Encoding:

So you give a positive voltage a one and a negative voltage a zero?

Non-Return to Zero:

I can do it that way or vice versa, depending on how I'm implemented, but I always stick to the rules of that implementation. I am a slim encoding technique. After all, I require only half the bandwidth you require.

Manchester Phase Encoding:

A little extra bandwidth is worth the price. I have built-in clocking. I make sure the data gets there, and I can spot errors. Can you do that?

Non-Return to Zero:

I like to keep the encoding process simple. Clocking is overrated.

Manchester Phase Encoding:

What happens when you have a whole bunch of bits in a row? Say you're trying to send a whole bunch of zeroes?

Non-Return to Zero:

What sort of crazy standard would allow for a bunch of bits in a row?

Manchester Phase Encoding:

Ethernet, for one. If you have a bunch of bits in a row. The signal sits there at the same voltage level for a long time. Without a clock, the sending device and the receiving device will get out of sync.

Non-Return to Zero:

I don't get caught up in all that high-falutin' stuff. Economy and simplicity is the name of my game.

Manchester Phase Encoding:

I use self-clocking. I give a network more bang for the buck. You'd be good for writing data to a hard drive, but you just don't cut it on a network, do you?

Non-Return to Zero:

Data should stay home. All that crazy travel over cables is unnecessary and fraught with problems.

Manchester Phase Encoding:

That's what I thought you might say.

Network cards handle encoding

Encoding is handled by the Network Interface Card, or NIC, inside the computer. It handles and decodes digital signals, and is in charge of all the messaging ins and outs on the computer.

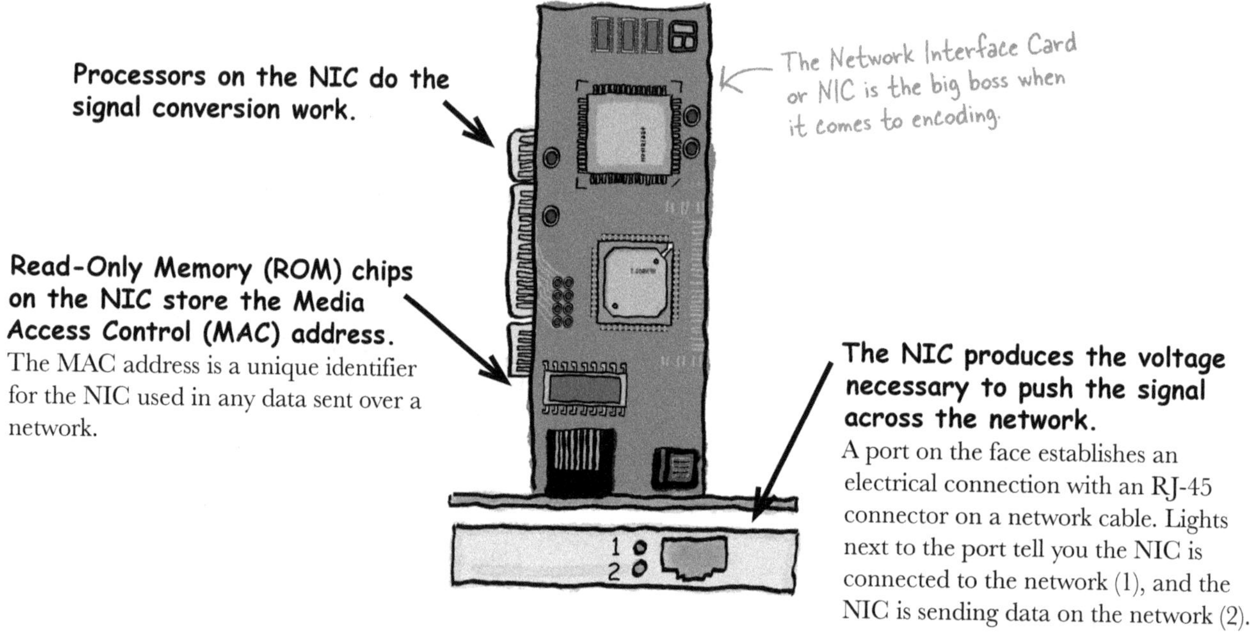

Processors on the NIC do the signal conversion work.
The Network Interface Card or NIC is the big boss when it comes to encoding.
Read-Only Memory (ROM) chips on the NIC store the Media Access Control (MAC) address.
The MAC address is a unique identifier for the NIC used in any data sent over a network.
The NIC produces the voltage necessary to push the signal across the network.
A port on the face establishes an electrical connection with an RJ-45 connector on a network cable. Lights next to the port tell you the NIC is connected to the network (1), and the NIC is sending data on the network (2).
1
2

So how does the NIC encode the data?

The NIC starts by taking the message that needs to be sent across the network. It then turns the message into binary numbers, a series of 0's and 1's. After that, it encodes these numbers, and sends corresponding voltage signals through an attached network cable.

This is a top secret message

The NIC takes the message, encodes it, and then sends it as a signal across the network.

So if we know what the signal is, how do we find the original message?

To get the message, reverse the encoding

To find out what the message is, we need to decode the rogue network signal. Here's what we need to do.

1. **Take the rogue signal.**
The signal is the series of voltage changes that's been transmitted along the cable. The message is hidden inside it.

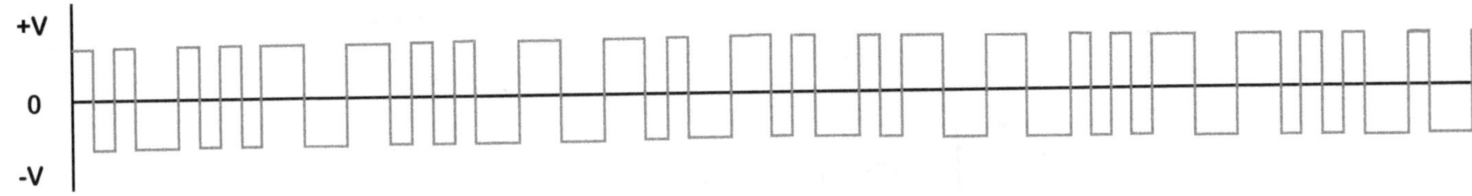

2. **Divide the signal into equal slices using a clocking mechanism.**
By this we mean a device that pulses regularly. The clock provides a regular heartbeat.

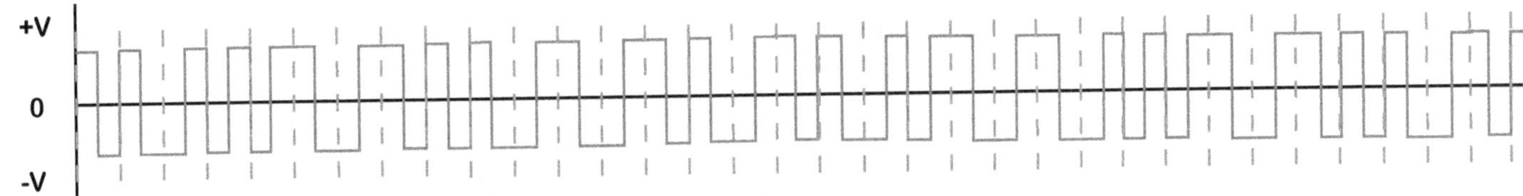

3. **Convert the signal into a series of 0's and 1's.**
To do this, look at the voltage level where the clock pulse meets the signal. The voltage level at this point determines whether the value is a 0 or a 1.

So how do we decode the signal?

The way in which we find the stream of 0's and 1's depends on the method used to encode the signal in the first place. So how do we know what this is?

The Ethernet standard tells hardware how to encode the data

So what sort of encoding scheme does the rogue signal use?

The signal is transmitted over Ethernet. This is a standard that engineers and manufacturers use when designing computers and network gear, and the protocol includes features such as Manchester phase encoding. So if the signal is sent using the Ethernet protocol, it uses Manchester encoding.

Let's look at how this works:

The protocol for 10BaseT Ethernet specifies that the signal will be encoded using Manchester encoding.

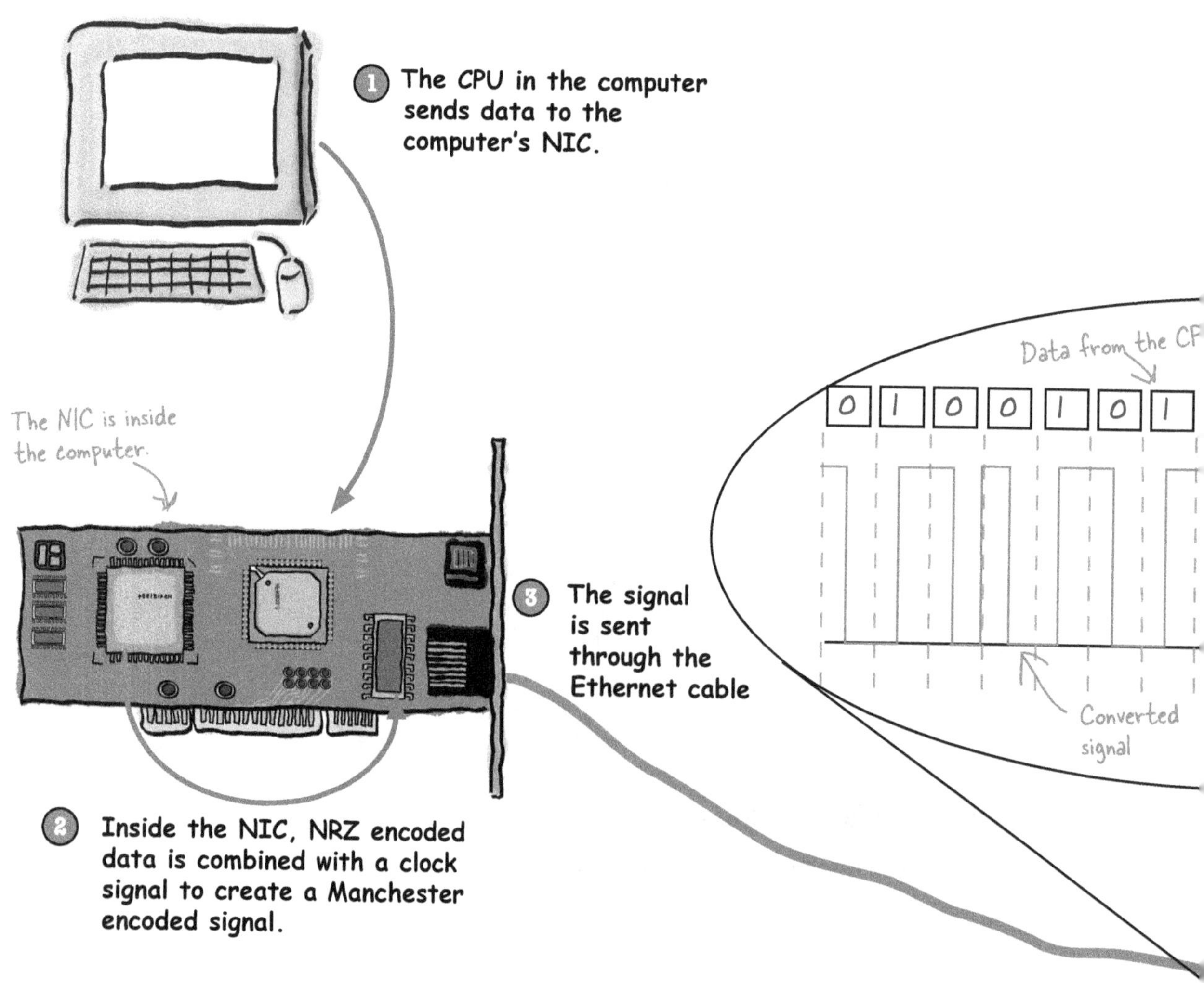

1 The CPU in the computer sends data to the computer's NIC.
The NIC is inside the computer.
2 Inside the NIC, NRZ encoded data is combined with a clock signal to create a Manchester encoded signal.
3 The signal is sent through the Ethernet cable
Data from the CP
0 1 0 0 1 0 1
Converted signal

In NRZ encoding, the binary data is represented by the high and low voltage levels; high is a 1, low is a 0. In Manchester encoding, it is the TRANSITION to a voltage that represents data.

You don't have to know the exact details of how encoding works.

What is important for you to understand is that data in a computer is represented one way but is encoded into a signal when it is transmitted on a network.

0 1 1 1 0 0 1

6 The CPU in the computer gets data from the computer's NIC.

4 The signal is received by the NIC.

5 Inside the NIC, the received Manchester encoded signal is converted in to NRZ. The NIC then lets the CPU know it has data.

there are no Dumb Questions

Q: Why do we need to encode and decode signals?

A: If we don't encode and decode signals, they come in as raw waveforms, i.e. 1's & 0's represented by voltages. We can't do much with such waveforms. We encode and decode signals so that we have a way to carry data on the signal. Networking is all about sending messages, so encoding and decoding are crucial to networking.

Q: Why don't we just encode data in one way and stick to that?

A: Different encoding methods have different advantages. Some encoding methods are more efficient. Some methods have better error correction. Over time, better and better encoding methods come about. These methods offer different advantages and disadvantages over others.

Q: What is error correction?

A: Any time you send data on a network, you can run into problems with that data. Different encoding methods allow for detection and correction of those problems. Error correction helps maintain the integrity of your data.

Q: How many different kinds of data encoding are there?

A: Data encoding comes in many flavors: American Standard Code for Information Interchange (ASCII), Binary Coded Decimal (BCD), Differential Manchester Encoding (DME), Extended Binary Coded Decimal Interchange Code (EBCDIC), Feedback Shift Register (FSR), Manchester Phase Encoding (MPE), Non Return to Zero (NRZ), Non Return to Zero Invertive (NRZ-I), Return to Zero (RZ), and Unicode. Some older encoding schemes in networking are Manchester, NRZ, and NRZ-I.

Q: Older schemes? What is being used now in networking?

A: 4B/5B and 8B/10B are used for Fast Ethernet and Gigabit Ethernet. The 4B/5B scheme uses 5 bits to represent the 4 bit numbers and 10 bits to represent 8 bit numbers. This is done to assure that there is a transition at some point.

Q: As a network professional, I just need to know how to connect stuff. Why should I learn all of this math and physics?

A: Networking is all about sending messages (data) over a carrier (signals). To diagnose problems, a good mechanic needs to know all the aspects of how an engine works. Similarly, a networking professional needs to know how data is packaged to understand how to completely troubleshoot a network.

Q: Where do I go if I want to find out more about the Ethernet protocol?

A: The Ethernet protocol was written by the Institute of Electrical and Electronics Engineers (IEEE). You can find a whole lot more about the IEEE Ethernet working group and its publications at the following sites:

http://grouper.ieee.org/groups/802/3/
http://standards.ieee.org/getieee802/

One of your colleagues at the Head First Spy Agency.

So we know that the signal uses Manchester encoding because it's Ethernet. But how does that help us decode the message from the mole?

If we know how a signal's encoded, that means we can decode it.

Knowing that the signal uses Manchester encoding means that we know the series of 1's and 0's that the signal represents. What we need to do next is translate this into something more meaningful. To do this, we need to understand how to translate binary numbers.

the Scholar's Corner

Manchester Encoding a method used in networking, which turns electric signals into data formats that a computer can read. The difference between Manchester and other binary encoding methods is that Manchester encodes data based on a change in the signal. The direction of the change in the signal determines whether the bit is a "0" or a "1."

A more formal definition appears in Federal Standard 1037C, Glossary of Telecommunications Terms. You can find this document at the following url:

http://www.its.bldrdoc.gov/fs-1037/fs-1037c.htm

A quick guide to binary

The first thing you need to know about binary numbers is that they aren't based on 10 digits (0 to 9); they're based on 2 digits, 0 and 1. Here's how binary digits work:

0
1
Forget all about your other fingers, you only need two of them for binary.

If you see a binary number like 0 or 1, this is the same as a decimal number 0 or 1. But how do we write a number like 2 in binary?

Binary is a base 2 system. This means that each digit in a binary number represents an increasing power of 2. The right-most digit in the binary number represents 2^0, the next represents 2^1, the next 2^2 and so on.

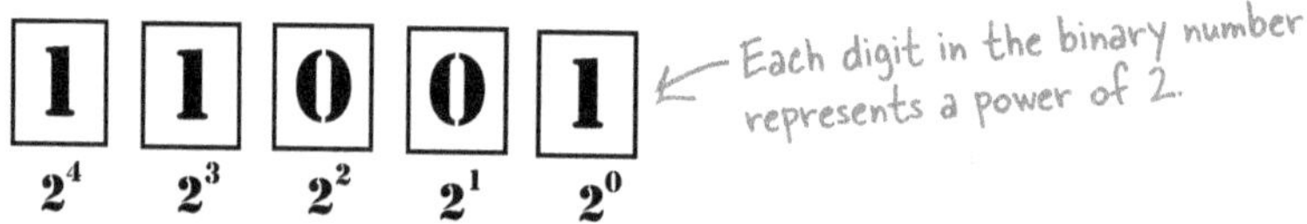

So how do we convert a binary to decimal?

To convert from binary, here's what you need to do.

1. **Multiply each digit in the binary number by the corresponding power of 2.**

2. **Add the whole lot up together.**

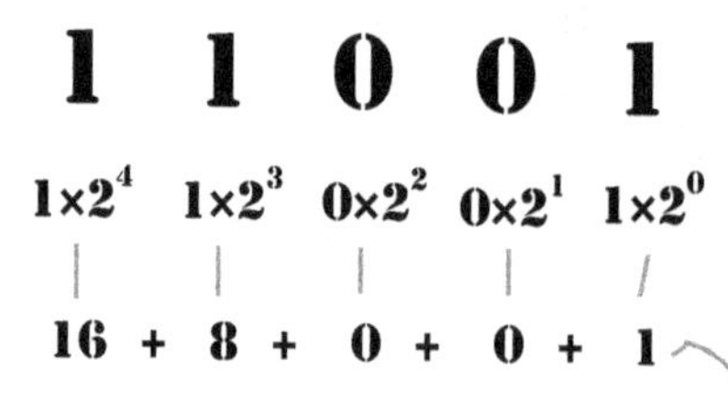

So 11001 in binary is the same as 25 in decimal.

And there's your decimal number equivalent.

Your job is to play the computer and convert the binary numbers below into decimal. We've done the first one for you.

1	0	1	1	1		0	1	
128 +	0 +	32 +	16 +	8 +	0 +	0 +	1 =	185
1	0	1	0	1	0	0	1	
+	+	+	+	+	+	+	=	
0	1	0	1	1	0	0	0	
+	+	+	+	+	+	+	=	
	0	0	1		1	1	0	
+	+	+	+	+	+	+	=	
1	1	1	1	1	1	1	0	
+	+	+	+	+	+	+	=	

BE the Computer Solution

Your job is to play the computer and convert the binary numbers below into decimal. We've done the first one for you.

1		0		1		1		1		0		0		1		
128	+	0	+	32	+	16	+	8	+	0	+	0	+	1	=	185

1		0		1		0		1		0		0				
128	+	0	+	32	+	0	+	8	+	0	+	0	+	1	=	169

0		1		0		1		1				0		0		
0	+	64	+	0	+	16	+	8	+	0	+	0	+	0	=	88

0		0		0		1		1		1		1		0		
0	+	0	+	0	+	16	+	8	+	4	+	2	+	0	=	30

1		1		1		1		1		1		1		0		
128	+	64	+	32	+	16	+	8	+	4	+	2	+	0	=	254

Sharpen your pencil

Try converting the signal below into binary and then into decimal. Use the Manchester encoding method to convert the signal.

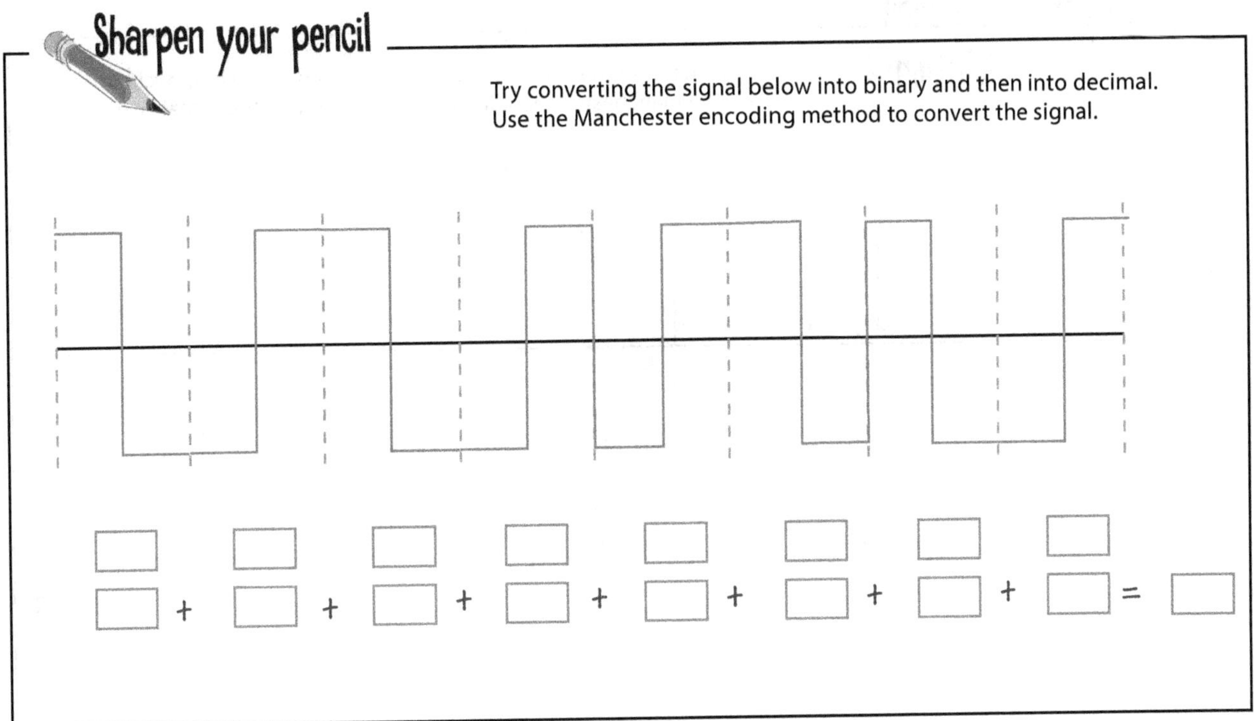

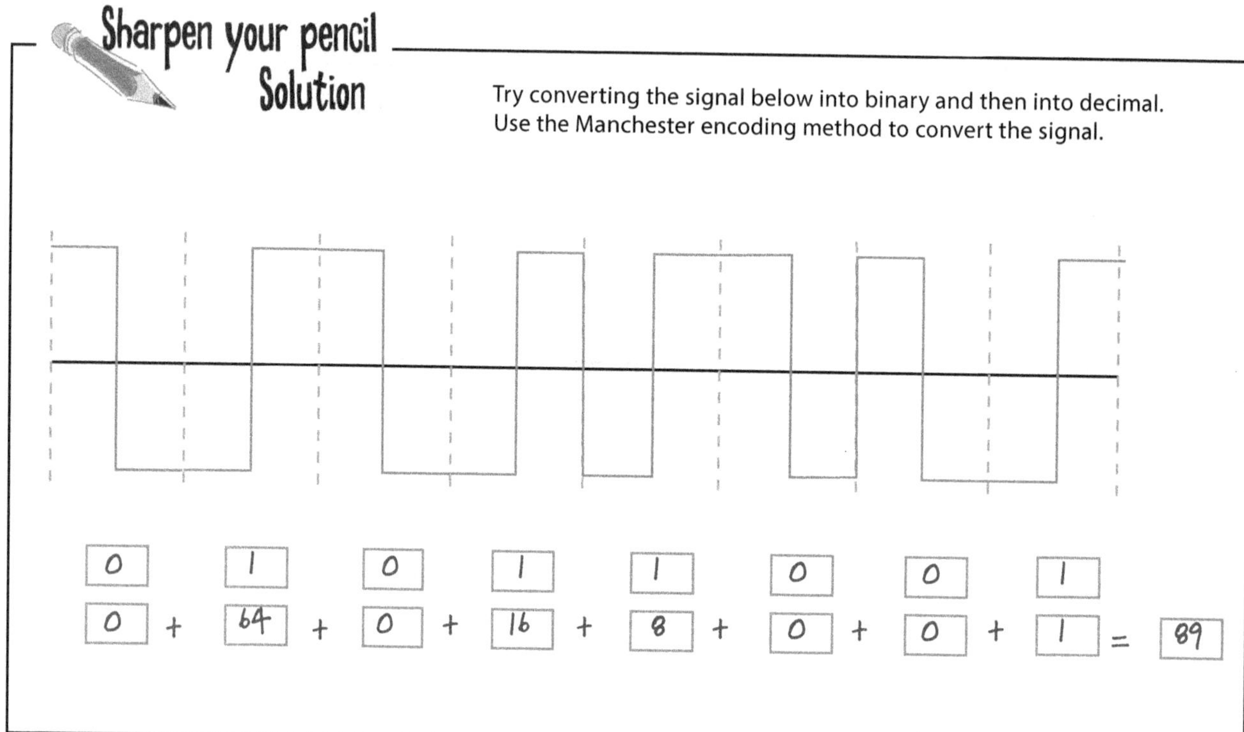
Sharpen your pencil
Solution
Try converting the signal below into binary and then into decimal.
Use the Manchester encoding method to convert the signal.
0 1 0 1 1 0 0 1
0 + 64 + 0 + 16 + 8 + 0 + 0 + 1 = 89

So are you telling me we can only send messages as numbers? That's a bit lame. What about text?

We can convert the numbers into letters.

So far we've looked at how we convert the signal into binary, and from binary to decimal. What we really want to do though is convert the signal into something more meaningful such as words. So how can we turn numbers into characters? The answer lies with ASCII...

there are no Dumb Questions

Q: Why don't computers just use decimals like humans do?

A: Computers use binary because it's more convenient to implement with electronics. Electricity is easier to deal with when it's in two states, like on-off, high-low, positive-negative. If we had to represent ten numbers at the signal level, we'd have to represent ten states. To do so, we'd need expensive, highly-sensitive electronics. We'd also have to account for errors in state and spend huge chunks of time error-correcting and troubleshooting. Binary is way easier and way cheaper to use.

Q: Where will I use binary in a day-to-day networking job?

A: The most common place you'll use binary as a network professional is in subnetting (which we cover in a later chapter). Subnetting can seem like magic if you don't understand the binary behind it. If you want to monitor packets on a network, binary can help you understand the data more completely. In the end, understanding binary makes you a better networking professional.

Q: Can you add, subtract, multiply, and divide binary numbers?

A: You can do all of the same operations we do with decimal numbers. You just need to learn some special rules to do so.

Q: Can't I just do binary on some sort of calculator?

A: On a Macintosh computer, you can use the Calculator app. When you open the app, choose "View > Programmer" and you've got a calculator that will do binary. For other operating systems, you can find and download a good programmer's calculator. You can also search the Internet for web-based binary converters.

Computers read numbers, humans read letters

We can convert a signal into numbers, but what can we do when we need text? We use something called the American Standard Code for Information Interchange (ASCII). Computers use this format when transferring text messages to one another.

In computer-speak, each binary digit is called a ***bit***, and eight bits together form a ***byte***.

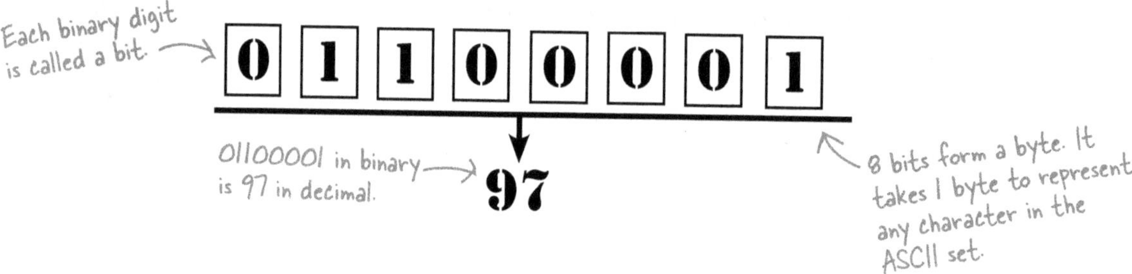
Each binary digit is called a bit.
0 1 1 0 0 0 0 1
01100001 in binary is 97 in decimal.
97
8 bits form a byte. It takes 1 byte to represent any character in the ASCII set.

Each byte needs to be translated to an ASCII character. To do this, we convert each byte into its decimal equivalent, and then look up the corresponding ASCII in an ASCII table, just like the one in Appendix ii.

To get the ASCII code that corresponds to a decimal, the computer uses a table much like this one.

Decimal	ASCII
97	a
98	b
99	c

So the ASCII character represented by 01100001 is the letter a.

But isn't there an easier way?

The trouble with translating bytes into ASCII characters in this way is that the 0's and 1's quickly become overwhelming. It can be fiddly converting bytes into decimal numbers, and this means it's easy to make mistakes. So is there an easier way?

BANG!
Watch it!

There is another character encoding scheme.

Another major character encoding scheme is Unicode. It allows for millions of characters.

Wouldn't it be dreamy if I could convert binary numbers into ASCII in some easier way than converting to decimal, and not have to juggle quite so many 1's and 0's? But I know it's just a fantasy...

Hexadecimal to the rescue

There's a handier way of converting a byte into ASCII. Instead of looking up a decimal number in an ASCII table, we can look up its hexadecimal equivalent instead.

Hexadecimal numbers are based on 16 digits, 0-15:

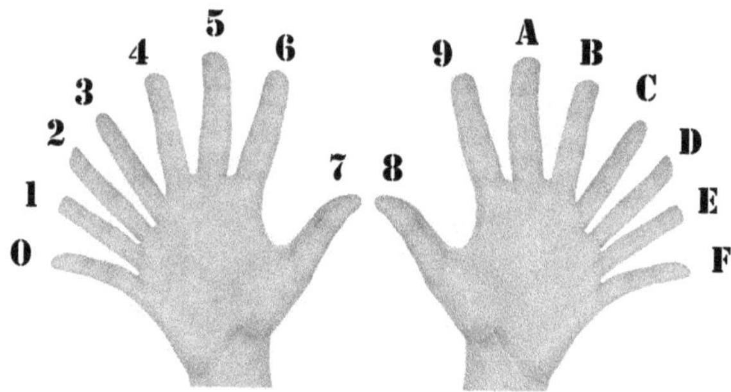

So if you see a hexadecimal number like B, you know that it just means 11 in decimal.

Hex is a base 16 system, which means that each digit represents an increasing power of 16. The right-most represents 16^0, the next represents 16^1, and so on.

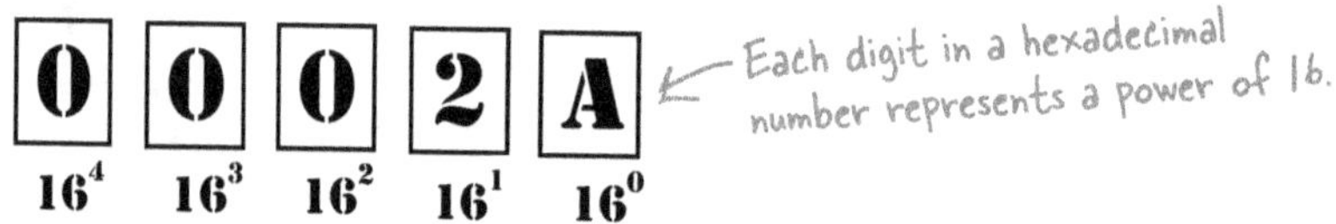

So how do we convert a hexadecimal to decimal?

To convert a hexadecimal number to a decimal, take each digit in the hexadecimal number, multiply it by the power of 16 it represents, and then add the whole lot up together.

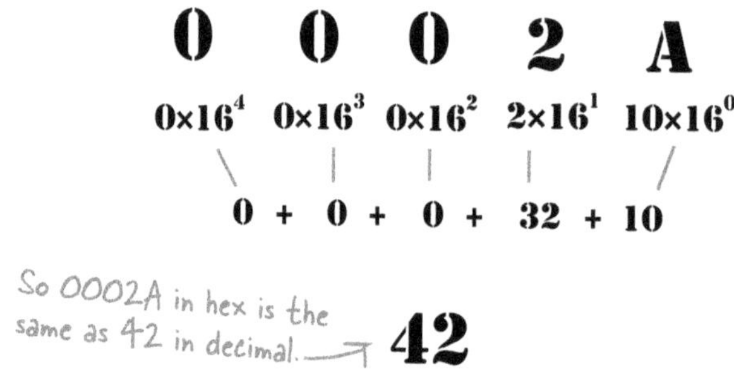

We can convert to ASCII using hex

Once you learn to use hexadecimal, you realize just how cool it is. Hex and binary make great partners, which simplifies conversions between binary and ASCII. Hex is like a bridge between the weird world of binary and our world (the human, readable world).

Here's what we do:

1. **Break the byte in half.**
Each half-byte is called a ***nibble***. *[Note from Editor: you're kidding, right?]*

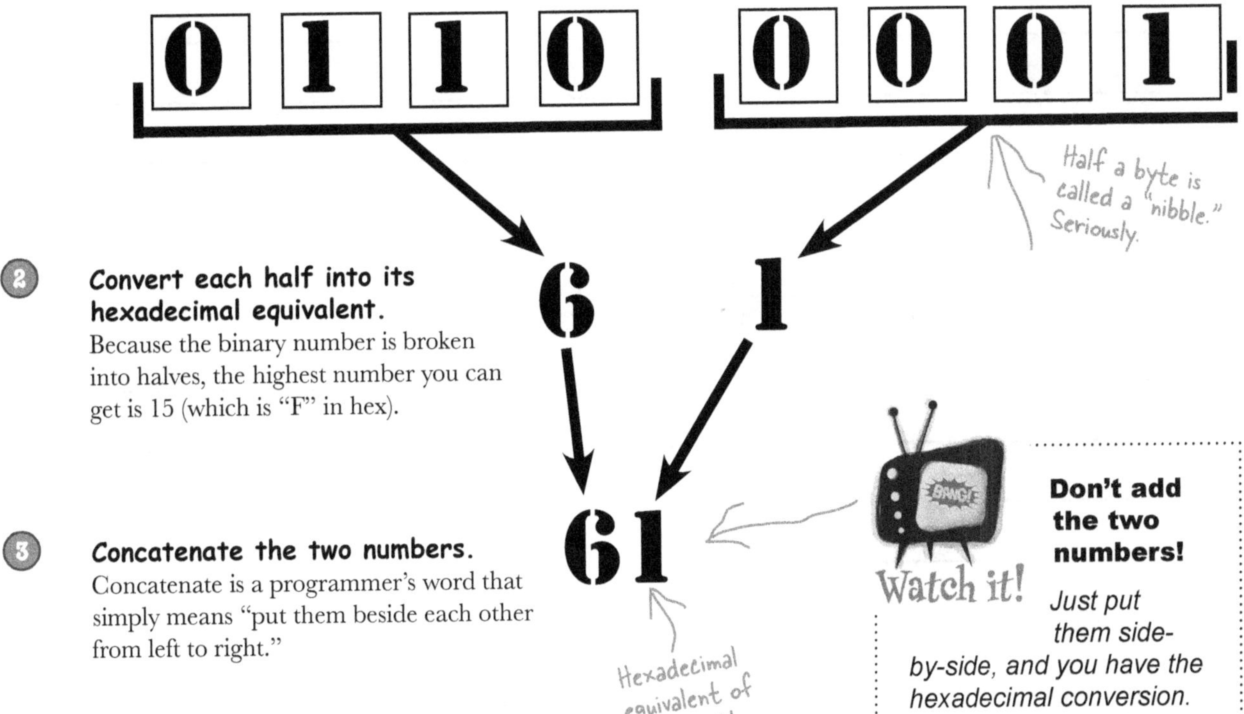

2. **Convert each half into its hexadecimal equivalent.**
Because the binary number is broken into halves, the highest number you can get is 15 (which is "F" in hex).

3. **Concatenate the two numbers.**
Concatenate is a programmer's word that simply means "put them beside each other from left to right."

Watch it!

Don't add the two numbers!

Just put them side-by-side, and you have the hexadecimal conversion.

4. **Look the number up in an ASCII table.**
The table to the right is just a sample. To find common ASCII codes, use the handy ASCII conversion table we've provided in Appendix ii.

Decimal	Hexadecimal	ASCII
97	61	a
98	62	b
99	63	c
100	64	d
101	65	e

We know it's strange at first, but trust us, this little trick makes conversion to ASCII faster.

The messages below are written in binary, decimal, and hexadecimal. Practice your decoding skills by deciphering the message.

Binary

01000011 01101111 01101101 01110000 01110101 01110100 01100101 01110010 01110011 00100000 01110011 01110000 01100101 01100001 01101011 00100000 01100010 01101001 01101110 01100001 01110010 01111001 00100000 01100001 01101110 01100100 00100000 01110011 01101111 00100000 01110011 01101000 01101111 01110101 01101100 01100100 00100000 01101110 01100101 01110100 01110111 01101111 01110010 01101011 00100000 01110000 01110010 01101111 01110011 00101110 00001101 00001010 00001101 00001010

Decimal

Hint: Use the ASCII table in Appendix ii to lookup the ASCII code.

69 118 101 110 32 100 101 99 105 109 97 108 115 32 99 97 110 32 98 101 32 101 110 99 111 100 101 100 32 97 115 32 65 83 67 73 73 46

Hexadecimal

48 65 78 61 64 65 63 69 6d 61 6c 20 70 61 63 6b 73 20 61 20 6c 6f 74 20 6f 66 20 76 61 6c 75 65 20 69 6e 74 6f 20 61 20 6c 69 74 74 6c 65 20 73 70 61 63 65 2e

BE the Computer

Your job is to play the computer and convert the binary numbers below into hexadecimal.

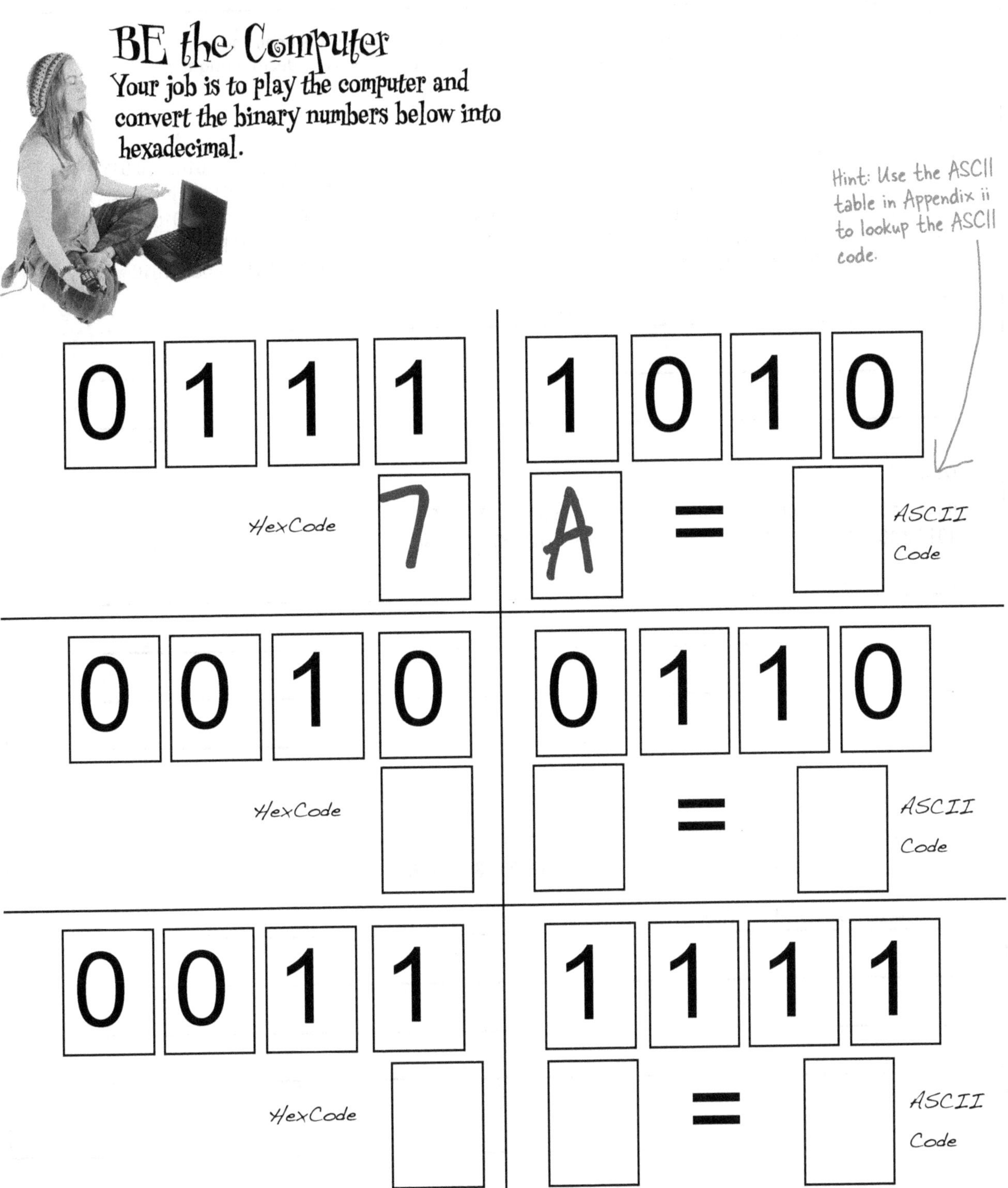

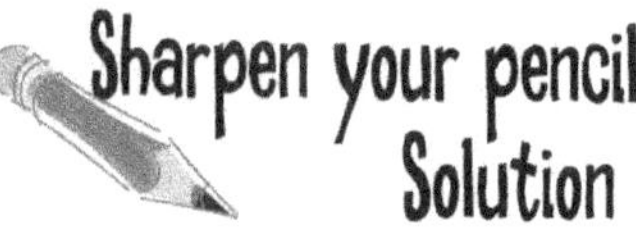

Solution

The messages below are written in binary, decimal, and hexadecimal. Practice your decoding skills by deciphering the message.

Binary

01000011 01101111 01101101 01110000 01110101 01110100 01100101 01110010 01110011 00100000 01110011 01110000 01100101 01100001 01101011 00100000 01100010 01101001 01101110 01100001 01110010 01111001 00100000 01100001 01101110 01100100 00100000 01110011 01101111 00100000 01110011 01101000 01101111 01110101 01101100 01100100 00100000 01101110 01100101 01110100 01110111 01101111 01110010 01101011 00100000 01110000 01110010 01101111 01110011 00101110 00001101 00001010 00001101 00001010

Computers speak binary and so should network pros.

Decimal

69 118 101 110 32 100 101 99 105 109 97 108 115 32 99 97 110 32 98 101 32 101 110 99 111 100 101 100 32 97 115 32 65 83 67 73 73 46

Even decimals can be encoded as ASCII.

Hint: Use the ASCII table in Appendix ii to lookup the ASCII code.

Hexadecimal

48 65 78 61 64 65 63 69 6d 61 6c 20 70 61 63 6b 73 20 61 20 6c 6f 74 20 6f 66 20 76 61 6c 75 65 20 69 6e 74 6f 20 61 20 6c 69 74 74 6c 65 20 73 70 61 63 65 2e

Hexadecimal packs a lot of value into a little space.

Sharpen your pencil

Try converting the signal below into binary and then into decimal.
Use the full Manchester phase encoding method to convert the signal.

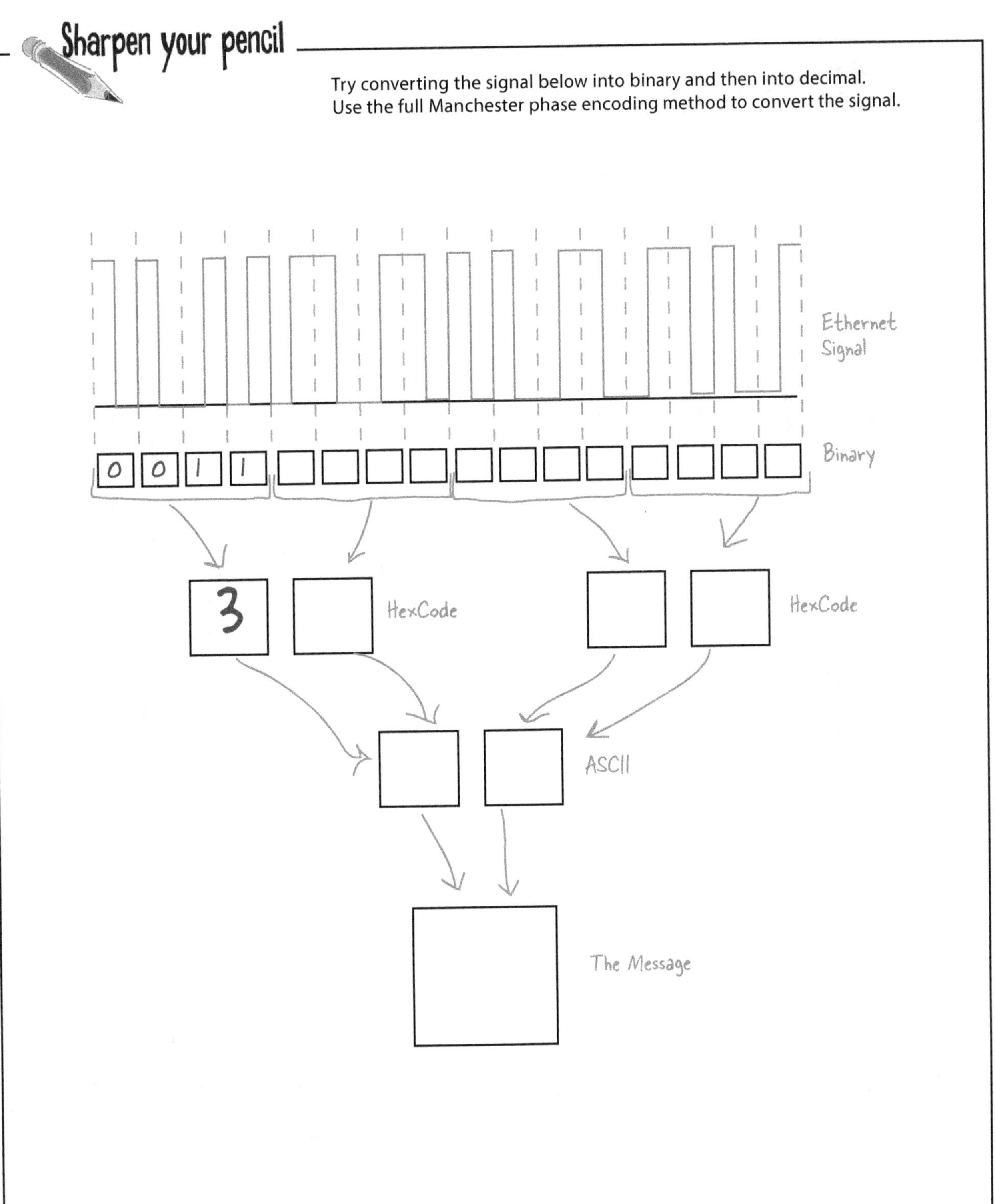

BE the Computer Solution

Your job is to play the computer and convert the binary numbers below into hexadecimal and then into ASCII.

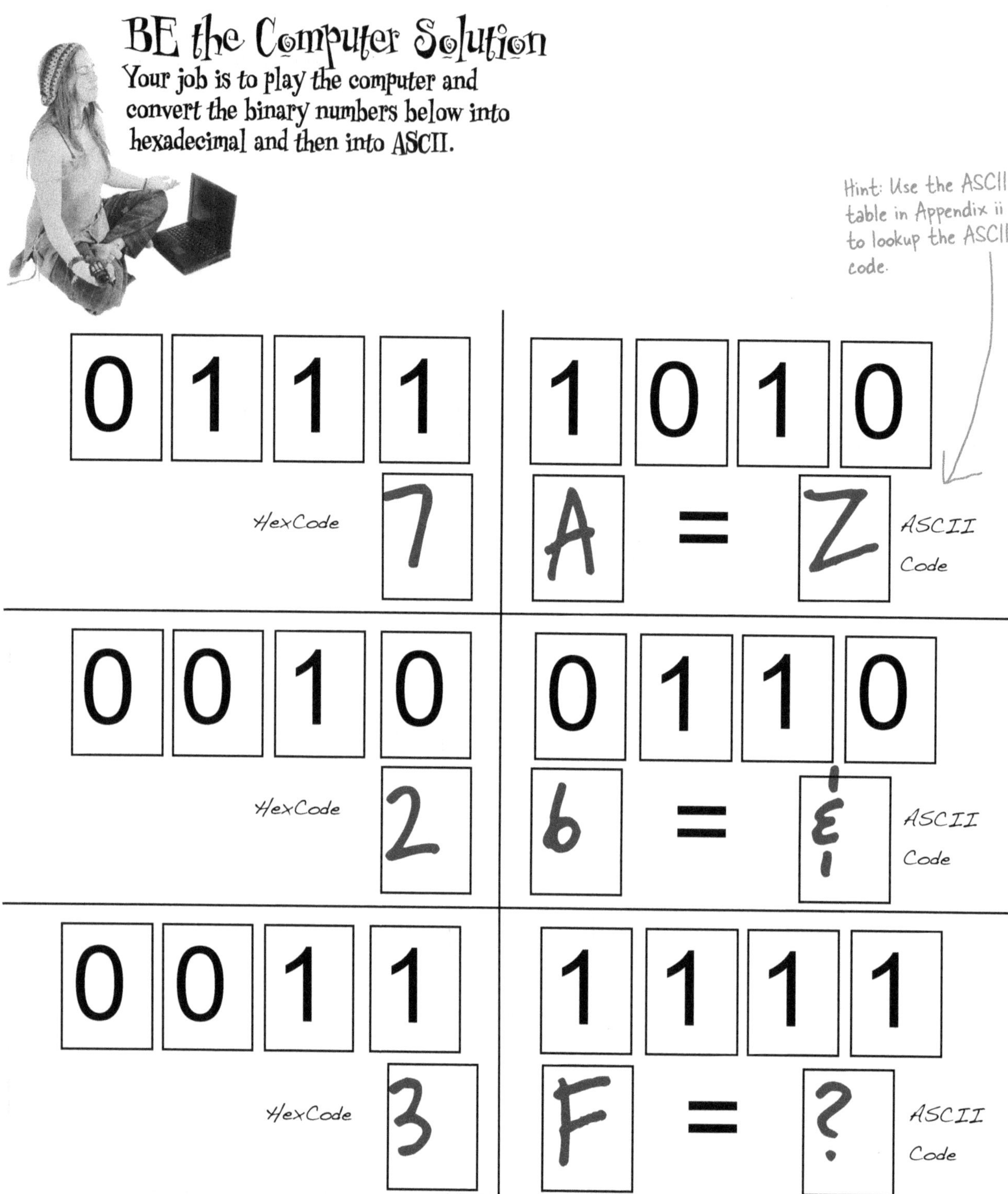

Sharpen your pencil Solution

Try converting the signal below into binary and then into decimal. Use the full Manchester phase encoding method to convert the signal.

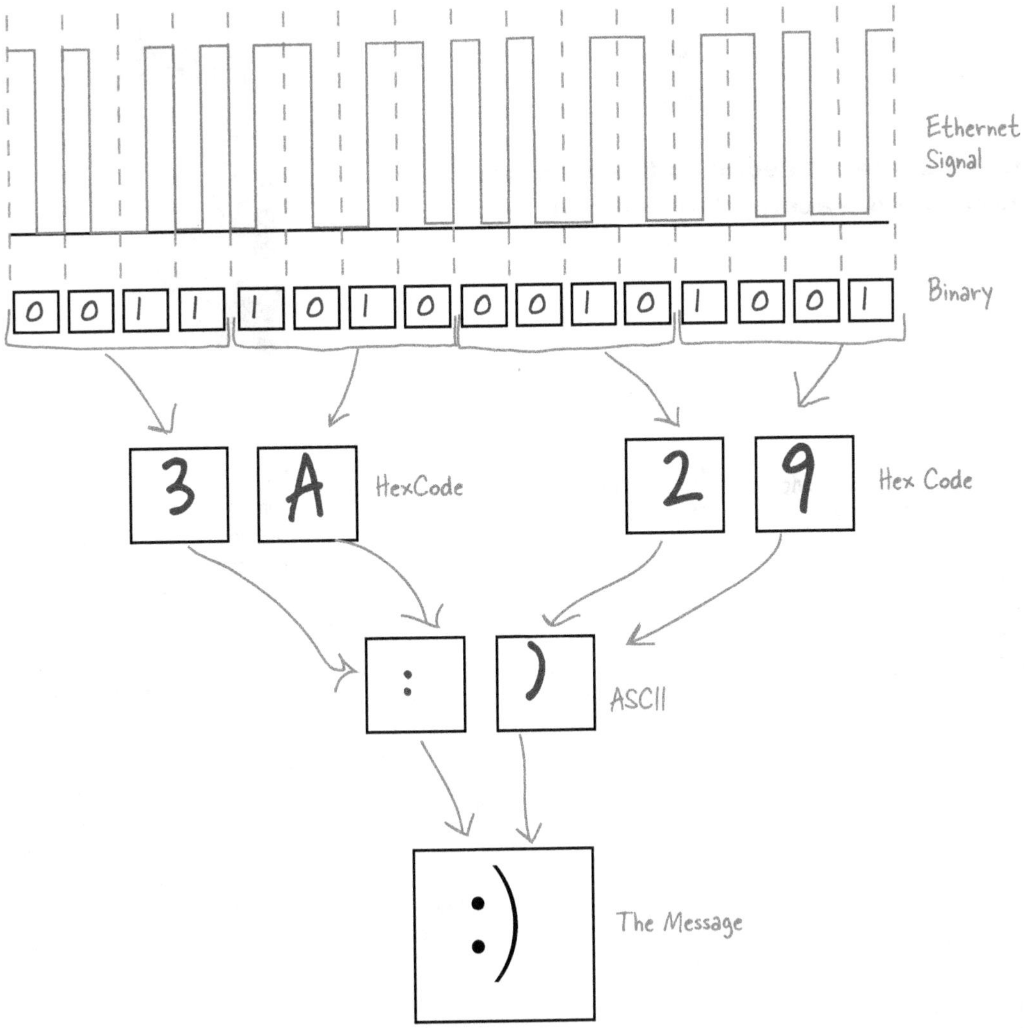

Ethernet Signal

Binary

0	0	1	1	1	0	1	0	0	0	1	0	1	0	0	1

HexCode: 3 A

Hex Code: 2 9

ASCII: :)

The Message: :)

Back at the spy agency...

So far we've looked at encoding techniques for finding out what message the mole is sending. So what progress have we made in interpreting the signal?

I've tried decoding the binary, but the ASCII makes no sense. I wonder what's wrong?

It's not just a matter of decoding the binary; we have to consider the appropriate protocol too...

there are no Dumb Questions

Q: Does it take a long time to encode Manchester, hex, and ASCII data?

A: Computers encode data at high speeds (like faster than we can blink), but it is dependent on hardware and how it's engineered. Obviously, the newest network gear is faster than the old stuff. The transmission media has a big impact on speed, too. For instance, fiber-optic cable allows for x speed. Whereas Ethernet cable allows for X speed depending on whether we're dealing with 10 mbps, 100 mbps, or 1000 mbps.

Q: Ethernet goes at different speeds?

A: Yes, the original Ethernet was 10Mbps, but engineers quickly figured out how to get more speed, and that quest has never ended. You can purchase Ethernet equipment right now that can go as fast as 10Gbps.

Q: So do all speeds of Ethernet use Manchester Encoding?

A: Good Question. No, they don't. 100 Mbps, or Fast Ethernet, uses the 4B5B encoding scheme. The simplest way to think about this encoding scheme is that 5 bits are used to transmit 4 bits of data.

Gigabit Ethernet, 1000Mbps or 1Gbps, uses an 8B10B encoding scheme. Gigabit Ethernet also uses all 4 pairs of wire in a cable.

Q: So how do these encoding schemes help the various devices stay in sync?

A: By using an encoding scheme, a device sending data on a network "embeds" its clock into the signal. The clock is what determines the 1's & 0's. Imagine if there was just a string of 0's using the NRZ encoding scheme. This means that there is just a low voltage. A device receiving this signal would not know if this was really the signal or if there was a break in the line.

A signal with the clock embedded in the signal allows the receiver to properly decode the signal because the data is in the transitions of voltages and not in just the voltage level.

Q: Doesn't a computer have to do all this encoding and decoding?

A: You might think that, but the engineers that designed this stuff are really smart people. They figured out how to create hardware that can do this encoding/decoding very fast. This is built into the network cards.

Protocols define the structure of a message

In order to effectively communicate, network devices use protocols, a set of guidelines, or rules, for the network conversation. These procotols cover such things as how fast data can be sent and how data will be structured when it's sent.

Most protocols define a size limit for messages, which means that the messages need to be broken into separate packages and labeled with information about where the message came from and where it's headed.

Network messages come in two kinds of packages: frames and packets.

Sharpen your pencil

Redraw frame protocol #2 so that it matches protocol #1.

Frame Procotol #1

Preamble	Destination MAC address	Source MAC address	EtherType	Payload	CRC Checksum

Frame Procotol #2

Payload	Destination MAC address	EtherType	CRC Checksum	Source MAC address	Preamble

Answers on page 156.

Why would it be important for the destination address to come near the front of a frame?

Frames and Packets Up Close

A frame is a logical structure of bits that organizes network traffic so every device knows how to read the information inside of it. Inside the frame is another structure called a packet. It's the real meat of the frame.

Let's take a look:

This is a frame, a logical structure of bits.
Length in Bytes:
7
1
6
6
Preamble
Start of Frame
Destination MAC address
Source MAC address
The preamble is made up of 7 bytes that each look like this: 10101010. This regular pattern of bits allows the communicating network devices to synchronize their clock pulses.
The SOF is one byte long and ends with two ones: 10101011. The SOF tells the receiving device that the crucial content of the frame is on its way.
The Destination MAC address is the hardware address of the next network device to which the packet is traveling.
The Source MAC address is the hardware address of the last device that sent the frame.

To give you a sense of how much information is packed into ONE frame, we've written a frame in binary below.

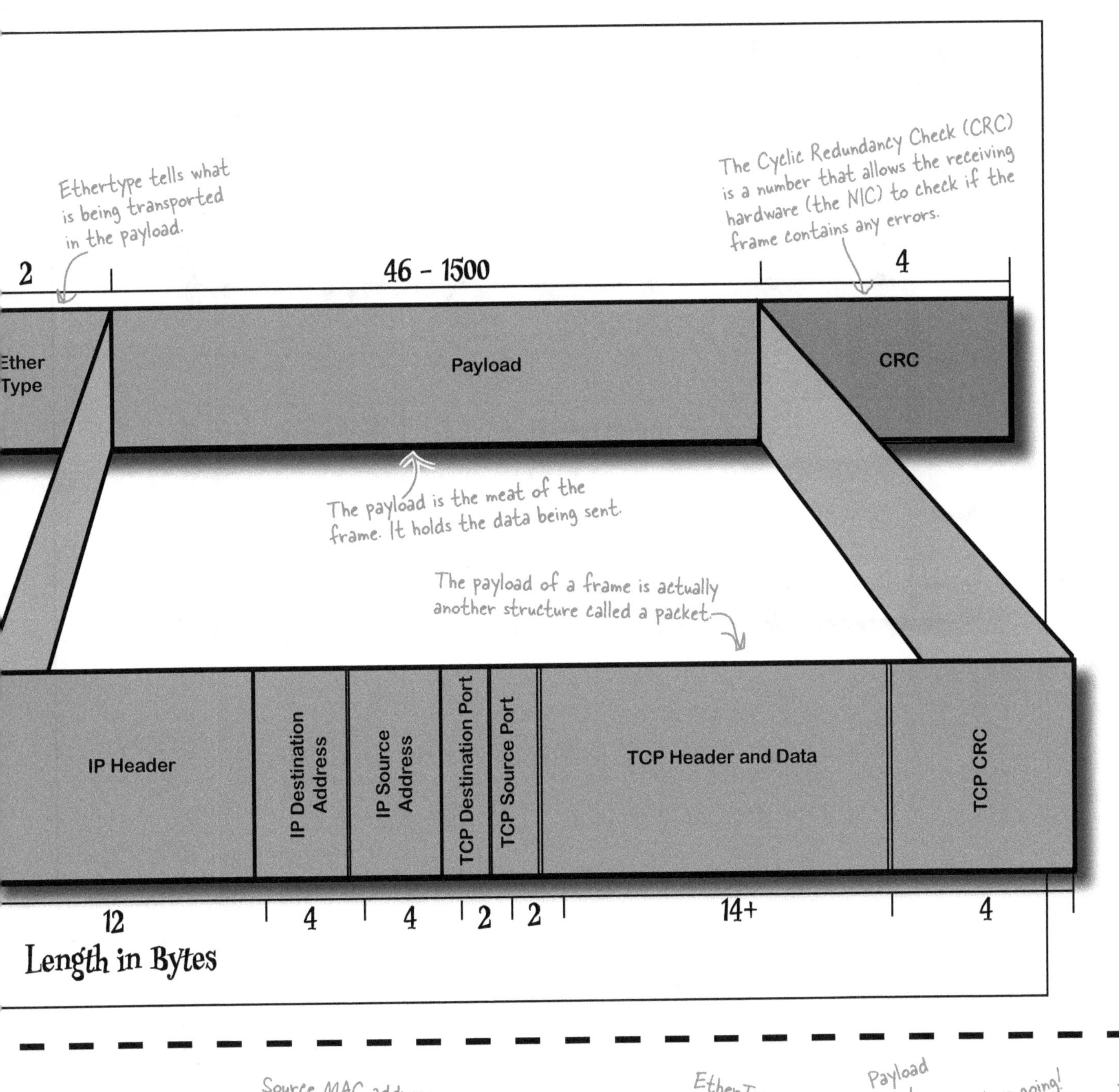

Ethertype tells what is being transported in the payload.
2
46 - 1500
The Cyclic Redundancy Check (CRC) is a number that allows the receiving hardware (the NIC) to check if the frame contains any errors.
4
Ether Type
Payload
CRC
The payload is the meat of the frame. It holds the data being sent.
The payload of a frame is actually another structure called a packet.
IP Header
IP Destination Address
IP Source Address
TCP Destination Port
TCP Source Port
TCP Header and Data
TCP CRC
12
4
4
2
2
14+
4
Length in Bytes
Source MAC address
EtherType
Payload
Keep going!

10011000 00000000 00010010 00110111 00111111 01101100 10101010 10111110 11101110 10101010 10101010

Sharpen your pencil Solution

From page 153.

Redraw frame protocol #2 so that it matches protocol #1.

Frame Procotol #1

Preamble	Destination MAC address	Source MAC address	EtherType	Payload	CRC Checksum

Frame Procotol #2

Payload	Destination MAC address	EtherType	CRC Checksum	Source MAC address	Preamble

Redrawn

Preamble	Destination MAC address	Source MAC address	EtherType	Payload	CRC Checksum

Payload (continued)

10101010 10101010 10101010 10101010 10101010 10101010 10101010 10101011 00000000 00100101 01000010 1111

Sharpen your pencil

Build a frame in the space below. The source address is 00 12 13 34 51 25, the destination address is 00 12 13 34 20 19. The Ethertype is 08 00, the data is 68 65 6c 6c 6f, and the CRC is 01 03 35 76. (Don't worry about the preamble.)

More to go...

011 10011000 00000000 00010010 00110111 00111111 01101100 10101010 10111110 1110110 10101010 10101010

Sharpen your pencil Solution

Build a frame in the space below. The source address is 00 12 13 34 51 25, the destination address is 00 12 13 34 20 19. The Ethertype is 08 00, the data is 68 65 6c 6c 6f, and the CRC is 01 03 35 76. (Don't worry about the preamble.)

Destination Address	Source Address	EtherType	Payload	CRC
00 12 13 34 20 19	00 12 13 34 51 25	08 00	68 65 6c 6c 6f	01 03 35 76

there are no Dumb Questions

Q: How can I find the MAC address on my computer?

A: On a Macintosh, go to "System Preferences." In the search entry box in the upper right, type `Ethernet ID` and hit "Return." The next window you see will show your Ethernet ID, which is really just another name for your MAC address.

On a Windows machine, go to "Start > Run." Type `cmd` and you will open the command line utility. Type `ipconfig/all` and the MAC address will appear in the output.

If you are a Unix or Linux user, open a command prompt window and enter `sudo /sbin/ifconfig -a`. The MAC address will show under "hwaddr" or "ether."

Q: Can I change my MAC address?

A: The company that manufactured the NIC in your computer burned it into a ROM chip on your NIC. Unless you're an electrical engineer with access to ROM burning equipment, it will be pretty hard to change the MAC address. You can, however, fake out others on the network by "spoofing" your MAC address. Typically this requires a software utility. We don't recommend MAC address spoofing because many companies regard it as a security violation and it could result in legal action.

Q: Are MAC addresses just random numbers or do they mean something?

A: The structure of a MAC address means something to manufacturers of network hardware. The first half of the MAC address is a special code assigned to the manufacturer of the hardware; the last half of the address is a number the manufacturer uses to number the devices they produce

Q: Is someone in charge of giving out MAC addresses?

A: The Institute of Electrical and Electronics Engineers Registration Authority is in charge of issuing MAC addresses.

Q: Will we ever run out of MAC addresses?

A: Not right away. There are 2^{48} or 281,474,976,710,656 possible MAC addresses. The IEEE does not expect to exhaust the address space until 2100. I guess we'll worry about it in 2099.

Payload (continued)

10101010 10101010 10101010 10101010 10101010 10101010 10101010 10101011 00000000 00100101 01000010 1111111

Sharpen your pencil

Back to our frame!

Try your hand at decoding the beginning part of one of the captured frames.

You may find it helpful to draw some lines where the various frame parts start.

Preamble bytes not shown

32512272E32A001E8D62014B08002112467842 3468f42f13654eb4ab ...

Destination MAC address 32 51 ______

Source MAC address ______

EtherType ______

First 15 Bytes of Payload ______

634A2C7244561A3E5621173308001 4624c2a4e8b42f213a112981ea345

Destination MAC address 63 4A ______

Source MAC address ______

EtherType ______

First 15 Bytes of Payload ______

Finally! After three pages of bytes, we reached the end of our frame.. To depict the largest Ethernet frame possible, we'd need to keep typing bytes for 57 more pages.

CRC Checksum

10011000 00000000 00010010 00110111 00111111 01101100 10101010 | 10111110 11101110 10101010 10101010

Sharpen your pencil Solution

Back to our frame!

Try your hand at decoding the beginning part of one of the captured frames.

You may find it helpful to draw some lines where the various frame parts start.

010101010101010101032512272E32A001E8D62014B080021124678423468f42f13654eb4ab2e

Destination MAC address: 32 51 22 72 E3 2A

Source MAC address: 00 1E 8D 62 01 4B

EtherType: 08 00

First 15 Bytes of Payload: 21 12 46 78 42 34 68 f4 2f 13 65 4e b4 ab 2e

0101010101010101010634A2C7244561A3E56211733080014624c2a4e8b42f213a112981ea345

Destination MAC address: 63 4A 2C 72 44 56

Source MAC address: 1A 3E 56 21 17 33

EtherType: 08 00

First 15 Bytes of Payload: 14 62 4c 2a 4e 8b 42 f2 13 a1 12 98 1e a3 45

Network frames have lots of layers

Encoding and decoding signals allows us to ship data efficiently. Frames give that data structure, but does a frame give us enough structure to package our data?

A network frame contains nested structures that allow us to pack and unpack the data efficiently. Like a series of nested dolls, each smaller structure is enclosed by the next largest structure.

The payload of a frame is actually a structure nested within the frame. We call it a packet, and the EtherType field lets us know what type of packet the payload contains.

The Ethernet frame encapsulates the smaller structures.
The packet with IP Header fits in the larger structure of the frame.
TCP or some other sub-packet fits into the larger structure of the IP packet.
Our message fits inside the larger structure of the packet.
TCP = Transmission Control Protocol
IP = Internet Protocol
This nested packaging allows messages to be packed and unpacked without losing the integrity of the data.

We have to do a bit more digging into this frame before we can get to the actual message.

Your friendly packet field guide

Packets come in several different types. You can see that there is a lot of information packed inside these packets. All of those "fields" contain information that helps the packet get across the network. You will notice that many of the same fields exist in the three packet types shown here.

UDP Packet - Protocol Type 17

UDP is used for streaming data such as music and videos.

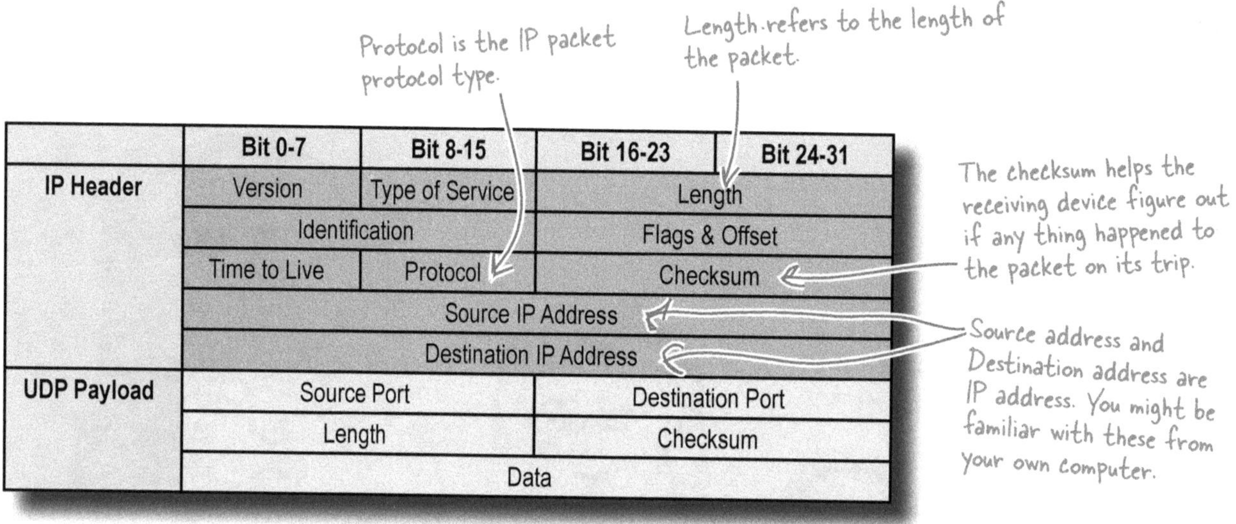

Protocol is the IP packet protocol type.
Length refers to the length of the packet.
Bit 0-7
Bit 8-15
Bit 16-23
Bit 24-31
IP Header
Version
Type of Service
Length
Identification
Flags & Offset
Time to Live
Protocol
Checksum
Source IP Address
Destination IP Address
UDP Payload
Source Port
Destination Port
Length
Checksum
Data
The checksum helps the receiving device figure out if any thing happened to the packet on its trip.
Source address and Destination address are IP address. You might be familiar with these from your own computer.

The message is in here

ICMP Packet - Protocol Type 1

ICMP is used for testing network connections using the `ping` program.

The IP header contains the IP addresses of the destination device, the source IP address, the protocol of the packet it is in front of, and its length. → IP Header

	Bit 0-7	Bit 8-15	Bit 16-23	Bit 24-31
IP Header	Version	Type of Service	Length	
	Identification		Flags & Offset	
	Time to Live	Protocol	Checksum	
	Source IP Address			
	Destination IP Address			
ICMP Payload	Type of Message	Code	Checksum	
	Identifier		Sequence Number	
	Data			

This is decimal 6, in a packet this would be in hex!

TCP Packet - Protocol Type 6

TCP is used for most IP network communications that require a reliable connection. By reliable, we mean that no information is lost.

	Bit 0-7	Bit 8-15	Bit 16-23	Bit 24-31
IP Header	Version	Type of Service	Length	
	Identification		Flags & Offset	
	Time to Live	Protocol	Checksum	
	Source IP Address			
	Destination IP Address			
TCP Payload	Source Port		Destination Port	
	Sequence Number			
	Acknowledgement Number			
	Header Length	Flags	Window	
	Checksum		Urgent Pointer	
	Options			
	Data			

All this information is what makes TCP a reliable protocol.

Geek Bits

There are many different types of IP protocols, around 139 of them. These are just three of the most common ones.

You can find a full list of IP protocols here:

http://www.iana.org/assignments/protocol-numbers/

there are no Dumb Questions

Q: Why are there so many different IP packet types?

A: The main reason is that there are many different types of communication that happens via IP. For example, routers exchanging route information or other protocol type such as IPX encapsulated inside of an IP packet.

Q: How many are there?

A: The current size of the protocol field in an IP header is 8 bits, which gives us 2^8 or 256 possible types of IP packets. There are currently about 139 registered IP protocols.

Q: Aren't packets and frames really the same thing?

A: No. We call data transmitting over Ethernet frames. Inside those frames, in the data field, are packets. Generally frames have to due with the transmission protocol, i.e., Ethernet, ATM, Token Ring, etc. But, as you read more about networking, you will see that there is some confusion on this.

Q: A guy in my office calls packets datagrams. Are they the same?

A: Not really. Packets refer to any data sent in as packets. Whereas datagrams are used to refer to data sent in packets by an unreliable protocol such as UDP or ICMP.

Q: So packets are inside frames; is there some type of data structure inside the packet?

A: Great question. Yes. This is usually an application specific protocol. Remember protocol simply means a set way of structuring information that is agreed upon by the parties involved. So when a web browser request a web page from a web server, it uses the http protocol to request that page, and the server responds with the data using the http protocol. When a server sends email, it uses the smtp protocol. There are many different application type protocols.

Sharpen your pencil

Decoding our packet!

Find the protocol number, destination and source IP addresses in the packet then use the table to decode the protocol type. This will help us find where the data starts.

Our Frame

Bit 0-7	Bit 8-15	Bit 16-23	Bit 24-31
45	00	00 51	
15 ac		00 00	
40	01	86 20	
c0 a8 01 2f			
cc 3e cb 0d			
08	00	ee 02	
f6 6e		00 07	
00 00 00 00 00 00 00 00 68 74 74 70 3a 2f 2f 77 77 77 2e 68 66 6e 65 74 77 6f 72 6b 69 6e 67 2e 63 6f 6d 2f 6d 65 64 69 61 2f 70 61 63 6b 65 74 2e 68 74 6d 6c			

Packet Type: ____________

Destination IP Address: ____________

Source IP Address: ____________

Data: ____________

Sharpen your pencil Solution

Decoding our packet!

Find the protocol number, destination and source IP addresses in the packet then use the table to decode the protocol type. This will help us find where the data starts.

Our Frame

Bit 0-7	Bit 8-15	Bit 16-23	Bit 24-31
45	00	00 51	
15 ac		00 00	
40	01	86 20	
c0 a8 01 2f			
cc 3e cb 0d			
08	00	ee 02	
f6 6e		00 07	
00 00 00 00 00 00 00 00 68 74 74 70 3a 2f 2f 77 77 77 2e 68 66 6e 65 74 77 6f 72 6b 69 6e 67 2e 63 6f 6d 2f 6d 65 64 69 61 2f 70 61 63 6b 65 74 2e 68 74 6d 6c			

Packet Type: ICMP (0x01)

Destination IP Address: 204.62.203.13

Source IP Address: 192.168.1.47

Data: ????

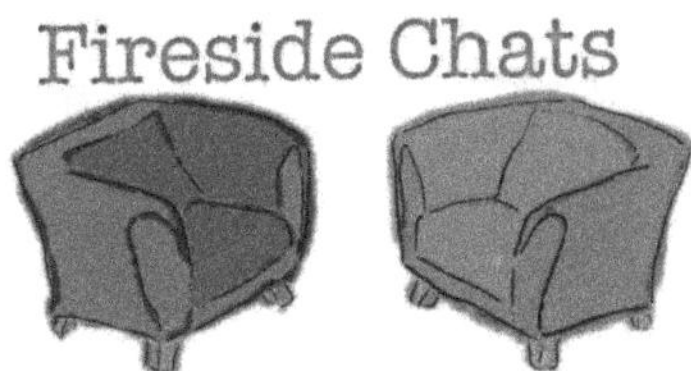

Tonight's talk: **TCP vs. UDP**

TCP Packet:

Well hello UDP. How are you doing?

UDP Packet:

Not bad, how you doing?

TCP Packet:

I heard you had some dropped packets the other day. What is that all about?

UDP Packet:

What do you mean "dropped packets"?

TCP Packet:

I mean packets that did not get from point A to point B.

UDP Packet:

How would I know if packets get anywhere?

TCP Packet:

Exactly my point. You see I can tell when a packet does not get from one point to another. The packets sent using me as a protocol have information in them that the sender enters which lets the receiver know if there are any lost packets.

UDP Packet:

Well why is it that most of the streaming stuff on the Internet, such as music or movies, is sent using me as a protocol? What do you have to say to that?

TCP Packet:

I guess lost packets don't mean much for that type of information then. But a lost packet with a database search or server command could be devastating. It could ruin the entire data set sent. So I protect it.

UDP Packet:

I will tell you the cost: performance. I can send data much faster than you because I have much lower overhead.

TCP Packet:

I guess the choice is one of reliability versus performance.

UDP Packet:

It is never an easy decision...

So can we decode the secret message?

So far we've looked at how frames are structured, how to tell which part of the frame contains the data, and how to convert the data into ASCII. So is that everything we need to decode the message the mole sent?

Well... nearly.

I think there's a problem. It doesn't look like the whole message is in the packet.

The entire message may need more than one frame.

Sometimes messages are spread across frames. So why's that?

An Ethernet frame can hold about 1500 bytes of data. So any data that is larger than that will have to be broken apart.

There's another reason too. In order to have a reliable transfer of data, the sender and receiver communicate using the TCP protocol on how the transfer is going. If there are errors in the packets, the sender will notify the receiver and it will resend the packets that had errors. Imagine if there was one large packet with all the data. If the connection is poor it might never get sent.

To reassemble the entire message, we need to collect together all the frames, making sure they're in the right order.

So what do we mean by the right order? Why should they be out of order? Let's take a look.

We've got all the right packets... but not necessarily in the right order

Individual packets on a large network with multiple routers can take different routes to get to the destination. Some paths are longer or have lower bandwidth and take longer for the packet to transit. These means that the packets could arrive at the destination out of order.

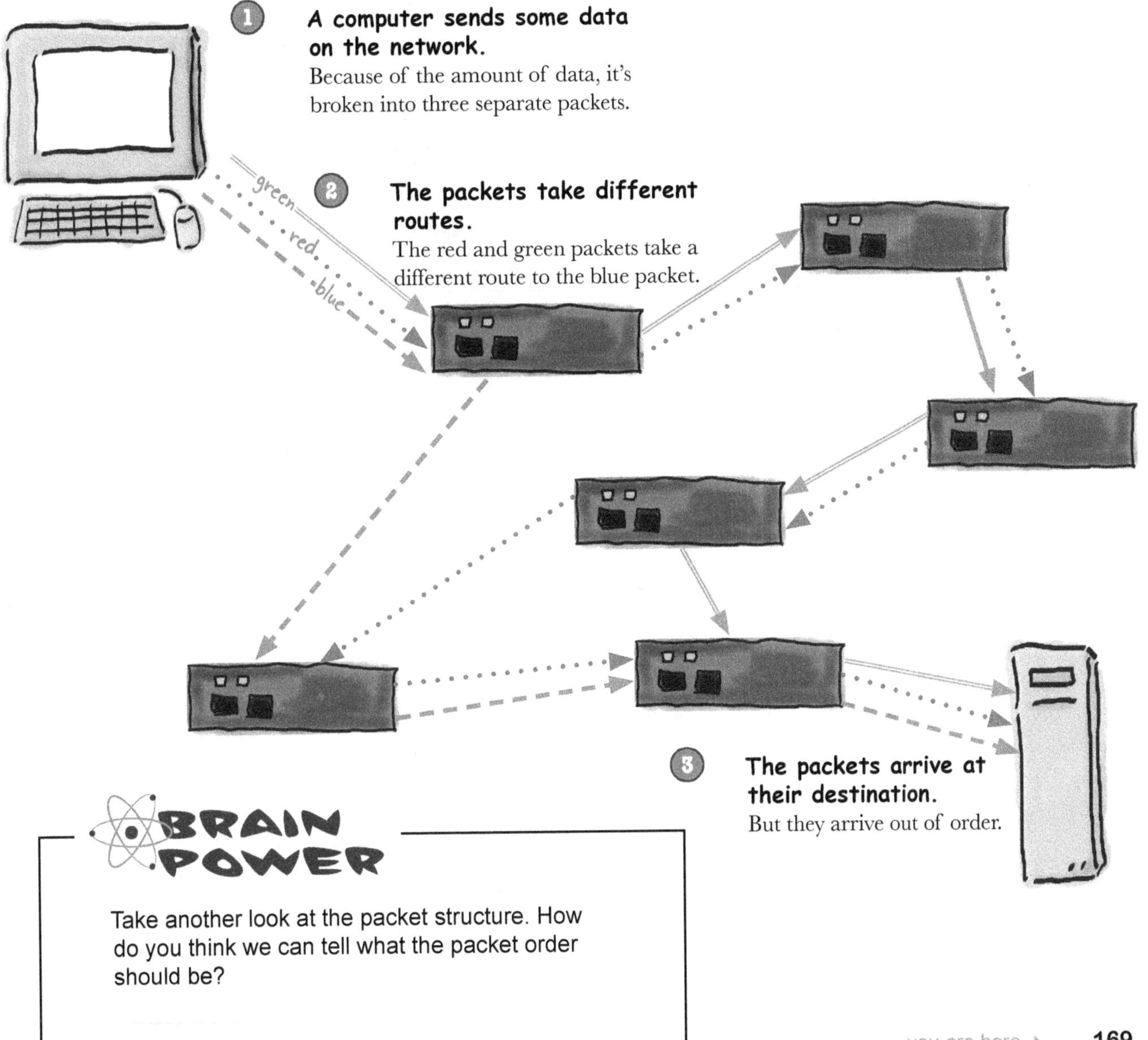

1. **A computer sends some data on the network.** Because of the amount of data, it's broken into three separate packets.

2. **The packets take different routes.** The red and green packets take a different route to the blue packet.

3. **The packets arrive at their destination.** But they arrive out of order.

BRAIN POWER

Take another look at the packet structure. How do you think we can tell what the packet order should be?

The packet tells you the correct order

Each packet contains a sequence number, and it's this sequence number that tells you the correct order of the packets. This means that you can use the sequence number inside a packet to put all the packets back together in the right order. So if we can decode the packets in the right order, we'll have the secret message.

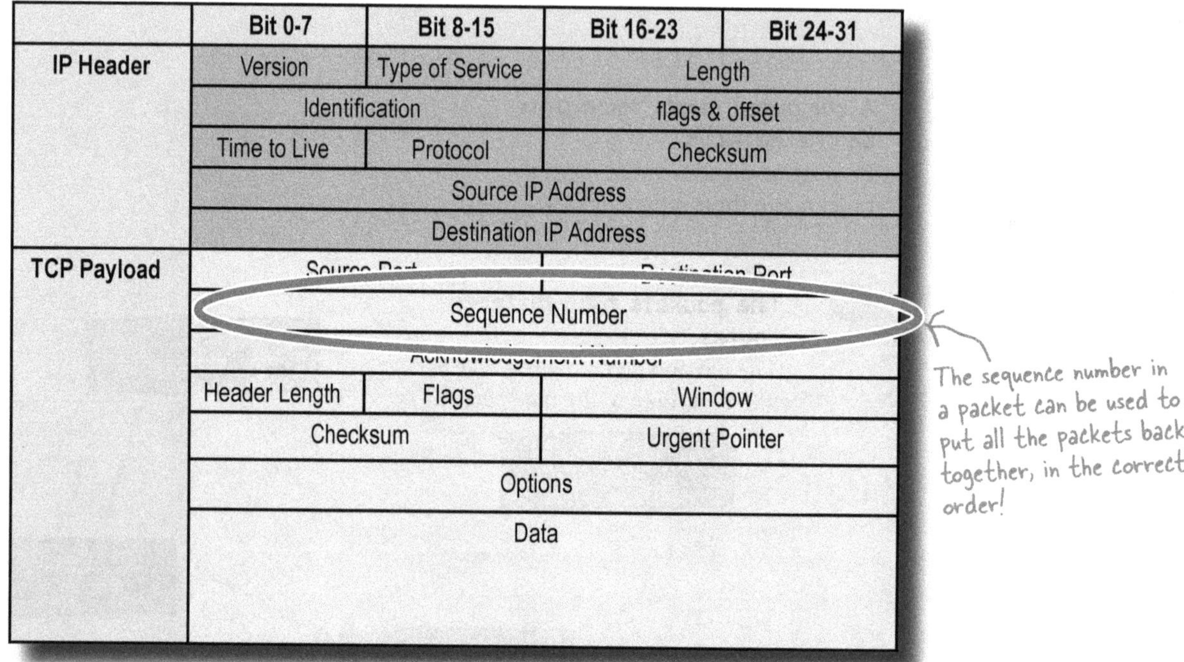

Bit 0-7
Bit 8-15
Bit 16-23
Bit 24-31
IP Header
Version
Type of Service
Length
Identification
flags & offset
Time to Live
Protocol
Checksum
Source IP Address
Destination IP Address
TCP Payload
Sequence Number
Header Length
Flags
Window
Checksum
Urgent Pointer
Options
Data
The sequence number in a packet can be used to put all the packets back together, in the correct order!

Geek Bits

The server sends packets to a particular application based on the port number. As an example, it knows which messages are emails by looking at the destination port in the packet.

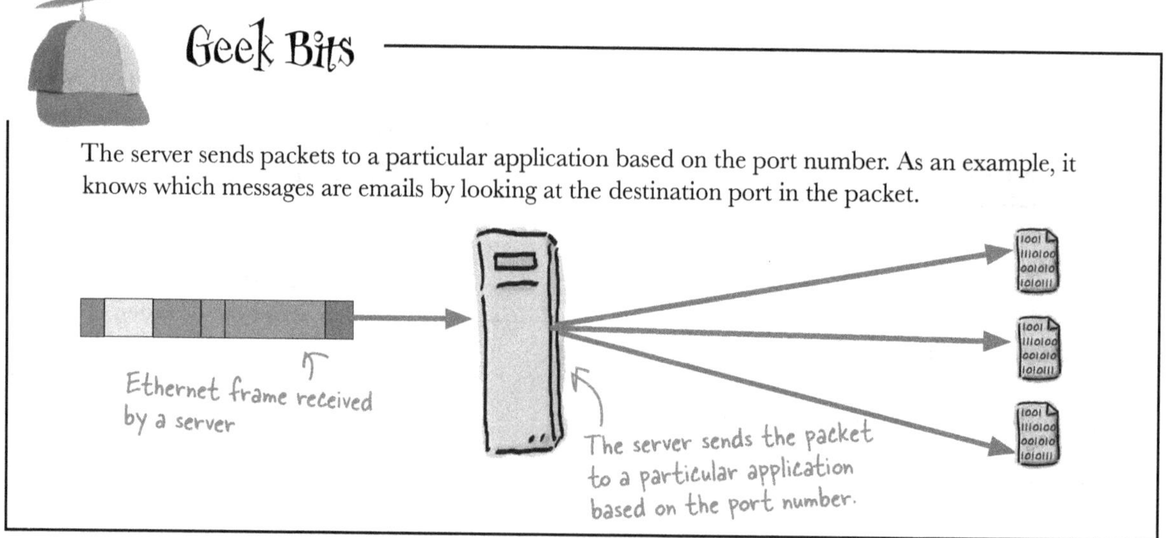

Sharpen your pencil

Finally, we move in to find the message.

Use the sequence number to put the individual packets in order, then translate the hex data into ASCII. Read the message!

08	00	ee 02
f6 6e		00 0D
6e 20 73 65 6c 6c 20 74 68 65 6d 2c 20 74		

08	00	ee 02
f6 6e		00 0C
20 49 20 74 68 69 6e 6b 20 77 65 20 63 61		

08	00	ee 02
f6 6e		00 0E
68 65 79 27 72 65 20 77 6f 72 74 68 20 73		

08	00	ee 02
f6 6e		00 0A
49 20 68 61 76 65 20 74 68 65 20 73 65 63		

08	00	ee 02
f6 6e		00 0F
6f 6d 65 74 68 69 6e 67 2e		

08	00	ee 02
f6 6e		00 0B
72 65 74 20 64 6f 63 75 6d 65 6e 74 73 2e		

Sharpen your pencil Solution

Finally, we move in to find the message.

Use the sequence number to put the individual packets in order, then translate the hex data into ASCII. Read the message!

I have the sec

08	00	ee 02
f6 6e		00 0A
49 20 68 61 76 65 20 74 68 65 20 73 65 63		

ret documents.

08	00	ee 02
f6 6e		00 0B
72 65 74 20 64 6f 63 75 6d 65 6e 74 73 2e		

I think we ca

08	00	ee 02
f6 6e		00 0C
20 49 20 74 68 69 6e 6b 20 77 65 20 63 61		

n sell them, t

08	00	ee 02
f6 6e		00 0D
6e 20 73 65 6c 6c 20 74 68 65 6d 2c 20 74		

hey're worth s

08	00	ee 02
f6 6e		00 0E
68 65 79 27 72 65 20 77 6f 72 74 68 20 73		

omething.

08	00	ee 02
f6 6e		00 0F
6f 6d 65 74 68 69 6e 67 2e		

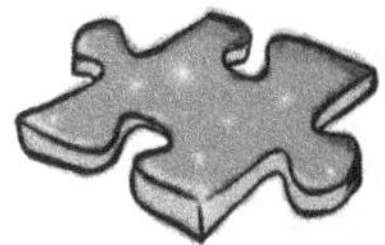

Networkcross

Take some time to sit back and give your right brain something to do. It's your standard crossword; all of the solution words are from this chapter.

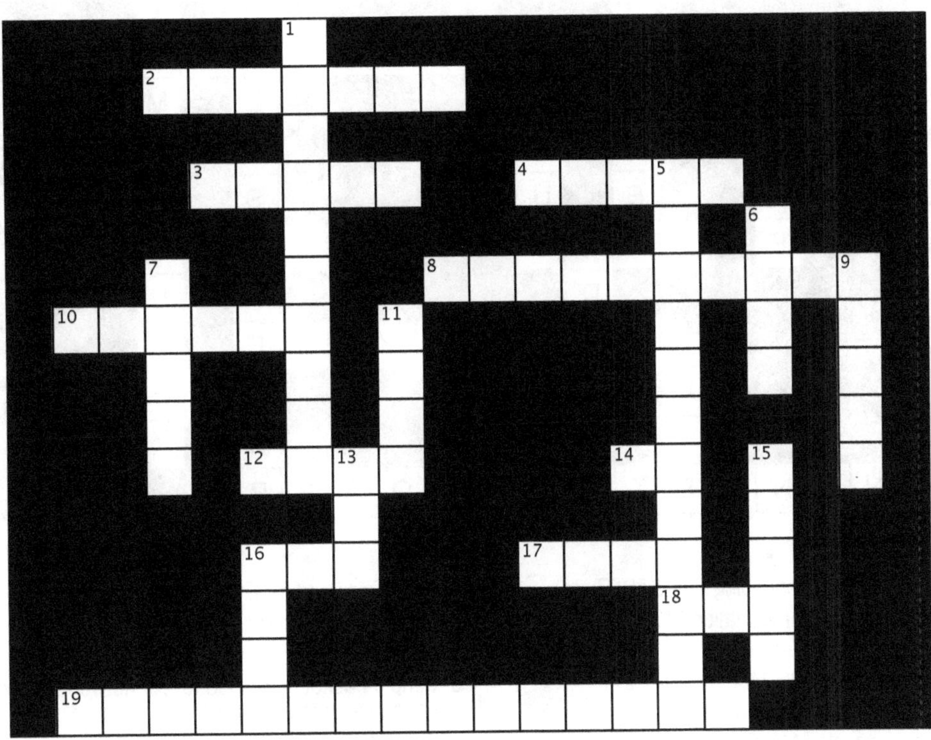

Across

2. Which Ethernet uses 8B10B encoding?
3. American Standard Code for Information
4. Protocols are ___________.
8. Hello written in ASCII hex code.
10. Packets are inside ________.
12. 1011 X-NOR 1010 equals 1110
14. 0100100001101001 in ASCII
16. Connection Oriented Connection Protocol
17. 1010 base 2 in decimal equals A.
18. Used by computers to connect to a network.
19. NRZ

Down

1. Encoding used for Ethernet 10Mbs
5. Manchester Encoding uses this boolean operation.
6. Simple packet type used to test network connections.
7. 1010 OR 0000 equals 1000
9. Hex is base 15
11. 1001 AND 1111 equals 1001
13. Connectionless Protocol Type
15. What is embedded with data in a Manchester signal?
16. You can do math such as adding and subtracting with binary numbers.

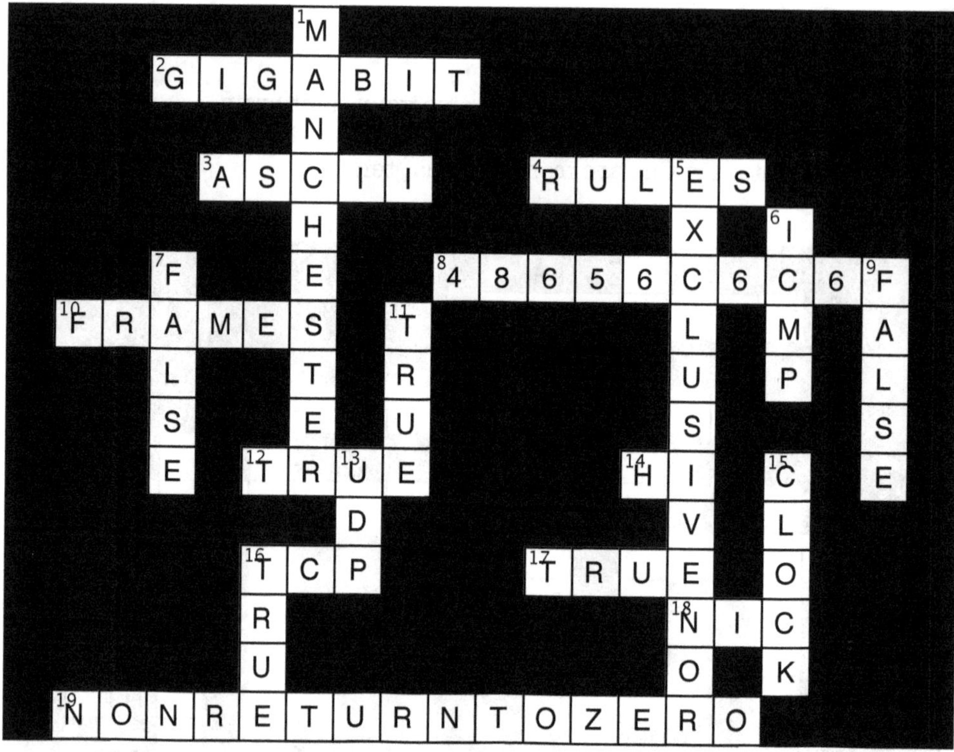

Across

2. Which Ethernet uses 8B10B encoding? [GIGABIT]
3. American Standard Code for Information [ASCII]
4. Protocols are ___________. [RULES]
8. Hello written in ASCII hex code. [48656C6C6F]
10. Packets are inside ________. [FRAMES]
12. 1011 X-NOR 1010 equals 1110 [TRUE]
14. 0100100001101001 in ASCII [HI]
16. Connection Oriented Connection Protocol [TCP]
17. 1010 base 2 in decimal equals A. [TRUE]
18. Used by computers to connect to a network. [NIC]
19. NRZ [NONRETURNTOZERO]

Down

1. Encoding used for Ethernet 10Mbs [MANCHESTER]
5. Manchester Encoding uses this boolean operation. [EXCLUSIVENOR]
6. Simple packet type used to test network connections. [ICMP]
7. 1010 OR 0000 equals 1000 [FALSE]
9. Hex is base 15 [FALSE]
11. 1001 AND 1111 equals 1001 [TRUE]
13. Connectionless Protocol Type [UDP]
15. What is embedded with data in a Manchester signal? [CLOCK]
16. You can do math such as adding and subtracting with binary numbers. [TRUE]

5 network devices and traffic

How Smart is Your Network?

Everyone in the office thinks I'm crazy, but I swear it's watching us! I warned them, and they'll find out soon enough. This network is too smart!

A network can never be too smart.

Networks need as much intelligence as you can pack into them, but **where does that intelligence come from**? The answer is from its network devices. In this chapter, we'll look at how **hubs, switches and routers** use their innate **intelligence** to move packets around a network. We'll show you how these devices **think**, why they're so **useful**, and we'll even take a peek at what network traffic looks like using **packet analyzing software**. Keep reading, and we'll show you **how to super-charge your network**.

You've decoded the secret message...

You're a crackerjack network technician for the Head First Spy Agency. You've successfully decoded a secret message from the rogue signal, so what's next?

...but how do we know who sent it?

Even though we've decoded one of the messages the mole sent, we don't know who sent it. And if we don't know who's sending rogue messages, how can we prevent it from happening?

We need to somehow track down who the mole is—but how? All we have to go on is the rogue signal we used to decode the message. Can we somehow use that to help us sniff out the mole?

Label each part of the frame below and write some notes about which part of the frame might be important in catching the mole on our network.

Notes: ....

....

....

....

....

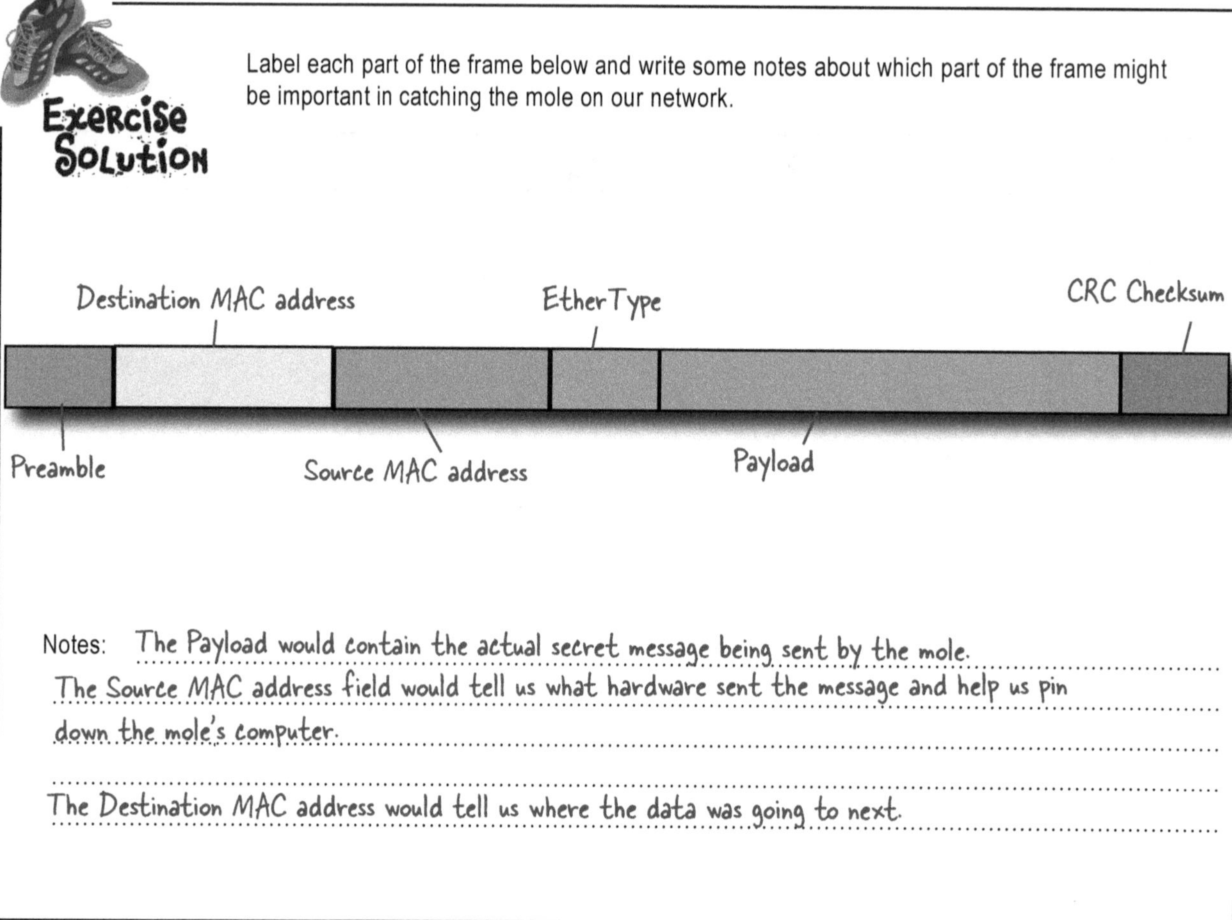

Label each part of the frame below and write some notes about which part of the frame might be important in catching the mole on our network.

Notes: The Payload would contain the actual secret message being sent by the mole.

The Source MAC address field would tell us what hardware sent the message and help us pin down the mole's computer.

The Destination MAC address would tell us where the data was going to next.

The packet information tells us where the packet came from

When we decoded the message earlier, we saw that each packet contains the source MAC address. In other words, it contains the MAC address of the hardware that sent the packet.

You can find a MAC address stamped on the NIC card inside a computer. MAC addresses are six bytes long, or 48 bits. Typically they are written in hexadecimal format and separated by colons or dashes, like this: 0f:2b:5d:e7:a3:eb.

Geek Bits

It's not just PCs that have MAC addresses. Many internet-capable video game systems have a console that will show you the MAC address of the device.

The frame is sent from one NIC to another.

The Destination MAC address is the hardware address of the next network device the frame is going to.

The Source MAC address is the hardware address of the last network device from which the frame was sent.

We don't need the rest of the frame elements for now.

Preamble	Destination MAC address	Source MAC address	...

The MAC address of the hardware that sent the rogue message is 00:00:0C:65:4e:12. So how can we use this to tell us who the mole is?

That's easy. We find the computer with that MAC address, and then see who uses it. Chances are, the mole is the person who uses the computer that sent the messages. Right?

Let's see if this works.

So who's the mole?

Here's a list of all the MAC addresses at the company you're investigating. So who uses the computer that sent the rogue signal?

The MAC address that sent the rogue signal is 00:00:0C:65:4e:12. But where is it in the list?

Person	Location	IP	MAC
Mike D.	Admin	192.168.100.34	00:1f:f3:53:fe:ae
Sue T.	Front Desk	192.168.100.45	00:1f:f3:53:fe:28
Ed G.	Shipping	192.168.100.32	00:1f:f3:53:f:18
Kyle M.	IT	192.168.100.2	00:1f:f3:54:27:d2
Debbie Y.	IT	192.168.100.3	00:1f:f3:86:fe:2a
Carol C.	Admin	192.168.100.4	00:1f:f3:23:4f:1a
Server	IT	192.168.100.100	00:1f:f3:23:4f:27
Alice O.	Sales	192.168.200.4	00:1f:f3:53:f:3a
Taylor S.	Sales	192.168.200.5	00:1f:f3:53:f:4f

Unfortunately, the source MAC address of the signal isn't in the list, even though the list of computers is up to date. But why?

I wonder... the list contains MAC addresses for computers, but what if the source MAC address belongs to some other sort of hardware? If that was the case, it wouldn't be on the list.

Other types of hardware have MAC addresses.

Let's take a look at the network and see if we can see what's going on.

There's more to networks than computers

The company network isn't just comprised of computers and servers. There's also network devices such as hubs, switches and routers. Hubs and switches work on the local area network (LAN) or intranet, and routers allow us to set up wide area networks (WANs) or internets.

The Internet is not the same thing as an internet.

The Internet refers to the big interconnected space we use to send data around the world. The term "internet" refers to at least two intranets connected together by a router.

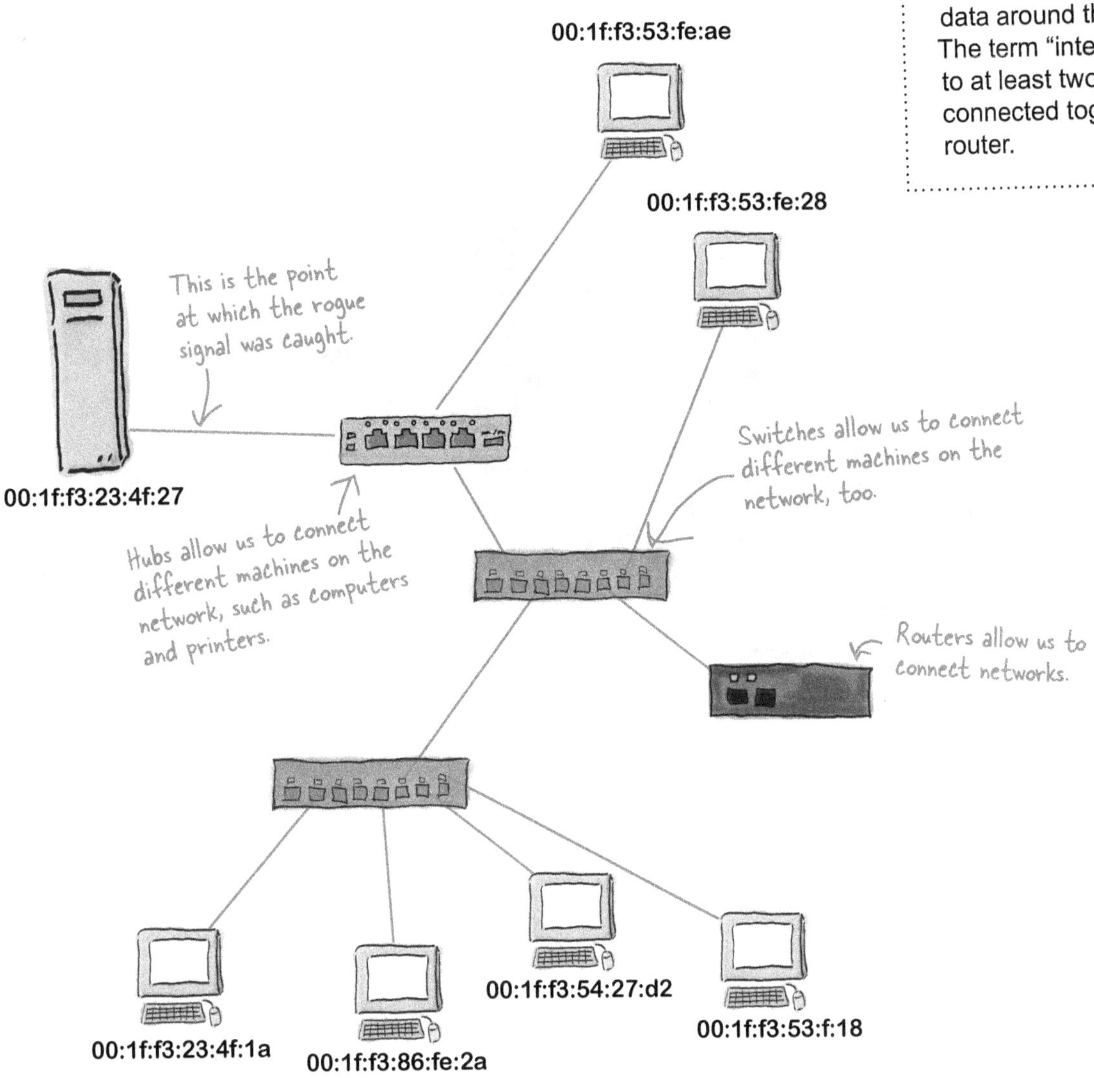

00:1f:f3:53:fe:ae

00:1f:f3:53:fe:28

This is the point at which the rogue signal was caught.

00:1f:f3:23:4f:27

Switches allow us to connect different machines on the network, too.

Hubs allow us to connect different machines on the network, such as computers and printers.

Routers allow us to connect networks.

00:1f:f3:54:27:d2

00:1f:f3:53:f:18

00:1f:f3:23:4f:1a

00:1f:f3:86:fe:2a

Hubs Up Close

As we've said before, hubs allow us to connect the different machines we want on our network, like computers and printers, for example. It simply takes an incoming signal, copies it to all its other ports, and broadcasts it. A hub is sometimes called a repeater because it repeats the incoming signal using no digital intelligence such as memory or a processor.

Here's what a hub looks like inside:

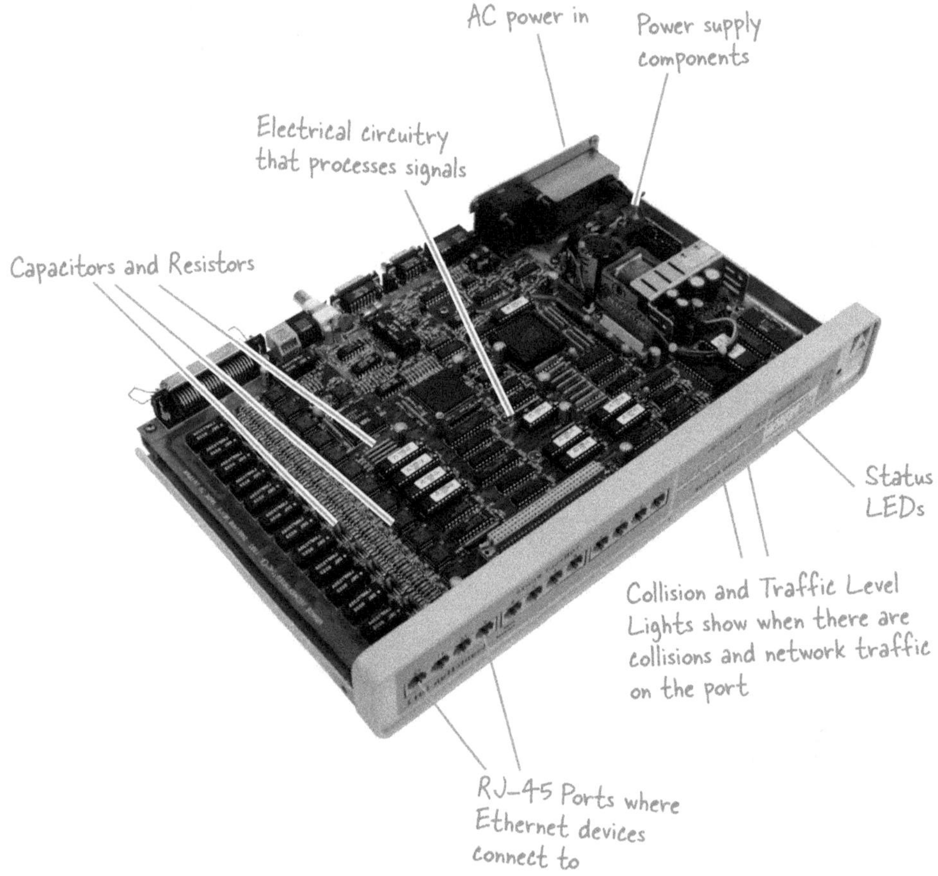

Hubs are dumb

A hub is a dumb device because it doesn't understand network data, and it doesn't know about or store MAC addresses. It simply repeats incoming signals on all ports, without making any changes to the signal before broadcasting it.

Hubs don't change the MAC address

So how does this help us trace the rogue signal?

The last device that the packet came through before it was intercepted was a hub. As a hub simply transmits signals as it receives them and has no real understanding of network data, it doesn't make any change to the source MAC address. It keeps the source MAC address as it was when it received the packet.

BANG!
Watch it!

There is no way to tell that a packet was broadcast from a hub.

You just have to know your network layout and what nodes are connected to hubs.

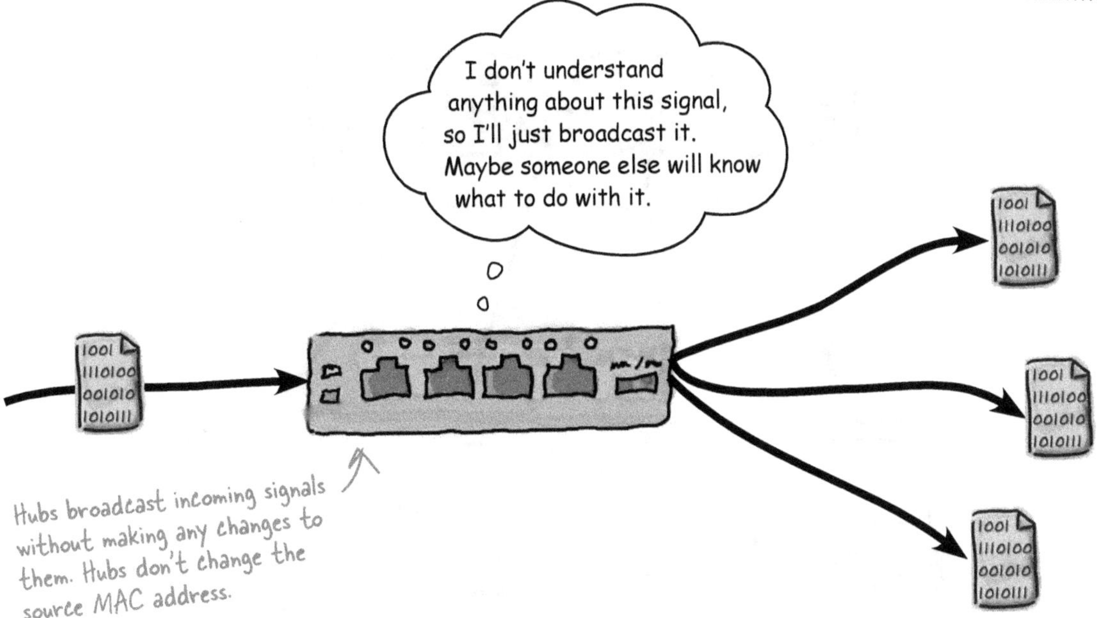
I don't understand anything about this signal, so I'll just broadcast it. Maybe someone else will know what to do with it.
1001
1110100
001010
1010111
Hubs broadcast incoming signals without making any changes to them. Hubs don't change the source MAC address.

So which device sent the packet to the hub?

As the hub makes no changes to the source MAC address, this means that the source MAC address must belong to the device that passed the signal to the hub. We need to look beyond the hub to sniff out the mole.

BRAIN POWER

Hubs contain no processors. What does this tell you about how the hub processes signals?

A hub sends signals, and sends them everywhere

A hub receives incoming signals and sends them out on all the other ports. When several devices start sending signals, the hub's incessant repetition creates heavy traffic and collisions. A collision happens when two signals run into one another, creating an error. The sending network device has to back off and wait to send the signal again.

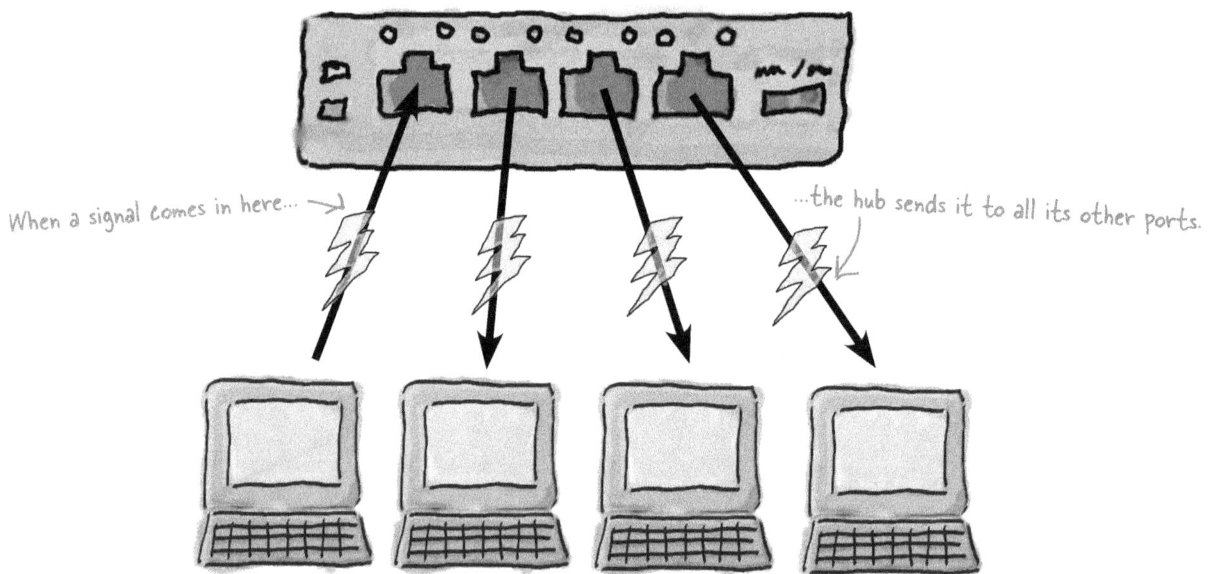

When a signal comes in here...
...the hub sends it to all its other ports.

Hubs think in terms of electricity

A hub contains no processors, and this means that a hub has no real understanding of network data. It doesn't understand MAC addresses or frames. It sees an incoming networking signal as a purely electrical signal, and passes it on.

So what next?

A hub is really just an electrical repeater. It takes whatever signal comes in, and sends it out on all the other ports.

So what passed the signal to the hub?

So far we've seen that the signal passed through a hub, but we don't know which network device passed the signal to the hub. Let's go back to the network diagram, this time looking at what other devices are connected to the hub.

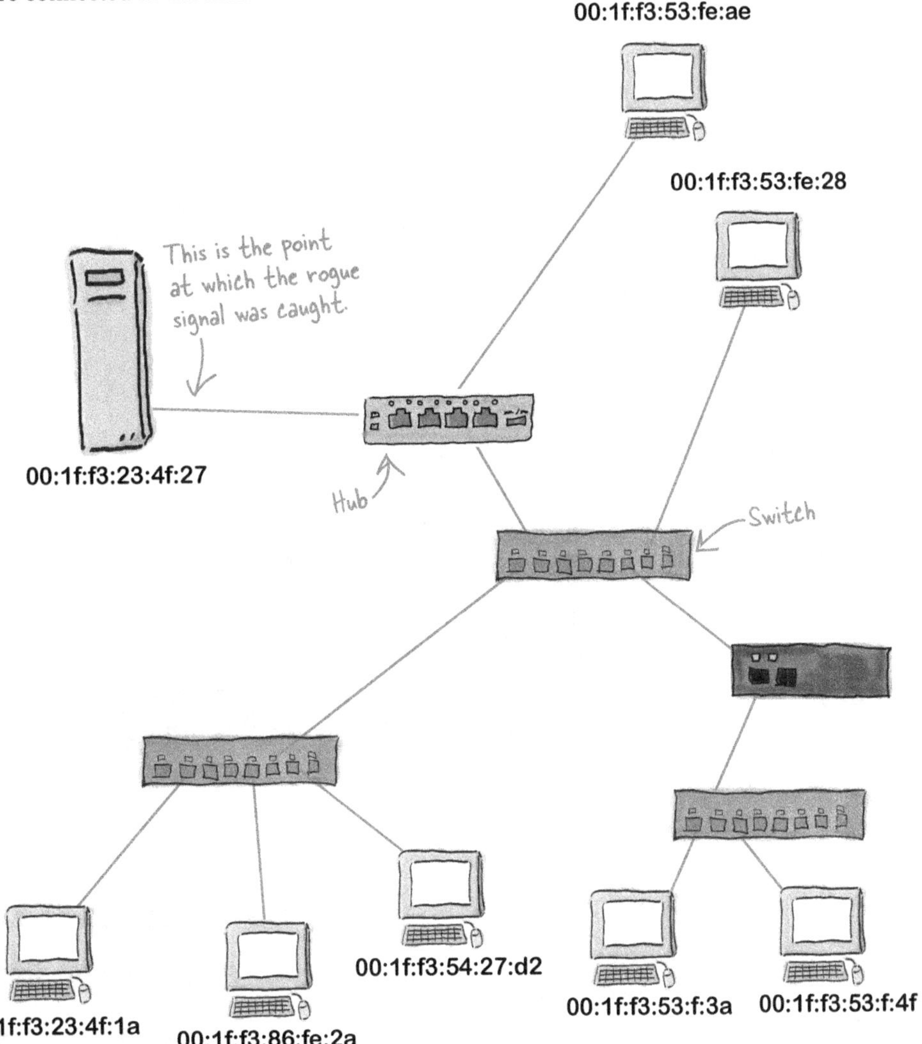

The hub has two devices connected to it that could have sent the signal, a computer and a switch. As the computer MAC address doesn't match the one we're looking for, we know the computer didn't send the signal; it must have been the switch.

So how do switches function?

A switch sends frames, and only sends them where they need to go

Switches avoid collisions by storing and forwarding frames on the intranet. Switches are able to do this by using the MAC address of the frame. Instead of repeating the signal on all ports, it sends it on to the device that needs it.

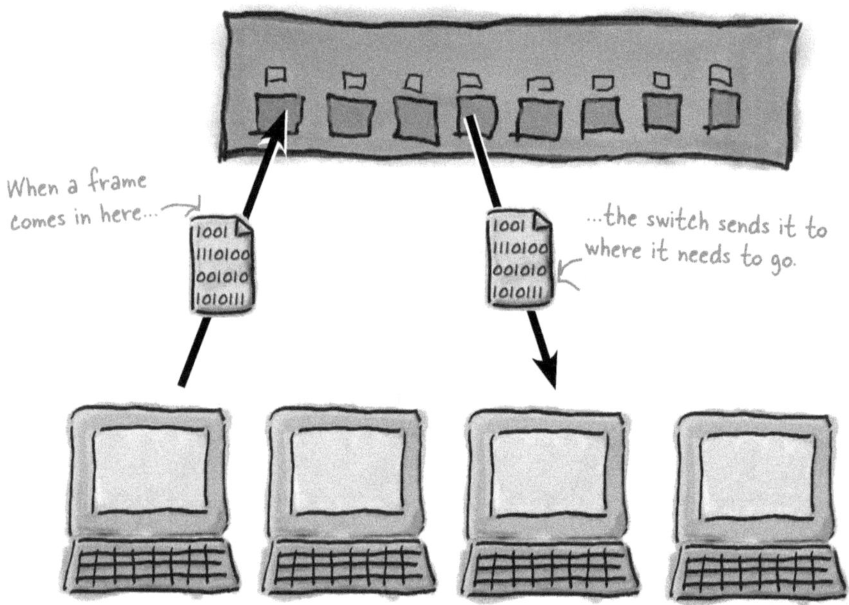

Switches think in terms of frames

A switch contains processors, RAM, and ASICS, and this means that a switch can properly process network data. It understands MAC addresses and frames, which means that it can deal intelligently with any incoming networking signal. It can work out where the signal needs to go, and deals with it accordingly.

A switch reads the signal as a frame and uses the frame's information to send it where it's supposed to go.

Switches Up Close

Just like a hub, a switch allows us to connect the different machines we want on our network, like computers and printers, for example.

Here's a look inside a switch:

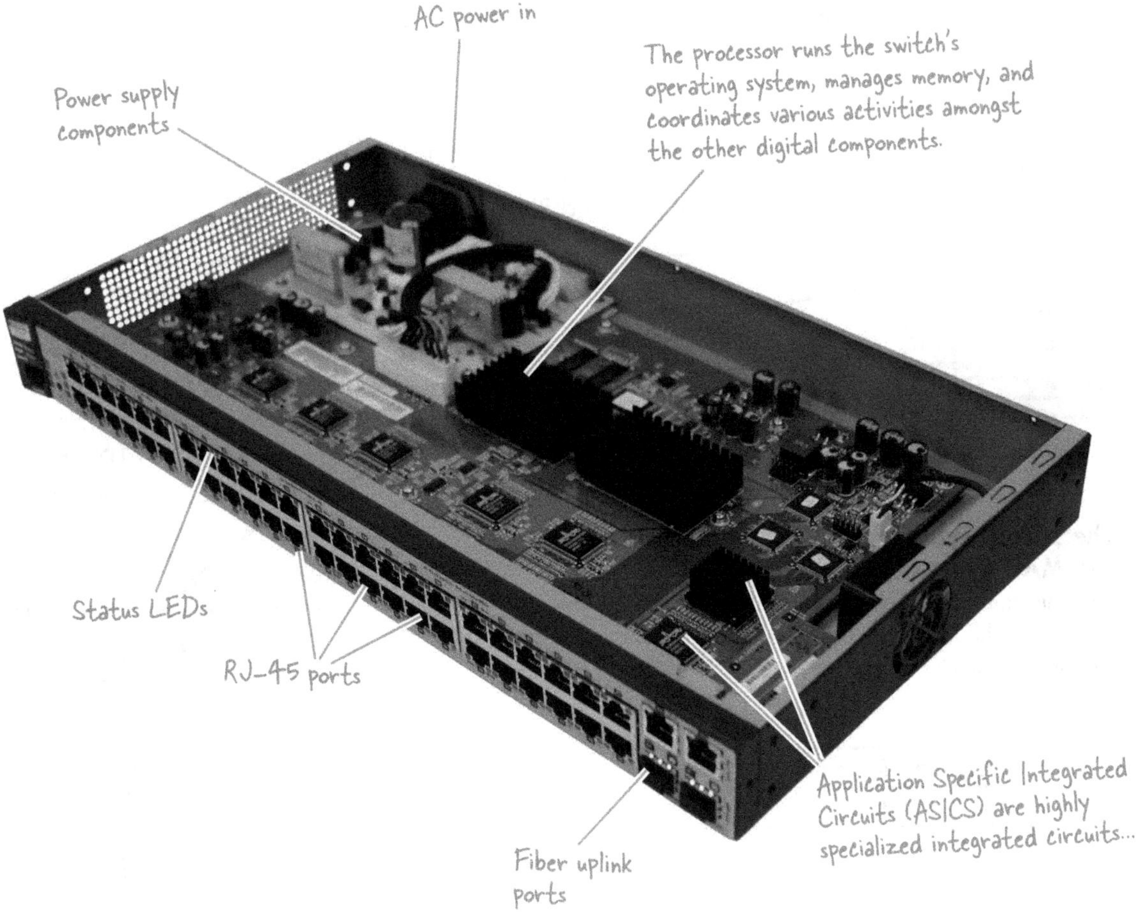

AC power in

The processor runs the switch's operating system, manages memory, and coordinates various activities amongst the other digital components.

Power supply components

Status LEDs

RJ-45 ports

Application Specific Integrated Circuits (ASICS) are highly specialized integrated circuits...

Fiber uplink ports

Switches are smart

There's a big difference in how hubs and switches deal with signals. A switch can process signals as frames, and also understands MAC addresses. Instead of repeating incoming signals on all ports, a switch can store packets and forward them to their destinations.

Let's take a closer look at this.

Switches store MAC addresses in a lookup table to keep the frames flowing smoothly

1. **The source workstation sends a frame.**
   A frame carries the payload of data and keeps track of the time sent, as well as the MAC address of the source and the MAC address of the target.

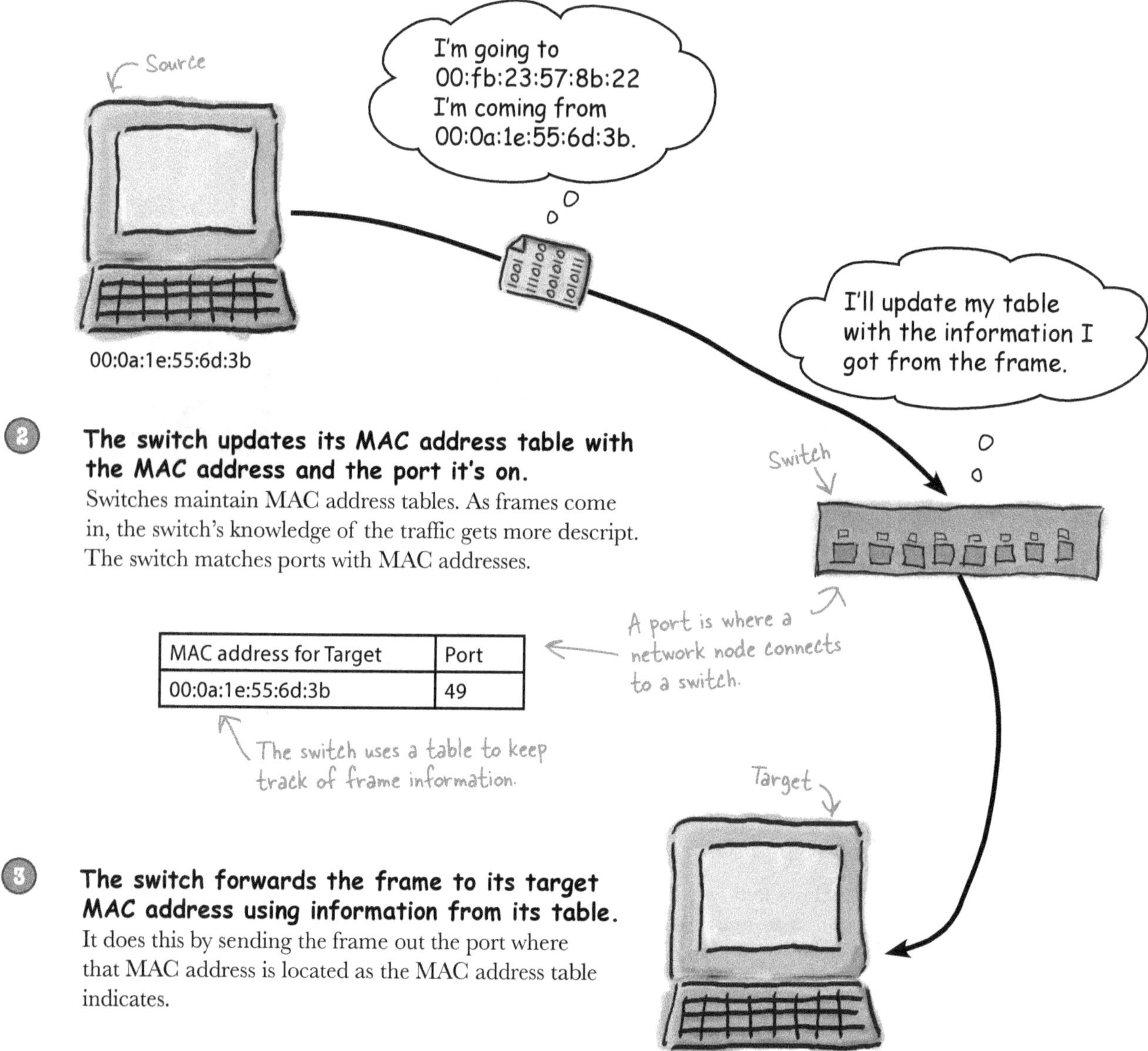
Source
00:0a:1e:55:6d:3b
I'm going to
00:fb:23:57:8b:22
I'm coming from
00:0a:1e:55:6d:3b.
I'll update my table with the information I got from the frame.
Switch
A port is where a network node connects to a switch.
The switch uses a table to keep track of frame information.
Target
00:fb:23:57:8b:22

2. **The switch updates its MAC address table with the MAC address and the port it's on.**
   Switches maintain MAC address tables. As frames come in, the switch's knowledge of the traffic gets more descript. The switch matches ports with MAC addresses.

MAC address for Target	Port
00:0a:1e:55:6d:3b	49

3. **The switch forwards the frame to its target MAC address using information from its table.**
   It does this by sending the frame out the port where that MAC address is located as the MAC address table indicates.

BE the Switch

Your job is to play the switch and update the lookup table based on the frame information shown. Follow the arrows to match the Mac Address with the port. We did the first one for you.

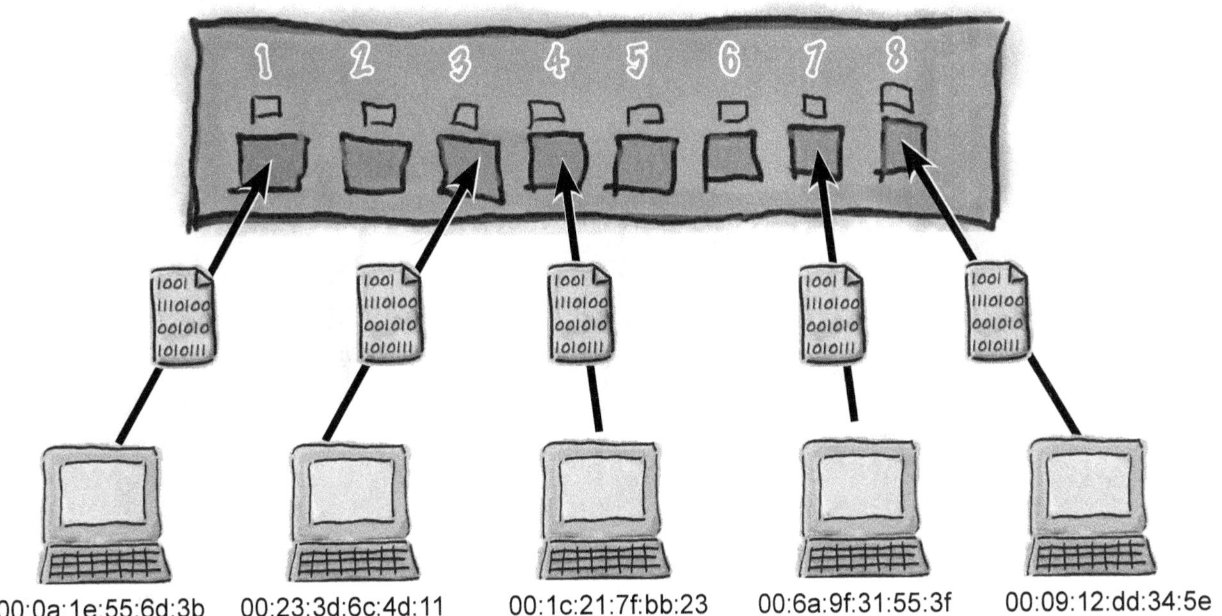

MAC address	Port
00:0a:1e:55:6d:3b	1

BE the Switch

Your job is to play the switch and update the lookup table based on the frame information shown. Follow the arrows to match the Mac Address wth the port. We did the first one for you.

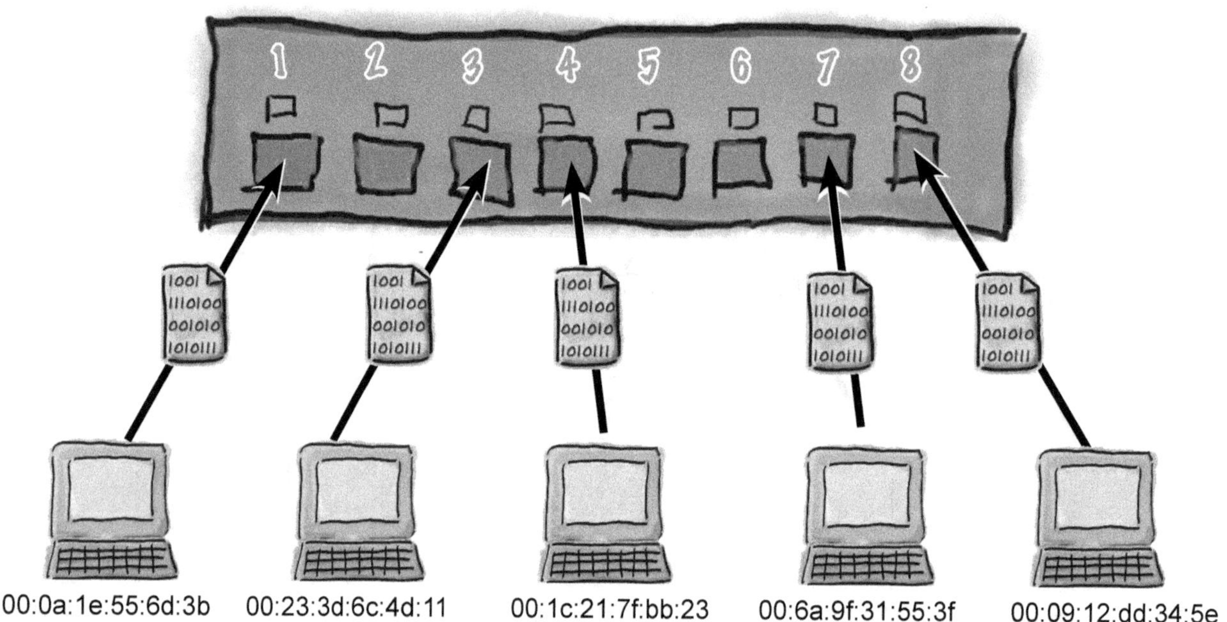

MAC address	Port
00:0a:1e:55:6d:3b	1
00:23:3d:6c:4d:11	3
00:1c:21:7f:bb:23	4
00:6a:9f:31:55:3f	7
00:09:12:dd:34:5e	8

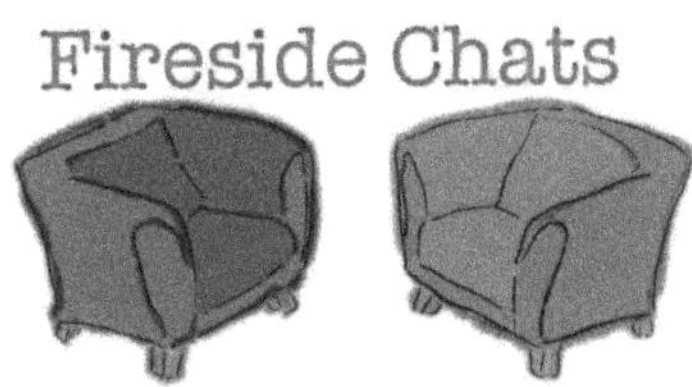

Tonight's talk: **Hub vs. Switch**

Hub:

Alright, Switch, I'm getting tired of you calling my intelligence into question.

Switch:

Could you repeat that?

Hub:

I'm getting tired of... are you making fun of me?

Switch:

Just a little joke on your other name.

Hub:

So they call me a repeater, so what?

Switch:

Well, that's where all your problems lie. The fact that you repeat every little thing that comes into your ports on ALL of your other ports makes for a real slow network.

Hub:

Okay, I repeat signals, other than that we're pretty similar.

Switch:

No we're not. You work in signals. I work in frames.

Hub:

I like power more than data. That's why I work with electricity exclusively.

Switch:

I'm a computer. I have my own operating system.

Hub:

Well, I connect computers together.

Switch:

But you don't do it efficiently. You bombard all of your ports with unnecessary network traffic.

Hub:

I like to make sure that every device on the network gets a heads-up about traffic.

Switch:

But it's all unnecessary noise. I send frames exactly where they need to go. I have built-in digital logic and can read information from frames and use it to send data accurately.

Hub:

But I'm cheaper. Can't beat me at that can you?

Switch:

I'm worth every penny. Put just one of me in a network run entirely by you, and I can up the speed and the bandwidth of the network the minute someone turns me on.

The switch has the information...

Since the switch stores MAC addresses, we should be able to connect to the switch and look at its table.

Will this get us the information we need to find the mole?

1. **Connect your computer to the switch with a serial cable.** You will use this to communicate with the switch.

Low end switches do not generally have serial ports on them.

2. **Open a terminal program such as Hyperterminal, and get to the command prompt of the switch. Type in the commands below:**

File Edit Window Help WhichSwitchIsWhich

```
switch# show mac-address

 Status and Counters - Port Address Table

  MAC Address   Located on Port
  ------------- ---------------
  000074-a23563 49
  0001e6-70f1bb 44
  0001e6-7673f6 42
  0001e6-800044 37
  0001e6-81cb6b  5
  0001e6-8f0a86 12
#
```

The MAC address of a computer or other network device connected to the switch.

The port number on the switch that the device is connected to.

How long do you think a switch keeps MAC addresses in its table?

The command above was for a HP ProCurve Switch.

Other brands of switches may have slightly different commands to see the MAC address table.

Here are all the MAC address tables. I can't see the rogue MAC address in any of the tables.

Frank: So do you think the switches aren't picking up the MAC address?

Jim: No, the problem is that the switches clear out those MAC address tables in about three minutes.

Frank: Clear them out?

Jim: Yea, if a network device stops transmitting, the switch just deletes the entry to keep the table size small.

Frank: So where does that leave us with finding this rogue machine?

Jim: Well I've looked at all the PCs and did not find the rogue address.

Frank: What's next?

Jim: I think we need to capture the network traffic and look for traffic with that source MAC address. I can then get back into the switches to find that address and narrow it down to a port on a switch.

Frank: That sounds like a good plan. How are you going to capture traffic?

Jim: I need to find some software...

We can use software to monitor packets

If you need to monitor network traffic and capture packet information, there's some great software out there that will do exactly what you need— software like Wireshark. To monitor traffic, you install the software on a workstation, and then plug the workstation into the network at the point you want to monitor. The software then gives you information about the packets that pass the workstation.

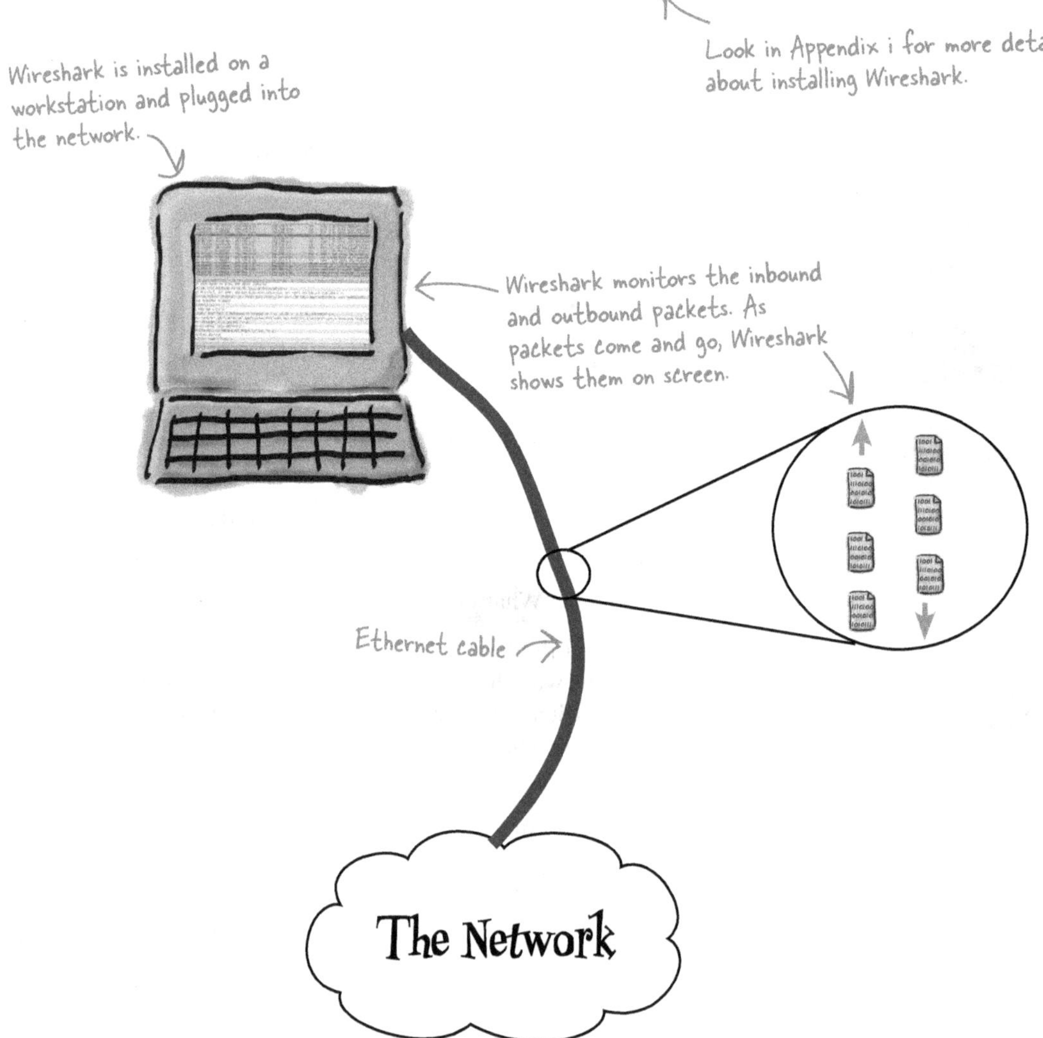

Look in Appendix i for more details about installing Wireshark.
Wireshark is installed on a workstation and plugged into the network.
Wireshark monitors the inbound and outbound packets. As packets come and go, Wireshark shows them on screen.
Ethernet cable
The Network

Let's use Wireshark to monitor traffic on the switch. That way we can pick up any more rogue signals the mole sends, and find out what network device sends them to the switch.

Let's hook Wireshark up to the switch

So how do we get Wireshark to monitor network traffic going through the switch? Follow these instructions, and you're sorted.

1. **Connect your computer to the switch with a serial cable.**
   You will use this to communicate with the switch.

2. **Open a terminal program such as Hyperterminal and get to the command prompt of the switch. Type in the commands below.**

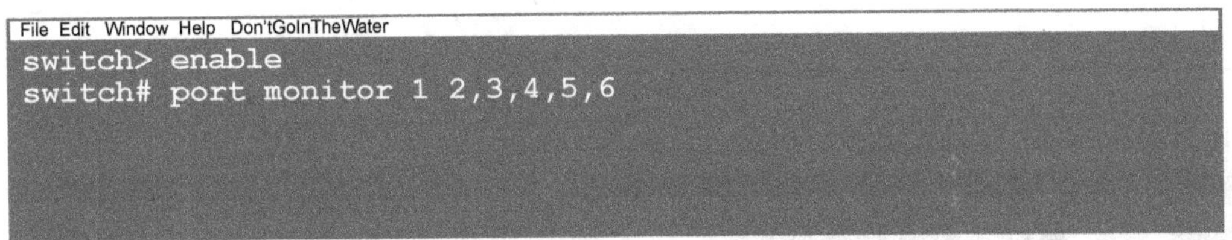

3. **Hook up your computer to port 1 on the switch with an Ethernet cable.**
   You will use this to capture network traffic.

4. **Startup Wireshark and capture some network traffic.**

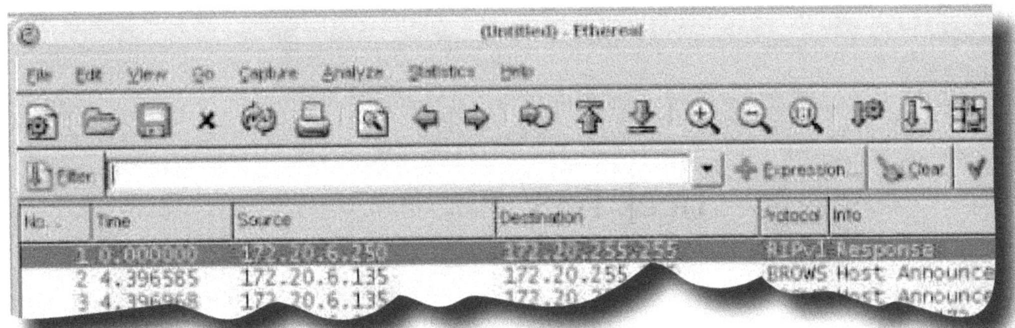

So what does Wireshark actually tell us?

Wireshark gives us traffic information

Wireshark shows us all the network traffic that the computer is seeing from the switch it is connected to. We can filter the output and look for specific frames if we wish.

What would you like to use for a filter?

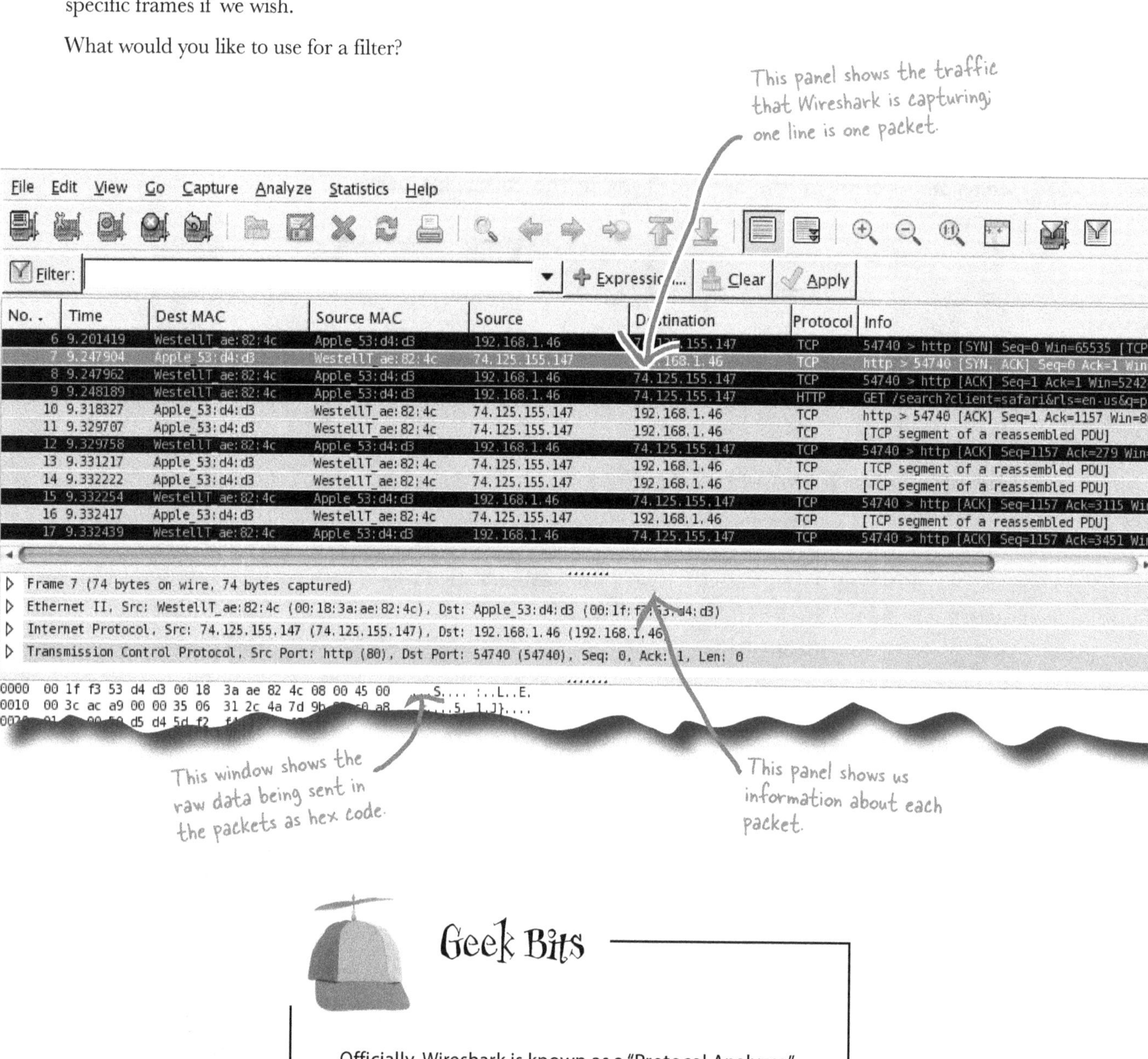

Officially, Wireshark is known as a "Protocol Analyzer."

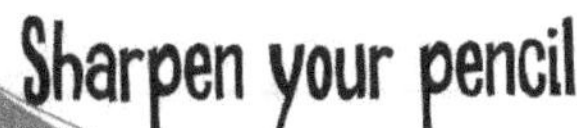

Below is a part of the packet information from Wireshark. Circle the device that sent this packet.

No.	Time	Dest MAC	Source MAC
1821		Apple_:23:4f:27	Cisco_65:4e:12

Wireshark is figuring out the equipment manufacturer from the first part of the MAC address and showing us that part.

00:1f:f3:53:fe:ae

00:1f:f3:53:fe:28

This is the point at which the rogue signal was caught.

00:1f:f3:23:4f:27

Hub

00:0b:cd:e7:1a:5e

00:00:0C:65:4e:12

00:0b:cd:e7:33:12

00:1f:f3:54:27:d2

00:1f:f3:53:f:3a

00:1f:f3:53:f:4f

00:1f:f3:23:4f:1a

00:1f:f3:86:fe:2a

Sharpen your pencil Solution

Below is a part of the packet information from Wireshark. Circle the device that sent this packet.

No.	Time	Dest MAC	Source MAC
1821		Apple_:23:4f:27	Cisco_65:4e:12

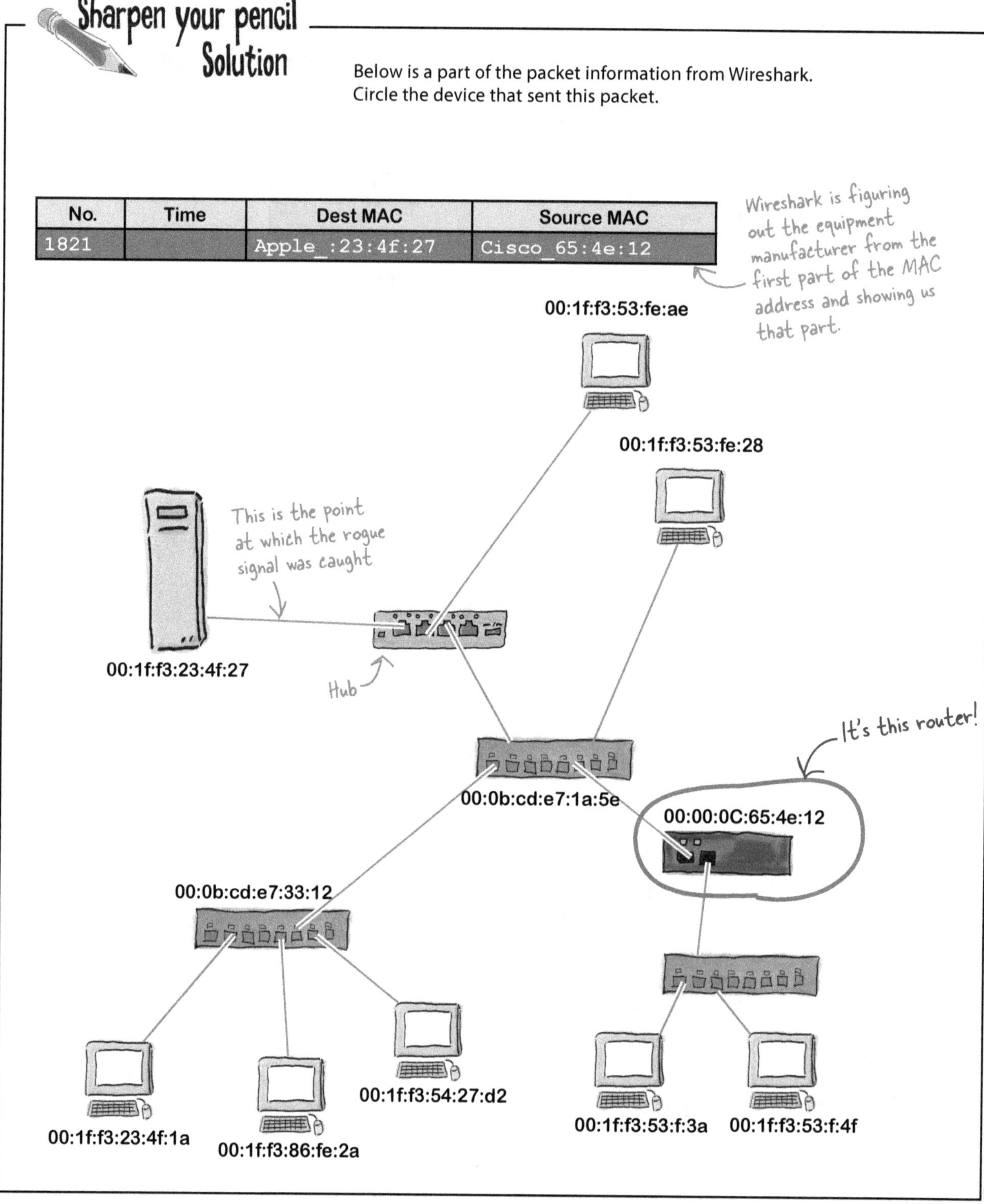

Routers have MAC addresses too

If network traffic comes from a router, we can only see the router's MAC address. All the workstations behind that router make up what we call an IP subnet. All a switch needs to look at to get frames to their destination is the MAC address. A router looks at the IP address from the incoming packet and forwards it if it is intended for a workstation located on the other network.

1. **The source workstation sends a frame to the router.** It sends it to the router since the workstation the traffic is meant for is behind the router.

2. **The router changes the source MAC address to its MAC address and changes the destination MAC address to the workstation the traffic is meant for.**

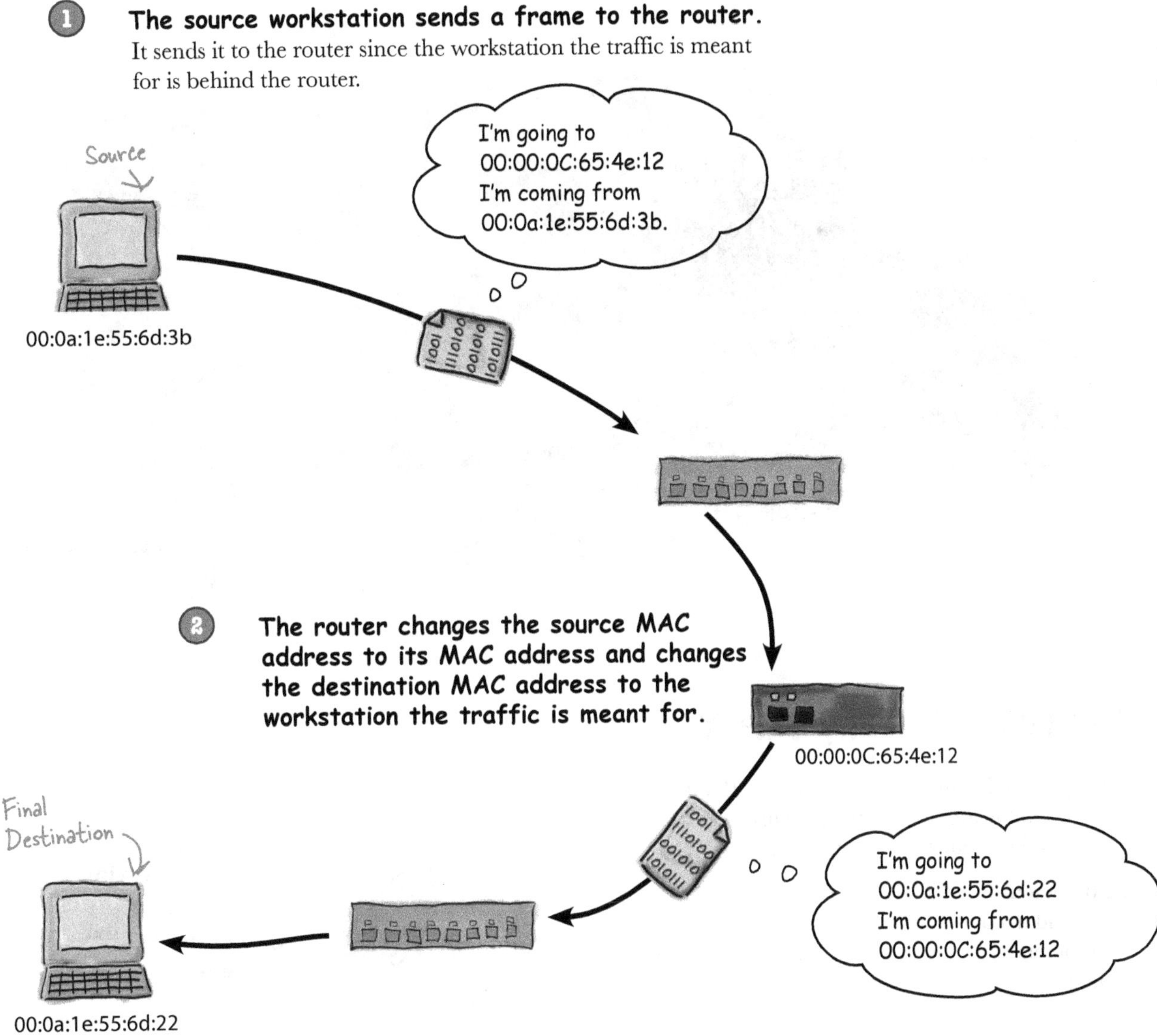

Source
I'm going to
00:00:0C:65:4e:12
I'm coming from
00:0a:1e:55:6d:3b.
00:0a:1e:55:6d:3b
00:00:0C:65:4e:12
Final Destination
I'm going to
00:0a:1e:55:6d:22
I'm coming from
00:00:0C:65:4e:12
00:0a:1e:55:6d:22

Routers Up Close

Routers are the high end networking devices of a network. They are the devices that connect the network together. The Internet is built using routers like this one.

Let's take a look inside.

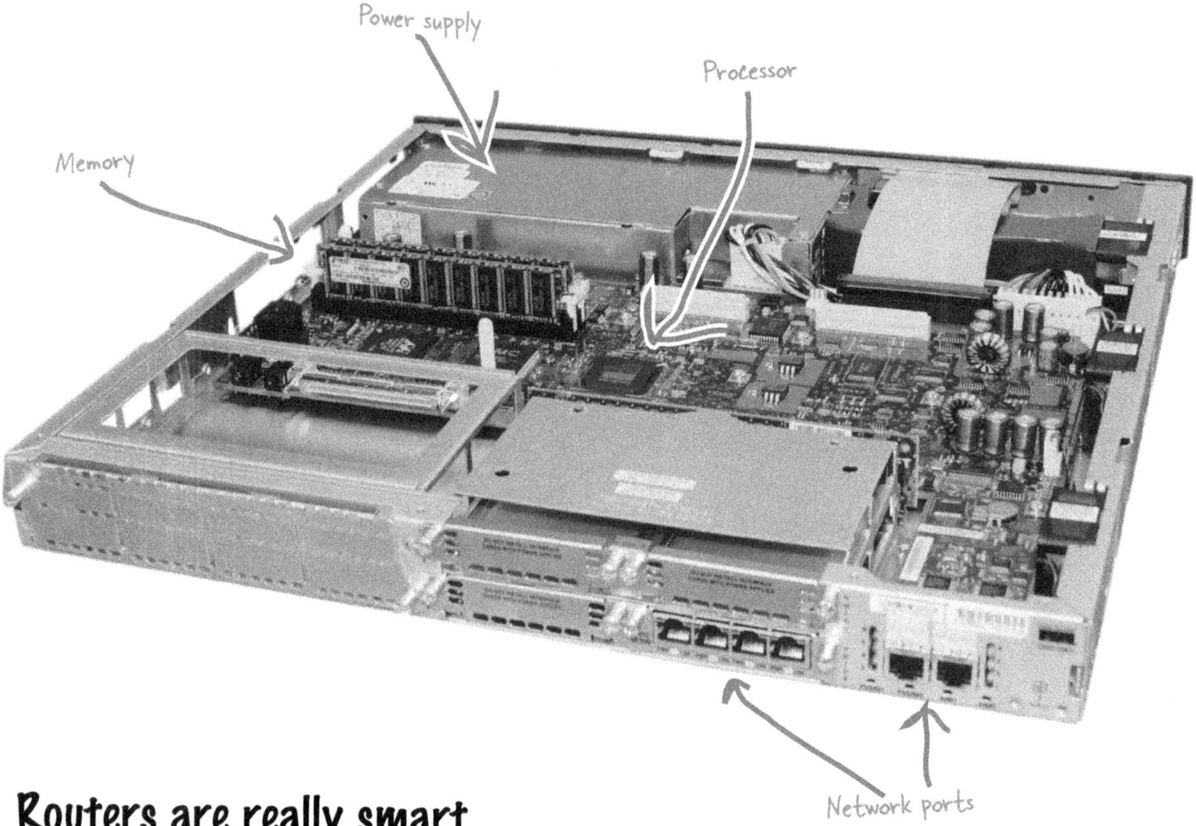

Power supply

Processor

Memory

Network ports

Routers are really smart

They have to be smart because they use IP addresses to move traffic around a network. This takes some processor horsepower to accomplish.

Also, routers have far less network ports because they tend to connect to other routers or to switches. Computers are generally not connected directly to a router.

We will be covering much more on routers in the next two chapters.

We're closing in!

We've isolated the rogue packets to a small part of our network behind a router. So how do we find the mole?

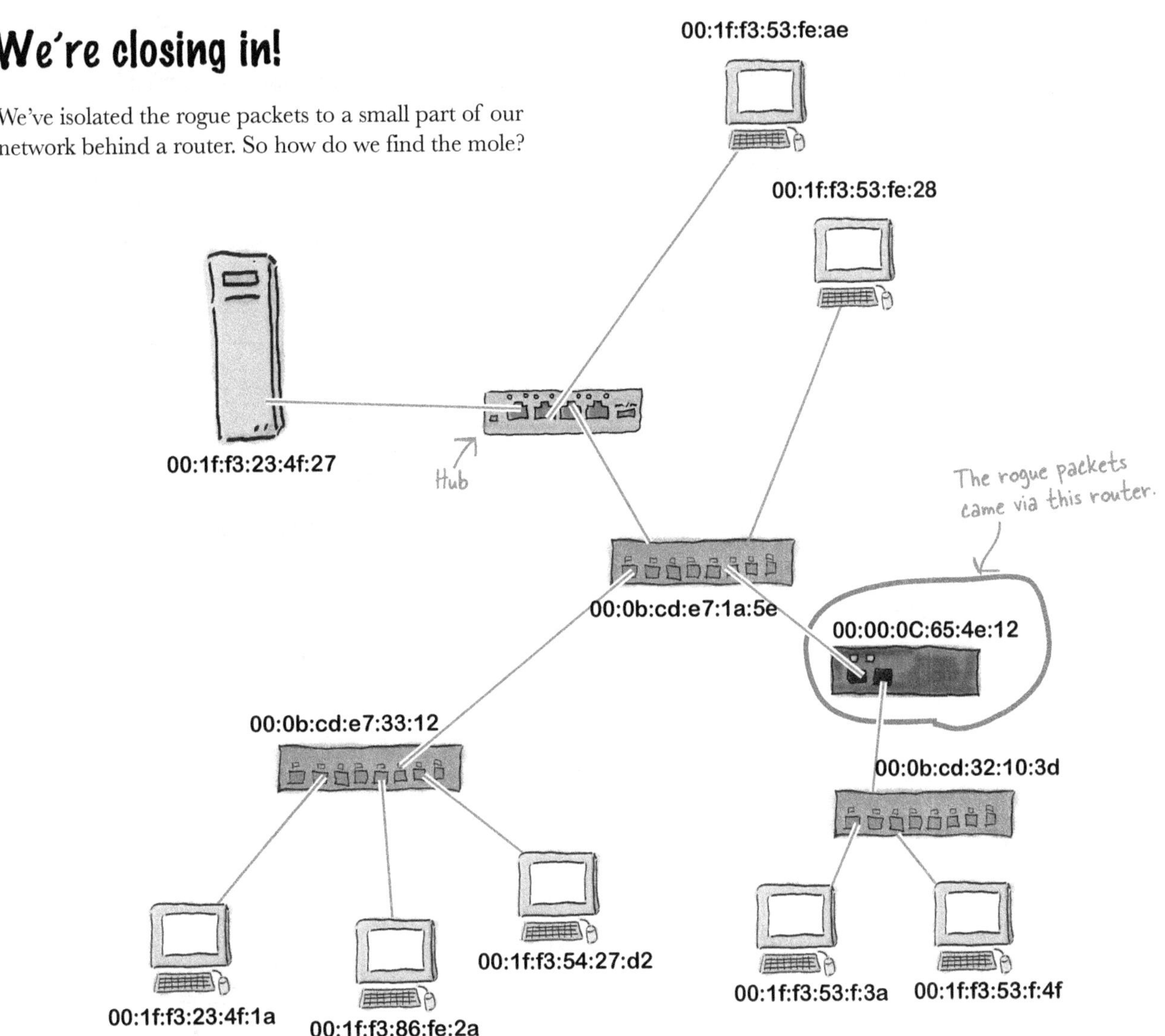

Exercise

Write down your next step(s) to find the workstation that the rogue packets are coming from.

....

....

....

Write down your next step(s) to find the workstation that the rogue packets are coming from.

Connect to the switch that is behind the router and look at its MAC address table. Find the rogue MAC address by finding the one that does not appear in your list of company MAC addresses. The switch's table will also tell us the port that the rogue address is connected to and lead us to the mole's location.

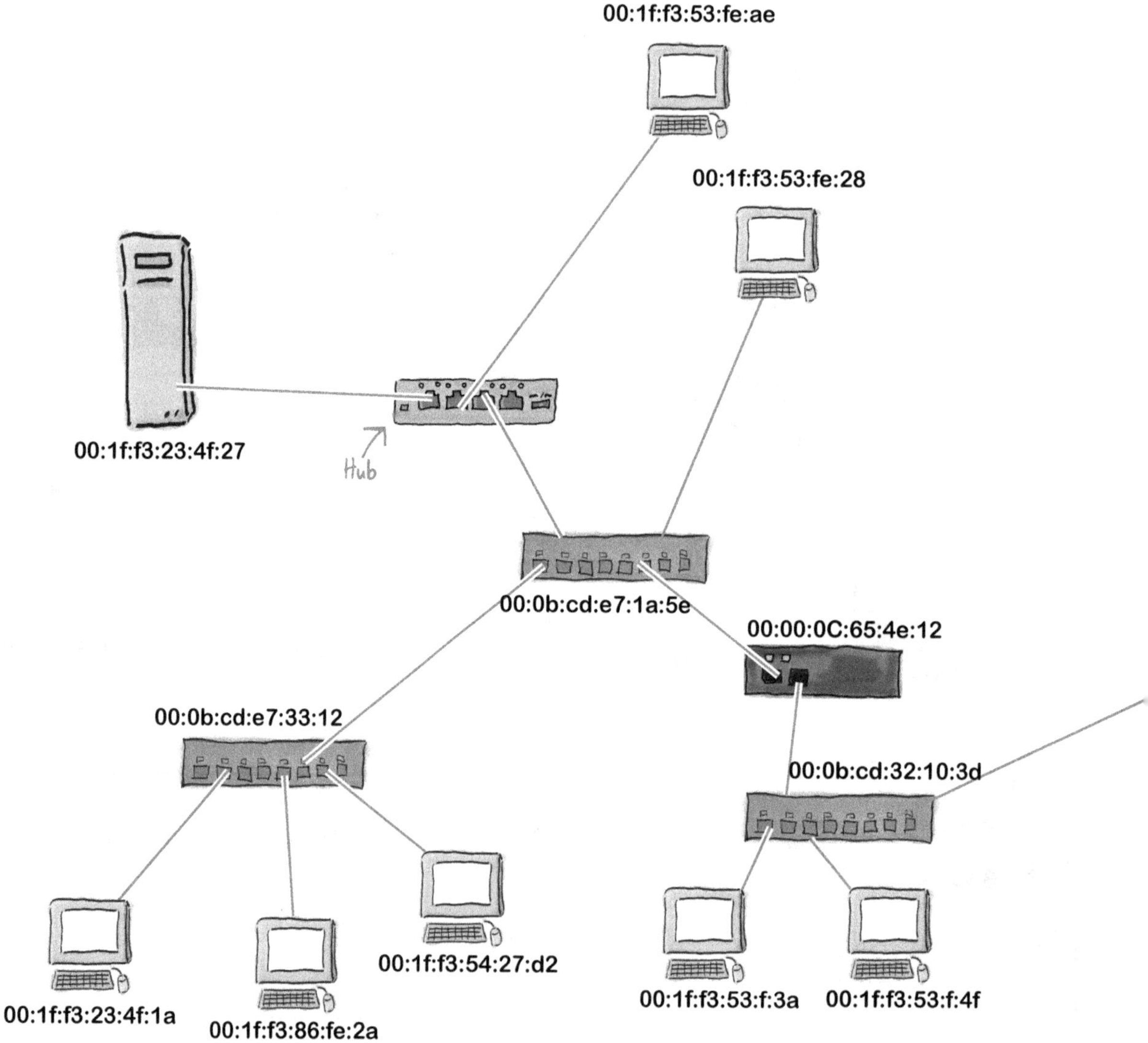

00:1f:f3:53:fe:ae

00:1f:f3:53:fe:28

00:1f:f3:23:4f:27

Hub

00:0b:cd:e7:1a:5e

00:00:0C:65:4e:12

00:0b:cd:e7:33:12

00:0b:cd:32:10:3d

00:1f:f3:54:27:d2

00:1f:f3:23:4f:1a

00:1f:f3:86:fe:2a

00:1f:f3:53:f:3a

00:1f:f3:53:f:4f

You've found the mole!

Thanks to your networking skills, we've found the mole. He's connecting a laptop to a switch that's sitting behind the router. Well done!

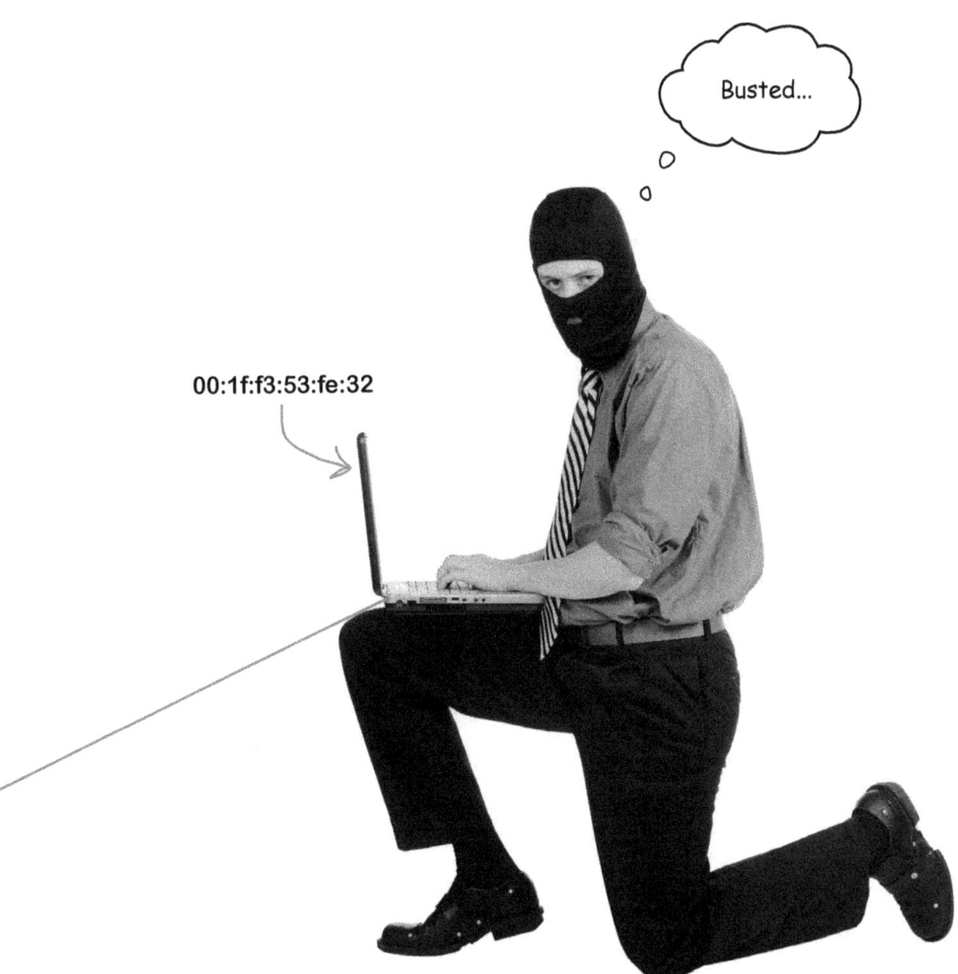

6 connecting networks with routers

Bringing Things Together

I thought we had such a great connection...

Need to a get a network connection to a place far, far away?

So far, we've shown you the ins and outs of how you get a single network up and running. But what do you do if you need to **share resources with some other network**? That's where routers come into their own. Routers specialize in seamlessly **moving network traffic** from **one network to another**, and in this chapter you'll learn exactly how they do that. We'll show you how to **program** your router, and how the router itself can help you **troubleshoot any problems**. Keep reading, and you'll find it's out of this world...

Networking ~~Walking~~ on the moon

Houston, this is Moonbase. The Network Pro has landed.

The Moonbase is a NASA command center that's been set up on the moon, and they need to establish a video connection with the International Space Station (ISS). There's just one problem—there's no network on the Moonbase to allow them to communicate with it.

Think you can help them out?

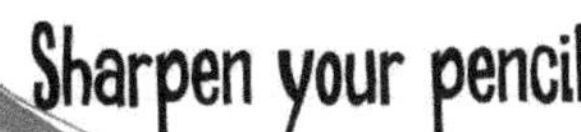

Start your moon network by connecting up the devices below into a network that will allow communications on the Internet using the radio.

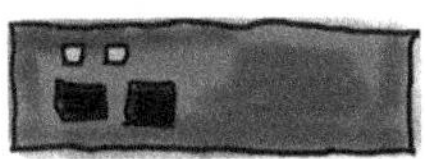

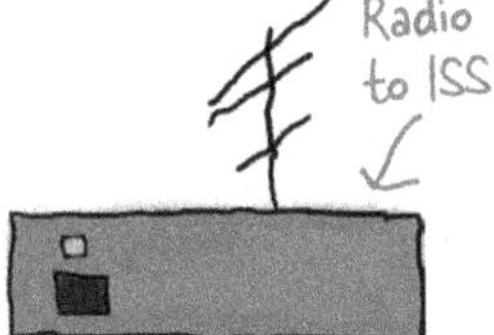

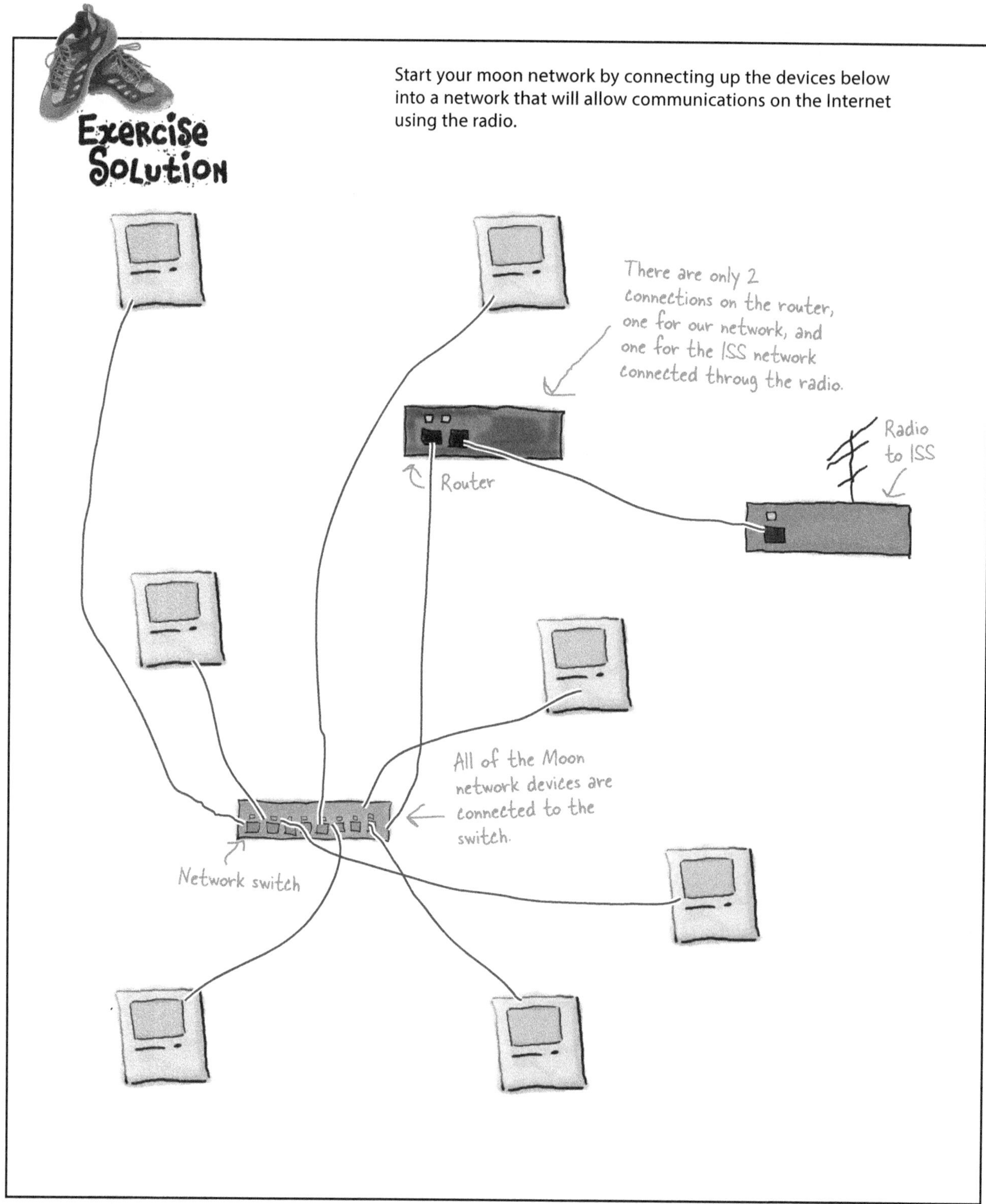
Exercise Solution
Start your moon network by connecting up the devices below into a network that will allow communications on the Internet using the radio.
There are only 2 connections on the router, one for our network, and one for the ISS network connected throug the radio.
Router
Radio to ISS
All of the Moon network devices are connected to the switch.
Network switch

We need to connect two networks together

So how do you generally connect two networks together? The first thing you need is a working local area network (LAN). Second, you need a connection to that other network. This could be a Cat 5 cable or fiber or even a radio link. Finally, you need a router to connect the 2 networks. The router connects the networks *physically* as well as *logically*.

The physical network is the hardware such as the cables, switches, hubs, and routers.

The logical network is the network addressing stuff.

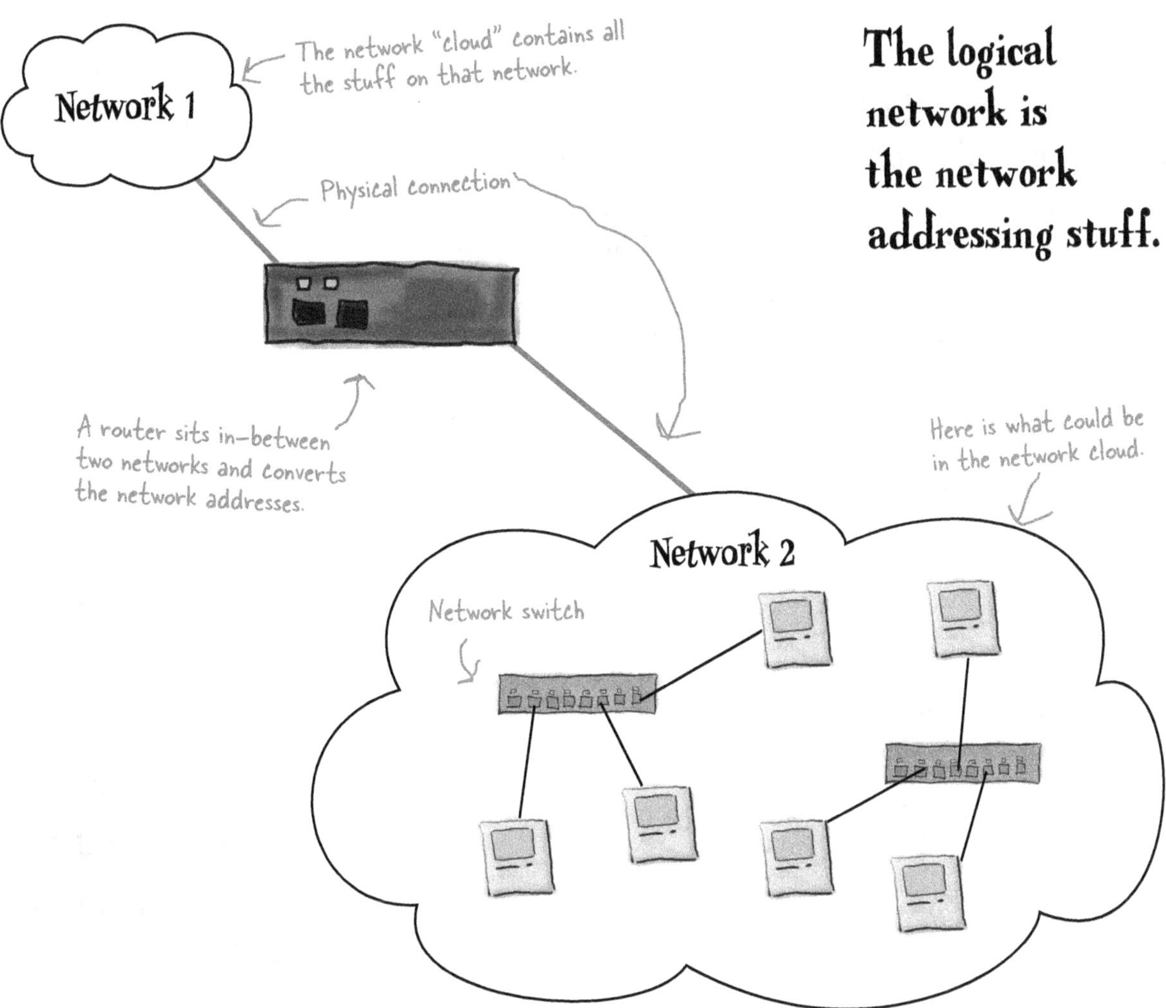

Network 1
The network "cloud" contains all the stuff on that network.
Physical connection
A router sits in-between two networks and converts the network addresses.
Here is what could be in the network cloud.
Network 2
Network switch

The Moonbase and ISS networks are now connected with a router. So is everything working?

The light's on, but nobody's home

The LEDs on the Moonbase switch are flashing, but unfortunately, there's still no video connection with the ISS.

The lights on the switch are flashing, but we're not getting through to the ISS. So what's up?

What do you think the flashing LEDs have to do with traffic on the network?

Remember from the previous chapter, that data sent on an Ethernet network travel as discrete units called frames. The LEDs flashing let you know that a particular port is sending or receiving network traffic in the form of these frames. The frames are directed where to go based on the MAC address inside the frame.

So, the LEDs represent network traffic.

But does that mean your network is working?

How would you find out?

Remember, every network device on an Ethernet network has to have a MAC address if it is going to send and receive network traffic.

How would you go about monitoring conversations on the network? What would you use?

there are no Dumb Questions

Q: So why do we have to use a router? Can't the switch connect to the radio?

A: We have to use a router when we connect two networks. The router acts as a "translator" between the two networks. Simple switches do not have the brains for this.

Q: What is the router "translating"?

A: In simply terms: network addresses. The two different networks are like 2 different cities. The router moves the data from one network to another.

Q: So do I always need to connect a computer to a switch?

A: To a switch or to a hub, but never directly to a router.

Q: But I have a DSL router at home, and my computer is directly connected to it. What is that all about?

A: Good observation. There are switches that have routing capability and routers that have switched ports. There is not a real clear line between the two devices. It is more about their primary function. Now, in large networks, there are switching routers. These have software that allow them to work as routers on switched ports. They are great to use and make building large sophisticated networks straightforward, but they are very expensive.

Q: So the difference betweeen my home DSL router and an enterprise switching router is the software?

A: The big difference is the hardware horsepower. Your home DSL router probably uses a small embedded processor or microcontroller which does all the processing. Switching routers and heavy duty routers have specialized processors with individual processors on each port. The name of the game is the speed at which is can move packets. Your home DSL router probably has a throughput of about 20 Mbps (Megabits per second), whereas a high end switching router can have a throughput of hundreds of Gbps (Gigabits per second) or more.

Let's see what traffic is on our network!

A packet sniffer program like Wireshark can show you the network traffic between devices. Wireshark can help you find out when devices are trying to communicate but can't for some reason.

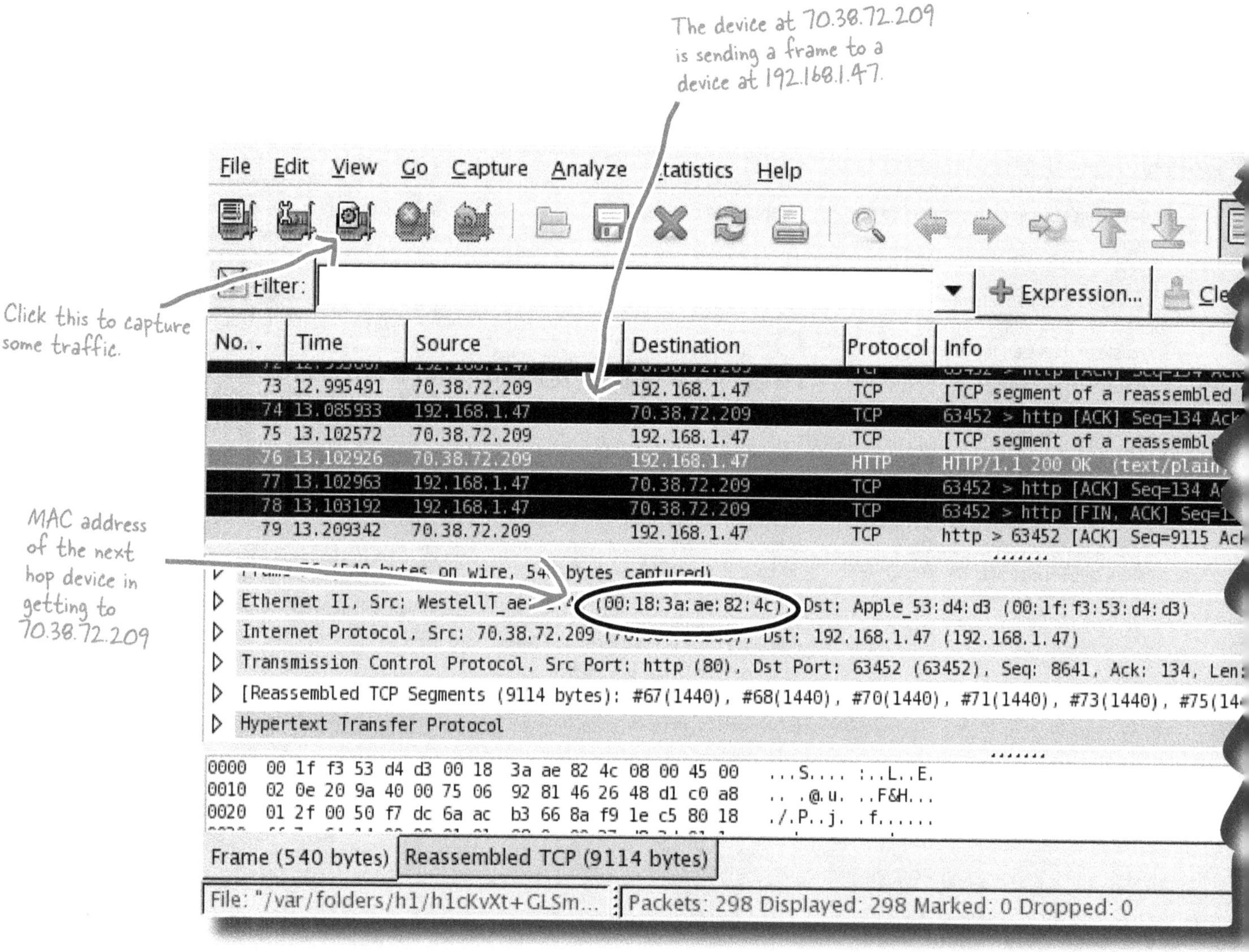

The device at 70.38.72.209 is sending a frame to a device at 192.168.1.47.

Click this to capture some traffic.

MAC address of the next hop device in getting to 70.38.72.209

File Edit View Go Capture Analyze Statistics Help

Filter: Expression... Cle

No.	Time	Source	Destination	Protocol	Info
73	12.995491	70.38.72.209	192.168.1.47	TCP	[TCP segment of a reassembled
74	13.085933	192.168.1.47	70.38.72.209	TCP	63452 > http [ACK] Seq=134 Ack
75	13.102572	70.38.72.209	192.168.1.47	TCP	[TCP segment of a reassembl
76	13.102926	70.38.72.209	192.168.1.47	HTTP	HTTP/1.1 200 OK (text/plain
77	13.102963	192.168.1.47	70.38.72.209	TCP	63452 > http [ACK] Seq=134 A
78	13.103192	192.168.1.47	70.38.72.209	TCP	63452 > http [FIN, ACK] Seq=1
79	13.209342	70.38.72.209	192.168.1.47	TCP	http > 63452 [ACK] Seq=9115 Ack

```
Ethernet II, Src: WestellT_ae:82:4c (00:18:3a:ae:82:4c), Dst: Apple_53:d4:d3 (00:1f:f3:53:d4:d3)
Internet Protocol, Src: 70.38.72.209 (70.38.72.209), Dst: 192.168.1.47 (192.168.1.47)
Transmission Control Protocol, Src Port: http (80), Dst Port: 63452 (63452), Seq: 8641, Ack: 134, Len:
[Reassembled TCP Segments (9114 bytes): #67(1440), #68(1440), #70(1440), #71(1440), #73(1440), #75(14
Hypertext Transfer Protocol
```

```
0000  00 1f f3 53 d4 d3 00 18  3a ae 82 4c 08 00 45 00   ...S.... :..L..E.
0010  02 0e 20 9a 40 00 75 06  92 81 46 26 48 d1 c0 a8   .. .@.u. ..F&H...
0020  01 2f 00 50 f7 dc 6a ac  b3 66 8a f9 1e c5 80 18   ./.P..j. .f......
```

Frame (540 bytes) | Reassembled TCP (9114 bytes)

File: "/var/folders/h1/h1cKvXt+GLSm... | Packets: 298 Displayed: 298 Marked: 0 Dropped: 0

What would you see if a device was trying but failing to have a network conversation?

Here's captured network traffic from the switch. There's lots of traffic here, but it's not making any sense.

Frank: What are all these different from and to addresses in this packets?

Jim: Those are IP addresses.

Frank: What are those used for?

Jim: Well, this is a TCP/IP network, and those are the network addresses of the various devices on the network.

Frank: Why are they all different?

Jim: They have to be unique on the network, like a telephone number is unique.

Frank: I get that, but some of these numbers are really different.

Jim: Oh yeah! I didn't notice that. It seems there are a couple of conversations going on, but none of the machines using the one type of address are talking with the other machines.

Frank: I bet they are on a different TCP/IP network!

Jim: So how can we get them to talk with each other?

Watch it!

Only network nodes with the same IP network address can communicate across a switch.

A switch can only deal with MAC addresses. A router is needed to connect two different IP networks.

MAC address versus IP address

So why can't a MAC address be used to move traffic from one network to another?

It's all in the numbers...

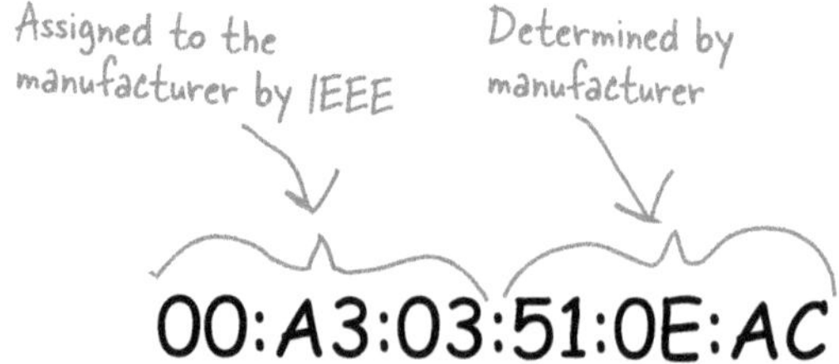

A MAC address is assigned to every device connected to an Ethernet network. In your computer, that is the network card. The beginning part of the MAC address designates the manufacturer. The later part, the manufacturer increments, so all their products have unique MAC addresses. It is like a social security number, in that you really can't tell where a person lives just by looking at it.

There is no way to store network information in the MAC address. Each address is specific and unique to the piece of hardware it is assigned to.

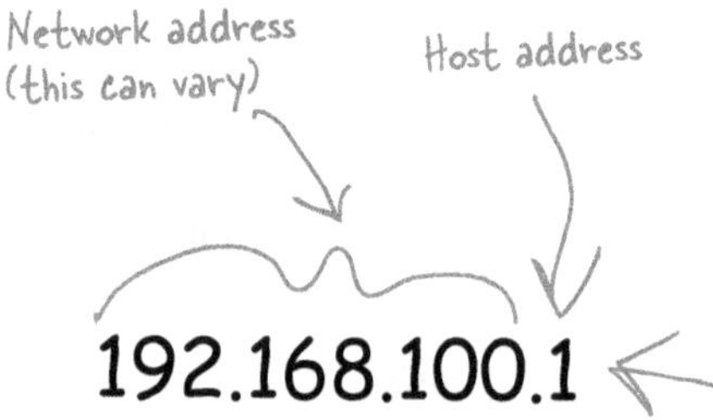

A IP address is made up of a network address and a host address. The host part is the unique bit assigned to a particular network device. It is much like a phone number. which has a country code, area code, and local calling area—finally, your unique individual number.

The ability to create groups of IP address, called IP networks is built into the number itself.

This is the network address of the above IP address.

192.168.100.0/24

The /24 tells us that the first 24 bit, or 3 bytes, are the network address and is called the subnet mask.

Geek Bits

Each network device on a TCP/IP network needs to have an IP network address, a unique address on the network. But how do you find what it is?

If you're running Mac OS X, open up the Terminal application from your Utilities folder, and type `ifconfig`. This same command works on Linux as well.

If you're running Windows XP, 2000, or Vista, click Start, then Run, and then type `cmd`. When the command window appears, type `ipconfig`.

IP addresses give our networks a sense of location, and network nodes a sense of belonging to that location

IP addresses are used to create an address space so that different networks can communicate with each other, much like area codes relate to different geographical areas. The IP address then gives a unique network and specific address to each and every network node.

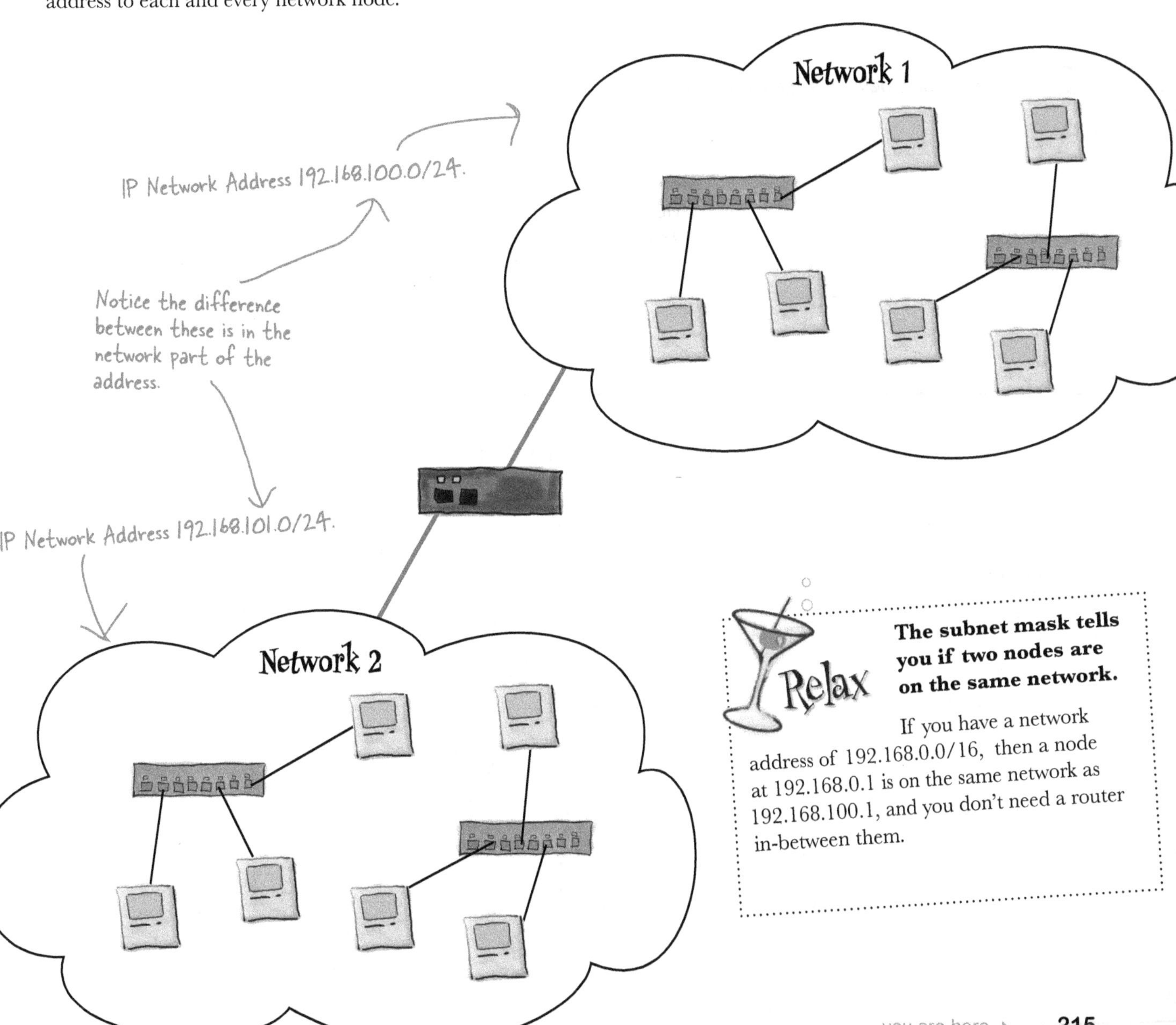

Network 1
IP Network Address 192.168.100.0/24.
Notice the difference between these is in the network part of the address.
IP Network Address 192.168.101.0/24.
Network 2
Relax
The subnet mask tells you if two nodes are on the same network.
If you have a network address of 192.168.0.0/16, then a node at 192.168.0.1 is on the same network as 192.168.100.1, and you don't need a router in-between them.

We retrieve IP addresses using the MAC address and the Address Resolution Protocol (ARP)

Here's what happens when a network device needs to send some data via a switch on a TCP/IP network. The device has to find out the MAC address using the IP address. It does by using ARP.

1 A network device sends an ARP request to the switch.

2 The switch broadcasts the ARP request to all devices.

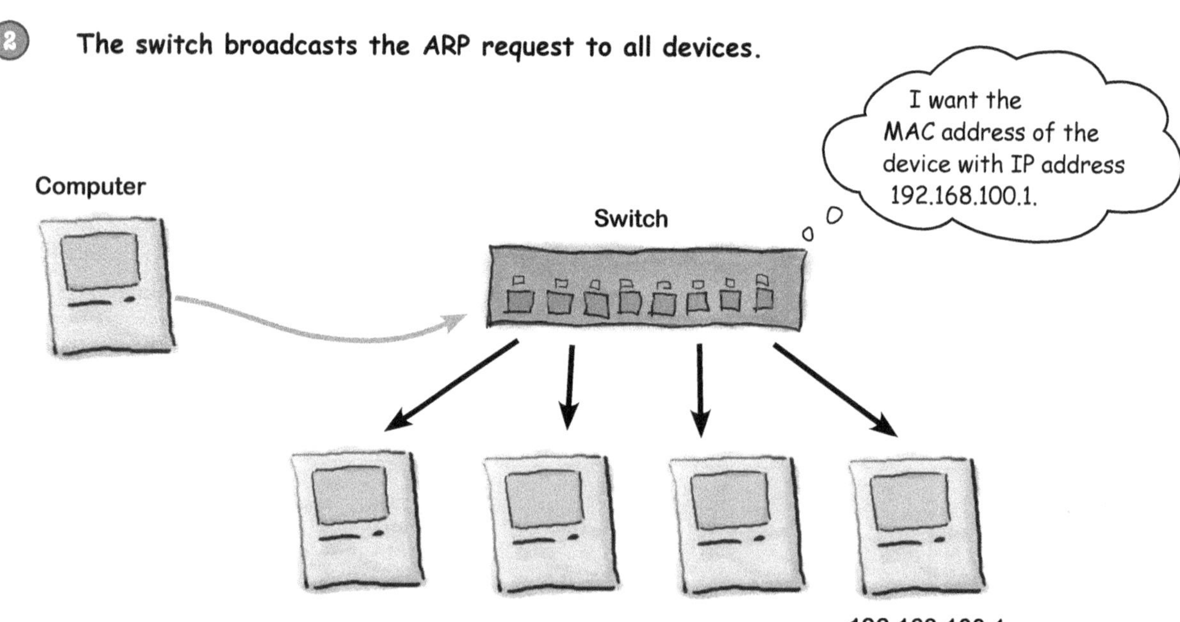

3 The device with the appropriate IP address makes an ARP response back to the switch.

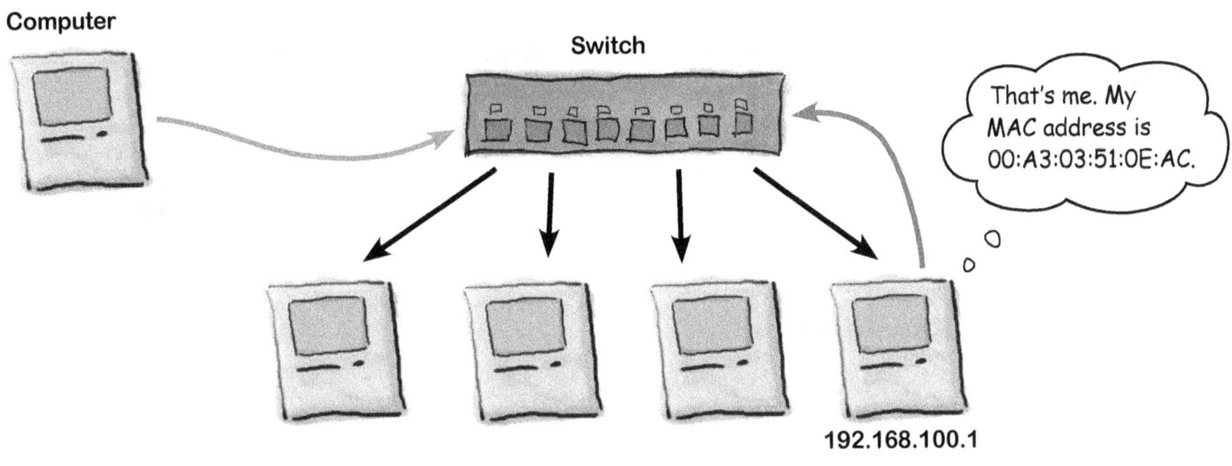

4 The switch relays the ARP response back to the network device.

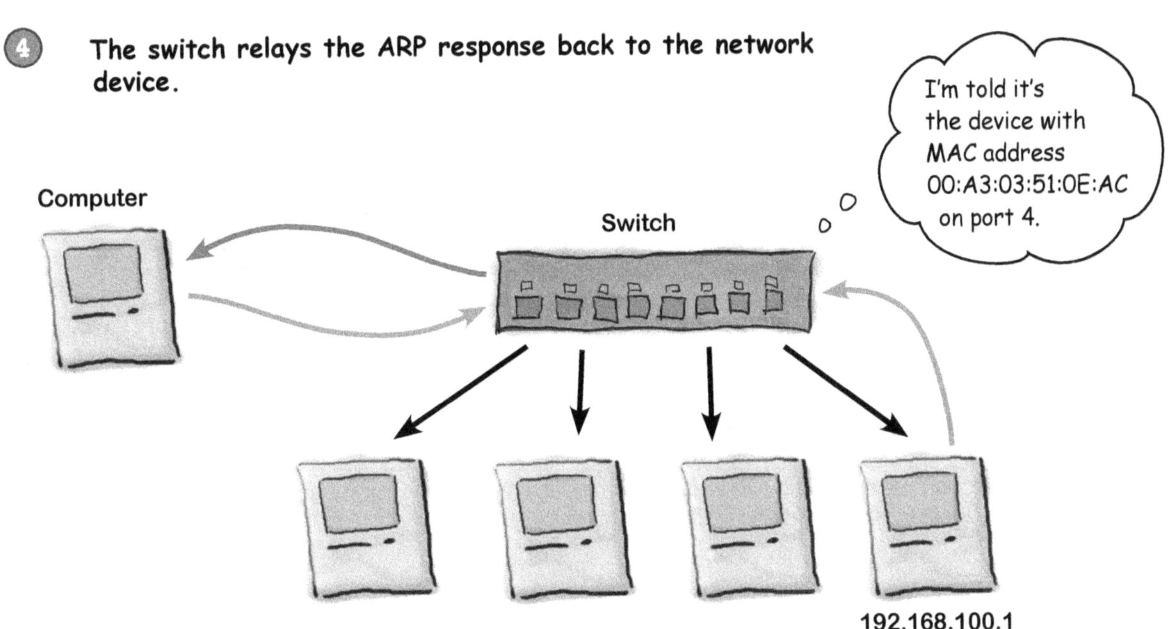

there are no Dumb Questions

Q: I thought I just needed a MAC address for a frame to get somewhere.

A: That's all an Ethernet frame needs to get somewhere. But, remember from the previous chapter that Ethernet frames contain things called packets, and these contain data in the form of protocols. In the case of TCP/IP networks, we need IP addresses to move the packets between networks.

Q: If my computer has an IP address, why does it need a MAC address too?

A: A computer can talk multiple network protocols on the same network. For example, on my Mac here, it is talking TCP/IP and Appletalk on the same Ethernet line. So the MAC address allows the Ethernet frames to move between network devices like routers and switches. The network protocols allow the computer to talk to devices on other networks.

Q: What is an IP address used for?

A: Every computer connected to the Internet has to have an IP address. It may not be a public address, or it might share a public address with other computers, but it will have some type of IP address.

Q: What do you mean "public" IP address?

A: There are some IP network addresses designated as private addresses. The rest are public. Public means that they are routable, whereas private addresses are not routable, i.e., the main routers of the Internet will not move packets from one network to another if they have private IP addresses.

Q: Who designated which IP addresses were public versus private?

A: Good question. When the TCP/IP protocol was developed, the designers recognized the need to reserve some addresses for use as private networks. These addresses have their own RFC, which is RFC 1918. This designates the private address ranges.

Q: So how do you get an IP address?

A: Another great question. At home your computer gets its public address from your ISP. A computer at a large business or university would get it from the network administrator who keeps track of all the IP addresses.

Q: So how do ISPs, businesses, and universities get IP addresses?

A: In the US, Canada, and nations in the Caribbean, the American Registry for Internet Numbers (ARIN) manages the IP address space. There are four other registry authorities for other regions of the world. You can look at **http://www.arin.net/community/countries.html** to find the Registry that manages each country's IP space.

Q: Can anyone get IP address space?

A: There are certain requirements to get IP address space. Having the need (i.e., lots of computers that need to be on the Internet) is probably the biggest requirement. But there are others as well.

Sharpen your pencil

Below is some captured network traffic. There are several network conversations shown. Write down six pairs of communicating network nodes.

No.	Time	Destination	Source	Protocol	info
221	11.424	70.13.31.201	192.168.100.1	TCP	http > 53605 [ACK] Seq 1 ...
222	11.443	192.168.100.1	70.13.31.201	HTTP	GET /index.html
223	11.453	192.168.100.2	192.168.100.3	TCP	http > 53634 [ACK] Seq 1 ...
224	11.489	192.168.100.3	192.168.100.2	TCP	[TCP segment of of reassembled PDU]
225	12.1	192.168.100.2	192.168.100.1	HTTP	continuation or non-HTTP traffic
226	12.25	192.168.100.1	192.168.100.2	TCP	http > 53285 [ACK] Seq 1 ...
227	12.354	11.48.124.65	192.168.100.3	ICMP	Echo (ping) request
228	12.410	192.168.100.1	70.13.31.201	TCP	http > 53654 [ACK] Seq 1 ...
229	12.478	192.168.100.3	11.48.124.65	ICMP	Echo (ping) reply
230	12.499	11.48.124.65	192.168.100.3	TCP	http > 53876 [ACK] Seq 1 ...
231	12.542	11.48.124.65	192.168.100.3	HTTP	continuation or non-HTTP traffic
232	12.611	192.168.100.1	70.13.31.201	TCP	http > 52348 [ACK] Seq 1 ...
233	12.619	192.168.100.3	11.48.124.65	TCP	continuation or non-HTTP traffic
234	12.759	192.168.101.1	192.168.100.1	SSH	SSH Encrypted request packet len=48
235	12.841	11.48.124.65	192.168.100.3	TCP	http > 53285 [ACK] Seq 1 ...
236	12.879	192.168.100.1	192.168.101.1	SSH	SSH Encrypted response packet len=48
237	12.91	11.48.124.65	192.168.100.3	TCP	http > 53285 [ACK] Seq 1 ...
238	12.934	192.168.101.1	192.168.100.1	SSH	SSH Encrypted request packet len=48
239	12.98	192.168.100.3	11.48.124.65	TCP	http > 53285 [ACK] Seq 1 ...
240	13.02	192.168.100.1	192.168.100.3	TCP	http > 53285 [ACK] Seq 1 ...
241	13.223	192.168.100.1	70.13.31.201	TCP	http > 53285 [ACK] Seq 1 ...
242	13.451	192.168.100.3	192.168.100.1	TCP	http > 53285 [ACK] Seq 1 ...
243	13.518	192.168.100.3	192.168.100.1	HTTP	continuation or non-HTTP traffic

Pair 1 192.168.100.1 ____________ ____________

Pair 2 ____________ ____________

Pair 3 ____________ ____________

Pair 4 ____________ ____________

Pair 5 ____________ ____________

Pair 6 ____________ ____________

Exercise Solution

Below is some captured network traffic. There are several network conversations shown. Write down six pairs of communicating network nodes.

	No.	Time	Destination	Source	Protocol	info
pair 1	221	11.424	70.13.31.201	192.168.100.1	TCP	http > 53605 [ACK] Seq 1 ...
	222	11.443	192.168.100.1	70.13.31.201	HTTP	GET /index.html
pair 5	223	11.453	192.168.100.2	192.168.100.3	TCP	http > 53634 [ACK] Seq 1 ...
	224	11.489	192.168.100.3	192.168.100.2	TCP	[TCP segment of of reassembled PDU]
pair 3	225	12.1	192.168.100.2	192.168.100.1	HTTP	continuation or non-HTTP traffic
	226	12.25	192.168.100.1	192.168.100.2	TCP	http > 53285 [ACK] Seq 1 ...
pair 4	227	12.354	11.48.124.65	192.168.100.3	ICMP	Echo (ping) request
pair 1	228	12.410	192.168.100.1	70.13.31.201	TCP	http > 53654 [ACK] Seq 1 ...
pair 4	229	12.478	192.168.100.3	11.48.124.65	ICMP	Echo (ping) reply
	230	12.499	11.48.124.65	192.168.100.3	TCP	http > 53876 [ACK] Seq 1 ...
	231	12.542	11.48.124.65	192.168.100.3	HTTP	continuation or non-HTTP traffic
pair 1	232	12.611	192.168.100.1	70.13.31.201	TCP	http > 52348 [ACK] Seq 1 ...
pair 4	233	12.619	192.168.100.3	11.48.124.65	TCP	continuation or non-HTTP traffic
pair 2	234	12.759	192.168.101.1	192.168.100.1	SSH	SSH Encrypted request packet len=48
pair 4	235	12.841	11.48.124.65	192.168.100.3	TCP	http > 53285 [ACK] Seq 1 ...
pair 2	236	12.879	192.168.100.1	192.168.101.1	SSH	SSH Encrypted response packet len=48
pair 4	237	12.91	11.48.124.65	192.168.100.3	TCP	http > 53285 [ACK] Seq 1 ...
pair 2	238	12.934	192.168.101.1	192.168.100.1	SSH	SSH Encrypted request packet len=48
pair 4	239	12.98	192.168.100.3	11.48.124.65	TCP	http > 53285 [ACK] Seq 1 ...
pair 6	240	13.02	192.168.100.1	192.168.100.3	TCP	http > 53285 [ACK] Seq 1 ...
pair 1	241	13.223	192.168.100.1	70.13.31.201	TCP	http > 53285 [ACK] Seq 1 ...
pair 6	242	13.451	192.168.100.3	192.168.100.1	TCP	http > 53285 [ACK] Seq 1 ...
	243	13.518	192.168.100.3	192.168.100.1	HTTP	continuation or non-HTTP traffic

Each conversation is color-coded

Pair 1	192.168.100.1	70.13.31.201
Pair 2	192.168.100.1	192.168.101.1
Pair 3	192.168.100.2	192.168.100.1
Pair 4	11.48.124.65	192.168.100.3
Pair 5	192.168.100.2	192.168.100.3
Pair 6	192.168.100.1	192.168.100.3

So what's the problem with the Moonbase?

So far we've seen that the computers on the Moonbase network are communicating using IP addresses rather than MAC addresses. So why aren't the Moonbase and ISS able to communicate?

Well, it looks like individually each network is working. The trouble is, the two networks aren't communicating with **each other**. I wonder whether the network traffic isn't being communicated somehow?

Maybe he's right.

So far we've looked at how switches behave on IP networks. But what if the problems aren't to do with the switch, but with how the traffic passes from one network to the other? What device should we look at next?

Take another look at the network diagram for the Moonbase. What device controls how traffic is handled between the two networks?

How do we get network traffic to move between networks?

The problem is that a node on one network does not know how to send ***frames*** to a node on another network. A router knows how to move traffic from one network to another.

But how does it do this? Doesn't it have to know about both networks, or at least how to get to the outside network?

Also, how does a network node know to send traffic bound for another network to its router?

We need to program a router to know about the networks it is connected to, and know how to get to other networks.

Network devices have a default gateway in their network setup. This is the router's IP address. It is where the devices send all network traffic bound for other networks.

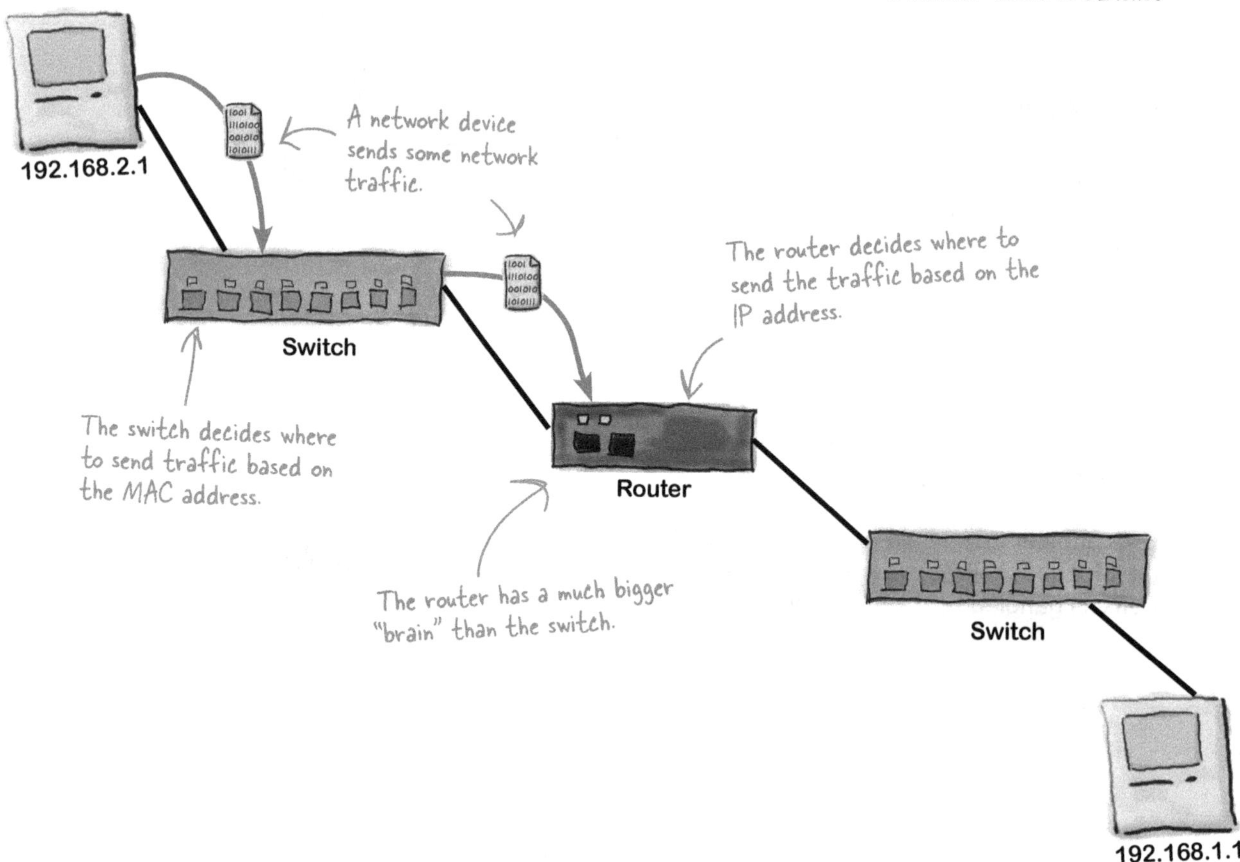

192.168.2.1
A network device sends some network traffic.
Switch
The router decides where to send the traffic based on the IP address.
The switch decides where to send traffic based on the MAC address.
Router
The router has a much bigger "brain" than the switch.
Switch
192.168.1.1

So why can't you just
use a switch to move
data between networks?

Remember, the only addresses the switch understands are MAC addresses.

An Ethernet switch just looks at the MAC address of a frame and forwards that frame to the correct device. It does not modify the frame in any way.

The router has to actually take the packet out of the frame, get the IP address, then modify the frame MAC address if it needs to send it on to a device on another network.

Let's take a closer look at this.

How the router moves data across networks

Computers are not generally connected directly to a router.

Usually there is a switch or hub in-between them.

Here's what happens if a network device wants to send network traffic to another network device located on a different IP network. It needs to send this traffic via a router.

1. **The sending device sends an ARP request for the MAC address of its default gateway.**

2. **The router responds with its MAC address.**

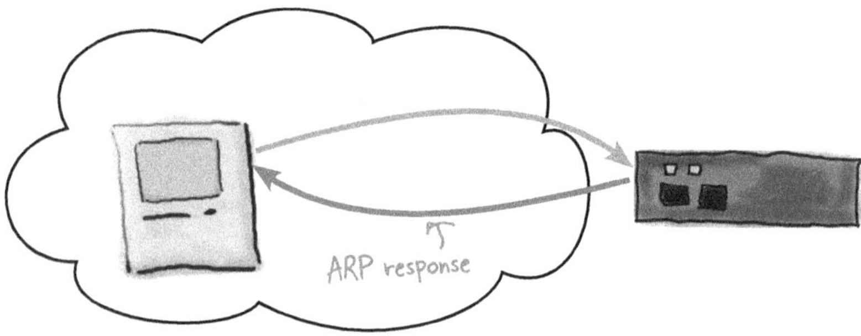

3. **The sending device sends its traffic to the router.**

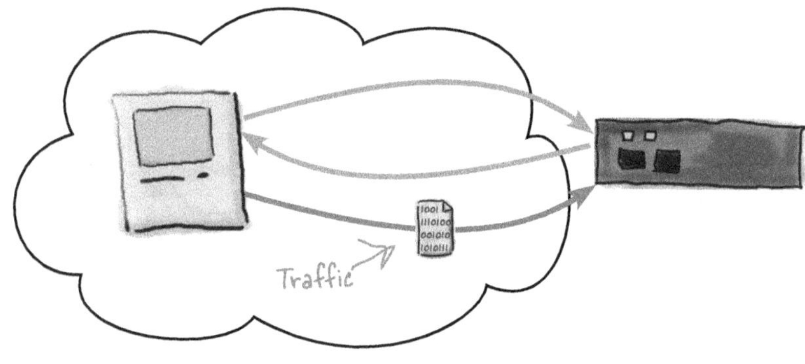

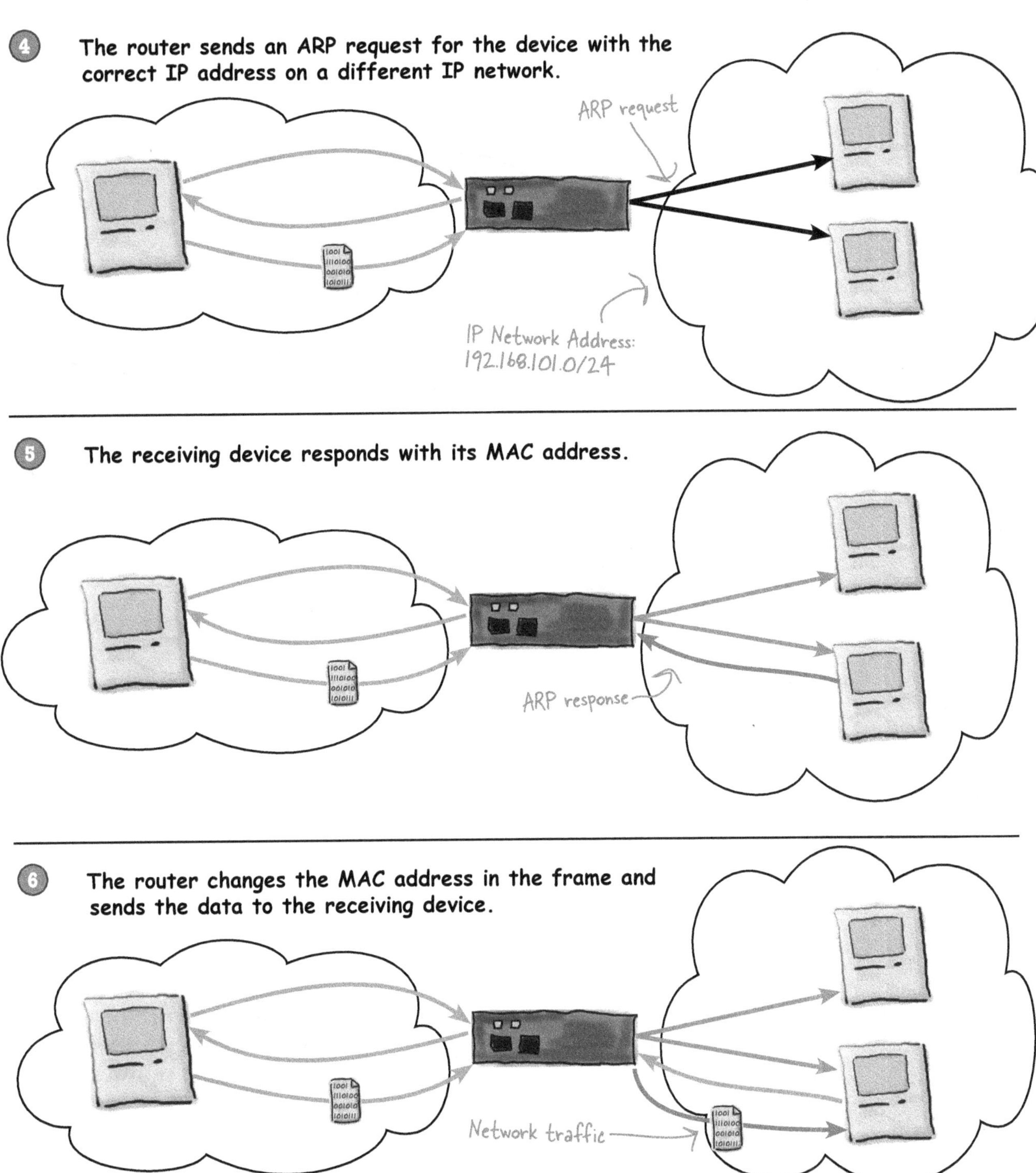
4
The router sends an ARP request for the device with the correct IP address on a different IP network.
ARP request
1001
1110100
001010
1010111
IP Network Address:
192.168.101.0/24
5
The receiving device responds with its MAC address.
ARP response
6
The router changes the MAC address in the frame and sends the data to the receiving device.
Network traffic

Back to the Moonbase problem

From the captured network traffic, we can see that devices on the same network are communicating, but devices with different IP network addresses are not. What makes the IP addresses different?

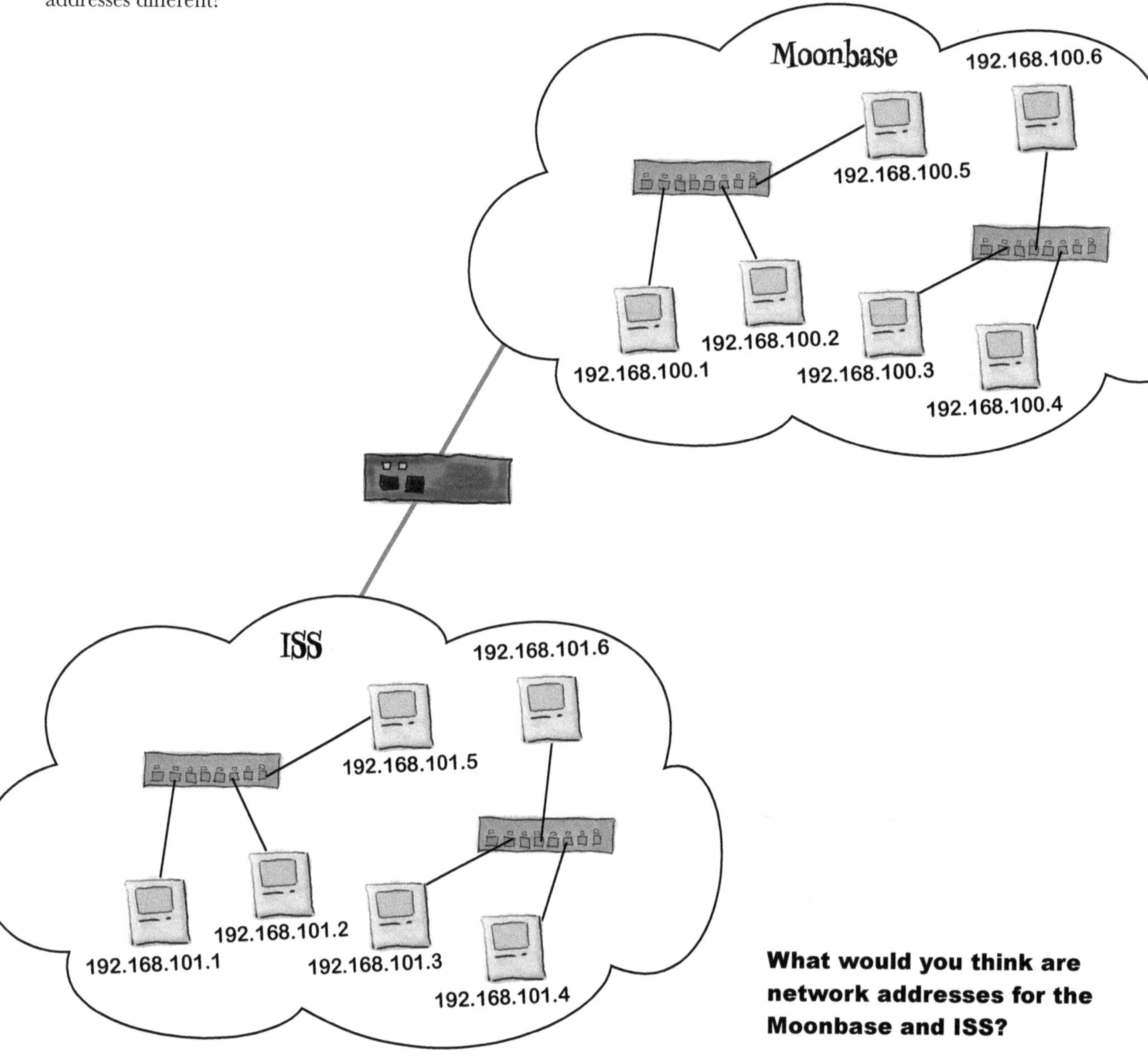

What would you think are network addresses for the Moonbase and ISS?

The secret of IP numbers is...

An IP address is made up of 4 to 8 bit binary numbers which are called octets or bytes. But the real secret is that an IP address is just half of the IP network address. The other part is the subnet mask. The mathematical combination of the IP address and subnet mask is what a router uses to determine the network of some packet it received.

An IP address has 4 octets. Each octet can represent 256 individual bits. So 4 octets of 256 each means that this type of number can potentially represent 2^32 or 4,294,967,296 individual addresses.

In decimal...

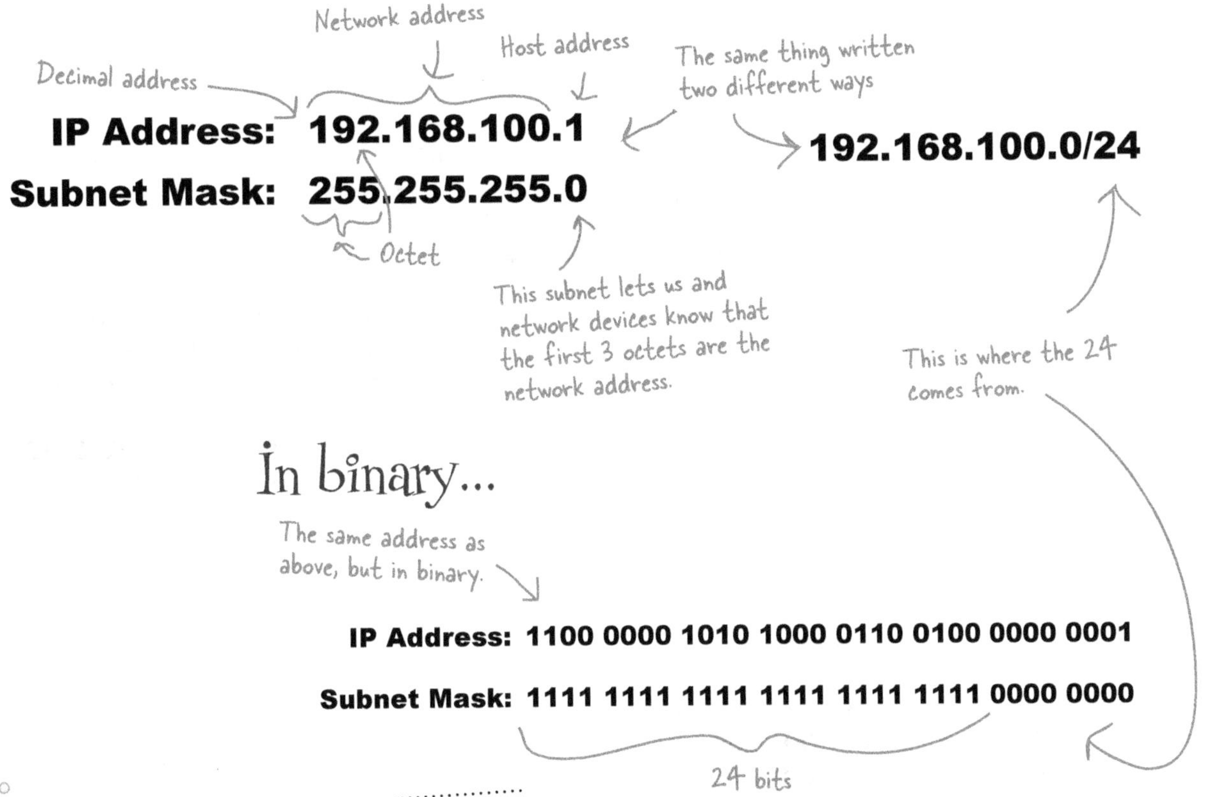

Network address

Host address

Decimal address

The same thing written two different ways

IP Address: 192.168.100.1

Subnet Mask: 255.255.255.0

192.168.100.0/24

Octet

This subnet lets us and network devices know that the first 3 octets are the network address.

This is where the 24 comes from.

In binary...

The same address as above, but in binary.

IP Address: 1100 0000 1010 1000 0110 0100 0000 0001

Subnet Mask: 1111 1111 1111 1111 1111 1111 0000 0000

24 bits

Relax

This is just a first look at IP addressing.

We're introducing IP addressing to you here so we can talk about routers. You will learn much more on IP addressing in upcoming chapters.

Routers connect networks by doing the math...

What type of math do you think a router uses to determine when it needs to route a packet to another network?

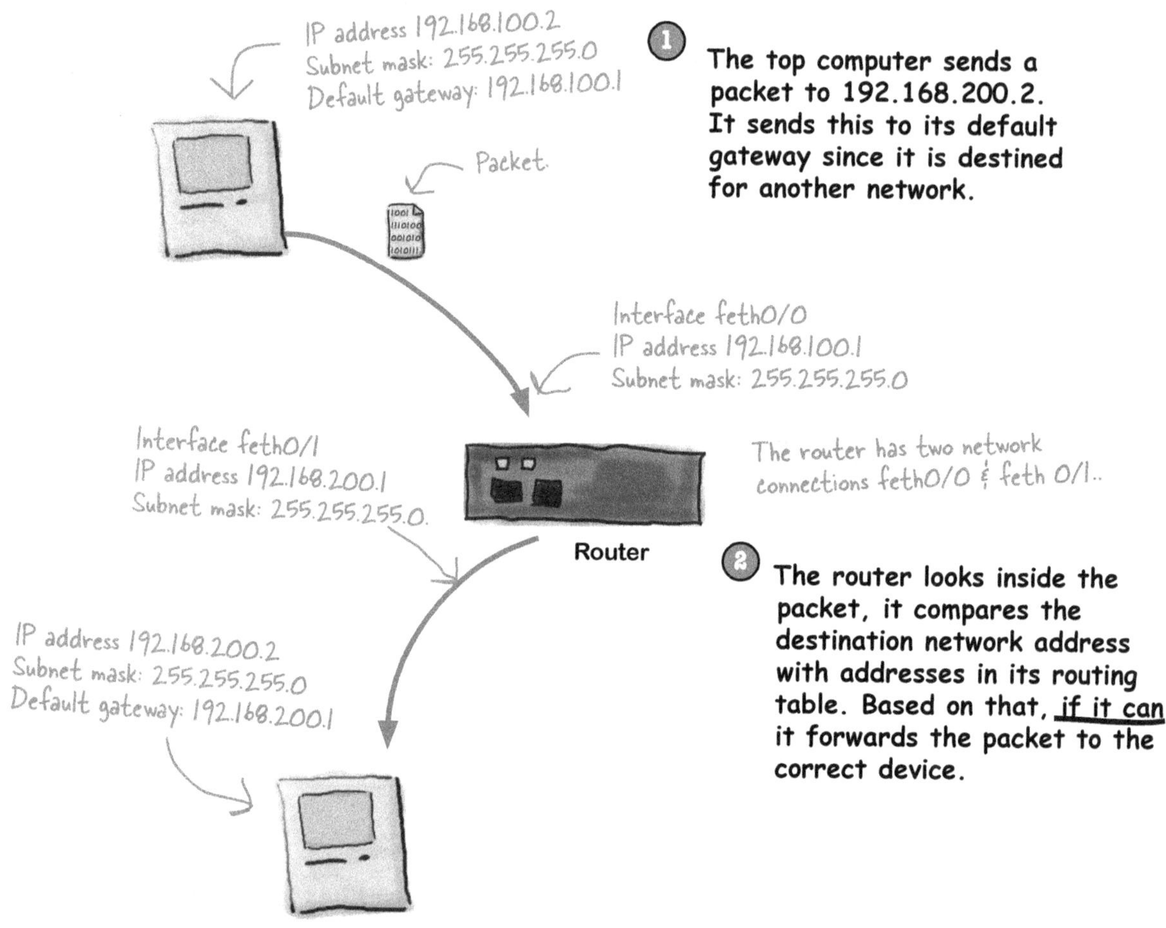

1. The top computer sends a packet to 192.168.200.2. It sends this to its default gateway since it is destined for another network.

2. The router looks inside the packet, it compares the destination network address with addresses in its routing table. Based on that, if it can, it forwards the packet to the correct device.

3. The computer receives the packet from the router. The router has changed the destination MAC address to the receiving computer's MAC and the source MAC address to the router's.

BE the Router

Your job is to play router and circle which packets in the trace below need to be moved from one network to another.

No.	Time	Destination	Source	Protocol	info
221	11.424	70.13.31.201	192.168.100.1	TCP	http > 53605 [ACK] Seq 1 ...
222	11.443	192.168.100.1	70.13.31.201	HTTP	GET /index.html
223	11.453	192.168.100.2	192.168.100.3	TCP	http > 53634 [ACK] Seq 1 ...
224	11.489	192.168.100.3	192.168.100.2	TCP	[TCP segment of of reassembled PDU]
225	12.1	192.168.100.2	192.168.100.1	HTTP	continuation or non-HTTP traffic
226	12.25	192.168.100.1	192.168.100.2	TCP	http > 53285 [ACK] Seq 1 ...
227	12.354	11.48.124.65	192.168.100.3	ICMP	Echo (ping) request
228	12.410	192.168.100.1	70.13.31.201	TCP	http > 53654 [ACK] Seq 1 ...
229	12.478	192.168.100.3	11.48.124.65	ICMP	Echo (ping) reply
230	12.499	11.48.124.65	192.168.100.3	TCP	http > 53876 [ACK] Seq 1 ...
231	12.542	11.48.124.65	192.168.100.3	HTTP	continuation or non-HTTP traffic
232	12.611	192.168.100.1	70.13.31.201	TCP	http > 52348 [ACK] Seq 1 ...
233	12.619	192.168.100.3	11.48.124.65	TCP	continuation or non-HTTP traffic
234	12.759	192.168.101.1	192.168.100.1	SSH	SSH Encrypted request packet len=48
235	12.841	11.48.124.65	192.168.100.3	TCP	http > 53285 [ACK] Seq 1 ...
236	12.879	192.168.100.1	192.168.101.1	SSH	SSH Encrypted response packet len=48
237	12.91	11.48.124.65	192.168.100.3	TCP	http > 53285 [ACK] Seq 1 ...
238	12.934	192.168.101.1	192.168.100.1	SSH	SSH Encrypted request packet len=48
239	12.98	192.168.100.3	11.48.124.65	TCP	http > 53285 [ACK] Seq 1 ...
240	13.02	192.168.100.1	192.168.100.3	TCP	http > 53285 [ACK] Seq 1 ...
241	13.223	192.168.100.1	70.13.31.201	TCP	http > 53285 [ACK] Seq 1 ...
242	13.451	192.168.100.3	192.168.100.1	TCP	http > 53285 [ACK] Seq 1 ...
243	13.518	192.168.100.3	192.168.100.1	HTTP	continuation or non-HTTP traffic

BE the Router Solution

Your job is to play router and circle which packets in the trace below need to be moved from one network to another.

No.	Time	Destination	Source	Protocol	info
[illegible]	11.424	70.13.31.201	192.168.100.1	TCP	http > 53605 [ACK] Seq 1 ...
[illegible]	11.442	192.168.100.1	70.13.31.201	HTTP	GET /index.html
223	11.453	192.168.100.2	192.168.100.3	TCP	http > 53634 [ACK] Seq 1 ...
224	11.489	192.168.100.3	192.168.100.2	TCP	[TCP segment of of reassembled PDU]
225	12.1	192.168.100.2	192.168.100.1	HTTP	continuation or non-HTTP traffic
226	12.25	192.168.100.1	192.168.100.2	TCP	http > 53285 [ACK] Seq 1 ...
227	12.354	11.48.124.65	192.168.100.3	ICMP	Echo (ping) request
228	12.410	192.168.100.1	70.13.31.201	TCP	http > 53654 [ACK] Seq 1 ...
229	12.478	192.168.100.3	11.48.124.65	ICMP	Echo (ping) reply
230	12.499	11.48.124.65	192.168.100.3	TCP	http > 53876 [ACK] Seq 1 ...
231	12.542	11.48.124.65	192.168.100.3	HTTP	continuation or non-HTTP traffic
232	12.611	192.168.100.1	70.13.31.201	TCP	http > 52348 [ACK] Seq 1 ...
233	12.619	192.168.100.3	11.48.124.65	TCP	continuation or non-HTTP traffic
234	12.759	192.168.101.1	192.168.100.1	SSH	SSH Encrypted request packet len=48
235	12.841	11.48.124.65	192.168.100.3	TCP	http > 53285 [ACK] Seq 1 ...
236	12.879	192.168.100.1	192.168.101.1	SSH	SSH Encrypted response packet len=48
237	12.91	11.48.124.65	192.168.100.3	TCP	http > 53285 [ACK] Seq 1 ...
238	12.934	192.168.101.1	192.168.100.1	SSH	SSH Encrypted request packet len=48
[illegible]	12.98	192.168.100.3	11.48.124.65	TCP	http > 53285 [ACK] Seq 1 ...
240	13.02	[illegible]	192.168.100.3	TCP	http > 53285 [ACK] Seq 1 ...
[illegible]	13.223	192.168.100.1	70.13.31.201	TCP	http > 53285 [ACK] Seq 1 ...
242	13.451	192.168.100.3	192.168.100.1	TCP	http > 53285 [ACK] Seq 1 ...
243	13.518	192.168.100.3	192.168.100.1	HTTP	continuation or non-HTTP traffic

Did you get this one? The IP network address is all the numbers except for the one after the third period.

The Router Exposed

This week's interview:
How do you move that network traffic?

Head First: How are you doing this morning?

Router: Busy as ever moving those packets. Seems everyone is doing something on the Internet these days.

Head First: Packets? I thought routers move frames around.

Router: Well, I see the frames, but really they are all packets to me. I have to take them apart and put them back together after all.

Head First: That must really slow things down. Can't you just take a peek at the MAC address and send the frame on its way. You really should try that. I think it might help with the speed of the Internet.

Router: That's all well and good when you are dealing with one network, but I have to move data from one network to others, and a MAC address just does not let me do that. There is no network information in a MAC address. It is like knowing a house number and street name, but not the city, state, or country.

Head First: Isn't that how switches move frames around a network?

Router: Key word there is A NETWORK.

Head First: So a switch cannot route network traffic, is that what you are saying?

Router: That is exactly what I am saying. They do not even have the proper software to deal with routing.

Head First: But if we installed software on a switch, it could route then?

Router: Then it would be called a router, wouldn't it?

Head First: I guess you're right. But aren't there network devices that do switching and routing?

Router: Yes there are. These are very expensive enterprise router/switches. They can have both behaviors. The can also route packets using other information besides IP addresses.

Head First: Oh you mean like other network protocols?

Router: Yes. They can also be very fast because they can combine switching and routing into something called Layer 3 Switching. This essentially means moving routing into the hardware like switching is.

Head First: So we've heard that you run the Internet. Is that true?

Router: The Internet is built on the back of routers. These routers are called backbone routers. So, yes, it's true.

Head First: Well thank you for the interview. Have fun moving those ... packets ... around.

Router: It was enjoyable to talk to you as well.

For each IP address/subnet pair, write down the network part of the IP address and the host part of the IP address.

IP Address	Subnet Mask	Network Address	Host Address
192.168.100.1	255.255.255.0	192.168.100	1
192.168.100.1	255.255.0.0		
10.10.0.103	255.0.0.0		
192.154.234.2	255.255.0.0		
203.54.2.23	255.255.255.0		
204.67.212.22	255.255.0.0		

there are no Dumb Questions

Q: What is with the number 255? Why can't it be a larger number?

A: 256 is the decimal number that 8 bits or 2^8 can represent. The standard for TCP/IP address was written using 32 bits divided into 4-8 bit groups. We start counting at 0, so that gives us 255 as the highest number.

Q: That makes for a lot of addresses. But I have read that the Internet is running out of addresses. How can that be with so many available?

A: Part of the problem is that historically IP address space has been given out in several different size chunks called Classes. These are Class A, B, and C. The scheme is rather wasteful, so many addresses may not be in actual use. Plus there are many reserved addresses, such as the private IP address spaces.

All of these issues plus the fact that there are a lot of devices connected to the Internet, means that the pool of available IP addresses is pretty limited and getting smaller.

Q: So is the Internet doomed?

A: No, there are some smart people out there. They have designed a new IP address space called IPv6. The old one that we are talking about is called IPv4. This new address space has about 3.4×10^{38} addresses available. Plus it has some other mechanisms designed in to help manage the address space.

Q: When is the Internet going to move to that address space?

A: It is happening as we speak. For about 10 years, a very slow transition has been happening. All of the routers, switches, computers, etc. that are connected to the Internet have to be upgraded to support IPv6, or they have to be replaced. This takes a boat-load of money and time.

Q: Back to the subnet, why is it called a mask?

A: The subnet is used as a mask on the IP address to see either the host address or the network address, depending on what it needed. The mask is just like a Halloween mask with eye holes. The mask blocks all of your face except for your eyes. In the case of a subnet, the 255 are all ones, so if you use the boolean AND operator to combine the IP address and subnet mask, you get just the network address without the host part. This is what the router uses to know if it needs to route a packet.

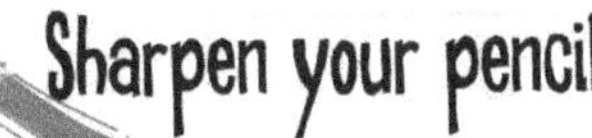

Based on the routing table below, decide whether or not it is routable, and if so, on which interface it will send the packet.

This is how a router stores routing information.

Routing Table

```
D    204.62.204.0/24 [90/30720] via 209.137.230.22, 5w0d, FastEthernet0/0
D    204.62.205.0/24 [90/30720] via 209.137.230.124, 5w3d, FastEthernet0/0
     209.137.230.0/25 is subnetted, 1 subnets
C       209.137.230.0 is directly connected, FastEthernet0/0
C    204.62.201.0/24 is directly connected, FastEthernet0/1
C    172.17.0.0/16 is directly connected, FastEthernet0/1
D    172.16.0.0/16 [90/30720] via 209.137.230.3, 5w3d, FastEthernet0/0
D    172.19.0.0/16 [90/30720] via 209.137.230.124, 5w3d, FastEthernet0/0
D    172.18.0.0/16 [90/30720] via 209.137.230.22, 5w0d, FastEthernet0/0
D    204.62.203.0/24 [90/30720] via 209.137.230.3, 5w3d, FastEthernet0/0
```

Network address — Next router's address — Router's interface

Destination	Source	Routable	Interface
172.16.10.1	204.62.201.12	Yes	FastEthernet0/0
192.168.100.1	204.62.201.12		
204.62.201.12	204.62.201.13		
10.52.1.18	172.17.0.3		
172.17.0.3	172.16.0.3		
172.17.0.3	172.17.0.4		
204.62.205.15	204.62.201.54		
172.19.152.42	204.62.201.57		
172.17.0.57	204.62.204.81		

For each IP address/subnet pair, write down the network part of the IP address and the host part of the IP address.

IP Address	Subnet Mask	Network Address	Host Address
192.168.100.1	255.255.255.0	192.168.100	1
192.168.100.1	255.255.0.0	192.168	100.1
10.10.0.103	255.0.0.0	10	10.0.103
192.154.234.2	255.255.0.0	192.154	234.2
203.54.2.23	255.255.255.0	203.54.2	23
204.67.212.22	255.255.0.0	204.67	212.22

Based on the routing table below, decide whether or not it is routable, and if so, on which interface it will send the packet.

Destination	Source	Routable	Interface
172.16.10.1	204.62.201.12	Yes	FastEthernet0/0
192.168.100.1	204.62.201.12	No	FastEthernet0/0
204.62.201.12	204.62.201.13	Yes	
10.52.1.18	172.17.0.3	No	FastEthernet0/0
172.17.0.3	172.16.0.3	Yes	FastEthernet0/1
172.17.0.3	172.17.0.4	Yes	
204.62.205.15	204.62.201.54	Yes	FastEthernet0/0
172.19.152.42	204.62.201.57	Yes	FastEthernet0/0
172.17.0.57	204.62.204.81	Yes	FastEthernet0/1

Back at the Moonbase...

So far we've connected the Moonbase and ISS networks together using a router. The trouble is, we've only connected the two networks together physically, and not logically. In order for the two networks to talk to each other, we need to sort out the logical connection too. In other words, we need to tell the router how the IP addresses of the two networks relate, and to do this, we need to learn how to program the router.

Sound difficult? Don't worry, just turn the page, and we'll show you how it's done.

Are you ready to program the router?

1. **Connect a computer to the router with a serial cable**
   Most routers allow you to connect to them with a serial cable. These days you can get a USB to serial cable, then use a terminal program to actually type commands into the router.

2. **Get to the enable or programming mode of the router**
   Routers have several modes. The first generally being a read-only mode. In order to program it, you must get it into the programming mode. That generally means first typing a command such as `enable` to get into a privileged mode, then `configure terminal` to actually program it.

3. **Select the interface to setup**
   Now you have to select the interface that you want to setup. This means the physical connection such as Ethernet or serial. A router should have at least 2 interfaces in order to route anything. In the Cisco IOS the command `interface feth0/0` will select the first or "zero" fast Ethernet port on the first or "zero" fast Ethernet card.

4. **Set the address and start the interface**
   The first command, `ip address 192.168.100.1 255.255.255.0`, sets the ip address and subnet mask of the interface. The second command, `no shutdown`, tells the router that the interface is in use.

5. **Select the second interface**
   Type the command `exit`, then the command `interface feth0/1`. This will switch us to the other interface so we can set it up too.

6. **Set the address and start the second interface**
   The first command, `ip address 192.168.101.1 255.255.255.0`, sets the ip address and subnet mask of the second interface.

7. **Exit from programming mode and save our setup**
   Type `exit` twice, then `write mem` to save our configuration to non-volatile memory. Our router is now configured to route between the 192.168.100.0 and 192.168.101.0 networks.

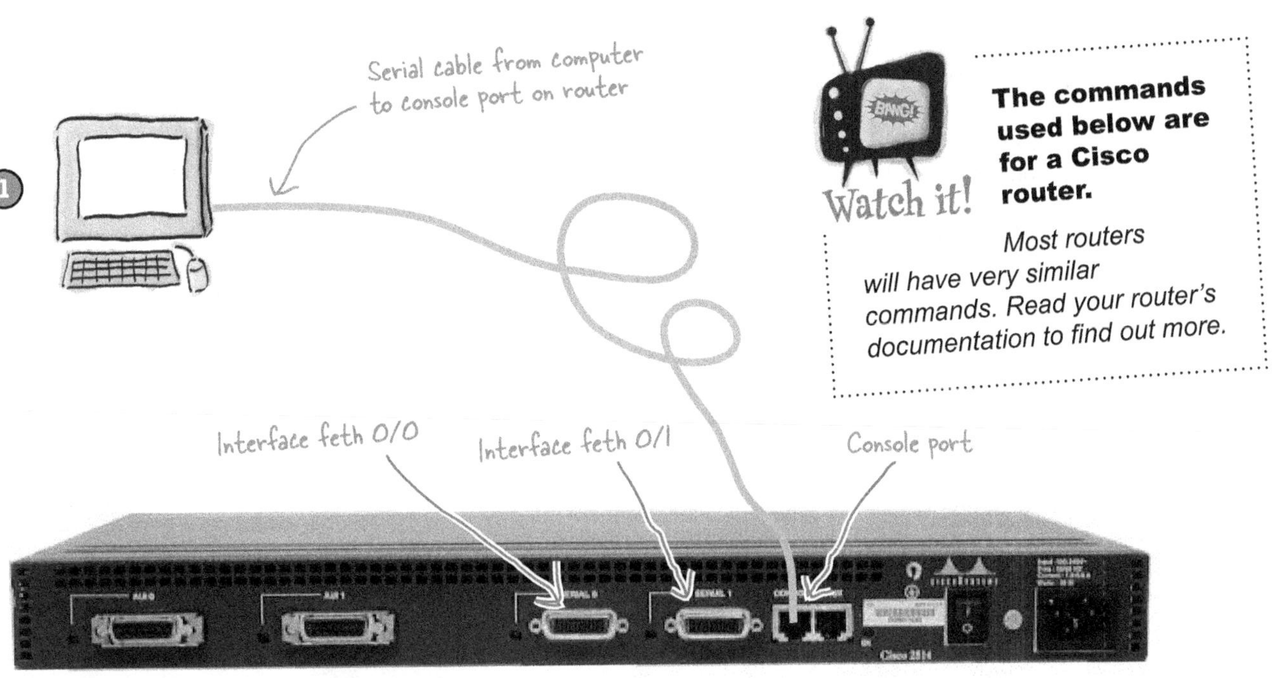

Watch it!

The commands used below are for a Cisco router.

Most routers will have very similar commands. Read your router's documentation to find out more.

File Edit Window Help There'sNoAtmosphere

```
router> enable
router# configure terminal
router(config)#interface feth0/0
router(int-feth0/0)#ip address 192.168.100.1 255.255.255.0
router(int-feth0/0)#no shutdown
router(int-feth0/0)#exit
router(config)#interface feth0/1
router(int-feth0/1)#ip address 192.168.101.1 255.255.255.
router(int-feth0/1)#exit
router(config)#exit
router#write mem
```

(Margin markers: 2 = enable / configure terminal; 3 = interface feth0/0; 4 = ip address / no shutdown; 5 = exit / interface feth0/1; 6 = ip address 192.168.101.1; 7 = exit / exit / write mem)

So what did this do?

You just created this router config file!

On the previous page, when you exited the configuration mode, the router wrote all those commands to the "running-configuration" file. When you typed the `write mem` command, you saved the running-configuration to the startup-configuration which is generally stored in flash memory.

```
!
ver 12.3
!
interface FastEthernet0/0
   ip address 192.168.100.1 255.255.255.0
   no shutdown
!
interface FastEthernet0/1
   ip address 192.168.101.1 255.255.255.0
!
end
```

Comment

Version of the router operating system

Your configuration commands

Lets the router operating system know that this is the end of the config file

So has this sorted out all the problems?

Routers can download their configuration files from network file servers like tftp servers. You can also create a configuration file with a text editor then upload it to the router using the same type of service.

Well, the router is all hooked up and the interfaces configured. But is still doesn't look like there's any Internet traffic.

Frank: I can see the computers are trying to send traffic, but the router just doesn't seem to be doing anything with that traffic.

Jim: I wonder whether it's a problem with the router configuration. What do you think?

Frank: It looks OK to me, but I don't really know that much about router configurations.

Jim: We could do with a way of getting diagnostic information from the router. Something like that could really help us out here.

Frank: Routers are pretty intelligent, so there must be some sort of command that will show us information on the interfaces.

So how do we get diagnostic information from the router?

Let the router tell us what's wrong...

You can get a lot of information from routers. Sometimes too much. What is important is to find *useful* information. At first looking at all the statistics can be a bit overwhelming, but most problems tends to be rather simple ones. So look for the "low hanging fruit."

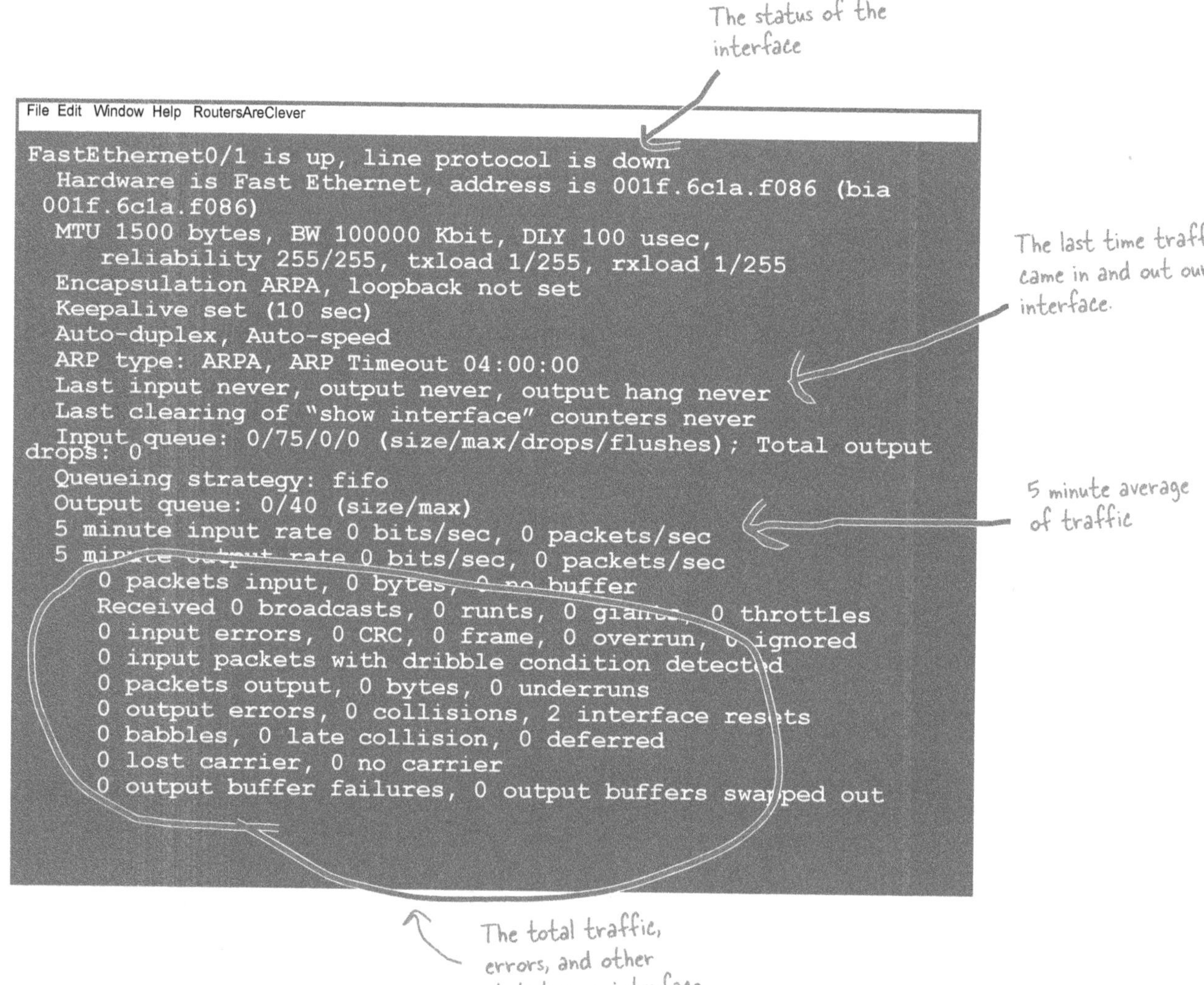

The status of the interface
File Edit Window Help RoutersAreClever
FastEthernet0/1 is up, line protocol is down
Hardware is Fast Ethernet, address is 001f.6c1a.f086 (bia 001f.6c1a.f086)
MTU 1500 bytes, BW 100000 Kbit, DLY 100 usec,
reliability 255/255, txload 1/255, rxload 1/255
Encapsulation ARPA, loopback not set
Keepalive set (10 sec)
Auto-duplex, Auto-speed
ARP type: ARPA, ARP Timeout 04:00:00
Last input never, output never, output hang never
Last clearing of "show interface" counters never
Input queue: 0/75/0/0 (size/max/drops/flushes); Total output drops: 0
Queueing strategy: fifo
Output queue: 0/40 (size/max)
5 minute input rate 0 bits/sec, 0 packets/sec
5 minute output rate 0 bits/sec, 0 packets/sec
0 packets input, 0 bytes, 0 no buffer
Received 0 broadcasts, 0 runts, 0 giants, 0 throttles
0 input errors, 0 CRC, 0 frame, 0 overrun, 0 ignored
0 input packets with dribble condition detected
0 packets output, 0 bytes, 0 underruns
0 output errors, 0 collisions, 2 interface resets
0 babbles, 0 late collision, 0 deferred
0 lost carrier, 0 no carrier
0 output buffer failures, 0 output buffers swapped out
The last time traffic came in and out our interface.
5 minute average of traffic
The total traffic, errors, and other statistics on interface

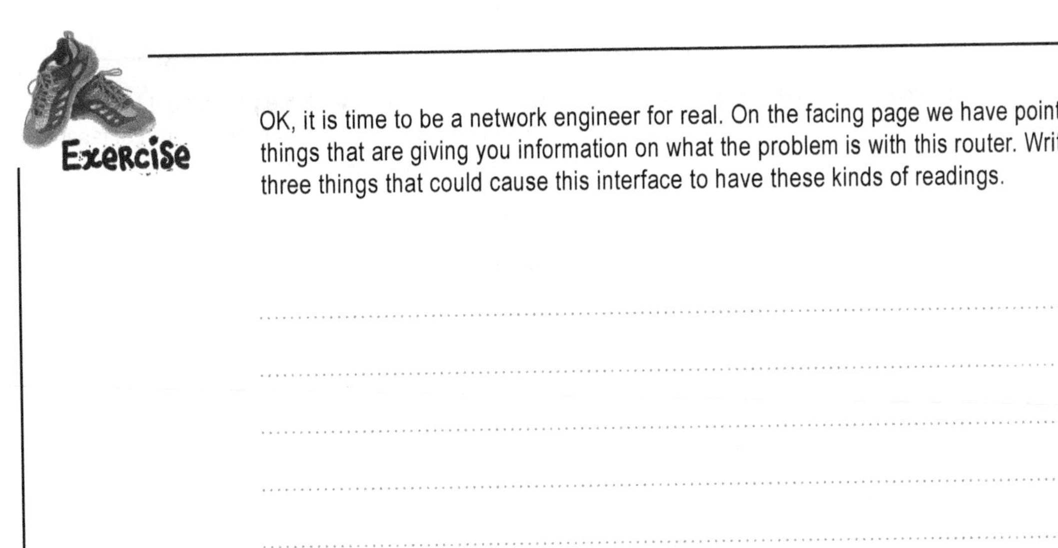

Exercise

OK, it is time to be a network engineer for real. On the facing page we have pointed out four things that are giving you information on what the problem is with this router. Write down at least three things that could cause this interface to have these kinds of readings.

there are no Dumb Questions

Q: Do routers have anything configured when they are new?

A: When you get a new router, there is no configuration on it at all. You have decided how to connect the router up and how it is going to connect between networks.

Q: Does it matter which network interface it's connected to?

A: It depends on the physical network cabling. If you are connecting 2 Ethernet networks, then it really does not matter. However, if you are connecting an Ethernet network to another network through a T-1 line, then you must use a serial interface.

Q: Routers can have more than one interface type?

A: Routers come with many different network interface types. This includes Ethernet, Token Ring, serial, wireless, ATM, DSL. The list goes on and on. If there are bits traveling on a physical media, there is a router to move those bits to another physical media.

Q: Can a single router have multiple interface types?

A: Yes, as many as you are willing to pay for. Also, a router can have different physical media (fiber, copper, radio waves) for a given protocol like Ethernet. Ethernet can travel over fiber or copper lines.

Q: What are the most common router problems?

A: Most router problems are related to a problem with physical media. Once a router is configured properly, generally the only thing that will cause problems is broken cables, disconnected cables, interference, etc. When a network with routers is configured, it can run for years without issues.

OK, it is time to be a network engineer for real. On the facing page we have pointed out four things that are giving you information on what the problem is with this router. Write down at least three things that could cause this interface to have these kinds of readings.

There is no traffic, so for some reason the interface is not getting traffic.

1. The cable could be broken
2. It could be a bad connector
3. The device on the other end could be down
4. The interface could be shutdown (look at the config file you created!)

Hello from the ISS. I guess you got the video conferencing working. I'm just finishing up some work here...

7 routing protocols

It's a Matter of Protocol

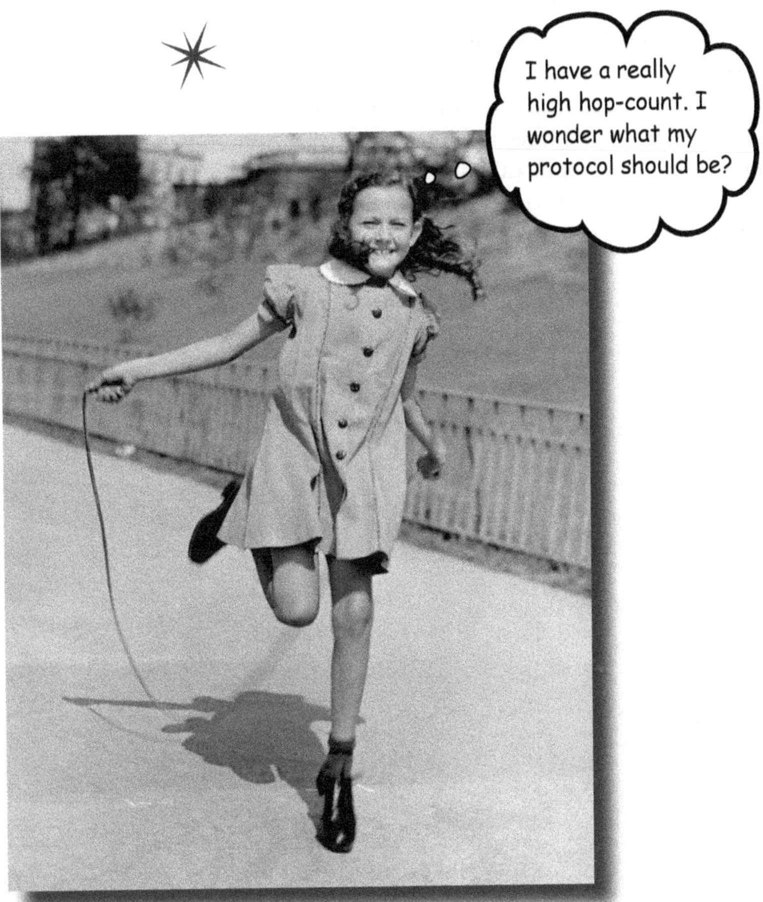

I have a really high hop-count. I wonder what my protocol should be?

To build big networks, you need to use routers and they have to talk to each other.

Routers need to exchange routes with each other. They use various routing protocols to exchange routes. In the chapter, you will first see how to manually enter a route, then you will learn how to implement the simple RIP routing protocol. Finally you will learn how to setup EIGRP, an advanced routing protocol.

Houston, we have a problem...

So far, you've successfully hooked up the Moonbase network so that it can communicate with the ISS. There's just one problem: there are actually *20* bases on the moon, and all the different moonbases need to keep in contact with each other through their network links in case they get into trouble. So is this possible?

When the international community started building the moonbases, they wisely decided to run fiber optic cables to all of the different moonbases. Each moonbase is directly connected to at least one other moonbase, and indirectly connected to all the others through the web of fiber optic cables. As an example, Moonbase 1 is directly connected to three other moonbases, and indirectly connected to all 20 others.

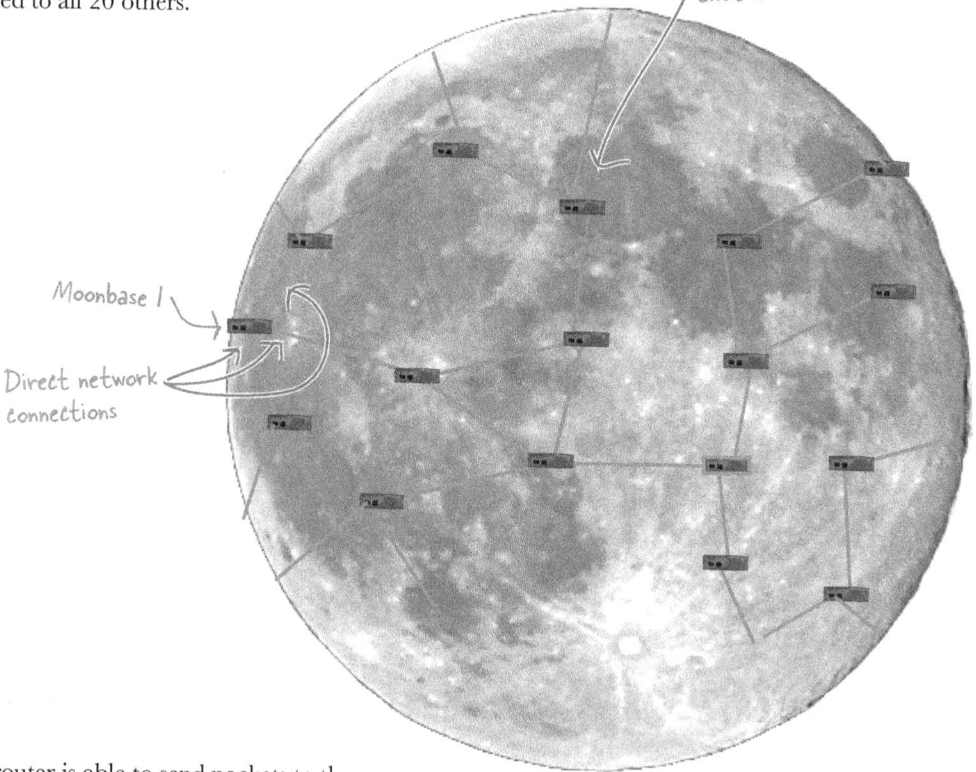

Moonbase 1 is indirectly connected to this router via another router.
Moonbase 1
Direct network connections

The Moonbase 1 router is able to send packets to the moonbases it's directly connected to, but it can't communicate with any of the other 18 moonbases it's only connected to indirectly.

So how do we get routers to communicate with each other when they're not directly connected?

Routing tables tell routers where to send packets

When two routers share a common IP network space or network address, they can automatically route packets to each other. But what about when routers aren't connected to each other directly?

When routers aren't directly connected to each other, they need to know how to send packets to the other router. They get this information from routing tables, tables which are stored in the memory of the router.

We can see routes in the table using the show command

To see the route table on a router, you need to use the `show` command. On a typical router such as a Cisco, you would run the `show ip route` command.

These codes tell you how the router knows about the routes.

File Edit Window Help TheAngelsHaveThePhoneBox

```
router1#show ip route
Codes: C - connected, S - static, R - RIP, M - mobile, B - BGP
       D - EIGRP, EX - EIGRP external, O - OSPF, IA - OSPF inter area
       N1 - OSPF NSSA external type 1, N2 - OSPF NSSA external type 2
       E1 - OSPF external type 1, E2 - OSPF external type 2
       i - IS-IS, su - IS-IS summary, L1 - IS-IS level-1, L2 - IS-IS level-2
       ia - IS-IS inter area, * - candidate default, U - per-user static
route
       o - ODR, P - periodic downloaded static route

Gateway of last resort is 209.137.230.1 to network 0.0.0.0

D     204.62.205.0/24 [90/30720] via 209.137.230.124, 2d18h, FastEthernet0/0
      209.137.230.0/25 is subnetted, 1 subnets
C        209.137.230.0 is directly connected, FastEthernet0/0
C     204.62.201.0/24 is directly connected, FastEthernet0/1
C     172.17.0.0/16 is directly connected, FastEthernet0/1
D     172.16.0.0/16 [90/30720] via 209.137.230.3, 2d19h, FastEthernet0/0
D     172.19.0.0/16 [90/30720] via 209.137.230.124, 2d18h, FastEthernet0/0
D     204.62.203.0/24 [90/30720] via 209.137.230.3, 2d19h, FastEthernet0/0
S*    0.0.0.0/0 [1/0] via 209.137.230.1
router1#
```

Let's take a look at what the contents of the routing table actually mean.

Each line represents a different route

The route table is a type of address book for the router. It looks at a packet's destination IP address, then looks that up in its routing table. Based on that lookup, it sends the packet to the right place.

Each line in the routing table has two parts. The first part is a letter which tells how the route was established. The second part tells the router how to get to the route. The route table is constantly kept up-to-date by the router so it knows where to send packets.

The destination IP network

Whether the network is directly connected, or accessed indirectly via another router

The address of the interface, or the other router

```
D     204.62.204.0/24 [90/30720] via 209.137.230.22, 09:52:06, FastEthernet0/0
D     204.62.205.0/24 [90/30720] via 209.137.230.124, 4d12h, FastEthernet0/0
C     209.137.230.0 is directly connected, FastEthernet0/0
C     204.62.201.0/24 is directly connected, FastEthernet0/1
C     172.17.0.0/16 is directly connected, FastEthernet0/1
D     172.16.0.0/16 [90/30720] via 209.137.230.3, 7w0d, FastEthernet0/0
D     172.19.0.0/16 [90/30720] via 209.137.230.124, 4d12h, FastEthernet0/0
D     172.18.0.0/16 [90/30720] via 209.137.230.22, 09:52:06, FastEthernet0/0
D     204.62.203.0/24 [90/30720] via 209.137.230.3, 7w0d, FastEthernet0/0
S*    0.0.0.0/0 [1/0] via 209.137.230.1
```

How the router got the route

How does a router **learn** about routes if they are not entered or directly connected?

The letter tells you how
they get in there, but
what do the letters mean?

Routes in a table come from several sources.

When you assign an IP address to an interface, this automatically places an entry in the routing table for that IP network. These are the routes that are **directly connected** and have a C in the front of their table entry. Routes that are entered by hand are static and have a S in front of them. Finally routes that are learned have different letters based on how the route was learned.

The simplest way to get routes into a table is just type them in. Those are called static routes because they don't change unless you change them.

These letters tell you how the particular network route got into the table.

Route table

```
D    204.62.204.0/24 [90/30720] via 209.137.230.22
D    204.62.205.0/24 [90/30720] via 209.137.230.12
C    209.137.230.0 is directly connected, FastEth
C    204.62.201.0/24 is directly connected, FastEt
C    172.17.0.0/16 is directly connected, FastEth
D    172.16.0.0/16 [90/30720] via 209.137.230.3, 7
D    172.19.0.0/16 [90/30720] via 209.137.230.124,
D    172.18.0.0/16 [90/30720] via 209.137.230.22,
```

So how do we enter routes?

The first thing you need to do is get a connection to the router. You can either ssh into the router via the network or connect with a serial cable. You did this in Chapter 6.

1. **At the router's console, issue the command `enable`**
   This puts the router into the privileged mode. You will probably need a password.

2. **At the router's console, issue the command `config t`**
   This puts the router into configuration mode.

3. **Type `ip route 192.168.102.0 255.255.255.0 eth0/1 192.168.101.1`**
   This command enters a static route for the 192.168.102.0 network into the route table. This network is reached via the eth0/1 interface, and the router that can deal with that network is 192.168.101.1.

4. **Type `exit`**
   This exits the router from configuration mode.

5. **Type `write memory`**
   This saves our new configuration to memory.

Routes help routers figure out where to send network traffic

So you need to enter all the network addresses that you want your router to be able to send traffic to.

You can't possibly enter all the networks of the world into your router's table.

You have to set a default gateway. This is the location, another router, where your router sends all the traffic it does not know where to send.

Sharpen your pencil

Here are three routers. See if you can fill in the two missing IP addresses on the lines in the routing tables below to get the packets flowing between the computers via the routers.

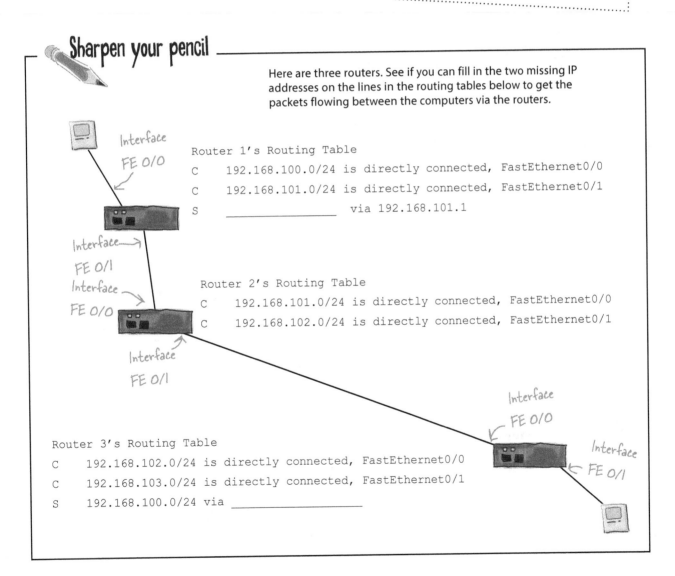

Interface FE 0/0

Interface FE 0/1

Interface FE 0/0

Interface FE 0/1

Interface FE 0/0

Interface FE 0/1

```
Router 1's Routing Table
C    192.168.100.0/24 is directly connected, FastEthernet0/0
C    192.168.101.0/24 is directly connected, FastEthernet0/1
S    ________________    via 192.168.101.1
```

```
Router 2's Routing Table
C    192.168.101.0/24 is directly connected, FastEthernet0/0
C    192.168.102.0/24 is directly connected, FastEthernet0/1
```

```
Router 3's Routing Table
C    192.168.102.0/24 is directly connected, FastEthernet0/0
C    192.168.103.0/24 is directly connected, FastEthernet0/1
S    192.168.100.0/24 via ____________________
```

Sharpen your pencil Solution

Here are three routers. See if you can fill in the two missing IP addresses on the lines in the routing tables below to get the packets flowing between the routers.

For the client connected to this router to send traffic to the other client, this router needs to know how to send traffic to the 192.168.102.0 network.

Interface FE 0/0

Interface FE 0/1

Router 1's Routing Table

```
C    192.168.100.0/24 is directly connected, FastEthernet0/0
C    192.168.101.0/24 is directly connected, FastEthernet0/1
S    192.168.102.0/24    via 192.168.101.1
```

Interface FE 0/0

Interface FE 0/1

Router 2's Routing Table

```
C    192.168.101.0/24 is directly connected, FastEthernet0/0
C    192.168.102.0/24 is directly connected, FastEthernet0/1
```

Interface FE 0/0

Interface FE 0/1

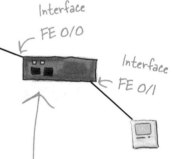

Router 3's Routing Table

```
C    192.168.102.0/24 is directly connected, FastEthernet0/0
C    192.168.103.0/24 is directly connected, FastEthernet0/1
S    192.168.100.0/24 via 192.168.102.1
```

For the client connected to this router to send traffic to the other client, this router needs to know how to send traffic to the 192.168.100.0 network.

Watch it!

Computers are not generally connected directly to a router.

Usually there is a switch or hub in-between them.

Exercise

Create routing tables from scratch for each router in the network below.

```
Router 1's Routing Table
C       ________________   is directly connected,
C       ________________   is directly connected,
S       ________________   via 192.168.1.2
S       ________________   via 192.168.4.1
```

```
Router 2's Routing Table
C       ________________   is directly connec
C       ________________   is directly connec
S       ________________   via 192.168.1.1
S       ________________   via 192.168.2.2
```

```
Router 4's Routing Table
C       ________________   is directly conne
C       ________________   is directly conne
S       ________________   via 192.168.4.2
S       ________________   via 192.168.3.1
```

```
Router 3's Routing Table
C       ________________   is directly connec
C       ________________   is directly connect
S       ________________   via 192.168.2.1
S       ________________   via 192.168.3.2
```

Exercise Solution

Create routing tables from scratch for each router in the network below.

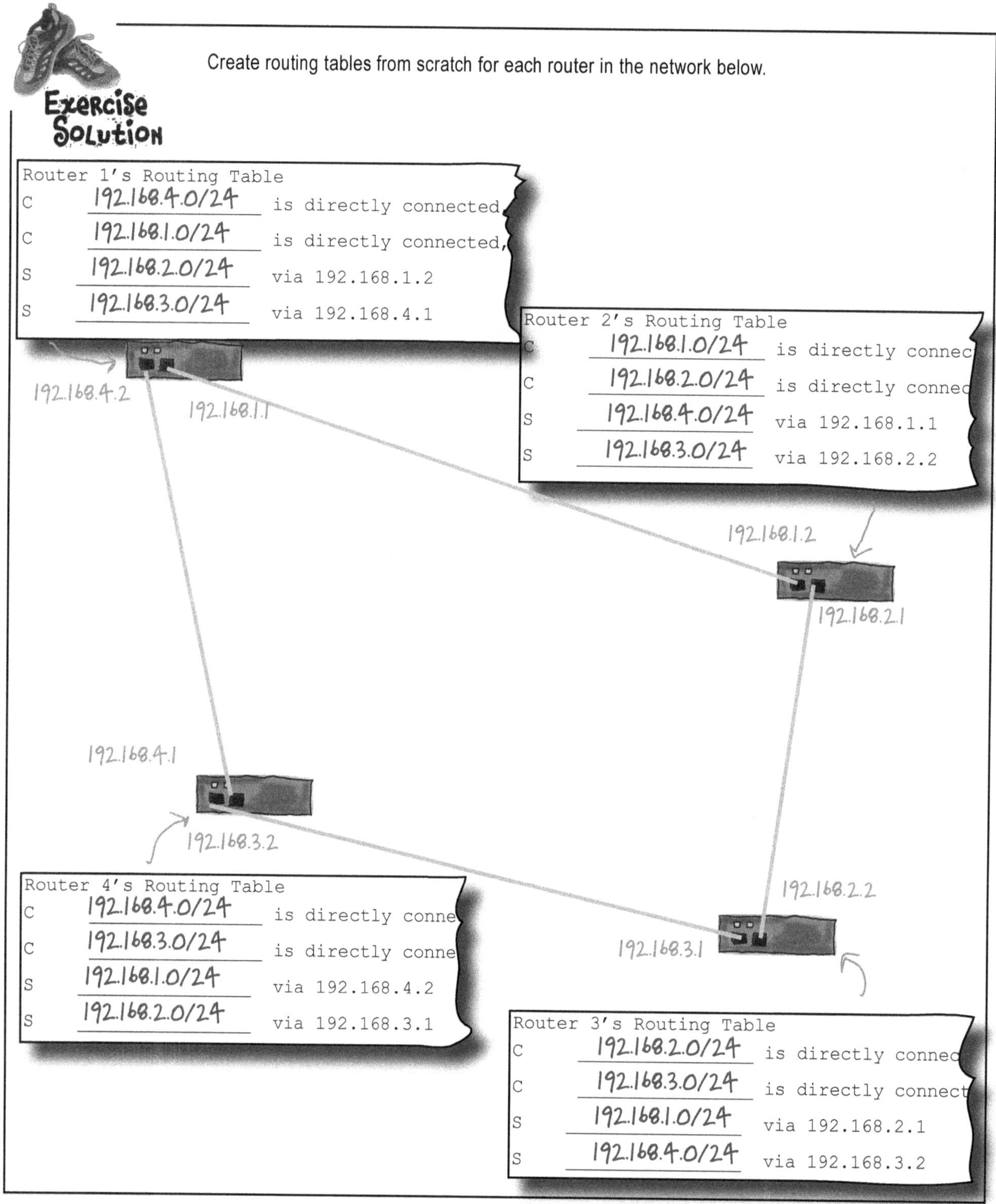
Router 1's Routing Table
C 192.168.4.0/24 is directly connected,
C 192.168.1.0/24 is directly connected,
S 192.168.2.0/24 via 192.168.1.2
S 192.168.3.0/24 via 192.168.4.1
Router 2's Routing Table
C 192.168.1.0/24 is directly connec
C 192.168.2.0/24 is directly connec
S 192.168.4.0/24 via 192.168.1.1
S 192.168.3.0/24 via 192.168.2.2
192.168.4.2
192.168.1.1
192.168.1.2
192.168.2.1
192.168.4.1
192.168.3.2
192.168.2.2
192.168.3.1
Router 4's Routing Table
C 192.168.4.0/24 is directly conne
C 192.168.3.0/24 is directly conne
S 192.168.1.0/24 via 192.168.4.2
S 192.168.2.0/24 via 192.168.3.1
Router 3's Routing Table
C 192.168.2.0/24 is directly connec
C 192.168.3.0/24 is directly connect
S 192.168.1.0/24 via 192.168.2.1
S 192.168.4.0/24 via 192.168.3.2

So are the moonbases now connected?

Let's try sending a message from a computer at Moonbase 1 to a computer on Moonbase 3 and see what happens.

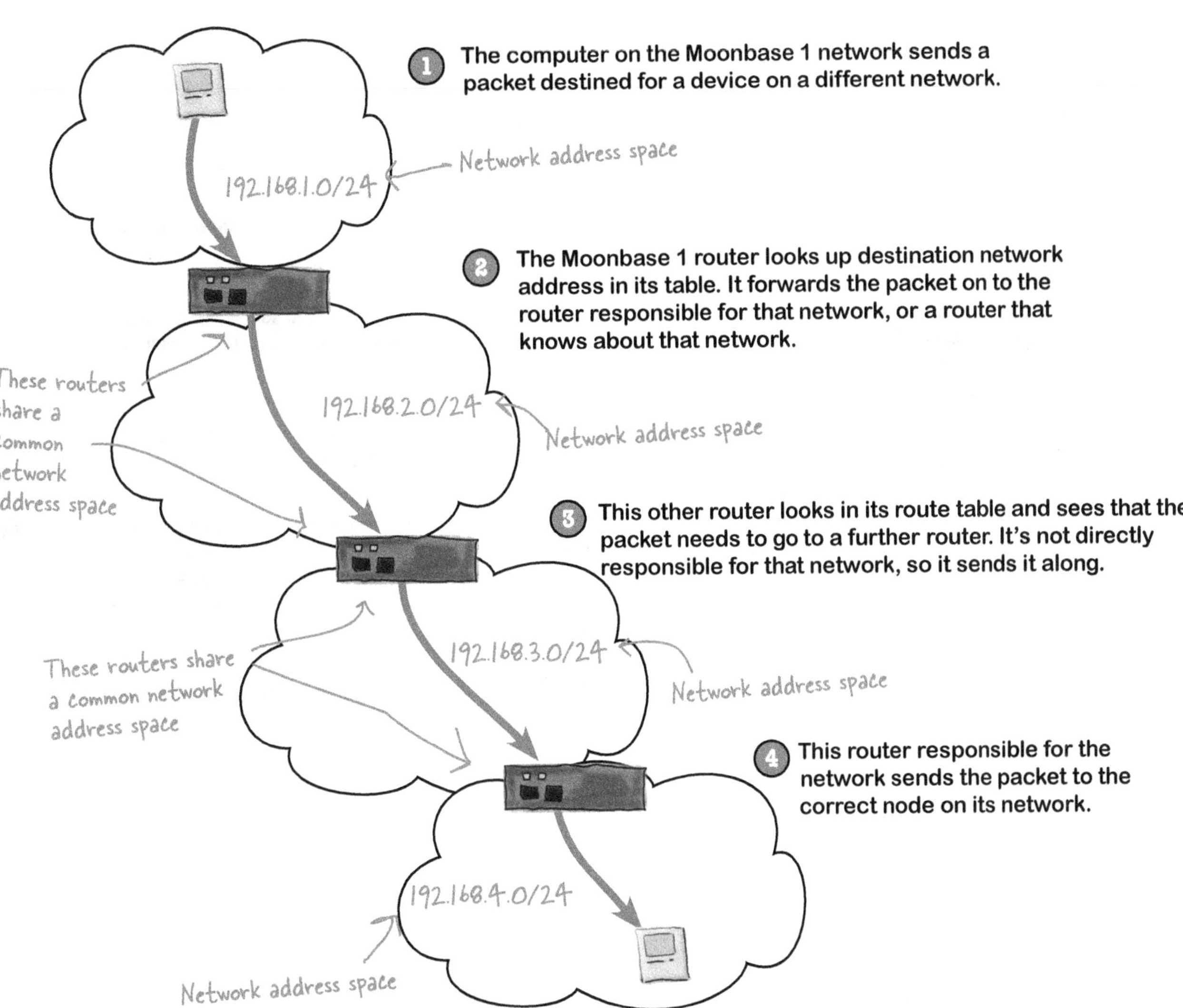

1 The computer on the Moonbase 1 network sends a packet destined for a device on a different network.
192.168.1.0/24
Network address space
2 The Moonbase 1 router looks up destination network address in its table. It forwards the packet on to the router responsible for that network, or a router that knows about that network.
These routers share a common network address space
192.168.2.0/24
Network address space
3 This other router looks in its route table and sees that the packet needs to go to a further router. It's not directly responsible for that network, so it sends it along.
These routers share a common network address space
192.168.3.0/24
Network address space
4 This router responsible for the network sends the packet to the correct node on its network.
192.168.4.0/24
Network address space

there are no Dumb Questions

Q: What do you mean by interface?

A: Interfaces are the physical network connections that a router has installed. These can be Ethernet RJ-45 type connectors, serial connectors, or even fiber optic connectors.

Q: What is the 0/0 and 0/1 in the interface name?

A: The first 0 represents the interface card in a router. Many routers support multiple interface cards, and each card can have multiple connections. So the second number represents that actual interface on a given interface card. So 0/1 refers to the number 1 interface on the number 0 card installed in the router. If the router has other cards, you could see interface numbers like 1/1.

Q: In the "via" bit, do I need to specify something that the router's directly linked to?

A: When you enter a static route, you need to specify the IP address of the router that will handle that network route. It is optional to enter the interface number as well.

Q: Does the routing table just contain IP addresses of routers? What about other devices?

A: Yes, it contains only IP addresses of other routers. Remember, the route table tells the router where to send network traffic to another network. So it is saying "to send network traffic to network X, you have to send it via router V, which knows how to send traffic to network X.

No other device addresses are entered into a route table.

Back on the moon...

Moonbase 1 calling Moonbase 16, can you hear me? Hello? Anybody there? Hellooooooo!

Moonbase 1 still has problems

The Moonbase 1 routing table has been populated with all the static routes to the other moonbases, but unfortunately, network traffic isn't getting through to one particular moon base. So what's wrong?

How do we troubleshoot routes if the data isn't getting through?

So how do we troubleshoot bad routes?

If there's a problem on an interface, the router can tell you whether the interface is up or down. But there isn't really much it can tell you about a static route. It doesn't know if the route is up or down; all it knows is that it can't send traffic via it when it is down. Fortunately, there's something that can help you—the **ping** command.

The ping command tells you if the network and host are reachable.

We can start with the ping command

The `ping` command is a great command line utility that can help you troubleshoot bad routes. It basically tells you whether or not the network and host are reachable. To use the ping command, type `ping` at a command prompt, followed by the IP address you want to check.

Here's an example:

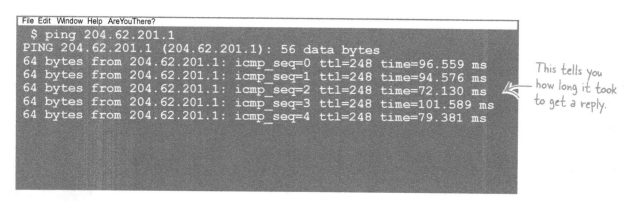

```
File Edit Window Help AreYouThere?
 $ ping 204.62.201.1
PING 204.62.201.1 (204.62.201.1): 56 data bytes
64 bytes from 204.62.201.1: icmp_seq=0 ttl=248 time=96.559 ms
64 bytes from 204.62.201.1: icmp_seq=1 ttl=248 time=94.576 ms
64 bytes from 204.62.201.1: icmp_seq=2 ttl=248 time=72.130 ms
64 bytes from 204.62.201.1: icmp_seq=3 ttl=248 time=101.589 ms
64 bytes from 204.62.201.1: icmp_seq=4 ttl=248 time=79.381 ms
```

This tells you how long it took to get a reply.

So how does the ping command work?

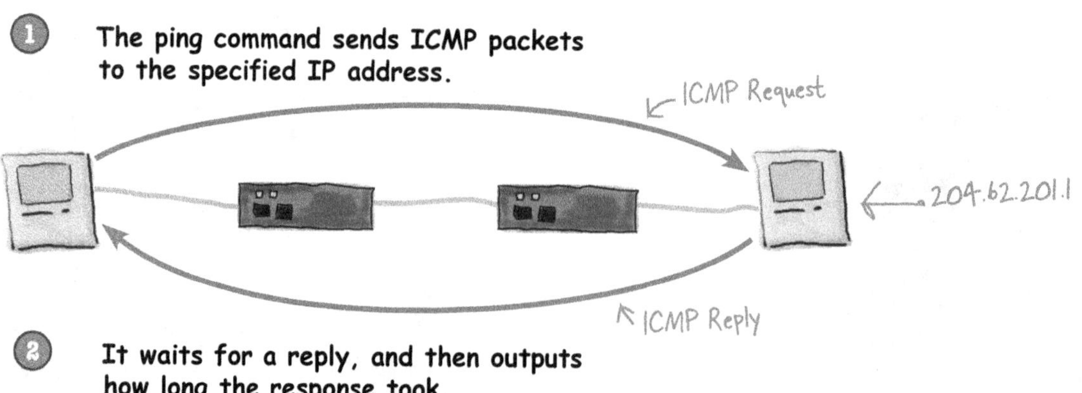
1 The ping command sends ICMP packets to the specified IP address.
ICMP Request
204.62.201.1
ICMP Reply
2 It waits for a reply, and then outputs how long the response took.

The traceroute command is useful too

The traceroute command traces the route that the packets take to get to the destination IP address. This route is represented by the IP addresses of the routers in-between the sending host and the destination IP address.

Here's an example:

The traceroute command shows you the route your packets take to get to an IP address.

```
File Edit Window Help WhereDidItGo?
$ traceroute 204.62.201.70
traceroute to 204.62.201.1 (204.62.201.1), 64 hops max, 40 byte packets
 1  204.62.203.254  1.318 ms  0.750 ms  0.688 ms
 2  209.137.230.2  1.460 ms  1.243 ms  1.153 ms
 3  204.62.201.70  0.890 ms !<10>  0.832 ms !<10>  0.833 ms !<10>
```

1. Traceroute from client A sends a block of three packets with a value of 1 in their time-to-live (TTL) field to client D.

2. Router B responds with a ICMP packet back to the client A because the packets have a TTL of 1.

3. Traceroute from client A then sends a second block of three packets with a value of 2 in their time-to-live (TTL) field to client D. Router B changes the packets TTL to 1 and sends them on the Router C.

4. Router C responds with a ICMP packet back to the client A because the packets have a TTL of 1.

5. Traceroute from client A then sends a third block of three packets with a value of 3 in their time-to-live (TTL) field to client D. Router B changes the packets' TTL to 2 and sends them on the Router C, which changes the packets' TTL to 1 and sends them on to client D. Client D sends an IMCP packet back to client A.

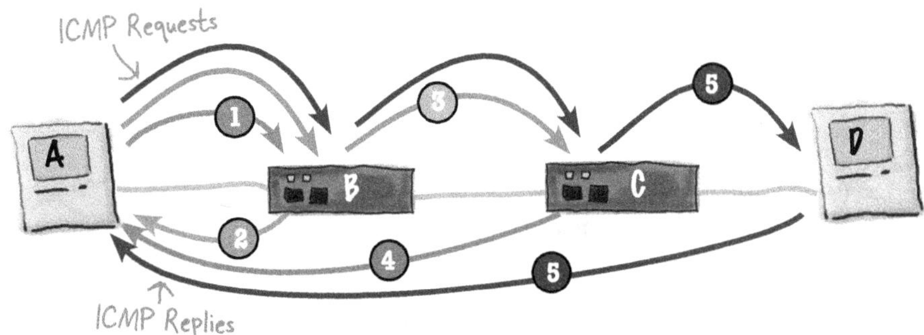

Let's see if we can use these tools to help us troubleshoot the Moonbase 1 routes.

there are no Dumb Questions

Q: Can I ping any IP address on the Internet?

A: Yes, you can. Whether you get a reply is another question. Many times firewalls block ping packets. So you will not see any reply in that case.

Q: When I ping some of the example addresses in the book, sometimes I get a response, and sometimes I don't.

A: Remember private IP addresess back in Chapter 6? Well most of the addresses we use in the book are private IP addresses. On your home network, some of these might be used by your local router, or your ISP might be using them as well.

Q: It seems like you could write a program to constantly ping some devices on the network and alert you when the pings fail. Would this be a cool tool or what!

A: There are many tools like this. Nmap is one such tool. Nagio is another. Nmap is a network scanner. You enter in a range of IP addresses to scan, and it lets you know if there is a machine there or not. Nagios is more of a monitoring tool like you described above. It can alert you when devices go off line.

Q: Can I control how many ping packets I send?

A: Good question. Yes, you can. Many ping program have different options that control how many packets you send or even what information is inside the ping packets. Type ping --help or ping /h to find out more.

Q: Are those times on the return ping packets very important?

A: A good network engineer learns what the various ping times around her network are. We are not saying you should memorize them, but you should have a good feel for what the times should be roughly. That way, when things go out of whack, with some simple pinging, you can tell what is and isn't behaving properly.

Q: Isn't traceroute a fancy ping?

A: Well traceroute sends ICMP packets just like ping does, but it is doing something totally different in that it sends out those series of packets to get the routers to respond in-between you and the destination.

Q: Sometimes my traceroutes seem to hang up then all of a sudden start going again. What is that all about?

A: If you are having traceroute look up the DNS names of the routers, sometimes those routers don't have DNS entries, so your ping command has to wait for the DNS request to timeout. This can take a bit. Plus, if it is doing this on a number of routers, it can really take some time. Run the traceroute command with the -n flag to turn off DNS lookups.

Q: Sometimes I see a little star when I run the traceroute command. Does the little star mean that the router is down?

A: No, often it means that the routers is configured to not respond to ICMP packets. This is done as a security measure.

Q: So each router along the path to the destination has to respond for my command to work?

A: No, traceroute will just timeout the packets going to that device and move on to the next one until it gets to the destination.

Q: How does it know when it gets to the destination?

A: Simple, it just keeps incrementing the TTL of the ICMP packets until it gets a response from the destination IP address.

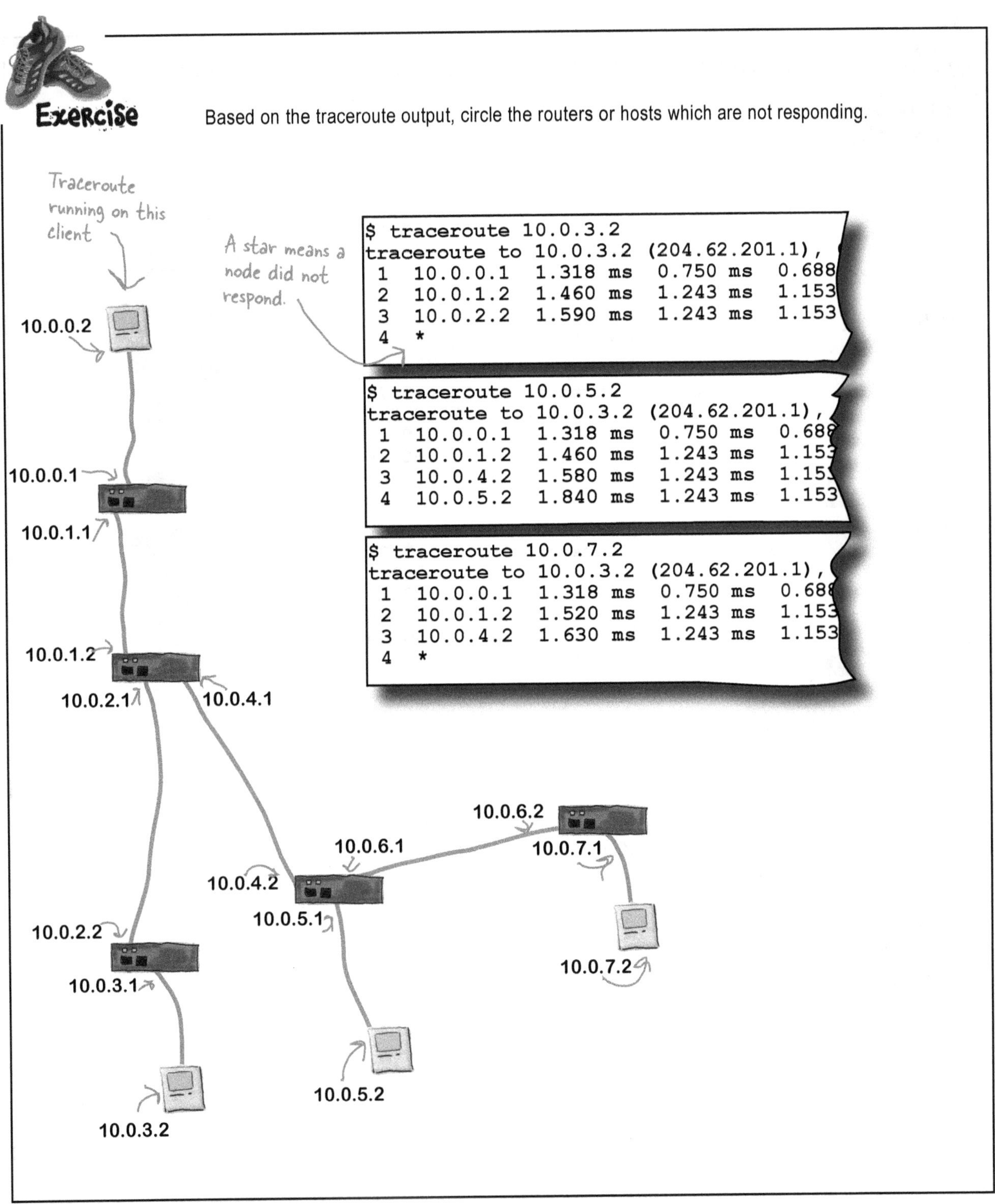
Exercise
Based on the traceroute output, circle the routers or hosts which are not responding.
Traceroute running on this client
A star means a node did not respond.
$ traceroute 10.0.3.2
traceroute to 10.0.3.2 (204.62.201.1),
1 10.0.0.1 1.318 ms 0.750 ms 0.688
2 10.0.1.2 1.460 ms 1.243 ms 1.153
3 10.0.2.2 1.590 ms 1.243 ms 1.153
4 *
$ traceroute 10.0.5.2
traceroute to 10.0.3.2 (204.62.201.1),
1 10.0.0.1 1.318 ms 0.750 ms 0.688
2 10.0.1.2 1.460 ms 1.243 ms 1.153
3 10.0.4.2 1.580 ms 1.243 ms 1.153
4 10.0.5.2 1.840 ms 1.243 ms 1.153
$ traceroute 10.0.7.2
traceroute to 10.0.3.2 (204.62.201.1),
1 10.0.0.1 1.318 ms 0.750 ms 0.688
2 10.0.1.2 1.520 ms 1.243 ms 1.153
3 10.0.4.2 1.630 ms 1.243 ms 1.153
4 *
10.0.0.2
10.0.0.1
10.0.1.1
10.0.1.2
10.0.2.1
10.0.4.1
10.0.6.2
10.0.6.1
10.0.7.1
10.0.4.2
10.0.5.1
10.0.2.2
10.0.3.1
10.0.7.2
10.0.5.2
10.0.3.2

Exercise Solution

Based on the traceroute output, circle the routers or hosts which are not responding.

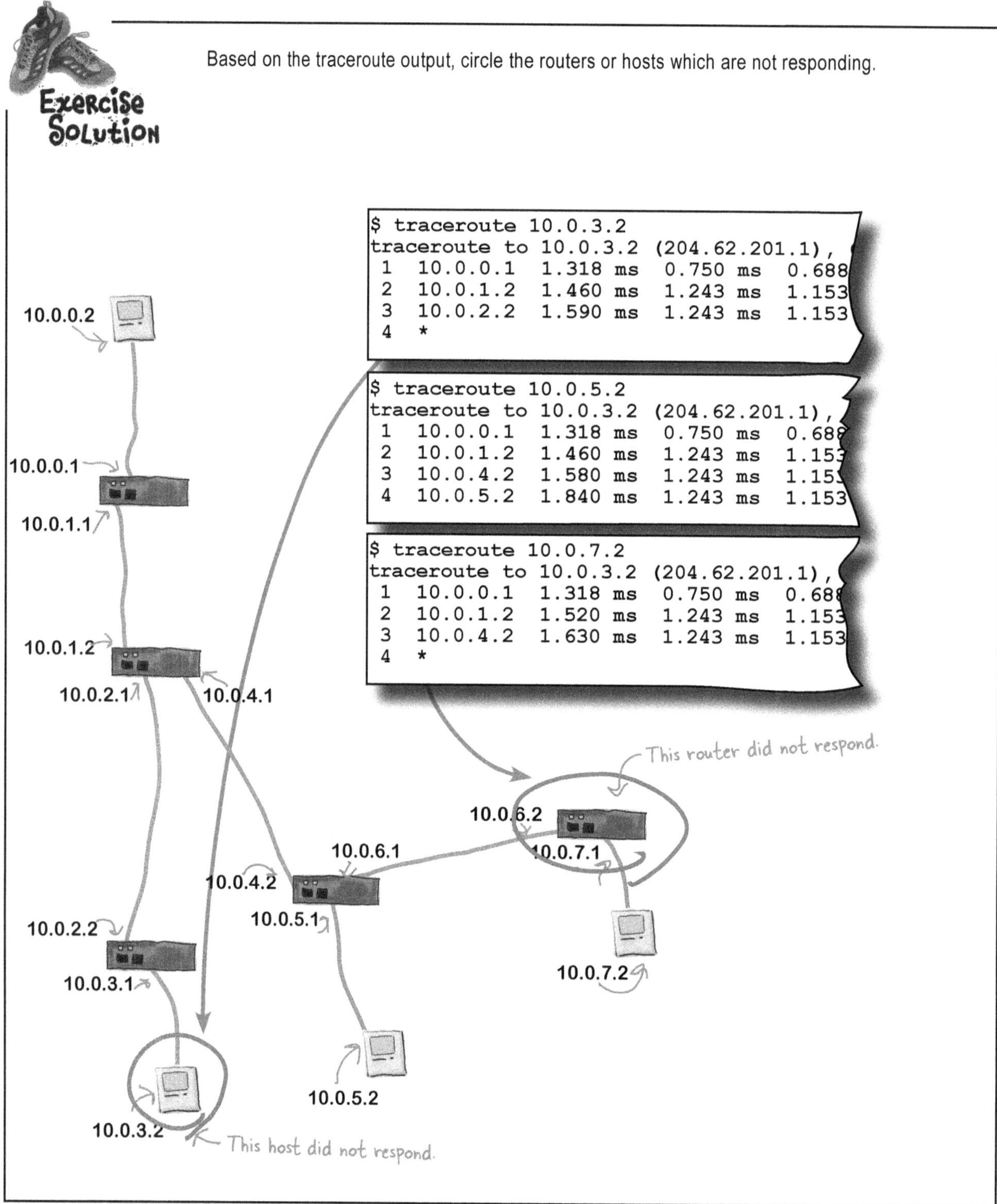

$ traceroute 10.0.3.2
traceroute to 10.0.3.2 (204.62.201.1),
1 10.0.0.1 1.318 ms 0.750 ms 0.688
2 10.0.1.2 1.460 ms 1.243 ms 1.153
3 10.0.2.2 1.590 ms 1.243 ms 1.153
4 *
$ traceroute 10.0.5.2
traceroute to 10.0.3.2 (204.62.201.1),
1 10.0.0.1 1.318 ms 0.750 ms 0.688
2 10.0.1.2 1.460 ms 1.243 ms 1.153
3 10.0.4.2 1.580 ms 1.243 ms 1.153
4 10.0.5.2 1.840 ms 1.243 ms 1.153
$ traceroute 10.0.7.2
traceroute to 10.0.3.2 (204.62.201.1),
1 10.0.0.1 1.318 ms 0.750 ms 0.688
2 10.0.1.2 1.520 ms 1.243 ms 1.153
3 10.0.4.2 1.630 ms 1.243 ms 1.153
4 *
10.0.0.2
10.0.0.1
10.0.1.1
10.0.1.2
10.0.2.1
10.0.4.1
This router did not respond.
10.0.6.2
10.0.7.1
10.0.6.1
10.0.4.2
10.0.5.1
10.0.2.2
10.0.3.1
10.0.7.2
10.0.5.2
10.0.3.2
This host did not respond.

So what's the problem with the network connection?

Unfortunately for Moonbase 1, it looks like Moonbase 16 and Moonbase 17 changed the network address their routers were using. As the Moonbase 1 router only had the old network addresses in the routing table as a static route, this meant that the router no longer knew where to send network traffic destined for these two networks.

So how do we fix this?

When there are changes to routes, you have to modify those routes in your router's route table to keep it current.

Well, that's easy. All we have to do is change the route in the routing table for the changed network addresses.

Static routes don't change automatically.

This means that if you have static routes in your routing table, you need to change them manually

What sorts of problems do you anticipate with this?

The network address changes keep on coming...

Unfortunately, they aren't the only moonbases to change their network addresses. With all the growth on the moon, other moonbases are changing their network configurations too. Before too long, Moonbase 1 is swamped with notifications from other moonbases that their network addresses have changed too.

To: Moonbase 1
Subject: Network changes
From: Moonbase 19
Just to let you know that we're now routing 10.1.67.0/24 instead of 10.0.28.0/24.
To: Moonbase 1
Subject: Network changes
From: Moonbase 13
To: Moonbase 1
Subject: Network changes
From: Moonbase 6
To: Moonbase 1
Subject: Network changes
From: Moonbase 10
Just to let you know that we're now routing 10.0.84.0/24 instead of 10.0.5.0/24.
that we're now routing 10.32.12.0/24
These are all static routes. How on earth can I keep up with making all these changes? Isn't there a better way?

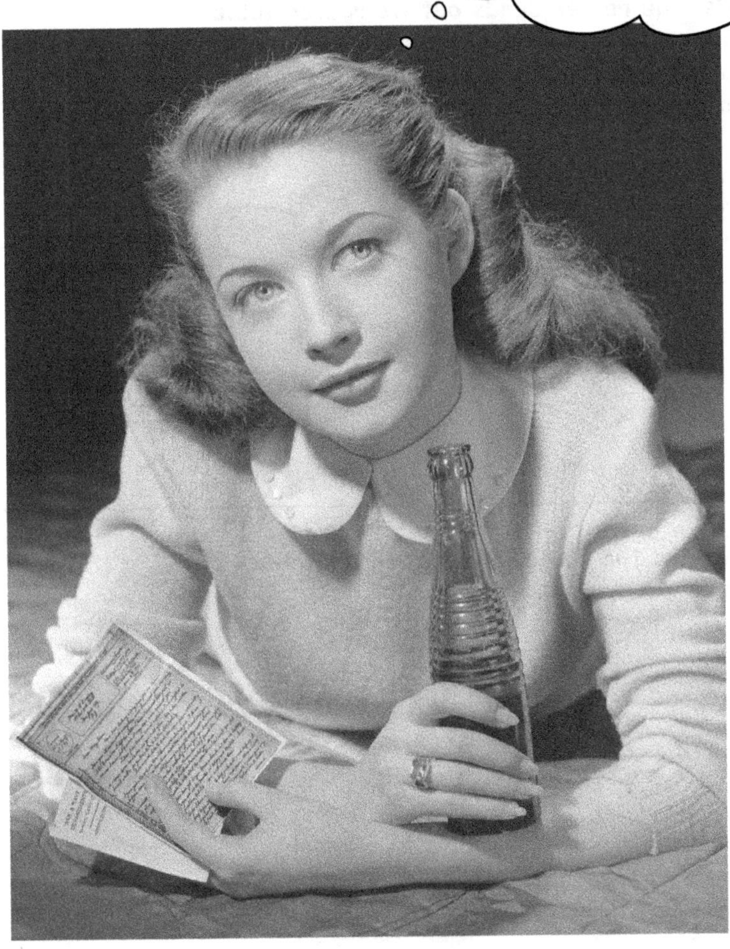
Wouldn't it be dreamy if we didn't have to update routing tables for every change in network configuration, but routers could just talk to each other and exchange route changes automatically? But I know it's just a fantasy...

Use RIP to get routes to update themselves

If you want to make your life easy, invest some time in getting a dynamic routing protocol running on your network. RIP, or Routing Information Protocol, is one such dynamic routing protocol. RIP is a way for routers to share network addresses. Routers use RIP to talk to each other, sharing their route information and allowing them to keep their route tables up-to-date.

Every 30 seconds, the router sends out its router table.
It sends out its entire route table to all other routes in the form of RIP update packets. This means that any changes that have been made to the routing table since the last time are included.

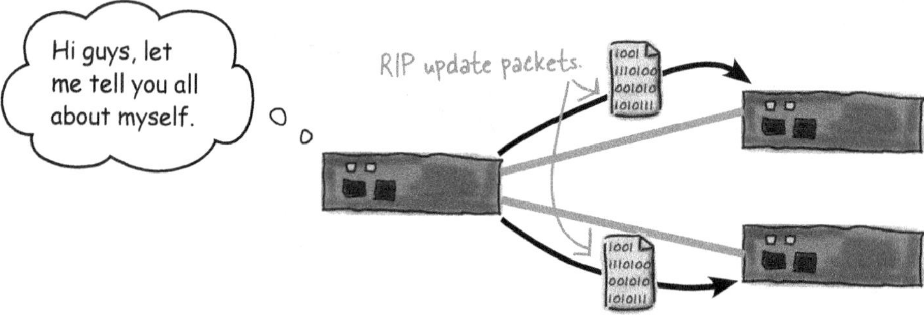

Other routers receive the route information and check their route tables.

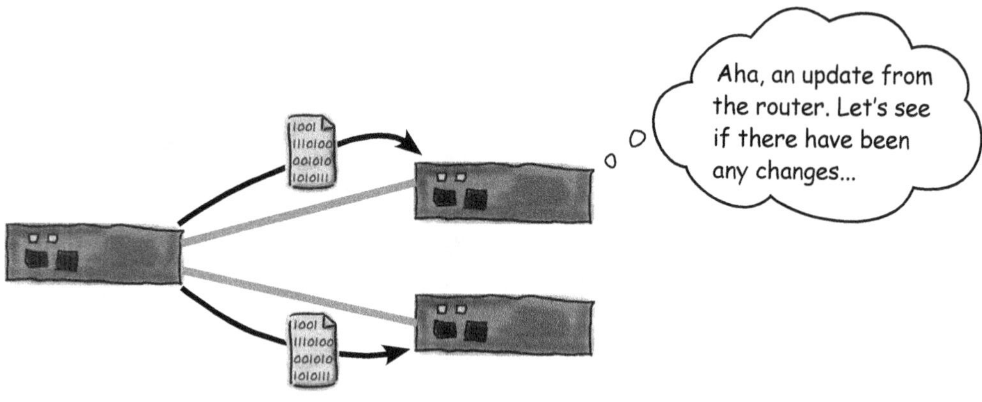

3 **The other routers update their own routing tables with any changes.**

Any new routes are added, existing routes are updated, and deleted routes are removed.

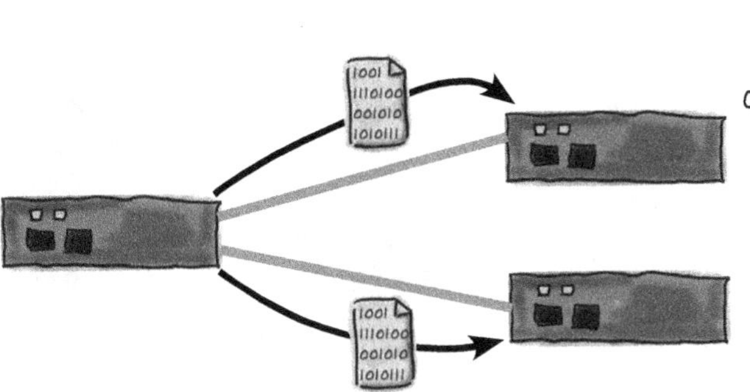

Hi guys, let me tell you all about myself.
1001
1110100
001010
1010111
Oh brother, off he goes again...
Oh man, he's changed again. I'd better change my routing table.

4 **After 30 seconds, the process begins again.**

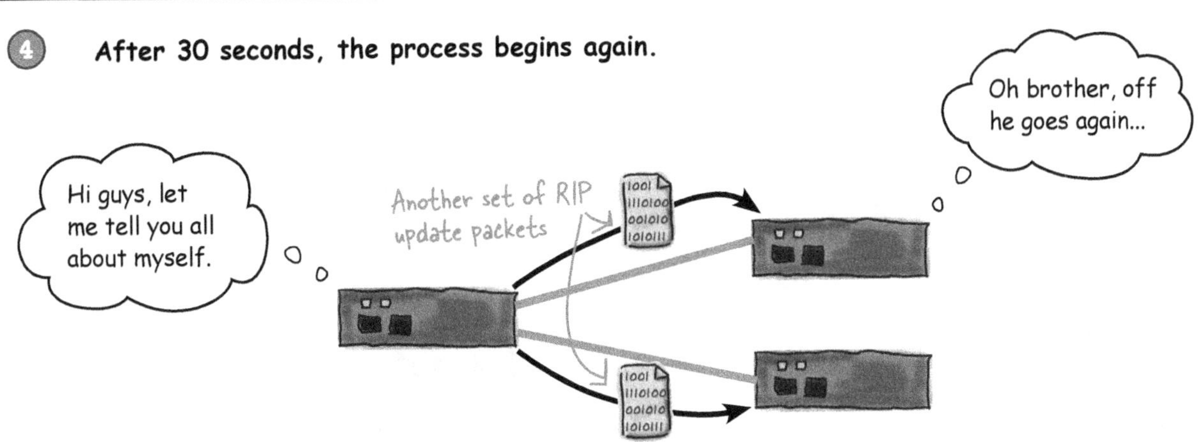

So what does this mean for Moonbase 1?

By implementing RIP across all the moonbases, we no longer have to maintain static routes for all the indirectly connected routers. Instead, we can let the routers maintain the routes for us—which makes life much easier.

Based on the changes in the network, circle the router(s) which would **send out** changes to their route table(s).

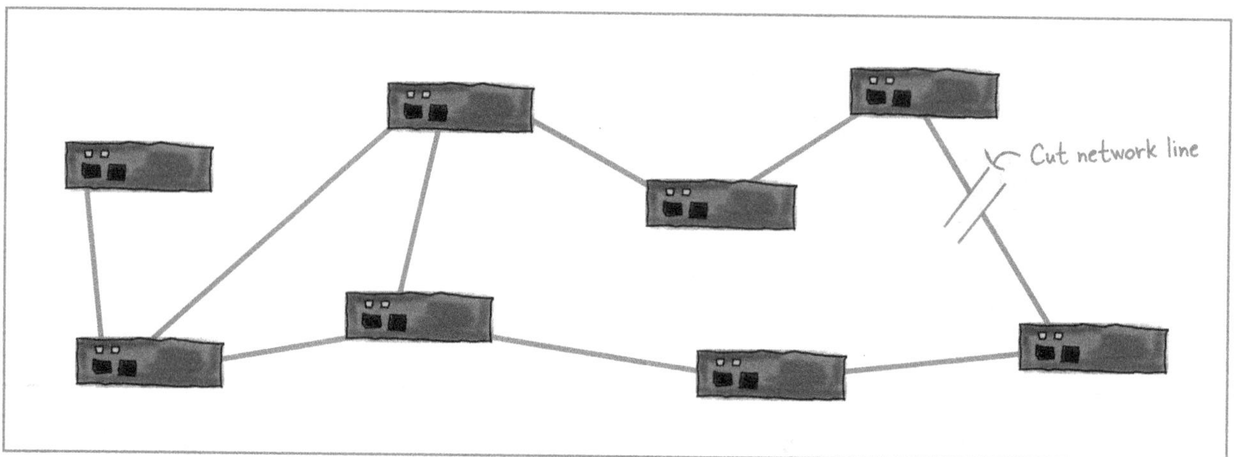

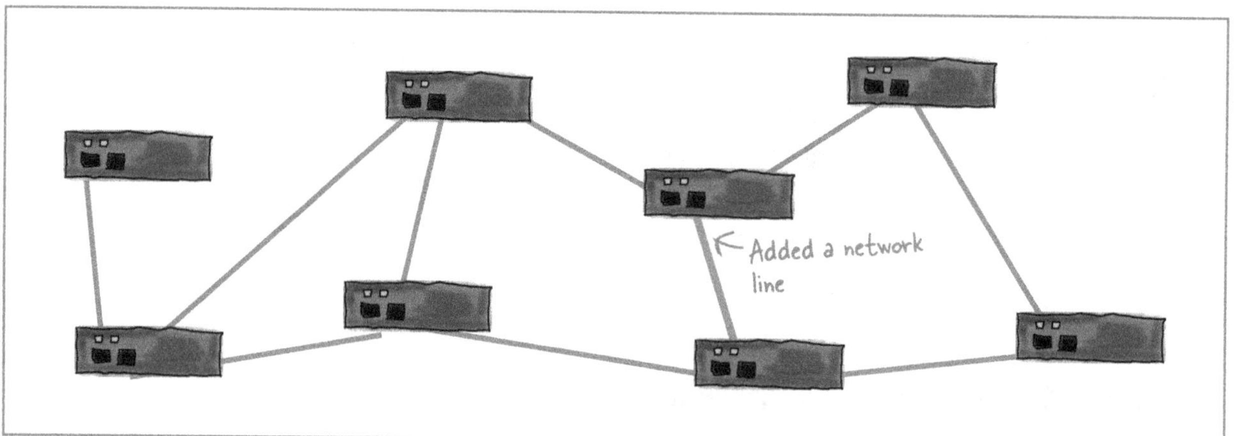

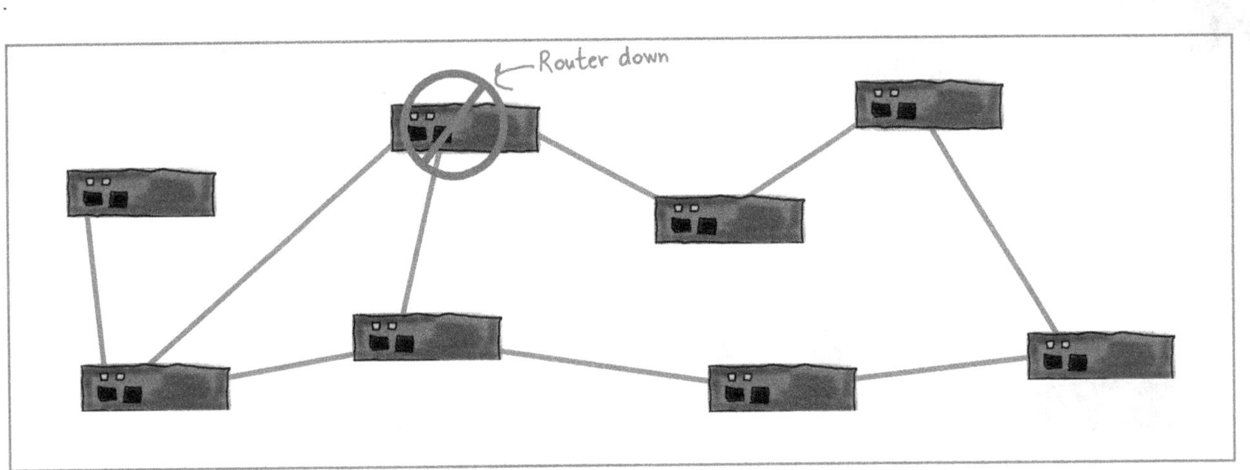
Router down

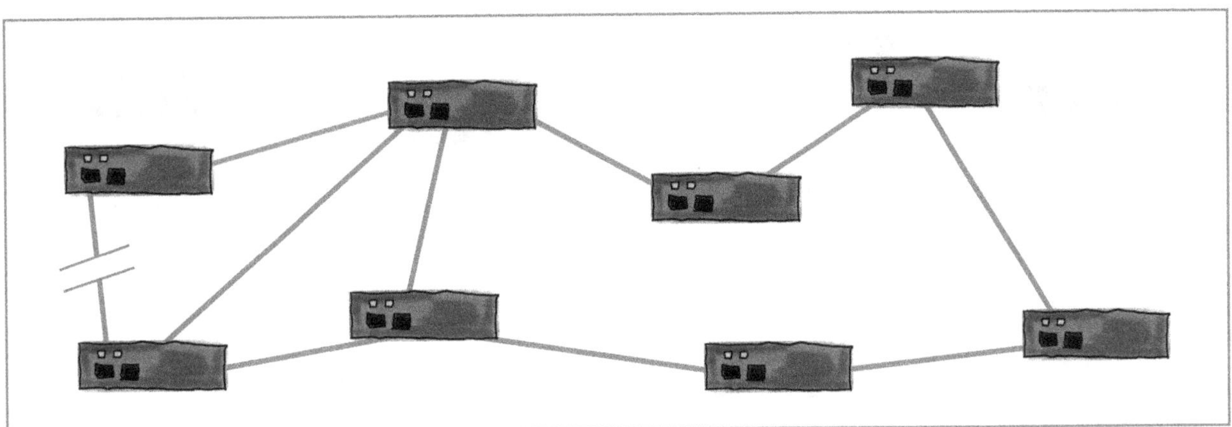

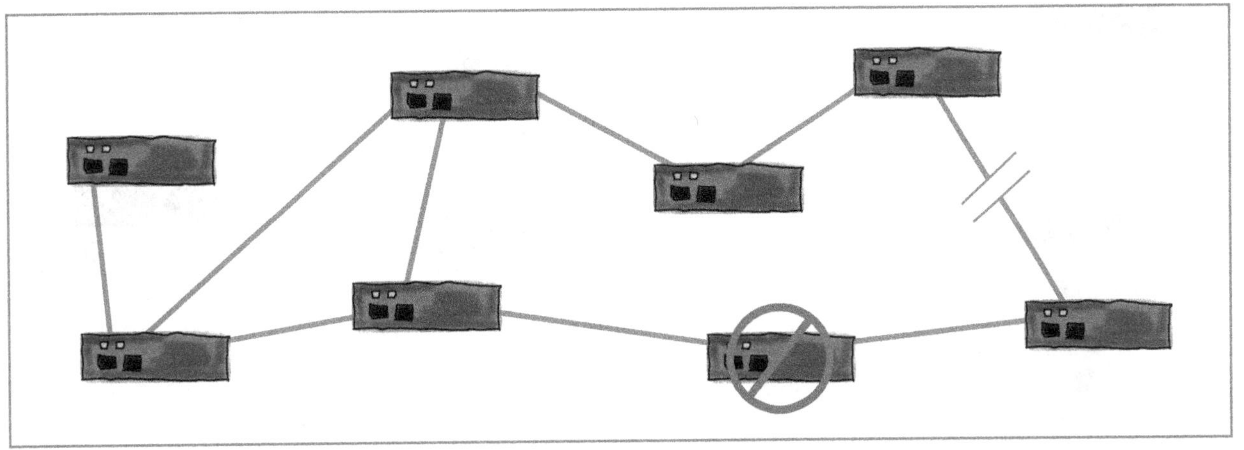

Based on the changes in the network, circle the router(s) which would **send out** changes to their route table(s).

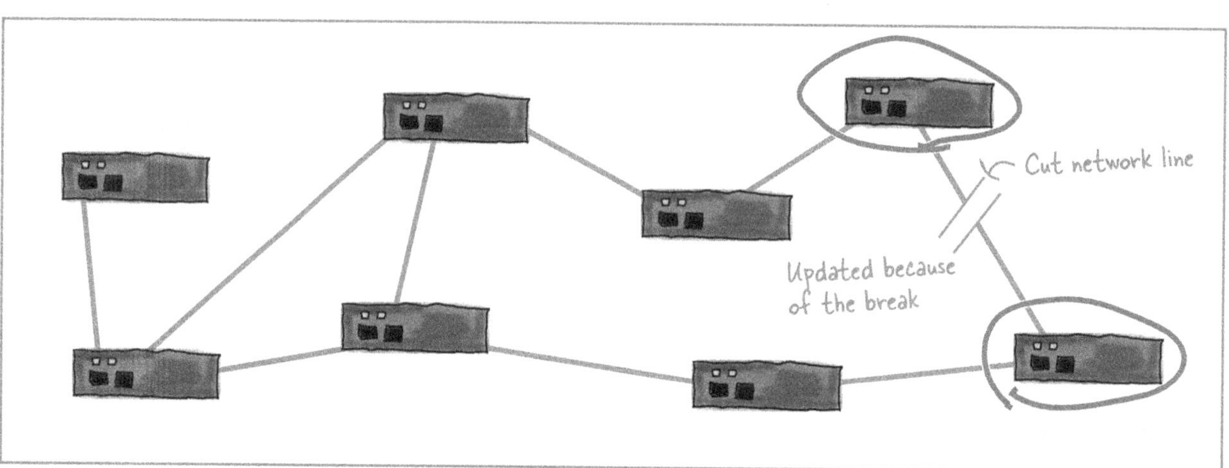

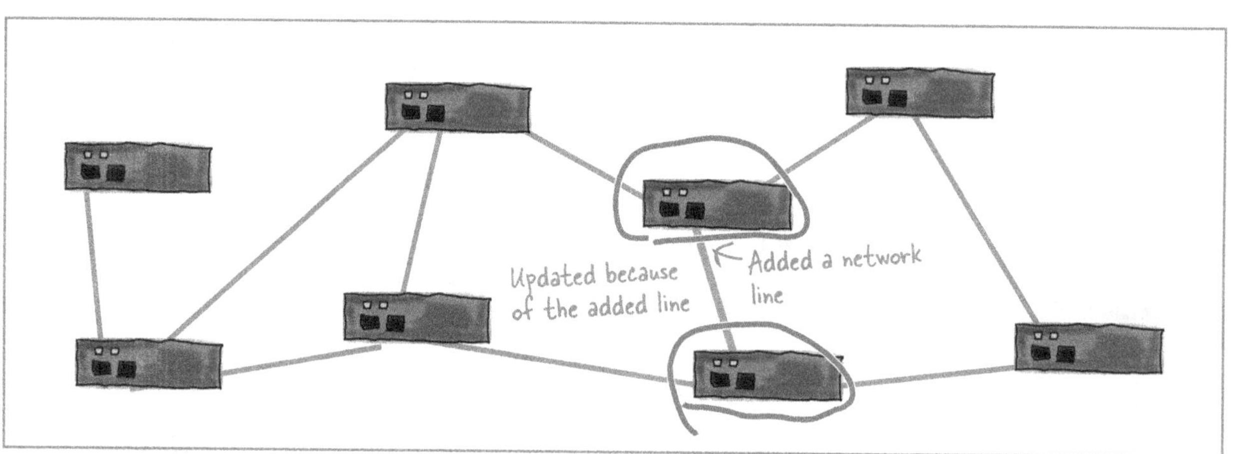

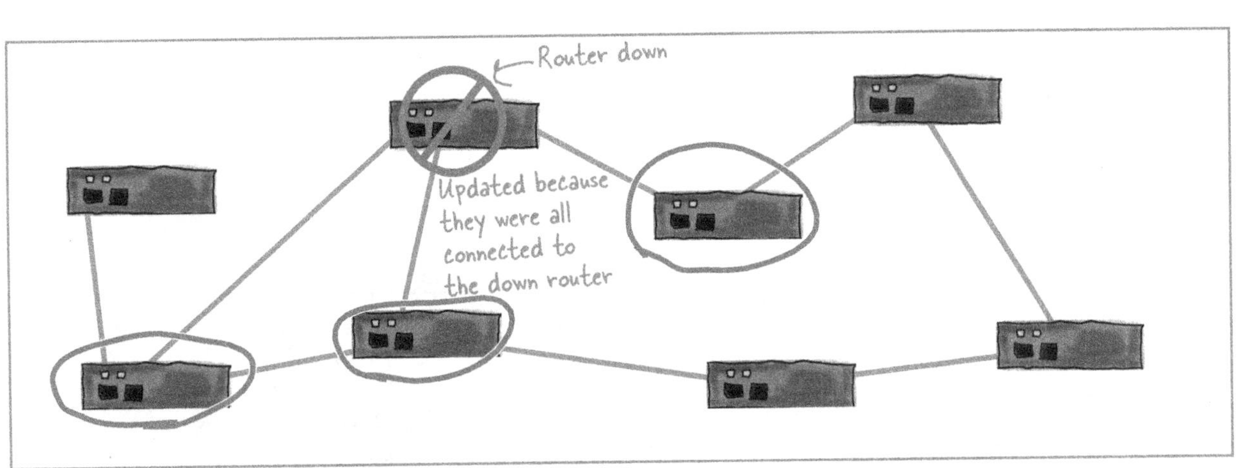
Router down
Updated because they were all connected to the down router

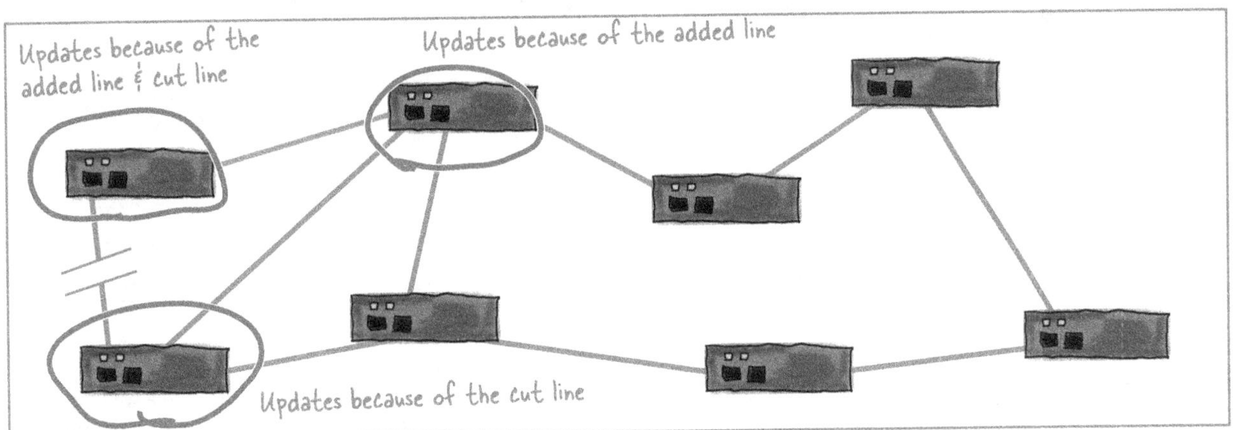
Updates because of the added line & cut line
Updates because of the added line
Updates because of the cut line

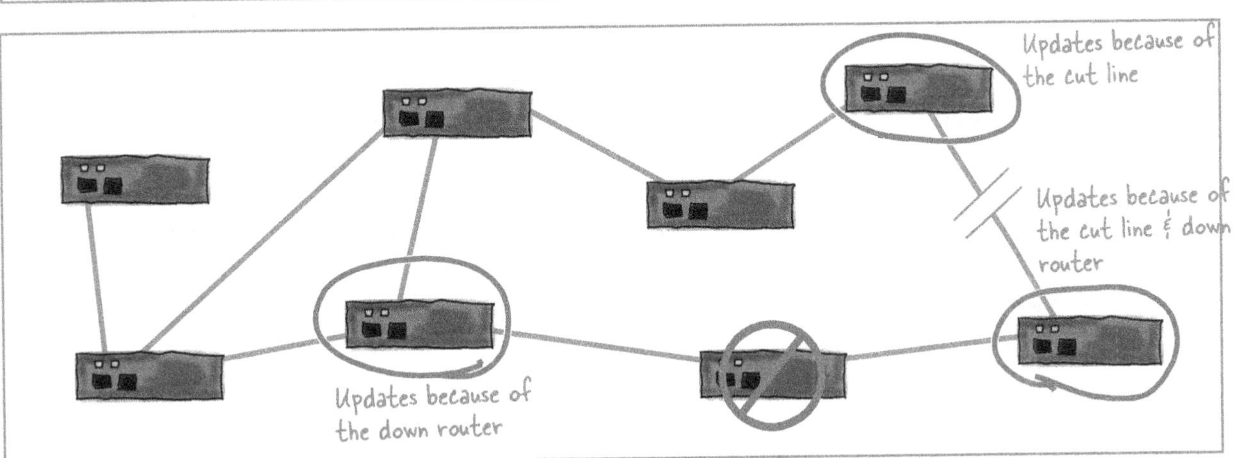
Updates because of the cut line
Updates because of the cut line & down router
Updates because of the down router

So how do we set up RIP?

Setting up RIP on a router is really simple. You enter the config mode on the router, then we enter the router rip configuration. When you add some networks, the router turns on RIP. Remember to save your changes with the write memory command when you exit the command mode.

These two lines add these networks to route table as networks that this router will route for.

File Edit Window Help RoutingInformationProtocol

```
router1#config t
router1(config)#router rip
router1(config-router)#network 192.168.1.0
router1(config-router)#network 192.168.2.0
router1(config-router)#exit
router1(config)#exit
router1#write memory
```

there are no Dumb Questions

Q: Does every type of router run RIP?

A: Just about any router you will come across will have a version of RIP available.

Q: Is RIP a program running on the router?

A: You could say that. It is an mixture of software running, a network protocol to communicate route information, and the configuration files. Depending on the type of router, it usually is some software function in the OS of the router.

Q: How do you guard against someone hooking their own router up and sending bad routes?

A: There is really nothing to prevent that with the RIP v1 protocol. In RIP v2 there is simple password authentication, but those passwords are sent in plaintext, so if someone is connected to your network, they could probably get these.

Some routers have mechanisms such as peers that allow you to control which routers you receive updates from.

Q: It seem like it could take a while for routers to share all their changes if there are more than a few routers with lots of changes.

A: Yes, that is one of RIPs problems. This is called convergence. Since a router broadcasts its router table every 30 seconds, it could take minutes for a change to propagate around even a small network.

But there's still a problem...

Unfortunately, there's now a problem getting data to Moonbase 20. So what's the problem?

Here's the output from the traceroute command:

File Edit Window Help Yikes

```
$ traceroute 192.168.116.1
Unable to reach destination address
```

Take a look at the output above. What do you think the problem is? What could you look at on your router to help figure out this problem?

There are too many hops

Given a choice, the RIP protocol always chooses the route with the fewest number of routers in its path, or the fewest number of "hops." We call the number of hops in a route the hop-count.

Unfortunately, the maximum number of hop-counts that the RIP protocol allows is 15—and it takes more than 15 hops to get to Moonbase 20.

The Hop-Count is the number of routers a packet must "hop" through to get to a particular IP network.

So RIP always chooses the route with the lowest hop-count. But what about the speed of the line, doesn't that make a difference?

RIP can only use the hop count to find the best route.

RIP doesn't know the speed of a particular network line, so it treats all lines equally. This means that if there are two possible routes to a particular nework, RIP will choose the one with the lowest hop count, even if the other route is really fast.

RIP views these two routes as the same, even though one's quicker than the other.

Slow network line

Slow network line

Fast network line

Fast network line

BE the Router

Your job is to play router and use the RIP route table to figure out which route you'd send a packet down.

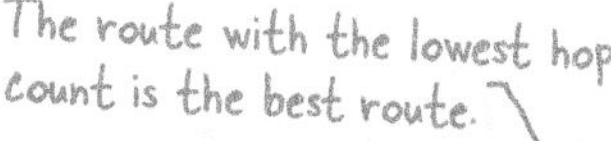
The route with the lowest hop count is the best route.

Network	Router IP	Hop Count
192.168.2.0/24	192.168.1.2	1
192.168.3.0/24	192.168.1.2	2
192.168.3.0/24	192.168.2.1	3
192.168.4.0/24	192.168.2.1	2
192.168.5.0/24	192.168.2.1	3
192.168.6.0/24	192.168.3.1	4
192.168.6.0/24	192.168.2.1	5
192.168.7.0/24	192.168.3.1	2
192.168.8.0/24	192.168.3.1	2
192.168.8.0/24	192.168.2.1	6
192.168.9.0/24	192.168.3.1	3

Packet Destination IP	IP of Router to Send Packet To
192.168.2.2	192.168.1.2
192.168.3.12	
192.168.8.99	
192.168.5.6	
192.168.7.211	
192.168.9.154	
192.168.6.176	
192.168.4.201	
192.168.7.154	
192.168.8.12	
192.168.2.23	

BE the Router Solution

Your job is to play router and use the RIP route table to figure out which route you'd send a packet down.

The route with the lowest hop count is the best route.

Network	Router IP	Hop Count
192.168.2.0/24	192.168.1.2	1
192.168.3.0/24	192.168.1.2	2
192.168.3.0/24	192.168.2.1	3
192.168.4.0/24	192.168.2.1	2
192.168.5.0/24	192.168.2.1	3
192.168.6.0/24	192.168.3.1	4
192.168.6.0/24	192.168.2.1	5
192.168.7.0/24	192.168.3.1	2
192.168.8.0/24	192.168.3.1	2
192.168.8.0/24	192.168.2.1	6
192.168.9.0/24	192.168.3.1	3

Packet Destination IP	IP of Router to Send Packet To
192.168.2.2	192.168.1.2
192.168.3.12	192.168.1.2
192.168.8.99	192.168.3.1
192.168.5.6	192.168.2.1
192.168.7.211	192.168.3.1
192.168.9.154	192.168.3.1
192.168.6.176	192.168.1.2
192.168.4.201	192.168.2.1
192.168.7.154	192.168.3.1
192.168.8.12	192.168.3.1
192.168.2.23	192.168.1.2

So what do we do? I mean, we can't just redesign the RIP protocol. Are there any other routing protocols we can use instead?

There are other routing protocols.

Earlier in the chapter, we had you use the RIP protocol, which works fine for a network with a small number of routers and paths, but it just does not scale. There are several other advanced IP routing protocols available. These include OSPF, IGRP, EIGRP, and BGP. IGRP and EIGRP are Cisco proprietary routing protocols. IGRP is now considered obsolete. It was replaced by EIGRP, but you may come across it here and there. These protocols are only available on Cisco routers. OSPF and BGP are routing protocols that are standards based and run on many different brands of routers.

But, which one do you choose?

If you are running all Cisco routers on your network, then using EIGRP is probably best. But if you have to interact with routers from other manufactures, then OSPF (Open Shortest Path First) and BGP (Border Gateway Protocol) are best. *Also, if you are hooking a router into an existing network, you will need to use the routing protocol that the rest of the routers are using.*

Geek Bits

You can find more information on RIP and OSPF by looking at RFC 1058, 2453, and 2328. Information on EIGRP can be found at Cisco's website:

http://tinyurl.com/cb6ny9

The routing protocol zoo

So what are the differences between the routing protocols? Let's take a look.

RIP

Advantages
It's easy to setup.
It's great for interoperability, as not all routers support OSPF and EIGRP.
Router discoverability. Routers broadcast their changes, and other routers listen.

Disadvantages
It can be too chatty. Routers broadcast every 30 seconds, so there can be a lot of traffic.
RIP trusts the information it receives from other routers without authentication.
RIP is slow to converge. When routes change, it takes a while for those changes to propagate across a network.
Its only metric is the hop count.

OSPF

Advantages
There are lots of metrics to adjust.
It needs authentication. It doesn't trust information sent from an unauthenticated router.
It's fast to converge. When routes change, they are quickly propagated across a network.
It's widely supported by different brands of routers.

Disadvantages
It can be complex to setup.
It needs lots of router memory

EIGRP

Advantages
There are lots of metrics to adjust.
It needs authentication.
It's fast to converge.
It's easy to setup.

Disadvantages
It only works on Cisco Routers.
It needs lots of router memory.

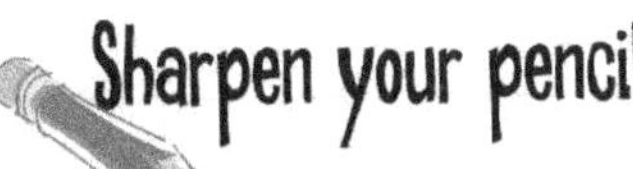

Choose a routing protocol for the four different network scenarios presented below.

Network #1 is a small network with only 3 routers. It has a fixed Internet connection with a default gateway provided by an ISP. Two of the routers are Cisco and one is a Juniper. There are not many changes to this network

- ◯ **RIP**
- ◯ **OSPF**
- ◯ **Static Route Tables**
- ◯ **EIGRP**

Network #2 is a large network with 600 routers. It has a 2 Internet connections. Most of the routers are Cisco, but there are a number of Extreme Network routers. This network has frequent changes to its topology.

- ◯ **RIP**
- ◯ **OSPF**
- ◯ **Static Route Tables**
- ◯ **EIGRP**

Network #3 is a medium size network with 83 routers. It has a fixed Internet connection with a default gateway provided by an ISP. All of the routers are Cisco. There are multiple paths amongst the routers.

- ◯ **RIP**
- ◯ **OSPF**
- ◯ **Static Route Tables**
- ◯ **EIGRP**

Network #4 is a medium size network with 15 routers. It has a fixed Internet connection with a default gateway provided by an ISP. The routers are all different brands. There are not many changes to this network.

- ◯ **RIP**
- ◯ **OSPF**
- ◯ **Static Route Tables**
- ◯ **EIGRP**

Sharpen your pencil Solution

Based on the information below, choose a routing protocol and write down your reason for choosing one over the others.

Network #1 is a small network with only 3 routers. It has a fixed Internet connection with a default gateway provided by an ISP. Two of the routers are Cisco and one is a Juniper. There are not many changes to this network

- ○ RIP
- ● Static Route Tables
- ○ OSPF
- ○ EIGRP

Since there aren't many changes and there are only 3 routers, it makes sense to just setup some static routes on each router.

Network #2 is a large network with 600 routers. It has a 2 Internet connections. Most of the routers are Cisco, but there are a number of Extreme Network routers. This network has frequent changes to its topology.

- ○ RIP
- ○ Static Route Tables
- ● OSPF
- ○ EIGRP

With a larger network, we need a better protocol than RIP, mostly because of the convergence problems RIP has. So OSPF is a good choice since not all the routers are Ciscos.

Network #3 is a medium size network with 83 routers. It has a fixed Internet connection with a default gateway provided by an ISP. All of the routers are Ciscos. There are multiple paths amongst the routers.

- ○ RIP
- ○ Static Route Tables
- ○ OSPF
- ● EIGRP

Again, RIP is not the best choice for a network of this size and complexity. Since all the equipment is Cisco, you can implement EIGRP.

Network #4 is a medium size network with 15 routers. It has a fixed Internet connection with a default gateway provided by an ISP. The routers are all different brands. There are not many changes to this network.

- ● RIP
- ○ Static Route Tables
- ○ OSPF
- ○ EIGRP

We could probably use any of the routing protocols for this scenario. RIP would be the easiest, but OSPF would work as well.

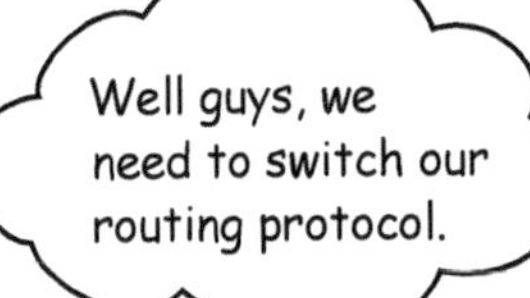

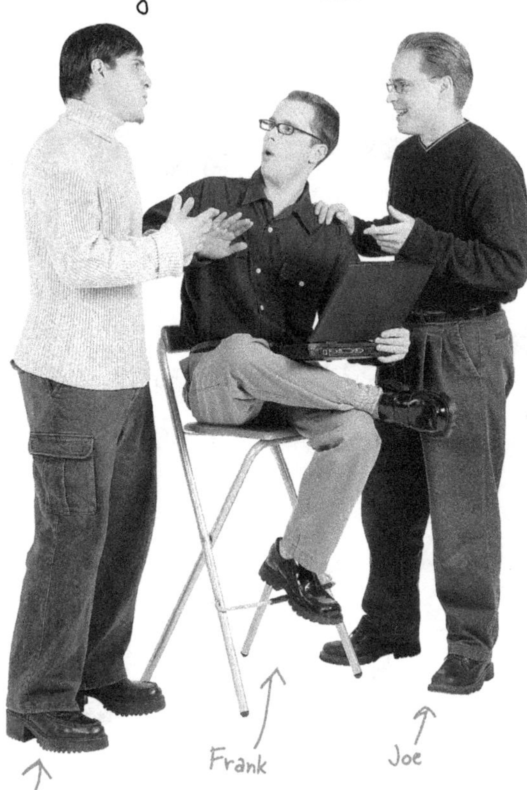

Frank: Why is that, what is wrong with RIP?

Jim: Just too many moonbases to hook-up. Some of the bases are more then 15 hops away from us, and that does not work with RIP.

Joe: So what are our choices?

Jim: OSPF or EIGRP.

Frank: What's the difference?

Jim: OSPF is an open standard for routing, and most routers support it. It is fast to converge to boot.

Joe: Well that sounds good; let's use OSPF.

Frank: But what about EIGRP?

Jim: EIGRP is comparable to OSPF. The fact that it only runs on Cisco hardware is probably the big downside.

Frank: Well Cisco got the moonbase equipment contract, so all the routers are Ciscos. That's not an issue.

Joe: Are there network techs up here that have experience with one or the other?

Jim: I know a couple of techs at the other bases have experience with EIGRP. They say it is pretty easy to setup.

Joe: I say that we go with EIGRP. It sounds like we have people that can help get it going, and it is a straightforward setup. Sound good?

Frank: Sounds good!

Jim: I'll get it going...

EIGRP Up Close

So what makes EIGRP so great? Let's take a look.

Neighbors

A router running the EIGRP protocol knows its neighboring routers and shares routes with them. Neighbors can be statically entered (a good security measure), or a router can discover its neighbors with EIGRP HELLO packets.

1. When our router, running EIGRP, starts up, if it does not have static neighbors, it will send a multicast HELLO packets out on all its connected interfaces.

2. When a neighboring connected router receives a HELLO packet, if the ASN and subnet from the sending router match, it will return a reply packet containing all the routes it knows.

3. Our router will return a short ACK packet to let the neighbor know it received the routes.

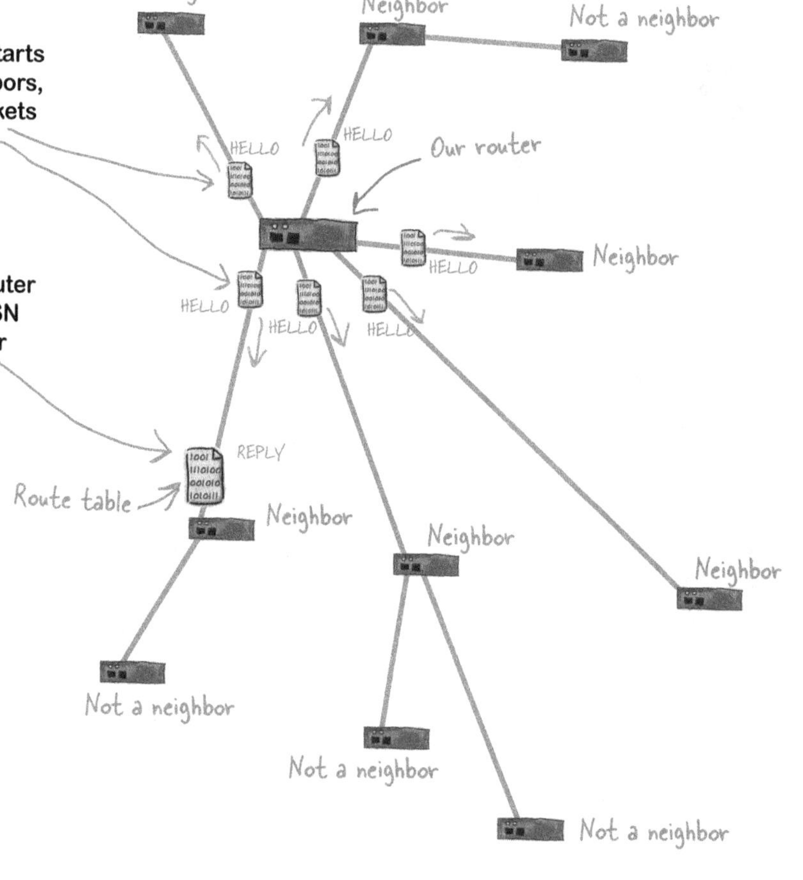

In order for routers to be neighbors, they must share a common IP subnet and a Autonomous System Number (ASN).

EIGRP uses the Diffusing Update Algorithm

The Diffusing Update Algorithm (DUAL) is a way of calculating routes when there are changes to a network topology. It helps keep routes **loop free**.

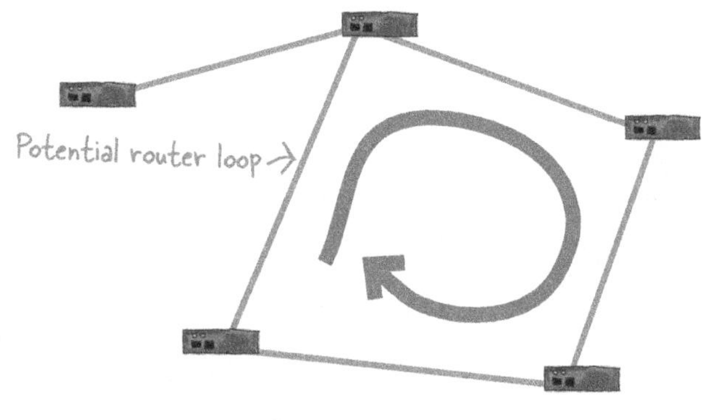

A router loop is where packets would just go from one router to the next and never get anywhere. They just go around the circle.

EIGRP uses the Reliable Transport Protocol to send its information

RTP assures that EIGRP route information a router sends reliably gets to its neighboring routers in the correct order with no errors.

A network is said to "converge" when all the routers have the correct routing information for the network.

EIGRP only sends route updates when there are changes

A router only updates other routers when it has a change in the network topology it is connected to. This allows for very fast convergence of a network.

So how do we setup EIGRP?

Setting up EIGRP on a router is pretty straightforward. You enter the config mode, then enter the router EIGRP configuration. When you add some networks in here, the router turns on EIGRP. You will need to add the neighbor routers that this router will exchange EIGRP route information with. Remember to save your changes with the write memory command when you exit the command mode.

```
File Edit Window Help MoreHopsWithEIGRP
router1#config t
router1(config)#router eigrp 1
router1(config-router)#network 192.168.1.0
router1(config-router)#network 192.168.2.0
router1(config-router)#neighbor 192.168.2.2
router1(config-router)#neighbor 192.168.1.3
router1(config-router)#exit
router1(config)#exit
router1#write memory
```

there are no Dumb Questions

Q: How does a router know when a route goes down with EIGRP?

A: Great question. When a router detects that one of its interfaces goes down, like a broken cable or a router dies, it sends out an EIGRP update with that route being down. That way all the routers get the message and adjust their route tables.

Q: OK, the big question is, what do I do if not all my routers are Ciscos?

A: If you don't want to run RIP (who could blame you), then OSPF is your choice. It is widely supported, even on Cisco equipment.

Q: Is OSPF much different than EIGRP?

A: Yes and no. It has very similar performance to EIGRP, but it is conceptually very different. Also its setup can be a bit more complex.

Q: So why doesn't everyone use EIGRP?

A: Because it is Cisco's proprietary routing protocol, and they have not licensed it to anyone else that we know of.

Q: Does someone own OSPF?

A: Nope, OSPF is an open standard. Any router manufacturer can implement it on their routers.

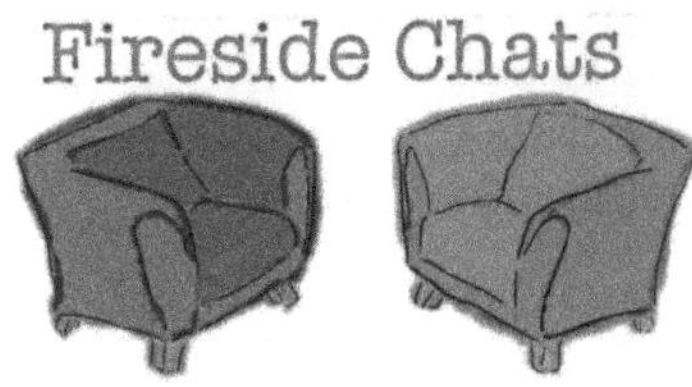

Tonight's talk: **RIP vs. EIGRP**

RIP: Hey youngster, how are you doing?

EIGRP: Well, I am not really that young. I am based on IGRP after all. And that was developed in 1986. Now where were you developed?

RIP: My RFC was written in 1988, but I was in development a lot earlier than that. But that is all besides the point. I want to talk about setup with you. I mean I just need to know the network address and the router's IP address, and I can get down to business. You know what I mean?

EIGRP: Man you sure are chatty. Do you talk this much all the time?

RIP: Yes, like every 30 seconds I send out my entire route table, keeping everyone on the network up-to-date.

EIGRP: Ah, well I just think it is easier to let the other routers know when one of my routes changes.

RIP: Well I don't really worry about that. I mean, I don't deal with that many other routers.

EIGRP: Yes, I have heard you have a 15 hop count limit. Mine is 244.

RIP: WOW! You can deal with some really big networks then.

EIGRP: And because I just send out changes to routes, the network converges really fast.

RIP: There still is the setup issue.

EIGRP: Not really, you just have to know what you are doing when you set me up. No newbies.

RIP: I don't think I like that last comment...

Long Exercise

Based on this network diagram of router connections, finish the EIGRP configuration. Because of security concerns, we want to statically enter this router's neighbors.

```
router eigrp 1
 network 192.168.1.0
 network
 network
 network
 network
 neighbor 192.168.1.2 FastEthernet0/0
 neighbor
 neighbor
 neighbor
 neighbor
```

```
router interface configuration
 interface FastEthernet 0/0
  ip address 192.168.1.1
interface FastEthernet 0/1
  ip address 192.168.2.1
interface FastEthernet 0/2
  ip address 192.168.3.1
interface FastEthernet 0/3
  ip address 192.168.4.2
interface FastEthernet 0/4
  ip address 192.168.5.1
```

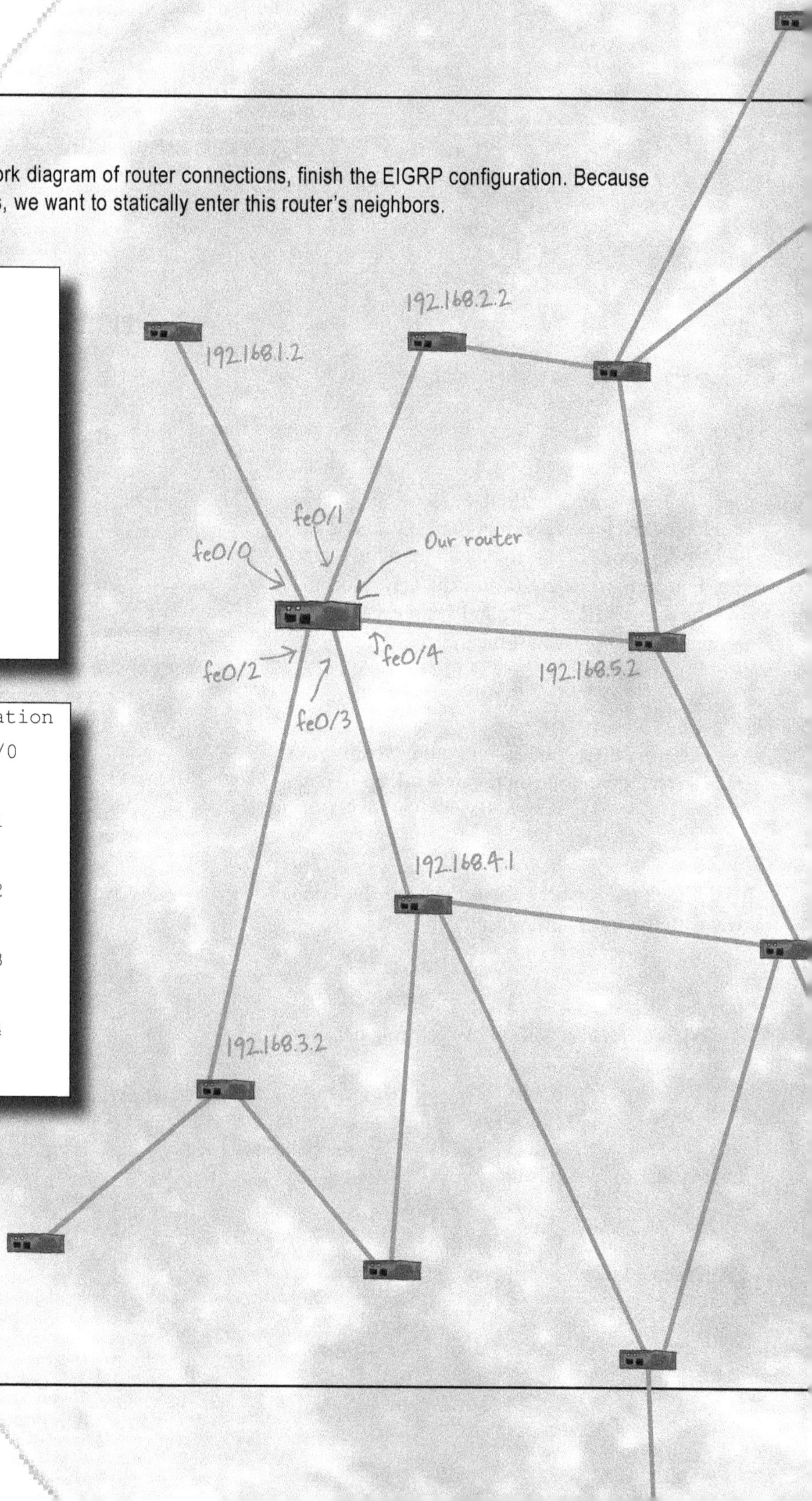

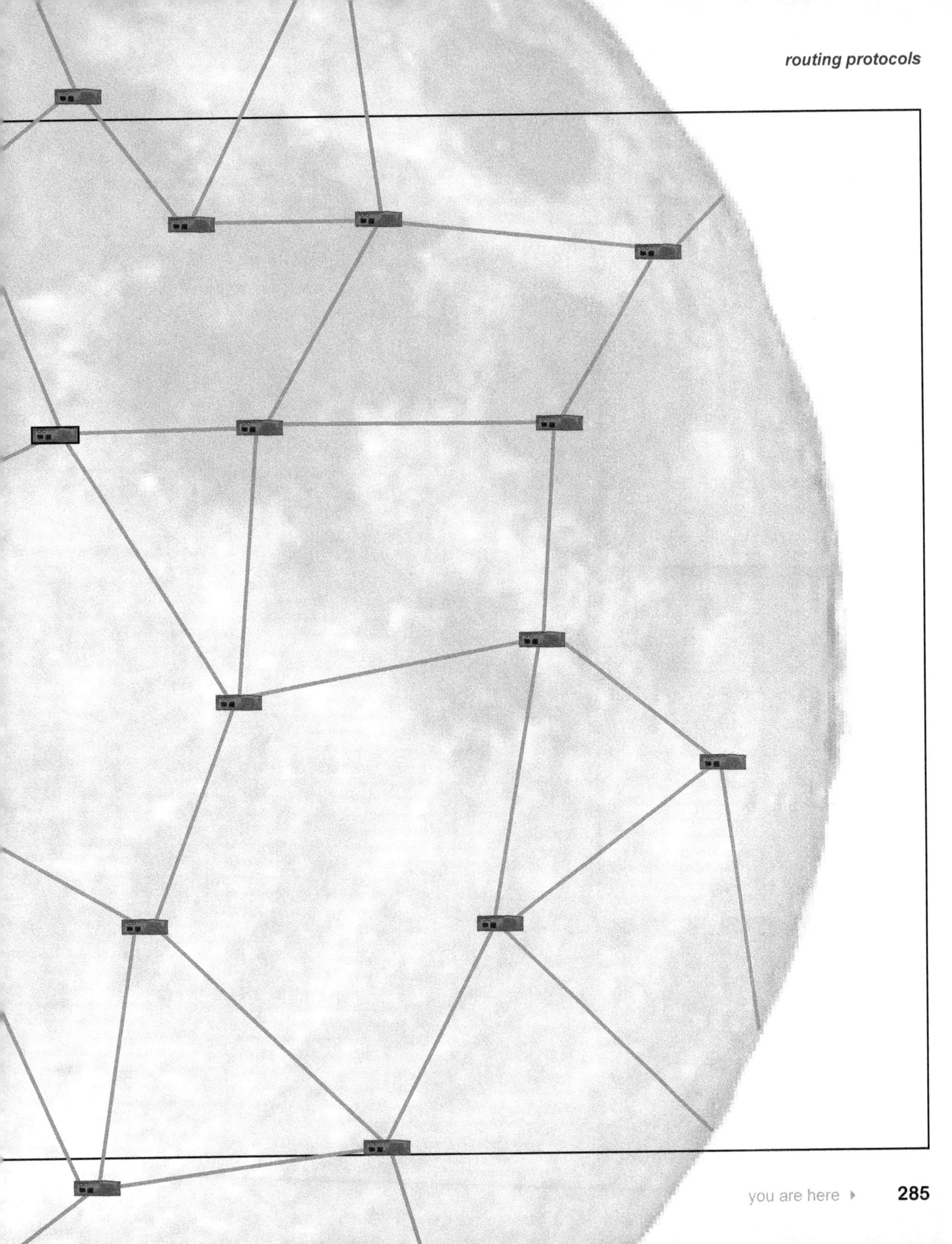

Based on this network diagram of router connections, finish the EIGRP configuration. Because of security concerns, we want to statically enter this router's neighbors.

```
router eigrp 1
 network 192.168.1.0
 network 192.168.2.0
 network 192.168.3.0
 network 192.168.4.0
 network 192.168.5.0
 neighbor 192.168.1.2 FastEthernet0/0
 neighbor 192.168.2.2 FastEthernet0/1
 neighbor 192.168.3.2 FastEthernet0/2
 neighbor 192.168.4.1 FastEthernet0/3
 neighbor 192.168.5.2 FastEthernet0/4
```

```
router interface configuration
 interface FastEthernet 0/0
  ip address 192.168.1.1
interface FastEthernet 0/1
  ip address 192.168.2.1
interface FastEthernet 0/2
  ip address 192.168.3.1
interface FastEthernet 0/3
  ip address 192.168.4.2
interface FastEthernet 0/4
  ip address 192.168.5.1
```

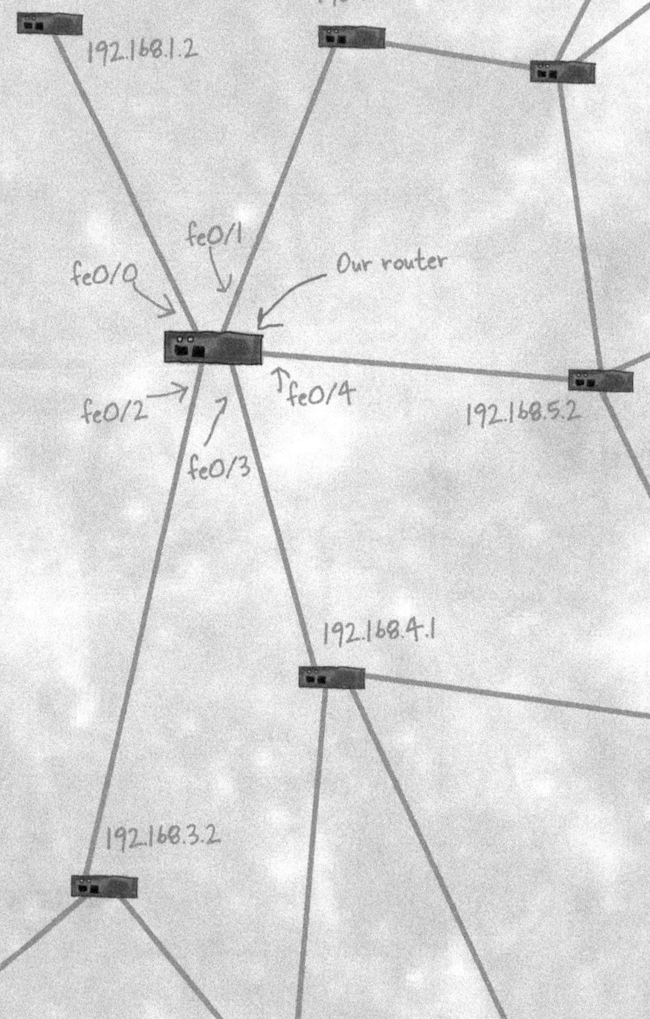

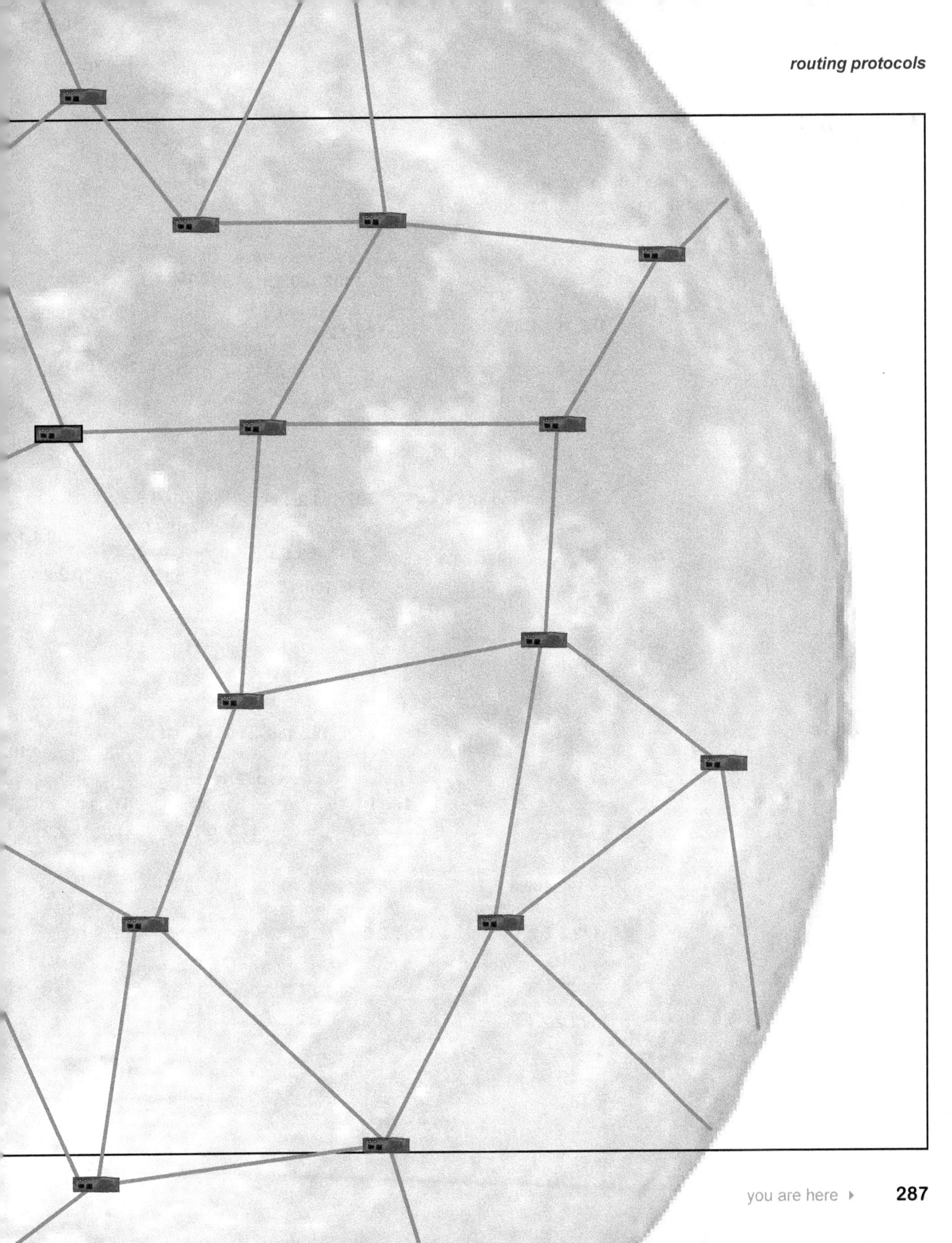

We have lift off!

Thanks to your efforts, all of the moon bases are now able to communicate with each other through their individual network devices. Congratulations!

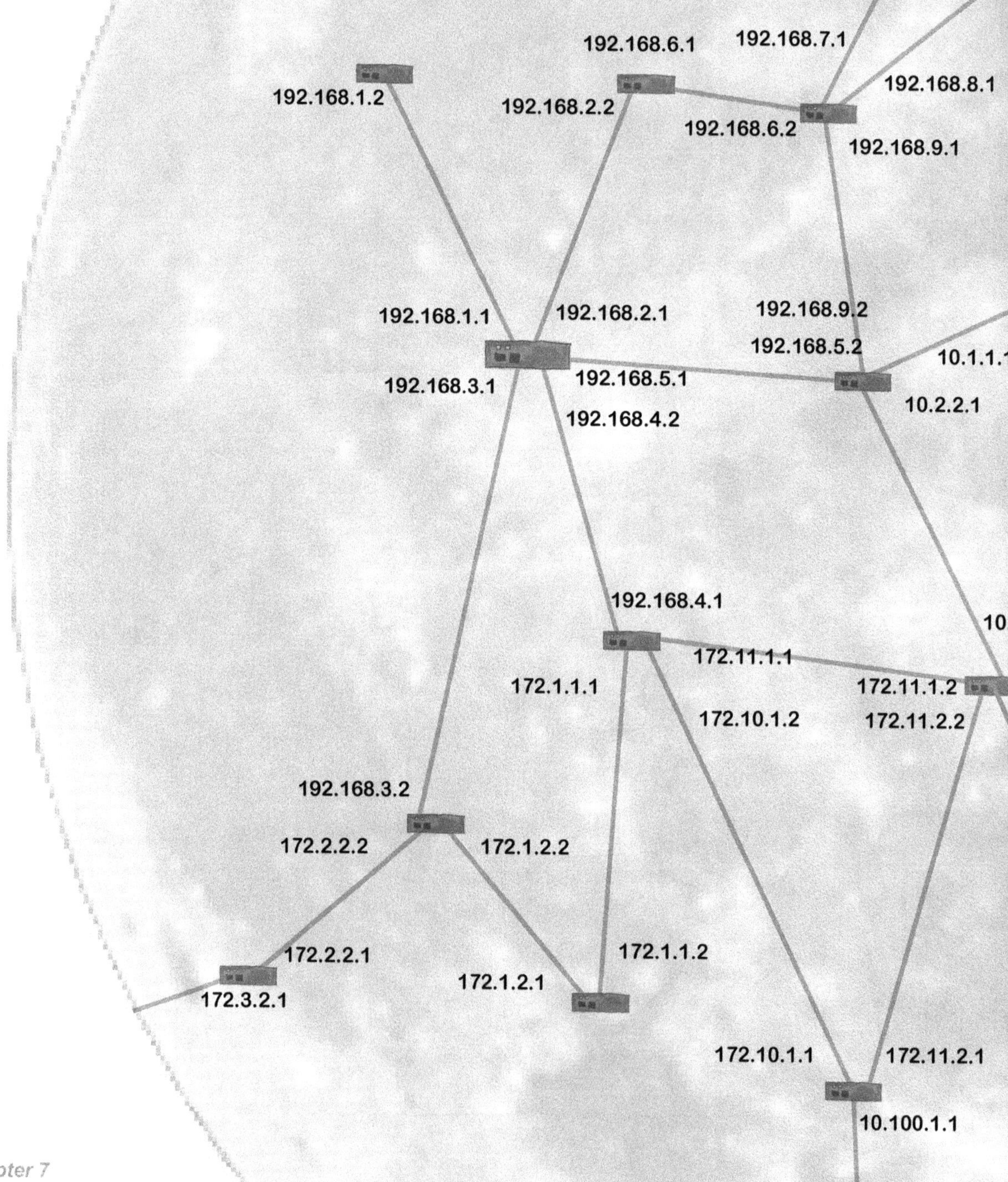

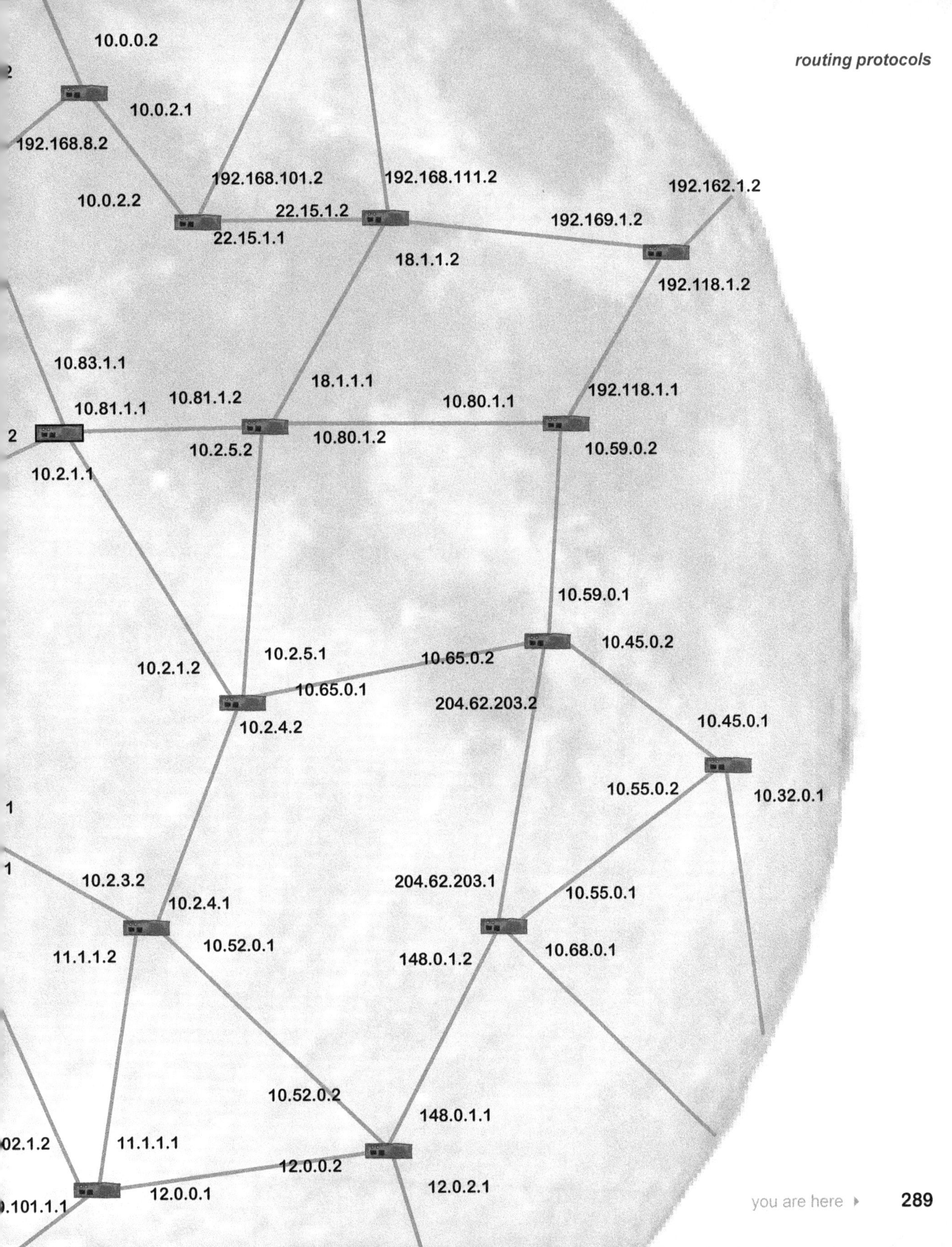
10.0.0.2
10.0.2.1
192.168.8.2
192.168.101.2
192.168.111.2
192.162.1.2
10.0.2.2
22.15.1.2
192.169.1.2
22.15.1.1
18.1.1.2
192.118.1.2
10.83.1.1
18.1.1.1
10.81.1.2
10.80.1.1
192.118.1.1
10.81.1.1
10.80.1.2
10.2.5.2
10.59.0.2
10.2.1.1
10.59.0.1
10.45.0.2
10.2.5.1
10.65.0.2
10.2.1.2
10.65.0.1
204.62.203.2
10.2.4.2
10.45.0.1
10.55.0.2
10.32.0.1
10.2.3.2
204.62.203.1
10.55.0.1
10.2.4.1
10.52.0.1
11.1.1.2
148.0.1.2
10.68.0.1
10.52.0.2
148.0.1.1
11.1.1.1
12.0.0.2
12.0.2.1
12.0.0.1

8 the domain name system

Names to Numbers

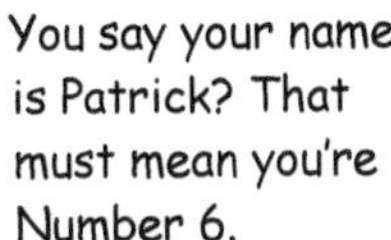

You say your name is Patrick? That must mean you're Number 6.

You probably don't even think about it, but when you type a URL into a browser, how does your computer find an IP address for that server?

In this chapter you will discover the world of Internet domains. You will find out how there are 13 root servers that deal out domain name information for the entire Internet. You will also install and configure your own DNS server.

The Head First Health Club needs a website

The Head First Health Club prides itself on its ability to find the perfect class for everyone. Whether you want to learn how to swim, practice martial arts, or get your body into shape, it has just the right class.

Unfortunately, competition between the different health clubs is fierce. In a bid to attract more customers, the CEO has decided that the Head First Health Club needs to have a website.

A strong web presence will be great for business. We'll be able to advertize all our classes and services. Can you set us up on the Internet?

The CEO already has web page developers handling the actual web pages that need to go on the site, and web servers for the site itself. What *you* need to do is get a domain for the website.

So what's a domain?

Hello, my domain name is...

Even if you've never heard of a domain name, you've seen and used a zillion of them; you know... google.com, yahoo.com, amazon.com, headfirstlabs.com, and maybe a few you wouldn't want us to mention.

So what's a domain name? Well, it's really just a unique name that's used to locate your site. Here's an example:

This is the host name. It's the name of a specific server IN the domain.

This part is the domain name.

www.hfhealthclub.com

This is called a fully qualified domain name (FQDN) because all the parts are present. It's basically the name of the website.

The domain ending is the top level domain name. There are different ones for different purposes: .com, .org, .gov; and also for different countries: .co.uk, .co.jp, and so on. You need to pick the one that best fits you.

The main reason why you should care about domain names is that it gives you a unique, specific, and memorable name for your site.

There's one other thing you should know. Domain names are controlled be a centralized authority (called ICANN) to make sure that only one person at a time uses a domain name. Also, you pay a small annual registration fee to keep your domain name (you knew it was coming).

So how do we get a domain name?

The easy answer is to go to a domain registrar and step through the process of searching for an unused domain name that you would like to register. Some offer great tools to manage your domain names and extra tools for web pages, email, and other servers. But like most things, that comes at a price. You really need to shop around and find the best deal and service for what you need.

Here's a list of some of the top domain registrars you might want to try out. *[Note from Marketing: are they paying us for this?]*

```
EuroDNS.com
godaddy.com
tucows.com
Sibername.com
Dotster.com
```

These are taken from a list of the top domain registrars in 2008, but there are plenty of others to choose from.

FQDN

Stands for Fully Qualified Domain Name. An example is:

www.hfhealthclub.com

It's basically the name of the website you'd type into your browser.

Let's go buy a domain name

The Health Club CEO likes the domain `hfhealthclub.com`, and a quick search reveals that it's available to buy. Before too long, you've bought up the domain and linked it to the Health Club web server. When the web page developers have deployed the web pages onto it, you're good to go.

there are no Dumb Questions

Q: Why is it called a "domain name" rather than a "website name"?

A: Because they are different things. If you look at www.hfhealthclub.com, that's the web server's name that is hosting that website, but only the "hfhealthclub.com" part is the domain name. You could also create other websites that use the same domain name, like corporate hfhealthclub.com or employees.hfhealthclub.com. So the domain name is something you can use for a lot of websites.

Q: But I thought www.hfhealthclub.com was the name of a website?

A: Yes and no. With regards to DNS, it is the name of a specific web server. A given web server can host lots of different websites, and it uses the domain name to decide which website to serve out.

Q: If I was going to get the domain name for the Health Club, wouldn't I want to get the name www.hfhealthclub.com? Everyone seems to use websites with the "www" at the front.

A: Again, don't confuse a domain name with a web server's name: hfhealthclub.com is a domain name, while www.hfhealthclub.com is the name of a web server. Buying a domain is like buying a piece of land—let's say 100mainstreet.com. On that land, you can set up as many web servers as you like, for example, home.100mainstreet.com, toolshed.100mainstreet.com and outhouse.100mainstreet.com. So www.hfhealthclub.com is just one web server in the hfhealthclub.com domain.

Q: What if I don't have my own web servers?

A: In that case, you can use those of a hosting company. They often have package deals for hosting web pages, registering domain names, and so on. Your best bet is to figure out what you need, and then shop around for the best deal.

Q: What's so great about a domain name anyway? Do I really need one? My hosting company says I can just use their name, www.dirtcheaphosting.com.

A: If that meets your needs, there's nothing wrong with using their name, But (and it's a big but) here's the disadvantage: should you ever want to choose another hosting company, or should that hosting company go out of business, then everyone who knows your site will no longer be able to easily find it. If, on the other hand, you have a domain name, you can just take that with you to your new hosting company. Your users will never even know you've switched.

Q: I don't know how to develop web pages. Is that a problem?

A: Not at all. We're assuming that a separate group of web page developers are doing the web page development and deploying it to the server. If, on the other hand, you're interested in learning more about how web pages are developed, *Head First HTML with CSS & XHTML* is a great starting point.

Let's try browsing to `www.hfhealthclub.com` and see what happens.

The bright and shiny Head First Health Club website with its very own domain name.

This looks great! This is bound to bring in more customers.

So everything's working well... right?

Uh-oh! We're in trouble

Everything seemed to be going well, but before too long, a customer reported a problem.

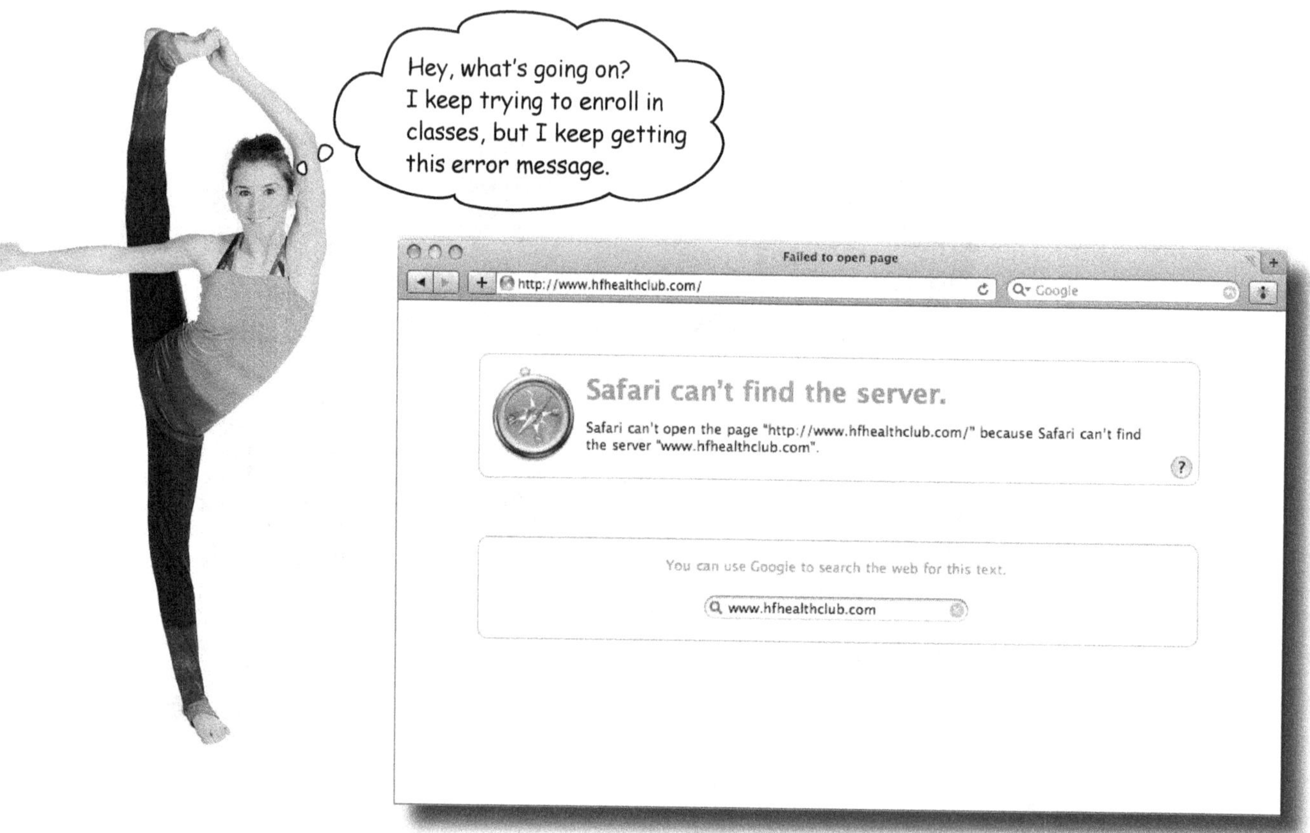

And she's not the only one

Before too long, the Head First Health Club is getting lots of complaints of intermittant problems and timeout issues.

So what could the problem be? And what can we do to fix it?

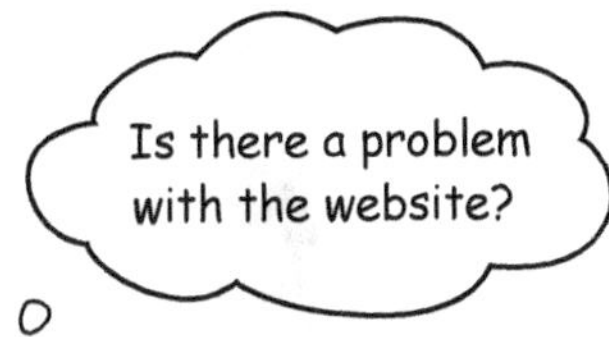
Is there a problem with the website?

Jim
Frank
Joe

Frank: No, I saw what the developers have done; it looks great.

Jim: Well I can't seem to get to it, and we have had some customer complaints as well.

Joe: I know the web server is running. I was just looking at it this morning. There were no errors or anything on it.

Jim: What else could be the problem?

Frank: I am trying to pull it up right now on my browser, and I am just getting an error.

Jim: That does not sound good.

Joe: What error message does the browser give?

Jim: It says it can't find the server www.hfhealthclub.com.

Frank: Sounds like our domain is not available, or at least that server's domain name is not available.

Joe: Did our domain registrar update the DNS records for the new web server?

Introducing the DNS

Before we look at how the client can find the web pages on www.hfhealthclub.com, we need to take a look at how DNS works. So what's that?

DNS stands for Domain Name System. It translates fully qualified domain names that are meaningful to humans into IP addresses that computers understand. It's a bit like an address book for the Internet that tells clients where to access resources.

The DNS relies on name servers

The translation between domain name and IP address is made possible because of a hierarchy of name servers. By a name server, we mean a server that can give an answer to a DNS query. So if we want to know which IP address is mapped to domain www.hfhealthclub.com, the name servers can tell us.

Let's take a closer look at this.

How the DNS sees your domain

You can think of the DNS as being like an upside down tree. The name servers are like the branches, and the leaves are like the domains. To get to a particular domain or leaf, we trace our way through the relevant name servers (branches) to get to where we want to be.

Let's look at www.hfhealthclub.com as an example.

1. **We start off with the DNS root servers.**
The DNS root servers look at what the top level domain (tld) name is to see where the address can be looked up from. In our case it's .com, so the DNS root servers direct us to the more specialized .com servers.

Each tld, like .com or .edu, has its own set of name servers.

2. **Next there's the .com tld servers.**
The .com top level domain (tld) servers know all about the .com domains. They see we need hfhealthclub.com, so they pass us along to the relevant name server.

3. **Then there's the hfhealthclub.com name server.**
The hfhealthclub.com name server knows about all the hosts and sub-domains of hfhealthclub.com. It sees we want www.hfhealthclub.com, so it passes us along to the web server.

4. **And here's the Health Club web server.**
This is the web server that's mapped to the the fully qualified domain name of www.hfhealthclub.com.

So how does the client use this to get to the domain?

DNS Magnets

Take a look at the following fully qualified domain names:

www.apple.com

en.wikipedia.org

oreilly.com

icann.org

Your job is to use the magnets below to say what the top level domain name, domain name, and host name is for each one.

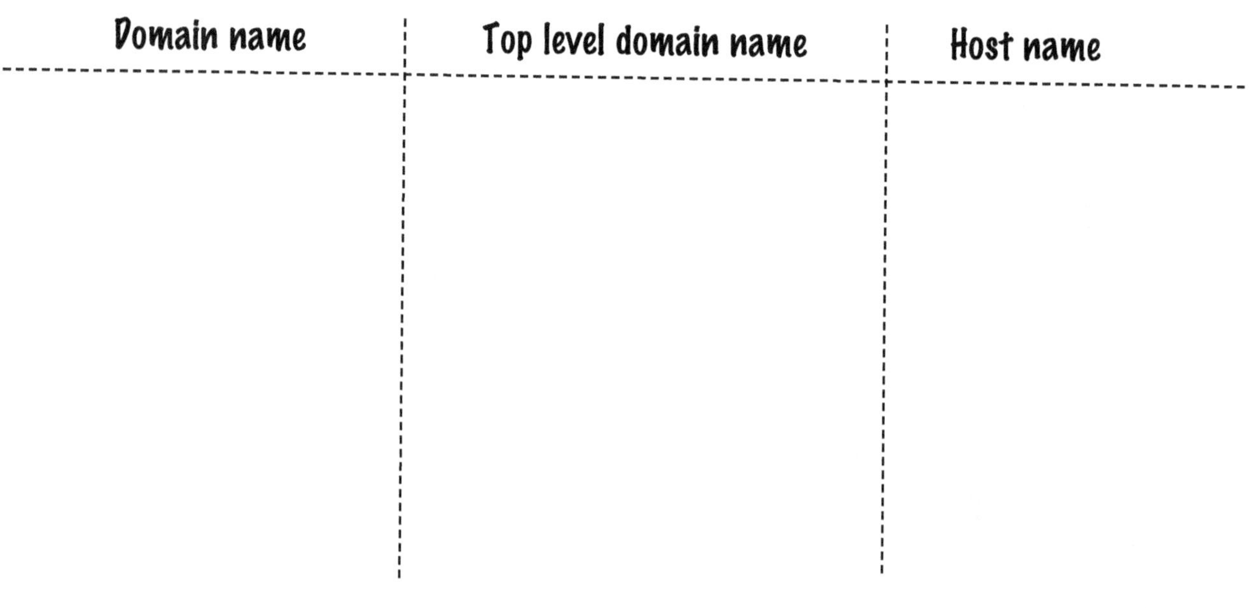

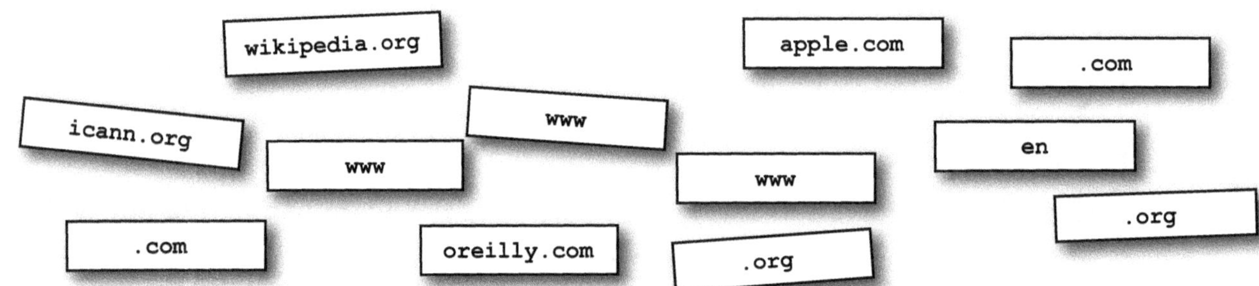

BE the Domain Name System

Your job is to play the domain system and fill in what happens in each step of the process of resolving a domain name when a client requests an name to be resolved to an IP address.

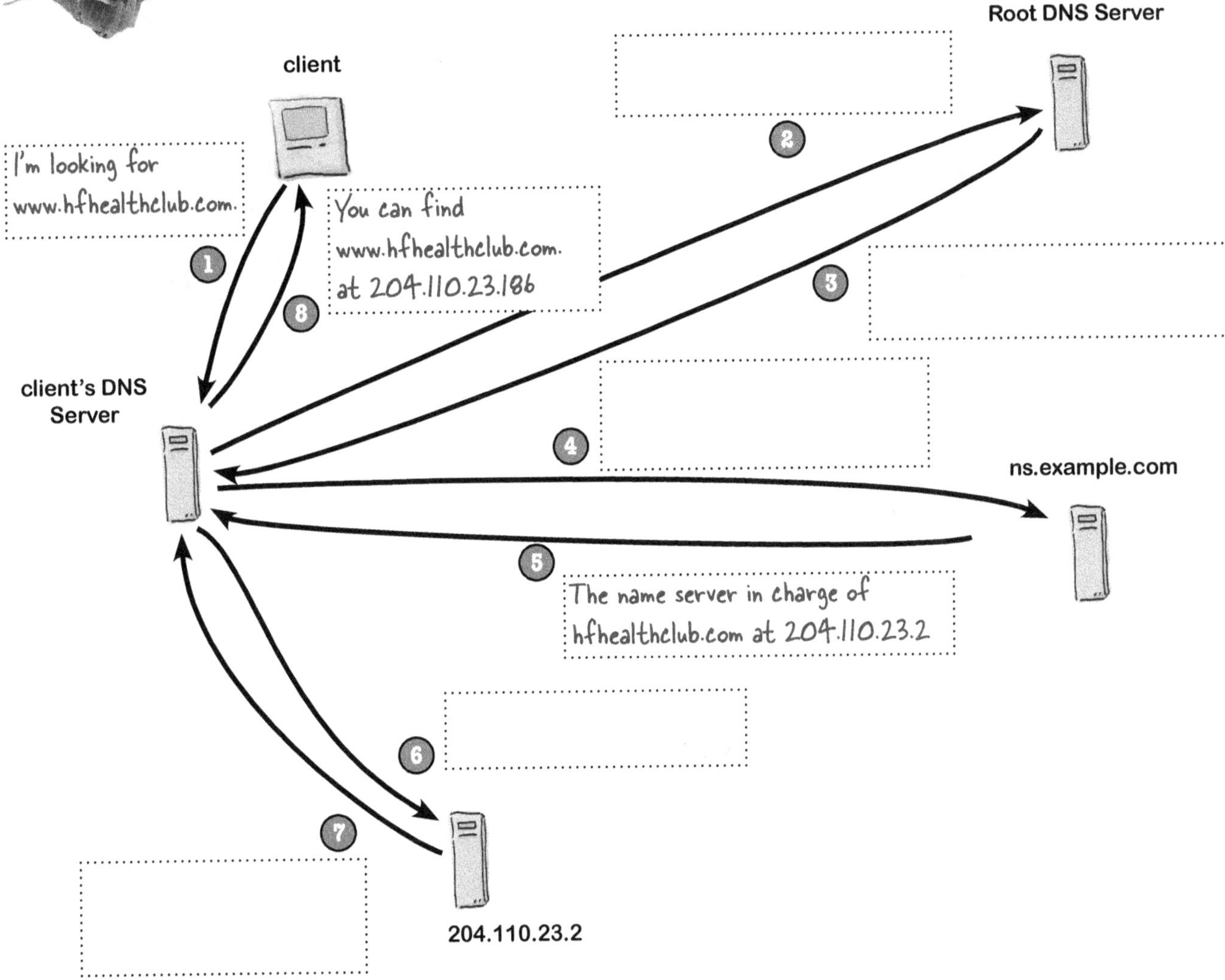

Root DNS Server
client
I'm looking for www.hfhealthclub.com.
2
You can find www.hfhealthclub.com. at 204.110.23.186
1
3
8
client's DNS Server
4
ns.example.com
5
The name server in charge of hfhealthclub.com at 204.110.23.2
6
7
204.110.23.2

DNS Magnets Solution

Take a look at the following fully qualified domain names:

www.apple.com

en.wikipedia.org

oreilly.com

icann.org

Your job is to use the magnets below to say what the top level domain name, domain name, and host name is for each one.

Domain name	Top level domain name	Host name
apple.com	.com	www
wikipedia.org	.org	en
oreilly.com	.com	
icann.org	.org	

www

www

BE the Domain Name System Solution

Your job is to play the domain system and fill in what happens in each step of the process of resolving a domain name when a client requests an name to be resolved to an IP address.

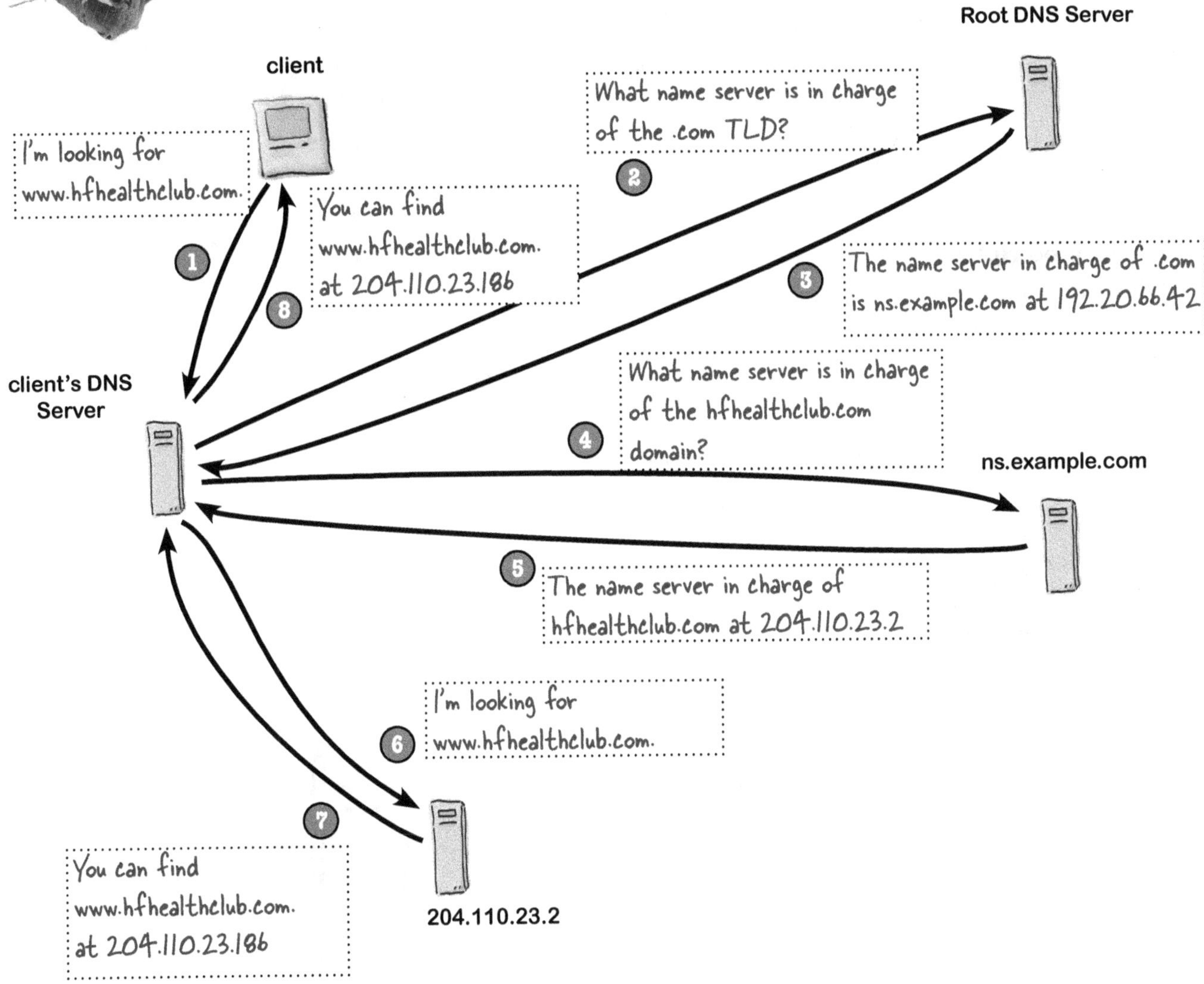
Root DNS Server
client
What name server is in charge of the .com TLD?
I'm looking for www.hfhealthclub.com.
You can find www.hfhealthclub.com. at 204.110.23.186
The name server in charge of .com is ns.example.com at 192.20.66.42
client's DNS Server
What name server is in charge of the hfhealthclub.com domain?
ns.example.com
The name server in charge of hfhealthclub.com at 204.110.23.2
I'm looking for www.hfhealthclub.com.
You can find www.hfhealthclub.com. at 204.110.23.186
204.110.23.2

So how does this affect the Health Club?

So far we've seen how the DNS relies on name servers, and how the name servers resolve IP addresses. But why might this be causing a problem for the Health Club? Why are the customers getting server timeout errors?

I wonder if people get errors because of the name servers? They were getting server timeout errors, and if the hfhealthclub.com name server is down, that might explain it.

He may be right.

When a client tries to browse to a particular domain, it needs to know which IP address the domain name represents. The client gets this from the name server.

If the name server is down, this means that the client has no way of knowing how to get to the website at www.hfhealthclub.com. This means that anyone trying to reach the website will get errors.

So we're doomed, right? We don't own those name servers, so there's nothing we can do.

We can replace the name server with our own.

At the moment the Health Club is using the domain registrar's name servers, but there's an alternative. Instead of using the name servers of the domain registrar, we can take control and setup our own instead. There are pros and cons to this approach, but if the current name servers are causing a problem for the Health Club, it might be the way to go.

So how do we set up our own name server?

Sharpen your pencil

Write down some more pros and cons of running your own name servers.

Pros ....

....

....

....

Cons ....

....

....

....

Sharpen your pencil Solution

Write down some more pros and cons of running your own name servers.

Pros
When you want to make a change in your DNS, there is no waiting around for it to take effect.
You can gain a really thorough understanding of how your DNS service is working.
You can immediately correct any problems that come up.

Cons
You have to perform sys admin duties not only on the DNS service but on the host operating system as well. This means updates, etc.
You have to purchase hardware and possibly licensing for the server OS.
You have to house the hardware somewhere.

First install a DNS name server...

A DNS name server is basically just an application that runs on an operating server. That means you have to have a server running Windows Server OS, Mac OS X Server, or a Linux variant. There are hardened servers that just do DNS. For some of these, you purchase subscriptions to keep the server up-to-date.

The most commonly used DNS server on the Internet is BIND. Installing BIND is relatively simple, but there's something else we need to do too. We need to configure the name server so that it can translate fully qualified domain names into IP addresses.

We've put some instructions on how to install the BIND DNS server in Appendix iii.

...then configure the name server

Your name server uses something called a DNS zone file that translates a FQDN to an IP address. Let's look at an example.

Since name servers are public, we can take a look at other name servers to see how they are configured using a command called dig. Go through the following steps to bring up details of the O'Reilly web servers. What do you think the output means?

On a Windows system you need to download dig from http://members.shaw.ca/nicholas.fong/dig/

1. **Open a terminal (cmd) window.**

2. **Type dig ns.oreilly.com www.oreilly.com any**

3. **This will return the records for the O'Reilly web servers. The A stands for Address.**

4. **You should see somewhere in the output:**

```
;; ANSWER SECTION:
www.oreilly.com.    21600  IN    A     208.201.239.36
www.oreilly.com.    21600  IN    A     208.201.239.37
;; AUTHORITY SECTION:
oreilly.com.        21600  IN    NS    ns.oreilly.com.
oreilly.com.        21600  IN    NS    b.auth-ns.sonic.net.
oreilly.com.        21600  IN    NS    a.auth-ns.sonic.net.
oreilly.com.        21600  IN    NS    c.auth-ns.sonic.net.
```

Since name servers are public, we can take a look at other name servers to see how they are configured using a command called dig. Go through the following steps to bring up details of the O'Reilly web servers. What do you think the output means?

1. **Open a terminal (cmd) window.**

2. **Type dig ns.oreilly.com www.oreilly.com any**

   dig command allows us to lookup domain information.

3. **This will return the records for the O'Reilly web servers. The A stands for Address.**

4. **You should see somewhere in the output:**

```
;; ANSWER SECTION:
www.oreilly.com.      21600   IN    A     208.201.239.36
www.oreilly.com.      21600   IN    A     208.201.239.37
;; AUTHORITY SECTION:
oreilly.com.          21600   IN    NS    ns.oreilly.com.
oreilly.com.          21600   IN    NS    b.auth-ns.sonic.net.
oreilly.com.          21600   IN    NS    a.auth-ns.sonic.net.
oreilly.com.          21600   IN    NS    c.auth-ns.sonic.net.
```

Means Internet class record (IN)

Means host address (A)

Their 2 web servers' IP addresses.

Means name server (NS)

Servers' FQDNs

These are BIND configuration file acronyms.

A bunch of BIND configuration file acronyms are playing the party game "Who am I?" They give you a clue, and you try to guess who they are, based on what they say. Assume they always tell the truth about themselves. If they happen to say something that could be true for more than one guy, then write down all for whom that sentence applies. Fill in the blanks next to the sentence with the names of one or more attendees.

Tonight's attendees:

SOA, CNAME, IN, MX, A, NS, PTR

	Acronym
I specify hosts used for handling email.	________
I designate a host address.	________
I point to a domain name.	________
I designate a name server.	________
I mark off the start of a zone of authority.	________
I define an alias.	________
I designate an Internet class record.	________

Who am I?

A bunch of BIND configuration file acronyms are playing the party game "Who am I?" They give you a clue, and you try to guess who they are, based on what they say. Assume they always tell the truth about themselves. If they happen to say something that could be true for more than one guy, then write down all for whom that sentence applies. Fill in the blanks next to the sentence with the names of one or more attendees.

Tonight's attendees:

SOA, CNAME, IN, MX, A, NS, PTR

	Acronym
I specify hosts used for handling email.	MX
I designate a host address.	A
I point to a domain name.	PTR
I designate a name server.	NS
I mark off the start of a zone of authority.	SOA
I define an alias.	CNAME
I designate an Internet class record.	IN

Pool Puzzle

Your **job** is to take Bind elements from the pool and place them into the blank lines in the Health Club Bind configuration file. You may **not** use the same Bind element more than once, and you won't need to use all the Bind elements. Your **goal** is to make a complete Bind configuration that will properly serve out IP addresses.

Hint: You'll need to use some of the BIND configuration file acronyms from the previous exercise.

```
$ORIGIN hfhealthclub.com
$TTL 86400
@      IN     _____   dns1.hfhealthclub.com.   hostmaster.hfhealthclub.com. (
                      2001062501 ; serial
                      21600      ; refresh after 6 hours
                      3600       ; retry after 1 hour
                      604800     ; expire after 1 week
                      86400 )    ; minimum TTL of 1 day

       IN   _____   ________________________
       IN   _____   dns2.hfhealthclub.com.
       IN   _____   10      _______________.

            IN        _____        10.0.1.5
server1     IN        _____        10.0.1.5
www         IN        _____        10.0.1.6
mail        IN        _____        _______________
dns1        IN        _____        10.0.1.2
dns2        IN        _____        10.0.1.3
```

Note: each thing from the pool can only be used once!

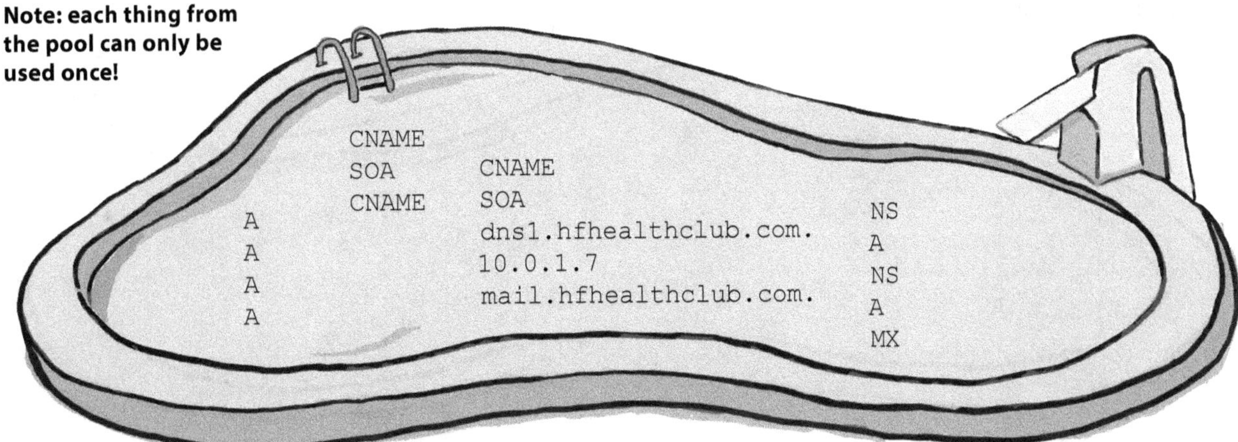

Pool Puzzle Solution

Your **job** is to take Bind elements from the pool and place them into the blank lines in the Health Club Bind configuration file. You may **not** use the same Bind element more than once, and you won't need to use all the Bind elements. Your **goal** is to make a complete Bind configuration that will properly serve out IP addresses.

```
$ORIGIN hfhealthclub.com
$TTL 86400
@       IN      SOA     dns1.hfhealthclub.com.   hostmaster.hfhealthclub.com. (
                        2001062501 ; serial
                        21600      ; refresh after 6 hours
                        3600       ; retry after 1 hour
                        604800     ; expire after 1 week
                        86400 )    ; minimum TTL of 1 day

        IN      NS      dns1.hfhealthclub.com.
        IN      NS      dns2.hfhealthclub.com.
        IN      MX      10      mail.hfhealthclub.com.

                IN      A       10.0.1.5
server1         IN      A       10.0.1.5
www             IN      A       10.0.1.6
mail            IN      A       10.0.1.7
dns1            IN      A       10.0.1.2
dns2            IN      A       10.0.1.3
```

Note: each thing from the pool can only be used once!

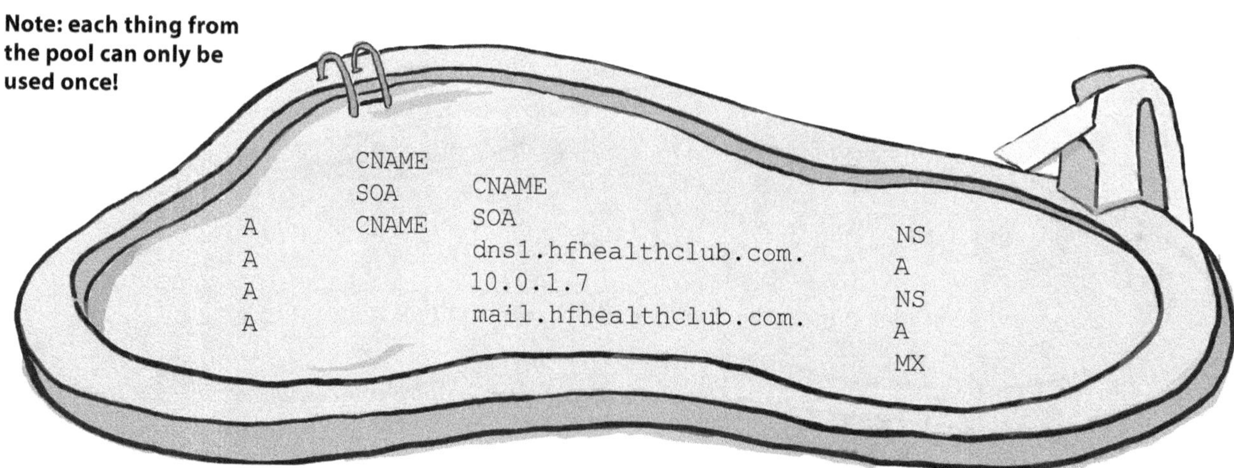

This week's interview:
DNS Nameserver

Head First: Good morning! How are you?

DNS Nameserver: I don't recognize that request.

Head First: Excuse me? I was just saying good morning and asking how you are doing.

DNS Nameserver: My apologies. I am so used to answering requests for names. I sometimes just can't seem to do anything else. I am great this morning.

Head First: So what is it like being a DNS nameserver? Busy all the time?

DNS Nameserver: Yes.

Head First: OK .... Could you speak a little more to what kind of things you do?

DNS Nameserver: Yes, I get requests for IP addresses. Other computers send me a FQDN for the domain that I am responsible for, and I return an IP address. I do other requests as well.

Head First: What would be some other request types?

DNS Nameserver: I do a lot of NS and MX types. The NS type is when they are looking for my or my partner's IP addresses. The NS stands for NameServer. The MX type is for email servers for our domain. When I get a request of that type, I return the IP address of the email server responsible for our domain.

Head First: Are there other types of DNS records that you deal with?

DNS Nameserver: Oh yes, I also deal with PTR records. These are fun because there are a reverse lookup. The computers making these requests give me an IP address, and I return a FQDN to them.

Head First: Why would a computer want to do that?

DNS Nameserver: You can tell if a computer is lying about who they are. It is very easy to say you are email.somewhere.com, but your IP address will not match. A reverse lookup enables someone to verify that you are who you say you are.

Head First: Are there other things that you do besides this?

DNS Nameserver: Besides this? My kin and I are the heart of the Internet. Without us you would not be able to get to your precious online shopping or news websites. You would have to memorize all those IP addresses. But we make it so easy; you just type in a name and voilà, there it is.

Head First: I am sorry, that is not what I meant to say. I was asking more about other things you do with regards to DNS.

DNS Nameserver: My apologies. I go off sometimes. I think one cool thing I do is load-balancing. I can load balance a web server by doing a round robin lookup. How that works is that I have the IP addresses of several web servers, and I rotate amongst them to distribute the workload.

Head First: Thank you for taking the time to answer my questions.

The anatomy of a DNS zone file

So what's really going on inside the Health Club DNS zone file? Let's take a close look at the file:

DNS Zone File

```
$ORIGIN hfhealthclub.com
$TTL 86400
@       IN      SOA     dns1.hfhealthclub.com.     hostmaster.
hfhealthclub.com. (
                        2001062501 ; serial
                        21600      ; refresh after 6 hours
                        3600       ; retry after 1 hour
                        604800     ; expire after 1 week
                        86400 )    ; minimum TTL of 1 day
        IN      NS      dns1.hfhealthclub.com.
        IN      NS      dns2.hfhealthclub.com.
        IN      MX      10      mail.hfhealthclub.com.
                IN      A       10.0.1.5
server1         IN      A       10.0.1.5
www             IN      A       10.0.1.6
mail            IN      A       10.0.1.7
dns1            IN      A       10.0.1.2
dns2            IN      A       10.0.1.3
```

Start of Authority - SOA this says that dns1 is a primary name server of the hfhealthclub.com domain

This information lets other name servers know when this file has changed and how long to cache the info.

Whatever follows this is a nameserver.

Whatever follows this is an email server.

Hosts in this domain

Whatever follows this is an Internet class record.

Whatever follows this is an IP Address.

The best way to interpret this is to start reading from the bottom of the DNS zone file upwards.

The last set of lines in the file tell us that there are five servers that the name server knows about. These servers have IP addresses 10.0.1.5, 10.0.1.6, 10.0.1.7, 10.0.1.2 and 10.0.1.3, and they're known by host names server1, www, mail, dns1 and dns2. These are all within the domain hfhealthclub.com.

The next batch of lines tell us that dns1 and dns2 are name servers, while mail is used as a mail server.

Finally, the top of the file tells us that the primary name server for domain hfhealthclub.com is dns1.

Every host name needs an IP address.

Every host name in a zone file needs to have an IP address or a CNAME record pointing to another host.

Here's what the DNS zone file tells us about the Health Club servers

So how do we visualize this? Here are the servers described in the zone file.

Name Servers

There are two name servers, 10.0.1.2 and 10.0.1.3. These are known as dns1 and dns2 within the domain hfhealthclub.com. The main name server is dns1.

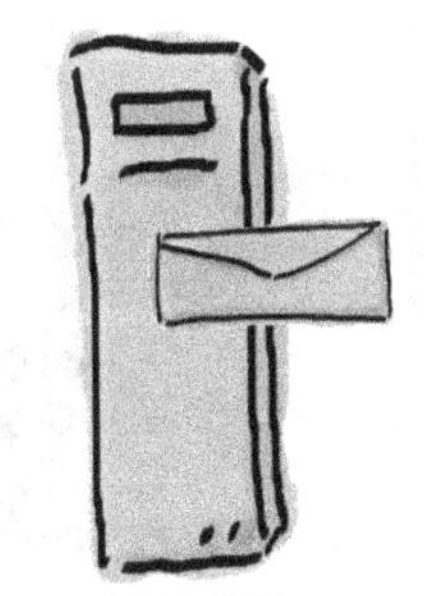

Mail Server

There's one mail server, 10.0.1.7. This has a host name of mail within the domain hfhealthclub.com.

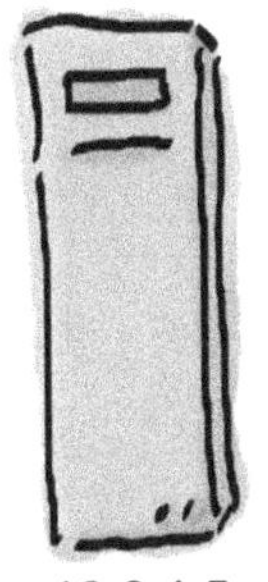

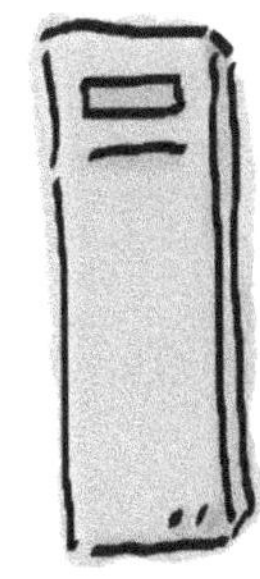

Other Servers

There are two other servers mentioned in the DNS zone file. The first of these is 10.0.1.5 and is known as server1. The second is 10.0.1.6 and is mapped to www. This is the server you get if you browse to www.hfhealthclub.com, so it's the server that holds the Health Club website.

Test Drive

The DNS zone file has been configured as a name server for the Health Club, and the domain registrar notified. In the future, all DNS queries relating to hfhealthclub.com will come via the Health Club name server.

So what effect has adding our own name server had on the Health Club website?

It looks like adding the name server has solved the problem.

Before too long, business is booming, and more and more customers are signing up for classes. But then something weird happens to email...

The Health Club can't send emails

When the DNS server was up and running, everything was great... until someone tried to send an email.

Yikes! This doesn't look good...

```
From: bendy.girl1234@googlemail.com
Subject: Automated Reply

To whom it may concern.

This is an automated reply. The attached email was received
from your IP address (10.0.1.7) but because Reverse DNS was
not enabled at this address, our email policies do not allow
us to forward your email to the orders section. Continued
attempts to re-send this email without RDNS enabled will be
futile and may result in legal action.
Hope this finds you well.

Marvin the Corporate SMTP Agent

Original email follows...
```

Ever since the name server was swapped over, the Health Club has been unable to send emails to their customers, even though they're still able to receive them. This means that they can't send email confirmations to their customers about classes they're interested in, and that's bad for business.

So what do you think the problem could be?

The Health Club uses email addresses in the form <name>@hfhealthclub.com. What do you think the problem might be?

So what's the problem?

The DNS server we've set up allows people to find our IP addresses from fully qualified domain names like this:

Reverse DNS (RDNS) let's you find a domain for an IP address.

www.hfhealthclub.com → 10.0.1.7

The trouble is, the DNS server doesn't allow us to do a Reverse DNS lookup. So what's that?

Reverse DNS lookup allows us to find a fully qualified domain name from an IP address like this:

10.0.1.7 → www.hfhealthclub.com

So why is this a problem? Why didn't the recipient's email system simply pass on the email?

Email servers use RDNS to fight SPAM

SPAM email is a huge problem on the Internet, and email servers have to do a lot of work to protect themselves from being submerged under a pile of junk mail. One common trick that they use is to check the domain name of the email server that sent them the email.

So why would they do that?

Well, the main reason is they need to be sure that the email comes from a reliable source. A spammer might decide to set up an email server on their PC at home. They could then make a connection to the Internet and flood the world with millions and millions of pieces of junk email.

So how does a reverse DNS lookup prevent this from happening?

Check your sources with reverse DNS

To prevent that from happening, email servers look at the IP address of the server that sent the message and do a ***Reverse DNS lookup*** to see which domain the message came from.

If the email message comes from a domain that's on a blocked list, then the email will be rejected.

smtp.spamulike.com? Not very likely. You can go away!

But it will *also* be rejected if the sending server's reverse DNS lookup IP address does not match its real IP address. Spammers try to do this by using a fake domain name.

Look, you aren't really who you say you are. Go away!

In this way Reverse DNS is used to **challenge** the sending server. It's key to preventing chaos on the email system.

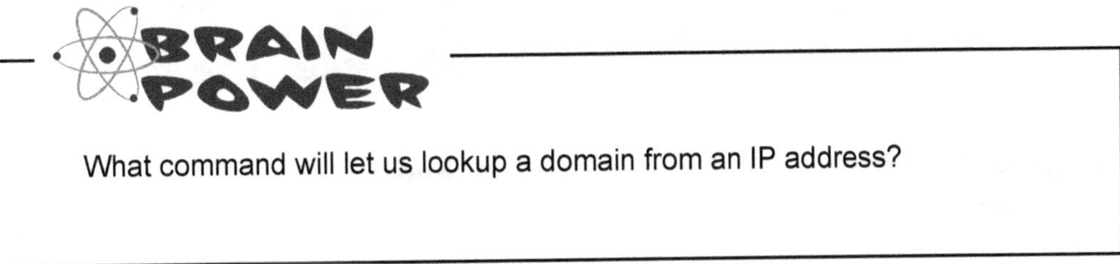

What command will let us lookup a domain from an IP address?

The dig command can do a reverse DNS lookup

We've already used a command that can perform a Reverse DNS lookup—the **dig** command.

The name dig stands for **Domain Information Groper**, and it's your window to the DNS system. It lets you interrogate DNS servers by asking just about any question.

You already know that you can find an IP address from a domain name by using the dig command:

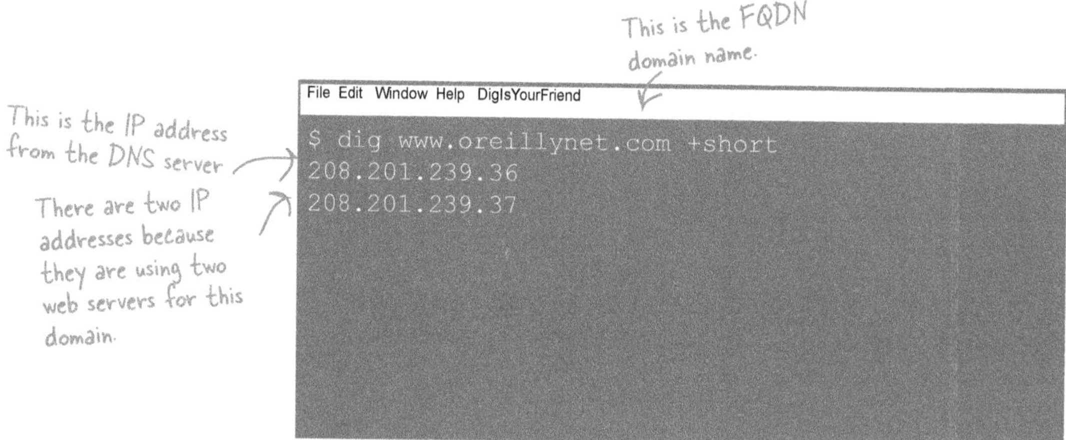
This is the FQDN domain name.
This is the IP address from the DNS server
There are two IP addresses because they are using two web servers for this domain.
File Edit Window Help DigIsYourFriend
$ dig www.oreillynet.com +short
208.201.239.36
208.201.239.37

You can use the dig to go the other way too:

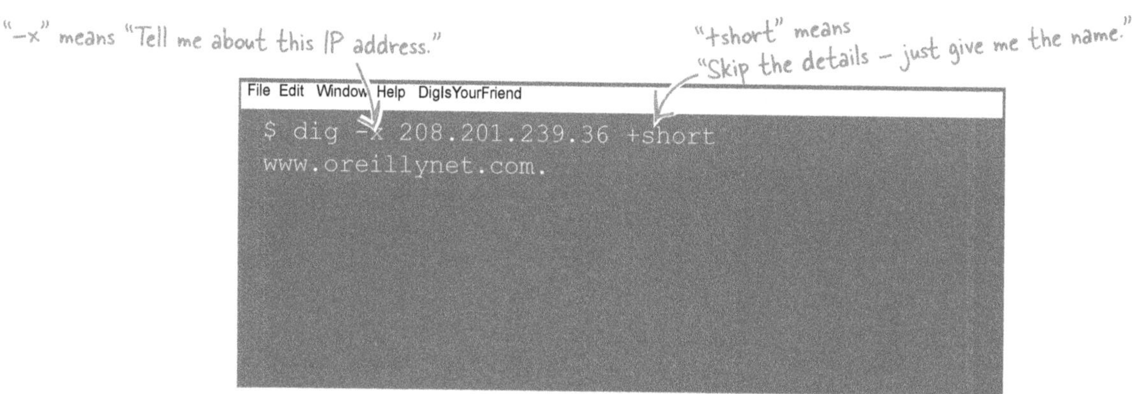
"-x" means "Tell me about this IP address."
"+short" means "Skip the details - just give me the name."
File Edit Window Help DigIsYourFriend
$ dig -x 208.201.239.36 +short
www.oreillynet.com.

So what happens if we try to do a Reverse DNS lookup on our new server?

Watch it!

10.0.1.7 is a private IP address, and the below command will not work in real life.

10.0.1.7 is not assigned to any domain, so the dig command will not return anything if you try this at home.

So are we able to do a reverse DNS? Let's try it and find out.

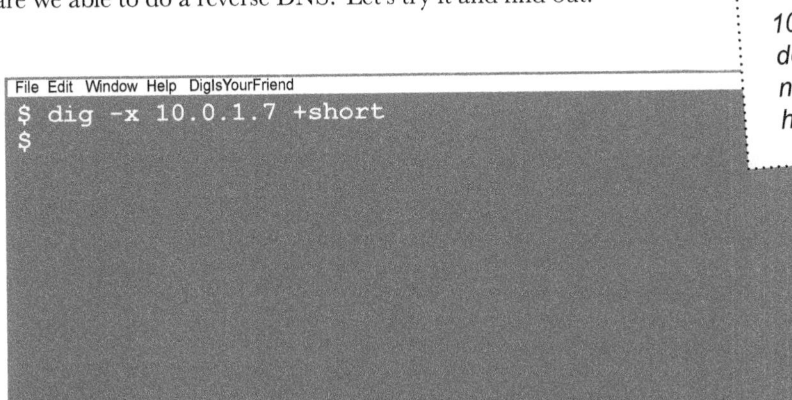


```
$ dig -x 10.0.1.7 +short
$
```

Oh dear—the command didn't return anything. This means that the reverse DNS isn't working.

So how can we fix it?

there are no Dumb Questions

Q: Why didn't the dig command return the domain that the ping command asked about?

A: Sometimes DNS servers associate several domain names with a particular IP address. That allows large companies like Google to give hundreds and thousands of servers the same IP "www.google.com".

Q: Why would they want to do that?

A: Scalability. They can spread millions of requests across thousands of servers.

Your name server has another important zone file...

That is the reverse lookup zone file. This is where all the PTR or pointer records go. Your name server uses this file to do DNS lookups using an IP address to return a FQDN.

```
$ttl 38400
1.0.10.in-addr.arpa. IN SOA skc.edu. hostmaster.1.0.10.in-addr.arpa. (
    2007080609
    10800
    3600
    604800
    38400 )
1.0.10.in-addr.arpa. IN NS dns1.hfhealthclub.com.

5     IN    PTR   www.hfhealthclub.com.
```

So in order to do reverse DNS lookups, we need to make changes to this file.

```
$ttl 38400
1.0.10.in-addr.arpa. IN SOA skc.edu. hostmaster.1.0.10.in-addr.arpa. (
    2007080609
    10800
    3600
    604800
    38400 )
1.0.10.in-addr.arpa. IN NS dns1.hfhealthclub.com.

5     IN    PTR   www.hfhealthclub.com.
7     IN    PTR   mail.hfhealthclub.com
```

This line will allow our name server to answer reverse DNS lookups for our mail server.

BE the Domain Name System

Your job is to play the domain system and fill in what happens in each step of the process of a reverse DNS lookup.

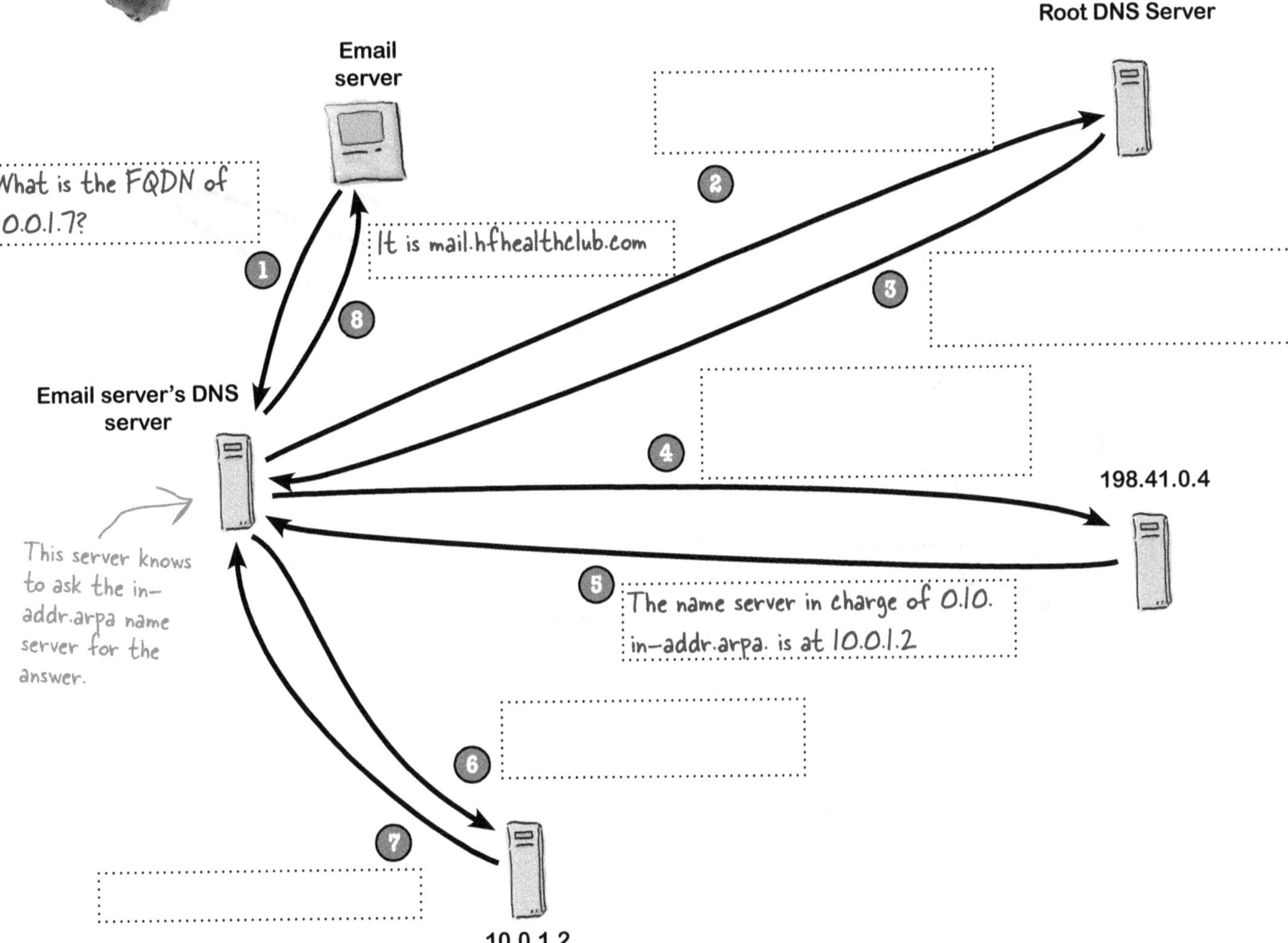

Root DNS Server
Email server
What is the FQDN of 10.0.1.7?
1
It is mail.hfhealthclub.com
8
2
3
Email server's DNS server
4
198.41.0.4
This server knows to ask the in-addr.arpa name server for the answer.
5
The name server in charge of 0.10.in-addr.arpa. is at 10.0.1.2
6
7
10.0.1.2

BE the Domain Name System Solution

Your job is to play the domain system and fill in what happens in each step of the process of a reverse DNS lookup.

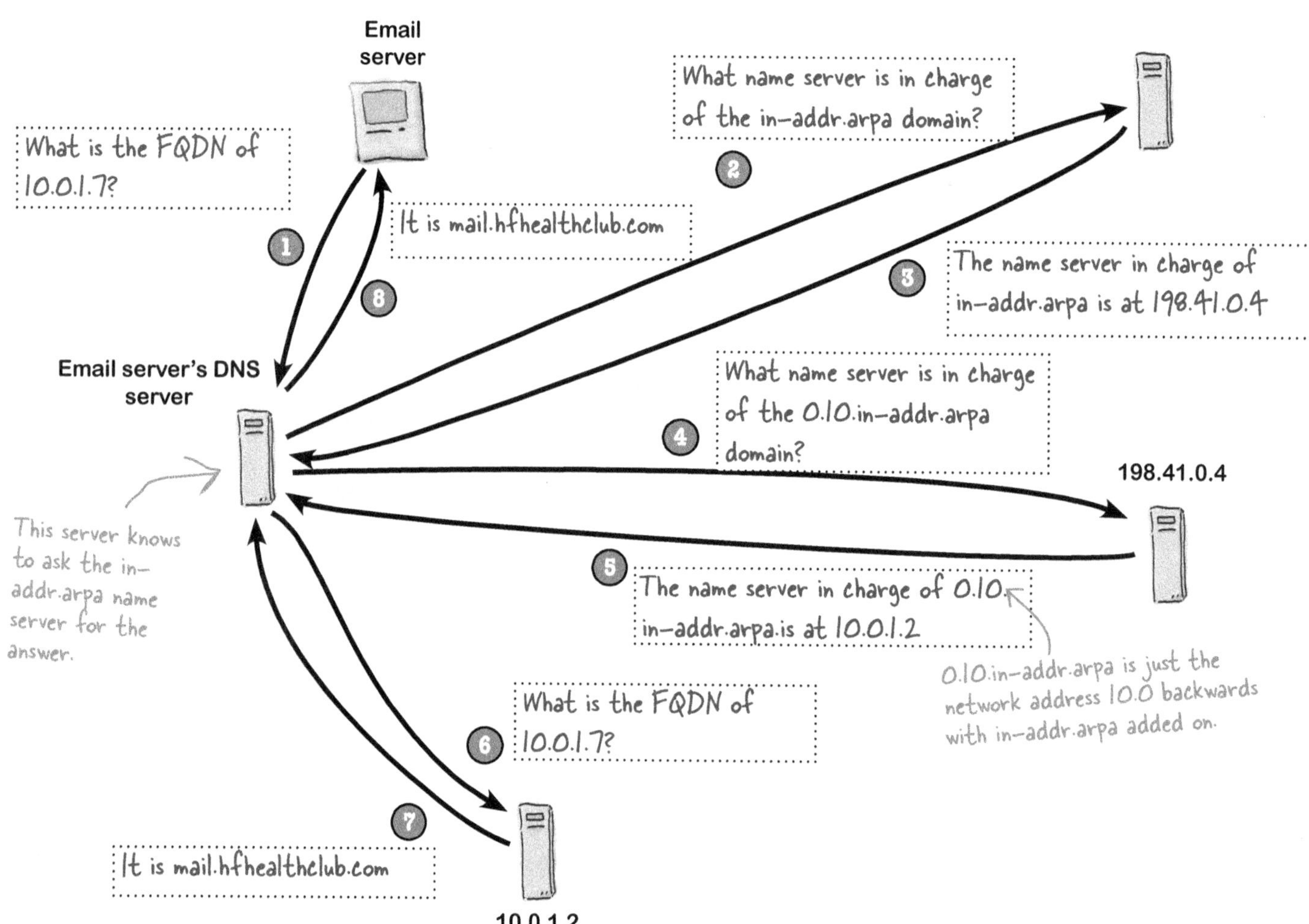

Email server
What is the FQDN of 10.0.1.7?
1
It is mail.hfhealthclub.com
8
What name server is in charge of the in-addr.arpa domain?
2
The name server in charge of in-addr.arpa is at 198.41.0.4
3
Email server's DNS server
This server knows to ask the in-addr.arpa name server for the answer.
What name server is in charge of the 0.10.in-addr.arpa domain?
4
198.41.0.4
5
The name server in charge of 0.10.in-addr.arpa.is at 10.0.1.2
0.10.in-addr.arpa is just the network address 10.0 backwards with in-addr.arpa added on.
What is the FQDN of 10.0.1.7?
6
7
It is mail.hfhealthclub.com
10.0.1.2

What's up with the
backwards IP addresses?
They are backwards, right?

Backward IP addresses allow the name servers to work from the top down.

They start with the root DNS servers (the in-addr.arpa part) and work their way down the IP network address until they find the name server responsible for that particular IP network.

dns1.hfhealthclub.com is responsible for this part.

in-addr.arpa at arin.net is responsible for this part.

0.10.in-addr.arpa

This is a FQDN—a very special one.

Why wouldn't an IP address in the normal order work for reverse DNS lookups?

Test Drive

Let's try doing a reverse DNS lookup again using dig.

File Edit Window Help DigIsYourFriend

```
$ dig -x 10.0.1.7 +short
www.hfhealthclub.com
$
```

The Reverse DNS is working! That means your server now works both ways—it's made the link from the FQDN to the IP address:

www.hfhealthclub.com → 10.0.1.7

And by using Reverse DNS, it's also made the link from the IP address to the FQDN:

10.0.1.7 → www.hfhealthclub.com

So has this fixed the email problem?

The emails are working!

Following your change, the Health Club can successfully send emails to their customers, which means that they can send email confirmations telling customers which courses they are enrolled in. Before too long, all of their classes are filled to capacity.

9 monitoring and troubleshooting

Listen to Your Network's Troubles

Listening to your network can save you lots of heartache!

Well, you have your network up and running. But like anything, it needs to be monitored and maintained. If it's not, one day it will just stop working, and you will have no idea why. You will discover in this chapter various tools and techniques to help you listen to your network and understand what is going on with it, so you can deal with any problem before it becomes a bigger problem.

Pajama Death are back on tour

Punk band Pajama Death have a large and dedicated fan base, and they've just announced their latest world tour. Tickets go on sale in just two hours, and fans are already lining up to buy prized tickets. The ticket agency expects it to be a sell-out, but there's just one problem: can their network cope with the strain?

Guys, the network's up and down like a freaking yo-yo. If you don't get it sorted by the time the Pajama Death tickets go on sale, I'll come around your houses and stomp on all your toys. Got it?

So here's your challenge...

The ticket agency needs to be up and running in two hours time, which means that you need to troubleshoot the immediate problems. What's more, you need to make sure that the network remains stable. You need to deal with network problems before they become bigger problems. Think you can do it?

So where would you start troubleshooting a misfiring network?

Since you have made it this far in this book, you know there are many things that can go wrong on a network. Anything from bad or disconnected cables, switch and router issues, and even individual computer issues. Troubleshooting network issues requires a methodical approach. If you just start running around with your network analyzer, plugging and unplugging connections, you will find troubleshooting a very exhausting and frustrating endeavor.

Getting information from your network is the key to successful troubleshooting.

Sharpen your pencil

In the space below, write down a few things you would check in your network troubleshooting process.

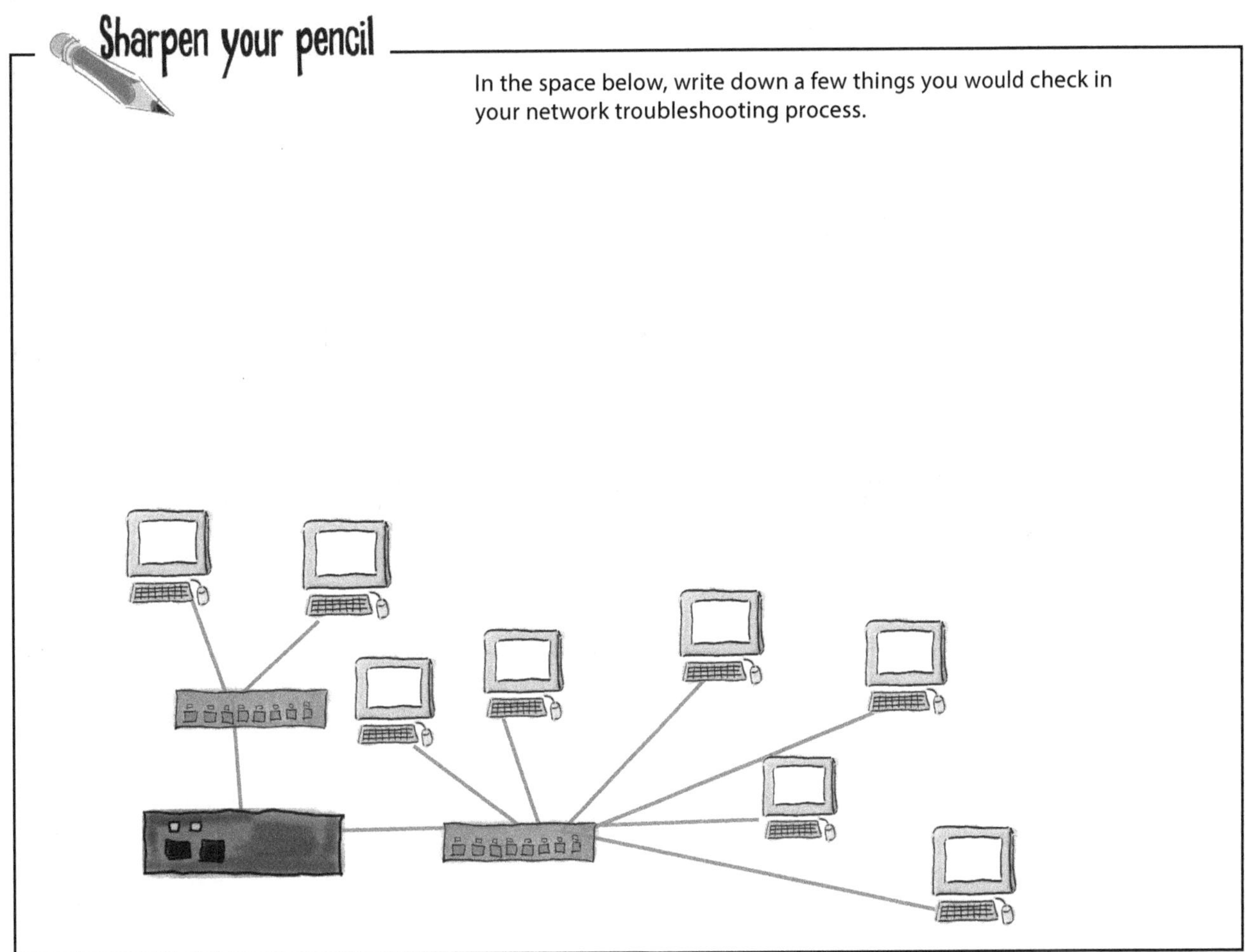

Sharpen your pencil Solution

In the space below, write down a few things you would check in your network troubleshooting process.

Ask user to demonstrate the problem.
Check for loose or disconnected cables on the computer with the problems.
Ask around to other people. Is the problem just one person, one area, or the entire network?
Check the router and switches to make sure they are on and running properly.
See if you can ping various devices and clients on the network.

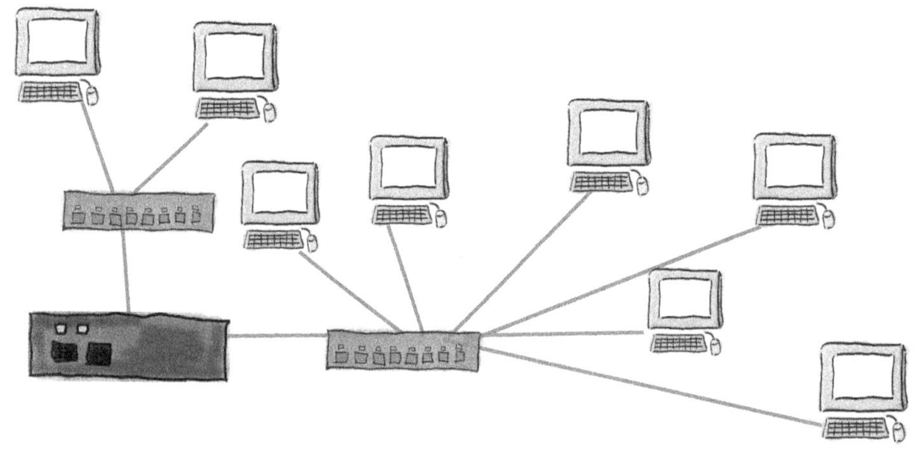

Start troubleshooting your network problems by checking in with your network devices

You want to start troubleshooting network problems by gathering information from your devices. In chapter 5 and 6, you learned the ping command and how to communicate with a switch and a router. You can use those tools to troubleshoot your network.

1. **Start off by pinging the IP addresses of the computer's default gateway.**
   If you can do this without the ping timing out, then you know that the network is working minimally.

   As an example, ping 192.168.1.1

2. **Connect a computer to the router with a serial cable or via SSH or telnet.**
   SSH is the preferred way to access your devices, although sometimes devices only support telnet. That way, you do not have to run all over the place with a cable. Besides, SSH is more secure than telnet.

   You did this back in chapter 6.

3. **Use the appropriate commands (like `show`) to look at a device's status and counters.**
   Routers and switches can collect lots of information that is very valuable in troubleshooting your network. The most common command is the **`show`** command. It shows you various counters and status information on your devices.

4. **Interpret the statistics to gain some insight on how your network is behaving.**
   This is the hardest part, how to interpret that data. You will want to start looking at the obvious things, like interfaces being down or ports with excessive errors. After that, you have to become more of a detective and look at traffic volume. Often you will have to look at information from multiple devices in order to form an opinion.

Troubleshoot network connectivity with the ping command

The ping command is the best tool to get a quick read on the overall status of your network and individual devices on your network. It can tell you whether or not your network is functioning, or whether a particular device is on the network.

The ping command can be used to ping anything with an IP address, including other computers.

If you can ping, you get timings

Here's what the output of a successful ping looks like. It tells you how long it takes your device to respond to the ping. Comparing these times with what you'd expect to get can give you some useful diagnostics.

```
Terminal — bash — 85×23
~ $ ping -c 5 -v 192.168.1.1
PING 192.168.1.1 (192.168.1.1): 56 data bytes
64 bytes from 192.168.1.1: icmp_seq=0 ttl=64 time=0.582 ms
64 bytes from 192.168.1.1: icmp_seq=1 ttl=64 time=0.575 ms
64 bytes from 192.168.1.1: icmp_seq=2 ttl=64 time=0.576 ms
64 bytes from 192.168.1.1: icmp_seq=3 ttl=64 time=0.574 ms
64 bytes from 192.168.1.1: icmp_seq=4 ttl=64 time=0.590 ms

--- 192.168.1.1 ping statistics ---
5 packets transmitted, 5 packets received, 0% packet loss
round-trip min/avg/max/stddev = 0.574/0.579/0.590/0.006 ms
~ $
```

The time here is how long it takes your ping to get to the device. It's useful to know how long this should take.

But what if you can't ping?

If a ping command fails, this means that you can't get to the device at the specified IP address. If you can't ping anything, you've got BIG problems. If you just can't ping one device, that really narrows down what you have to look at.

```
Terminal — ping — 80×24
Last login: Tue Mar 31 09:31:11 on ttys000
~ $ ping 192.168.21.1
PING 192.168.21.1 (192.168.21.1): 56 data bytes
```

Yikes! If you get this sort of message, you need to do more investigating.

If the ping fails, check the cables

So what do you do if you can't ping anything?

The first thing to do is check your computer's network cables and network configuration. Try the ping command from another computer. If your computer's stuff checks out and the ping command on the other computer fails as well, then you need to physically go to the network devices.

So what sorts of things do you need to look out for?

Did the power go out?

Is the computer even connected to the network?

Did a construction worker rip up a cable?

Did a critical network device fail?

Did the janitor pull the plug?

Did a circuit breaker blow?

These are all real things that happen to your network, so look out for them.

What other tools on a computer could you use to help troubleshoot network problems (especially if the computer is connected to the network and still not working)?

Long Exercise

Look at the ping output below and circle the devices that are causing problems on the network.

File Edit Window Help PingIsYourFriend

```
ping 192.168.1.2
64 bytes from 192.168.1.2: icmp_seq=0 ttl=64 time=0.590 ms
ping 192.168.1.3
ping: sendto: Host is down
ping 192.168.1.1
64 bytes from 192.168.1.1: icmp_seq=0 ttl=64 time=0.290 ms
ping 192.168.1.4
64 bytes from 192.168.1.4: icmp_seq=0 ttl=64 time=0.450 ms
ping 192.168.1.5
ping: sendto: Host is down
ping 192.168.1.6
64 bytes from 192.168.1.4: icmp_seq=0 ttl=64 time=0.560 ms
ping 192.168.2.2
64 bytes from 192.168.1.4: icmp_seq=0 ttl=64 time=0.720 ms
ping 192.168.2.3
ping: sendto: Host is down
ping 192.168.2.4
ping: sendto: Host is down
```

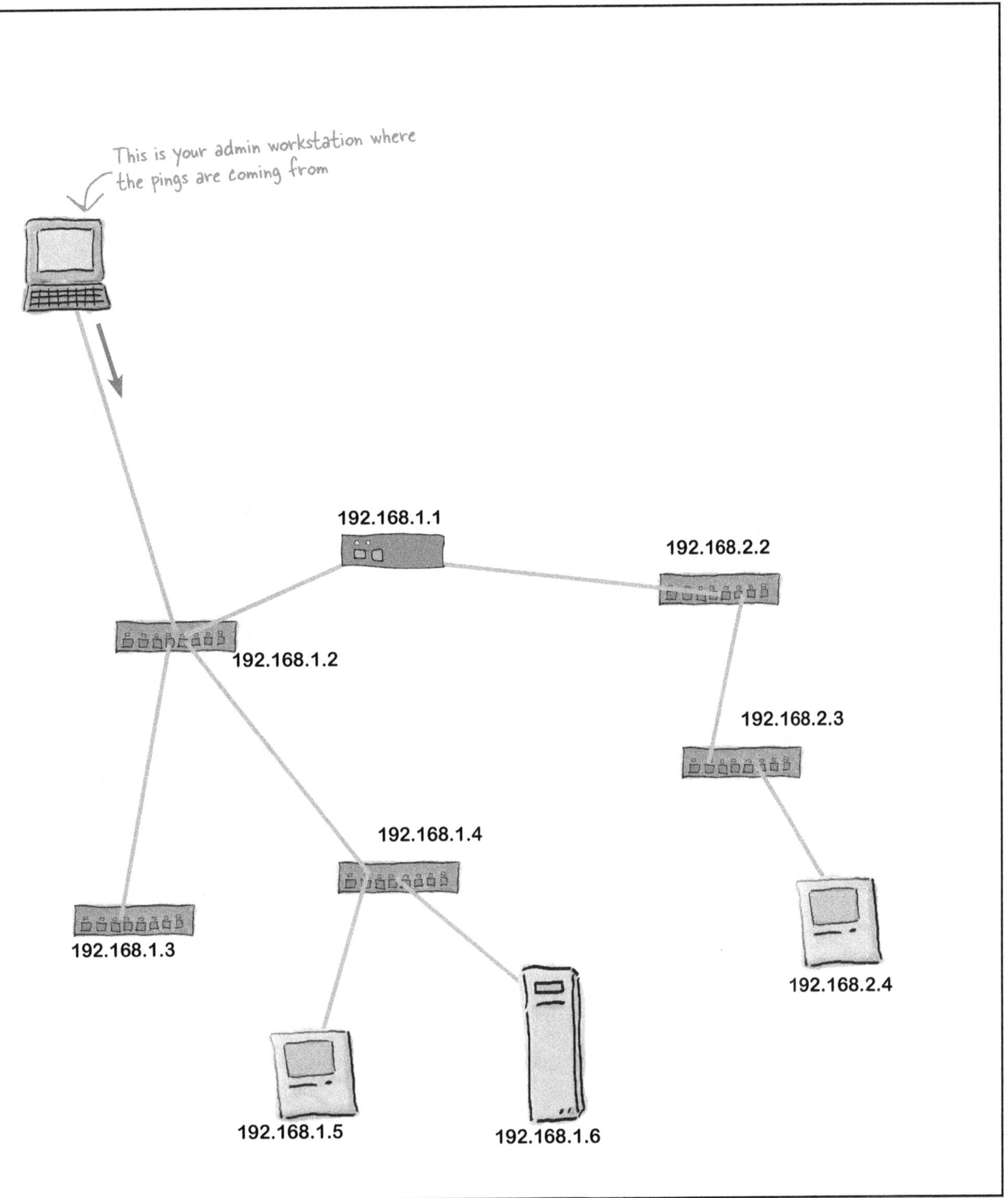
This is your admin workstation where the pings are coming from
192.168.1.1
192.168.2.2
192.168.1.2
192.168.2.3
192.168.1.4
192.168.1.3
192.168.2.4
192.168.1.5
192.168.1.6

Long Exercise Solution

Look at the ping output below and circle the devices that are causing problems on the network.

File Edit Window Help PingIsYourFriend

```
ping 192.168.1.2
64 bytes from 192.168.1.2: icmp_seq=0 ttl=64 time=0.590 ms
ping 192.168.1.3
ping: sendto: Host is down
ping 192.168.1.1
64 bytes from 192.168.1.1: icmp_seq=0 ttl=64 time=0.290 ms
ping 192.168.1.4
64 bytes from 192.168.1.4: icmp_seq=0 ttl=64 time=0.450 ms
ping 192.168.1.5
ping: sendto: Host is down
ping 192.168.1.6
64 bytes from 192.168.1.4: icmp_seq=0 ttl=64 time=0.560 ms
ping 192.168.2.2
64 bytes from 192.168.1.4: icmp_seq=0 ttl=64 time=0.720 ms
ping 192.168.2.3
ping: sendto: Host is down
ping 192.168.2.4
ping: sendto: Host is down
```

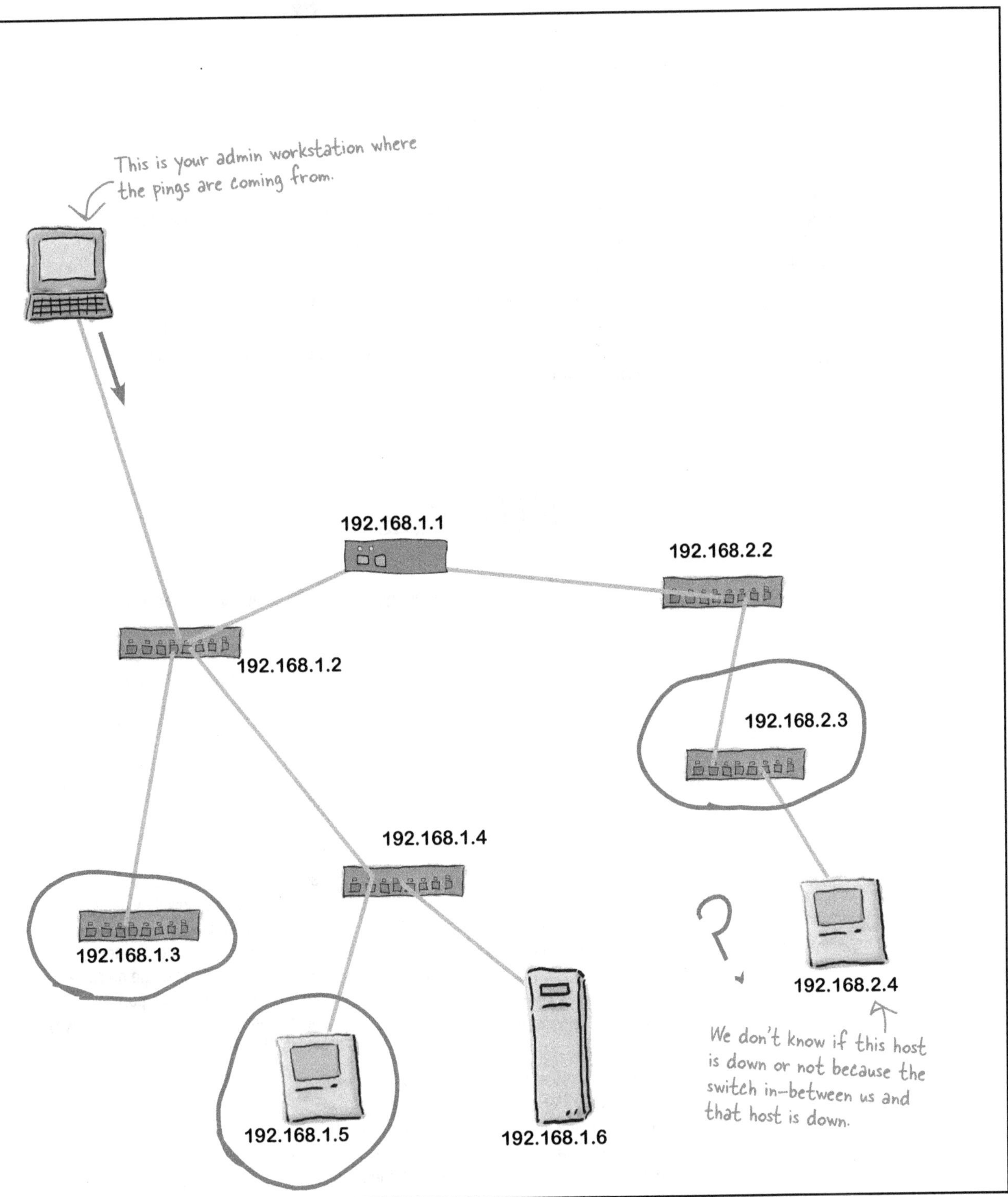
This is your admin workstation where the pings are coming from.
192.168.1.1
192.168.2.2
192.168.1.2
192.168.2.3
192.168.1.4
192.168.1.3
?
192.168.2.4
We don't know if this host is down or not because the switch in-between us and that host is down.
192.168.1.5
192.168.1.6

But what if we need more information than ping can give us? What then?

Sometimes ping just doesn't give you enough information to work with.

The ping command is very effective in helping you with connectivity issues. But when it comes to network issues such as slowdowns or sporadic connectivity, ping does not help much. We need to pull out the big guns and talk to the switches and routers themselves.

there are no Dumb Questions

Q: What kind of information can a switch give me?

A: It can give you the number of frames going in and out of particular ports. It can give error rates on its various ports. It can tell you if a port has an active client or not.

Q: How about a router?

A: A router is a whole other animal when it comes to information. Even a mid-range router will give you an incredible amount of information. This includes packet counts, error rates, and interface status, just like a switch. But it can also give you the status of routing and even the status of other routers.

Q: Can computers give me this type of information?

A: Yes, they can. Most modern operating systems can collect information. Some of it is easily accessible from the command line or from logs that the OS keeps. It is similar information to what a switch collects.

Q: Is the ping command available on all computer operating systems?

A: The ping command is available on just about every computer and router operating system out there.

Q: Is there any time the ping command will not work?

A: Yes, a router can be configured to block the ICMP packets. ICMP is the packet type that the ping command uses. If a router is blocking these, you will not see anything until the command times out, then you will get an error.

Q: Can a computer block a ping?

A: Yes, pings can be blocked by computers as well. The firewall can be configured to just ignore ping requests and drop them without responding.

Q: Why would you want to block pings?

A: One of the techniques that hackers use is that of scanning a network for hosts. One of the tools they use is the ping command or software that acts like a ping command. If your computer or router responds to a ping, then the hacker knows that there is a device at a particular IP address and can start figuring out a way to get into the system.

Get started with the show interface command

The `show interface` command is the best command to get started with. It will give you the most concentrated information on the status of your device's network connection. It works on most network devices, including switches and routers.

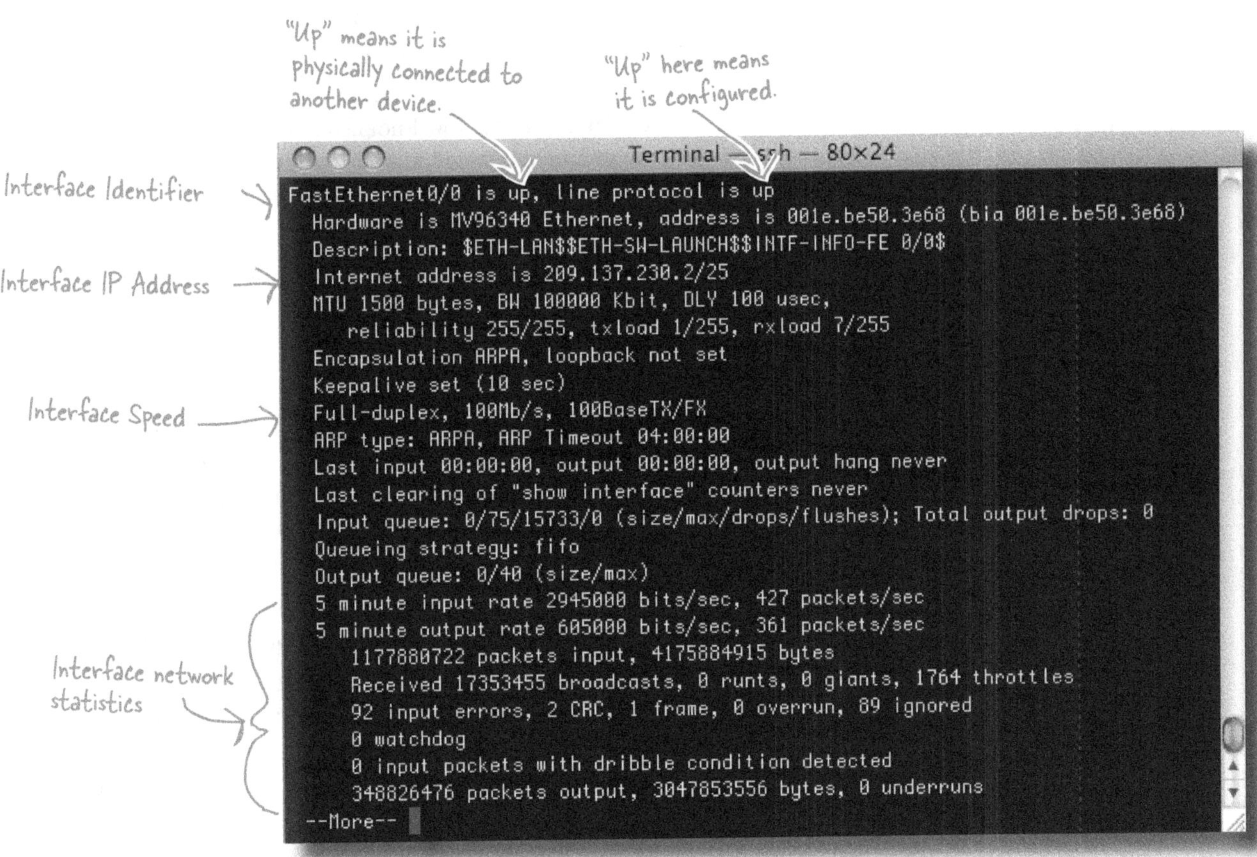

"Up" means it is physically connected to another device.
"Up" here means it is configured.
Interface Identifier
Interface IP Address
Interface Speed
Interface network statistics
Terminal — ssh — 80×24
FastEthernet0/0 is up, line protocol is up
Hardware is MV96340 Ethernet, address is 001e.be50.3e68 (bia 001e.be50.3e68)
Description: $ETH-LAN$$ETH-SW-LAUNCH$$INTF-INFO-FE 0/0$
Internet address is 209.137.230.2/25
MTU 1500 bytes, BW 100000 Kbit, DLY 100 usec,
reliability 255/255, txload 1/255, rxload 7/255
Encapsulation ARPA, loopback not set
Keepalive set (10 sec)
Full-duplex, 100Mb/s, 100BaseTX/FX
ARP type: ARPA, ARP Timeout 04:00:00
Last input 00:00:00, output 00:00:00, output hang never
Last clearing of "show interface" counters never
Input queue: 0/75/15733/0 (size/max/drops/flushes); Total output drops: 0
Queueing strategy: fifo
Output queue: 0/40 (size/max)
5 minute input rate 2945000 bits/sec, 427 packets/sec
5 minute output rate 605000 bits/sec, 361 packets/sec
1177880722 packets input, 4175884915 bytes
Received 17353455 broadcasts, 0 runts, 0 giants, 1764 throttles
92 input errors, 2 CRC, 1 frame, 0 overrun, 89 ignored
0 watchdog
0 input packets with dribble condition detected
348826476 packets output, 3047853556 bytes, 0 underruns
--More--

The interface's network statistics are a gold mine of troubleshooting information

You can tell how busy the network connected to a particular interface is by looking at the number of packets being input and output from that interface. After looking at this a couple of times, you will be able to judge whether the number is of the correct magnitude. You can also see any errors. Some errors are normal, but high error counts should lead you to investigate the portion of your network connected to that particular interface.

Cisco Show Command Exposed

This week's interview:
Can you tell us all you know about the hardware you are running on?

HeadFirst: It is great to get a chance to talk with you. How are you doing today?

Show Command: What specific part of today are you asking about? I can tell you about many aspects of my day.

HeadFirst: OK, I was just trying to make some small talk. But to get started, what can you tell me about the network device you are running on?

Show Command: You need to be a little more specific than that. I can tell you things about the interfaces, the system itself, the software version, the IP statistics, the TCP statistics, the IP routing statistics, the processor's information and statistics, the SNMP statistics, the startup and running configurations, the...

HeadFirst: Whoa, whoa! That is a lot of information. What would you recommend if I wanted to know how the devices' interfaces are doing?

Show Command: That would be "show interfaces." With that command I will show you whether the interface is connected to another device, whether it is configured or not, the interface's IP address and subnet, and network statistics about the interface.

HeadFirst: Will you tell me about all the interfaces?

Show Command: If you just ask me to show interfaces, I will give all that information I just mentioned all the interfaces that are on the device—even if they are not configured.

HeadFirst: Great, is there anything else that you can tell me that might help troubleshoot network problems?

Show Command: I can tell you about IP statistics with the show ip traffic command. I'll give you all sorts of information about the various IP protocols the device is running, including traffic amounts and various errors.

HeadFirst: Now I noticed that you like to have commands issued in a very certain way. Can you tell me a little more about that?

Show Command: Sure, obviously you have to type "show" then follow it with what you are interested in. For example, "show interface," which we already talked about. But, you can get more specific information by adding modifiers after that initial command.

HeadFirst: Can you give me an example?

Show Command: OK, say you want to see the the EIGRP routes in the device route table. You would type "show ip route eigrp." Then I would display all the EIGRP routes that are in the table.

HeadFirst: That's cool! So what if I don't know what command to type?

Show Command: Easy, type show. I will display a list of commands with descriptions. Then if you find a particular command, then you can type "show ip," and I will display the commands available under the ip command.

HeadFirst: Thanks for the interview. You are indeed a valuable command to learn.

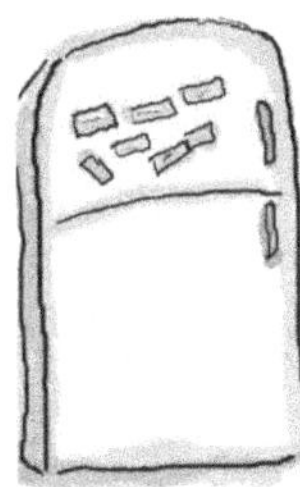

Show Command Magnets

The show command from the Cisco IOS is a hierarchy command. You build a show command by walking down a tree until you get to the information you need. Arrange the magnets into the proper structure.

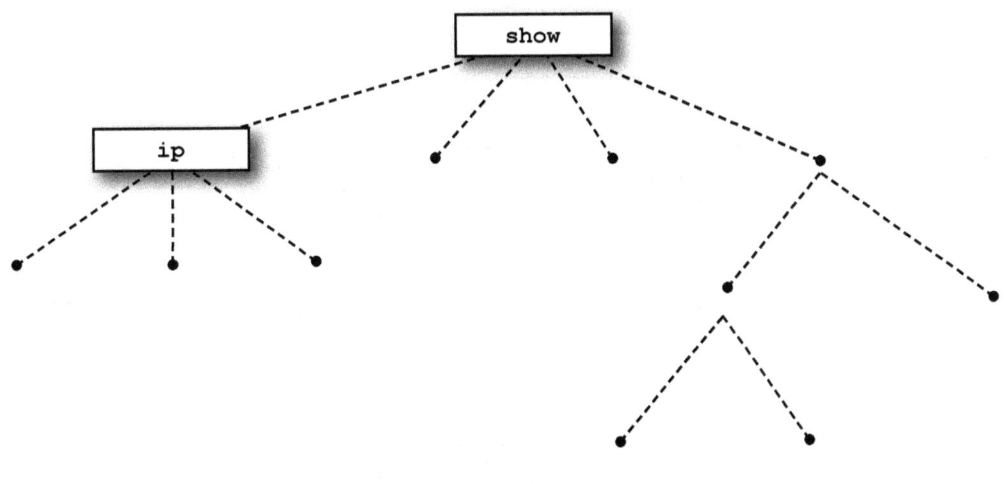

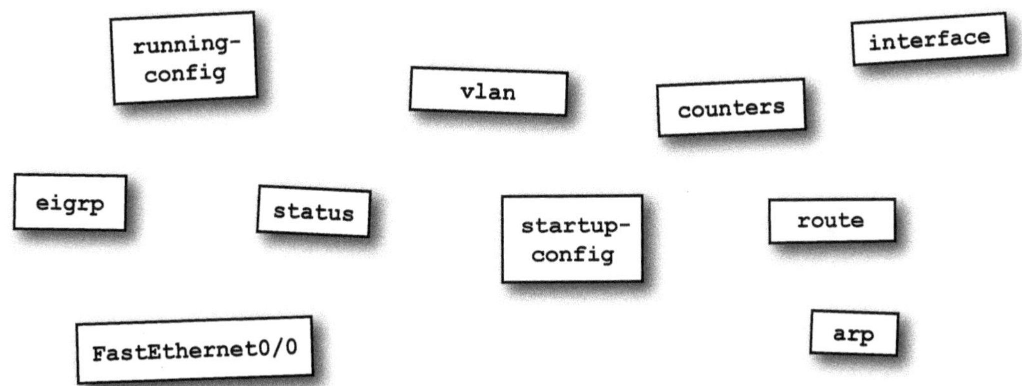

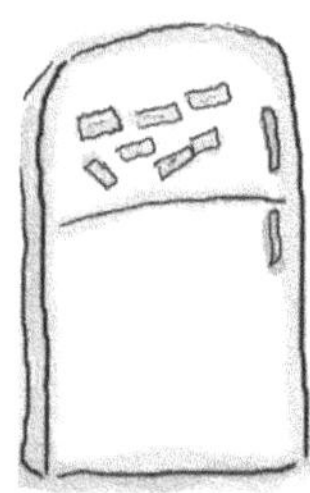

Show Command Magnets Solution

The show command from the Cisco IOS is a hierarchy command. You build a show command by walking down a tree until you get to the information you need. Arrange the magnets into the proper structure.

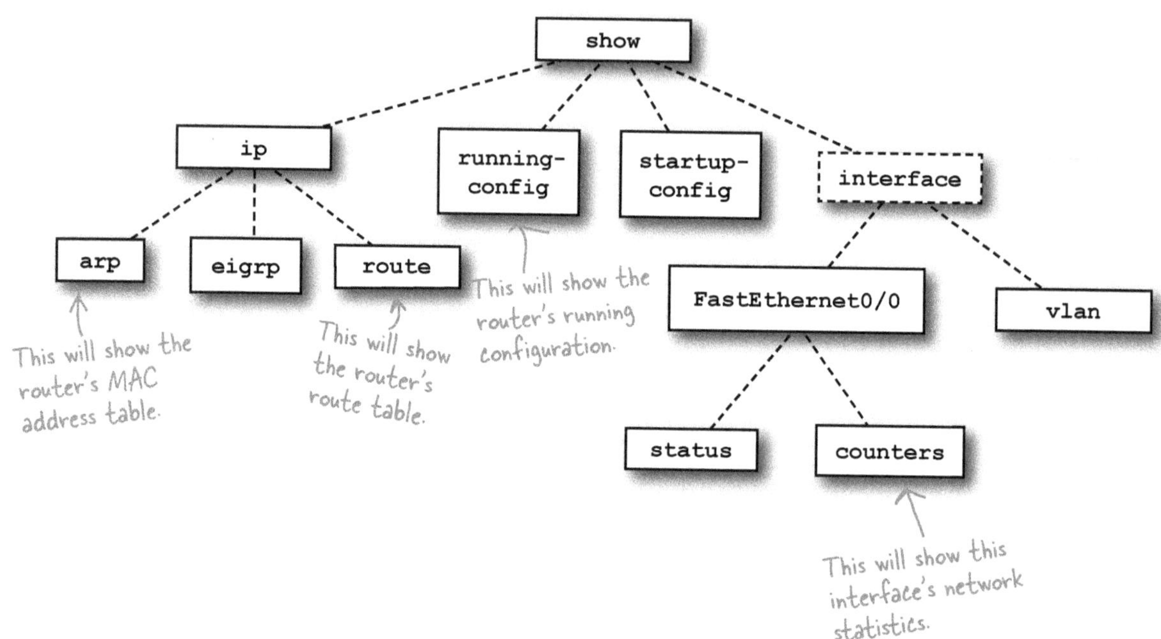

The ticket network's still not fixed

Time's ticking on, and the ticket agency network still has problems. So what's causing the hold up?

This is really serious! We can't get to all of the network devices with SSH or telnet. That means I have to run round hooking my laptop up to each one of them to find out what's wrong. It's taking me forever, and the Pajama Death tickets go on sale soon. What can we do?

How can we quickly troubleshoot networks without SSH or telnet?

The trouble with SSH and telnet is that they're not always available. While we could visit each network device and connect a laptop to it to get diagnostics, this approach is time-consuming and inefficient. So is there a better way of troubleshooting the network?

SNMP to the rescue!

SNMP (Simple Network Management Protocol) is a way to talk to your network devices and get all kinds of information from them **without having to connect each device to a laptop.** You can use a software program to automatically question any or all your network devices every so often. This allows you to check on their health and their workloads. The protocol uses simple commands to access a database of information on the target device.

The information database of an SNMP managed device is called the MIB (Management Information Base).

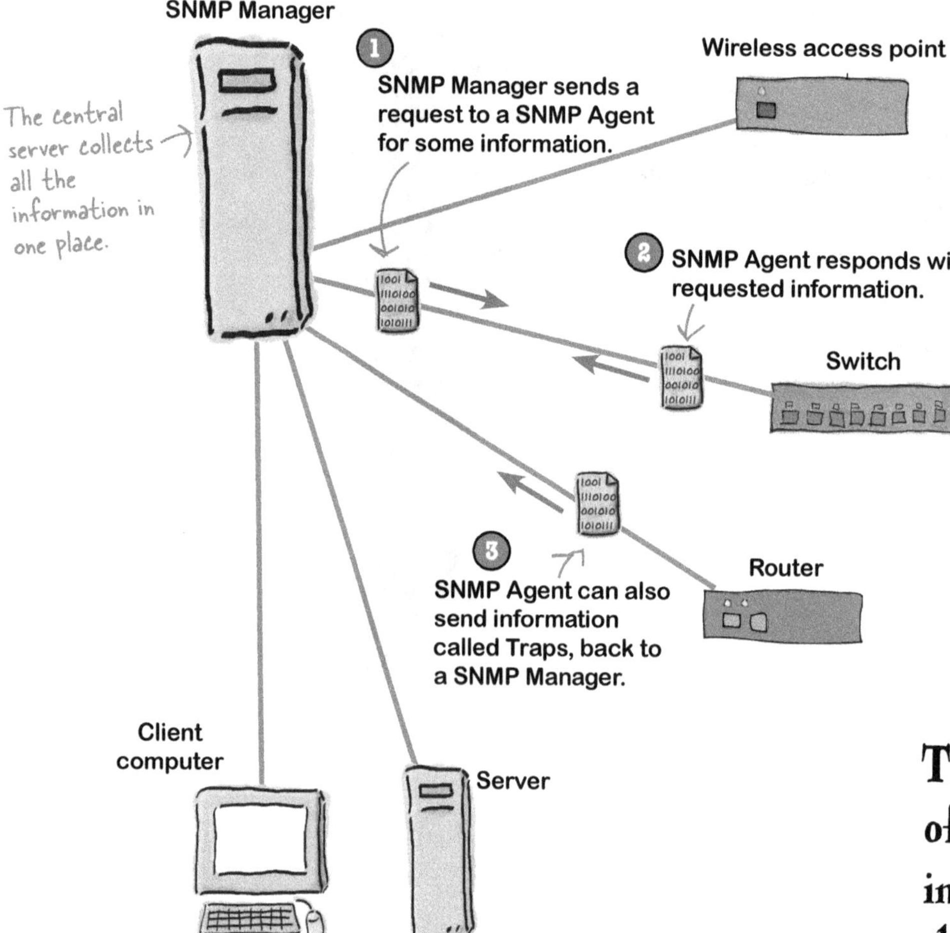

SNMP Manager
The central server collects all the information in one place.
1 SNMP Manager sends a request to a SNMP Agent for some information.
Wireless access point
2 SNMP Agent responds with requested information.
Switch
3 SNMP Agent can also send information called Traps, back to a SNMP Manager.
Router
Client computer
Server

The object identifier of information stored in the MIB is called the OID.

SNMP is a network admininistrator's communication tool

SNMP has been designed so simple software such as scripts can be used to query different information from a network device. It uses a simple set of commands to retrieve and set information. SNMP gets a bit complicated in the implementation of the MIBs. There are standardized sets of MIBs that are available to network equipment manufacturers to implement in their devices. As long as a manufacturer has implemented the MIB properly, there usually isn't a problem retrieving information via SNMP. The problems occur when network devices have custom MIBs. Then in order to read this information, a network administrator has to include the modified SNMP template on the SNMP requester so it knows the correct OID to ask for from the SNMP agent.

Did you know that there are three versions of SNMP? SNMP v1, SNMP v2, and SNMP v3.

SNMP v2 is just an expanded version of SNMP v1.

SNMP v3 is a whole rewrite of the protocol. It has authentication built into the protocol.

So what prevents just anybody from getting to that information? It is secure, right?

SNMP does allow some access control

SNMP does have one feature allowing you to control access. When you setup SNMP on a network device, you can create a group name that can have read-only access and a group name that can have read-write access. The problem is that **the group name is the password.** That's not a very good scheme, so that's why SNMP version 3 has an authentication system built into it.

Most devices default with public being the group to have read-only access.

So how do we set up SNMP?

How to configure SNMP on a Cisco device

Let's take a look at how to get a basic setup of SNMP on a Cisco device. You'll need to type these commands at the device command line in config mode.

A basic setup of SNMP is all you need to access lots of handy information.

1. **Start SNMP service on router.**
   Actually, there's no specific command for this. The first snmp-server command you enter, regardless of the command, will enable the SNMP service on the device.

2. **Create a community access control for SNMP.**
   To do this, type the command:

   ```
   snmp-server community public ro
   ```

   This will give public read-only access.

3. **Set some basic system info.**
   To set up your contact information, type the command:

   ```
   snmp-server contact yourname
   ```

   To set up the location of the device, type the command:

   ```
   snmp-server location place
   ```

4. **Save your setup.**
   To save your config setup, type the commands:

   ```
   exit
   write memory
   ```

Setting up SNMP on a non-Cisco is really similar to this.

Other network devices are configured in a similar fashion—just check your device documentation for the specifics.

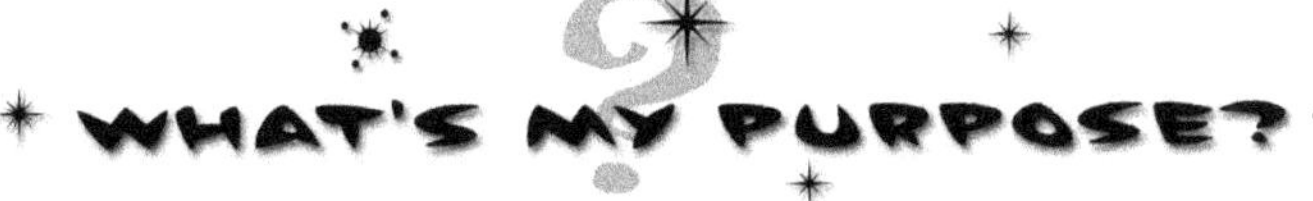

Match each SNMP command to what it does.

GET	Retrieves some information from the SNMP managed device
SET	Retrieves information from the SNMP managed device that is the value of the next OID in the tree.
GET-NEXT	A command the managed device sends to the agent with some information.
GET-RESPONSE	This is the information that the SNMP agent requested.
TRAP	Allows the SNMP agent to change a value on the managed device.

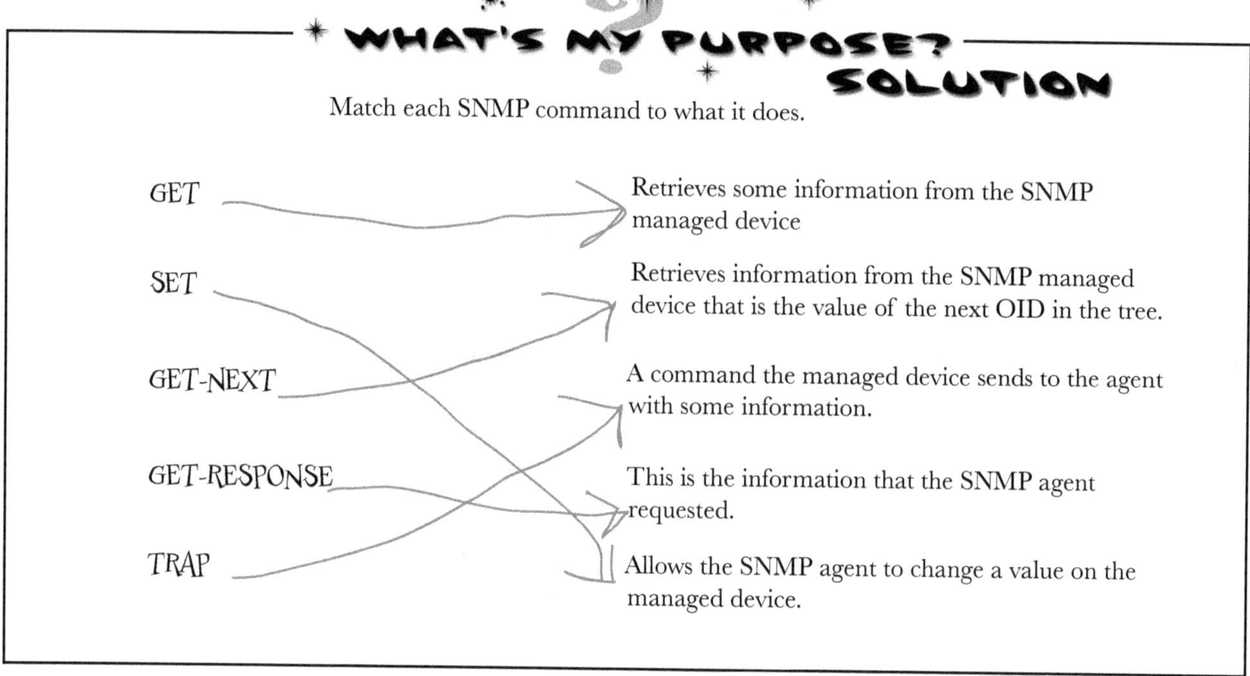
WHAT'S MY PURPOSE? SOLUTION
Match each SNMP command to what it does.
GET
SET
GET-NEXT
GET-RESPONSE
TRAP
Retrieves some information from the SNMP managed device
Retrieves information from the SNMP managed device that is the value of the next OID in the tree.
A command the managed device sends to the agent with some information.
This is the information that the SNMP agent requested.
Allows the SNMP agent to change a value on the managed device.

there are no Dumb Questions

Q: Can I tell a device what type of information I want to receive from it via SNMP?

A: No, the MIB is essentially coded and, in some cases, in the hardware. So you really can't have a device collect different information from what the manufacturer decided to put into the MIB.

Q: Why do the OIDs have such odd and complex names?

A: The first thing that makes them complex is that no spaces are allowed in an OID. So they looked all crammed together. Second, there are so many types of information that people want to collect; that leads to some pretty complex names.

Q: Is a OID the whole name of the information I want to get?

A: No, the entire name is from the top of the tree down. And the name is actually a number like .1.3.6.1.2.1.2.2.1.2.

Q: How do I find anything? These numbers don't tell me what I am looking at.

A: Good question. Like we said, many of these OIDs and MIBs are standard. So you can look up the standards, RFC1213, and it will tell you all the OIDs that this MIB has.

Q: Is there software to help me manage SNMP?

A: There is open source software like Nagios and MRTG available to help monitor your network. There is also tons of commercial software available. Some of these have great network maps with traffic flows and colored network devices. The big network monitoring centers of ISPs use software like this to keep tabs on their networks via SNMP.

Q: What's a Trap?

A: A Trap is a message that a SNMP end device sends to the SNMP manager. It is just a message sent because the Agent has trapped an event and is configured to send that trapped event message to the SNMP manager.

Sharpen your pencil

Circle the OIDs from the MIB tree below that could help you to troubleshoot a network problem?

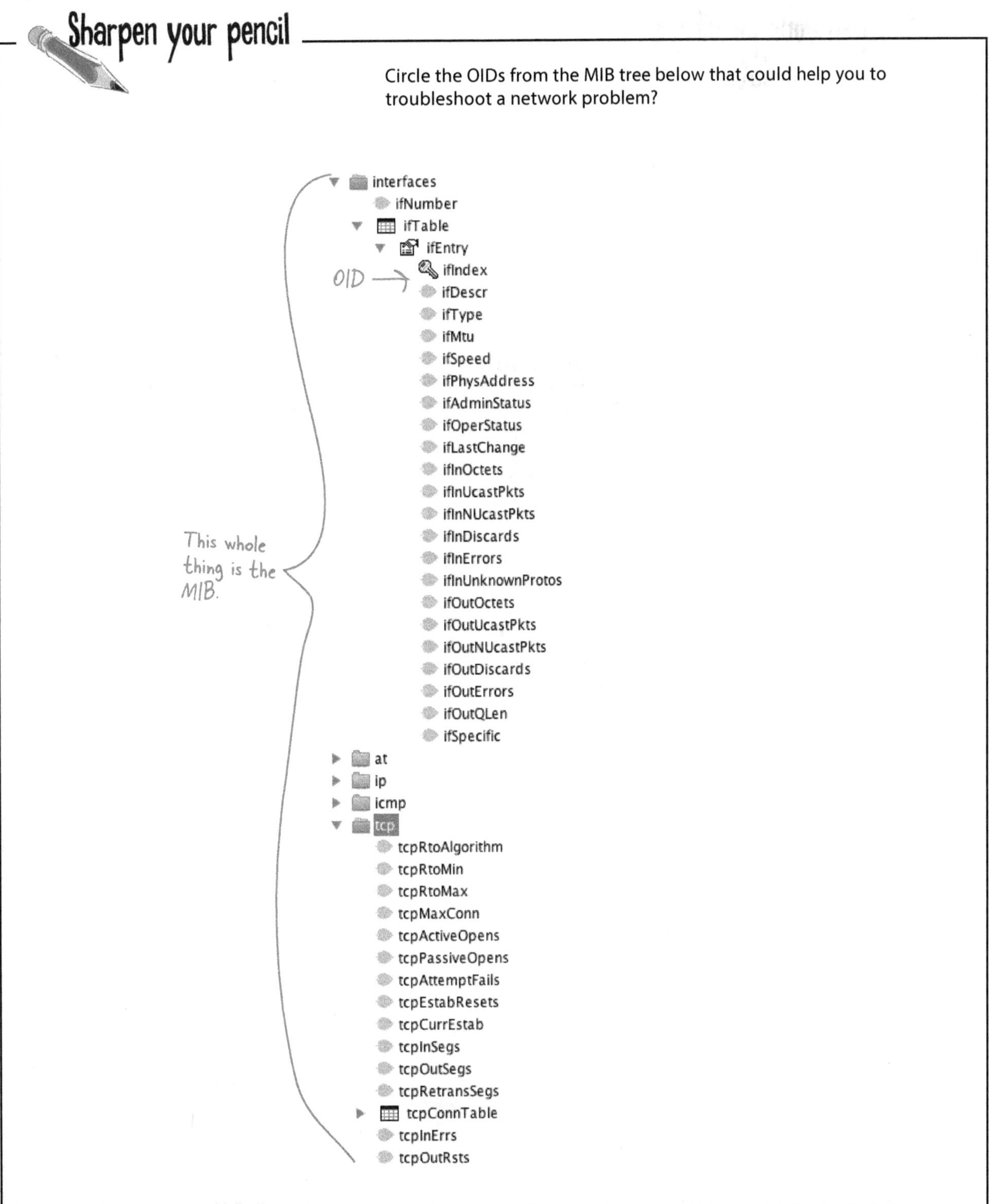

Sharpen your pencil Solution

Circle the OIDs from the MIB tree below that could help you to troubleshoot a network problem?

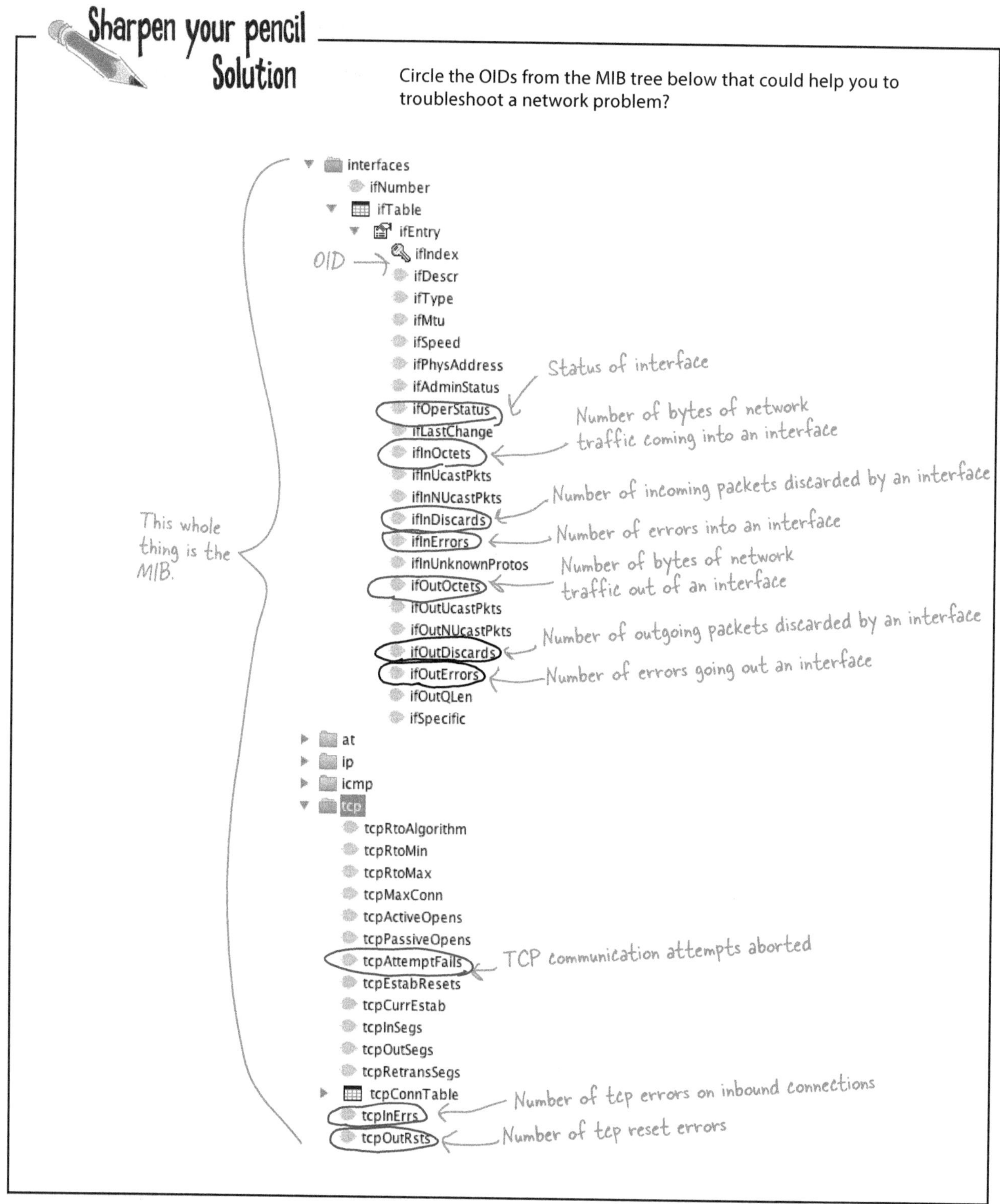

One hour to go...

There's one hour to go before the Pajama Death tickets go on sale. Unfortunately, the ticket agency network still has problems...

SNMP has helped me clear up some of the network problems, but there are other diagnostics we can only get from the server logs. I can't get to these using SNMP. Are we back to connecting to each device? There's not much time left, and the boss knows where I live...

SNMP gets most of the information, but not all of it.

A lot of the time, network devices send errors to a console or to a log, and these errors are often not accessible via SNMP. So how can we gain access to this logged information?

Are we back to connecting to each device individually?

Get devices to send you their problems

There is a tool that devices can use to send their errors to a central server called a syslogd. The d stands for daemon, which is a little service program running on a server.

Instead of a network device sending error messages to a console screen, it can send them to the syslogd server. This means that instead of checking the local log files on each individual device, we can just check the syslogd server.

A syslogd daemon allows you to have all sorts of network devices send information to that server. That information normally would have being written to a local log file on that device.

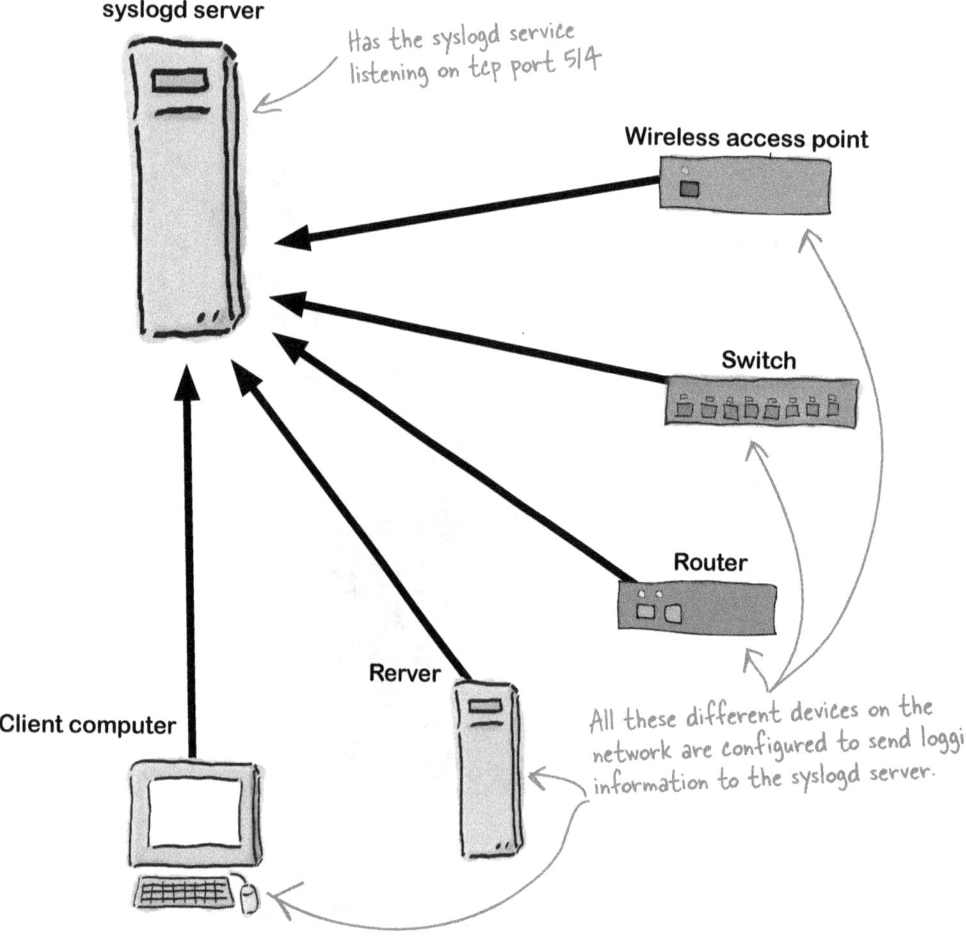
syslogd server
Has the syslogd service listening on tcp port 514
Wireless access point
Switch
Router
Rerver
Client computer
All these different devices on the network are configured to send logging information to the syslogd server.

So how do we set up syslogd?

How to configure syslogd on a Cisco device

Setting up syslogd on a non-Cisco is very similar to this.

Other network devices are configured in a similar fashion—just check your device documentation for the specifics.

Let's take a look at how to set up syslogd on a Cisco device. You'll need to type these commands at the device command line in config mode.

1. **Set up timestamping on the logs.**
   To do this, type the command:

   ```
   service timestamps log datetime localtime
   ```

   This will put date and time stamps on each log entry in the format specified.

2. **Stop the logging to the console and monitor.**
   To turn off logging to the console window, type:

   ```
   no logging console
   ```

   To turn off logging to the non-console windows, type:

   ```
   no logging monitor
   ```

3. **Set up the router to send logging to the syslogd server.**
   To replace the logging IP address with your syslogd server's IP address, type:

   ```
   logging 192.168.100.1
   ```

4. **Set the logging level.**
   To set the router to send log messages that are just warnings, or worse, to the syslogd server, type:

   ```
   logging warning
   ```

   ← There is a whole scale of log severity from 0-Emergency to 7-Debug.

5. **Save your setup.**
   To save your config setup, type the commands:

   ```
   exit
   write memory
   ```

Watch it!

Only use the debug level when you need to debug.

It can really tax a router's memory and processor.

So now that syslogd has been configured, how do we access the logs?

How do you tell what's in the logs?

One of the great things about syslogd is that you can get applications that watch the logs. Whenever an interesting logged event is received, it can fire off a message to the network admin.

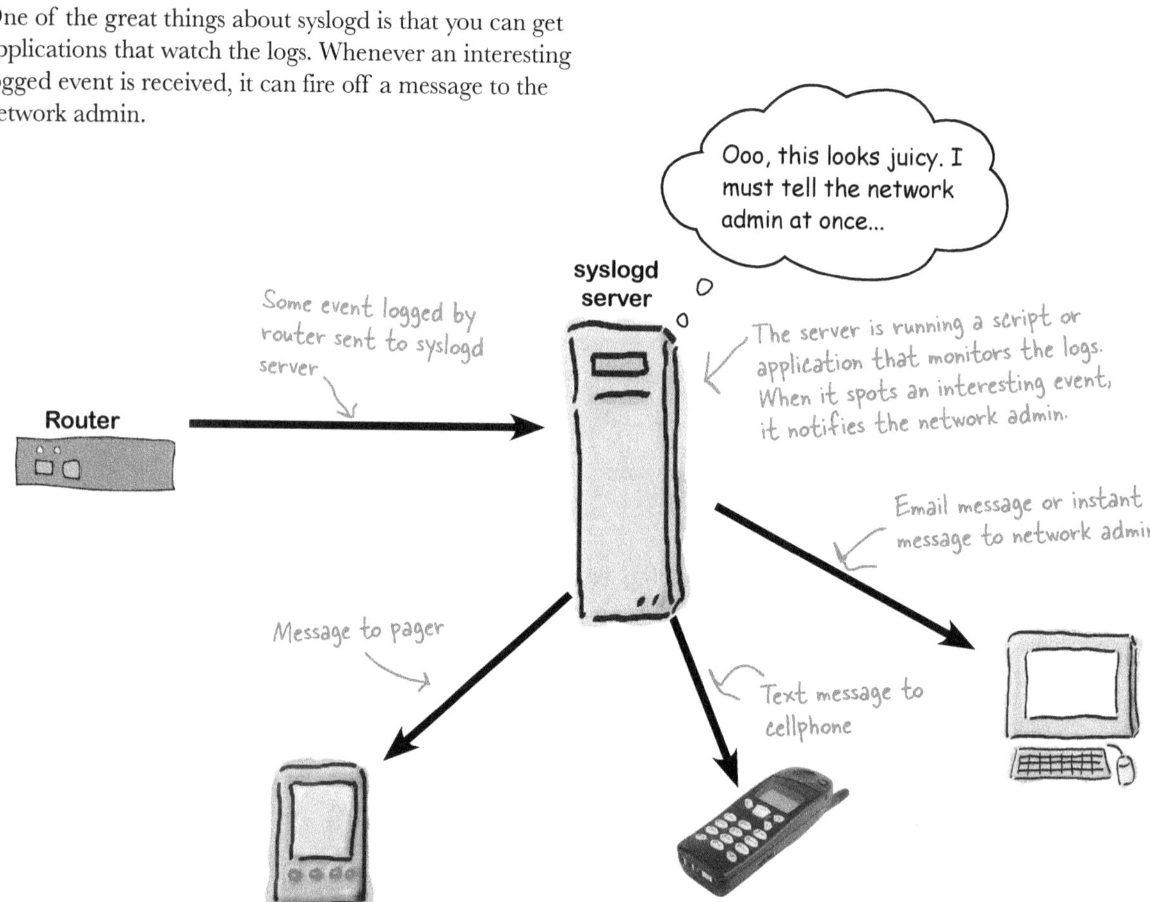

syslogd lets you fix problems before they're problems

The beauty of syslogd is that you can get devices to alert you to events that might lead to severe network difficulties in the future. This means that you can effectively deal with problems before they happen—making your network much more stable as a result. As an example, if a router tells you that its power supply voltage is fluctuating, you can replace it before it becomes a huge problem.

You can usually choose which messages are sent to the network admin via which devices. So how do you choose?

BE the Syslogd Messenger

Your job is to play the messenger program on the syslogd server and decide which messages get sent to the network admin. Next to each logged event choose whether it should be texted via cellphone or just an email. The cellphone is for higher priority issues.

Text Message	Email Message	Ignore	
☐	☐	☐	1649.12 EVENT: Router 3 has excessive TCP Errors on FE0/0
☐	☐	☐	1652.54 EVENT: Server 1 has low memory
☐	☐	☐	1653.22 EVENT: Router 1 has a low temperature alarm
☐	☐	☐	1655.84 EVENT: Port 3 on Switch 12 is Down
☐	☐	☐	1656.21 EVENT: Router 6 has power fluctuations
☐	☐	☐	1701.81 EVENT: Port 6 on Switch 12 is Down
☐	☐	☐	1701.96 EVENT: Router 3 has excessive TCP Errors on FE0/0
☐	☐	☐	1702.14 EVENT: Port 18 on Switch 12 is Down
☐	☐	☐	1702.19 EVENT: Router 3 has excessive TCP Errors on FE0/0
☐	☐	☐	1704.50 EVENT: Router 4 rebooted
☐	☐	☐	1705.11 EVENT: Port 9 on Switch 12 is Down

BE the Syslogd Messenger Solution

Your job is to play the messenger program on the syslogd server and decide which messages get sent to the network admin. Next to each logged event choose whether it should be texted via cellphone or just an email. The cellphone is for higher priority issues.

Text Message	Email Message	Ignore	Event
☐	☑	☐	1649.12 EVENT: Router 3 has excessive TCP Errors on FE0/0
☑	☐	☐	1652.54 EVENT: Server 1 has low memory
☐	☐	☑	1653.22 EVENT: Router 1 has a low temperature alarm
☐	☐	☑	1655.84 EVENT: Port 3 on Switch 12 is Down
☑	☐	☐	1656.21 EVENT: Router 6 has power fluctuations
☐	☐	☑	1701.81 EVENT: Port 6 on Switch 12 is Down
☐	☑	☐	1701.96 EVENT: Router 3 has excessive TCP Errors on FE0/0
☐	☐	☑	1702.14 EVENT: Port 18 on Switch 12 is Down
☐	☑	☐	1702.19 EVENT: Router 3 has excessive TCP Errors on FE0/0
☑	☐	☐	1704.50 EVENT: Router 4 rebooted
☐	☐	☑	1705.11 EVENT: Port 9 on Switch 12 is Down

Errors like this need to be investigated, but they are not emergencies. (1649.12)

This could be critical. (1652.54)

Not really an issue. (1653.22)

Probably someone shutting down their computer for the day. (1655.84)

This could be critical. (1656.21)

This is a BIG deal! (1704.50)

Too much information can be just as bad as not enough

Getting just the right information sent to you is the real challenge when it comes to syslogd. It takes some tuning to get just the right information flowing. So when you set up the different message systems, don't just turn it all on; think it through carefully.

I can't believe how many messages I am getting about network events. What does all this mean? I am sooooo tired. I really need to get a handle on this...

What you need is relevant information

The thing that's most important is that you get information that lets you know when there are real problems. And remember that low priority events can be emailed to you, rather than sent as a high priority text message to your cellphone or pager.

So how do you choose what's relevant?

How do you know which events are important?

If your network devices are getting lots of network type errors, i.e., tcp or frame errors, something is going wrong on your network. Generally this means some hardware is failing. Other important errors include interfaces going down, routes flapping (going up and down), and hardware health issues such as power supply voltages, temperatures, and memory.

Once you know what events are normal on your network, you'll be able to fine-tune the messages you receive so that only things that aren't normal are messaged to you. In the meantime, here's a quick guide:

High Priority Events
Power supply voltages
Case & processor temperatures
High network error rates
Memory errors
Interface status changes
Many of these mean that some hardware is failing or on the verge of failing. You need to do something about these real quickly.
High network traffic
Changes to configuration
Low temperature
Unable to reach some website on Internet
These events are less likely to cause huge problems on your network, so you probably won't need an urgent message.
Low network traffic
Low Priority Events

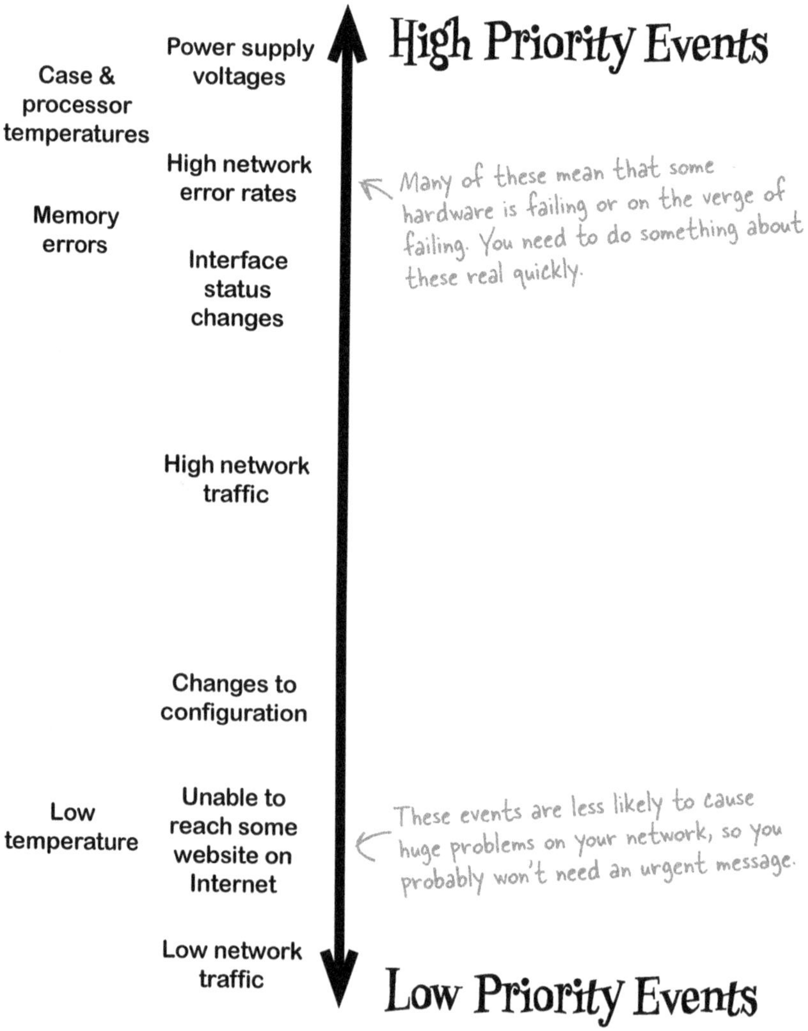

Pajama Death's a sell-out!

Thanks to your network troubleshooting, the Pajama Death tickets went on sale without a hitch. Ticket sales were so successful that the entire tour sold out in record time, and the syslogd messages helped the network guys react to high priority events before they became problems.

The CEO of the ticket agency is so impressed with the help you've given them that he's given you front row tickets to opening night.

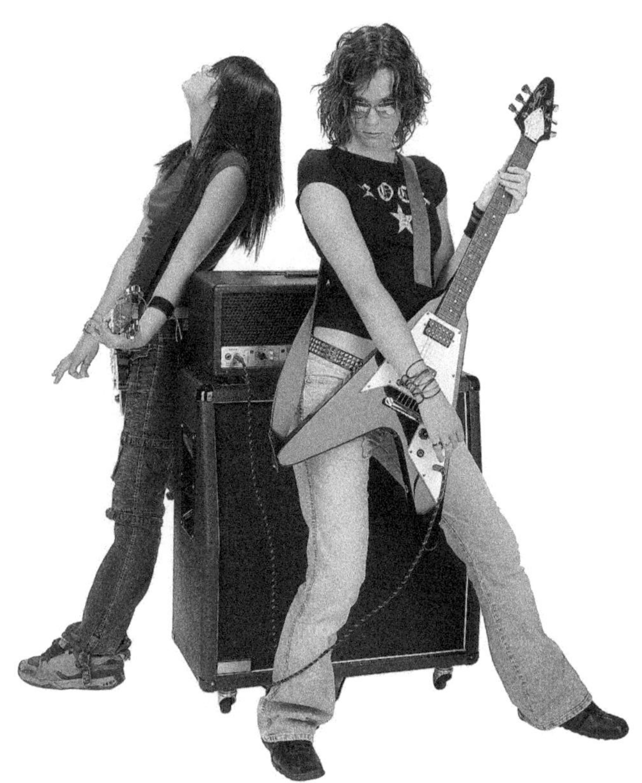

10 wireless networking

Working Without Wires

I wish I could hook up to the Internet without connecting these wires all the time...

Surfing the Internet without wires is great!

This chapter will show you all the things that you need to think when setting up a wireless access point. First you need to consider the physical location, because radio waves can be blocked. Second, we introduce some more network acronyms, NAT and DHCP. But don't worry, we'll explain them, so at the end of the chapter you will be able to have one great wireless network up and running.

Your new gig at Starbuzz Coffee

Starbuzz Coffee has made a name for itself as the fastest growing coffee shop around. If you've seen one on your local corner, look across the street; you'll see another one.

The Starbuzz CEO has a great idea for enticing new customers into his coffee shops. He'll offer free in-store Internet access to all Starbuzz customers.

It's perfect. People will come in to surf the Internet, and they'll order more coffee while they're here. But I don't want any ugly cables about the place. We're going **wireless**!

Starbuzz Coffee needs a wireless hotspot

What the CEO needs is an open wireless access point that his customers can use to access the Internet. In other words, he needs a wireless hotspot. His customers will be able to bring their laptops along to his coffee shops and get an automatic connection to the Internet. What's more, the back office staff will be able to access it too.

So how do we set up a wireless access point?

Wireless access points create networks using radio waves

Let's start by looking at how wireless access points work.

When you use a wireless access point to create a network, computers are connected through radio waves instead of Ethernet cables. The access point itself has to have a wired network connection, but all other devices link into it wirelessly. So if you have a wireless network capable laptop, you're free to roam, just as long as you're in range.

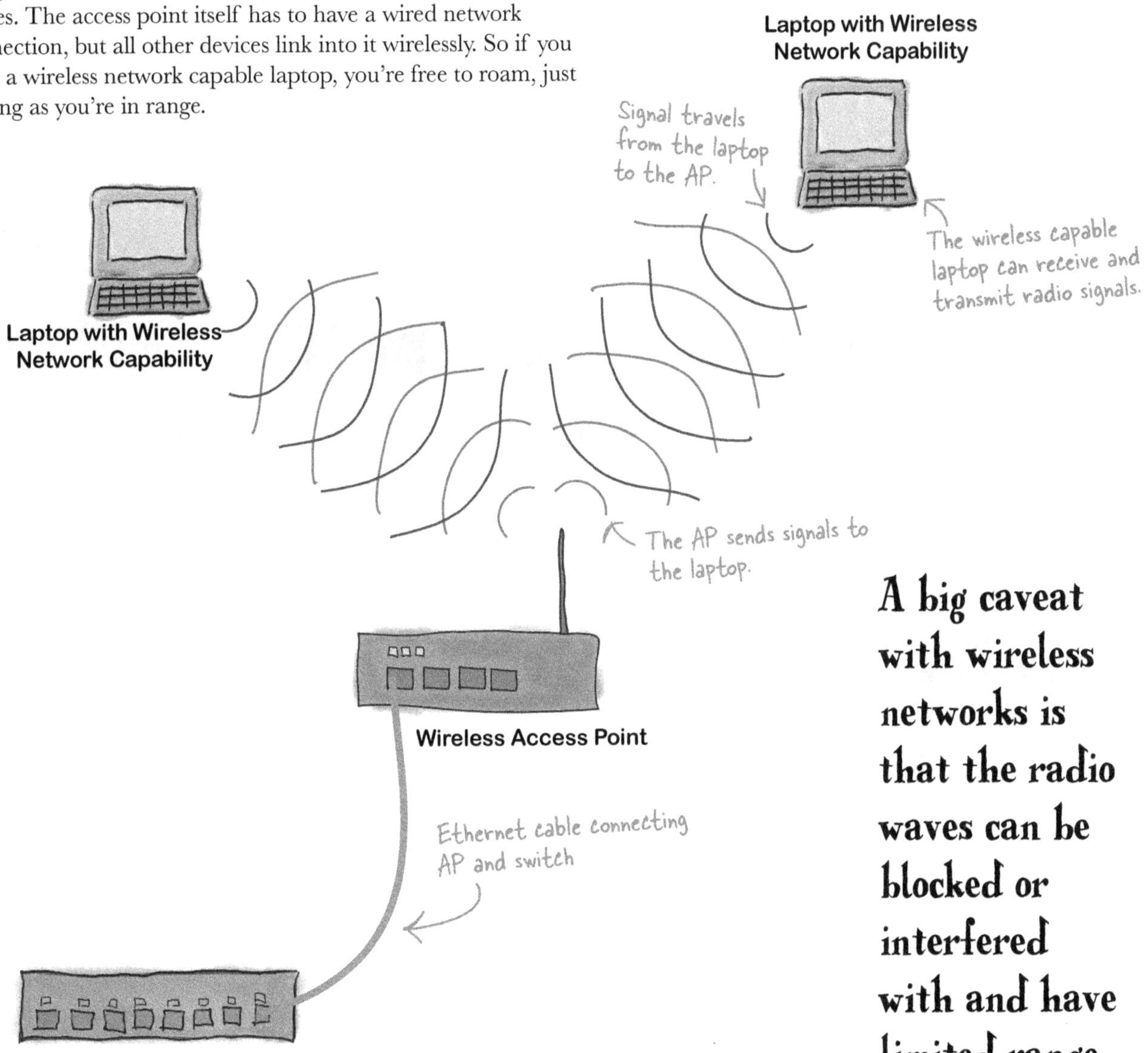

Laptop with Wireless Network Capability

Signal travels from the laptop to the AP.

The wireless capable laptop can receive and transmit radio signals.

Laptop with Wireless Network Capability

The AP sends signals to the laptop.

Wireless Access Point

Ethernet cable connecting AP and switch

A big caveat with wireless networks is that the radio waves can be blocked or interfered with and have limited range.

So how do we install a wireless access point?

Let's fit the wireless access point

Physically fitting a wireless access point is actually pretty simple. Once you have you have your wireless access point device, just take it out of the box, put it somewhere nice and safe where the radio waves can't get blocked, and hook it up to your network.

Here's what a typical wireless access point looks like:

Watch it!

If your access point has a WAN port and LAN ports, plug the network connection to the WAN port.

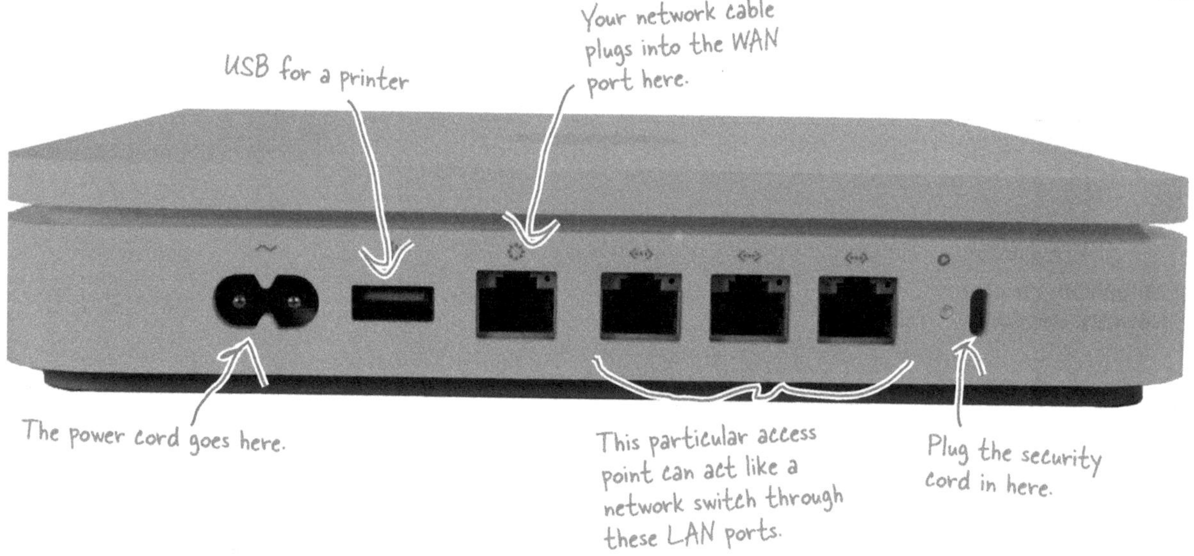
USB for a printer
Your network cable plugs into the WAN port here.
The power cord goes here.
This particular access point can act like a network switch through these LAN ports.
Plug the security cord in here.

So where should we put the Starbuzz Coffee wireless access point?

BRAIN POWER

Take a look round your house or workplace. What sorts of things can you see that might get in the way of a wireless network? What other devices might interfere with it?

Here's a floor plan of one of the Starbuzz Coffee shops. Where would you put the access point? Draw in where you think the best position for it is.

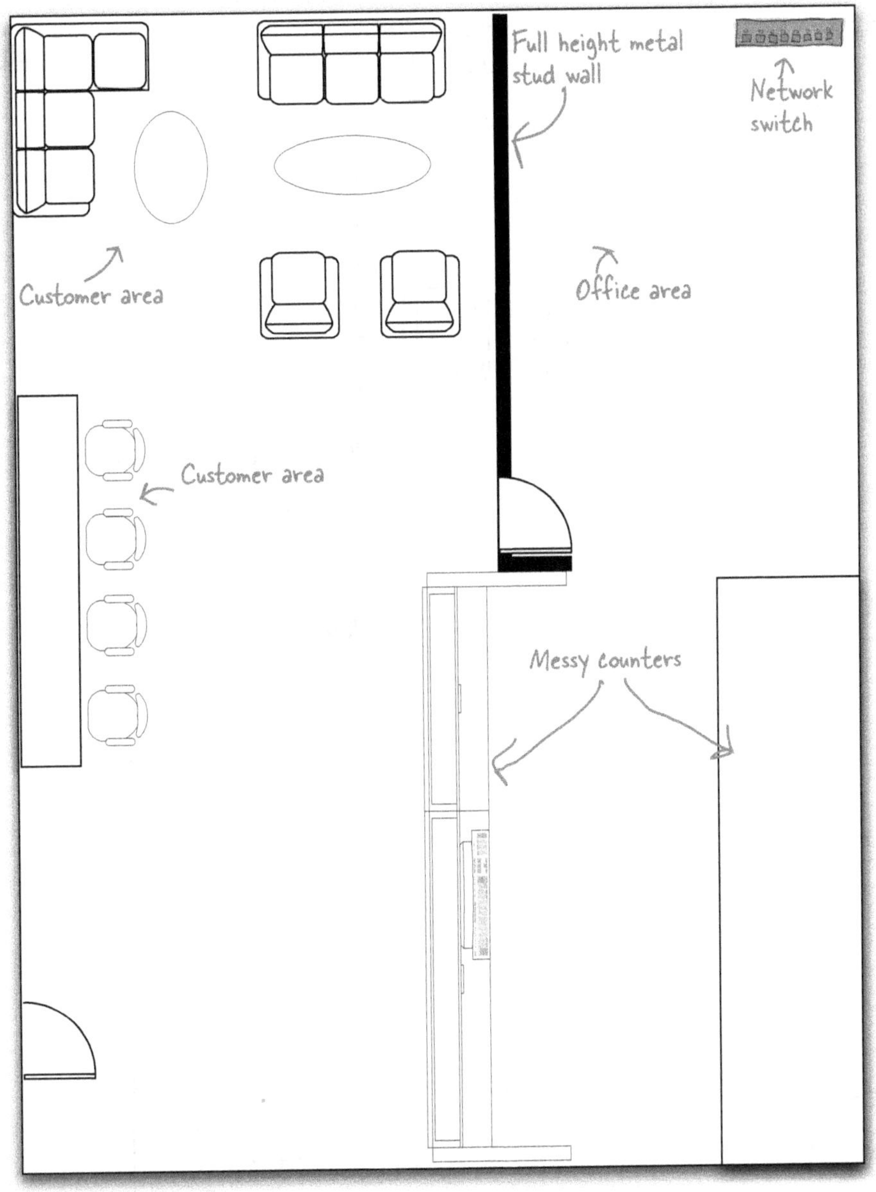

Exercise Solution

Here's a floor plan of one of the Starbuzz Coffee shops. Where would you put the access point? Draw in where you think the best position for it is.

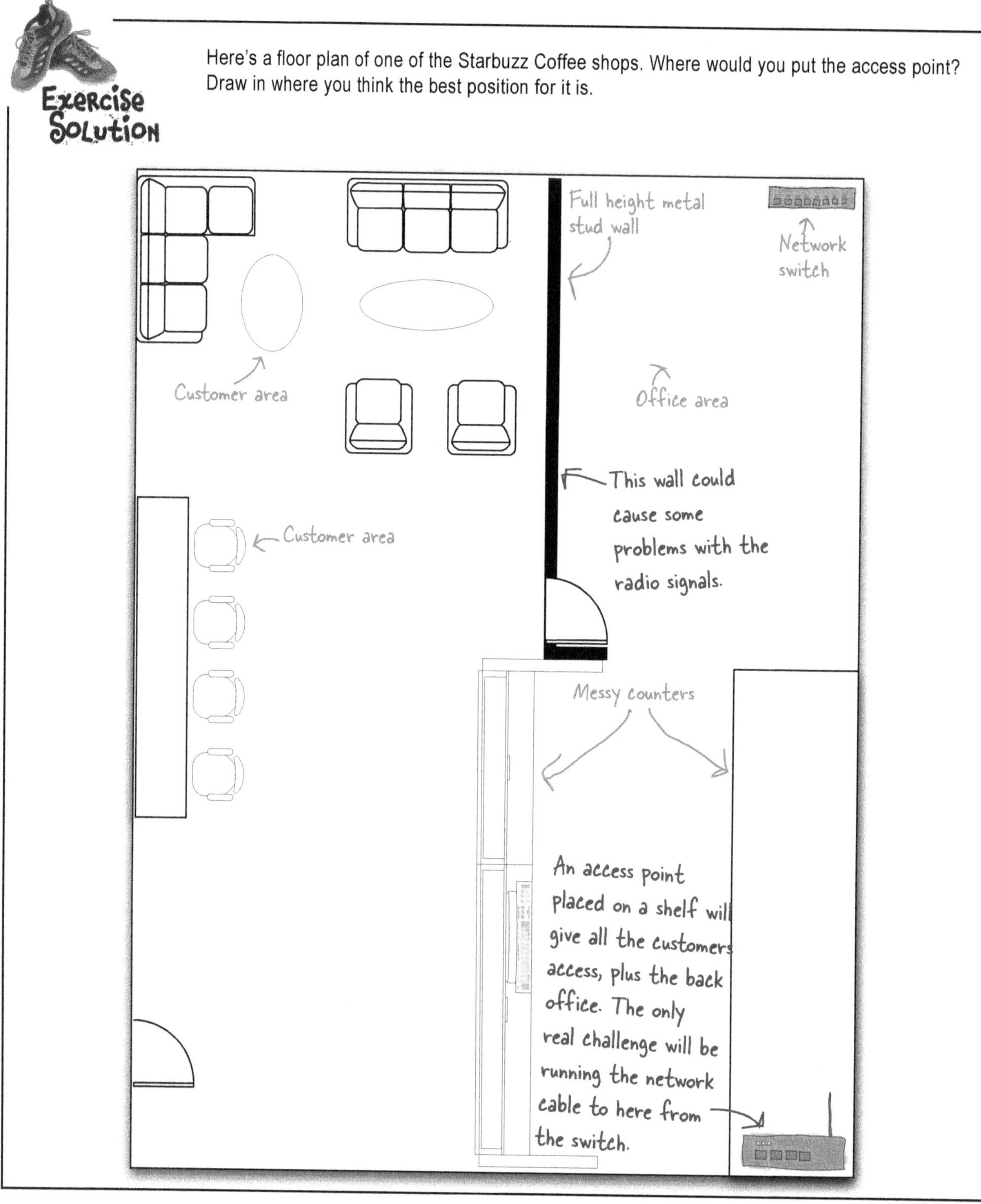

Full height metal stud wall
Network switch
Customer area
Office area
This wall could cause some problems with the radio signals.
Customer area
Messy counters
An access point placed on a shelf will give all the customers access, plus the back office. The only real challenge will be running the network cable to here from the switch.

there are no Dumb Questions

Q: So a 802.11G wireless card in, say, a laptop can only talk to an 802.11G access point?

A: Yes, but most wireless cards and built-in wireless interfaces can access multiple types of access points.

Q: Why are there old access points that don't support newer protocols around still?

A: Because someone invested money in them and does not want to spend the money to replace them.

Q: Can a single access point talk to different wireless clients with different standards?

A: Most of the time this is true. Many access points can "speak" different wireless standards at the same time. Many times you can turn this off because usage of older wireless standards can slow down the new standards.

Q: Can one brand of wireless card, say a Dell, connect to an access point of another company, like Apple?

A: Yes, as long as they are using the same wireless standard, they will communicate together fine.

Q: Are inexpensive access points just as good as the expensive ones?

A: Depends. If the features are the same, then you really have to look at the quality of the components. They are inexpensive for a reason. Many of the more expensive access points have additional features such as printer and external hard drive support.

Q: Why would you connect a hard drive to an access point?

A: An access point with an external hard drive attached to it provides a Network Attached Storage unit. Anyone with wireless access can store file on that hard drive.

Test Drive

The wireless access point's all hooked up, so let's put it to the test. Let's try connecting a computer to it and see what happens.

1. **Turn on the wireless networking on the computer.**
   In some older machines, this may have to be installed. But most modern operating systems have wireless ready to go.

2. **Connect to the access point.**
   Essentially you should see a list of access points; select yours from the list to attach to it.

3. **Enter any password required.**
   Most access points have some type of security. Most of the time it is a password that you have to enter when you attach to the access point.

4. **Test your connection.**
   At this point you should be able to access network resources such as the Internet via the access point.

So is the wireless hotspot working okay?

You're kidding me, right? I can't get to any websites, not even starbuzzcoffee.com. How will my customers be able to surf?

So what went wrong?

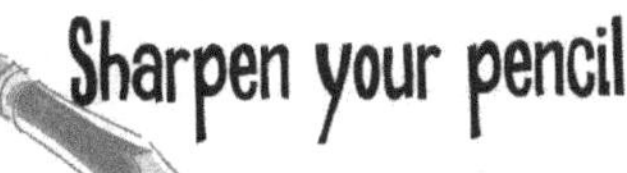

Why doesn't the wireless hotspot work? Based on the results, write down some things that you think may be going wrong.

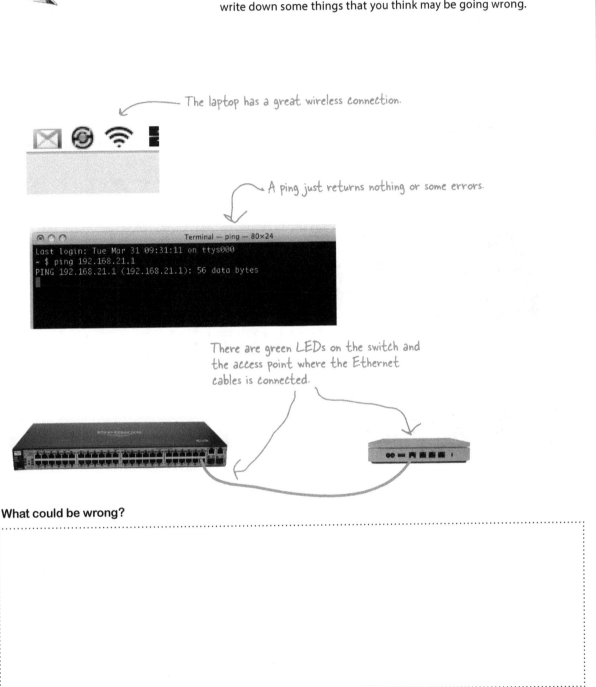

The laptop has a great wireless connection.

A ping just returns nothing or some errors.

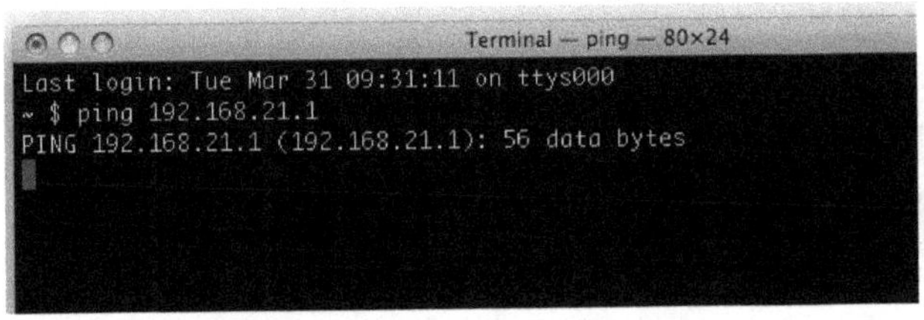

```
Terminal — ping — 80×24
Last login: Tue Mar 31 09:31:11 on ttys000
~ $ ping 192.168.21.1
PING 192.168.21.1 (192.168.21.1): 56 data bytes
```

There are green LEDs on the switch and the access point where the Ethernet cables is connected.

What could be wrong?

Sharpen your pencil Solution

Why doesn't the wireless hotspot work? Based on the results, write down some things that you think may be going wrong.

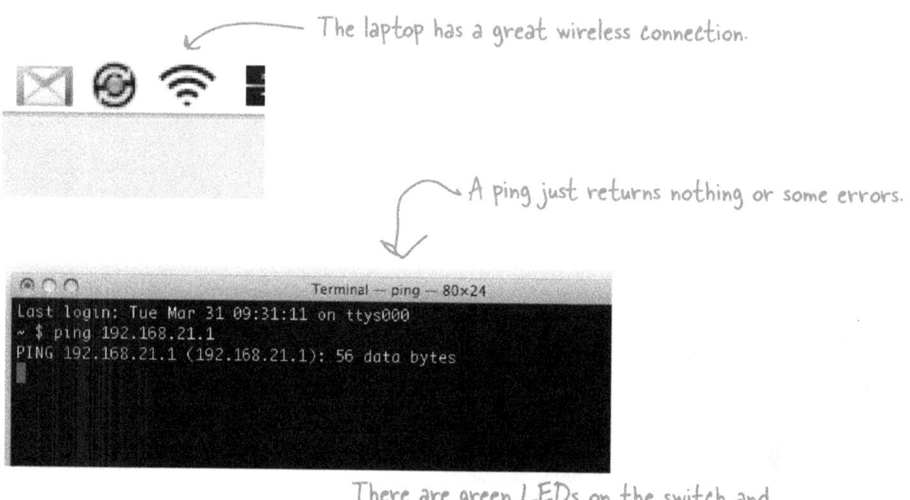
The laptop has a great wireless connection.
A ping just returns nothing or some errors.
Terminal — ping — 80×24
Last login: Tue Mar 31 09:31:11 on ttys000
~ $ ping 192.168.21.1
PING 192.168.21.1 (192.168.21.1): 56 data bytes

There are green LEDs on the switch and the access point where the Ethernet cables is connected.

What could be wrong?

Is the Ethernet cable plugged into the WAN port on the access point?

Is the problem bigger? Can computers hooked to the switch by Ethernet get on the network?

Is the access point configured with the correct IP address information?

Is the access point configured to give out addresses correctly?

What about the network configuration?

When we set up a wireless access point, it's not enough to just plug it in. We need to say which computers can use the wireless access point.

You're kidding me, right? You mean we have to tell the wireless access point which computers can **use** it? But that's **all the Starbuzz customers!** Why can't they just show up and use it?

Maybe she has a point.

The last thing you want to have to do is manually setup an IP address for every Starbuzz customer that walks into the shop. So what can we do?

Fortunately, there's a way round this, and it's called ***DHCP***.

So what's DHCP?

DHCP stands for Dynamic Host Configuration Protocol. It's a way of automatically allowing devices onto your network with no manual intervention on your part.

Here's how it works.

DHCP Discovery.
The client broadcasts to find available servers. To do this, it needs an IP address network interface configured to use DHCP.

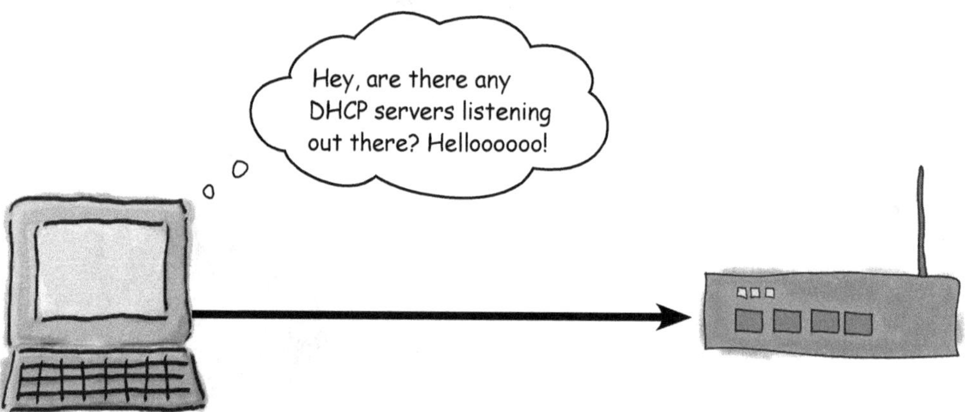

DHCP Offers.
The DHCP server in the wireless access point responds to the client broadcast by offering the client an IP address. The IP address is within a pre-defined range that the DHCP server has configured in its pool of available addresses.

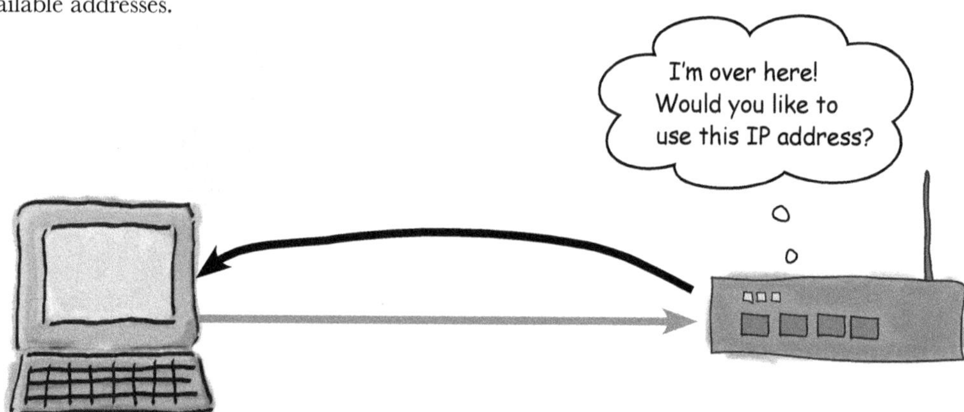

3 **DHCP Requests.**
The client broadcasts a DHCP request message, accepting the offer of the DHCP server.

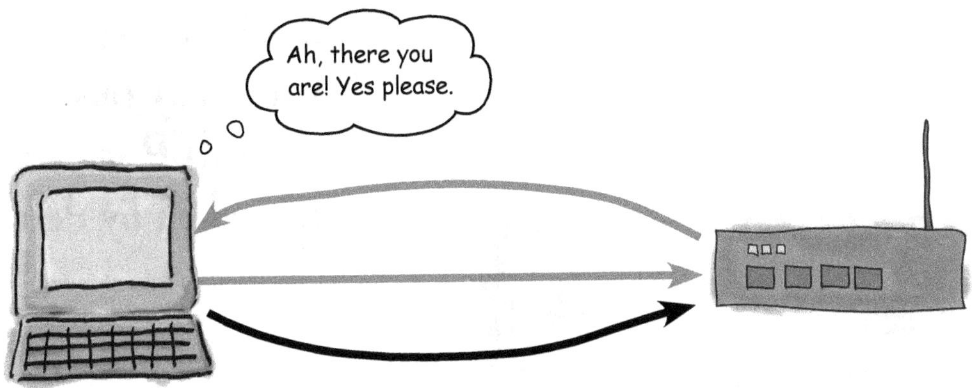

4 **DHCP Acknowledgement.**
The DHCP server sends a DHCPACK packet to the client. The packet gives the client the length of time it can hold and address (lease duration), and any other configuration details that are needed.

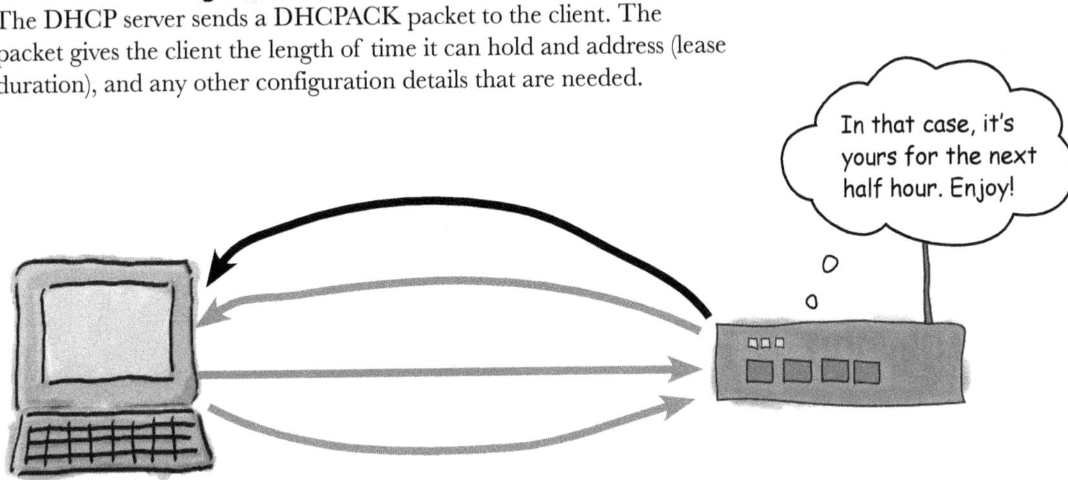

DHCP allocates IP addresses

DHCP makes our life easy by offering to clients IP addresses it has in its pool of available addresses. This sounds like just the sort of thing that Starbuzz Coffee needs, as it means clients will be able to come into the store, open up their laptops, and start surfing.

So how do we set up DHCP?

First make sure the client has DHCP turned on...

You configure this in the client's network configuration.

A wireless access point may come with the DHCP service turned on by default.

Windows

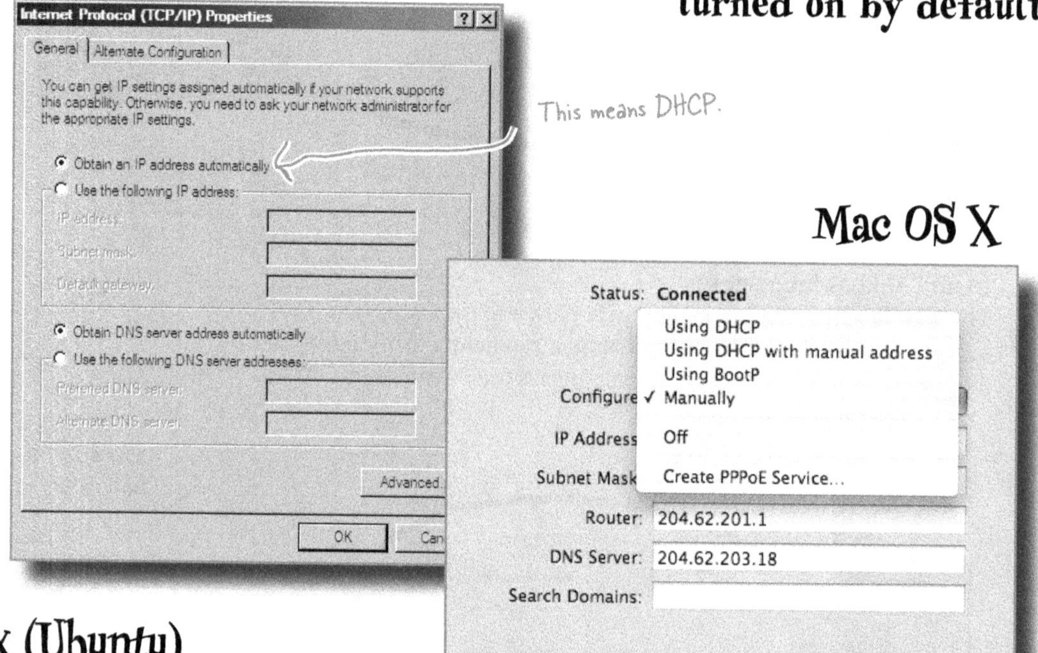

Linux (Ubuntu)

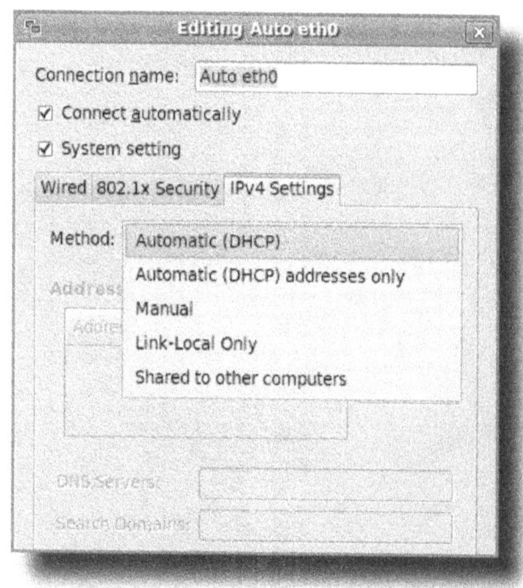

Second, make the wireless access point a DHCP server...

The first thing we need to do is turn on the DHCP service on the wireless access point. This tells the wireless access point that you want it to be a DHCP server.

The wireless access point may come with DHCP switched on by default, but in case it doesn't, here are the settings you need to change.

...and then specify an acceptable range of IP addresses

After you've told the wireless access point you want it to be a DHCP, you need to tell it which IP address ranges to give out. You also configure information such as the gateway and DNS name server addresses, and how long the client can keep hold of the IP address for.

The gateway and DNS are set in different places depending on the particular DHCP server.

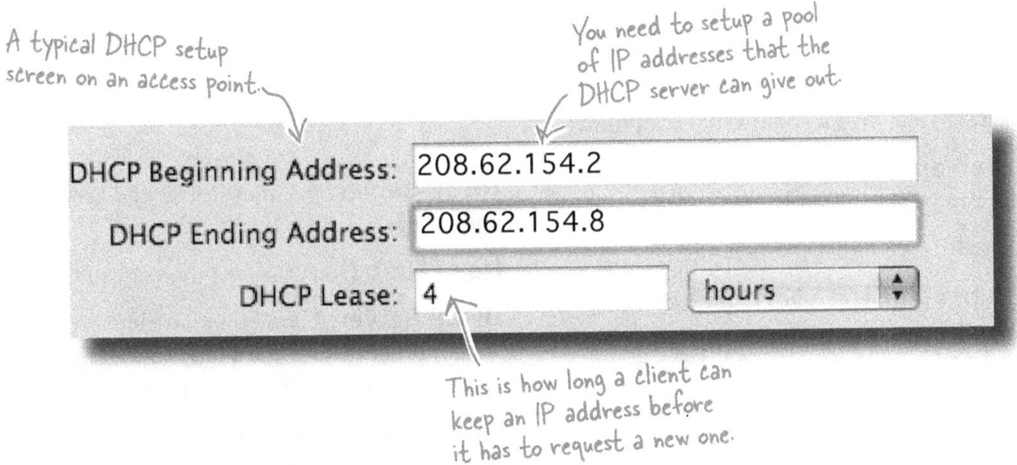

A typical DHCP setup screen on an access point.
You need to setup a pool of IP addresses that the DHCP server can give out.
DHCP Beginning Address: 208.62.154.2
DHCP Ending Address: 208.62.154.8
DHCP Lease: 4 hours
This is how long a client can keep an IP address before it has to request a new one.

there are no Dumb Questions

Q: What happens if there is more than 1 DHCP server on the network?

A: The client responds with a broadcast DHCP request. That broadcast contains the specific information from 1 DHCP server, so it is the only one that does anything with the request. So the protocol is written with multple DHCP servers in mind.

Q: Does a Windows client have to use a Windows DHCP server?

A: No. As long as the DHCP server meets the protocol standards, it will work fine with a Windows, Mac or Linux client, or even some other device looking for an IP address with DHCP.

Q: Can I control which machines get which IP addresses?

A: Yes, you can put into a special table the MAC addresses of those machines and what IP addresses they should be issued.

Q: What happens when a DHCP host runs out of IP addresses?

A: Good question. It just stops responding to any discovery broadcasts until some addresses free up.

Q: Can the IP addresses my DHCP host gives out be public IP addresses?

A: Yes. Just make sure that no other machine is using them and that they are routable.

Q: How long do clients get to keep an IP address?

A: That is called the lease. It is for whatever time you set it for. Typically it is a couple of hours to days.

The DHCP Server Exposed

This week's interview: Secrets of the DHCP Server

Head First: Hello.

DHCP Server: Hello, here is an IP address: 192.168.100.1, with a gateway of...

Head First: Hold on a second! What is all this?

DHCP Server: Oh sorry, I don't normally get into conversations outside of work.

Head First: So you work pretty hard?

DHCP Server: Man, it is just request after request after request. It never ends. It seems just as I give a client an IP address, they are back for another one.

Head First Server: Wow, it sounds like your lease time is set too low.

DHCP Server: Yea, that is what I think, but I really have no way of letting the network administrator know that other than logging it.

Head First: Let's hope she checks the logs once in a while. So do you ever deny a request for an IP address?

DHCP Server: Once in a while. The admin has a pretty good number of IP addresses in the pool. It meets the demand.

Head First: Do the clients get mad when they get denied?

DHCP Server: No, they just sit and keep trying and trying.

Head First: Don't they get mad at you?

DHCP Server: I don't offer anything to them, so they do not know that I am around. I keep my mouth shut until I have some addresses available.

Head First: That sounds like a smart thing to do. Well thank you for the interview, and we hope you get some time off soon.

So has setting up DHCP solved the problem?

The connection works! Before too long, the wireless access point is live, and people start flocking in even greater numbers to the Starbuzz Coffee shops.

Geek Bits

You can read more about DHCP by reading the RFC located at **http://www.faqs.org/rfcs/rfc2131.html**

This time it's personal

Things were going fine until one particularly busy day in the coffee shop...

Where's my internet connection, baby? I came in here to surf MeBay, and can I get there? No! Everyone else seems OK, so what's going on? Why are you doing this to me?
Wow... maybe too much coffee can be a bad thing.

Uh-oh! Everyone who came into the coffee shop before this guy is happily surfing the Internet. The trouble is, everyone who came in afterwards can't get a connection.

Why do you think the wireless access point won't let any new clients connect to the Internet?

Hint: Look back through the DHCP configuration for clues.

We've run out of IP addresses

Can you remember when we set DHCP up on the wireless access point? We configured a range of IP addresses that the DHCP server could allocate to clients. Our ISP only gave us 12 IP addresses and the other 5 are being used by other computers on Ethernet.

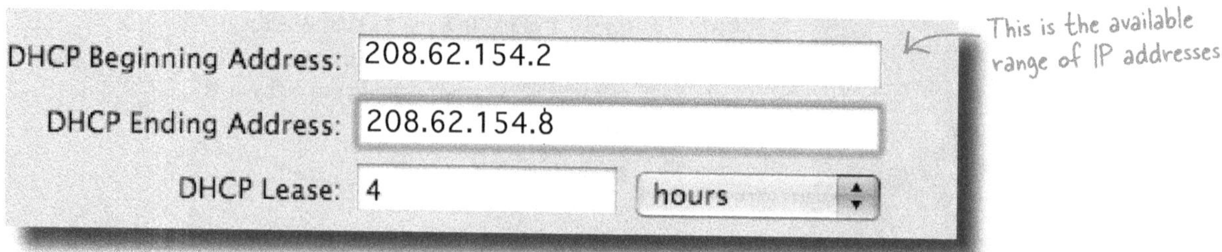

But what happens when we have more clients than available IP addresses? The DHCP server can only give out a limited range of IP addresses, and when it runs out, that's it. It can't offer any new clients a connection. So what can we do to get around this?

So it gives up? But that's ridiculous. There's gotta be a way around this, right?

We can get around the IP address problem by implementing NAT.

NAT stands for Network Address Translation, and it's something else we can enable on the wireless access point. With NAT enabled, we can use just about any IP address we want, and however many we need to.

So how does NAT work?

NAT works by reallocating IP addresses

Here's what happens when a client accesses a website using NAT.

1. **The client sends a packet to the wireless access point.**
In this case, it uses 192.168.1.1 for the source IP address on the packets.

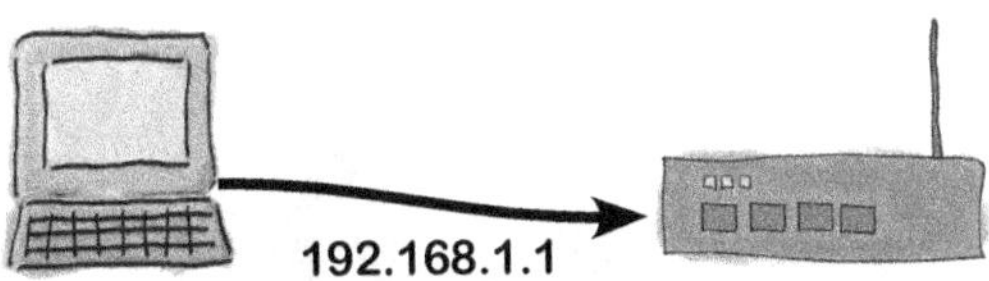

2. **The access point sends the packet on to the web server.**
But it changes the packet's source IP address to a public IP address such as 204.62.201.18, and records it in a table of inside addresses translated to outside communication streams.

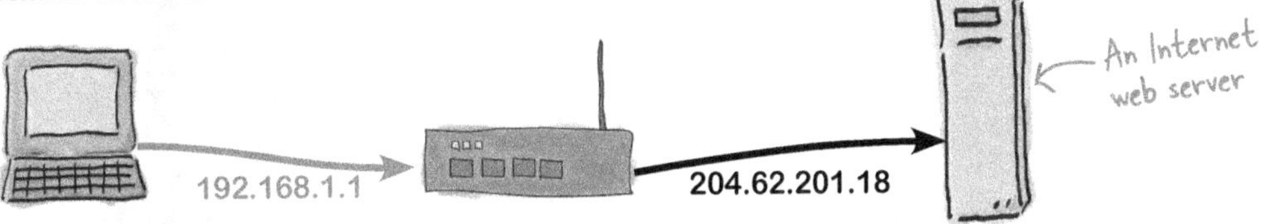

3. **The web server responds.**
It sends the requested information to the public IP address 204.62.201.18.

4. **The access point forwards the traffic to the client.**
But it changes the destination IP address of the packets back to the private 192.168.1.1 by checking its translation table.

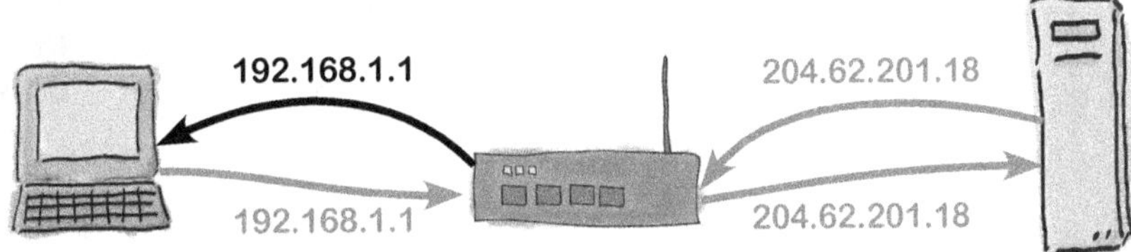

So how do we configure NAT?

Let's set up NAT on the Starbuzz wireless access point. Wireless access points sometimes come with NAT switched on by default, but in case yours doesn't, here's the setting you need to change:

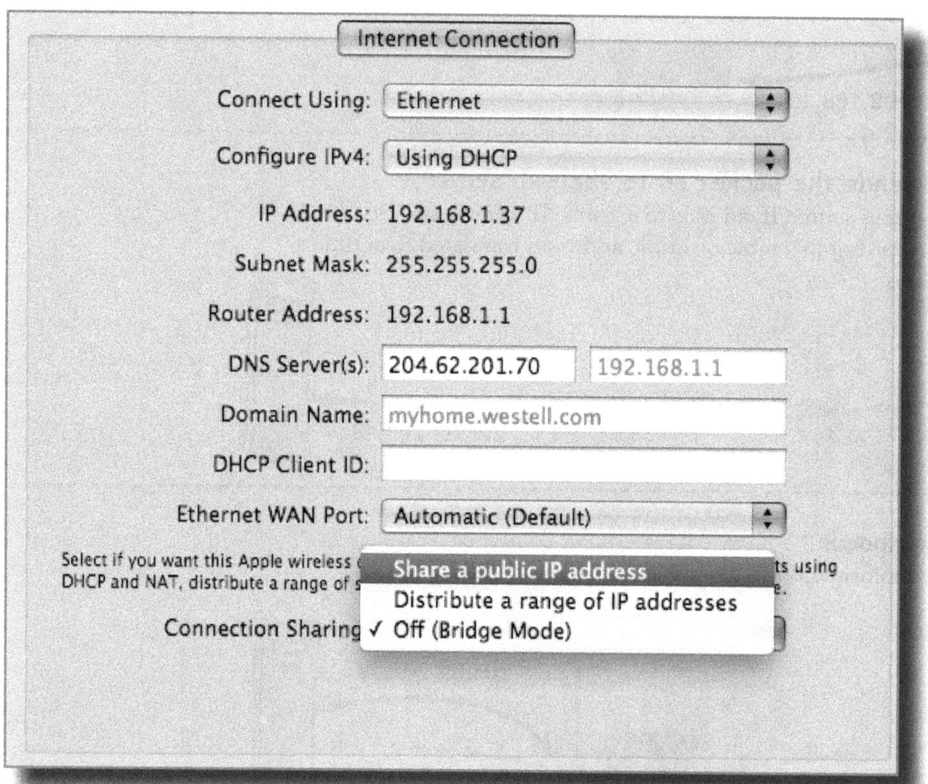

Configuring NAT on most access points consists of turning it on, and that's about it.

Each brand of access point has its own interface for doing this.

The concepts are the same, but the interface may look different.

Using the **NAT Table** below, fill in the inside client IP address on the **bottom table**. This is how a NAT device gets packets back to the original device hidden behind the NAT server.

NAT Table

Source IP	Destination IP	Source Port	Destination Port	NAT Port
192.168.1.1	204.24.254.12	1234	80	5102
192.168.1.1	204.24.254.12	2541	80	2348
192.168.1.2	12.4.51.84	8421	143	7412
192.168.1.10	72.54.84.32	11542	80	1028
192.168.1.1	84.51.25.8	421	80	7452
192.168.1.7	204.24.254.12	24154	80	12547
192.168.1.2	84.1.4.23	5478	143	24751

You fill out this part

Incoming Packets to Access Point

Source IP	Destination IP	Source Port	Destination Port	Inside Client IP Address
204.24.254.12	192.168.1.1	4214	2348	192.168.1.1
204.24.254.12	192.168.1.7	1124	12547	
72.54.84.32	192.168.1.10	42101	1028	
84.51.25.8	192.168.1.1	7511	7452	
204.24.254.12	192.168.1.1	5142	5102	
12.4.51.84	192.168.1.2	7421	7412	
84.1.4.23	192.168.1.2	2741	24751	

Using the **NAT Table** below, fill in the inside client IP address on the **bottom table**. This is how a NAT device gets packets back to the original device hidden behind the NAT server.

You fill out this part

Incoming Packets to Access Point

Source IP	Destination IP	Source Port	Destination Port	Inside Client IP Address
204.24.254.12	192.168.1.1	4214	2348	192.168.1.1
204.24.254.12	192.168.1.7	1124	12547	192.168.1.7
72.54.84.32	192.168.1.10	42101	1028	192.168.1.10
84.51.25.8	192.168.1.1	7511	7452	192.168.1.1
204.24.254.12	192.168.1.1	5142	5102	192.168.1.1
12.4.51.84	192.168.1.2	7421	7412	192.168.1.2
84.1.4.23	192.168.1.2	2741	24751	192.168.1.2

there are no Dumb Questions

Q: Do the IP addresses behind the NAT have to be private IP addresses?

A: No, they can be public. But why not use the private IP addresses. There are tons available.

Q: Do I have to set up the NAT table?

A: No, the device doing NAT uses this table for each and every packet that is going in and out of the device.

Q: Does NAT have to use the public address of the access point?

A: No, it can use other public addresses. You can create a pool of public addresses that can be used to send outside traffic.

Q: What happens if I need multiple web servers behind the NAT to be publicly accessible?

A: That is where the pool of public addresses comes in. On a device that can do advance NAT, you port map that public IP address and port 80 to the second NAT'd web server.

Q: What type of devices can do NATing?

A: Routers, firewalls, access points, some switches, servers.

Q: Is there a RFC that deals with NAT?

A: Of course. Doesn't is seem like there is a RFC for just about everything in networking? The original RFC on NAT is RFC 1631. Another one is RFC 3022, and finally there is RFC2663. Use your favorite search engine to look these up.

Q: Couldn't NATing cause problems with some network protocols?

A: Great question! It certainly can. There are some protocols that put IP addresses in other places inside a packet. A NAT device will not change these other IP addresses. This will cause connection problems for these protocols through a NAT device.

So has this fixed the problem?

After implementing NAT on the Starbuzz wireless access point, all of the customers are able to surf the Internet while inside the coffee shop, even on the busiest of days. That is, until one day...

Why can't my laptop get to the Internet? I know my laptop's old, but it's still wireless capable. I can surf the Internet through **any** wireless hotspot except this one. I'm going to tell all my friends not to come here.

So what went wrong this time?

There's more than one wireless protocol

The problem this time comes down to the age of the laptop and the available wireless protocols.

Wireless network started being developed in the late 1990's. The first standards were called 802.11A and 802.11B. In 2003, 802.11G came onto the scene. Lately, 802.11N equipment has become available. The big differences between the older versions and newer ones is speed, bandwidth, and range.

The problem is that ***all the standards are incompatible***, so, for example, 802.11G equipment will not talk to 802.11N access points. And if you're using an old laptop, you might not have the wireless protocol that the access point requires.

So what can we do?

Geek Bits

You can check out the various wireless standards at **http://en.wikipedia.org/wiki/802.11**

Most newer access point support multiple protocols

Hardware engineers are a smart bunch. They have built access points that support multiple wireless protocols; you just have to configure the access point to allow access via different protocols. On most access points, it's just a matter of selecting the right mode in order to turn on other protocols.

Watch it!

Just turn on the protocols you need.

Multiple wireless protocols on one access point is great, but there can be a performance hit.

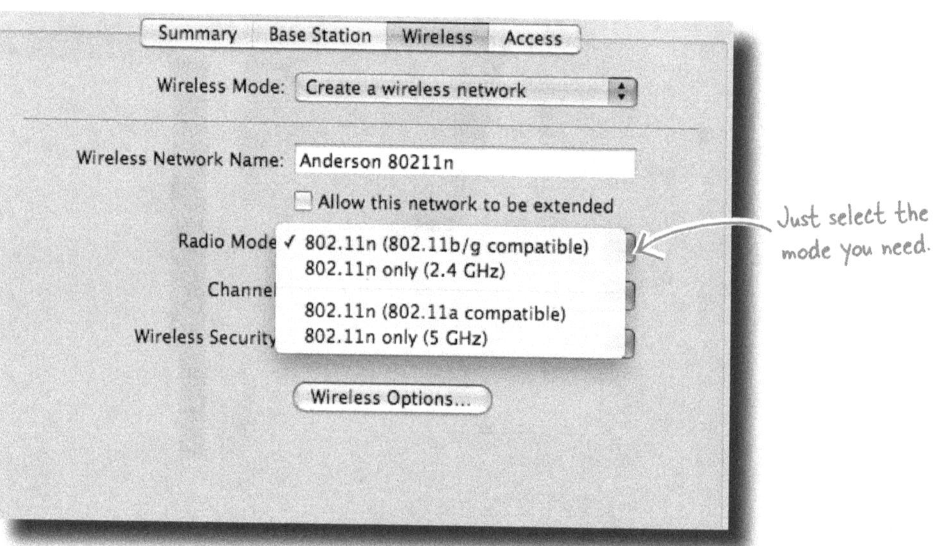

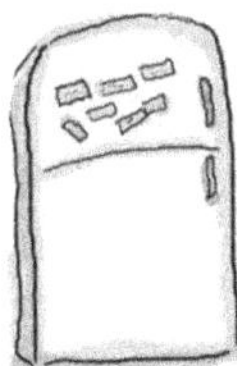

Wireless Standards Magnets

Drag the magnets onto the chart below where you think the wireless standards should go based on their performance.

802.11 N
802.11 B
802.11 G
802.11 A

600 Mbs
54 Mbs
11 Mbs
Speed
35 m
100 m
300 m
Range

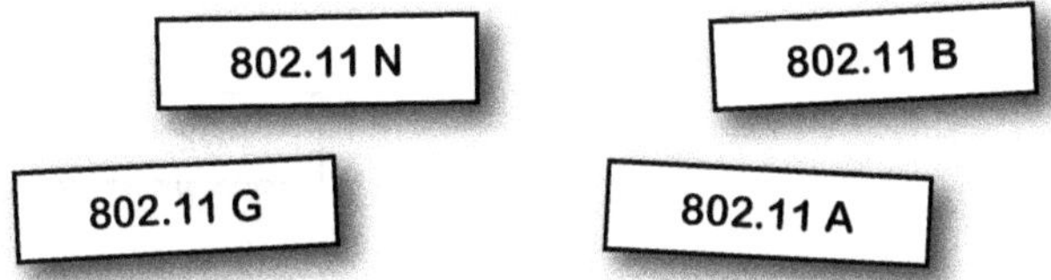

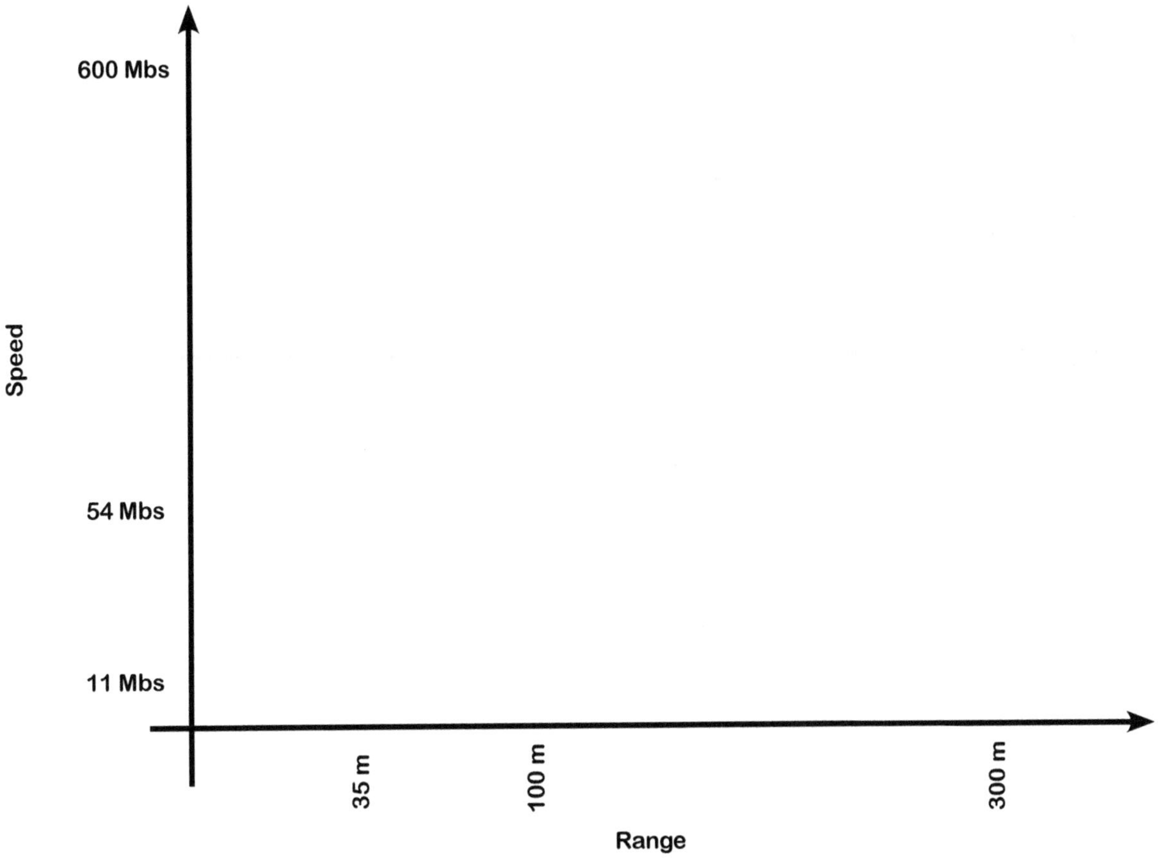

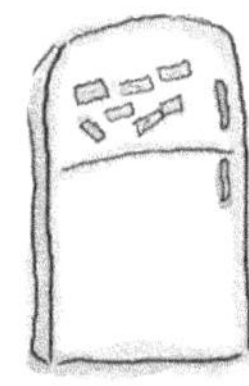

Wireless Standards Magnets Solution

Drag the magnets onto the chart below were you think the wireless standards should go based on their performance.

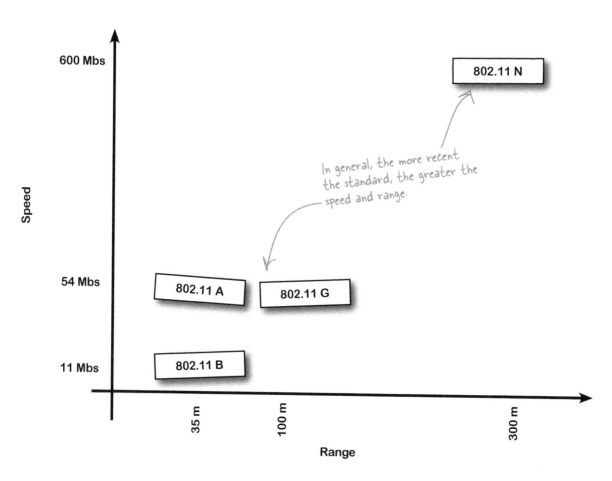

Test Drive

So how are the Starbuzz customers getting on?

Man, this is so cool! I'm coming here again.

So is the Starbuzz wireless access point sorted?

Well, nearly. There's just one more problem that needs to be figured out...

The central Starbuzz server needs to access the cash register

So far, we've looked at implementing the wireless access point so that it's set up for the Starbuzz customers. But there's another requirement too. There's a central Starbuzz server that needs to access the coffee shop cash register so that it can keep track of the daily profits.

It looks retro, but it has built-in wireless connectivity. Think you can sort it out?

What problems can you see with this?

Well, isn't this what we've been doing anyway? If the cash register is wireless enabled, can't it just get a connection?

This time it's the opposite situation.

Instead of a device inside the coffee shop needing a connection to the outside, a server from outside the coffee shop needs to establish a connection to a device inside the network.

So what's the problem? Let's take a look.

1. **The outside Starbuzz server sends a request for the cash register to the DHCP server.**

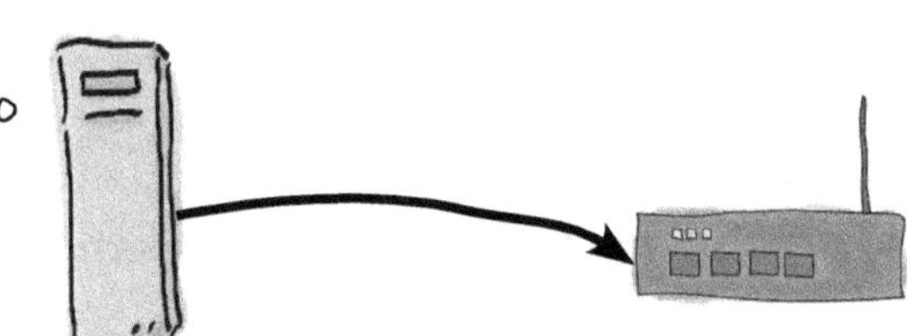

Hey, I'm after the cash register; can you pass this on?

2. **The DHCP server checks the address translation tables to see where to send the request.**
   But because the request wasn't instigated from inside the network, it doesn't know where to send the packets.

Cash register? Nope, I've no record of that, sorry.

So what's the way round this?

Port mapping to the rescue!

The way around this problem is to use port mapping. Port mapping means that we specify a port in the address translation table for a particular device, and any traffic that comes in on this port is forwarded to the corresponding device. It's essentially a very specialized form of routing using TCP and UDP port numbers instead of IP addresses to decide where to send packets.

Here's how it works:

The outside Starbuzz server sends a request for the cash register to the access point, specifying a particular port.
It sends its request to the public IP address of the access point.

Hey, I'm after the cash register; can you pass this on? It's on port 80.

The access point sees that it forwards port 1032 packets to the inside cash register.
But it changes the packets' destination IP address to the web server's private IP address.

Cash register? Yes, I know who you mean.

3 **The cash register responds.**
It sends the requested information to the access point.

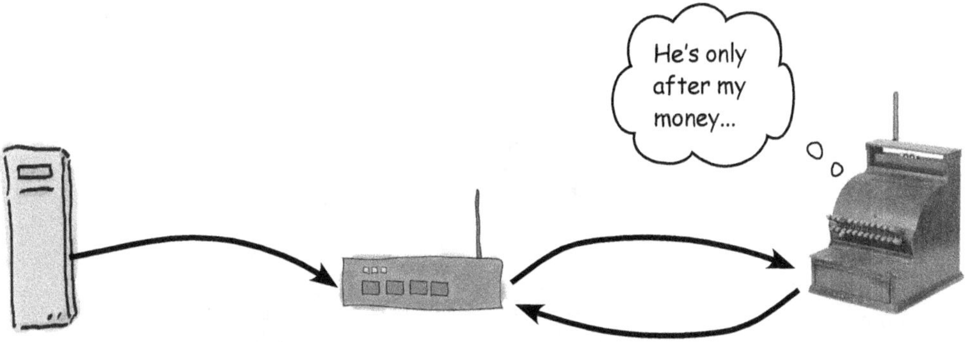

4 **The access point forwards traffic to the public computer.**
But it changes the source IP address of the packets back to the public IP address of the access point.

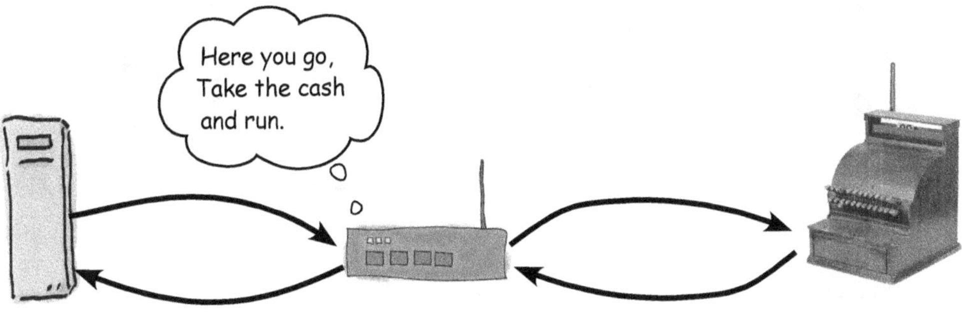

Here you go,
Take the cash
and run.

So port mapping is a bit like NAT in reverse

It's a way of making sure that devices outside of the internal network can get to devices inside.

So how do we configure port mapping?

Let's set up port mapping on the Starbuzz access point

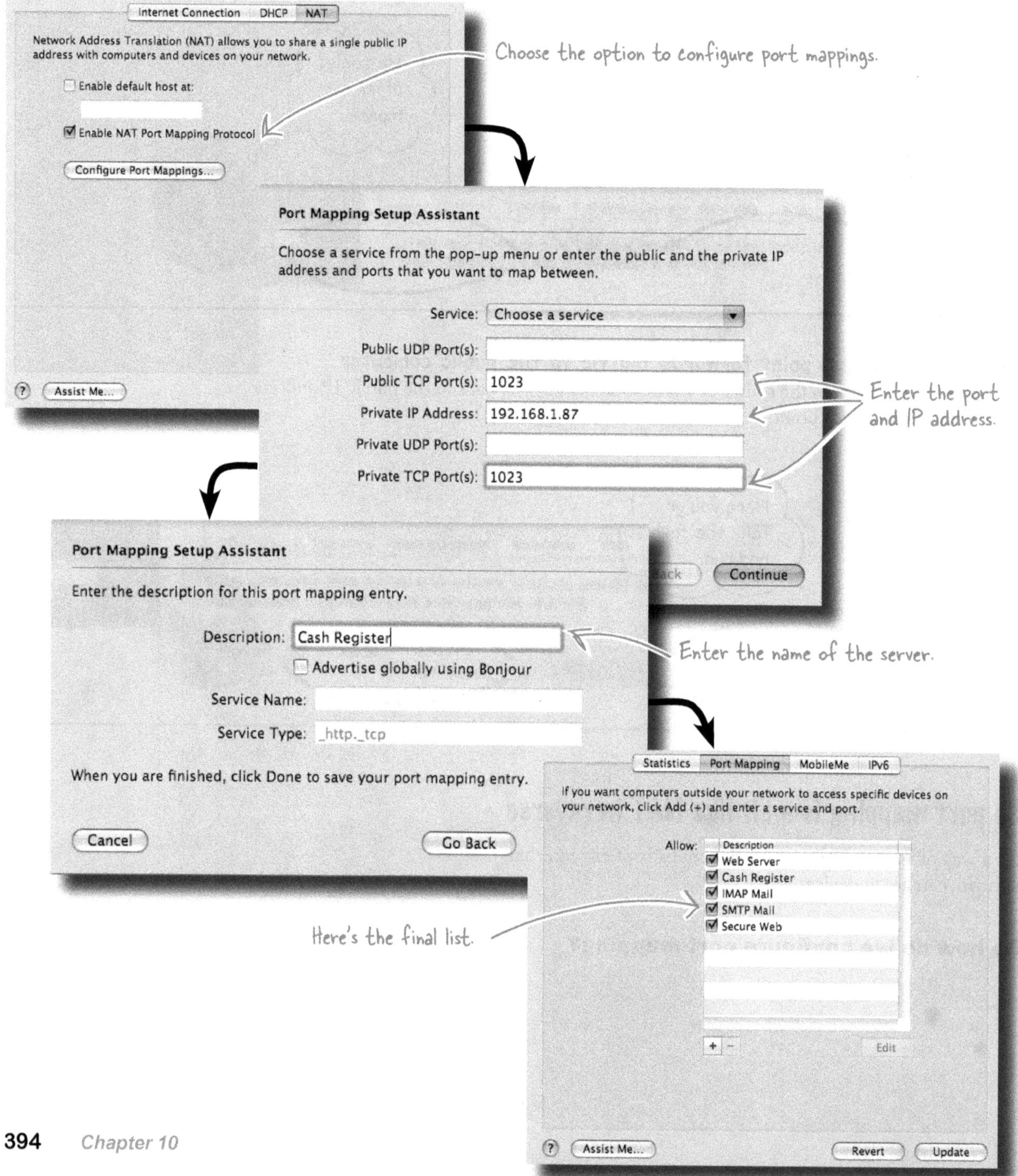

BE the Access Point

Your job is to play Access Point. Use the port forwarding table and decide where the incoming traffic goes. Write in the correct private IP address to send the traffic to.

Port Forwarding Table

Server Private IP Address	Port to forward	Service
192.168.1.2	80	Web
192.168.1.54	143	IMAP
192.168.1.87	1032	Cash Register
192.168.1.7	25	SMTP
192.168.1.2	443	Secure Web

206.252.212.2 is the public IP address of the access point.

You fill out this part.

Source IP	Destination IP	Destination Port	Inside Client IP Address
204.24.254.12	206.252.212.2	80	192.168.1.2
204.24.254.12	206.252.212.2	143	
72.54.84.32	206.252.212.2	80	
206.252.212.3	206.252.212.2	1032	
84.51.25.8	206.252.212.2	25	
204.24.254.12	206.252.212.2	25	
12.4.51.84	206.252.212.2	443	
84.1.4.23	206.252.212.2	24751	

The access point changes the destination IP address of each packet to this.

BE the Access Point Solution

Your job is to play Access Point. Use the port forwarding table and decide where the incoming traffic goes. Write in the correct private IP address to send the traffic to.

Port Forwarding Table

Server Private IP Address	Port to forward	Service
192.168.1.2	80	Web
192.168.1.54	143	IMAP
192.168.1.87	1032	Cash Register
192.168.1.7	25	SMTP
192.168.1.2	443	Secure Web

206.252.212.2 is the public IP address of the access point.

You fill out this part.

Source IP	Destination IP	Destination Port	Inside Client IP Address
204.24.254.12	206.252.212.2	80	192.168.1.2
204.24.254.12	206.252.212.2	143	192.168.1.54
72.54.84.32	206.252.212.2	80	192.168.1.2
206.252.212.3	206.252.212.2	1032	192.168.1.87
84.51.25.8	206.252.212.2	25	192.168.1.7
204.24.254.12	206.252.212.2	25	192.168.1.7
12.4.51.84	206.252.212.2	443	192.168.1.2
84.1.4.23	206.252.212.2	24751	DISCARD IT

OK, we tricked you, but the access point would probably just discard this packet since it has no ports mapped for this port.

The access point changes the destination IP address of each packet to this.

Wireless Security Up Close

You can control who can connect to your wireless access point two ways. One is to enter the MAC addresses into a table on the wireless access point and only allow those computers that have their MAC addresses in the table to connect. The second way is to use a password or some other form of authentication. There are several methods including WEP, WPA, and RADIUS. These are all forms of password authentication protocols. WEP and WPA rely on passwords that the access point and the client computer share. RADIUS is an outside service that the access point uses to confirm the credentials of a client computer trying to get connected.

there are no Dumb Questions

Q: So using port mapping will secure my server from hackers, right?

A: Nope. If you allow access to a server via port mapping, it is no different than if the server was sitting beyond the NAT with a public IP address.

Q: Isn't port mapping what firewalls do?

A: Yes, but firewalls use access control lists to decide who gets to talk to the server that is being NAT'd. Plus most firewalls have other safeguards in place.

Q: Can I change the port that a server talks on?

A: Yes, you can. But this is done on the server. So if you wanted to move a web server to port 1024, for example, that would be done on the configuration of the web server. The only thing you would do on the NAT server is change the port number to the new one.

Q: What I meant was can the NAT server change the port number?

A: Good question. On some NAT servers, they can port map to a different port. They can take traffic on port 80 and change it to a different port.

Q: Can port mapping work with any port?

A: Yes, it can. As long as there is a device behind NAT that will communicate on that port.

Q: Is port mapping limited to TCP, or does it work with other protocols, like UDP?

A: It works with just about any protocol. The issues are similar to regular NAT. If the packets contain addressing information that the NAT server does not change, it will break that particular protocol.

Q: Does port mapping work with DNS?

A: Yes, it would be the public IP address of the NAT server that would be a FQDN.

The wireless access point is a success!

Thanks to your skill in setting up the wireless access point, coffee sales within the coffee shop are soaring. More and more people are using the facilities to browse the Internet, which means that extra coffee is being sold in the store.

Added to this, you've also given the central Starbuzz server access to the state-of-the-art wireless cash register.

This wireless access point is awesome! I'm going to get one for each of the Starbuzz coffee shops. In the meantime, have a coffee on the house.

11 network security

Get Defensive

Come on now, Sweetie, open up the firewall and let the cereal packets in...

The network's a dangerous place to make a living.

Attackers lurk around every corner: rootkits, and script kiddies, and bots... oh my! You've got to buck up and harden your network, or the barbarians will crash the gates. In this chapter, we expose you to the seedy underworld of the network, where attackers spoof MAC addresses, poison your ARP cache, infiltrate your internets, sneak packets into your network, and trick your co-workers into coughing up their passwords. Get defensive, dude! Let's keep our precious data in and the interlopers out.

The bad guys are everywhere

You've put together crucial services like DNS, you've used troubleshooting to keep your network free of bugs, and you've set up a wireless network. The last thing you need now is someone infiltrating your network and messing up all the crucial data you have flying back and forth at top speeds.

As a network professional, you need to protect your networks from the bad guys and stop them from stealing information and launching deadly attacks on your servers.

It is not unusual to have a new server attacked within minutes of being turned on.

The evil impersonator

The evil attacker

And it's not just the NETWORK that gets hurt...

Eavesdroppers can be the worst. Not only are they trying to burn your business, they can hurt some of your good customers too. A double hit. If the eavesdropper is successful, he'll swipe your client's credit card information and charge up a storm.

The evil eavesdropper

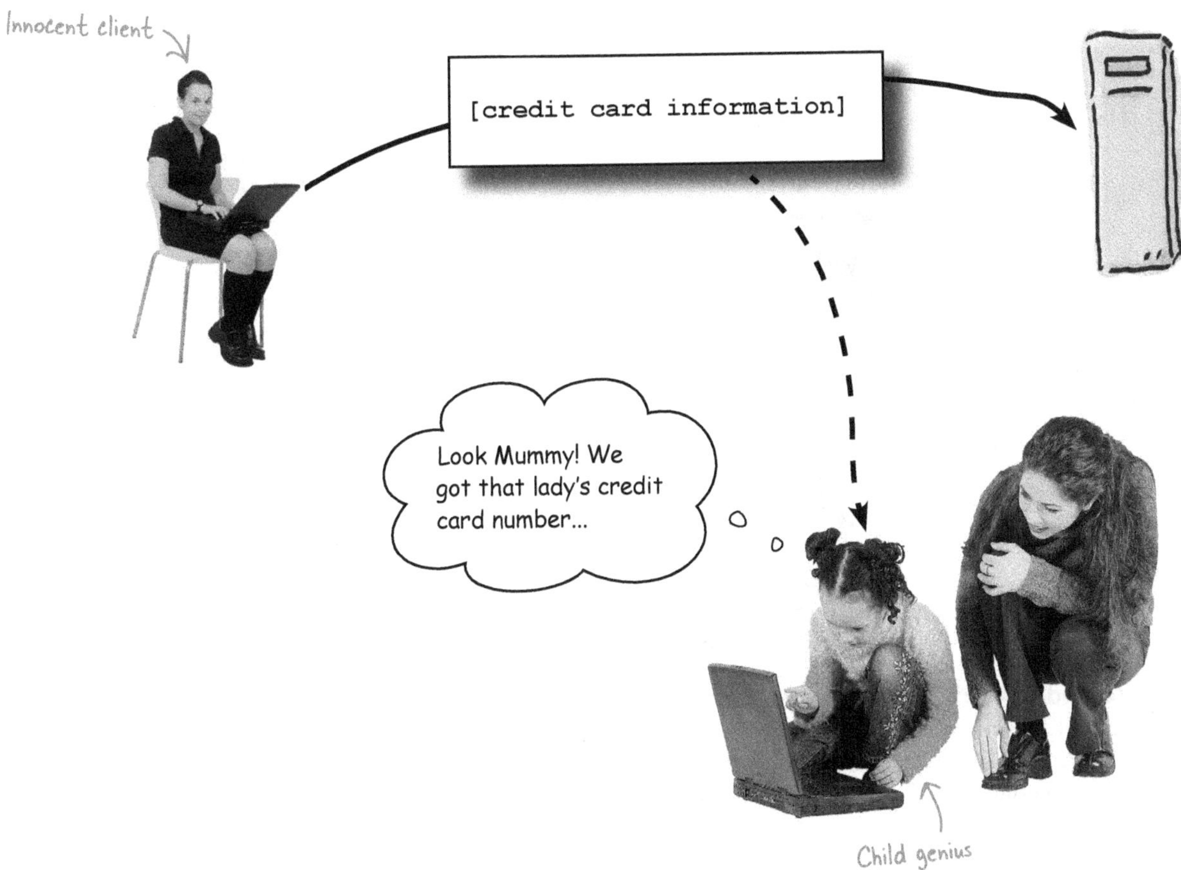
Innocent client
[credit card information]
Look Mummy! We got that lady's credit card number...
Child genius

So how can we protect our networks against bad guys like these?

The big four in network security

Network security helps you—the network professional—foil the bad guys. It basically boils down to four key areas:

1. **Harden your switches.**
   Your switches are vulnerable to MAC address spoofing and ARP poisoning.

To harden your network, you need to analyze the devices that make up your network and where those devices sit in the network topology.

2. **Harden your routers.**
   Out of the box, your routers are not secure. Turn on Access Control Lists and Port Security to keep attackers out.

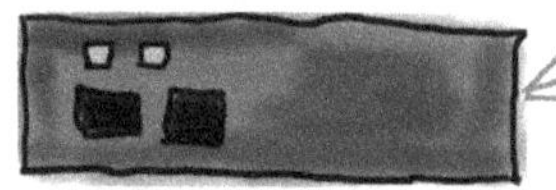

3. **Install a firewall.**
   A firewall is essential for keeping attackers out and crucial data in.

4. **Write and enforce a security policy.**
   All the cool technology stuff you do to protect your network means nothing if an attacker can get at your resources with "social engineering." A good security policy will help to avoid this.

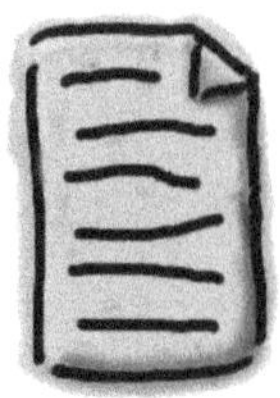

there are no Dumb Questions

Q: So are we talking about hackers?

A: We prefer the term "attacker" to "hacker." The old school use of the term hacker refers to ingenious problem-solvers rather than the creeps and criminals who infiltrate networks.

Exercise

Below you'll see our highly classified network diagram. Circle each of the devices that can be fooled by a spoofed MAC address. Cross out ones that won't be fooled.

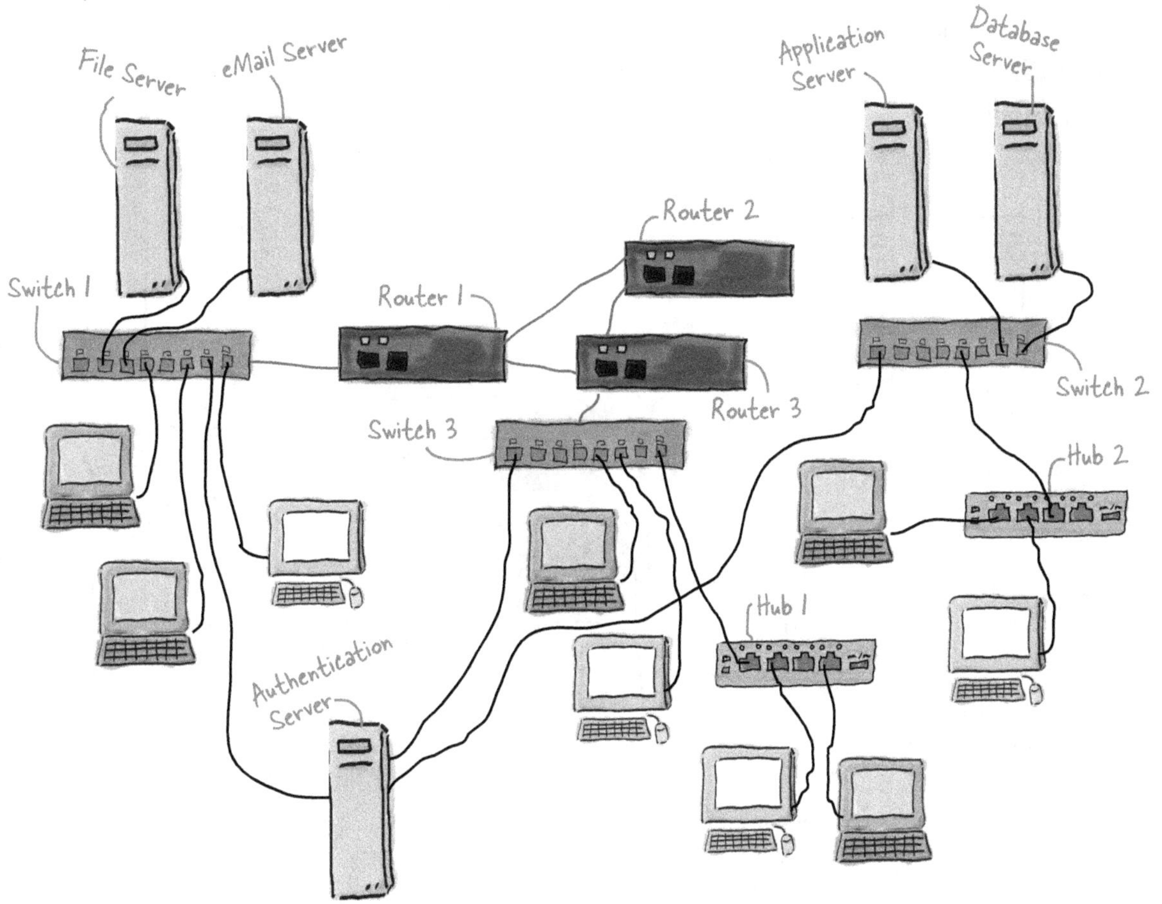

File Server
eMail Server
Application Server
Database Server
Router 2
Switch 1
Router 1
Router 3
Switch 2
Switch 3
Hub 2
Hub 1
Authentication Server

Why does MAC address spoofing pose a threat to network security?

Exercise Solution

Below you'll see our highly classified network diagram. Circle each of the devices that can be fooled by a spoofed MAC address. Cross out ones that won't be fooled.

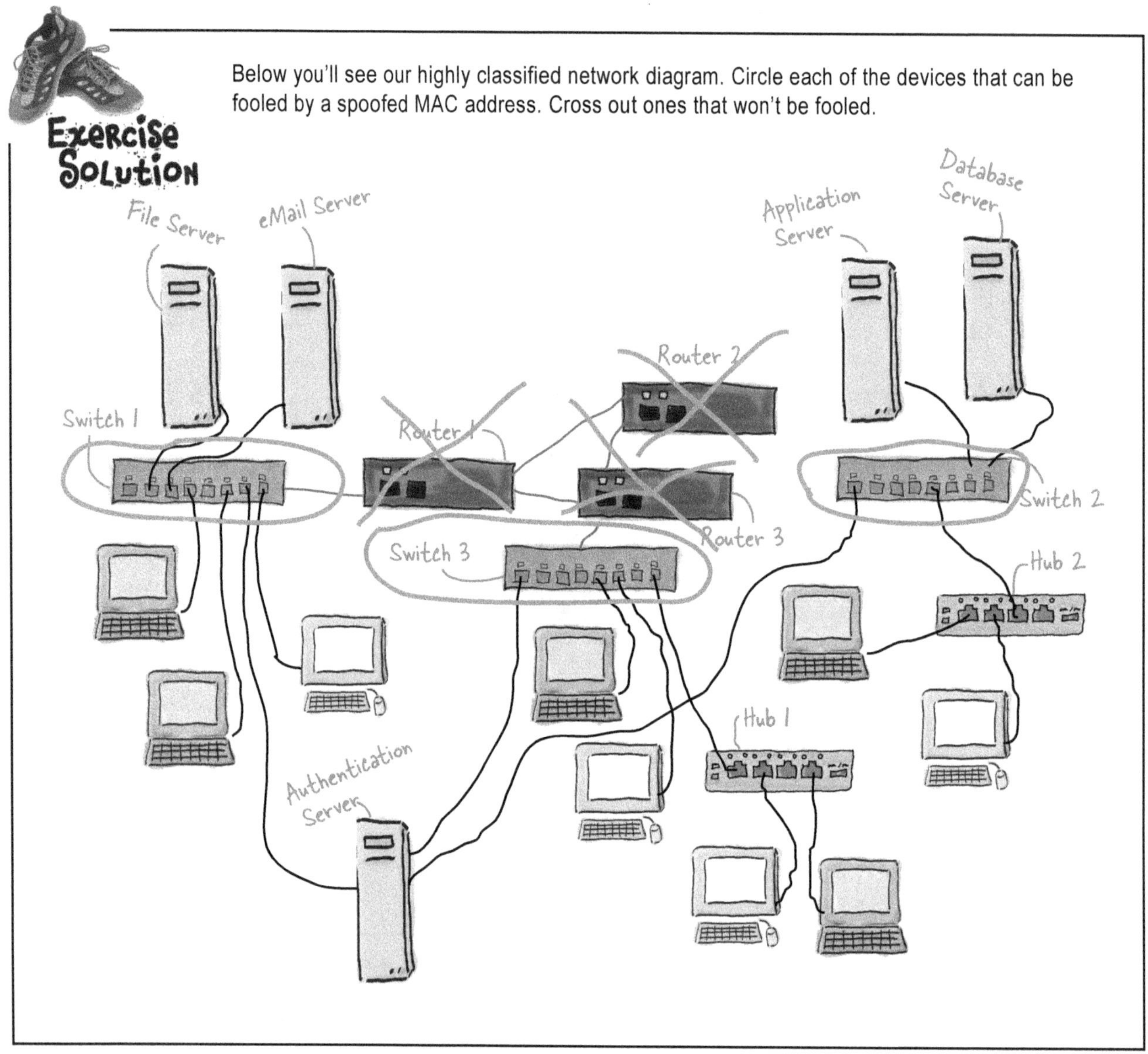

Defend your network against MAC address spoofing

MAC address spoofing is what happens when an attacker changes their MAC address so that it matches another device on the network. It allows an attacker to pretend that the hardware they're using belongs to someone else—like the boss.

By spoofing a MAC address, an attacker can pose as an approved network device and fool other devices into thinking that it's okay to send network traffic to, or receive traffic from, the spoofed device. So if the boss's computer has been spoofed, this means that the attacker can con the switch into sending it information that only the boss should see.

Here's how it goes:

1. **The attacker changes their MAC address to match that of the boss and requests information across the network.** The hardware looks like it belongs to the boss, even though it doesn't.

2. **The switch sees that a device with the boss's MAC address is requesting information and lets it through.**

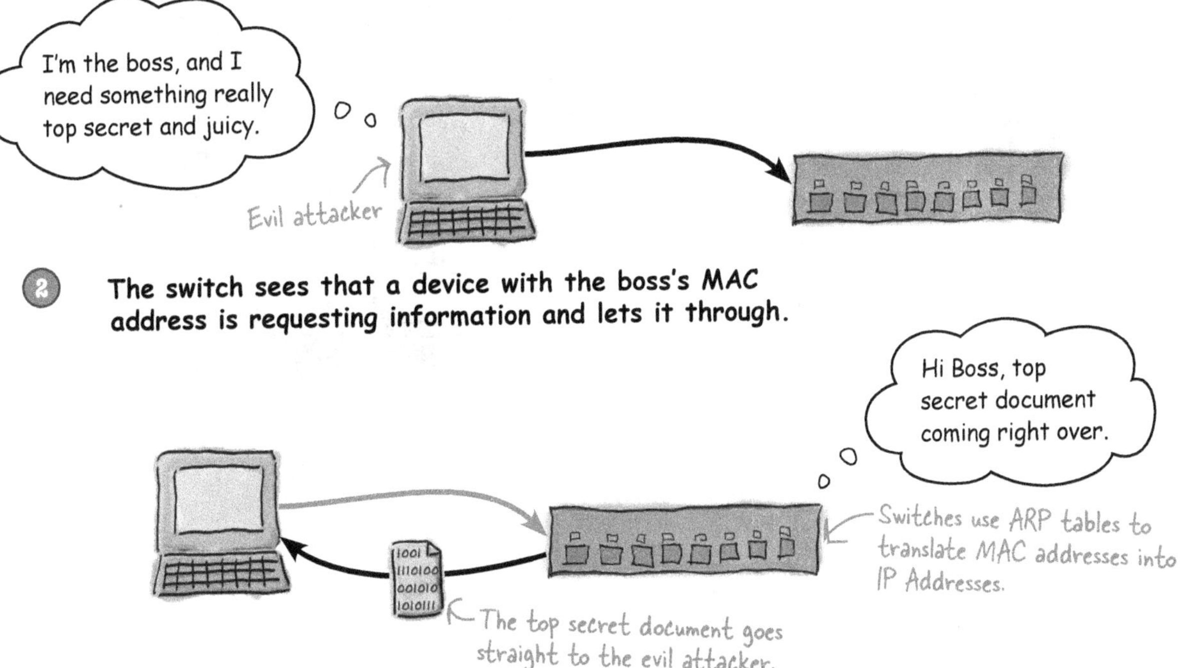

I'm the boss, and I need something really top secret and juicy.
Evil attacker
Hi Boss, top secret document coming right over.
Switches use ARP tables to translate MAC addresses into IP Addresses.
1001
1110100
001010
1010111
The top secret document goes straight to the evil attacker.

So how can we harden a switch against this sort of attack?

Long Exercise

Below is the vulnerable network. On the next page, redesign the network so that its resources can be hardened against MAC address spoofing.

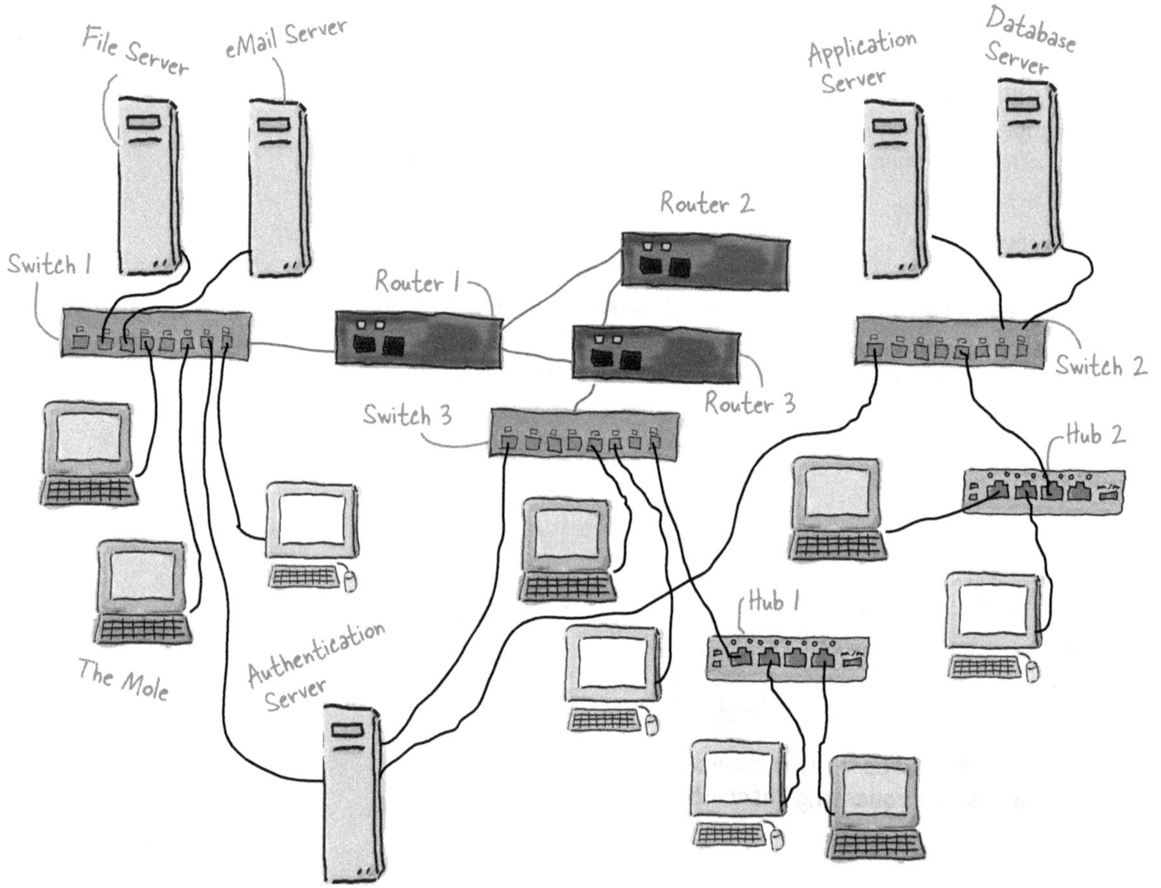

File Server
eMail Server
Application Server
Database Server
Router 2
Switch 1
Router 1
Router 3
Switch 2
Switch 3
Hub 2
Hub 1
The Mole
Authentication Server

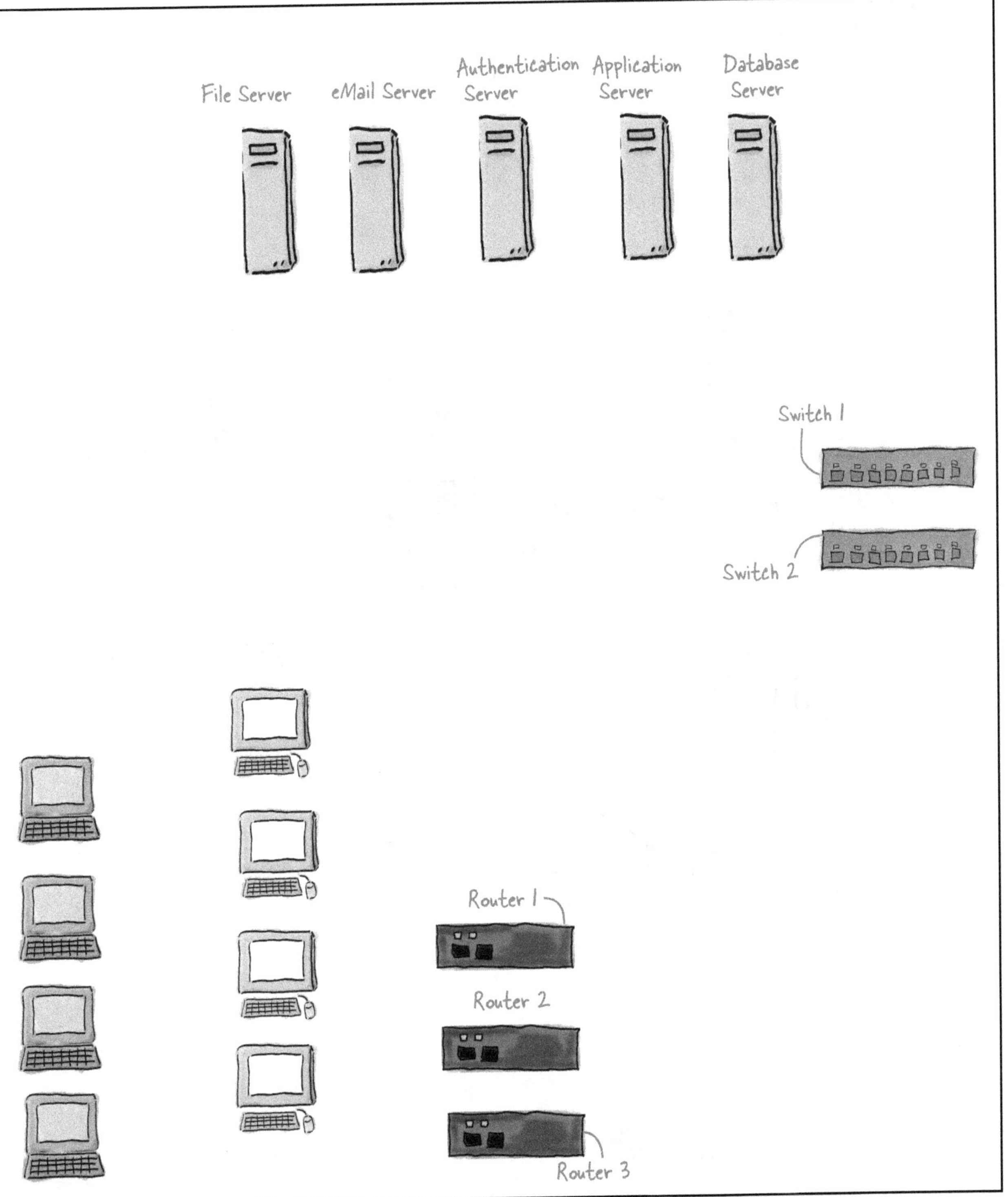
File Server
eMail Server
Authentication Server
Application Server
Database Server
Switch 1
Switch 2
Router 1
Router 2
Router 3

Below is the vulnerable network. On the next page, redesign the network so that its resources can be hardened against MAC address spoofing.

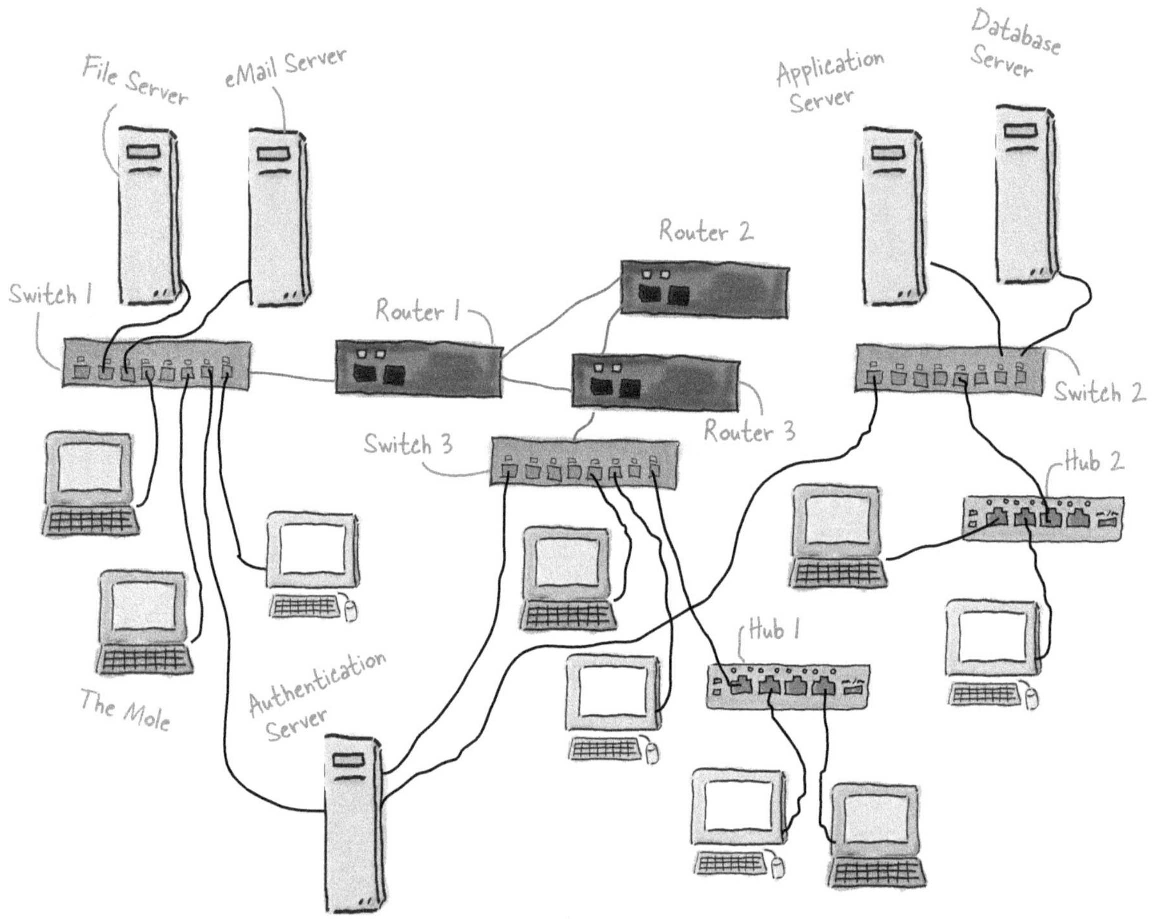

File Server
eMail Server
Application Server
Database Server
Router 2
Switch 1
Router 1
Router 3
Switch 2
Switch 3
Hub 2
Hub 1
The Mole
Authentication Server

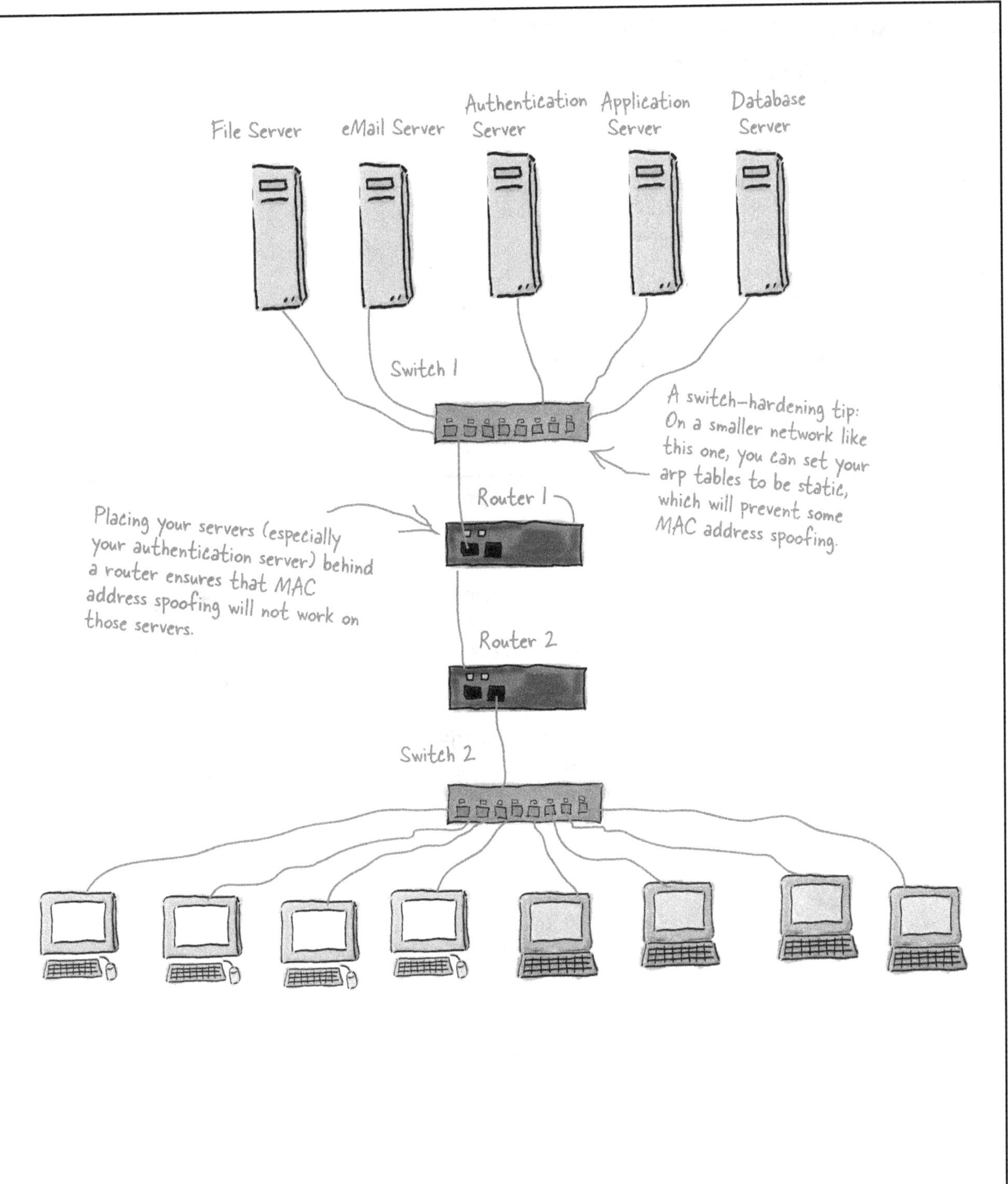

File Server
eMail Server
Authentication Server
Application Server
Database Server
Switch 1
A switch-hardening tip: On a smaller network like this one, you can set your arp tables to be static, which will prevent some MAC address spoofing.
Router 1
Placing your servers (especially your authentication server) behind a router ensures that MAC address spoofing will not work on those servers.
Router 2
Switch 2

So how do we defend against MAC address spoofing?

Switches are susceptible to MAC address spoofing, while routers are unaffected because they deal with IP addresses. Your key defense against MAC address spoofing is to place your servers (especially your authentication server) behind a router. This means that MAC address spoofing will not work on these servers.

Another defense for a smaller network is to set the switch ARP tables to be static. This will prevent some MAC address spoofing.

But there's more to network attacks than MAC address spoofing...

Five Minute Mystery

The Case of the Stolen Messages

At the offices of Yellow Pad Inc., manufacturers of fine legal pads, Talula works in cubicle 4. During her lunch hour, Talula likes to send instant messages to her sweetie, RJ, in cubicle 21. When she sends the messages, she signs them with her secret nickname, "Kung-Fu Princess," whereas RJ signs his with his secret nickname, "Kid Rye."

One morning, when Talula boots up her workstation, she sees a message on her screen that says, "Another device with the address 204.08.22.68 is connected to the network. Change your IP address to join the network."

The same day, the office busybody, Dwight, walks past RJ and asks him, "How's the Kung-Fu Princess, Kid Rye?"

When RJ tells Talula the story, she thinks a while and says, "I think I know how he did it, but we'll fix his wagon."

RJ asks, "How did Dwight find out our secret nicknames? And how are we going to fix him?"

How were the messages intercepted?

Defend your network against ARP poisoning attacks

Another sort of attack is the ARP (Address Resolution Protocol) poisoning attack that bad guys can use to completely bring down your network. Let's see how this works.

1. **The attacker sends a poisoned packet.**
The attacker broadcasts a packet with an IP address, along with a MAC address that's either faked or simply doesn't exist.

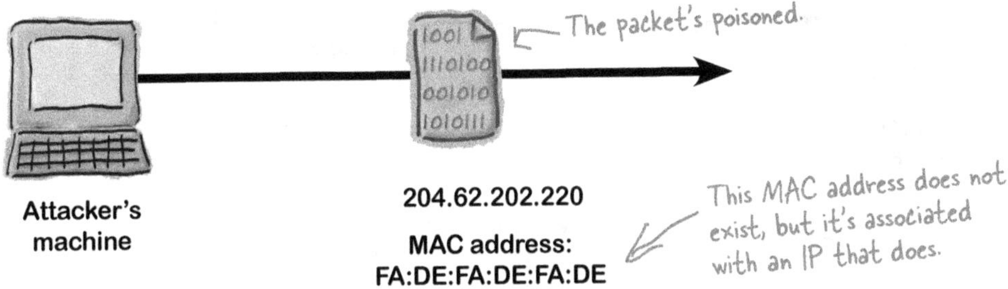
1001
1110100
001010
1010111
The packet's poisoned.
Attacker's machine
204.62.202.220
MAC address: FA:DE:FA:DE:FA:DE
This MAC address does not exist, but it's associated with an IP that does.

2. **Network devices update their ARP tables, which poisons them.**
Other workstations and network devices receive the broadcast packet and update their ARP tables (aka caches) with the bad information. Those devices are now using information that is poisoned, or intentionally corrupted.

All of these devices are now "infected."

3. **The exploit proceeds.**
Now that the AR tables are poisoned, the attacker can use one of three attack methods: Denial of Service, Man in the Middle, or MAC flooding.

Because the Address Resolution Protocol has no way of verifying whether a MAC address is valid, an intruder can "poison" a network device by giving it false information.

So what can we do about ARP poisoning attacks?

The key thing with this sort of attack is to harden your switch. Most switches have port security features which let you assign only one MAC address per port, and this is one of your best defences against this sort of attack. If the wrong MAC address comes into the wrong port, the switch won't let it through.

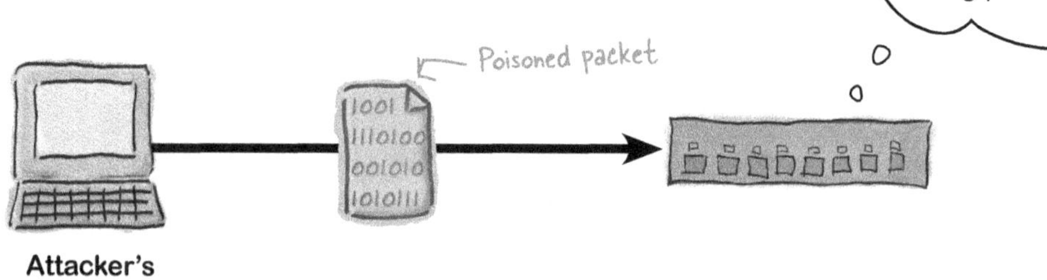
You say you're the boss? No way! You're through on the wrong port.
Poisoned packet
1001
111010
001010
101011
Attacker's machine

there are no Dumb Questions

Q: Is there any way to find out if someone is sending ARP poisoning attacks on my network.

A: An intrusion detection system (IDS), like Snort, will monitor your network for ARP requests that seem out of the ordinary.

Q: How does an attacker create a poisoned packet?

A: Programs like "Dsniff" come packaged with smaller apps like "arpspoof." Using arpspoof inside a switched network, the attacker can create and send poisoned ARP packets, which open up other exploit possibilities.

Q: Why won't MAC spoofing and ARP poisoning affect a router?

A: Good question. Remember that routers work at the IP Address level. Routers can't be fooled by these attacks the way switches can.

Q: You mentioned a few different types of ARP attacks. First off, what's a Denial of Service attack?

A: With an ARP-based DoS attack, you trick other devices on the network into sending traffic to an IP address that is valid, but you give it a MAC address that can't be found on the network. Once all of the ARP tables are poisoned, other machines on the network start sending traffic intended for the router to a device that doesn't exist. In effect, you isolate the local network from getting beyond the router in question.

Q: What about a Man in the Middle attack?

A: An attacker finds a way to intercept traffic intended for the router, or another workstation, and forwards it on to another device. It would be like changing your mailbox number so that the mailman believes your mailbox is actually your neighbor's. That way, you could get their mail before they do. You can then deliver the mail to your neighbor so that they never know what happened. However, you get a chance to filter through mail that was intended for your neighbor. You become the "man in the middle" between the mailman and your neighbor.

Q: And a MAC flooding attack?

A: You can eat up the switch's resources by overwhelming it with tons of ARP requests that ask for hardware (MAC addresses) that don't exist. You clobber the switch's memory.

The Case of the Stolen Messages

So how were the messages intercepted?

Five Minute Mystery Solved

Talula tells RJ, "Dwight used a 'man-in-the-middle' attack. He poisoned the ARP tables of the Yellow Pad, Inc. network by intercepting traffic that was supposed to go to my workstation, RJ."

RJ says, "How did you figure it out, Talula?"

Talula says, "I noticed this morning that when I booted up my machine, another machine on the network had the same IP address as mine. Then, when you told me what Dwight said, I realized that he had probably poisoned the ARP tables so that he could associate his MAC address with my IP address."

"Slow down," RJ says. "You know I'm not a techie, Talula."

Talula says, "Here's how it works, RJ: An attacker finds a way to intercept messages intended for another workstation, and forwards it on to another device. The attacker gets a chance to read your messages before you do. Then sends them on to you without your knowledge.

"I get it." RJ says, "So how are you going to fix him?"

"I already did." Talula says, "I performed a counter-attack by becoming the 'man-in-the-middle' and sending all of Dwight's network traffic to the boss. Won't the boss be surprised when she finds out how many hours a day Dwight spends playing Warlocks of Worldcrash?"

RJ says, "Darn your smart, Talula!"

It's all about the access, baby!

So far we've dealt with switch hardening, but that's not the only device we need to tighten security on. We need to tighten security on the router, too.

Big Bad Internet
Router
Switch
eMail Server
File Server
The only thing between me and the network is that sweet little router...

If an attacker can get past your router, then he's on your network!

If you don't have proper access controls in place on your router, then anyone can get into your network. They don't even have to spoof anything to do it.

Set up your router's Access Control Lists to keep attackers out

The meat-and-taters of hardening your router comes in the form of Access Control Lists (ACLs). An Access Control List is a simple table that a router uses to keep track of which IP Addresses are allowed to cross the router. You configure the table so that particular IP addresses are either allowed or denied access.

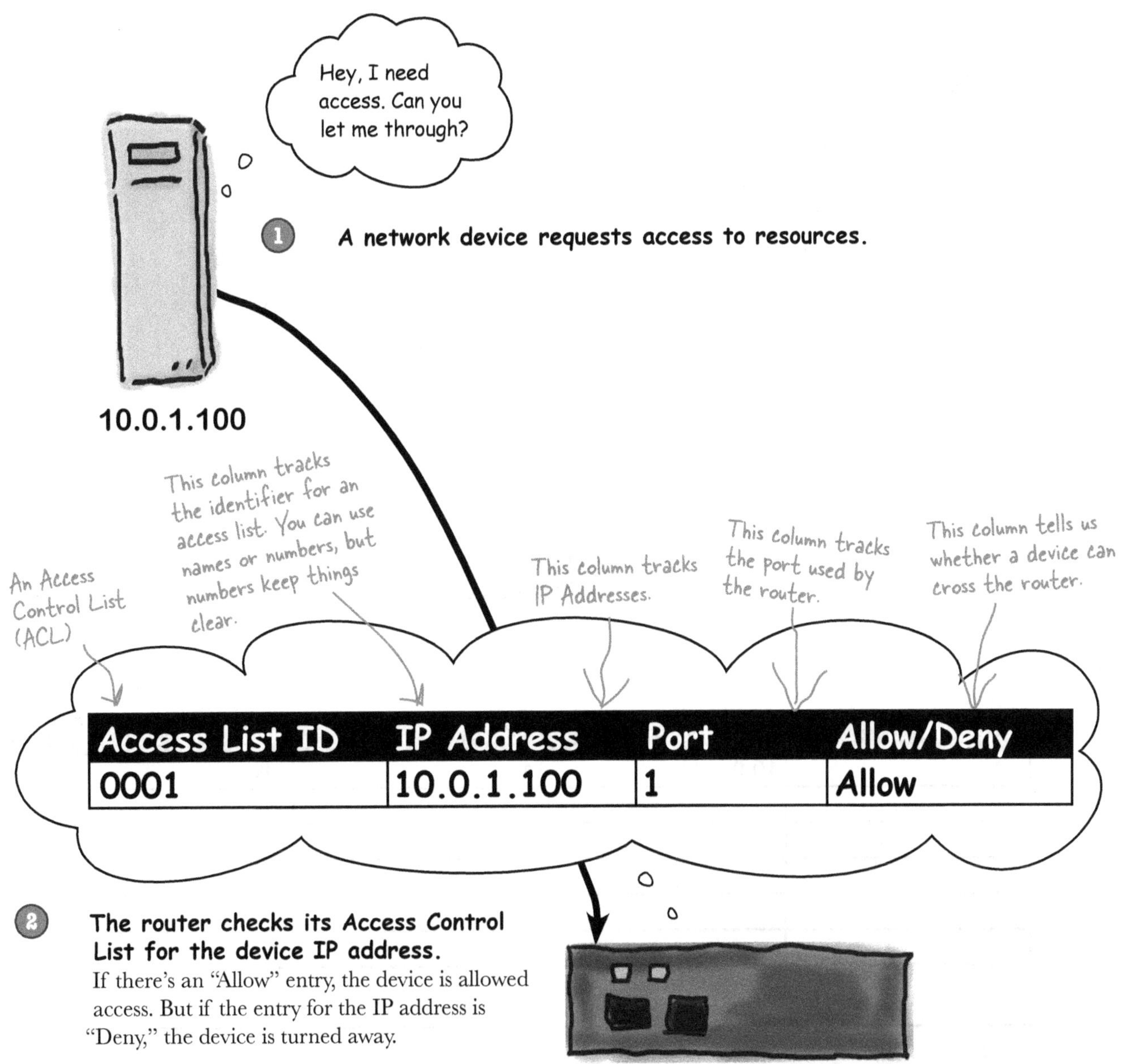
Hey, I need access. Can you let me through?
1 A network device requests access to resources.
10.0.1.100
An Access Control List (ACL)
This column tracks the identifier for an access list. You can use names or numbers, but numbers keep things clear.
This column tracks IP Addresses.
This column tracks the port used by the router.
This column tells us whether a device can cross the router.

Access List ID	IP Address	Port	Allow/Deny
0001	10.0.1.100	1	Allow

2 The router checks its Access Control List for the device IP address.

If there's an "Allow" entry, the device is allowed access. But if the entry for the IP address is "Deny," the device is turned away.

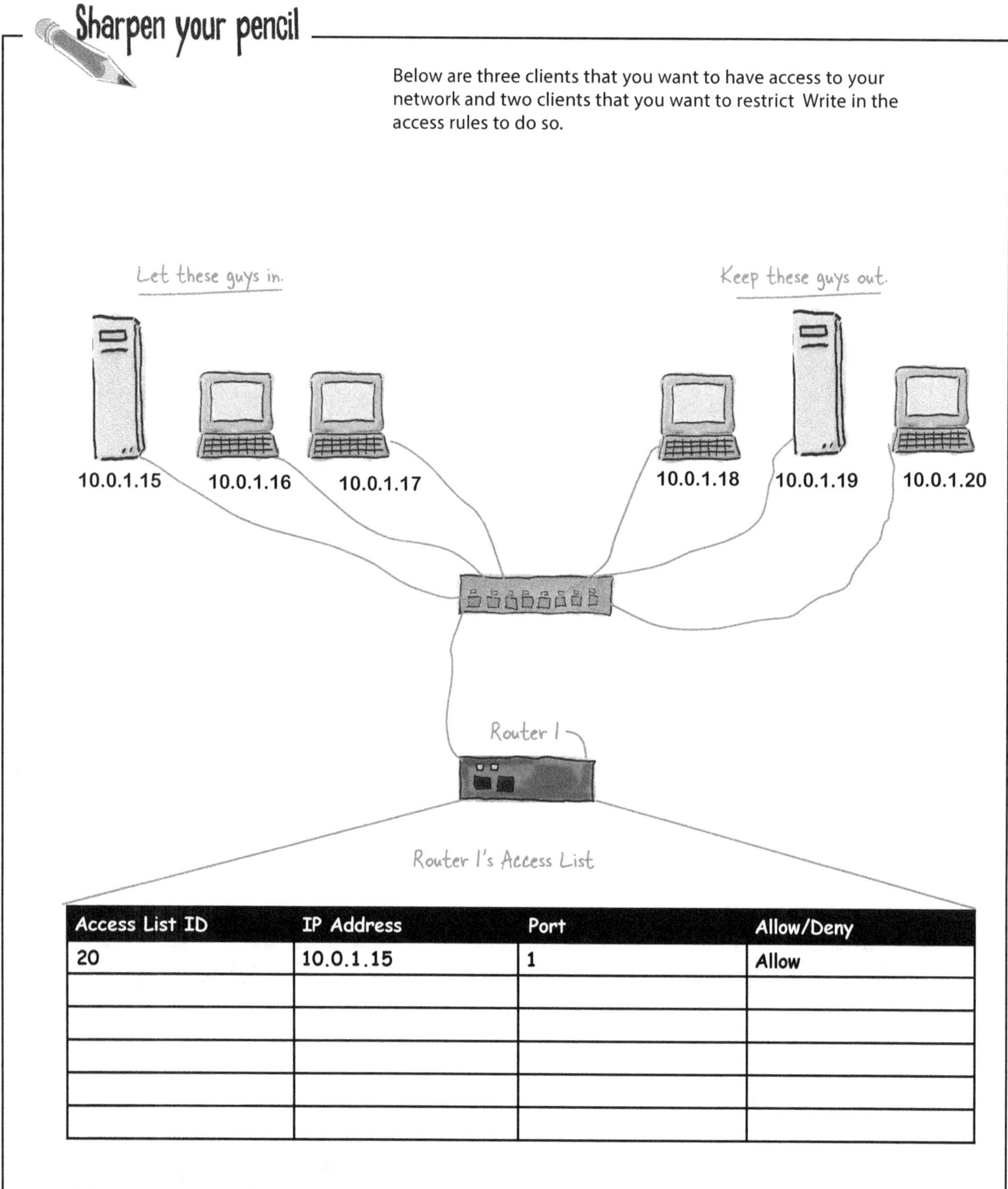

Below are three clients that you want to have access to your network and two clients that you want to restrict Write in the access rules to do so.

Access List ID	IP Address	Port	Allow/Deny
20	10.0.1.15	1	Allow

So how do we configure the Access Control List?

To set up permissions in the router Access Control List, you open up a terminal and use commands to configure the permissions. Here's an example:

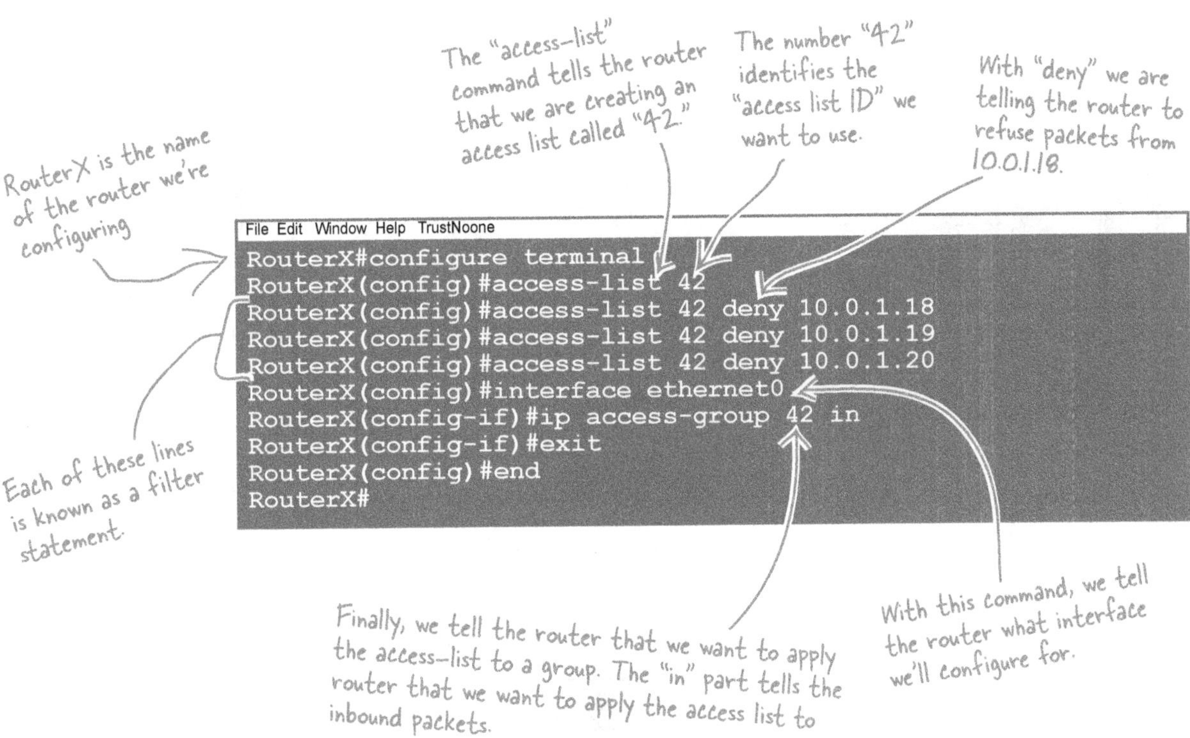

The "access-list" command tells the router that we are creating an access list called "42."
The number "42" identifies the "access list ID" we want to use.
With "deny" we are telling the router to refuse packets from 10.0.1.18.
RouterX is the name of the router we're configuring
File Edit Window Help TrustNoone
RouterX#configure terminal
RouterX(config)#access-list 42
RouterX(config)#access-list 42 deny 10.0.1.18
RouterX(config)#access-list 42 deny 10.0.1.19
RouterX(config)#access-list 42 deny 10.0.1.20
RouterX(config)#interface ethernet0
RouterX(config-if)#ip access-group 42 in
RouterX(config-if)#exit
RouterX(config)#end
RouterX#
Each of these lines is known as a filter statement.
Finally, we tell the router that we want to apply the access-list to a group. The "in" part tells the router that we want to apply the access list to inbound packets.
With this command, we tell the router what interface we'll configure for.

Most Cisco routers use a graphical user interface (GUI) app to control access lists.

We like to show you the command line interface (CLI) so that you understand how the command works at its most basic level.

Sharpen your pencil Solution

Below are three clients that you want to have access to your network and two clients that you want to restrict Write in the access rules to do so.

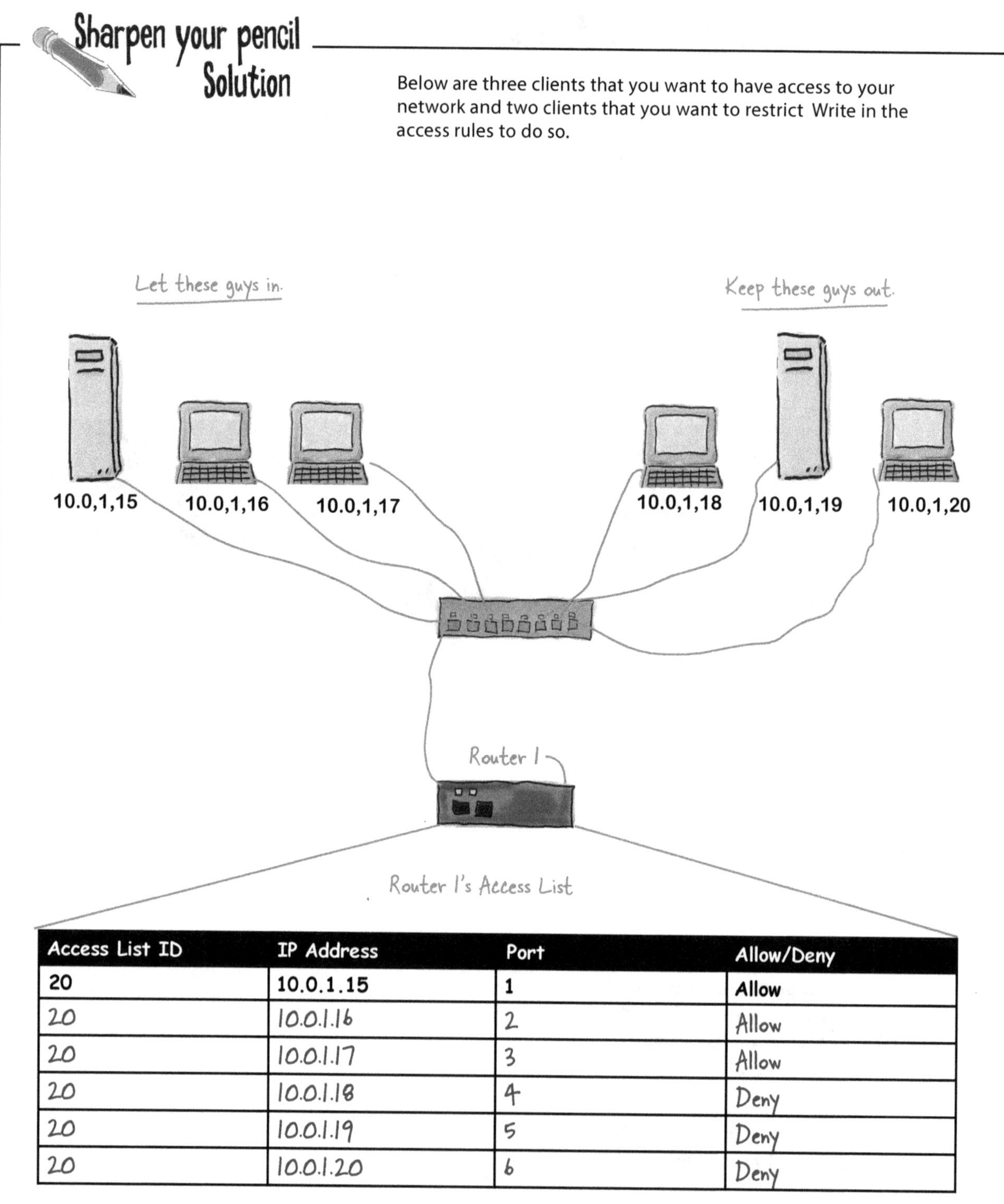

Access List ID	IP Address	Port	Allow/Deny
20	10.0.1.15	1	Allow
20	10.0.1.16	2	Allow
20	10.0.1.17	3	Allow
20	10.0.1.18	4	Deny
20	10.0.1.19	5	Deny
20	10.0.1.20	6	Deny

Ha, switch and router hardening won't stop me! I'm gonna bring your network to its knees from the outside.

You've hardened your switches and routers, but that's not enough.

If you're not careful, the bad guys will attack your network from the outside. You need to defend your network from dangerous outside influences with an effective firewall.

Firewalls filter packets between networks

A firewall filters packets that travel between networks by applying rules for access. Firewalls can be hardware devices, or they can be a piece of software on a device.

Cisco manufactures an older series of firewalls called "Pix Security Appliances" and a new series of firewalls called "Adaptive Security Appliances" (ASAs). A regular router can be set up as a firewal, and most Linux installers allow you to configure a workstation as a firewall. Tons of software apps offer you a software firewall solution. Our purpose here is not to tell you which kind to choose and use, but to explain how they work and how they protect your network.

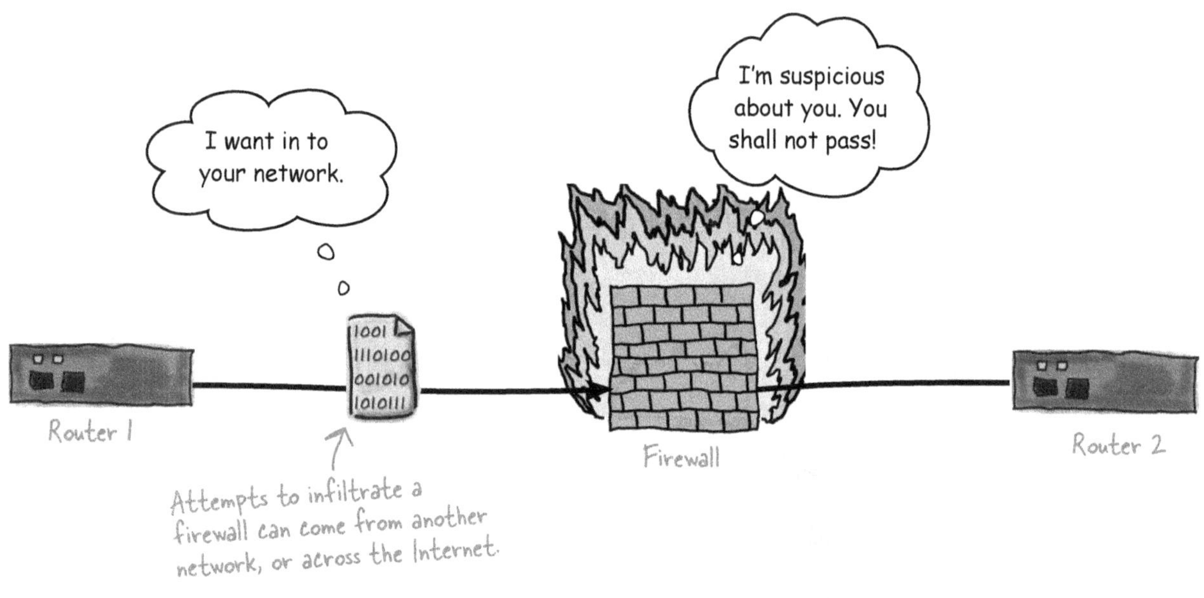

Attempts to infiltrate a firewall can come from another network, or across the Internet.

BRAIN POWER

What are the differences between software and hardware firewalls? Which type is more secure? Is there a difference between these types of firewalls and a firewall on a personal computer?

Packet-filtering rules!

So a firewall filters packets, but how does it do so? By applying rules that are a little bit like a router's ACLs. The big difference is that a router's ACL applies to an IP-based device, where a firewall's packet-filtering rules apply to ... well ... packets.

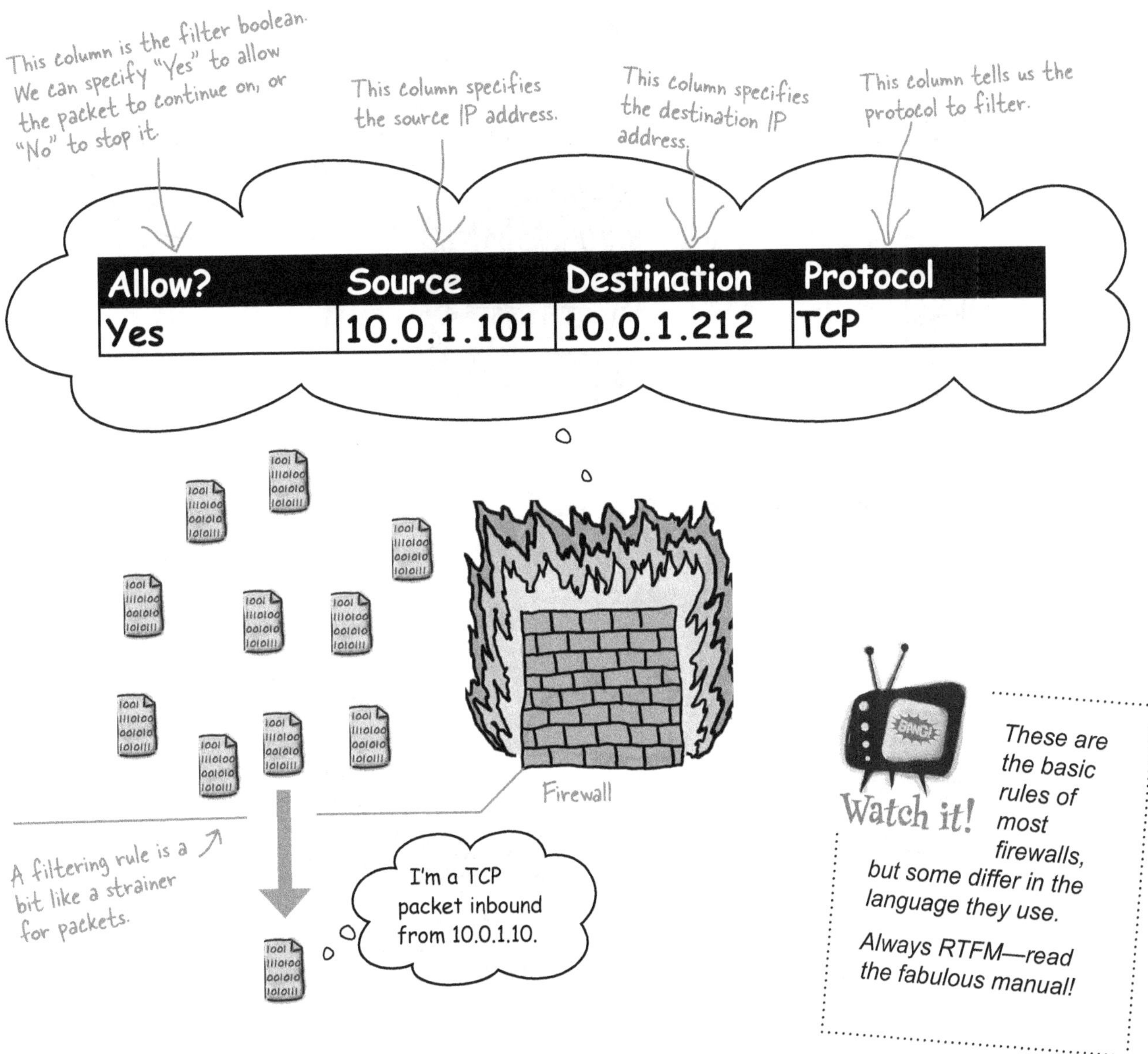

This column is the filter boolean. We can specify "Yes" to allow the packet to continue on, or "No" to stop it.
This column specifies the source IP address.
This column specifies the destination IP address.
This column tells us the protocol to filter.
Allow? | Source | Destination | Protocol
Yes | 10.0.1.101 | 10.0.1.212 | TCP
Firewall
A filtering rule is a bit like a strainer for packets.
I'm a TCP packet inbound from 10.0.1.10.
Watch it!
These are the basic rules of most firewalls, but some differ in the language they use.
Always RTFM—read the fabulous manual!

Master the static packet filter

A firewall uses static packet-filtering and stateful packet-filtering. Obviously, you should grasp the simple rules first. Then, we can get a bit more complex.

1. **Analyze the packet header.**
   The packet header contains all the information a firewall needs to apply its rules. Like a border security guard, the firewall gathers information on the travelers who want to get to one side or the other.

2. **Allow or deny access based on the rule.**

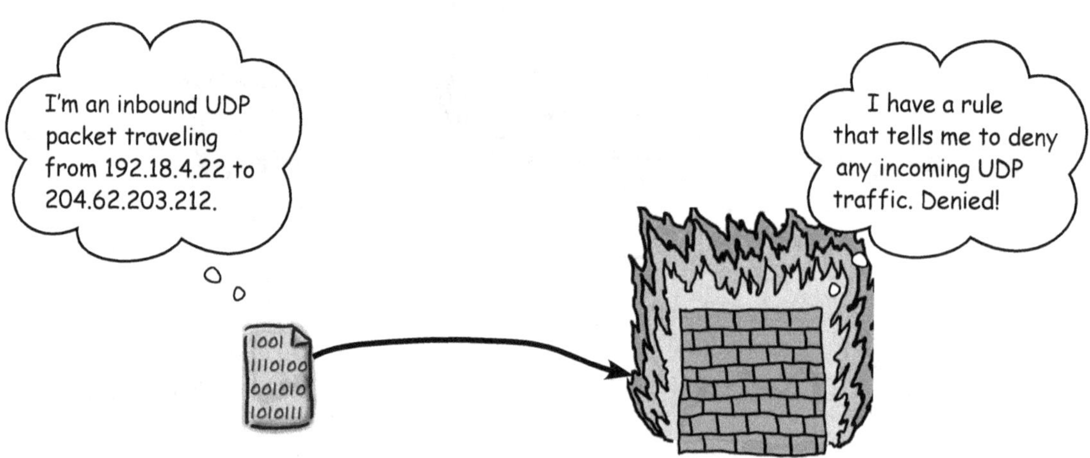

BE the Firewall

Your job is to play the Firewall and allow or deny packets based on the filtering rules shown. If a packet will make it through the firewall, complete the connection to the device on the other side. If the packet will be denied, put an "X" through it.

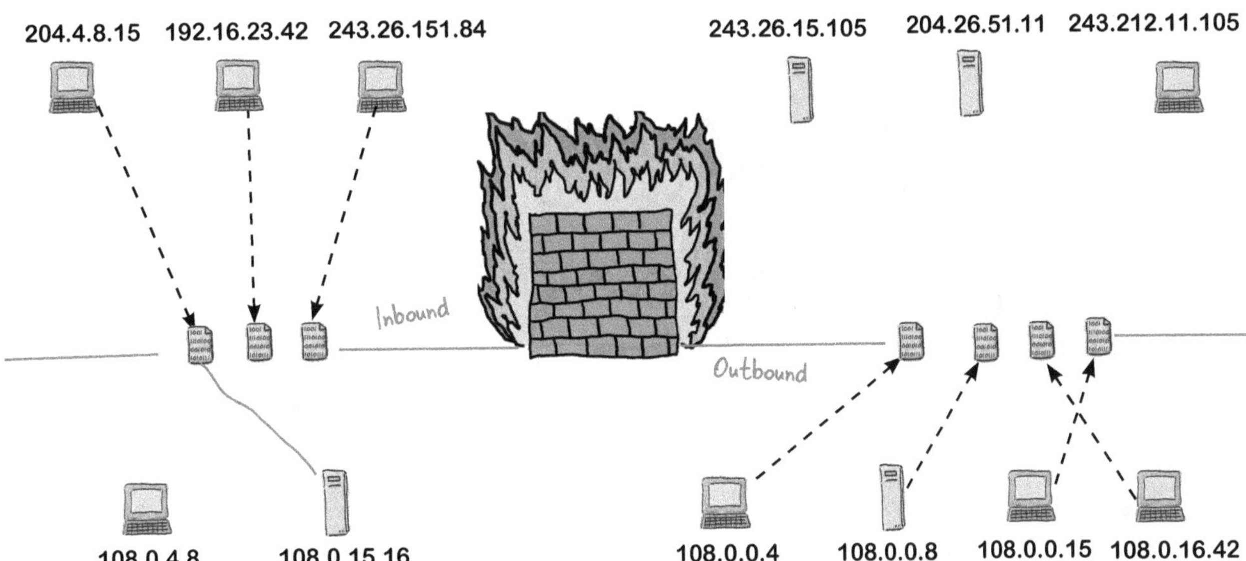

Allow?	Source	Destination	Direction
Yes	204.4.8.15	108.0.15.16	Inbound
No	108.0.0.4	243.26.15.105	Outbound
Yes	108.0.16.42	243.26.15.105	Outbound
Yes	108.0.0.15	243.212.11.105	Outbound
No	192.16.23.42	108.0.15.16	Inbound
Yes	243.26.151.84	108.0.4.8	Inbound
Yes	108.0.0.8	204.26.51.11	Outbound

BE the Firewall Solution

Your job is to play the Firewall and allow or deny packets based on the filtering rules shown. If a packet will make it through the firewall, complete the connection to the device on the other side. If the packet will be denied, put an "X" through it.

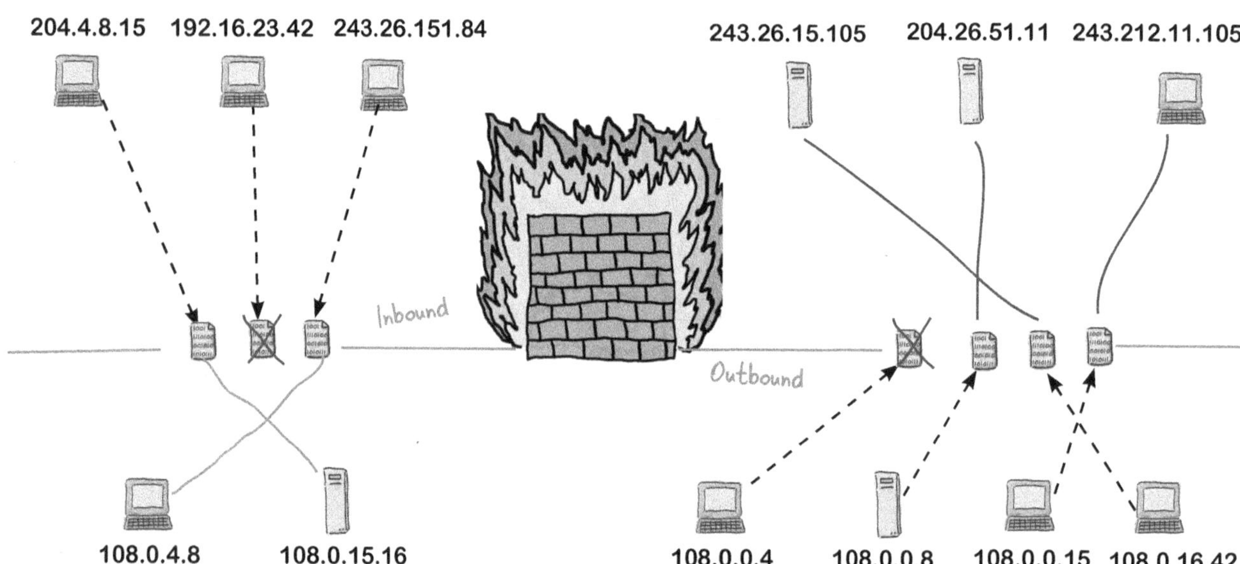

Allow?	Source	Destination	Direction
Yes	204.4.8.15	108.0.15.16	Inbound
No	108.0.0.4	243.26.15.105	Outbound
Yes	108.0.16.42	243.26.15.105	Outbound
Yes	108.0.0.15	243.212.11.105	Outbound
No	192.16.23.42	108.0.15.16	Inbound
Yes	243.26.151.84	108.0.4.8	Inbound
Yes	108.0.0.8	204.26.51.11	Outbound

Packet-filter, shmacket-
shmilter. I'll just use a dumb
little UDP packet to slip past
your simple filters.

Applying static packet filtering isn't enough.

Because static packet-filters rely on header information, they are often not descript enough to catch traffic cloaked in a simple protocol like UDP. So how do we defend against this little conundrum?

We need something that doesn't just analyze the packet's basic characteristics, but can also look at the packet's state. Enter, the stateful packet filter...

Get smart with stateful packet-filters

The problem with static packet filters is that their packet-filtering rules are static, meaning they can't be changed. Static packet filters use a simple table to check packets, and they have no way to remember which packets have come through and when. Hackers can take advantage of the amnesiac, rigid nature of static packet filters. Fortunately, we have a more dynamic way to firewall: the stateful packet filter.

1. **Analyze the packet header AND manage a state table.**
Like static packet filters, a stateful packet filter analyzes packet headers. However, a stateful packet filter adds some brains to its operations in the form of a state table, which allows it to keep track of which packets have come through and when.

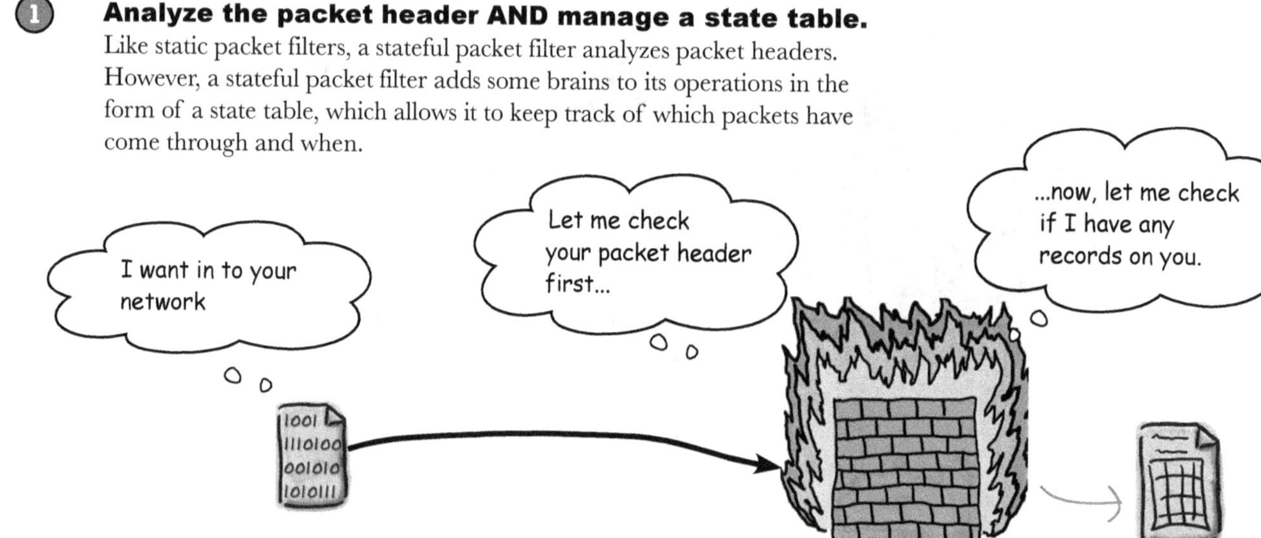

2. **Allow or deny access based on rules and the state.**

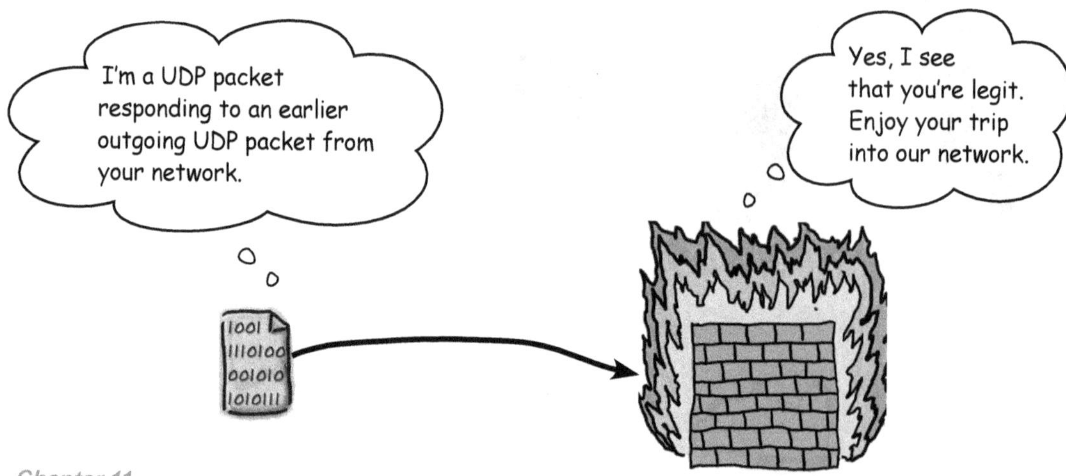

A bunch of security technologies, in full costume, are playing the party game "Who am I?" They'll give you a clue, and you try to guess who they are based on what they say. Assume they always tell the truth about themselves. Fill in the blanks to the right to identify the attendees.

Tonight's attendees:

Router Access Control List (ACL), Static Packet Filter, Stateful Packet Filter, Firewall, Switch, Honeypot, Intrusion Detection System (IDS), Antivirus Program

	Name
I am the night watchman of security technologies. I am always listening to network traffic.	____________
I am smarter than the static packet filter. I do pretty much the same thing but with some memory.	____________
I can use static MAC address tables to block MAC spoofing	____________
I set traps for hackers	____________
I look for computer viruses and worms, then I kill them.	____________
I give access based on destination and source IP addresses and port numbers.	____________
I deal with IP addresses and protocols coming through a router.	____________
I use various filters and rules to control access to networks.	____________

Who am I?

A bunch of security technologies, in full costume, are playing the party game "Who am I?" They'll give you a clue, and you try to guess who they are based on what they say. Assume they always tell the truth about themselves. Fill in the blanks to the right to identify the attendees.

Tonight's attendees:

Router Access Control List (ACL), Static Packet Filter, Stateful Packet Filter, Firewall, Switch, Honeypot, Intrusion Detection System (IDS), Antivirus Program

	Name
I am the night watchman of security technologies. I am always listening to network traffic.	IDS
I am smarter than the static packet filter. I do pretty much the same thing but with some memory.	Stateful Packet Filter
I can use static MAC address tables to block MAC spoofing	Switch
I set traps for hackers	Homeypot
I look for computer viruses and worms, then I kill them.	Antivirus Program
I give access based on destination and source IP addresses and port numbers.	Static Packet Filter
I deal with IP addresses and protocols coming through a router.	ACL
I use various filters and rules to control access to networks.	Firewall

Humans are the weakest link in your security chain

You've hardened your network, but you missed the most crucial element to security: the human beings that surround you. No matter how intense your security technology, if the human element breaks down, the attacker can hit you where you live.

Social engineering refers to the practice of using human interaction and trust to gain access to vital network resources.

I can talk your co-workers into anything. Your network doesn't stand a chance.
The social engineer can be charming and innocent on the surface, but underneath it's a different story.

So how do social engineers operate?

Let's take a look.

Gain trust.

The social engineer operates by, first of all, gaining the trust of people who have access. Like good con men, they work by appealing to basic human nature.

Hi, it's my first week, and the boss has asked me to look at a problem on the network. Can you help me?

2 **Gain access.**

Once the social engineer has gained trust, they use that trust to gain access. As an example, they might con or sweet talk an employee into giving them access to the wiring closet where the switch is located.

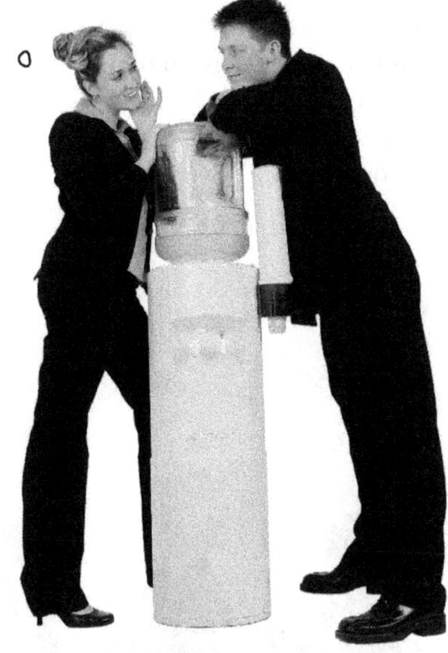

Oh no! I left my keys at home.
The boss will be so mad at me.
Can you let me in?

3 **Exploit what they want.**

Once the social engineer has gained access, they wreak havoc on the network, therby nullifying all the hard work you did securing the network.

Ha, I have full access
to the network.
Gullible or what...

Smash social engineering with a clear and concise security policy

The easiest way to defend against social engineering is to write a well-crafted security policy. A security policy describes how the company operates in regards to protecting access to its physical and logical assets. In other words, who can get into the wiring closets, who can login to routers and switches, and what rights must someone have to change things (read-only or admin).

An effective security policy is embraced by an organization; otherwise, it is just more useless policy.

The Chief Information Officer writes policy.
The Chief Executive Officer enforces the security policy by making it a priority of the company.
The Network Administrator enforces the security policy using firewalls, routers, and switches.
The Information Security Officer makes sure that the policy is effective by conducting audits and monitoring.
The System Administrator enforces the security policy on servers using passwords and file access permissions.
The Facility Manager controls access to physical assets, like server room and wiring closets, with door locks and other physical access control methods.
The Employees Make the security policy real by following it.

Sharpen your pencil

To get started on a security plan, start with controlling access to assets. Fill in the table below with who you think needs access to the assets listed, and how the assets should be secured.

Choose from these

- Network Admin
- Sys Admin
- Facility Manager
- Security Officer
- Public

- Network Admin
- Sys Admin
- Facility Manager
- Security Officer
- Employees

Asset	Needs Physical Security?	Needs to have network access to it controlled?	Who administers it?	Who can access it?
File Server	✓	✓	Sys Admin	Employees
Email Server				
Server Room				
Switch				
Router				
Wiring Closet				
Firewall				
Wireless Access Points				

Sharpen your pencil Solution

To get started on a security plan, start with controlling access to assets. Fill in the table below with who you think needs access to the assets listed, and how the assets should be secured.

Choose from these

- Network Admin
- Sys Admin
- Facility Manager
- Security Officer
- Public
- Network Admin
- Sys Admin
- Facility Manager
- Security Officer
- Employees

Asset	Needs Physical Security?	Needs to have network access to it controlled?	Who administers it?	Who can access it?
File Server	✓	✓	Sys Admin	Employees
Email Server	✓	✓	Sys Admin	Employees
Server Room	✓		Facility Manager	Network Admin, Sys Admin, Security Officer
Switch	✓		Network Admin	Network Admin
Router	✓		Network Admin	Network Admin
Wiring Closet	✓		Facility Manager	Network Admin
Firewall	✓		Network Admin	Network Admin, Security Officer
Wireless Access Points	✓		Network Admin	Employees

You've hardened your network

Congratulations! Through the course of this chapter, you've learned about various attacks that the bad guys can make on your network, and you've discovered a variety of techniques for keeping them out. You've seen how hardening your switches and routers prevents many attacks, and how your firewall guards your entire network against outside infiltration. Finally, you've seen how to deal with social engineering by implementing a good security policy.

Your network is in safe hands.

12 designing networks

You Gotta Have a Plan!

I love it when a plan comes together...

When it comes to networks, a good plan means everything.

You've learned an awful lot about networking since those early days in Chapter 1. You've learned how to implement physical cable networks, how wireless access points work, how to make the most of your intelligent network devices, and all sorts of troubleshooting techniques to get you out of the hairiest network dilemmas. It's now time for you to put everything you've learned into practice and see just how far you've traveled on your networking journey. We know you can do it!

Hey there! Are you ready for a new project? We need you to come up with a network design from scratch. Think you're up to the challenge?

Now you have to plan a network from scratch!

In an earlier chapter, you essentially reran some cables and put in some trays. But the challenge here is to plan all aspects of a network on a building that, at this point, is just a rough floor plan.

This is the best possible point to get going with your network design, when there is not even a blueprint yet, just an idea. You can make sure that the network you plan will meet the needs of the building's occupants and accomodate future growth.

The most important thing to do at this early stage is to talk to people. Talk to the future occupants, to the bosses, to the contractors, and to your IT people. Gather as much information as you can. Armed with all this information, you can make informed decisions about your network design.

A network design includes:

Physical layout of wire and network drops

Network hardware configuration

Logical network design

An implementation plan

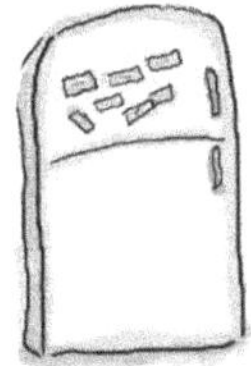

Action Plan Magnets

Let's hit the ground running and create an action plan. Drag each step for creating a network design into the correct slot. Pay attention to the order of the steps.

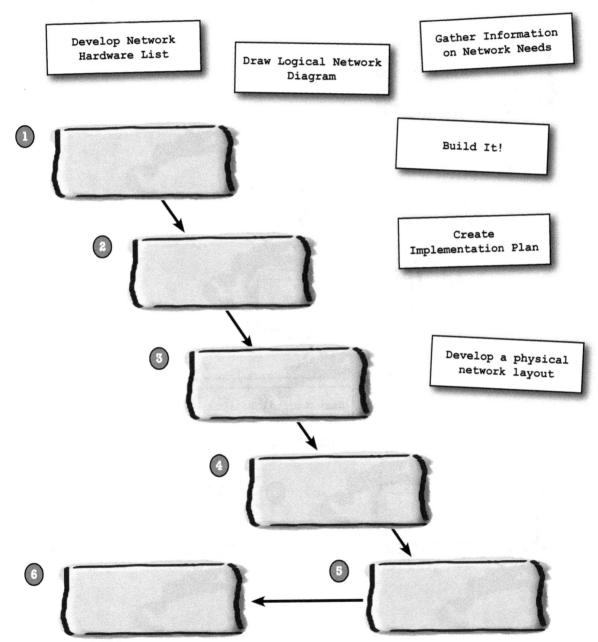

Develop Network Hardware List

Draw Logical Network Diagram

Gather Information on Network Needs

Build It!

Create Implementation Plan

Develop a physical network layout

1

2

3

4

5

6

Action Plan Magnets Solution

Let's hit the ground running and create an action plan. Drag each step for creating a network design into the correct slot. Pay attention to the order of the steps.

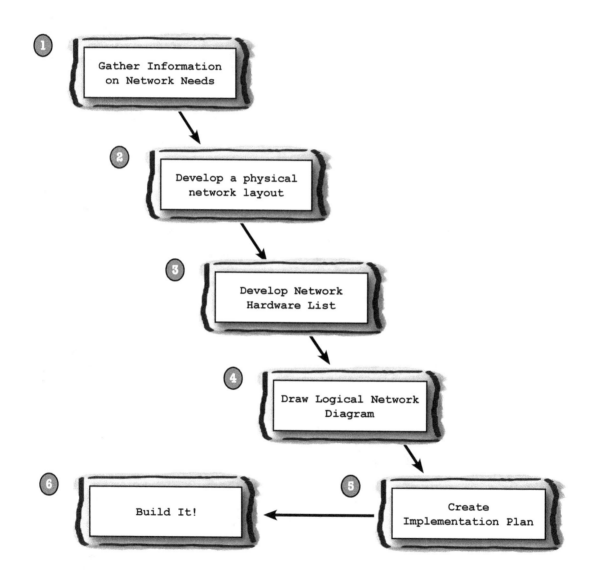

1. Gather Information on Network Needs
2. Develop a physical network layout
3. Develop Network Hardware List
4. Draw Logical Network Diagram
5. Create Implementation Plan
6. Build It!

You have to know what the needs are before you can plan

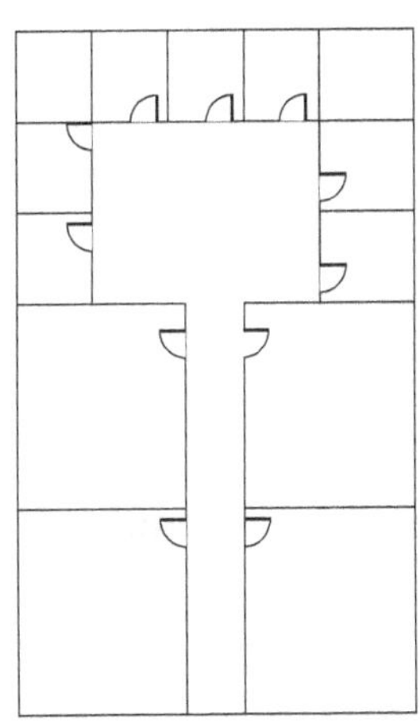

The first thing you need to do is gather requirements for your network. You have to be thinking in terms of network size, type, growth potential, equipment location, logical configuration, etc. This means that you have to be asking a lot of questions. Questions to the people in charge, questions to the users, and questions to the architects.

And remember to write it all down!

Exercise

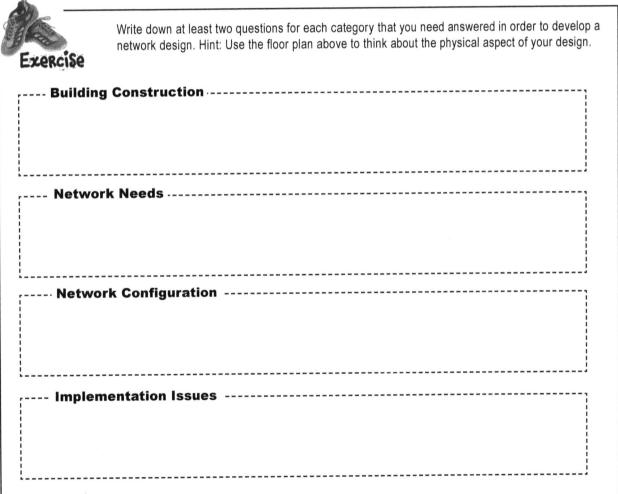

Write down at least two questions for each category that you need answered in order to develop a network design. Hint: Use the floor plan above to think about the physical aspect of your design.

Building Construction

Network Needs

Network Configuration

Implementation Issues

Write down at least two questions for each category that you need answered in order to develop a network design. Hint: Use the floor plan above to think about the physical aspect of your design.

Building Construction

Is there a basement?

Can wires run in the walls?

Where is the wiring closet to be located?

Can we use cable trays in the basement?

Network Needs

How many network nodes are needed in each room?

Do we need fiber or Cat-5e or Cat 6 cable?

Network Configuration

Does the building need just a switch or does it need a router too?

Do we need to put in a firewall?

How does it connect to the outside network or Internet?

Implementation Issues

When does the network need to be ready?

What is the budget?

Are we responsible for running the cables?

So you've developed your questions, now what?

You've got to ask them. First thing is to find out who all the stakeholders in the building are. This could include the people in charge, the users, the architects, and even the contractors. Talk to them all and ask them your questions.

And make sure you write it all down!

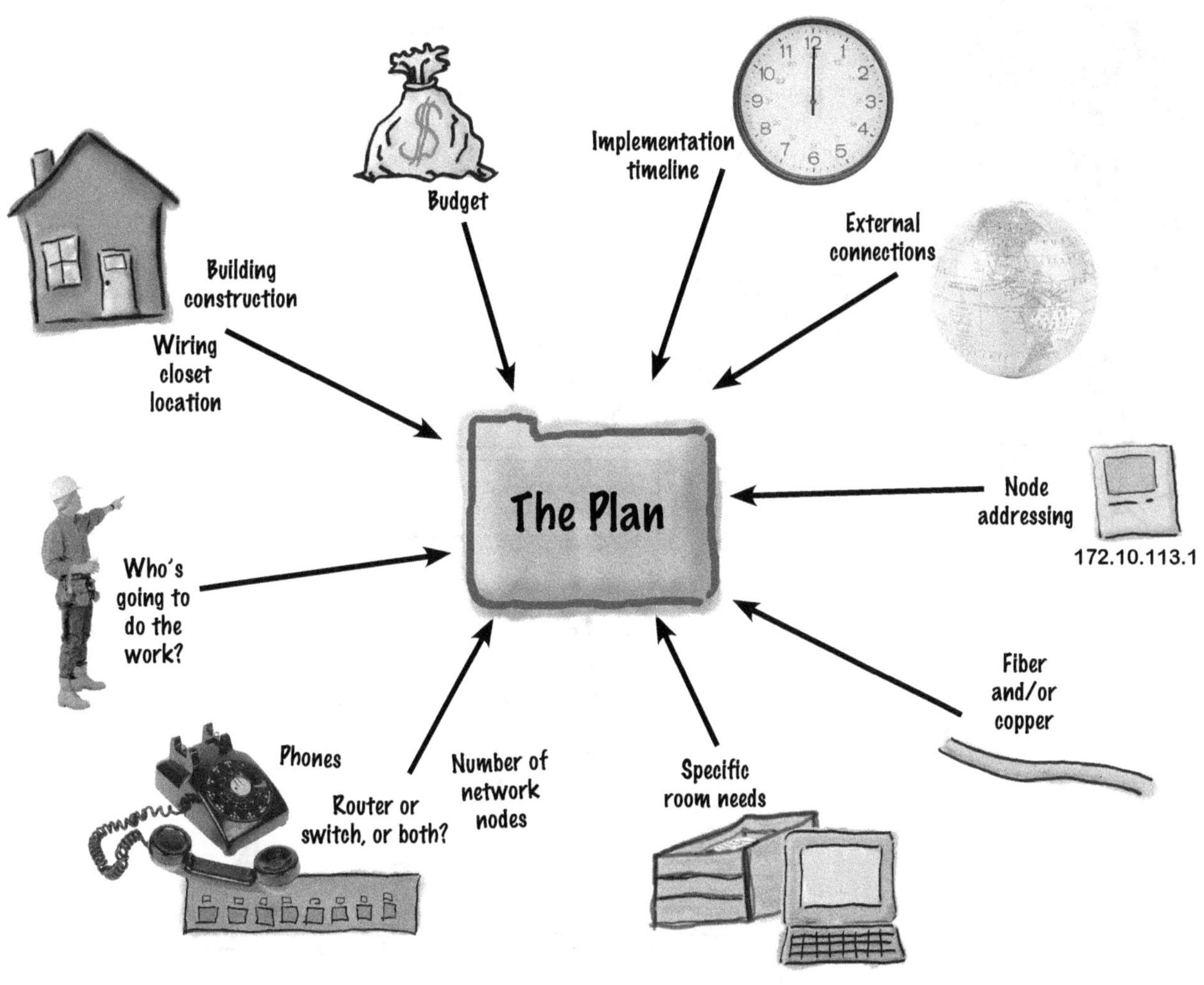

OK, I now have a great big file folder of information. So what's next?

Look at your action plan

The next step is to draw up a physical network plan. You can use a floor plan to get started. Your goal is to figure out where your cables are going to run and where your equipment is going to be located.

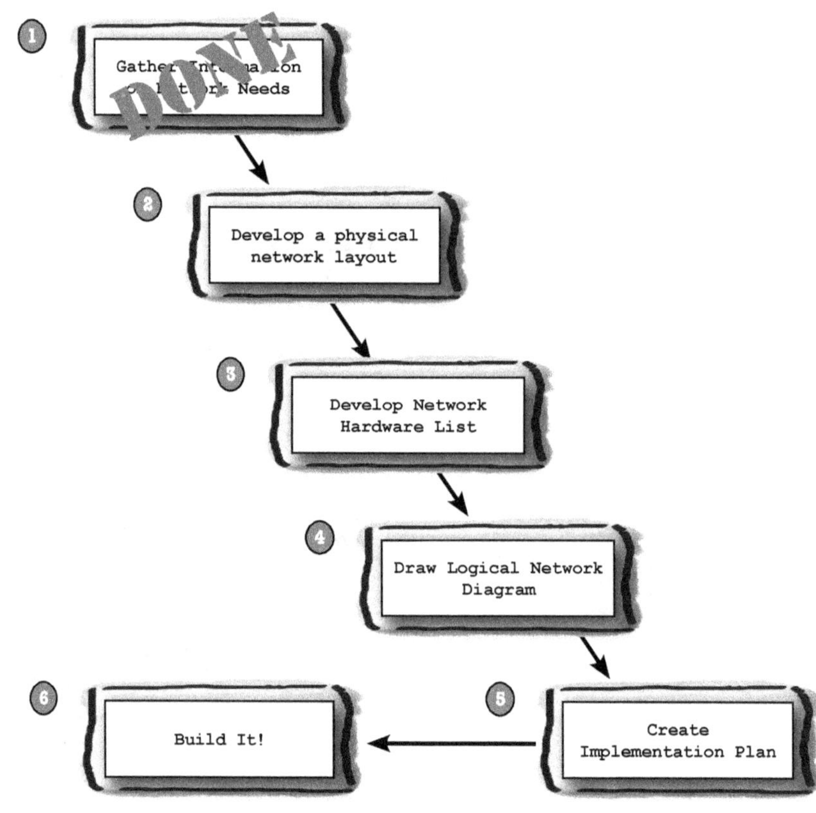

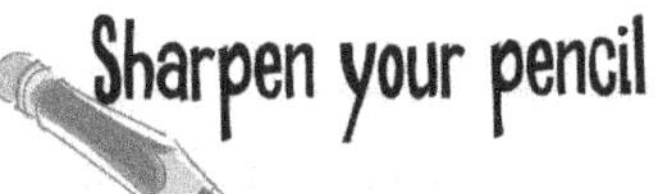

Use the network requirements to draw up a physical network diagram. Include network drops, switch location, and cable tray location.

Physical Network Needs & Information

Room 101 is the wiring closet; 110 is the mechanical room.
Rooms 102, 103, 113, 112, 111, & 109 have 1 computer and 1 phone each.
Room 108 will house a printer and a fax machine.
Room 107 will house a tech support area with 5 computers on the wall opposite the door.
Room 106, 105 & 104 will house 15 computers each. They will be in rows of 5 in the middle of the rooms.
Cat 5e will be used for all the connections.
The building just needs switches.
It will have a fiber network connection run from the main building under the wiring closet.
The building will have an 8′ crawlspace, so trays and wiring can go down there.
The CIO wants at least 3 network drops in each office.

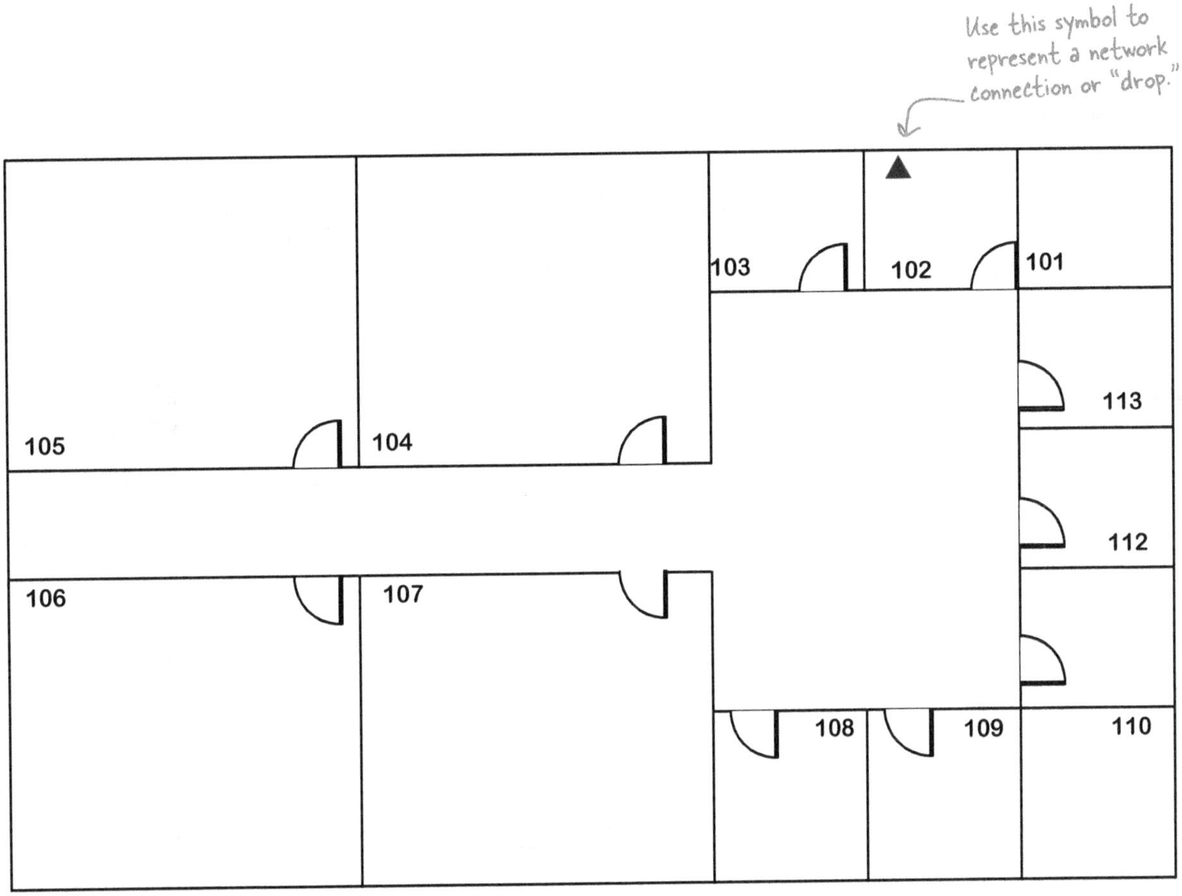

Use the network requirements to draw up a physical network diagram. Include network drops, switch location, and cable tray location.

Physical Network Needs & Information

Room 101 is the wiring closet; 110 is the mechanical room.
Rooms 102, 103, 113, 112, 111, & 109 have 1 computer and 1 phone each.
Room 108 will house a printer and a fax machine.
Room 107 will house a tech support area with 5 computers on the wall opposite the door.
Room 106, 105 & 104 will house 15 computers each. They will be in rows of 5 in the middle of the rooms.
Cat 5e will be used for all the connections.
The building just needs switches.
It will have a fiber network connection run from the main building under the wiring closet.
The building will have an 8′ crawlspace, so trays and wiring can go down there.
The CIO wants at least 3 network drops in each office.

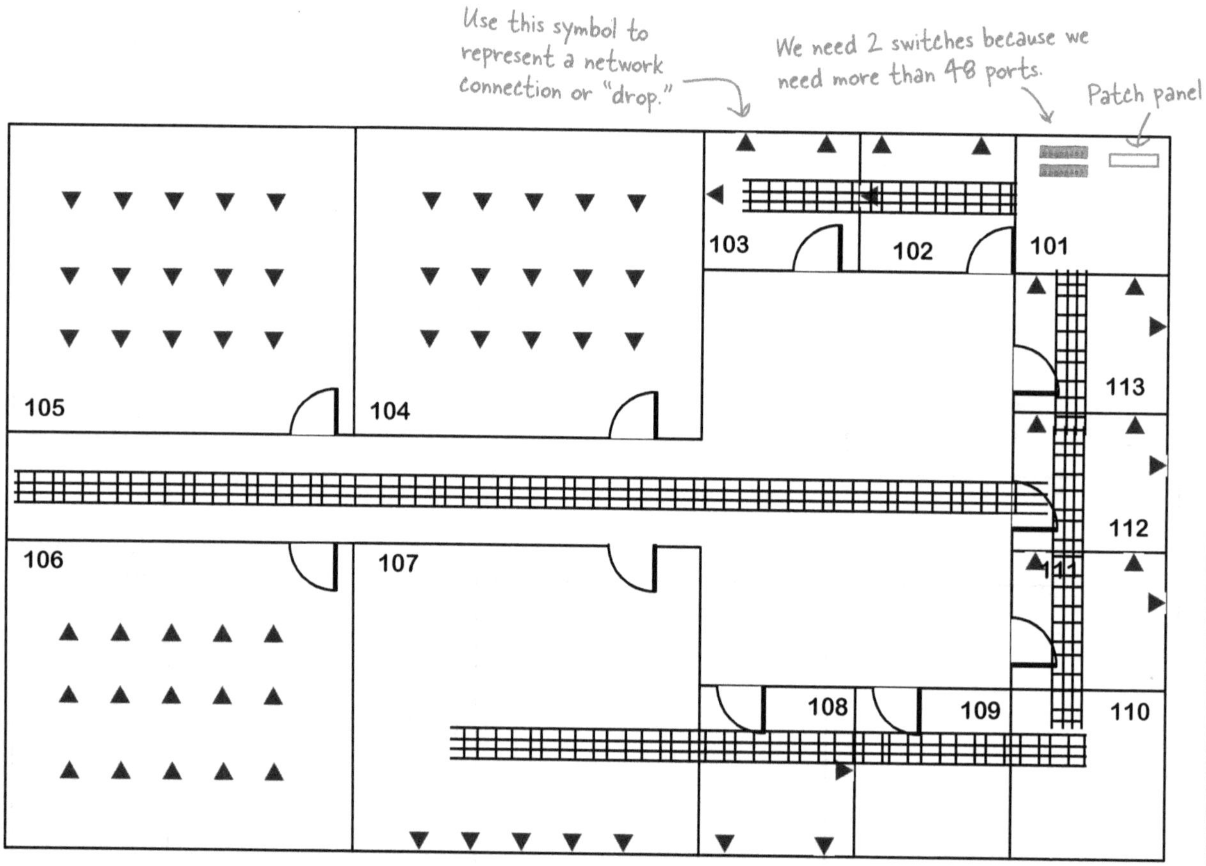

Use this symbol to represent a network connection or "drop."

We need 2 switches because we need more than 48 ports.

Patch panel

105 104 103 102 101 113 112 111 106 107 108 109 110

So you have a physical layout, what's next?

Well, our action plan is missing a step. There is something we need to do between 2 and 3. When you get your physical network diagram done, you need to compare it to the actual building to make sure everything will fit, but the building does not exist yet.

You need to review the building's blueprints!

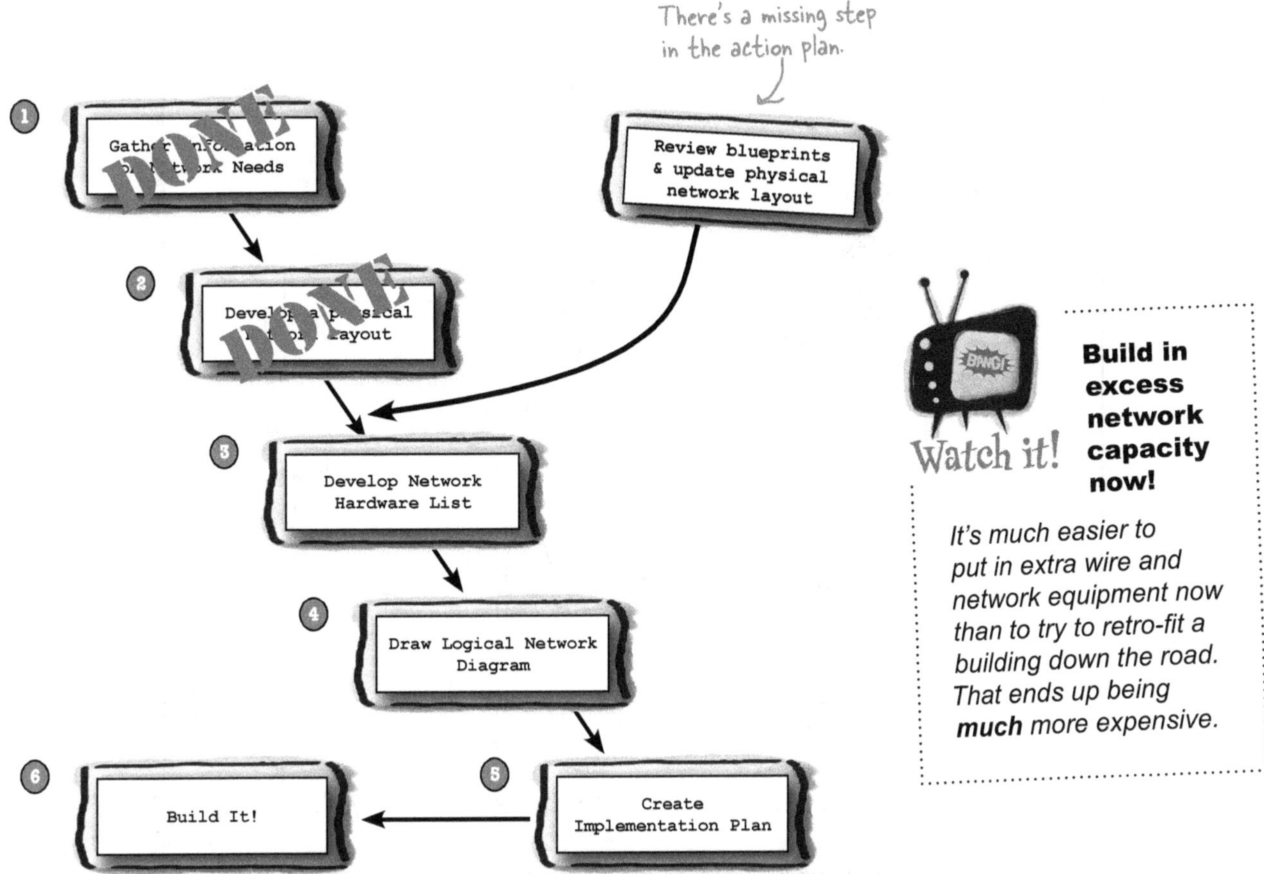
There's a missing step in the action plan.
1
DONE
Review blueprints & update physical network layout
2
DONE
3
Develop Network Hardware List
4
Draw Logical Network Diagram
5
Create Implementation Plan
6
Build It!
Watch it!
Build in excess network capacity now!
It's much easier to put in extra wire and network equipment now than to try to retro-fit a building down the road. That ends up being much more expensive.

Blueprints show everything in a building's design

A blueprint consists of many pages. They are generally broken down into sections corresponding to specific areas like framing, HVAC (heating, ventilation and air conditioning), plumbing, electrical, and surface covering, such as flooring. The electrical section is where network stuff usually is found.

You need to be familiar with all the pages to see how your design is impacted by the different parts of the building.

Be sure you read the notes for each section of the blueprint. Often these are located on the first page of the section.

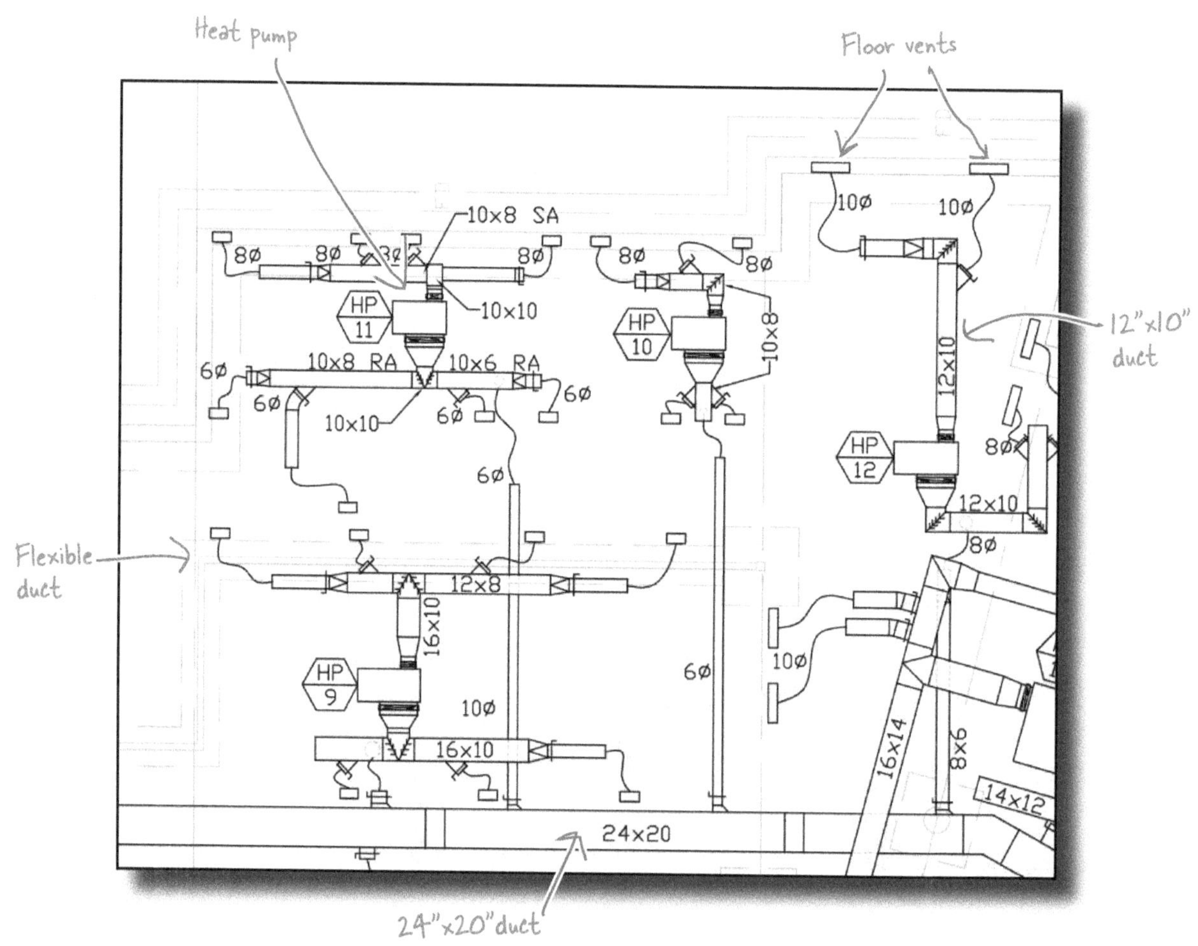

Most of this ductwork will hang via hangers from the floor joists, hanging down about 2'.

You may have to modify your network design based on what you see in the blueprints!

Many times, after reviewing blueprints, you will find that aspects of your network design conflict with parts of the building design. Frequently these involve the HVAC and plumbing components.

Watch it!

When the blueprint changes, your plan may change.

As construction of a building progresses, you will frequently find the blueprints have changed. You need to watch for these, and adjust your design accordingly.

Sharpen your pencil

Below are several areas that will be on a blueprint. Write down two things for each area that you need to check on the blueprint to assure that there are no conflicts with your plan.

Network Drops

Cables and Trays

Electrical Power & Lighting

Sharpen your pencil Solution

Below are several areas that will be on a blueprint and should match network your design. Write down two things for each area that need to be checked on the blueprint to assure they match your design to could cause your design issues.

Network Drops

The correct number of network drops
All the drops are in the correct location
The drops are accessible from below and not blocked by HVAC or plumbing

Cables and Trays

There is no HVAC ducting or equipment that is in the path of the cable trays and runs
There is no plumbing in the path of the cable trays or runs

Electrical Power & Lighting

There is adequate electrical power in the wiring closet
There is good lighting in the basement to facilitate cable tray installation and running the cable

there are no Dumb Questions

Q: So, if I work for a big company, there could be a lot of people that are going to use the new building. Do I talk to all of them?

A: No, but it is important to talk to a good cross section of people. The people at the top don't always know the nitty-gritty details of how stuff is working.

Q: But can't I rely on the architect and her engineers to design the network?

A: Sure, if you are willing to pay them lots of money. Often they have an idea of how things are, but only you and the people working with the network really know. The more time an architect and engineer spend interviewing people and gathering requirements, the more it costs you.

Q: You mentioned phones a couple of times. Do they use the same wire?

A: Yes, they do. Usually you terminate all the cables coming into wall boxes into a patch panel, regardless of whether a phone or computer gets connected to it. Then at the patch panel end, you connect it to either a phone system or a network switch.

Q: Aren't there phones that work on the network? Do I do anything different with those as far as cabling?

A: Yes, you are correct. These are called voice over IP phones, or VOIP. They use your regular network wiring. The only caveat is that certain phones require a voltage on the network cable to actually run. You can purchase special Ethernet switches that put power out over the network cable for these types of phones.

Q: You did not really mention how I should document my network plan. How should I do that?

A: Great question. When you are gathering requirements, you will collect information from all sorts of sources, including different types of documents such as speadsheets, memos, and emails.

When you are collecting the information, it is best to keep a folder on your computer as well as a paper folder with all your information. When you are ready to start documenting the plan, use a good word processor that can include graphics and tables so you can document all of your information nicely and professionally.

Q: What about network diagrams? How do I produce those?

A: There are a lot of graphics programs out there, including Microsoft Visio and OmniGroup OmniGraffle. These programs have the icons and tools to create professional diagrams. Whatever you do, do NOT try to use Word or some other word processing program to create diagrams. It will only end in disaster as your diagrams get more complex.

Q: What is the difference between a floorplan and a blueprint?

A: A floorplan is generally a rough idea of what a building should be. It is not used for anything except large scope planning, and maybe some space planning.

A blueprint is the actual guide for the various contractors on how to put the building together. As such, it has to be very detailed and specific. Often a blueprint will contain a floorplan as well.

Sharpen your pencil

Review the HVAC plans below and your physical network diagram to the left. Circle problems areas and write a list of problems that the HVAC system will cause your network design. Don't forget to think of solutions as well.

These are plans of the basement

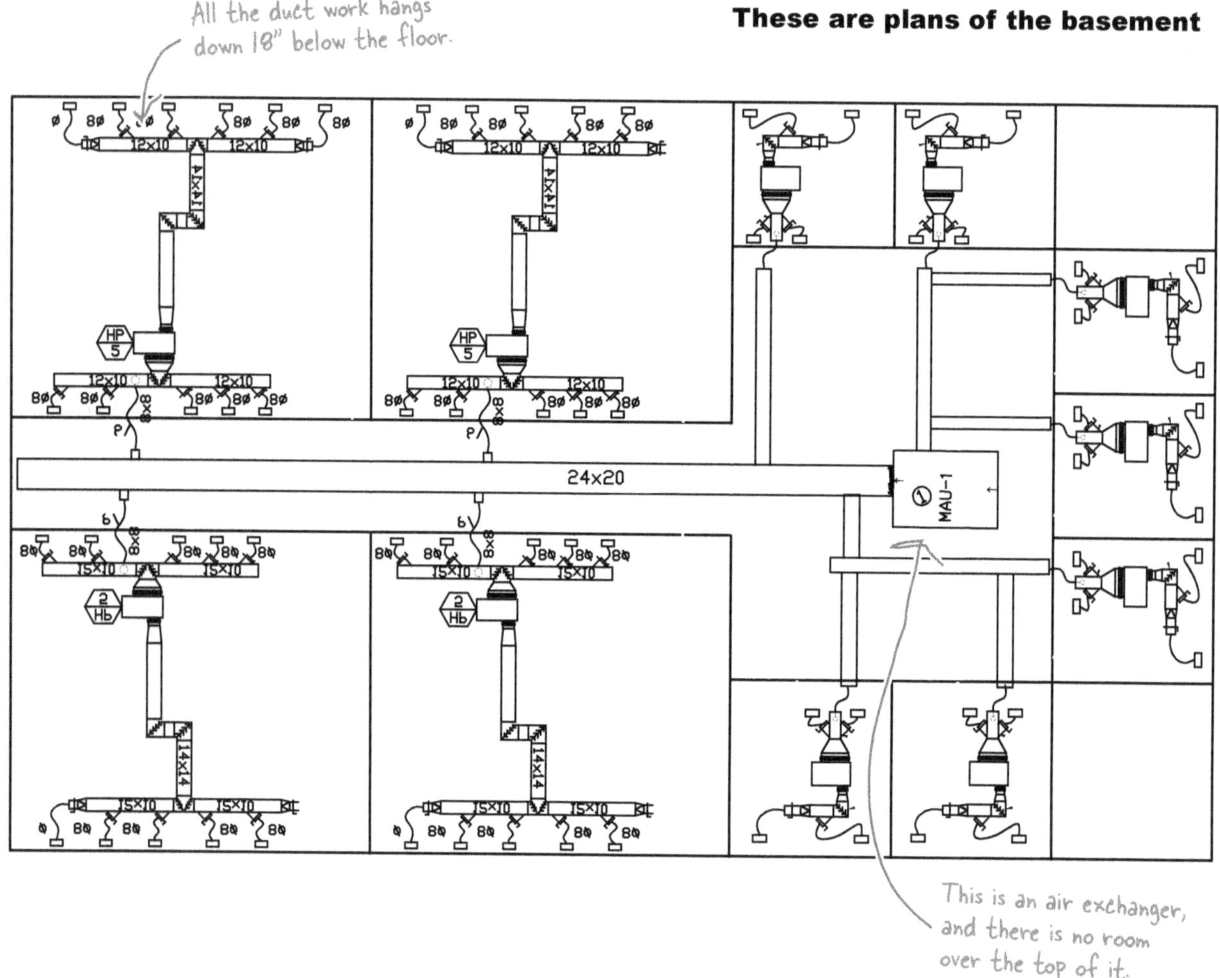

All the duct work hangs down 18" below the floor.
24x20
MAU-1
This is an air exchanger, and there is no room over the top of it.

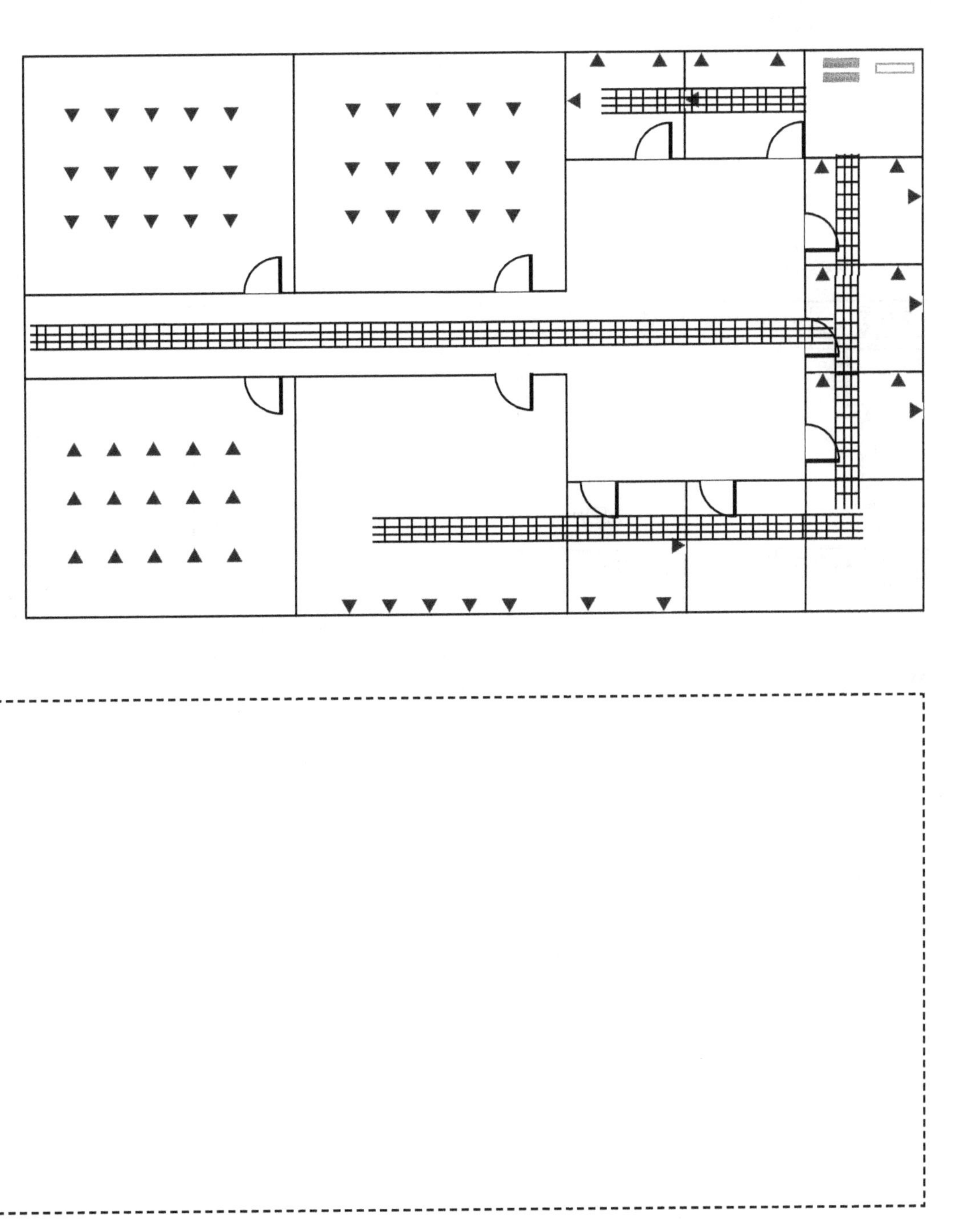

Sharpen your pencil Solution

Review the HVAC plans below and your physical network diagram to the left. Circle problems areas and write a list of problems that the HVAC system will cause your network design. Don't forget to think of solutions as well.

These are plans of the basement

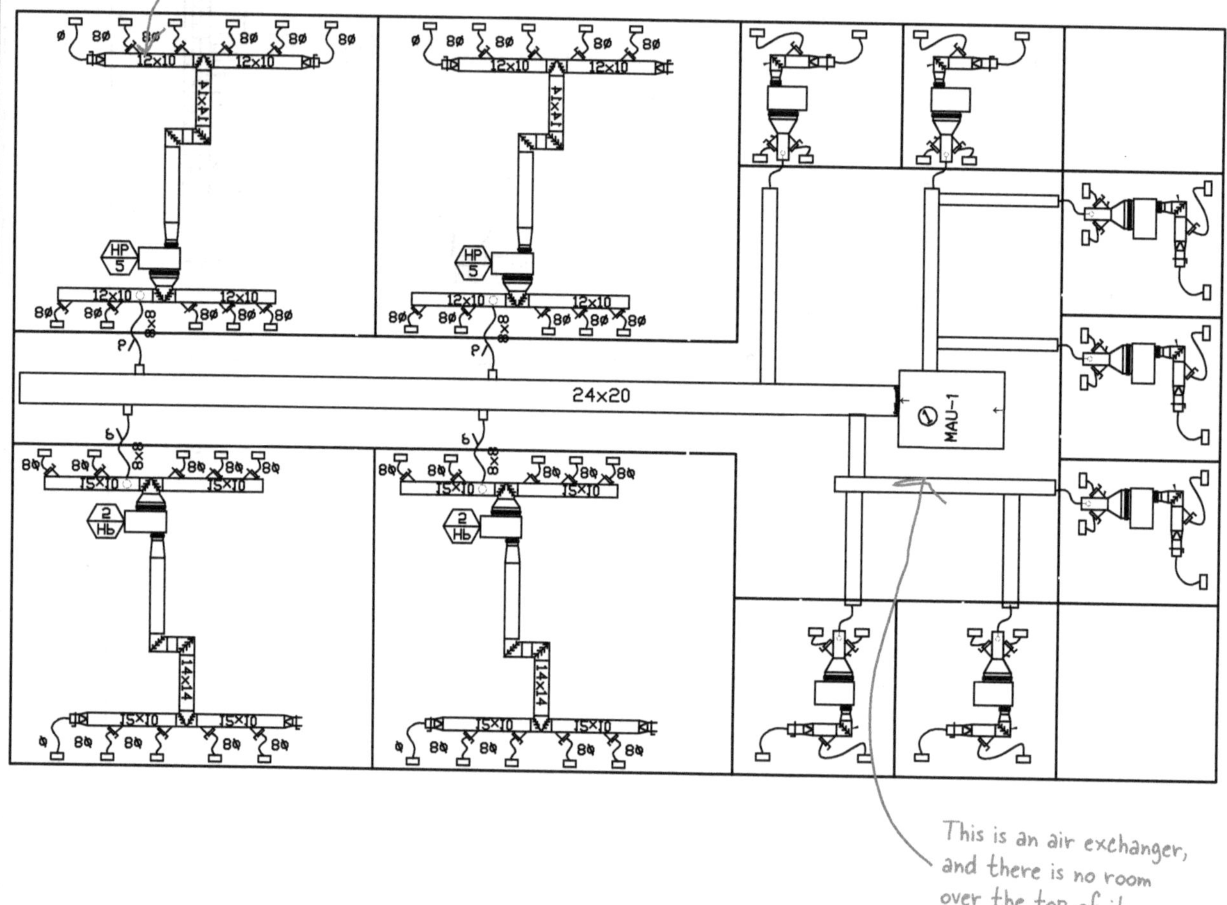

All the duct work hangs down 18" below the floor.
24x20
MAU-1
HP 5
2 HP
12x10
15x10
14x14
8x8
This is an air exchanger, and there is no room over the top of it.

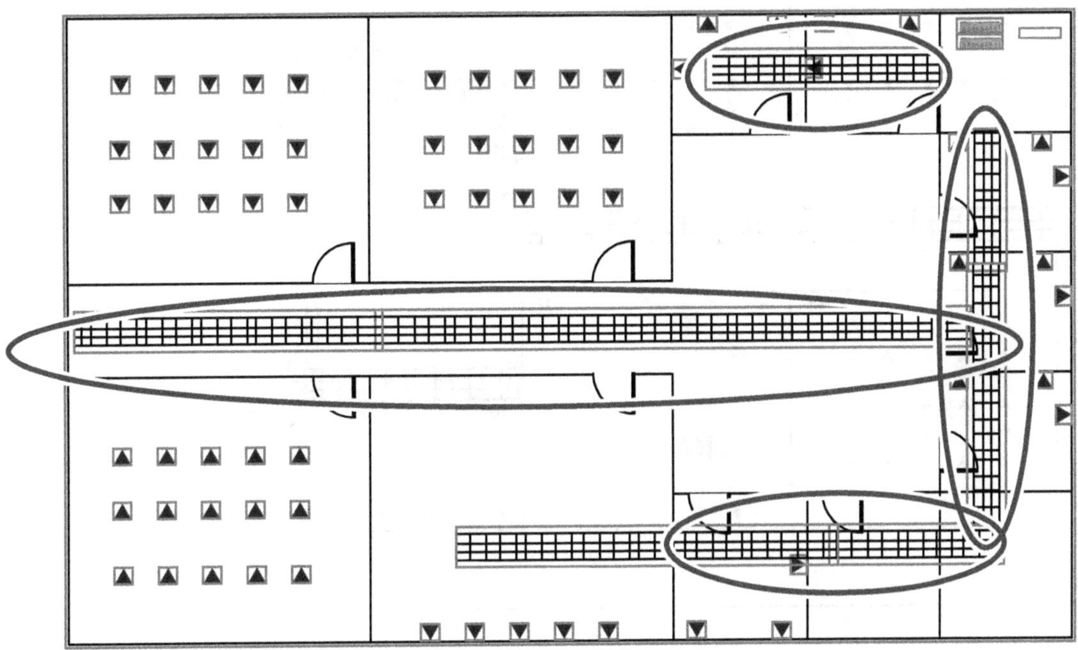

Problems:

All the cable trays appeared to be in the same area as HVAC ducting and equipment.
Some of the office network drops may be hard to access from below because of HVAC ducts.
The area under the central office area is filled up with an air exchanger, not leaving any room for cable trays.

Solutions:

The cable tray can be moved to one side or the other and hung down below the HVAC ducts.
The call centers on the top of the floor plan could be run straight into the wiring closet.
The flex tube from the wall boxes can be run out past the ductwork to ensure access.

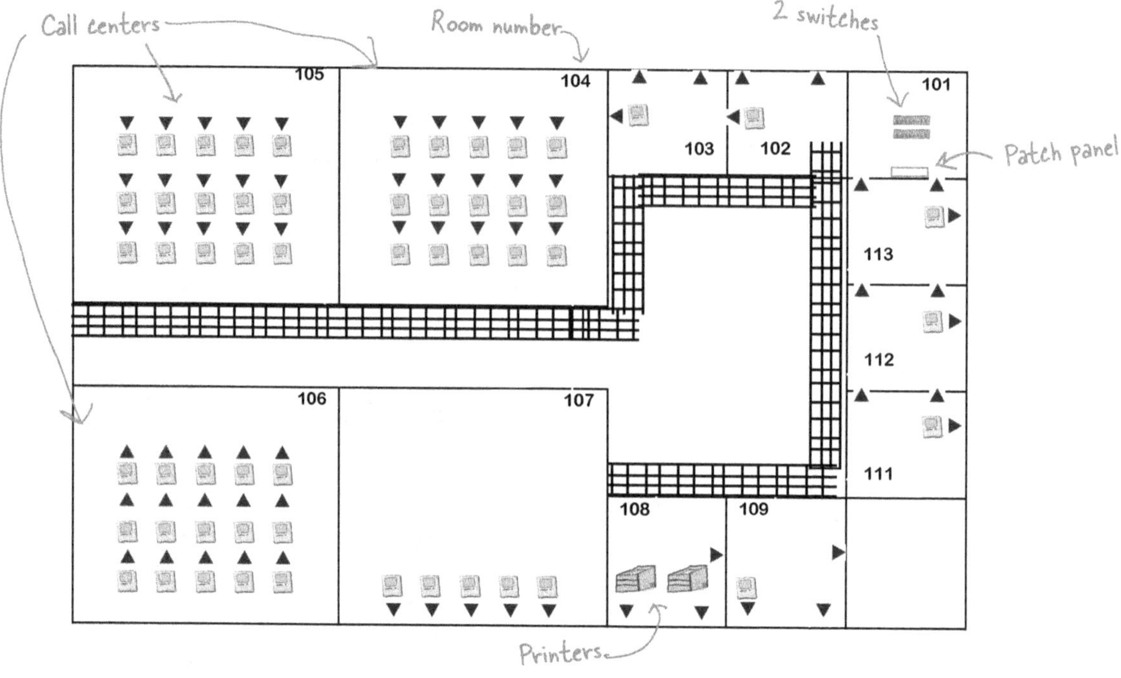

So you've got your physical network layout, what's next?

The next thing on the list is to develop an equipment list, but we think you can do that on your own. Just look at your physical layout and list the equipment you are going to need.

Let's move onto the next thing: a logical network diagram.

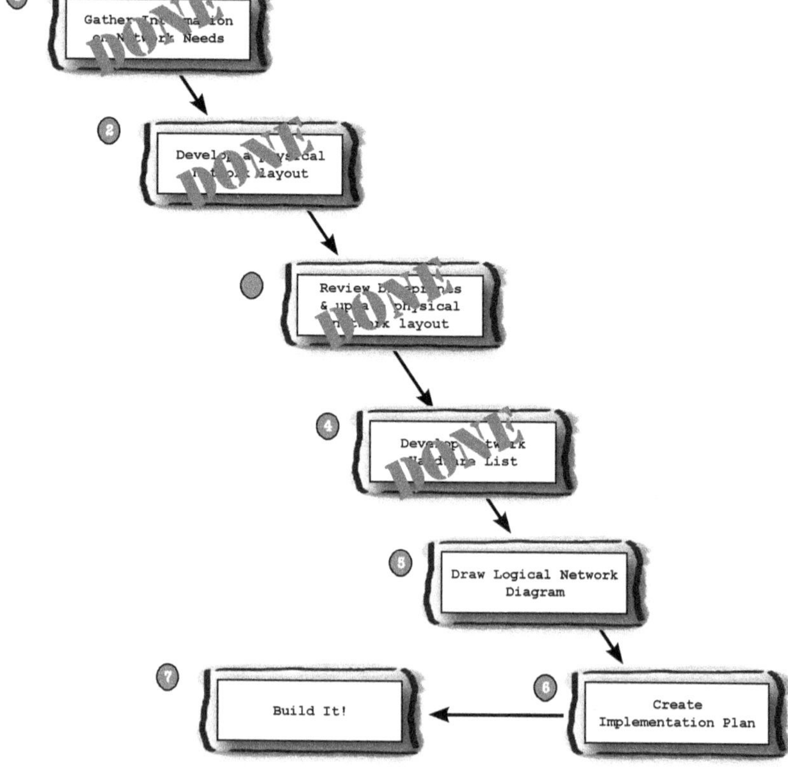

Using the physical network design on the left, complete the logical network design. Add network connections and IP addresses. The IP addresses use the office number and have the network address of 172.10. We've started the design for you.

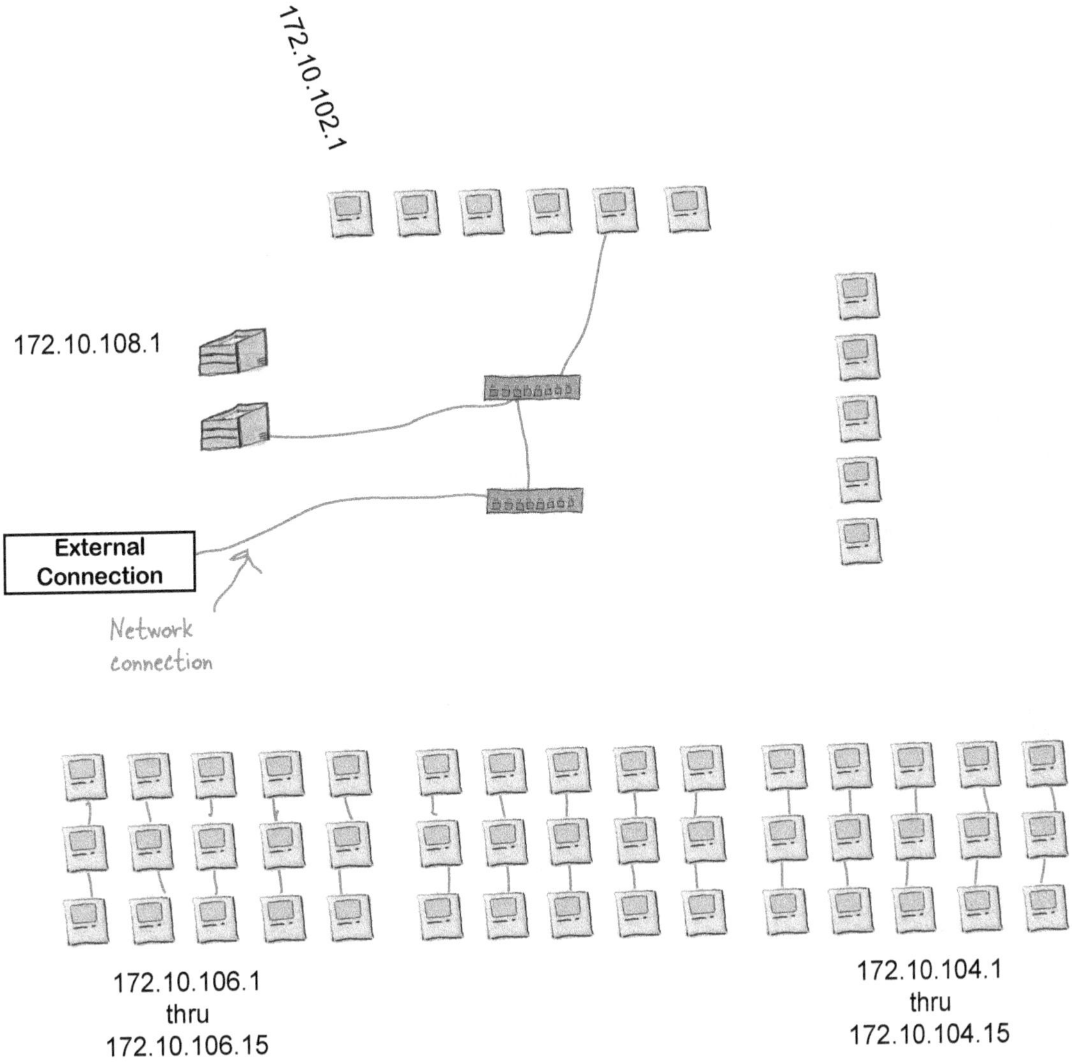

172.10.102.1

172.10.108.1

External Connection

Network connection

172.10.106.1
thru
172.10.106.15

172.10.104.1
thru
172.10.104.15

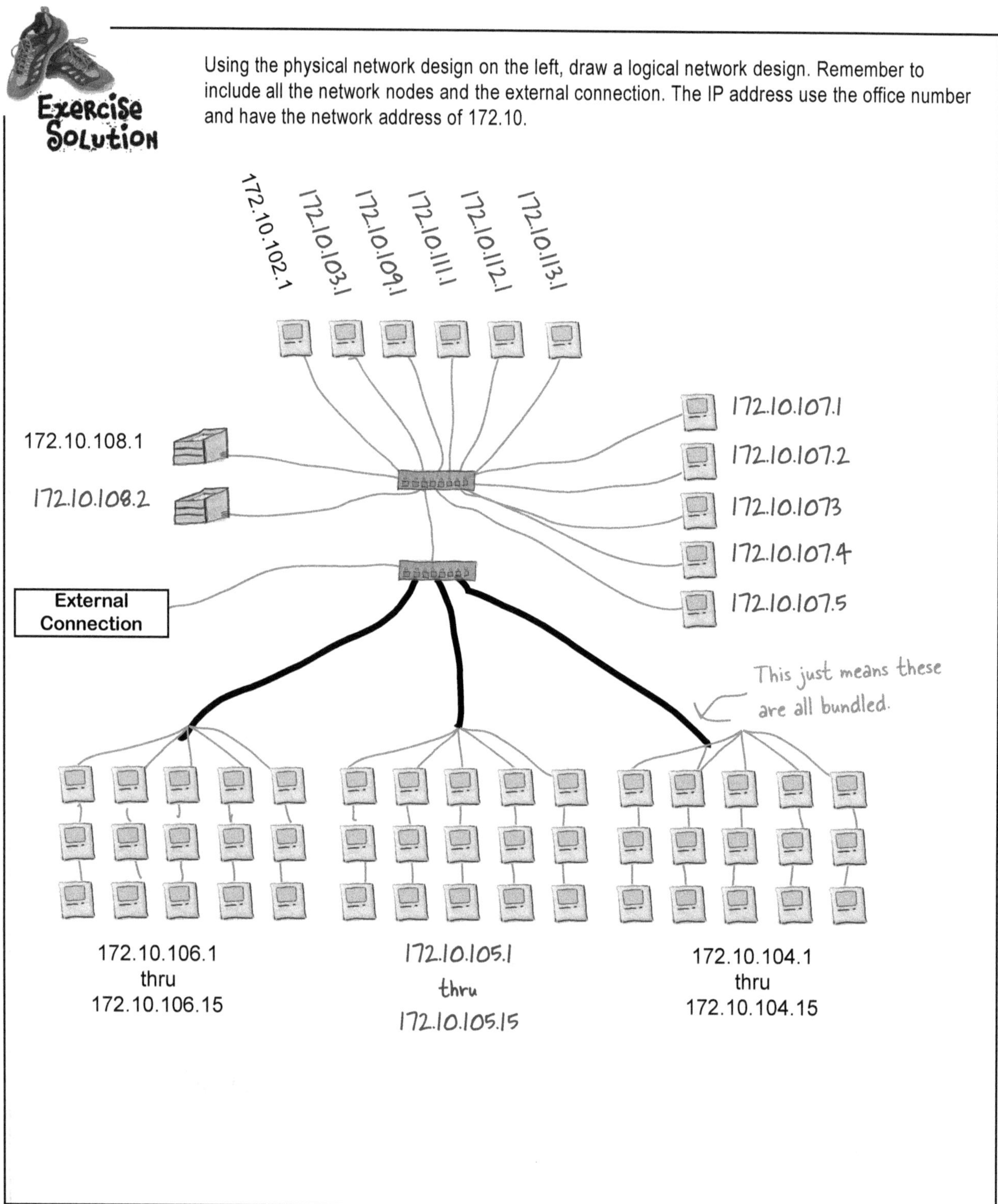
Exercise Solution
Using the physical network design on the left, draw a logical network design. Remember to include all the network nodes and the external connection. The IP address use the office number and have the network address of 172.10.
172.10.102.1
172.10.103.1
172.10.109.1
172.10.111.1
172.10.112.1
172.10.113.1
172.10.108.1
172.10.108.2
172.10.107.1
172.10.107.2
172.10.1073
172.10.107.4
172.10.107.5
External Connection
This just means these are all bundled.
172.10.106.1 thru 172.10.106.15
172.10.105.1 thru 172.10.105.15
172.10.104.1 thru 172.10.104.15

Hey, I've got a new requirement for you. Can you segment the network? You need to make sure that the call center computers can't see the admin computers.

You have got several options to segment this into two networks

1. You could put in a router, subnet the 172.10.0.0/16 network into two networks, and use access control lists to control the traffic.
2. You could put a firewall in to segment off the administrative computers.
3. You could get another external connection and disconnect the two switches from one another.

To decide between the choices, you have to look at cost of equipment, ongoing costs, ease of installation, and ease of maintenance.

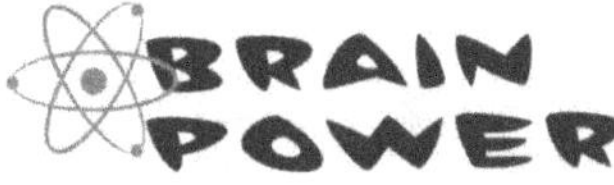

Why wouldn't putting the call center machines behind a firewall solve your problem?

Exercise

Redesign the network below and add a router in the appropriate place in the network. Make sure to change all the IP addresses to reflect that you have subnetted the 172.10.0.0/16 block. Also, use the third interface on the router to connect to the external connection. 172.5.1.2 will be used for that interface. Finally fill out the tables to the left with the appropriate information to complete the router configuration.

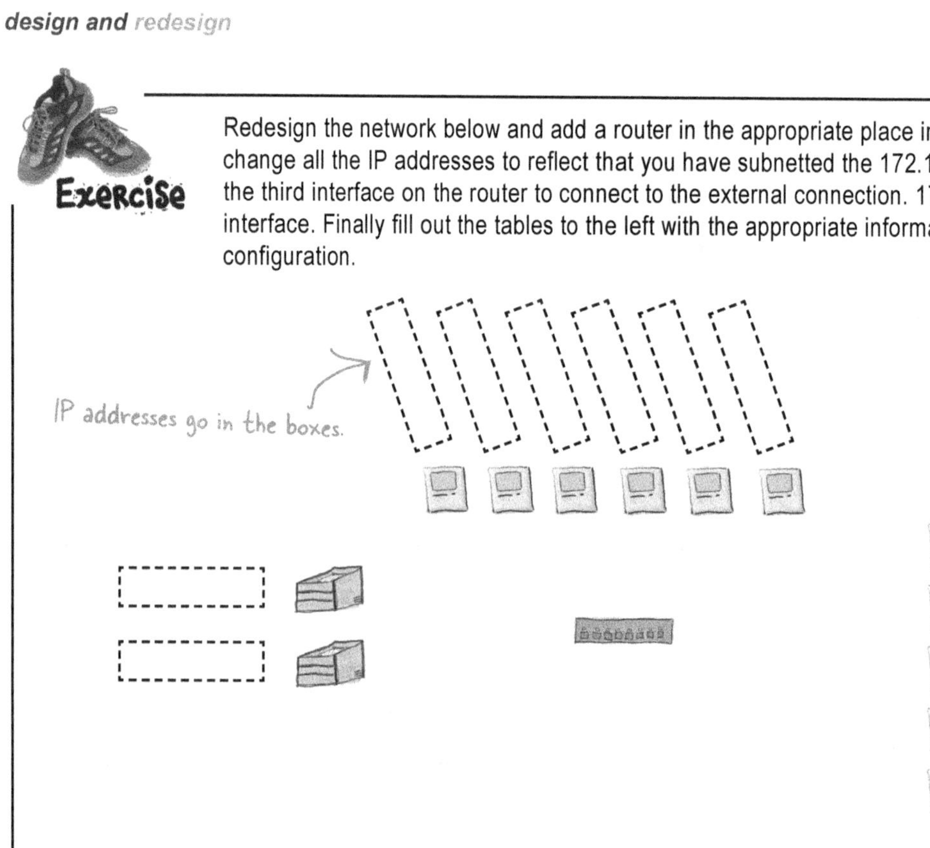

IP addresses go in the boxes.
External Connection

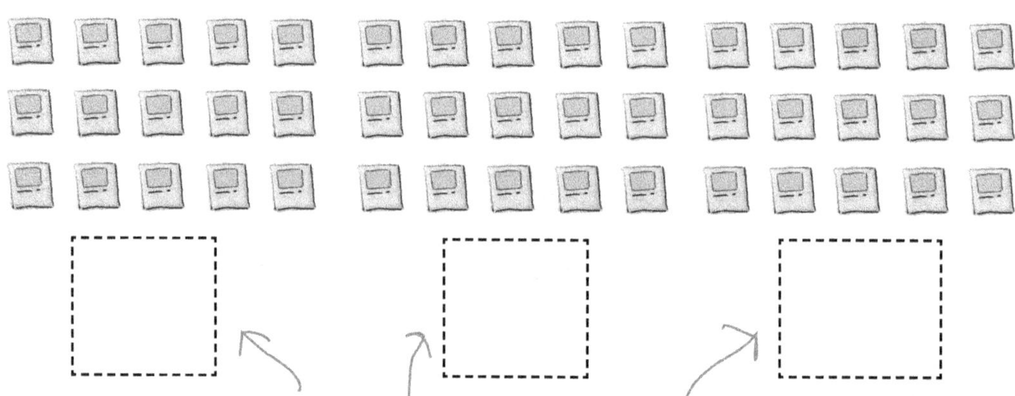

You'll have to use a network address that does not use the room number for these, since they will be subnetted.

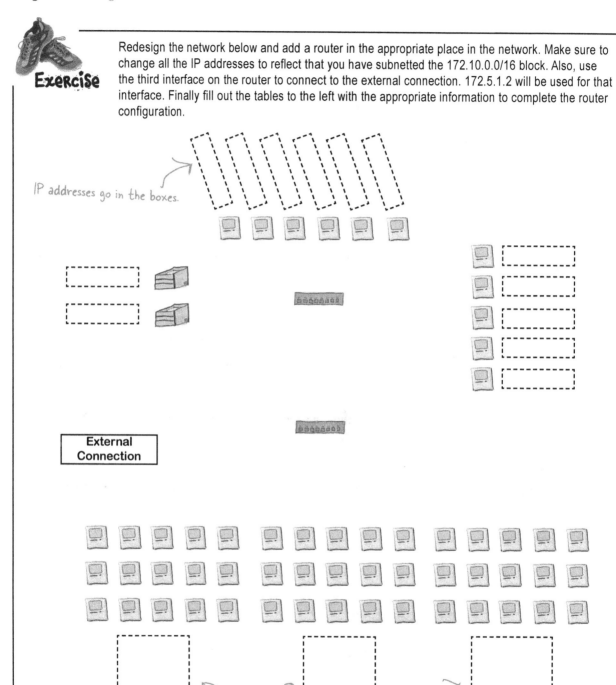

Router Configuration Tables

We covered subnetting in Chapter 6.

Search online for a subnet calculator to help you.

Subnets		
Network Address	Subnet Mask	Host Address Range

Router Interfaces				
Interface	IP Address	Subnet Mask	ACL List #	Area
FastEthernet0/0	172.5.1.2	255.255.0.0		External Connection
FastEthernet0/1				Admin
FastEthernet0/2				Call Centers

EIGRP Configuration	
Network	Interface
172.5.0.0	FastEthernet0/0

Access Control List			
Number	permit or deny	Network	Inverse Subnet Mask

Redesign the network below and add a router in the appropriate place in the network. Make sure to change all the IP addresses to reflect that you have subnetted the 172.10.0.0/16 block. Also, use the third interface on the router to connect to the external connection. 172.5.1.2 will be used for that interface. Finally fill out the tables to the left with the appropriate information to complete the router configuration.

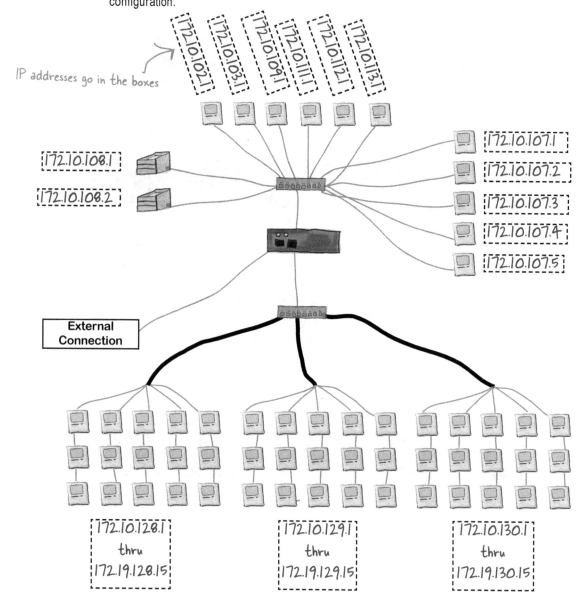

Configuration Tables

Subnets		
Network Address	Subnet Mask	Host Address Range
172.10.0.0	255.255.128.0	172.10.0.1 – 172.10.127.254
172.10.128.0	255.255.128.0	172.10.128.1 – 172.10.254.254

Router Interfaces				
Interface	IP Address	Subnet Mask	ACL List #	Area
FastEthernet0/0	172.5.1.2	255.255.0.0		External Connection
FastEthernet0/1	172.10.0.1	255.255.128.0	10	Admin
FastEthernet0/2	172.10.128.1	255.255.128.0		Call Centers

EIGRP Configuration	
Network	Interface
172.5.0.0	FastEthernet0/0
172.10.0.0	FastEthernet0/1
172.10.128.0	FastEthernet0/2

Access Control List			
Number	permit or deny	Network	Inverse Subnet Mask
10	deny	172.10.128.0	0.0.128.255

Finally, you need an implementation plan

Now that you've come up with a complete network diagram, you can move onto the final stage in designing a network. You need to create an implementation plan.

Your implementation plan is comprised of all the pieces needed to actually install your network.

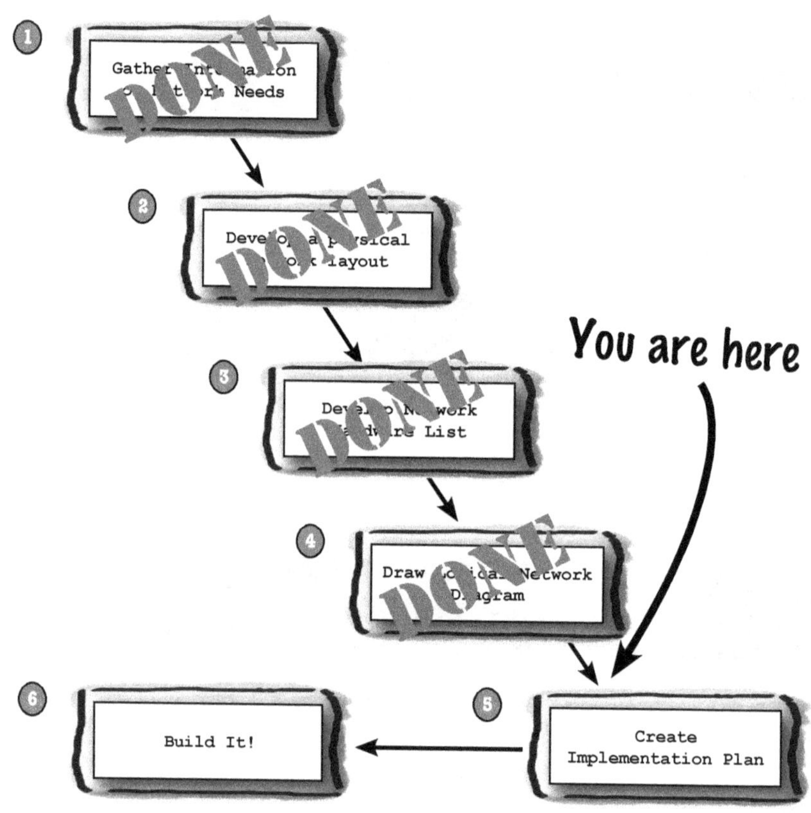

Sharpen your pencil

Write down at least four things that you will need to get this network installed. Think about people, equipment, time, etc.

Sharpen your pencil Solution

Write down at least four things that you will need to get this network installed. Think about people, equipment, time, etc.

1. People needed for installation
2. Installation timeline including deadline
3. Need to purchase the network equipment and other hardware
4. Installation process, who does what and order of installation

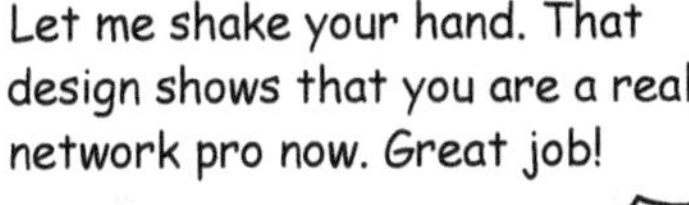

Let me shake your hand. That design shows that you are a real network pro now. Great job!

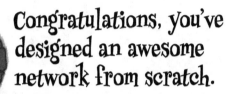

Congratulations, you've designed an awesome network from scratch.

You're there, at the end of the book. If you've stuck it out this far, then you are on your way to being a true network professional!

Leaving town...

It's been great having you here in Networkville!

We're sad to see you leave, but there's nothing like taking what you've learned and putting it to use. You're just beginning your networking journey, and we've put you in the driver's seat. We're dying to here how things go, so ***drop us a line*** at the Head First Labs website, **www.headfirstlabs.com**, and let us know how networking is paying off for **YOU**!

appendix i: leftovers

The Top Ten Things (we didn't cover)

Networking is such a huge subject, we couldn't hope to cover everything in just one book.

But before we turn you loose on the world, we want to add a few more things to your toolbox. Some of these things are in all the network books, so we thought we could squeeze them in here. Some of these things are higher level, and we want you to at least be familiar with the terminology and basic concepts. So before you put the book down, take a read through these tidbits.

#1 Network topologies

The topology of a network is the logical structure of the connections in a network. Here are three topologies you might encounter.

Star topology

When we talked about designing and wiring networks, we assumed that we were working with an Ethernet switch or hub in the middle. The topology or shape of this network is called a ***star***. A star is called that because all the network clients talk to the hub or switch in the middle.

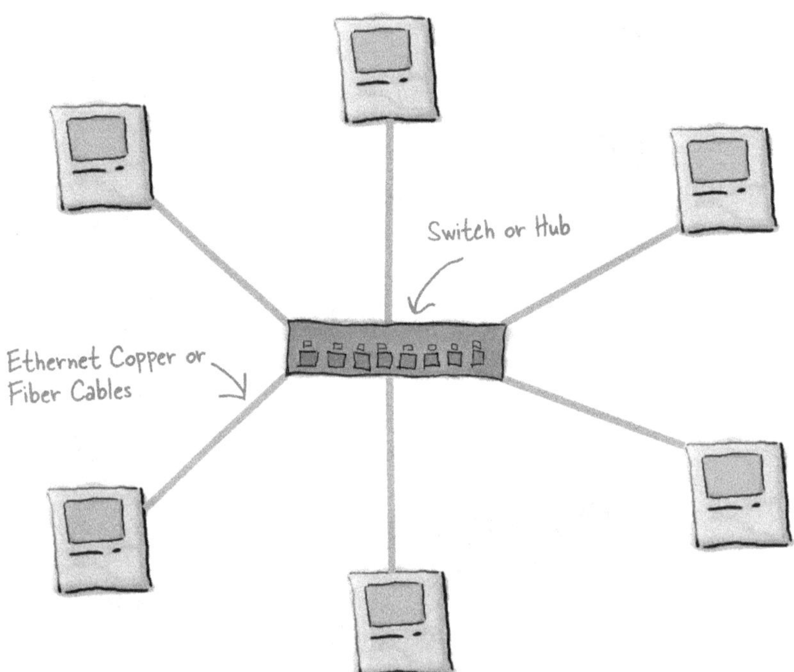

Bus topology

Another topology is the ***bus***. An Ethernet network using coax uses a bus topology. All the network nodes are connected to a shared cable, so there is no central device. Each node on the network deals with all the traffic.

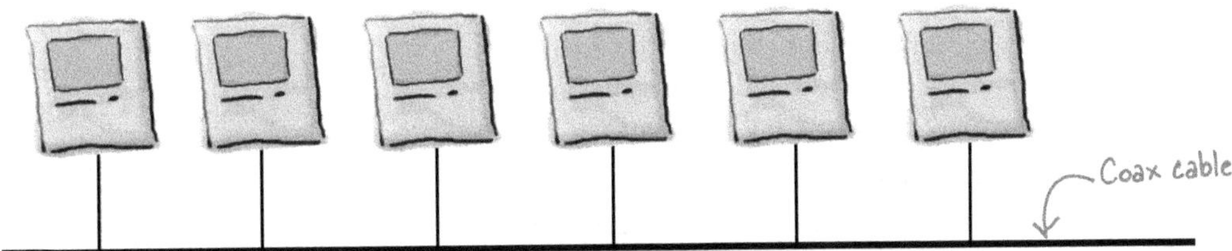

Token Ring topology

A third topology is the ***ring***. Token Ring is the most widely used ring technology. It was designed by IBM and is a proprietary technology, so it wasn't as widely adopted as Ethernet. Token Ring uses a "token" packet that is sent from client to client. The client holding the token is allowed to send network traffic.

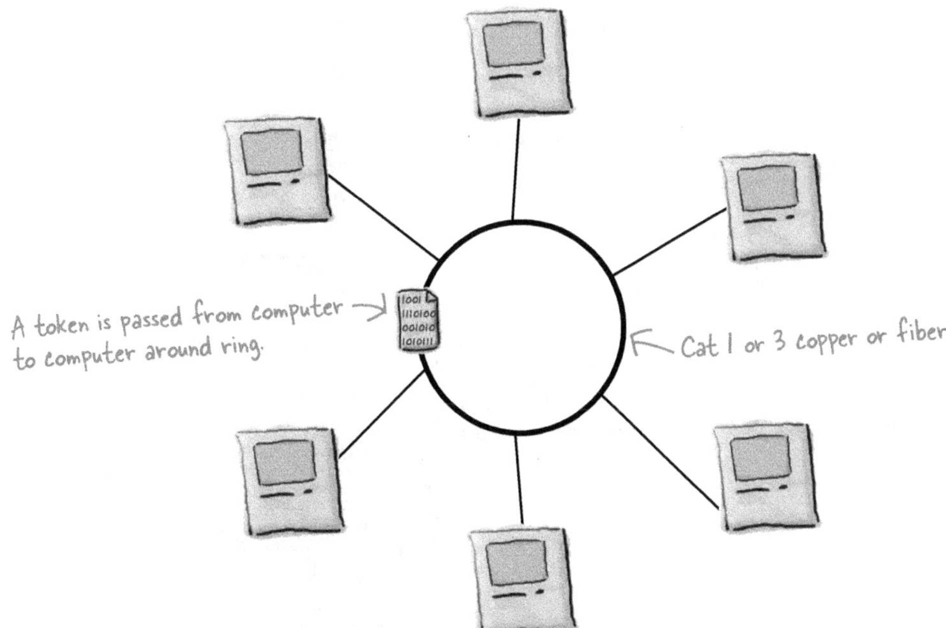

#2 Installing Wireshark

The first thing you need to do to get Wireshark running is download the appropriate package for your system. You can find these at `http://www.wireshark.org/download.html`

Windows Install

Installation on Windows is a typical installation. Start off by double-clicking on the Wireshark installer icon. The Windows installer starts, and you basically keep clicking on Next through the screens.

There are two screens to pay attention to. The first is the specific parts of Wireshark to be installed. You should leave the defaults checked unless you're confident you know what you're doing. The second screen to pay attention to is the WinPcap installation screen. This is a program used to capture network data, and you **must** install it. If you don't, Wireshark will not be able to capture traffic.

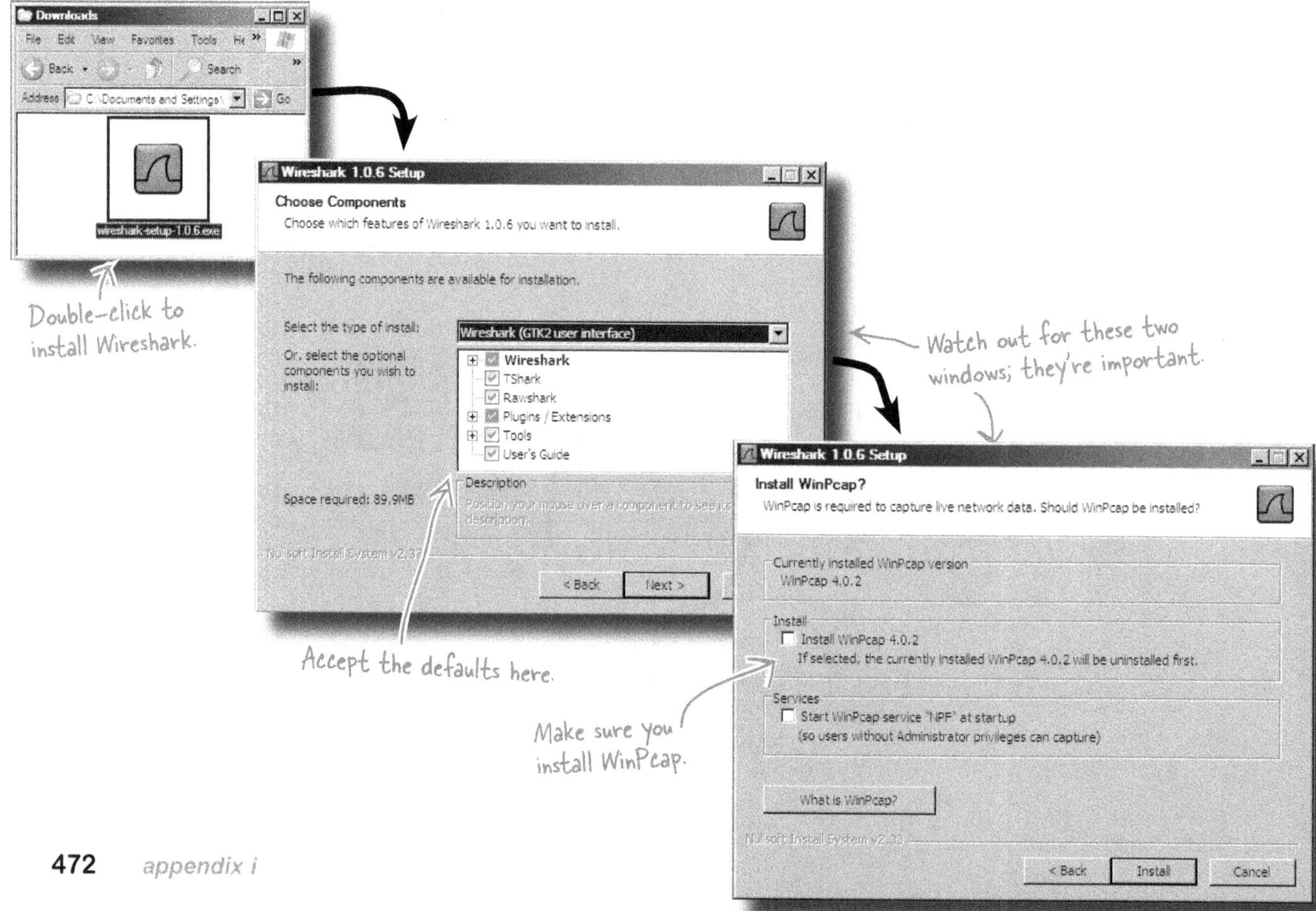

Mac OS X Install

Installation on Mac OS X is pretty straightforward. First you just drag the GUI portion of the application to your Applications folder. Second, you have to install a couple of command-line utilities. Finally, you need to change the permissions on some links that allow access to the network drivers.

A big caveat with the Mac OS X installation is that you need to have X11 installed. This is the GUI library that Wireshark uses. These can be found on the optional installs on your Mac OS X Installation DVD.

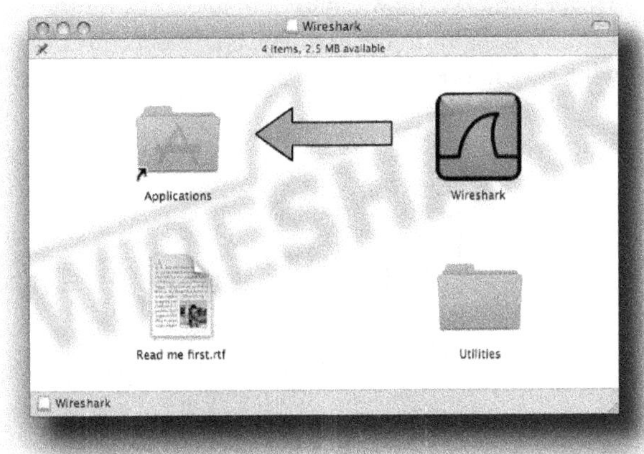

Linux Install (Ubuntu)

To install Wireshark on Linux, you have a few choices.

First, you can download the source code and compile it yourself. If you can do this, you don't need any more help from us.

The second choice is to download a pre-compiled package and install that. There are several listed on the Wireshark download webpage.

The third choice available for Ubuntu is to use the Add/Remove Software application located on the Applications menu. Do a search for Wireshark, making sure to select Show All available applications from the dropdown menu. You'll get a warning about community maintained software, but just click OK. It will ask you a few more things, but just click OK to those as well. You will have to enter your admin password.

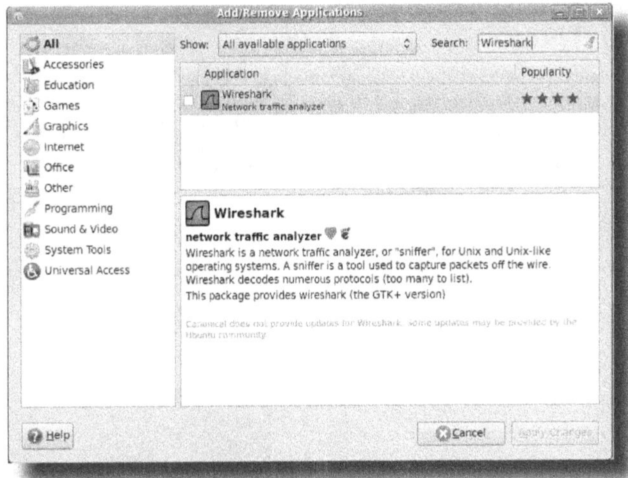

#3 How to get to the console or terminal

Windows

To get to the Windows command line, click on the Start button, and then select Run. In the text box, type **`cmd`**, and a command line window will open up.

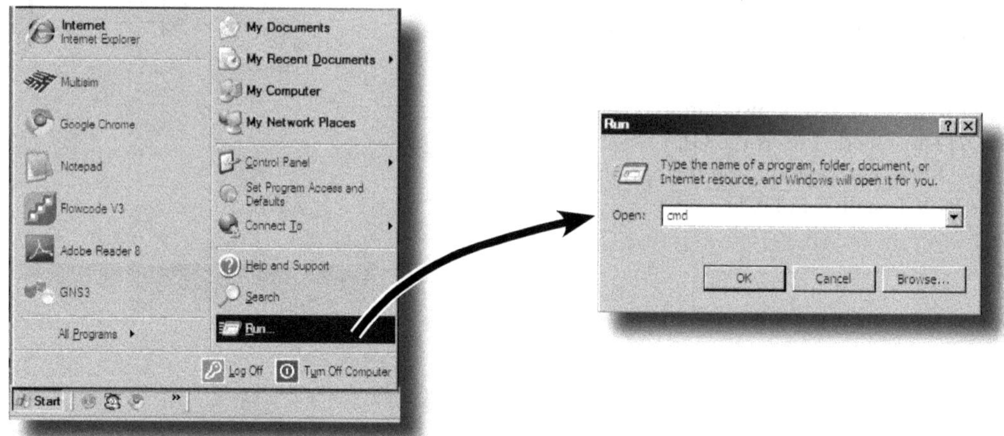

Linux

On Ubuntu, the Terminal application is accessed via the Accessories menu located under the Applications menu. On Fedora, it's located under the System Tools menu under the Application menu.

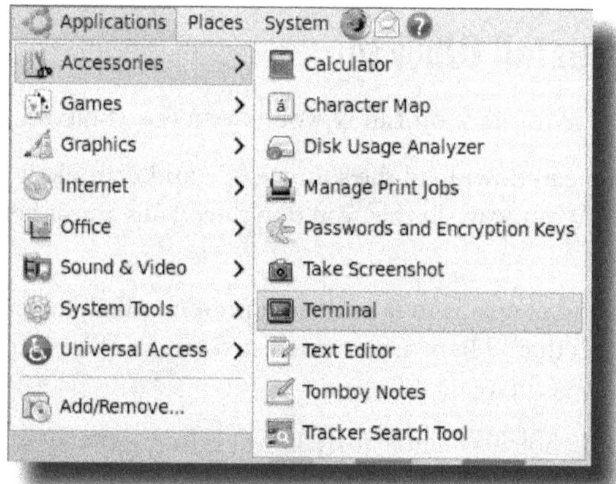

Mac OS X

Go to your Applications folder, and then go to Utilities. The Terminal application is within Utilities; just double-click on it to run it.

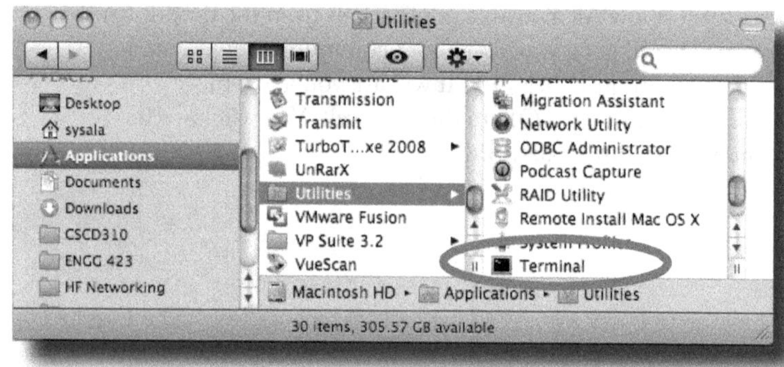

#4 The TCP Stack

You may have spent the whole book wondering "When are we going to get to the TCP stack?" Well, here it is.

The TCP/IP stack is the model of the protocols used in TCP/IP networking. It's called a stack because it's usually represented in a vertical stack of protocols. We covered several of these protocols, but we didn't put them in the context of the TCP/IP stack.

Many books start off by introducing the TCP/IP stack, but we chose to be different. The reason we did not present this is that there is no absolute model for TCP/IP, and we see this as a problem.

The model below is based on RFC 1122, but you'll see many models that are slightly different.

The application layer is where TCP/IP applications work. This includes ftp, smtp, telnet, etc.

The transport layer is where TCP works. This is to guarantee communications between two network nodes by providing error checking.

The Internet layer is the IP addressing layer. This is how nodes find each other.

This is the layer that connects the software to the hardware. This is often called the media-access layer.

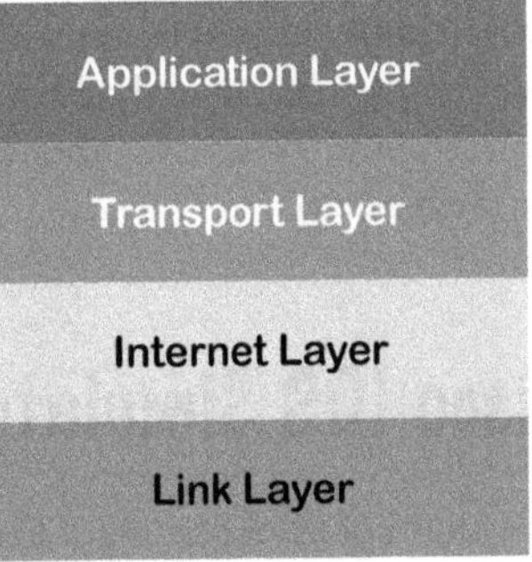

If you look back at Chapter 4, you will see how an Ethernet frame is built from all these parts. The Link layer corresponds to the frame parts; the Internet layer corresponds to the IP part of the frame; the TCP part of a packet corresponds to the TCP part of the frame. Not every TCP/IP packet type includes all the layers. Frames holding ICMP packets will only have the bottom two layers. This is just a way of viewing how the various parts of the TCP/IP protocol work together. It also gives guidelines to developers on how to write network applications and drivers that use TCP/IP.

For more information, take a look at
`http://tools.ietf.org/html/rfc1122`

#5 VLANS

Another hot topic that we didn't cover is VLANs. This stands for ***Virtual Local Area Networks***. It's a way for switches to form virtual networks. Specifically, the broadcast domain gets spread across multiple switches. This allows a network administrator to virtually separate hosts on the network as if they were on separate physical networks. A router is needed to move traffic between VLANs.

A network administrator would want to separate traffic for security and performance reasons. For security, you might want to keep certain servers from being accessed from certain parts of your network. As an example, a college might not want computers that students use to have access to administrative servers. A VLAN would allow those servers to be spread around campus, but wouldn't allow the student computers to see the traffic coming and going to those administrative servers. Splitting up the broadcast domains would reduce the amount of broadcast traffic on a given VLAN port.

VLANS are implemented by creating VLANs, and attaching ports to these VLANs. The packets created by hosts on VLANs are tagged by the switch that has VLANs setup. That way, other switches know which VLAN ports to send those packets out to.

#6 Cisco IOS Simulators

We know that not everyone has a Cisco or other brand of router sitting on their desk. You can obtain a cheaper used Cisco router for a few hundred dollars. This class of router would allow you to do most everything in this book and would allow you to work towards a Cisco Certification.

There are also software IOS simulators available, either for free or for purchase. Here is a list of a few of them:

Use these costs as a rough guide only.

Name	Cost	Caveats
Router Simulator	$29.95	
Network Simulator	$31.95	
MIMIC Virtual Lab CCNA	$99.00	
SemSim Router Simulator	$39.00	
Boson NetSim	starts at $199	
GNS3	Free	Need to purchase IOS images

#7 BGP

BGP stands for ***Border Gateway Protocol***. This is the routing protocol used by ISPs. It is unique in that it uses ASNs (Autonomous System Numbers) to route traffic instead of IP network addresses. The ASNs used by BGP are actually registered with one of the Internet registries such as arin.net.

Blocks of IP addresses are aggregated under an ASN. This aggregation of IP network addresses enables routers using BPG to hold the entire ASN route table of the Internet. In other words, if you get to the big leagues and manage a router using BGP, that router will have a route table of the *entire Internet*. Right now that table is about 200+ MBs.

BPG does not do automatic discovery of neighbors. You have to enter these neighbors yourself, and those neighbors have to setup your router as a neighbor as well. Also, encryption is generally used to exchange BGP routes. Entities that have multiple Internet connections and/or large blocks of IP network addresses are likely to be using BGP.

#8 VPN

Say you want to work from home on some sensitive company information. Wouldn't it be great if you could just hook up to your companies network to do that work? Well, VPNs allow you to do that. VPN stands for ***Virtual Private Network***. It has two parts, a special network configuration on the client computer and a VPN gateway on the network that you wish to connect into. A VPN allows a remotely located client to gain secure access to an internal network. The communication between a VPN client and gateway is encrypted to protect the communications.

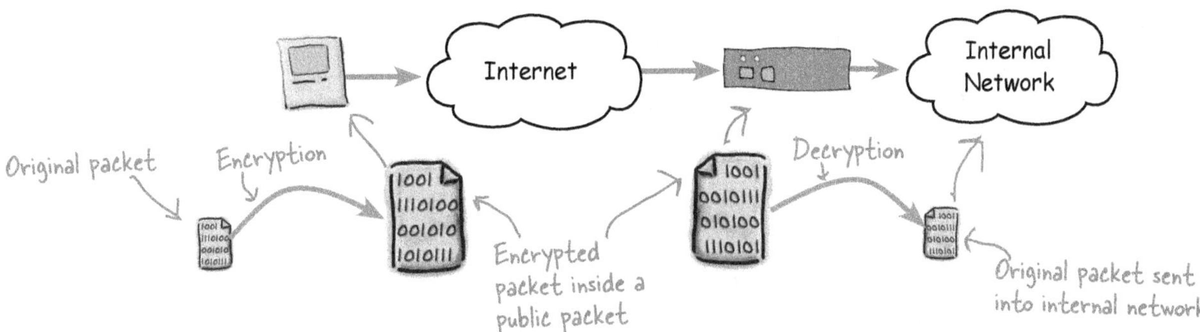

VPN works by encrypting the packets destined for the internal network. It then puts those encrypted packets into the data section of a regular TCP packet, sends that packet across the public network, and then the VPN gateway removes the encrypted packet, decodes it and sends it into the internal network.

There are also VPN Gateway to VPN Gateway connections which allow a small office to have internal network access to a parent company's network using a VPN gateway.

#9 Intrusion Detection Systems

With all the problems of people trying to get into your systems, wouldn't it be nice to be able to detect this type and activity and have it reported to you or, even better, take some kind of action?

Well, IDSs (Intrusion Detection Systems) do just this. These are generally special purpose servers that have the proper software to listen on your network for anomalous traffic. This could include scanning behavior, incorrect data on registered ports, or even denial-of-service attacks.

Although many firewalls incorporate IDS functions as well.

A popular open source package is ***snort***. Snort is similar to wireshark in that it can sniff network traffic. The difference is that it filters this traffic using various rules to look for this anomalous traffic using different patterns. There are many rules developed by network administrator in order to capture this bad traffic.

Some IDSs also allow actions to take place based on this kind of traffic. This action usually consists of implementing access lists on a router or firewall which block ports and/or IP addresses of the hosts creating the anomalous network traffic.

IDSs are great to have, but like anything, you can't just set it up and let it run. You have to actively manage and monitor it for it to be at its most effective on your network.

#10 Cisco Certification

The last big thing we didn't cover was network certifications. The biggest in terms of people with these certifications are the Cisco certifications. There are two main ones, CCNA and CCNP, with CCNA being the entry level network certification. Both of these certifications are obtained by taking one or more tests. In the case of the CCNP, there are three or four tests to take (two of the tests can be taken as a combined test).

The CCNA requires that you know a little more information than this book provides. The CCNP requires the same type of knowledge but in much greater depth. It also requires a lot more knowledge of switched networking and wide area networking using various telco technologies such as ISDN and T-1 lines.

There are other vendor specific certifications, but these two are the heavy hitters in the network cert world.

appendix ii: ascii tables

Looking Things Up

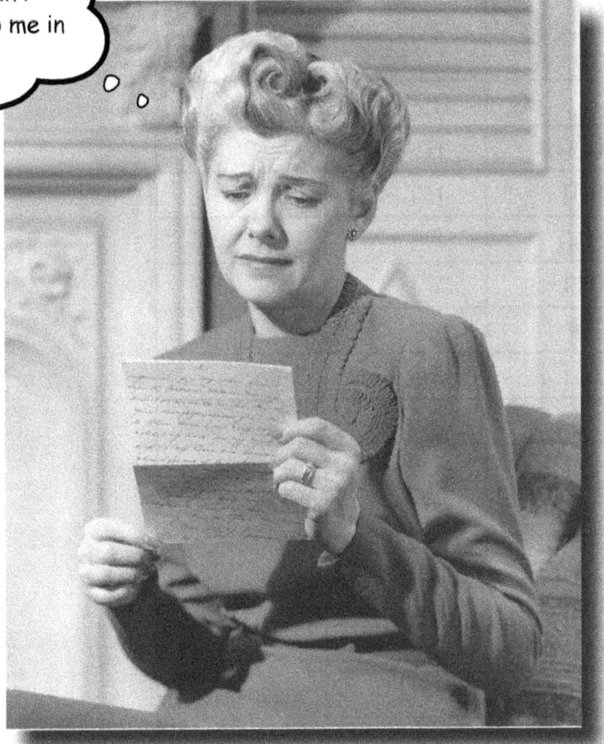

I wish he wouldn't keep writing to me in binary...

Where would you be without some trusty ASCII tables?

Understanding network protocols isn't always enough. Sooner or later, you're going to need to look up ASCII codes so you can understand what secrets are being passed around your network. In this appendix, you'll find a whole bunch of ASCII codes. Whether you prefer binary, hexadecimal, or good old decimal, we've got just the codes you need.

ASCII tables 0-28

In decimal, that is.

Just look up your decimal, hex or binary code here...

...and read off the character here.

0	0	0	NUL	
1	1	1	SOH	
2	2	10	STX	
3	3	11	ETX	
4	4	100	EOT	
5	5	101	ENQ	
6	6	110	ACK	
7	7	111	BEL	
8	8	1000	BS	
9	9	1001	HT	
10	0A	1010	LF	
11	0B	1011	VT	
12	0C	1100	FF	
13	0D	1101	CR	
14	0E	1110	SO	
15	0F	1111	SI	
16	10	10000	DLE	
17	11	10001	DC1	
18	12	10010	DC2	
19	13	10011	DC3	
20	14	10100	DC4	
21	15	10101	NAK	
22	16	10110	SYN	
23	17	10111	ETB	
24	18	11000	CAN	
25	19	11001	EM	
26	1A	11010	SUB	
27	1B	11011	ESC	
28	1C	11100	FS	

ASCII code tables 29-57

29	1D	11101	GS	
30	1E	11110	RS	
31	1F	11111	US	
32	20	100000	Space	
33	21	100001	!	
34	22	100010	“	
35	23	100011	#	
36	24	100100	$	
37	25	100101	%	
38	26	100110	&	
39	27	100111	‘	
40	28	101000	(	
41	29	101001	)	
42	2A	101010	*	
43	2B	101011	+	
44	2C	101100		
45	2D	101101	-	
46	2E	101110	.	
47	2F	101111	/	
48	30	110000	0	
49	31	110001	1	
50	32	110010	2	
51	33	110011	3	
52	34	110100	4	
53	35	110101	5	
54	36	110110	6	
55	37	110111	7	
56	38	111000	8	
57	39	111001	9	

ASCII code tables 58-87

58	3A	111010	:	
59	3B	111011	;	
60	3C	111100	<	
61	3D	111101	=	
62	3E	111110	>	
63	3F	111111	?	
64	40	1000000	@	
65	41	1000001	A	
66	42	1000010	B	
67	43	1000011	C	
68	44	1000100	D	
69	45	1000101	E	
70	46	1000110	F	
71	47	1000111	G	
72	48	1001000	H	
73	49	1001001	I	
74	4A	1001010	J	
75	4B	1001011	K	
76	4C	1001100	L	
77	4D	1001101	M	
78	4E	1001110	N	
79	4F	1001111	O	
80	50	1010000	P	
81	51	1010001	Q	
82	52	1010010	R	
83	53	1010011	S	
84	54	1010100	T	
85	55	1010101	U	
86	56	1010110	V	
87	57	1010111	W	

ASCII code tables 88-117

88	58	1011000	X	
89	59	1011001	Y	
90	5A	1011010	Z	
91	5B	1011011	[	
92	5C	1011100	\	
93	5D	1011101	]	
94	5E	1011110	^	
95	5F	1011111	_	
96	60	1100000	`	
97	61	1100001	a	
98	62	1100010	b	
99	63	1100011	c	
100	64	1100100	d	
101	65	1100101	e	
102	66	1100110	f	
103	67	1100111	g	
104	68	1101000	h	
105	69	1101001	i	
106	6A	1101010	j	
107	6B	1101011	k	
108	6C	1101100	l	
109	6D	1101101	m	
110	6E	1101110	n	
111	6F	1101111	o	
112	70	1110000	p	
113	71	1110001	q	
114	72	1110010	r	
115	73	1110011	s	
116	74	1110100	t	
117	75	1110101	u	

ASCII code tables 118-127

118	76	1110110	v	
119	77	1110111	w	
120	78	1111000	x	
121	79	1111001	y	
122	7A	1111010	z	
123	7B	1111011	{	
124	7C	1111100	|	
125	7D	1111101	}	
126	7E	1111110	~	
127	7F	1111111	Delete	

appendix iii: installing bind

Getting a Server to talk DNS

...so I installed a DNS server and BAM! All the problems were fixed.

Every good network professional needs a good DNS server.

And the most commonly used DNS server on the Internet is BIND. Installing BIND is fairly simple, but just in case you need some extra reassurance, here are some handy instructions on how to do it.

#1 Installing BIND on Windows (XP, 2000, Vista)

1. Download the installer from `https://www.isc.org/downloadables/11`
2. Unzip the file.
3. Run the **BINDInstall.exe** program located in the unzip directory.
4. Enter a password for your service and hit the Install Button.
5. Create a directory **C:\named\zones**
6. Create the file called **named.conf** (see an example below).
7. Create the file called **db.yourdomain.com** (see an example below).
8. Start it up!

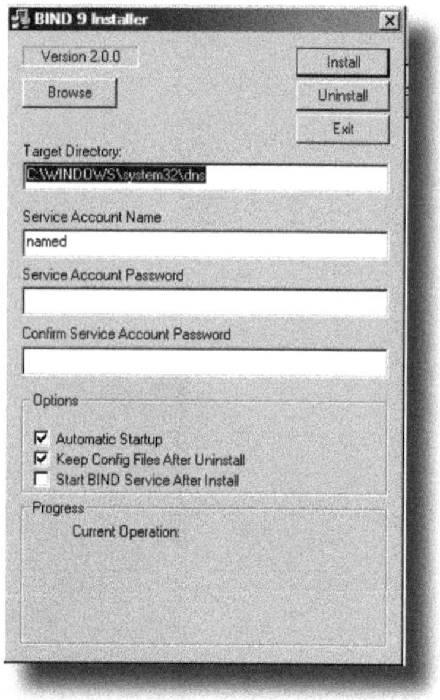

BIND 9 Installer

Version 2.0.0 | Browse | Install | Uninstall | Exit

Target Directory: C:\WINDOWS\system32\dns

Service Account Name: named

Service Account Password

Confirm Service Account Password

Options
- [x] Automatic Startup
- [x] Keep Config Files After Uninstall
- [ ] Start BIND Service After Install

Progress
Current Operation:

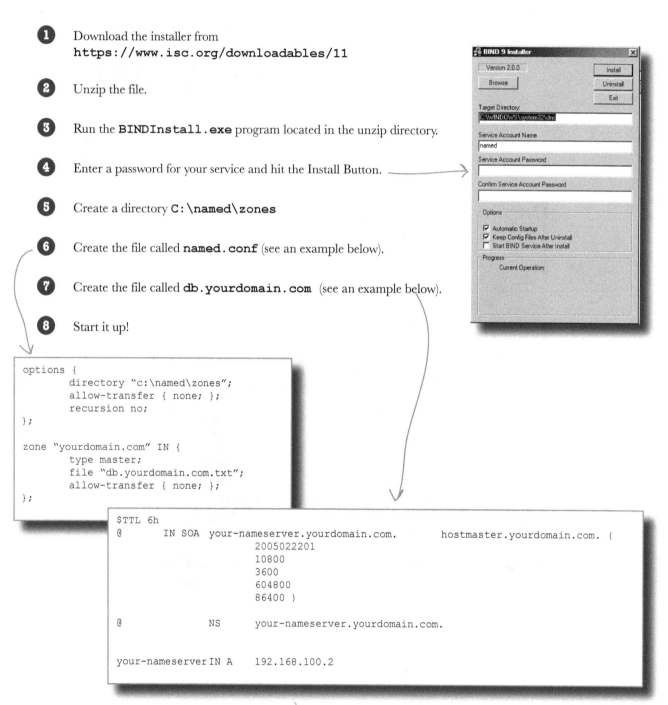

```
options {
        directory "c:\named\zones";
        allow-transfer { none; };
        recursion no;
};

zone "yourdomain.com" IN {
        type master;
        file "db.yourdomain.com.txt";
        allow-transfer { none; };
};
```

```
$TTL 6h
@       IN SOA  your-nameserver.yourdomain.com.       hostmaster.yourdomain.com. (
                        2005022201
                        10800
                        3600
                        604800
                        86400 )

@               NS      your-nameserver.yourdomain.com.


your-nameserver IN A    192.168.100.2
```

#2 Installing BIND Mac OS X Server

1. BIND is already installed on Mac OS X Server; just turn it on in Server Manager.
2. Use Server Manager to configure your domain.

#3 Installing BIND Mac OS X Client & Linux

1. Download the installer from `https://www.isc.org/downloadables/11`
2. Unzip the file.
3. Open a Terminal window.
4. Switch to the directory where the bind file unzipped.
5. Type `./configure`
6. Type **`make`**
7. Type **`sudo make`** `install`.
8. Edit the **`named.conf`** and create the **`db.yourdomain.com`** files. They should be located in the **`/etc`** directory.

With Ubuntu, the steps are much simpler.

Type

```
apt-get install bind9 dnsutils
```

to install BIND, then follow step 8 above.

Index

Numbers

4B/5B 134

8B/10B 134

8P8C connector 18

10Base-T Ethernet protocol 10

568A and 568B wiring standards 17

568A and 568B Wiring Standards Up Close 13

802.11G 369

A

access control lists (ACLs) 415–418
- configuring 417

access points 364–370
- radio waves 365
- warning 366

AC & DC voltage 99

Adaptive Security Appliances (ASAs) 420

Address Resolution Protocol (ARP) 216–217

appliances 71

ARP (Address Resolution Protocol) 216–217

ARP poisoning attacks 411–412

ASCII (American Standard Code for Information Interchange) 134

ASCII tables 479–484

ASN (Autonomous System Number) 280

B

bad connector 107

bad grounding 107

bandwidth 10
- CAT-5 cable 8
- Test Drive 9

Base-T 10

BGP (Border Gateway Protocol) 275, 477

Binary Coded Decimal (BCD) 134

binary format 141

BIND
- DNS (Domain Name System) 304–305, 306
- installing 485–488

blueprints 447–451
- versus floorplans 451

BNC connectors 23

bus networks 24

bus topology 471

C

Cablecross 36

cable improperly wired 90

cable management hardware 64–71
- cable protectors 67
- cable ties 67
- cable trays 67
- j-hooks 67
- raceway 67
- smurf tubes 67

Cable Management Hardware Up Close 67

cables
- CAT-5 6–10
  - fixing 11
- CAT-5e and CAT-6 10
- coaxial 20–35

crossover 18
crosstalk 107
labeler 74
plugged to wrong end 90
problems 87
protectors 67
repairing 5
ties 67
too long 90–91, 98
twisted pair 6
UTP 6

cable trays 67

CAT-5 cables 6–18
colors 8
fixing 11, 17
length 18
versus coaxial cables 23

CAT-5e and CAT-6 10

certifications 478

Cisco
Adaptive Security Appliances (ASAs) 420
certification 478
Cisco Show Command Exposed 342
IOS simulators 476
Pix Security Appliances 420
routers and ACLs 417
show ip route command 245
SNMP (Simple Network Management Protocol) 348
syslogd daemon 355

Cisco Show Command Exposed 342

cmd command 474

CNAME record 314

coaxial cables 20–35
connectors 29
inside 28
terminators 29
toner-tracer set 30–31
versus Cat-5 cables 23

Coconut Airways 2–50
(see also fixing physical networks)

connecting two networks 209
network traffic 222–225
Wireshark (see Wireshark)
(see also routers)

connector mis-wired 98

connectors 107
8P8C 18
BNC 23
coaxial cables 29
fiber-optic cables 38, 42, 47
LC 42
polish & epoxy 47
pre-built 47
RJ-45 6, 11–12
SC 42
ST 42
T-connectors 23

convergence 281

CRC Checksum 178

crimping tool 17

crossover cable 18

current 99

D

data encoding 152

datagrams 164

Denial of Service attack 412

designing networks 437–468
blueprints 447–451
equipment list 456–459
floorplans 444–446
floorplans versus blueprints 451
gathering information 441–443
implementation plan 464–466
router configuration tables 460–463, 462–465
VOIP (voice over IP phones) 451

Destination MAC Address 178, 179

device lists 54, 60

devices and traffic 175–204
Destination MAC Address 179
frames 179
hubs 182–185
internets 181
local area network (LAN) 181
monitoring packets 194–198
packets 179
Source MAC Address 179
switches 186–192
wide area networks (WANs) 181
devices, troubleshooting 333
DHCP (Dynamic Host Configuration Protocol) 374–378
IP addresses 375, 377
running out 380
DHCP Server Exposed 378
Differential Manchester Encoding (DME) 134
dig command 320, 321, 326
DNS (Domain Name System) 291–328
BIND 304–305, 306
email, sending 317–328
Reverse DNS (RDNS) 318–321
how it works 299
installing name server 304–305, 306
mail servers 315
Nameserver Exposed 313
name servers 315
obtaining domain name 293
pointer records 322
Reverse DNS (RDNS) 318–321
dig command 320, 321, 326
Test Drive 295
dig command 326
reverse DNS 321
zone file 316
zone file 314–315
pointer records 322
Domain Information Groper 320
DSL router 211
dynamic routing protocol 264–270

E

EIGRP 275–278
setting up 282
versus RIP 283
EIGRP Up Close 280–281
electrical lines 63
electrical repeater 184
electric motor 107
electrons 30–31
email, sending 317–328
Reverse DNS (RDNS) 318–321
equipment list 456–459
Ethernet
10 Base-T standard 10
frames 119
MAC addresses 210
speed 152
EtherType 178
Extended Binary Coded Decimal Interchange Code (EBCDIC) 134

F

Fast Ethernet 134
Feedback Shift Register (FSR) 134
fiber-optic cables 38–47
connectors 38, 42
fusion splicer 39–41
types 45–46
Fireside Chats
Hub vs. Switch 191
Manchester Phase Encoding vs. Non-Return to Zero 129
Multimeter versus Oscilloscope 104
Oscilloscope versus Logic Analyzer 116
RIP versus EIGRP 283
TCP vs. UDP 167
Toner & Tracer versus Multimeter 94

firewalls 402
- packet filtering 420–426
  - rules 421
  - stateful packet filters 426
  - static packet filter 422

Five Minute Mystery
- Case of the Meteorologist and the RJ-45 Connector 15
  - Solved 18
- Case of the Stolen Messages 410
  - Solved 413

fixing physical networks 1–50
- 8P8C connector 18
- 568A or 568B wiring standards 17
- 568A wire order 13
- 568B wire order 13
- BNC connectors 23
- CAT-5 cables 6–10, 11–12
  - colors 8
  - length 18
- Cat-5 versus coaxial cables 23
- coaxial cables 20–35
  - connectors 29
  - inside 28
  - terminators 29
  - toner-tracer set 30–31
- crimping tool 17
- crossover cable 18
- fiber-optic cable
  - types 45–46
- fiber-optic cables 38–47
  - connectors 38, 42, 47
  - fusion splicer 39–41
- repairing cables 5
- T-connectors 23
- terminators 23
- Test Drive
  - bandwidth 9

floorplans 56–63, 444–446
- versus blueprints 451

fluorescent :lights 71

FQDN (Fully Qualified Domain Name) 293

frames 119, 161, 161
- switches 186

fusion splicers 39–41
- warning 40

G

Geek Bits
- DHCP 378
- MAC addresses 179
- RIP, OSPF, and EIGRP 275
- TCP/IP network 214
- wireless standards 386
- Wireshark 196

GET command (SNMP) 350

GET-NEXT command (SNMP) 350

GET-RESPONSE command (SNMP) 350

Ghost Watch 52–84
- (see also planning network layouts)

Gigabit Ethernet 134

grounding 107

H

hackers 402

Head First Health Club 292–328
- (see also DNS (Domain Name System))

heat 59, 71

hertz 107

hop-counts 272

horizontal cable management tray 75

HP ProCurve Switch 192

hubs 182–185
- versus switches 191

Hubs Up Close 182

I

ICMP packets
- blocking 340
- TCP stack 475

IDSs (Intrusion Detection Systems) 478

ifconfig command 214

IGRP 275

implementation plan 464–466

internets 181

Internet versus internet 181

IOS simulators 476

IP addresses 214–218, 218
- DHCP 375, 377
  - running out of addesses 380
- number 255 232
- octets 227
- reallocating 380–384
- routers 222
- running out of 232
- versus MAC addresses 214

ipconfig command 214

IPv6 232

J

j-hooks 67

L

labeling cables 74

LAN analyzer 118–120, 120, 122

LC connector 42

lights on switches 210

Linux
- BIND, installing 487
- Terminal application 474

local area network (LAN) 181

logical network 209

logic analyzer 110–116, 120, 122
- oscilloscope 110
- versus oscilloscope 115, 116
- when useful 115

M

MAC addresses 179, 218
- ARP (Address Resolution Protocol) 216–217
- Ethernet network 210
- routers 199–200
- switches 188, 213
- versus IP addresses 214

MAC address spoofing 405–410, 412
- defending against 410

MAC flooding attack 412

Mac OS X
- Terminal application 474

Mac OS X Client
- BIND, installing 487

Mac OS X Server
- BIND, installing 487

mail servers 315

Manchester Phase Encoding (MPE) 129, 134

Man in the Middle attacks 412

megabits per second (Mbps) and megabytes per second (MBps) 10

MIB (Management Information Base) 346–347

Microsoft Visio 451

Mighty Gumball 86–124
- (see also troubleshooting)

misfiring network 331–333

monitoring packets 194–198

monitoring (see troubleshooting)

Moonbase 206–242, 244–290
- (see also routers; routing protocols)

motors 59

MRTG 350

multimeter 92, 98, 99, 122
- versus oscilloscope 104
- versus toner and tracer 94

multimode fiber 45–46

mutimeter 107

N

Nagios 350

Nameserver Exposed 313

name servers 315

NAT (Network Address Translation) 380–384
- configuring 382

NAT tables 383–384

network cable problems 87

network certifications 478

network speed 9

new buildings 63

No Dumb Questions
- 8P8C connector 18
- 802.11G 369
- access points 369
- AC & DC voltage 99
- ARP poisoning attacks 412
- bandwidth versus speed 10
- Base-T 10
- binary format 141
- cable too long 91
- CAT-5 cable 18
- CAT-5e and CAT-6 10
- coaxial networks 27
- crossover cable 18
- current 99
- data encoding 152
- datagrams 164
- Denial of Service attack 412
- device lists 60
- DHCP 377
- dig command 321
- domain name 294
- DSL router 211
- EIGRP 282
- electrical lines 63
- encoding data 134
- Ethernet speeds 152
- floorplans versus blueprints 451
- hackers 402
- hertz 107
- ICMP packets 340
- IP addresses 218
  - number 255 232
  - running out of 232
- LAN analyzer 120
- logic analyzer 120
- MAC addresses , 158
- MAC address spoofing 412
- MAC flooding attack 412
- Man in the Middle attacks 412
- megabits per second (Mbps) and megabytes per second (MBps) 10
- multimeter 99, 107
- NAT 384
- new buildings 63
- noise 107
- obstacles 60
- OID 350
- oscilloscope 107, 120
- OSPF 282
- packet types 164
- ping command 258, 340
- port mapping 397
- RIP 270
- routers 211
  - common problems 241
  - interface types 241
  - new 241
- routing tables 254
- running network cables on the floor 63

SNMP 350
subnet mask 232
toner and tracer 120
traceroute command 258
Trap 350
troubleshooting 340
VOIP (voice over IP phones) 451
walls 60, 63
wireless networking 369

noise 69, 98, 102–103, 107

Non Return to Zero Invertive (NRZ-I) 134

Non Return to Zero (NRZ) 129, 134

NRZ encoding 134

O

obstacles 56–63

Obstacles Up Close 59

OID 346, 350

OmniGroup OmniGraffle 451

oscilloscope 101–108, 120, 122
logic analyzer 110
versus logic analyzer 115, 116
versus multimeter 104

OSPF (Open Shortest Path First) 275–278, 282

P

packaging network data
binary format 141
data encoding 152
datagrams 164
Ethernet speeds 152
network frames 161
packet types 164

packet filtering 420–426
rules 421
stateful packet filters 426
static packet filter 422

packets 179
monitoring 194–198

packet sniffer programs 212

packet types 164

Pajama Death 330–362
(see also troubleshooting)

patch panels 75–77

Payload 178

physical networks 209
fixing (see fixing physical networks)

ping command 256, 258, 333–340
blocking 340

Pix Security Appliances 420

planning network layouts 51–84
appliances 71
cable labeler 74
cable management hardware 64–71
cable protectors 67
cable ties 67
cable trays 67
j-hooks 67
raceway 67
smurf tubes 67
device lists 54, 60
electrical lines 63
floorplans 56–63
fluorescent :lights 71
heat 59, 71
horizontal cable management tray 75
labeling cables 74
motors 59
new buildings 63
noise 69
obstacles 56–63
patch panels 75–77
punch down block 78
rodents 71
running network cables on the floor 63
showers 59

sinks 59
stairs 59
steps 55
stoves 59
toner 74
tracer 74
vibrations 59, 71
walls 59, 60, 63
water 59, 71
windows 59

pointer records 322

polish & epoxy connector 47

Pool Puzzle 311
Solution 312

port mapping 392–394

Preamble 178

pre-built connector 47

Protocol Analyzer. 196

punch down block 78

R

raceway 67

radio frequency interference 107

RADIUS 397

reallocating IP addresses 380–384

resistance 92–99, 102
defined 93

Return to Zero (RZ) 134

Reverse DNS (RDNS) 318–321
dig command 320, 326

RFC 1122 475

RG-62 networks 24

RIP (Routing Information Protocol) 264–270, 276–278
setting up 270
versus EIGRP 283

RJ-45 connectors 6, 11–12, 12

rodents 71

router configuration tables 460–463, 462–465

Router Exposed 231

router loop 281

routers 205–242
access control lists (ACLs) 415–418
configuring 417
Cisco 237
common problems 241
configuration files 238
connecting networks with math 228
DSL router 211
finding useful information 240
interface types 241
IP addresses 214–218, 222
MAC addresses 199–200
moving data across networks 224–225
new 241
programming 236–237
security 402
access control lists (ACLs) 415–418
troubleshooting 340
warning 250

Routers Up Close 200

routing protocols 243–290
BGP (Border Gateway Protocol) 275
dynamic routing protocol 264–270
EIGRP 275, 276–278
setting up 282
EIGRP Up Close 280–281
entering routes 248
hop-counts 272
IGRP 275
OSPF (Open Shortest Path First) 275, 276–278, 282
ping command 256, 258
RIP (Routing Information Protocol) 264–270, 276–278
setting up
RIP versus EIGRP 283
show ip route command 245
static routes 261–262
traceroute command 257, 258
troubleshooting bad routes 256–260

routing tables 245–247, 249–252

running network cables on the floor 63

S

SC connector 42

Scholar's Corner
- bandwidth 10
- speed 10

security 399–436
- ARP poisoning attacks 411–412
- big 4 402
- Denial of Service attack 412
- firewalls 402
  - packet filtering 420–426
- hackers 402
- MAC address spoofing 405–410, 412
  - defending against 410
- MAC flooding attack 412
- Man in the Middle attacks 412
- packet filtering 420–426
  - rules 421
  - stateful packet filters 426
  - static packet filter 422
- routers 402
  - access control lists (ACLs) 415–418
- social engineering 429–432
- switches 402
- wireless 397

SET command (SNMP) 350

show command 333, 341–344
- Cisco Show Command Exposed 342

showers 59

show interface command 341

show ip route command 245

signal quality 88

single mode fiber 45–46

sinks 59

smurf tubes 67

SNMP (Simple Network Management Protocol) 346–350
- configuring on Cisco device 348
- GET command 350
- GET-NEXT command 350
- GET-RESPONSE command 350
- SET command 350
- software 350
- Trap 350
- TRAP command 350

social engineering 429–432

Source MAC Address 178, 179

speed 9, 10

spoofing 405–410, 412
- defending against 410

Spy Agency 176–204

SSH 333

stairs 59

Starbuzz Coffee 364–398
- (see also wireless networking)

star topology 470

stateful packet filters 426

static packet filter 422

static routes 261–262

statistics, interpreting 333

ST connector 42

stoves 59

subnet mask 232

switches 186–192
- frames 186
- HP ProCurve Switch 192
- lights 210
- MAC addresses 188, 213
- security 402
- troubleshooting 340
- versus hubs 191

Switches Up Close 187

syslogd daemon 354–356
- Cisco 355
- log files 356

T

T-connectors 23, 24
TCP/IP network 214
  ARP 216–217
TCP/IP packets 475
TCP packets
  versus UDP packets 167
TCP stack 475
telnet 333
Terminal application 474
terminators 23, 29
token ring topology 471
toner and tracer 74, 87–91, 120, 122
  versus multimeter 94
toner-tracer set
  coaxial cables 30–31
topologies 470–471
traceroute command 257, 258
traffic
  moving between networks 222–225
  routes 249
  (see also devices and traffic)
Trap 350
TRAP command (SNMP) 350
troubleshooting 85–124, 329–362
  bad routes 256–260
  cable improperly wired 90
  cable plugged to wrong end 90
  cable too long 90–91, 98
  Cisco Show Command Exposed 342
  connector mis-wired 98
  LAN analyzer 118–120, 120, 122
  logic analyzer 110–116, 120, 122
  MIB (Management Information Base) 346–347
  misfiring network 331–333
  multimeter 92, 98, 99, 107, 122
  network devices 333
  noise 98
  oscilloscope 101–108, 120, 122
  ping command 333–340
    blocking 340
  relevant information 359–360
  resistance 92–99
  routers 340
  show command 333, 341–344
  show interface command 341
  SNMP (Simple Network Management Protocol) 346–350
  SSH 333
  statistics, interpreting 333
  summary 120
  switches 340
  syslogd daemon 354–356
  telnet 333
  toner and tracer 120, 122
twisted pair cable 6, 7

U

Ubuntu
  BIND, installing 487
  Terminal application 474
UDP packets
  versus TCP packets 167
Unicode 134
UTP cable 6

V

vibrations 59, 71, 107
VLANS (Virtual Local Area Networks) 476
VOIP (voice over IP phones) 451
voltage 102
  changes in signal 110
VPN (Virtual Private Network) 477

W

walls 59, 60, 63

Watch it!
  10.0.1.7 321
  access points 366
  blueprints 449
  Cisco routers 237
  configuring NAT 382
  debugging 355
  designing networks 447
  DNS zone file 314
  fusion splicers 40
  HP ProCurve Switch 192
  hubs 183
  Internet versus internet 181
  logic analyzer 110
  noise 69
  oscilloscope 101
  routers 213, 224, 250
  routing tables 249
  wireless protocols 386

water 59, 71

WEP 397

wide area networks (WANs) 181

windows 59

Windows
  BIND, installing 486
  command line 474

wireless networking 363–398
  802.11G 369
  access points 364–370
    radio waves 365
    warning 366
  cash register 390–394
  DHCP (Dynamic Host Configuration Protocol) 374–378
    IP addresses 375
  DHCP Server Exposed 378
  NAT (Network Address Translation) 380–384
  port mapping 392–394
  protocols 386
  RADIUS 397
  reallocating IP addresses 380–384
  Test Drive 389
    access points 370
  WEP 397
  WPA 397

Wireless Security Up Close 397

Wireshark 194–198, 212
  installing 472–473

WPA 397

wrapping objects. *See* Adapter Pattern, Decorator Pattern, Facade Pattern